Protecting Endangered Species in the United States

Protecting Endangered Species in the United States is a collection of original essays by economists, biologists, and political scientists with a common theme – protecting species at risk while safeguarding social order is a policy challenge that entangles biology, politics, and economics. Nearly 1,200 species are now listed as endangered or threatened under the Endangered Species Act (ESA) of 1973; only twelve have been removed from the list. Attempts at species recovery on public and private property lead the authors to examine the political realities that define the debate – who should pay the costs and receive the benefits and how interest group behavior affects the nature of endangered species protection. Although the ESA directs administrative agencies to list and protect species following scientific priorities, the collection addresses the economic choices that still must be confronted. These range from the protection potential of private markets to the design of incentive schemes to encourage conservation by private landowners.

Jason F. Shogren is the Stroock Distinguished Professor of Natural Resource Conservation and Management and Professor of Economics at the University of Wyoming. Before returning to his alma mater, he taught at Appalachian State, Iowa State, and Yale Universities. In 1997, Professor Shogren served as the senior economist for environmental and natural resource policy on the Council of Economic Advisors in the White House. Currently, he serves on the Science Advisory Board for the U.S. Environmental Protection Agency and the Intergovernmental Panel on Climate Change. He was an associate editor of the *Journal of Environmental Economics and Management*, and he is currently an associate editor of the *American Journal of Agricultural Economics*. Recent publications include the coauthored *Environmental Economics* (1996) and authored essays on risk, conflict, valuation, environmental policy, and experimental economics. Professor Shogren was invited to brief the western U.S. governors at their annual meeting in June 1999 on the political economy of endangered species on private land.

John Tschirhart is Professor of Economics, Director of the Public Utility Research and Training Institute, and past Chair of the Department of Economics and Finance at the University of Wyoming. His research is in microeconomics with an emphasis on natural resources and government regulation. It has been supported by the National Science Foundation, the U.S. Environmental Protection Agency, the U.S. Geological Survey, Los Alamos Laboratories and the Electric Power Research Institute. He was a Teaching Fellow at Australian National University and recently he has taken assignments from the World Bank to address public utility regulatory issues in Bolivia and from the United Nations to address solid waste problems in Kazakhstan. He has published in the *American Economic Review, American Political Science Review, Journal of Political Economy, Journal of Economic Literature, RAND Journal of Economics, Review of Economics and Statistics, Journal of Public Economics, Energy Journal, Journal of Economic Perspectives, Journal of Environmental Economics and Management, Journal of Theoretical Biology* and other outlets. He recently participated in an Earthwatch expedition gathering data on black rhinos in Kenya, and he lives in the foothills of the Rocky Mountains.

Protecting Endangered Species in the United States

Biological Needs, Political Realities, Economic Choices

Edited by

Jason F. Shogren
University of Wyoming

John Tschirhart
University of Wyoming

PUBLISHED BY THE PRESS SYNDICATE OF THE UNIVERSITY OF CAMBRIDGE
The Pitt Building, Trumpington Street, Cambridge, United Kingdom

CAMBRIDGE UNIVERSITY PRESS
The Edinburgh Building, Cambridge, CB2 2RU, UK
40 West 20th Street, New York, NY 10011-4211, USA
10 Stamford Road, Oakleigh, VIC 3166, Australia
Ruiz de Alarcón 13, 28014 Madrid, Spain
Dock House, The Waterfront, Cape Town 8001, South Africa

http://www.cambridge.org

First published 2001

Printed in the United States of America

Typeface Times Roman 10/12 pt.   *System* QuarkXPress 3.32 [NG]

A catalog record for this book is available from the British Library.

Library of Congress Cataloging in Publication Data

Protecting endangered species in the United States: biological needs, political realities,
economic choices/edited by Jason F. Shogren, John Tschirhart.
    p.cm.
  Includes bibliographical references (p.), and index
  ISBN 0-521-66210-9
    1. Endangered species – United States. 2. Nature conservation – Political aspects – United
States. 3. Nature conservation – Economic aspects – United States. I. Shogren, Jason F.,
II. Tschirhart, John.

QH76 .P755 2001
333.95′22′0973–dc21

ISBN 0 521 66210 9 hardback

To Deborah and Daniel, and Maija and Riley
May their days in nature be as good as ours

Contents

About the Authors

Terry Anderson

Terry Anderson is executive director of the Political Economy Research Center, a think tank focusing on market solutions to environmental problems located in Bozeman, Montana, a senior fellow at the Hoover Institution, Stanford University, and professor emeritus at Montana State University. His work has helped launch the idea of free market environmentalism and has prompted public debate over the balance between markets and government in managing natural resources. Anderson is the author or editor of twenty-four books, including *Sovereign Nations or Reservations? An Economic History of American Indians* (Pacific Research Institute 1995) and *Enviro-Capitalists: Doing Good While Doing Well* (Rowman & Littlefield Publishers, 1997), coauthored with Donald Leal. He has published widely in both professional journals and the popular press, including the *Wall Street Journal*, the *Christian Science Monitor*, and *Fly Fisherman*. Anderson received his Ph.D. in economics from the University of Washington in 1972. He has been a visiting scholar at Oxford University, the University of Basel, and Cornell University Law School. He was awarded a Fulbright Research Fellowship to Canterbury University and was a National Fellow at the Hoover Institution. Anderson is an avid outdoorsman who enjoys fishing, skiing, and ice climbing. He is a skilled bow hunter and has hunted throughout Montana and in Africa.

Amy Whritenour Ando

Amy Whritenour Ando received her Ph.D. in economics in 1996 from MIT, where she held a National Science Foundation Graduate Fellowship. She taught at the University of Virginia as a Lecturer in Economics for the academic year 1995–96, and was a research Fellow at Resources for the Future in the Quality of the Environment division from 1996 to 1999. She is now on the faculty at the University of Illinois. She has done empirical research on the political economy of the Endangered Species Act, and studies cost-effective methods of choosing and protecting land for conservation reserves. She is also involved in a program of research on motor-vehicle regulation. As part of that research, she has evaluated the efficiency of current inspection and maintenance programs designed to reduce mobile-source air pollution, and is embarking on a project to explore links between fuel-economy and emission-rate regulations, safety, and the shift in new-vehicle purchases from cars to light trucks.

Steven R. Beissinger

Steven R. Beissinger is a professor of conservation biology at the University of California, Berkeley. He received a Ph.D. from the University of Michigan, and was a NSF Postdoctoral Fellow in Environmental Biology at the National Zoo. His work centers on the conservation, behavior, and population ecology of birds, but he has also studied mammals, amphibians, and aquatic invertebrates. Beissinger's research includes field studies of endangered species (e.g., Snail Kites in the Everglades and Marbled Murrelets in the Pacific Northwest) and exploited birds (e.g., parrots in Venezuela), the use of computer models to determine risks of extinction and to evaluate recovery strategies, and continental level analyses of ecosystem conservation priorities. Dr. Beissinger is a Fellow of the American Ornithologists' Union, serves on the Editorial Boards of *Conservation Biology* and *Current Ornithology*, and is the senior editor of *New World Parrots in Crisis: Solutions from Conservation Biology* (Smithsonian Institution Press 1992).

David S. Brookshire

David S. Brookshire is Chair and Professor of Economics at the University of New Mexico, specializing in natural resource, natural hazard, and environmental economics. He performs studies pertaining to public policy issues in these areas and has also contributed to the development of the contingent valuation method for valuing environmental goods. Dr. Brookshire received his B.A. from San Diego State University in 1970, and a Ph.D. in Economics from the University of New Mexico in 1976. He served on the faculty of the University of Wyoming from 1976 to 1989, and was Policy Sciences Editor of *Water Resources Research* from 1987 to 1992. He has served on the Board of Directors of the Association of Environmental and Resource Economists, and as a panelist on ground subsistence for the Committee on Ground Failure Hazard of the National Research Council, and on earthquake loss estimation for the National Institute of Building Sciences.

Gardner Brown

Gardner Brown is Professor of Economics and Adjunct Professor in the Program for the Environment at the University of Washington. He has played a leading role in environmental and resource economics over three decades, with numerous professional articles in outlets such as the *American Economic Review*, the *Journal of Political Economy*, the *Review of Economics and*

Statistics, International Economic Review, and the *Journal of Environmental Economics and Management*. He has been a member of two National Academy of Science panels: the Ocean Studies Board, Committee on Fisheries and the Committee on Endangered Species. He has been a visiting professor at Stanford, Cambridge, and the Universities of Geneva, Aix-Marseilles, and Gothenburg; and a visiting research fellow at Woods Hole Oceanographic Institute and Beijer Institute. Specific areas of research include renewable resources, including predator-prey and meta population models; theory and application of nonmarket valuation methods; biodiversity; and the economics of antibiotic resistance.

David W. Cash

David Cash is a doctoral candidate in Public Policy at the John F. Kennedy School of Government at Harvard University, and a research fellow on the Global Environmental Assessment Project at the Belfer Center for Science and International Affairs. His research investigates the role of science in the development and implementation of environmental policy, focusing on (1) how scientific assessment of global environmental risks are linked to local decision making and local environmental risk management – with specific interest in how information and decision-making systems can best support the management of cross-scale environmental risks; (2) how participation is structured in environmental assessment processes and what influence participation has on the outcome of assessments; and (3) the role of science in endangered species and biodiversity conservation. David has also worked extensively with the U.S. Global Change Research Program/Office of Science and Technology Policy's U.S. National Assessment of Climate Change.

Don L. Coursey

Don L. Coursey is the Ameritech Professor and former dean of the Irving B. Harris Graduate School of Public Policy Studies at the University of Chicago. Coursey is an experimental economist whose research is concerned largely with eliciting reliable measures of preferences and monetary values for public goods. It has focused on comparisons of demand for international environmental quality, environmental legislation in the United States, and public preferences for environmental outcomes relative to other social and economic goals. Coursey's 1994 report "The Revealed Demand for a Public Good: Evidence from Endangered and Threatened Species" was widely noted for its analysis of public expenditures per animal on the endangered species list. His research indicated that federal expenditures reflect public preferences for large, familiar animals such as panthers, bald eagles, or grizzly bears rather than animals such as spiders, snails, or insects, regardless of each species' biological value in the ecosystem. Coursey has also consulted with NOAA in the wake of the Exxon *Valdez* oil spill to develop guidelines for environmental disasters. Coursey joined the faculty of the Harris School in 1993, received a

B.A. in mathematics and a Ph.D. in economics from the University of
Arizona, and has previously taught at the University of Wyoming and
Washington University in St. Louis. He has received the Burlington-Northern
Foundation Award for Distinguished Achievement in Teaching; the Greater
St. Louis Award for Excellence in University Teaching; and the John M. Olin
School of Business Teacher of the Year Award in 1989 and 1990.

Thomas D. Crocker

Thomas D. Crocker is J. E. Warren Distinguished Professor of Energy and
Environment in the Department of Economics and Finance at the University
of Wyoming. He was the first Director of the Institute and the School of
Environment and Natural Resources at Wyoming. His published research has
involved most areas of environmental economics, with a recent focus on
interactions of human capital formation and environmental states, endogenous risk, and the ways in which ecological and economic systems mediate
each other's responses to change. For twenty-four years, Tom Crocker has
been trying to use economics to connect the state of Maine to the University
of Wyoming. The effort is beginning to get a bit wearing. His current ambi-
tion is to continue that part of his program which involves writing in environmental economics, roaming around in the woods, drinking beer, and hanging
out with his wife and his friends.

J. R. DeShazo

J. R. DeShazo is assistant professor in the School of Public Policy and Social
Research at the University of California at Los Angeles. He holds a B.A. in
economics/history from the College of William and Mary, a M.Sc. in development economics from Oxford University, where he was a Rhodes Scholar, and
a Ph.D. in Urban Planning from Harvard University. His research has focused
on protected areas management, regulatory reform, environmental economics
and policy and economic development. He has worked for the EPA, NSF, the
United Nations, the World Bank, U.S. AID, the U.S. Geological Survey and
several foreign governments and non-profit organizations.

Boyd Gibbons

Boyd Gibbons is President of The Johnson Foundation in Racine, Wisconsin.
As Secretary of the President's first Council on Environmental Quality and
Deputy Secretary of the Interior in the Nixon administration, he was instrumental in helping develop many of the nation's environmental policies, giving
particular attention to the problems of land-use policy. A lawyer, Mr. Gibbons
was most recently Director of the California Department of Fish and Game,
responsible for administering, in that most contentious of states, the California
Endangered Species Act in coordination with the federal ESA. Under his
leadership, California DFG undertook mitigation banking and the use of other

innovative incentives in protecting habitat and species, including a massive multispecies effort covering nearly a half million acres of contested real estate in Southern California. Formerly at Resources for the Future and legislative assistant in the U.S. Senate, Boyd Gibbons was for many years a member of the Senior Editorial Staff of the *National Geographic* magazine. He has written numerous *Geographic* articles and two books of nonfiction: *Wye Island* and *The Retriever Game*. Described by William H. Whyte as a "first-rate social history... a fine study of a classic land-use encounter," *Wye Island* won the American Library Association's Award as one of the ten best books of 1977.

Rob Godby

Rob Godby is an Assistant Professor in the Department of Economics and Finance at the University of Wyoming. Rob grew up in central Ontario in a small town called Peterborough, and spent most summers vacationing in the old-growth forests near Temagami, in Northern Ontario. Both experiences made impressions on a young mind – Peterborough was a town where urbanites from Toronto flocked to spend weekends in their cottages on the many lakes near the city. To young eyes these cottage communities seemed like no escape from the city, only a continuation of it. In Temagami, Rob encountered his first taste of environmental conflict when loggers began to clear-cut the forests, and people he actually *knew* were arrested while protesting these activities. Still naive, Rob began studying economics in 1985 at Trent University in Peterborough as an undergraduate, hoping he could change the world somehow. This hope persisted during graduate studies at the University of Guelph and McMaster University. After graduation with a Ph.D., Godby began teaching at Laurentian University in Sudbury, Ontario, before coming to Wyoming. Not surprisingly, Rob's primary research interests are in environmental and macroeconomic policy. As trite as it sounds, Rob still hopes to someday help make the world a better place, even if only marginally.

Greg Hayward

Greg Hayward is Assistant Professor of wildlife biology at the University of Wyoming and Regional Wildlife Ecologist with the USDA Forest Service, Rocky Mountain Region. Greg's research focuses on the ecology of birds and mammals in subalpine forests with an emphasis on habitat relationships and population dynamics. He is also involved with conservation planning for certain Threatened and Endangered Species, most notable the Amur Tiger. His recent research is published in *Conservation Biology*, *Ecological Applications*, *Condor*, and other biological journals.

Robert Innes

Robert Innes is a Professor of Agricultural and Resource Economics at the University of Arizona. Innes was educated at the London School of

Economics and the University of California at Berkeley, where he received a
B.A. in Economics in 1981, an M.B.K. in 1984, and a Ph.D. in Agricultural
and Resource Economics in 1986. His research has focused on a variety of
issues in microeconomic theory, industrial organization, finance, agricultural
policy, environmental economics, and law. Innes has published more than
thirty academic papers, including articles in the *American Economic Review,
Journal of Law and Economics, Journal of Economic Theory, Quarterly
Journal of Economics, International Economic Review*, and *Journal of Public
Economics*. He has received awards for the Outstanding Ph.D. Dissertation
(1987), Quality of Research Discovery (1994), and Distinguished Policy
Contribution (1996) from the American Agricultural Economics Association,
and the Hicks-Tinbergen Medal for outstanding research from the European
Economic Association (1994). In 1994–95, Innes served as a Senior
Economist on the President's Council of Economic Advisers with responsibil-
ity for agricultural, natural resource, and international trade issues.

David Layton

David Layton is an Assistant Professor in the Department of Environmental
Science and Policy, at the University of California, Davis. He is also a member of the Graduate Groups in Ecology and in Statistics. After earning his
doctorate in Economics at the University of Washington, he was a postdoctoral fellow at the Center for Conservation Biology at Stanford University.
His research and teaching focus on issues in environmental policy and in nonmarket valuation. His policy work has considered the conservation of endangered species and the economics of emerging antibiotic resistant bacteria. His
work on nonmarket valuation focuses on developing econometric methods
suitable for Stated Preference surveys. His applications in this area include
valuing forest loss due to climate change, improving fish populations, the
northern spotted owl, costs of electric power outages, recreational fishing,
and beach recreation.

John B. Loomis

John Loomis has worked for twenty years as a natural resource economist,
first for two federal agencies (Bureau of Land Management and then
U.S. Fish and Wildlife Service) and more recently with two universities
(University of California, Davis and now Colorado State University). This has
provided an opportunity to understand what agencies actually do, as well as
to research ways to improve their performance. Dr. Loomis has published
more than 100 scientific journal articles and two books. Several of the journal
articles deal with estimating the economic benefits provided to society from
protection of threatened and endangered species and their habitats. This
research indicates that such benefits can be reliably measured and the benefits
are widely distributed over the entire U.S. population. How nonmarket

valuation techniques can be used to improve the efficiency in allocating natural resources is the focus of his *Integrated Public Lands Management* book.

Henry R. Maddux

Henry Maddux is currently the Director of the Upper Colorado River Endangered Fish Recovery Program, U.S. Fish and Wildlife Service. He has been working on Colorado River and other endangered fish issues since 1984. He started with the Fish and Wildlife Service in 1991, working on Great Basin and Colorado River endangered fish issues out of the Salt Lake City Ecological Service's Office. While there he was the June Sucker Recovery Team leader and served on the Virgin River Fishes Recovery Team. In 1995, he transferred to the Upper Colorado River Endangered Fish Recovery Program as Instream Flow Coordinator, becoming director in 1997. Henry has worked for both state and federal natural resource agencies, including serving as aquatic project leader for Arizona Game and Fish working in the Grand Canyon. Henry was born in Kingman, Arizona, and graduated from Death Valley High School in California. He has his Bachelor of Science in Fisheries from the University of Arizona and his Masters degree in fisheries from South Dakota State University. He now lives in Littleton, Colorado, and has been married for eighteen years.

Andrew Metrick

Andrew Metrick is an assistant professor of Finance at the Wharton School of the University of Pennsylvania. He received his B.A. in Economics and Mathematics in 1989 from Yale University and his Ph.D. in Economics from Harvard University in 1994. He has published articles in *The American Economic Review, The Quarterly Journal of Economics, The Journal of Finance, Land Economics*, and other academic journals.

Stephen M. Meyer

Stephen Meyer is Professor in Political Science at the Massachusetts Institute of Technology, having joined the MIT faculty in 1979. Professor Meyer's principal area of teaching and research is in public policy, focusing on U.S. domestic environmental policy. He directs the MIT Project on Environmental Politics and Policy. His forthcoming book *Environmentalism and Economic Prosperity*, which examines the economic impact of environmental regulation, will be published by MIT Press. Currently Professor Meyer serves as chairman of the Sudbury Conservation Commission, is a member of the Board of Directors of the Sudbury Valley Trustees, a participant of the Massachusetts Herpetological Atlas Project, and a member of the Massachusetts Division of Fisheries and Wildlife Non-Game Wildlife Advisory Board.

Norman Myers

Norman Myers is an independent scientist and a Fellow of Oxford University. He has an interdisciplinary background based on systems ecology and resource economics, with a Ph.D. from the University of California at Berkeley. He has spent twenty-four years in Africa, based mostly in Kenya and Ghana, traveling widely and repeatedly throughout the continent. He has also made extended visits to many parts of both Latin America and Asia. He undertakes research projects, development analyses and policy appraisals for the U.S. National Academy of Sciences (where he is a member), the World Bank, United Nations agencies, the White House, the MacArthur and Rockefeller Foundations, and the European Commission. He has served as a Visiting Professor at Harvard, Cornell, and Stanford Universities, also the Universities of California, Texas, and Michigan. He has published more than 250 scientific papers and more than 300 popular articles, together with fifteen books with total sales of more than one million copies. He was the first British scientist to be awarded the Volvo Environment Prize and the UNEP Sasakawa Environment Prize, and the second British scientist to receive a Pew Fellowship in Conservation and Environment. He has been awarded the Gold Medal of the World Wildlife Fund International and the New York Zoological Society, and the first Distinguished Achievement Award of the Society for Conservation Biology. In 1998, he was awarded a Queen's Honour with appointment to the Order of St. Michael and St. George, for "services to the global environment." He originated the hotspots thesis in the late 1980s; since then it has mobilized more than $400 million for biodiversity conservation.

William Noonan

William Noonan, Colorado Partners for Wildlife Coordinator, received a B.S. in Animal Ecology in 1980 from Iowa State University and started employment with the U.S. Fish and Wildlife Service in 1983, working with the Endangered Colorado River fishes. In 1985, he began a ten-year term as an Ecological Services staff biologist in the Colorado Field Office. In 1995, the Colorado Division of Wildlife and the USFWS initiated a four-year Intergovernmental Personnel Act agreement to establish a full-time coordinator for the Partners for Wildlife program in Colorado. The agreement ended in March 1999, and he continues to serve as Coordinator as a full-time U.S. Fish and Wildlife Service employee.

Clifford Nowell

Clifford Nowell received his Ph.D. in economics at the University of Wyoming in 1988. He is currently the Willard L. Eccles Professor of Economics and Chair of the Economics Department at Weber State

University in Ogden, Utah. His primary fields of inquiry are environmental economics, recreation demand, and the economics of education. He has participated on numerous environmental projects for agencies such as the Sierra Club, Henry's Fork Foundation, and the U.S. Forest Service. He is currently studying the recreation benefits associated with angling in and around Yellowstone National Park. His publications have appeared in journals such as *Ecological Economics, Land Economics, Southern Economic Journal, The Journal of Economic Behavior and Organization, The Review of Economics and Statistics, The Journal of Regulatory Economics*, and *The Journal of Economic Education*.

John Perrine

John D. Perrine is a Ph.D. candidate in the Ecosystem Sciences Division of the Department of Environmental Science, Policy, and Management at the University of California, Berkeley. His primary research area is resource utilization by red foxes and other medium-sized carnivores in the Sierra Nevada and Cascades Mountains of California. Prior to attending U.C. Berkeley, John was a policy analyst for Defenders of Wildlife, where he specialized on the ESA, international wildlife trade, and carnivore management on public lands.

Stephen Polasky

Stephen Polasky is the Fesler-Lampert Professor of Ecological/ Environmental Economics at the University of Minnesota, and formerly a Professor in the Department of Agricultural and Resource Economics at Oregon State University. Prior to OSU, he was an Assistant Professor in the Department of Economics at Boston College. He has served as a Senior Economist for environmental policy on the President's Council of Economic Advisers, and has been a Senior Visiting Research Fellow at the Marine Policy Center, Woods Hole Oceanographic Institution. He received his Ph.D. in economics from the University of Michigan in 1986 and a B.A. from Williams College in 1979. His research interests include biodiversity conservation, endangered species policy, common property, renewable and nonrenewable resources, and environmental regulation. His research has been published in such journals as *Biological Conservation, Journal of Environmental Economics and Management, International Economic Review,* and *Science*. He is currently serving as an Associate Editor for the *Journal of Environmental Economics and Management*.

Todd Schatzki

Todd Schatzki is an economist focusing on energy and environmental issues. His past work examines the optimal design of policy mechanisms; strategies to achieve cost-effective climate, air quality, and water quality programs; the effect of environmental policies on economic markets; and the role of real options in decision-making and optimal policy. This work has examined policies and economic impacts in the electric power, automotive, manufacturing, and fisheries industries, including economy-wide analyses. He has a Ph.D. in Public Policy from Harvard.

Stuart Shapiro

Stuart Shapiro received a Ph.D. in public policy from Harvard in 1999. He is currently working as a policy analyst for the Office of Management and Budget.

Jason F. Shogren

Jason Shogren is the Stroock Distinguished Professor of Natural Resource Conservation and Management, and Professor of Economics at the University of Wyoming. Before returning to his alma mater, he taught at Appalachian State, Iowa State, and Yale. In 1997, Shogren served as the senior economist for environmental and natural resource policy on the Council of Economic Advisers in the White House. He is currently a member of the International Panel on Climate Change. He was an associate editor of the *Journal of Environmental Economics and Management*, and is currently an associate editor of the *American Journal of Agricultural Economics*. Recent publications include *Environmental Economics* (Oxford University Press) and *Private Property and the Endangered Species Act* (University of Texas Press); and essays on risk, conflict, valuation, environmental policy, and experimental economics. Shogren was invited to brief the western governors at their annual meeting on the political economy of endangered species on private land.

Rodney B. W. Smith

Rodney Smith is an Associate Professor in the Department of Applied Economics at the University of Minnesota. He received his Ph.D. in agricultural economics at the University of Maryland, 1992. Journals in which he has published include the *American Journal of Agricultural Economics*, the *Journal of Environmental Economics and Management*, and *Land Economics*. Current research involves studies on the design of contracts and regulatory schemes under private information and hidden action, and natural resource policy.

John Tschirhart

John Tschirhart is Professor of Economics, Director of the Public Utility Research and Training Institute, and past Chair of the Department of

Economics and Finance at the University of Wyoming. His research is in microeconomics with an emphasis on natural resources and government regulation. It has been supported by the National Science Foundation, the U.S. Environmental Protection Agency, the U.S. Geological Survey, Los Alamos Laboratories and the Electric Power Research Institute. He was a Teaching Fellow at Australian National University and recently he has taken assignments from the World Bank to address public utility regulatory issues in Bolivia and from the United Nations to address solid waste problems in Kazakhstan. He has published in the *American Economic Review, American Political Science Review, Journal of Political Economy, Journal of Economic Literature, RAND Journal of Economics, Review of Economics and Statistics, Journal of Public Economics, Energy Journal, Journal of Economic Perspectives, Journal of Environmental Economics and Management, Journal of Theoretical Biology* and other outlets. He recently participated in an Earthwatch expedition gathering data on black rhinos in Kenya, and he lives in the foothills of the Rocky Mountains.

Gary Watts

Gary Watts is a natural resource and environmental economist with a private consulting practice located in Laramie, Wyoming. He specializes in economic issues and problems associated with water resource development and allocation. Over the past twenty years, he has directed dozens of applied research and policy studies in these areas for federal, state, and private institutions in the western United States. In recent years, he has assisted in quantifying federal reserve water rights on six Indian reservations in the Rocky Mountain region and has been involved in interstate water allocation studies in the Arkansas River and North Platte River Basins. He has been retained as an expert witness in numerous water rights litigation matters and has advised the Attorneys General of five western states on water-related issues. Mr. Watts has authored refereed journal articles on water issues in natural resource related journals, and is the author of numerous research reports. He is a member of the American Economic Association, the American Water Resources Association, and several other professional organizations.

Martin L. Weitzman

Martin L. Weitzman is Ernest Monrad Professor of Economics at Harvard University. He has worked in many areas of environmental economics. He was elected a fellow of the Econometric Society and a member of the National Academy of Arts and Sciences.

Acknowledgments

Thanks to the Bugas, Lowham, and Stroock endowments at the University of Wyoming for funding the conference "Social Order and Endangered Species Preservation" from which this volume originated. The citizens of Centennial provided true Wyoming hospitality during the conference. We thank Tom Crocker, Alison Del Rossi, Bruce Forster, Shelby Gerking, Rob Godby, Steve Horn, John Loomis, Chuck Mason, Bill Morgan, Tommy Stamland, and the College of Business, the College of Agriculture, and the Department of Economics and Finance for their support. We also appreciate Norman Myers' encouragement. Shogren thanks his friends and family, Deb, Maija, and Riley, for their fortitude during a very busy year of commuting between Centennial and Washington, D.C.

The Biodiversity Outlook

Endangered Species and Endangered Ideas

Norman Myers

I. INTRODUCTION

This Foreword will not venture into deep discussion of the major themes adumbrated in this book. Written by economists for the most part, they are not my "bag": I am not a card-carrying economist. Rather, I specialize in being a generalist. I am also one who prefers to side-step the usual practice of supplying new answers to established questions. I prefer to raise new questions. So I propose to try my hand with a number of fresh perspectives on endangered species, in the hope that they will serve to expand the policy purview for the issue. Some perspectives are not so much fresh as "fresh-ish" since they have been around, in principle at least, for some years, while receiving only moderate attention from ecologists and economists. Nor shall I focus on the United States after the manner of most contributors to this book. After spending lengthy periods in a dozen countries West, East, North, and South, I prefer to look at the endangered species question as manifested in the world at large, though many of the points apply specifically to the United States.

II. TRIAGE PLANNING FOR ENDANGERED SPECIES

We are far from possessing sufficient conservation resources – funds, scientific skills, and the like – to help all species in trouble. Even if resources were to increase several times over, we could not hope to save more than a proportion of all species at risk. When we allocate funds to safeguard one species, we automatically deny those funds to other species. We thereby express a preference for certain species over others. We may choose contingently rather than deliberately. But we choose. Current conservation practices imply – whether they intend it or not – that the majority of Earth's species are insufficiently worthy of preservation efforts except as incidental parts of ecosystems

I appreciate the many helpful comments on an early draft received from Gretchen Daily, David Duthie, Jennifer Hughes, Jeff McNeely, Dan Perlman, David Pimentel, Peter Raven, and Terry Root.

protected by parks and reserves. Yet it is among this "mystery majority" that most extinctions are occurring.

This raises a basic question. How shall we allocate our scarce resources with most methodical discretion? We have reached a stage where there is merit in determining which species are "most deserving" of a place on the planet. Agonizing as it will be to make choices between species – to implement a triage strategy – we should clearly make our conservation strategy as logically selective as possible.

We can make a start on the challenge through systematic analysis of biological factors, for instance, taxonomic distinctiveness, or those attributes that make some species more susceptible to extinction than others (e.g., sensitivity to habitat disruption or poor reproductive capacity). Then we can evaluate species for their ecological value as intrinsic components of ecosystems. Which species contribute to ecosystem workings more than others through, for example, energy flow or their role as keystone species? Are certain species essential to the survival of their ecosystems, and can some be regarded as superfluous? Although the disappearance of any species is to be deplored, the ecological loss can range from "regrettable but marginal" to "critical if not worse." Much the same applies to genetic and evolutionary values inherent in species. Thereafter we can consider economic values, and even political and sociocultural aspects of the situation. When we integrate all the various factors that tell for and against particular species, we shall have a clearer idea of where we can best apply our conservation efforts.

To some extent, we can finesse the dilemmas of species ranking by elevating the analysis to the level of premium ecosystems insofar as certain habitats, ecozones, and entire sectors of biomes are biotically richer than others. By safeguarding these areas, we can preserve more species than through protecting much larger areas in other biomes. Yet when we pitch our analysis at this broader-scope level, we still face agonizing choices. How do we choose between those ecosystems where safeguard efforts would be appropriate, helpful, or important, and those where they would be crucial (given that we cannot afford to preserve the whole lot)? How should we rank, say, key sectors of tropical forests, coral reefs, and wetlands in order of priority? This is a taxing challenge indeed.

Many hard, even harsh decisions will have to be made. Nobody cares for the prospect of deliberately consigning certain species or ecosystems to extinction. But insofar as we are undoubtedly doing that already, we might as well do it with as much selective discretion as we can muster. In other words, we should make our choices explicitly rather than implicitly: We should determine the future of species by design rather than by default. We have tried playing Noah and have goofed: Our Ark is too small. We are short of the sort of wisdom that would enable us to play God.

To reiterate the central point: The obvious response is to engage in a more methodical and science-based approach. After all, the question is not "Shall we attempt to apply triage?" It is "How shall we apply triage to better effect?" Hence the need for sustained analysis to determine which species and ecosystems shall be deemed most "worthy" of our conservation support. Yet even though the issue was raised fifteen years ago (Myers 1983) and has generated a fair amount of agreement in principle among the conservation community, it remains a black hole in practice because of the meager research directed at the issue.

III. EFFICIENT FUNDING AND BIODIVERSITY HOTSPOTS

For all that there is a severe shortage of conservation funding, monies are often spent with less than tight targeting. There is much scope to do a better job. Consider, for example, the "hotspots" strategy. These are areas that (a) feature exceptional concentrations of endemic species, and (b) face exceptional threat of imminent destruction (Myers 1988, 1990; Myers et al. 2000; see also Mittermeier, Mittermeier, and Myers 1999). Research of the late 1980s revealed that eighteen localities contained the sole habitats of at least 20 percent of all plant species in just 0.5 percent of Earth's land surface, these being areas that for the most part have already lost the bulk of their habitats. The hotspots thesis, as formulated in the late 1980s, has merited conservation priority to the extent that it has attracted $210 million of funding from the MacArthur Foundation over a period of ten years, plus substantial support from the W. Alton Jones Foundation, the Global Environment Facility, and private bodies such as Conservation International and the World Wildlife Fund–U.S. The total spent on hotspots to date is at least $400 million, the largest amount ever assigned to a single conservation measure. This sum is only 0.8 percent of the amount spent by governments during the same period on biodiversity, roughly $40 billion, together with $10 billion by international NGOs, these monies being assigned mainly to across-the-board activities rather than the sharply focused efforts advocated here. It is to be compared with the $250 million for the Pathfinder mission to Mars, which along with many other space probes has been justified largely on biodiversity grounds, namely, the search for extraterrestrial life.

The original hotspots assessment has been greatly expanded and refined recently. The list has been expanded from eighteen to twenty-five hotspots; in addition to plants, the focus has been extended to four vertebrate groups – mammals, birds, reptiles, and amphibians (fish have been omitted for lack of comprehensive data). The analysis also has been extended to consider factors such as area/species ratio and congruence among taxa. It now turns out that 44 percent of Earth's plant species and 35 percent of the four vertebrate categories are confined to 1.4 percent of Earth's land surface. Note, in addition, that conservation needs in terms of protected areas, ex-situ protection (zoos, herbaria, gene banks), and other traditional measures (though not including nontraditional measures such as reducing population pressures and poverty in developing countries of the tropics) amount to a sum sometimes estimated at $17 billion a year (e.g., McNeely, Harrison, and Dingwell 1994). By contrast, we could go far to safeguarding the hotspots and thus a large proportion of all species at risk for just $500 million a year, which is only 12.5 times the annual average over the past ten years. The traditional scattergun approach of much conservation activity, seeking to be many things to many threatened species and thus failing to be much to most, needs to be complemented by a silver bullet strategy in the form of hotspots with its emphasis on the most cost-effective measures.

This tightly targeted strategy could generate a handsome payoff in stemming the biotic crisis. It is often supposed that, were the global mass extinction to proceed virtually unchecked, somewhere between one-third and two-thirds of all species could well be eliminated within the foreseeable future (Raven 1990; Pimm et al. 1995; Wilson 1992). The hotspots analysis indicates that perhaps half of the overall problem could be countered through protection of hotspots covering an aggregate expanse of only a little over 2 million square kilometers. In short, the prospect of a mass extinction can be made far less daunting and much more manageable.

All this does not mean – I emphasize the point – that we should subject non-hotspot areas to benign neglect. They all have their biodiversity values. Nonetheless, I sometimes wonder if it is worthwhile to spend such large funds on biodiversity in my own country, Britain, when so much more is at stake and at greater risk elsewhere. After all, if Britain disappeared beneath the waves, the most species we would lose from the planet would not exceed a dozen, whereas we are losing several dozen every day in Amazonia and Borneo alone.

IV. THE MINI-MASS EXTINCTION SINCE 1950

It is sometimes supposed, at least implicitly, that the mass extinction of species is something that largely lies ahead of us, and so we still have time to talk about it, to analyze it, to plan for it, and to do lots of other things. Yet we are well into the opening phase of the mass extinction. Try a brief thought experiment. Consider the period since 1950, that is, since the time when humans began to increase their numbers and environmental effects with unprecedented impact. Guesstimate how many species have been eliminated to date. Suppose we have been losing species in just tropical forests during the 1990s at an average rate of 27,000 per year (a conservative estimate based upon a planetary total of 10 million) (Wilson 1992; see also Ehrlich and Daily 1993). Suppose too that during the 1980s and given the rate of tropical deforestation then (Myers 1980), the annual extinctions total was one-tenth as many as today, or 2,700 per year. Let us further suppose that during the 1970s, once again the rate averaged one-tenth as many, or 270 per year; and during the 1960s, 27 per year. The total for 1960–2000 comes to roughly 300,000 out of a planetary stock of 10 million, or 3 percent in total.

Of course this reckoning, if indeed it deserves that designation, is not so much preliminary and approximate as rough and ready in the extreme. It is even speculative – but surely not spurious. It is advanced with the sole purpose of getting a handle on how far we are already into a mass extinction episode. It shows that the biotic crisis has been working up momentum for a good while, and of course it could well maintain its momentum for a good while to come. This places a super premium on calculating how much time we have left to mobilize our conservation forces to best effect, bearing in mind the planning syndrome of the lily pond and the twenty-ninth day.

The upshot is that the main phase of the current mass extinction could overtake the biosphere sooner than we may anticipate. More significant still, the time left for us to stem and slow the process could be a lot less than we often suppose. This raises the most critical question of all for ecologists and economists alike, also political leaders, policy makers, and other lever pullers. What we should be asking ourselves is not whether we are now doing better than before (and in certain respects we are doing much better). There is only one question that ultimately counts: Are we doing enough? And if not, what more should we or could we be doing to help us get on top of the problem before it terminally gets on top of us? This could rank as the biggest research challenge of all. The literature offers scant clues to how we are making out. What sort of research agenda would we need to come to grips with this issue?

V. SPECIES AND THEIR POPULATIONS

There is more to the biotic crisis than sheer loss of species. The term "biodiversity" comprises life in its complete panoply. So we should consider populations as well as species – and with good practical cause. Any species has subgroups such as races; and subgroups of races are populations, or assemblies of individual organisms that resemble each other more than members of other populations. It is populations rather than species that supply the many environmental services that keep our ecosystems ticking along, and it is populations with their many environmental adaptations that maintain ecological stability around the world.

Obviously populations greatly outnumber species. Earth's 10 million species feature a rough total of 2.2 billion populations – and we are losing these populations at a rate of 43,000 per day, which is, proportionately, far faster than we are losing species (Hughes, Daily, and Ehrlich 1997). So perhaps it would make more sense for conservationists to focus on the mass extinction of populations. This is all the more an imperative insofar as it is populations that help maintain watershed functions, generate topsoil, disperse pollutants, regulate weather and climate, and provide the raw materials for new drugs, foods, and industrial products, among a host of other services. If the mass extinction proceeds unabated, it seems we are likely to lose perhaps half of all species and maybe 90 percent of all populations. Which will do more to undermine the environmental stability of the planetary ecosystem, and do it in what will surely be a world of environmental uproar?

The biggest service of biodiversity via populations is ecosystem resilience, being an amorphous attribute that has long resisted ecological quantification

(Tilman et al. 1997) and economic evaluation (Perrings et al. 1995). While we wait for uncertainties to be clarified on that one, we can be glad that certain brave analysts have attempted an economic assessment of the other and better known services. Estimates range from $2.9 trillion per year (Pimentel 1997) to $33 trillion per year (Costanza et al. 1997). Either way, environmental services are significantly valuable, and global natural product figures alongside global economic product. Hurrah for populations, unsung as they generally are.

VI. PROTECTED AREAS: NO LONGER THE FRONT-LINE STRATEGY?

Many conservation efforts are reactive and defensive in nature. They implicitly acknowledge that biodiversity habitats are being eaten away by the growth in human numbers and material aspirations; and they propose that a sound way to counter this process is to build bulwarks against the rising tide of human activities. "Parks are the answer, we must have more parks." True, there is massive reason to expand our networks of parks forthwith. Ecologists estimate we need at least twice as large an expanse, located far more strategically and much better protected. This is the case particularly in tropical forests, as well as coral reefs, wetlands, and other prime localities in the tropics with their ultrarich reservoirs of species.

Alas, many present parks are "paper parks." One-third of such areas in the tropics are already subject to encroachment by landless and impoverished peasants. During the past few decades, some 200 million landless peasants have found themselves squeezed out of traditional farmlands, and, feeling they have no other option if they are to keep putting supper on the table, they pick up machete and matchbox and head off toward the last unoccupied lands they know of, tropical forests. Or they take their digging hoes to savannahs and grasslands, often desertifying them. This is the greatest land-use change in human history, precipitated by the greatest migration ever to occur in such a short span of time – yet it remains almost entirely undocumented in overall terms, even to the extent that we have next to no idea of how fast their numbers may build up during the foreseeable future (Myers 1992). Driven by their desperation and poverty (cash incomes of less than $1 per day), these are marginal people in marginal environments. Often enough, the marginal environments are parks and other protected areas.

The displaced peasants, or "shifted cultivators" as I call them, are no more to be castigated for encroaching onto parks than soldiers are to be blamed for fighting wars. They know little of the ultimate pressures that drive them to do what they do, and even if they did understand they would be largely powerless to do otherwise. Meantime, we need more parks that are much better protected. No doubt about it.

What is in doubt is whether parks, together with other protected areas, can keep on doing as good a job as in the past. Setting aside a park in the overcrowded world of the late twentieth century is like building a sandcastle on the seashore when the tide is coming in deeper, stronger, and faster than ever. While building more and stronger sandcastles, we must also do more about the tide – to deflect it and reduce it. We must find ways to curb population growth, to relieve poverty, to cut back on environmentally harmful forms of consumption, and many other things as well – all things that we should be doing on plenty of other good grounds anyway.

For example, consider the Cape Peninsula stretching southward from Cape Town in South Africa. In its 475 square kilometers, little over half the size of New York City, there are 2,250 plant species, or one-seventh as many as in the United States and Canada combined. Of these species, almost 200 are endemic. Given its small expanse, it is a global epicenter of species richness. Although the new South African government has taken measures to protect it more than ever, it is threatened by the expansion of Cape Town's burgeoning populace. That threat could theoretically be countered by building a 20-meter high wall across the Peninsula just south of the city. But it would not keep out a still larger threat in the long run: global warming.

As the planet warms up and temperature bands move away from the equator toward the poles, they will be followed by vegetation bands. In the United States, the vegetation of Florida will be able to "migrate" toward the mid-Atlantic states and even farther northward if need be. True, the plant species will find it a tough trip, having to traverse farmlands, cities, and other forms of "development deserts." The Cape Peninsula's plants will have no place to go except into the sea. To save the Peninsula's flora, we shall need to do much more than support conservation on the spot. We shall need to tackle the main source of global warming: those countries that burn most fossil fuels, notably the country where people burn most per capita – the United States. Even if South Africans were to do a perfect job with their sandcastles, that would avail them little unless Americans play their part to tame the tide.

I often think of a future envisaged by Jeffrey McNeely (1990), head of biodiversity at the World Conservation Union. He proposes that in fifty years' time we may have no more protected areas, and for one of two reasons. First is that they will have been overtaken by landless peasants or global warming or other megathreats. Or, second, we shall have found ways to manage all our landscapes in such rational fashion that we shall automatically make provision for species habitats. It is a Heaven Forbid scenario versus a Golden Age scenario.

VII. ENVIRONMENTAL SURPRISES: DISCONTINUITIES AND SYNERGISMS

The need for a holistic or a biospherewide approach is all the more pertinent in light of some potential environmental surprises ahead. These surprises could prove to be so potent that they could cause the mass extinction to gather pace until it overwhelms the biosphere even more rapidly than is usually supposed. The surprises include environmental discontinuities with their ecological synergisms, both of which will surely become front-rank issues for conservation. The analytic rationale is grounded in the notion that the future is not going to be a simple extension of the past. We should anticipate that environmental discontinuities will become a prominent phenomenon, many of them arising from synergistic interactions between two or more environmental problems.

Both discontinuities and synergisms have the capacity (1) to be profoundly disruptive of ecosystems, ecological processes, biodiversity habitats, and species communities; and (2) to catch us unaware by overwhelming our anticipatory and preventive capacities. Indeed, the worst environmental problems ahead will often be the ones we have scarcely thought of. To cite Benjamin Disraeli, "What we anticipate does not regularly occur, while what we least expect often happens."

These surprises deserve priority attention from conservation practitioners. Yet a library computer check reveals few substantive efforts to broach them even in exploratory terms. They remain black holes of research. For some very preliminary and exploratory work on discontinuities, see Costanza and Cornwell (1992); Faber, Manstetten, and Proops (1992); and Schneider and Turner (1995); on synergisms, see Ehrlich (1986); Odum (1993); and Ricklefs (1990); and for a recent overview, see Myers (1996a).

Prominent examples of environmental discontinuities are acid rain, deforestation-derived declines in tropical rainfall, ozone-layer depletion, and global warming. Lesser instances include the bleaching of coral reefs, mass mortalities of dolphins and seals, phytoplankton blooms, cancer epizootics in fish, and miscellaneous population declines such as those of amphibians worldwide, the anchoveta fishery off the coast of Peru, passerine birds in the northeastern United States and Western Europe, and saguaro cactuses in the southwestern United States and northern Mexico.

We constantly claim to be surprised by the "sudden" onset of a discontinuity. Yet in the cases of global warming and ozone-layer depletion, our most advanced atmospheric models tend to discount, by virtue of their very structure, the possibility of discontinuities. We should anticipate, moreover, that as human communities continue to increase their numbers, consumption demands, and overexploitative technology – a redoubtable triad – they will exert ever-expanding pressures on ecosystems and natural resource stocks. In turn, certain of these ecosystems and stocks will prove increasingly less capable of supporting the needs of humans, let alone those of biodiversity. The plausible upshot is that environmental discontinuities will become more frequent. To illustrate the scope of potential impacts, the human triad can readily overwhelm the environmental underpinnings of agriculture, leading to a downturn in the capacity of agriculture to sustain human communities at their erstwhile level (Brown 1998; Pimentel et al. 1994). As a result, established farmlands will no longer be able to do their job of feeding humankind with its burgeoning numbers, notably in the Indian subcontinent and Sub-Saharan Africa. As a result, subsistence agriculture will increasingly encroach onto wildlands and biodiversity habitats.

As for synergisms, recall that while we are well aware of the main mechanisms of extinction, we tend to study these mechanisms in isolation from each other. We know much less and understand less still about the dynamic interplay between discrete mechanisms. Yet synergisms (literally, the uniting of energies) are unusually significant. For instance, a biota's tolerance of one stress tends to be lower when other stresses are at work. A plant that experiences depleted sunlight and hence reduced photosynthesis is unduly prone to the adverse effects of cold weather, and it thereby suffers more from the cold than would a plant enjoying normal growth and vigor. A similarly amplified effect operates the other way round as well (Mooney, Winner, and Pell 1991). In certain circumstances, a synergisms-induced outcome can be a whole order of magnitude greater than the simple sum of the component mechanisms. Among probable synergisms at work with respect to biodiversity are the impact of acid rain on logged forests, and global warming working in conjunction with ozone-layer depletion (for details, see Myers 1996a).

Synergisms in the biodiversity sphere, working collectively and with compounding impact, will surely lead to an extinction episode of greater scale than usually envisaged. They may also cause the episode to be telescoped in time, meaning that the full biotic crisis could arrive even sooner than anticipated. To the extent that we can discern some possible synergistic interactions, the better we shall start to understand some potential patterns and processes as the species extinction spasm works itself out – and the better we shall be able to anticipate and even prevent some of them.

VIII. PERVERSE SUBSIDIES

Next, consider a factor that rarely appears in the conservation debate: perverse subsidies. These subsidies are harmful to both the economy and the environment (Myers and Kent 1998). A notable example lies with marine fisheries, which have left numerous fish species on the edge of commercial if not biological extinction. The fisheries catch – well above sustainable yield – costs more than $100 billion a year to bring to dockside, whereupon it is sold for around $80 billion, the shortfall being made up with government subsidies. The result is depletion of major fish stocks and endangerment of certain species, plus bankruptcy of fishing businesses and much unemployment.

Perverse subsidies are prominent in five leading sectors: agriculture, fossil fuels/nuclear energy, road transportation, water, and fisheries. Subsidies for agriculture foster overloading of croplands, leading to erosion of topsoil, pollution from synthetic fertilizers and pesticides, release of greenhouse gases, and grand-scale loss of biodiversity habitat. Subsidies for fossil fuels aggravate pollution effects such as acid rain, urban smog, and global warming, with all the profound impacts these will generate for wildlands. Subsidies for road transportation promote pollution at local, national, and global levels, plus excessive road building with loss of landscapes. Subsidies for water encourage misuse and overuse of supplies that are increasingly scarce in many lands. As noted, subsidies for fisheries foster overharvesting of depleted fish stocks. Not only do these environmental ills entrain economic costs in themselves, but the subsidies serve as direct drags on the efficient functioning of economies overall. All help to deplete wildlands and thus to undermine species' habitats if not to threaten species directly.

Subsidies in these sectors are estimated to total around $1.9 trillion per year, and perverse subsidies almost $1.5 trillion. Plainly, perverse subsidies have the capacity to (a) exert a highly distortive impact on the global economy of $29 trillion, and (b) promote grand-scale injury to our environments. On both counts, they foster unsustainable development. Ironically, the total of almost $1.5 trillion is two and a half times larger than the Rio Earth Summit's budget for sustainable development – a sum that governments claimed could not be found at all. To the extent that we have reached a stage when we can save biodiversity only by saving the biosphere (for instance, by staving off global warming with its grand-scale disruption of natural environments), species habitats will be best preserved in a sustainably developed world. The perverse subsidies total is also three times larger than the annual cash incomes of the 1.3 billion poorest people, whose impoverished status causes them to degrade many tropical forests and savannahs.

If perverse subsidies were to be reduced, there would be a double dividend. First, there would be an end to the formidable obstacles imposed by perverse subsidies on sustainable development. Second, there would be a huge stock of funds available to give an entirely new push to sustainable development – funds on a scale unlikely to become available through any other source. In the case of the United States, for instance, they would amount to more than $300 billion, or more than the Pentagon budget. An American pays taxes of at least $2,000 a year to fund perverse subsidies, and pays another $1,000 through increased costs for consumer goods and through environmental degradation. Were just half of the world's perverse subsidies to be phased out, just half of the funds released would enable most governments to abolish their budget deficits at a stroke, to reorder their fiscal priorities in fundamental fashion, and to restore environments more vigorously than through any other single measure. They offer vast scope here to find funds to do a better job of protecting endangered species, and to stop other species from becoming endangered in the first place.

IX. FUTURE EVOLUTION

Finally, the biggest "fresh perspective" of all: If we allow the mass extinction to proceed virtually unchecked, the length of time it will take for evolution to generate replacement species with numbers and variety to match today's will be, so far as we can judge from recovery periods following mass extinctions of the prehistoric past, some 5 million years (Myers 1996b). This is twenty times longer than humans have been a species. Consider the numbers of our descendants who will be affected by what we do, or don't do, in the next few decades (or just the next decade, given the accelerating pace of the debacle?). Suppose too that the average global population during that period will be, say, only 2.5 billion people. The total affected will be 500 trillion, or 10,000 times more than all the people who have existed to date. Just 1 trillion is a large number; figure the length of time represented by 1 trillion seconds.

This raises all manner of questions in terms of fairness to future generations. The most far-reaching analyses of intergenerational justice (e.g., Rawls 1971; Weiss 1988) do not extend beyond a dozen generations. Here lies a lodestone of research for moralists and ethicists. In many respects it is a question that raises the issue way beyond conventional economics. But this is not to say there is not a role for economists. On the contrary, it highlights the urgency of economics research that points the way to more productive measures to slow the biotic debacle while we still have time. Time is probably the most valuable and scarcest of all our conservation resources. Hence I hail the chance to contribute to this fine book.

References

Brown L. R. 1998. The Future of Growth. In L. R. Brown et al. 1998. *State of the World 1998*. W. W. Norton, New York.

Costanza, R. and L. Cornwell. 1992. The 4P Approach to Dealing with Scientific Uncertainty. *Environment* 34: 12–20, 42.

Costanza, R. et al. 1997. The Value of the World's Ecosystem Services and Natural Capital. *Nature* 387: 253–60.

Ehrlich, P. R. 1986. *The Machinery of Nature*. Simon and Schuster, New York.

Ehrlich, P. R. and G. C. Daily. 1993. Population Extinction and Saving Biodiversity. *Ambio* 22: 64–68.

Faber, M., R. Manstetten, and J. O. R. Proops. 1992. Humankind and the Environment: An Anatomy of Surprise and Ignorance. *Environmental Values* 1: 217–42.

Hughes, J., G. C. Daily, and P. R. Ehrlich. 1997. Population Diversity: Its Extent and Extinction. *Science* 278: 689.

McNeely, J. A. 1990. The Future of National Parks. *Environment* 32(1): 16–20, 36–41.

McNeely, J. A., J. Harrison, and P. Dingwell. 1994. *Protecting Nature: Regional Review of Protected Areas*. IUCN, Gland, Switzerland.

Mittermeier, R. A., C. Mittermeier, and N. Myers. 1999. *Hotspots: Earth's Biologically Richest and Most Endangered Terrestrial Ecoregions*. CEMEX, Conservation International and Agrupacion, Sierra Madre, Monterrey, Mexico.

Mooney, H. A., W. E. Winner, and E. J. Pell, eds. 1991. *Response of Plants to Multiple Stresses*. Academic Press, New York.

Myers, N. 1980. *Conversion of Tropical Moist Forests*. National Academy Press, Washington, D.C.

— 1983. A Priority-Ranking Strategy for Threatened Species? *The Environmentalist* 3: 97–120.

— 1988. Threatened Biotas: "Hot Spots" in Tropical Forests. *The Environmentalist* 8: 187–208.

Myers, N. 1990. The Biodiversity Challenge: Expanded Hot-Spots Analysis. *The Environmentalist* 10: 243–56.

—— 1992. Tropical Forests: Present Status and Future Outlook. In N. Myers, ed. *Tropical Forests and Climate*: 3–32. Kluwer, Dordrecht, Netherlands.

—— 1993. Tropical Forests: The Main Deforestation Fronts. *Environmental Conservation* 20(1): 9–16.

—— 1996a. Two Key Challanges for Biodiversity: Discontinuities and Synergisms. *Biological Conservation* 5: 1025–34.

—— 1996b. The Biodiversity Crisis and the Future of Evolution. *The Environmentalist* 16: 1–11.

—— 1998. Emergent Issues of Environmental Economics: What We Should Be Analyzing Closely But Haven't Thought Enough About. *International Journal of Social Economics* 25(6/7/8), special issue: 1271–78.

Myers, N. and J. Kent. 1998. *Perverse Subsidies: Tax $s Undercutting Our Economies and Environments Alike*. International Institute for Sustainable Development, Winnipeg, Canada.

Myers, N., R. A. Mittermeier, C. Mittermeier, and G. A. B. da Fonseca. 2000. Biodiversity Hotspots for Conservation Priorities. *Nature* 403: 853–58.

Odum, E. P. 1993. *Ecology and Our Endangered Life-Support Systems*. Sinauer Associates, Sunderland, Mass.

Perrings, C., K.-G. Maler, C. Folke, C. S. Holling, and B. O. Jansson, eds. 1995. *Biodiversity Loss: Ecological and Economic Issues*. Cambridge University Press, Cambridge, U.K.

Pimentel, D. 1997. Economic and Environmental Benefits of Biodiversity. *BioScience* 47(11): 747–57.

Pimentel, D., R. Harman, M. Pacenza, J. Pecarsky, and M. Pimentel. 1994. Natural Resources and an Optimum Human Population. *Population and Environment* 16: 347–70.

Pimm, S. L., G. J. Russell, G. L. Gittleman, and T. M. Brooks. 1995. The Future of Biodiversity. *Science* 269: 347–54.

Raven, P. R. 1990. The Politics of Preserving Biodiversity. *BioScience* 40(10): 769–74.

Rawls, J. 1971. *A Theory of Justice*. Harvard University Press, Cambridge, Mass.

Ricklefs, R. 1990. *Ecology* (third edition). Freeman, San Francisco, Calif.

Schneider, S. H. and B. L. Turner III. 1995. Anticipating Global Change Surprise. In S. J. Hassol and J. Katzenberger, eds. 1994. *Elements of Change*, 130–45. Aspen Global Change Institute, Colorado.

Tilman, D., J. Knops, D. Wedin, P. Reich, M. Ritchie, and E. Siemann. 1997. The Influence of Functional Diversity and Composition on Ecosystem Processes. *Science* 277: 1300–02.

Weiss, E. B. 1988. *In Fairness to Future Generations: International Law, Common Patrimony and Intergenerational Equity*. Transnational Books, London, U.K.

Wilson, E. O. 1992. *The Diversity of Life*. Harvard University Press, Cambridge, Mass.

CHAPTER 1

The Nature of Endangered Species Protection

Gregory D. Hayward, Jason F. Shogren, and John Tschirhart

I. INTRODUCTION

During Earth's most recent 3.5 billion junkets around the Sun, its inhabitants have busied themselves adapting to myriad physical surroundings and finding niches within niches to carry out their life functions. In doing so, they established a bewildering number of species, each depending on thousands of fellow species for survival. Five times over the past 440 million years, the number of species crashed in mass extinctions initiated by exogenous shocks to their environments from meteorites, ice ages, and volcanic eruptions. After each shock, the number of species rebounded, and after the most recent shock 66 million years ago, the number rebounded to the 10 million or more species currently inhabiting Earth.

Today, these inhabitants are again experiencing a mass extinction, although many argue this event is not due to an exogenous shock, but to the endogenous activities of a single species. There is evidence that species are disappearing worldwide at rates 10 to 1,000 times greater than natural rates of extinction (Jablonski 1991; May, Lawton, and Stork 1995; National Research Council 1995; Pimm, Russell, and Gittleman 1995). A casual look at data in the contiguous United States reveals a telling correlation between human populations and threatened and endangered species. Table 1.1 displays a state-by-state tally of species on the endangered species list (ESA) along with the percentage change in state population densities from 1970 to 1997, which encompasses the period the ESA has been in existence. (Species data are from the DEMES database described in Chapter 19.) These data are plotted in Figure 1.1 and they suggest a positive relationship between human activity and species endangerment. Omitting the two outliers, California and Nevada, the correlation between population density change and listed species is 0.53.

We humans refer to our millions of fellow species as Earth's "biodiversity," and judging from some of our activities, one might think the purpose of all our forerunner species was to set the stage for human existence, and now that we are here, the forerunners are less important or even expendable. "Human beings . . . have become a hundred times more numerous than any

Table 1.1. *Endangered species and human population*

State	Number of species	Change in population density	State	Number of species	Change in population density
CA	192	62	AR	14	31
NV	31	248	MD	12	31
TN	80	37	LA	12	23
AL	78	25	PA	12	2
FL	74	117	ID	10	70
TX	64	74	NY	10	1
AZ	51	157	OK	9	30
VA	42	46	MA	9	7
GA	38	64	WI	8	17
NM	34	70	IA	8	2
KY	34	21	WY	7	44
NC	33	46	NH	6	60
UT	29	95	VT	6	33
OR	27	56	KS	6	15
IL	24	73	NJ	6	14
MS	24	24	DE	5	35
IN	21	14	MN	5	23
SC	18	46	NE	5	11
OH	18	5	CT	5	8
CO	17	76	MT	4	25
MO	15	16	ME	3	25
MI	15	10	SD	3	10
WV	15	4	RI	3	5
WA	14	65	ND	2	5

other land animal of comparable size in the history of life" (Wilson 1992). Accordingly, we now appropriate about 40 percent of the terrestrial food available for all species (Vitousek et al. 1986), and 45 percent of the fresh water (Postel, Daily, and Ehrlich 1996). But in truth, not only are forerunner species not expendable, but "biodiversity represents the very foundation of human existence" (Heywood 1995). For example, E. O. Wilson (1992) has argued that humans would likely not survive beyond a few months if invertebrates disappeared. Biodiversity provides ecosystem services such as filtering fresh water, generating soil, and disposing of waste; it provides marketable goods such as food, building materials, and medicines; it provides nonmarketable goods such as scenic vistas and wildlife observation; and it serves as cultural and spiritual sources for human expression (see, for example, Daily 1997; Daily et al. 1997; Perrings et al. 1995; and Roughgarden 1995).

Given these benefits, why is there an ongoing mass extinction? Ought not something as indispensable to human existence as biodiversity be preserved? The answer is captured by the classic paradox of value. Recall the diamond-water paradox from economics 101. Water is indispensable to human existence so its total value is infinite, yet its price is low. Diamonds are hardly

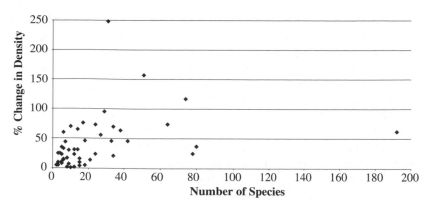

Figure 1.1 Species versus Population Density.

indispensable and their total value relative to water is low, yet their price is high. Price is related to incremental or marginal value and water has a low price, not because its total value is low, but because it is abundant and the value of an additional unit is low. Biodiversity is like water. With at least 10 million species, the large majority of which are uncatalogued and unknown to anyone, it appears abundant, and the marginal species has little value in the market (see, for example, Simpson, Sedjor, and Reid 1996). Biodiversity competes with many other goods that humans demand, and in using limited resources to secure these goods, we make trade-offs that may mean marginal units of biodiversity are sacrificed to increase the supply of other worthy goods such as children's health and education.

Furthermore, as a "good," biodiversity exhibits characteristics that cause its market value to understate its social value. First, biodiversity is a public good and as such it will be undersupplied, or oversacrificed, in the marketplace. Second, some of the important services biodiversity provides are not bought and sold by the pound on the market. There are positive externalities associated with biodiversity that are not reflected in its market value (Crocker and Tschirhart 1992). Third, substantial uncertainty exists about the benefits and resiliency of biodiversity. Only so much biodiversity can be sacrificed before it ceases to support human existence. But nobody knows exactly how or when we will cross the line. Plus the transition from support to collapse may not be smooth; a threshold might exist beyond which incremental sacrifices do not lead to incremental losses of support, but to swift collapse. Common sense suggests that we should err on the conservative side by protecting more biodiversity than would be justified in the absence of uncertainty.

In the United States, Congress passed the 1973 Endangered Species Act (ESA) in response to biodiversity loss. Among the ESA's purposes is ". . . to provide a means whereby the ecosystems upon which endangered species and threatened species depend may be conserved, [and] to provide a program for the conservation of such endangered and threatened species." The Act acknowledges that species have "ecological, educational, historical, recreational and scientific value" unaccounted for in the course of "economic growth and development" (ESA, Sec. 2). The ESA significantly broadened the scope of species protection. It makes every species, subspecies, and discrete populations (restricted to vertebrates) of plants and animals eligible for protection by being listed either as endangered or threatened (those likely to become endangered). At the time, this language seemed harmless enough, and the Act passed in 1973 with little or no opposition – 390 to 12 in the House of Representatives and 92 to 0 in the Senate. Not surprisingly, the list of endangered and threatened species has expanded from 114 in 1973 to over 1,200 in 2000. Plants make up two-thirds of the listed species.

As with many pieces of legislation, the ESA was a response to the market failures associated with the characteristics of biodiversity: it is a public good, it generates positive externalities, it has uncertain thresholds. And because the marketplace alone was unlikely to preserve all the biodiversity society desired, Congress mandated that it will be preserved legislatively. To this end, Congress initially stipulated that biological needs would be the sole criterion used for listing species or designating critical habitat. Economic criteria should play no explicit role. In fact, the Supreme Court ruled in *Tennessee Valley Authority v. Hill* that "it is clear from the ESA's legislative history that Congress intended to halt and reverse the trend toward species extinction – whatever the cost" (Souder 1993). In effect, the well-intentioned goal was to preserve the *total value* of biodiversity. But human activities and choices revolve around *marginal values*. Simply stating that the *totality* of biodiversity is to be preserved without specifying the *incremental* means to correct the market failures through incentives or establishing new markets was then and is now insufficient to ensure survival. The original ESA tried to repair the gap between the market value and the social value of biodiversity without an effective set of tools (see Clark, Reading, and Clarke 1994).

The situation was addressed to some degree with the 1978 ESA Amendments, which opened the door to account explicitly for economic considerations. The secretary of the interior was now allowed to "take into consideration the economic impact, and any other relevant impact, of specifying any particular area as critical habitat." And unless failure to designate habitat would lead to extinction, the secretary can exclude areas from critical habitat if the benefits of exclusion outweigh the benefits of designation. Nevertheless, the ESA still relied on legislative mandates to accomplish its goal, eschewing economic incentives. The political reality was that interest groups who envisioned their wealth being diminished or freedoms impinged by the mandates rallied against the Act, often in the courts and legislatures. As such, reauthorization of the ESA has been on hold since 1992. Several congressional bills that rewrite the ESA have been proposed, but none have survived the political infighting. This inaction testifies to the substantial costs that some interest groups foresee being burdened with (e.g., landowners), while other groups, looking toward stronger legislation, see the bills shortchanging preservation goals (e.g., environmentalists). No one sees a quick end to the ESA controversy.

This book collects a set of essays written by economists, biologists, and policy makers that address this tangle of biological needs, political realities, and economic choices associated with species protection. The essays focus primarily on the United States, where conflicts and opportunities are more sharply defined and extensively examined than elsewhere. In what follows, our introduction surveys the underlying currents behind these three themes. We first turn to biological needs.

II. BIOLOGICAL NEEDS

Effective protection of endangered species requires some measures of biological success and failure. To illustrate, consider the biological effectiveness of the ESA in the United States. How have species fared in the United States under the ESA? Table 1.2 shows that as of September 30, 1999, 477 animals and 716 plants in the United States are listed as endangered or threatened (U.S. Fish and Wildlife Service – USFWS – web page, www.fws.gov/r9endspp/endspp.html). Recovery plans guide the conservation efforts for 886 species; this includes 525 approved plans; some of the plans address conservation direction for multiple species. By 1997, the list included eight U.S. species of animals and plants designated recovered (Gordon, Lacy, and Streeter 1997), and seven species removed from the list because they were designated extinct. Beissinger and Perine (Chapter 4) provide much more detail about the endangered species list, along with a map of the United States showing the distribution of endangered and extinct species across the states. Cash et al. (Chapter 19) supply a comprehensive data set available on biological, political, and economic variables related to threatened and endangered species in the United States.

Based on this record, can we say the ESA has met its biological need of conserving endangered species? Assessing the biological effectiveness of the act is hotly debated among biologists and conservation managers (e.g., Franklin 1993; Losos 1993; NRC 1995; Gordon et al. 1997). Many conservation biologists regard the ESA as the most important piece of conservation legislation in U.S. history (Tracy and Brussard 1994). Others suggest that "the ESA has entirely failed to lead to the recovery of endangered or threatened species" (Gordon et al. 1997, 394). These critics contend that the problems are so profound and require such drastic revisions that a wholesale replacement of the ESA might be needed for real conservation.

Why do biologists within the conservation community have such differences of opinion? One reason is that conservation biologists differ in how they judge success. They continue to ask questions about the appropriate metric to evaluate biological effectiveness. Is the ESA effective if some proportion of listed species recover to the point where they can be delisted? Or is the act effective if it helps reverse the trend in species abundance prior to recovery? Or is it effective if it simply prevents listed species from becoming

Table 1.2. *Box score of threatened and endangered species (as of September 30, 1999)*

Group	Endangered U.S.	Endangered Foreign	Threatened U.S.	Threatened Foreign	Total species	Species with plans
Mammals	61	248	8	16	333	48
Birds	74	178	15	6	273	76
Reptiles	14	65	22	14	115	30
Amphibians	9	8	8	1	26	12
Fishes	69	11	42	0	122	91
Snails	18	1	10	0	29	20
Clams	61	2	8	0	71	45
Crustaceans	17	0	3	0	20	12
Insects	28	4	9	0	41	27
Arachnids	5	0	0	0	5	5
Animal Subtotal	356	517	121	37	1,035	366
Flowering Plants	550	1	135	0	686	530
Conifers	2	0	1	2	5	2
Ferns and Others	26	0	2	0	28	28
Plant Subtotal	578	1	138	2	719	560
Grand Total	934	518	263	39	1,754	886*

*There are 525 approved recovery plans – some plans cover more than one species, and some species have more than one plan.
Source: U.S. Fish and Wildlife Services. Division of Endangered Species (1999).

extinct? A broad interpretation of effectiveness may even include an evaluation of the degree to which the ESA encourages management actions that prevent species from declining to the point of being considered for listing.

The temporal scale chosen for analysis further complicates evaluating the ESA. Failure to acknowledge the mismatch between the temporal scales of the extinction process and implementation of the ESA is the cause for much disagreement. The retraction of a species' distribution, decline in abundance, and final extinction is a process that can take centuries. Following the degradation of critical habitat, the recovery of species dependent on that habitat can occur only following restoration of habitat conditions or change in other limiting factors. Natural processes of succession and time lags between habitat recovery and species response result in unavoidable delays in the conservation of endangered species. For instance, forest succession that leads to habitat conditions optimal for red-cockaded woodpeckers (*Picoides borealis*) occurs over decades. Furthermore, many of the species currently protected by ESA have experienced gradual retraction of geographic distributions and declines in abundance over the past 500 years associated with major changes in North American landscapes. Finally, natural or "background" extinction rates as established from the fossil record are estimates that provide average rates generally taken over thousands of years. Is twenty-five years long enough to judge the effectiveness of a law that begins with the difficult task of identifying species in imminent danger of extinction?

An objective evaluation of effectiveness is limited by circumstantial evidence. No controlled experiments have been conducted (Caughley and Gunn 1996). But despite this limit, we can build an argument for, or against, the effectiveness of ESA based on the record from the past twenty-five years. The most obvious evidence of success for the act, and the only evidence accepted by Gordon et al. (1997, 364), is the recovery of species "to the point at which protection is no longer required," at which point a species can be delisted. Only a handful of species have achieved the goal of recovery as established by the USFWS and been removed from the List of Endangered and Threatened Wildlife and Plants. In 1997, the list included a total of eight U.S. species of animals and plants designated recovered (Gordon et al. 1997, 381). Among these are the eastern states brown pelican (*Pelecanus occidentalis*), Utah's Rydberg milk-vetch (*Astragalus perianus*), and California gray whale (*Eschrichtius robustus*). Although abundance of these eight species clearly increased, it is not obvious whether actions resulting from ESA were significant in the conservation of these species (Gordon et al. 1997). Thus, the list of recovered species may not even represent an unmistakable piece of evidence regarding the effectiveness of the act.

With so few species achieving recovery and so many continuing to exist in a tenuous state, it might appear that the ESA has been ineffective in achieving its goals. Is this the case? Before species can recover, they must halt their slide toward extinction and then increase in numbers. If we examine the extent to which declines in abundance have been halted or reversed, the ESA begins to look more effective. A 1994 report to Congress (USFWS 1994) listed the status of threatened and endangered species as follows: 42 percent stable or improving, 34 percent declining, 1 percent extinct, and 23 percent unknown. Species downlisted from endangered to threatened include Aleutian Canada goose (*Branta canadensis leucopareia*), greenback cutthroat trout (*Salmo clarki stomias*), Virginia round-leaf birch (*Betula uber*), and bald eagle (*Haliaetus leucocephalus*).

Again, the conservation status of species identified as stable or improving may not all be a consequence of the ESA; the ultimate direct and indirect effects of the act are impossible to estimate. But the report suggests that the trend was in the right direction for a substantial proportion of taxa (42 percent) identified as critical conservation concerns by the ESA prior to 1994. If this pattern reflects reality, it suggests the ESA is having a significant positive influence on species and represents evidence of success. Similarly, evidence that 34 percent of taxa were declining identifies the cases in which the ESA did not reverse the trajectory since 1973.

While the ultimate goal of the ESA is to conserve species by achieving population sizes resistant to the threat of extinction, preventing extinction is a critical objective. Since 1973, at least seven animal and plant species have likely gone extinct in the United States. Conservation efforts clearly failed these species. Is the ESA tarred as a failure? Well, we have no way to evaluate how many species would be extinct today without the protection of the ESA. Quantifying precisely whether the ESA has held back a flood of extinctions is nearly impossible (NRC 1995). Historical trends, however, can provide some perspective. In North America, sixty-eight species of birds and mammals have been threatened with extinction since the sixteenth century, and 50 percent of them have gone extinct. "However, in the 14 cases where people have attempted to recover an endangered species, only 1 species (7 percent) has gone extinct" (Belovsky et al. 1994, 309). Looking at a broader range of taxa, it seems clear that extinction rates were lower during the years following passage of ESA than before. Whereas over 500 species were lost during the 200 years prior to the act, only seven documented extinctions occurred in the first twenty-one years after passage.

The effectiveness of ESA in slowing the rate of extinction is especially difficult to evaluate when we consider extinction in a broader temporal context. Extinctions have always occurred (Benton 1995). At least 90 percent of all species that have lived have disappeared (Myers 1979). Consequently, some might argue that we cannot and should not legislate to stop natural processes. Most scientists agree, however, that today's extinction rates go far beyond "background" levels. Caughley and Gunn (1996) calculated an average background extinction rate of 0.06 percent species lost every 1,000 years. The mass extinction of the dinosaurs translates into an extinction rate of one per 1,000 years (Myers 1979). One estimate for the last quarter of the twentieth century is more than 100 per day (Myers 1979). Even based on conservative estimates, today's extinction rates are 10–1,000 times background levels and future extinction rates could be even higher (Nott et al. 1995; Hunter 1996). Furthermore, the extinction rate is rapidly increasing (Nilsson 1983), and the extent and distribution of extinctions is unlike any previous major extinction period. Assuming human population stabilizes at 10–15 billion people in the next 50–100 years and that ecosystems stabilize concomitantly, Myers (1992) hypothesized that over 10 percent of Earth's biota will be lost in the next decade (an incredibly short period). This estimate is only slightly higher than estimates by ten other biologists summarized by Stork (1997). Given these discouraging estimates, the relative effect of ESA in stemming this tide during the past twenty-five years is especially difficult to estimate.

Most evaluations of species protection effectiveness focus on rates of recovery, rates of species extinction, or trends in abundance and status, or all three (e.g., Losos 1993; Tear et al. 1993; Gordon et al. 1997). But the most profound consequences of the ESA may be indirect, and the biological effectiveness may stem most strongly from these indirect consequences. One example of indirect effects can be seen in the administration of federal lands. With the ESA, federal land management agencies devoted more resources to evaluate alternative management actions on plants and animals without explicit market value. The U.S. Forest Service (USFS), for instance, initiated a sensitive species program to ensure that species do not become threatened or endangered through the agency's actions (USDA 1995). In 1996, the nationwide list of sensitive species for the USFS included 2,339 species: 5.6% birds, 4.4% mammals, 5.0% reptiles/amphibians/snails, 4.8% fish, 2.9% clams/crustaceans, 3.7% insects, and 73.6% plants (L. Fenwood pers. comm. 1996).

But in fact, the record of stabilization, improvement, recovery, and the rarity of extinction following ESA listing is quite surprising in light of the theoretical predictions regarding persistence of small populations. Small populations are threatened by both deterministic (e.g., habitat loss) and stochastic processes (e.g., demographic, genetic, and environmental shocks) (see Belovsky et al. 1994). The black-footed ferret's (*Mustela nigripes*) recovery history is a prime example of a species increasing in abundance only to succumb to stochastic, uncontrollable variables. Brown and Layton (Chapter 3) examine saving a species whose population has become small over just the last two decades – the black rhino (*Diceros bicornus*). Their work looks beyond the United States to show that innovative approaches might be necessary when stochastic processes threaten extinction. Poaching has been the major threat to the rhinos in recent years, and the authors propose policies that operate by changing a potentially stochastic process into a deterministic one.

Many subjective variables interfere with the ability to evaluate biological effectiveness. The best measure of progress in species conservation is unclear and difficult to quantify, and might well be species-specific. Because of the problems with small population demography, effective biological conservation must begin prior to species decline. Delays in developing and implementing recovery plans further imperil species. The lack of biological information on the abundance, distribution, and trends in species abundance further hampers the listing and recovery plan process (Tear et al. 1993, 1995).

Given this high level of uncertainty and risk, most conservation biologists want proactive efforts of habitat preservation while species are common, functioning parts of ecosystems (see Chapter 4 of this volume). Biologists argue that initiating proactive management of species before they reach extremely low population size can protect species without the expense of "emergency room tactics" (e.g., Scott et al. 1987). Quality habitat will also involve larger areas than is customary today, and should include multiple species (Losos 1993). In addition, any action should account for special demographic and genetic traits of small populations. For instance, Belovsky et al. (1994) found that 74 percent of the endangered species to go extinct were restricted to small areas, whereas only 35 percent of those that survived were restricted to small areas. And a better understanding of small population demography, patterns in species rarity, and restoration ecology will also improve the design of recovery plans.

But the actuality is that listing and delisting decisions are often not based on biological or demographic grounds but on political expediency. The mismatch in temporal scale between biological operations and human preferences makes this so. Perhaps biological ineffectiveness lies not with the ESA but because the act has been asked to accomplish too much too late (Tear et al. 1993; NRC 1995; Carroll et al. 1996; Belovsky et al. 1994; Bean 1986). As such, judging the success of species protection based on success or failures for individual species will depend in part on the political discourse on what is "too much" and what is "too late."

III. POLITICAL REALITIES

Biological needs usually demand long-term global thinking; *political realities* usually supply short-term local thinking. The resources society might devote to habitat protection and other biological needs as mandated by an act like the ESA exact an opportunity cost – lost resources that could have been used to satisfy other human demands for health and welfare. Broad scope and unfunded mandates fan the flame of controversy because species protection epitomizes the classic quandary of diffuse benefits and concentrated costs. The benefits of protecting endangered species accrue to the entire nation, while a sizable share of costs fall on private landowners or local industries. About half of the listed endangered species rely on private land for 80 percent of their habitat (Innes, Polasky, and Tschirhart 1998). Some landowners complain about the high costs of complying with the ESA, and they demand compensation for compliance; some defenders of the ESA go along with this compensation because they see it as a means to bring private land into the fold of species protection. But other landowners want nothing to do with compensation because they fear further public erosion of private control; and many pro-ESAers also eschew compensation because they see it as a plot to paralyze the act through the back door of underfunding (Shogren 1998).

And because governments at all levels are instrumental in allocating resources, interest groups inevitably fight against devoting resources to species protection or they compete for resources by lobbying legislatures, filing lawsuits, and even conducting illegal activities. Plus local, state, and federal agencies are pitted against one another over jurisdiction and resource availability. Three highly publicized examples of these interest group and government activities revolve around efforts to preserve the northern spotted owl (*Strix occidentalis*), to preserve various species of salmon in the Pacific Northwest, and to reintroduce the timber wolf (*Canis lupis*) to Yellowstone Park. Examples of less publicized activities include the following:

- In March 1999, the USFWS ordered New Jersey to close the North Brigantine Natural Area, located on an island north of Atlantic City, to four-wheel drive vehicles during the nesting season of the threatened piping plover (*Charadrius melodus*). The area is popular among people who drive onto the beach to fish, and Brigantine City plans to challenge the order.
- In July 1998, the Biodiversity Legal Foundation, the Endangered Species Network, and other environmental groups sued to overturn

the U.S. Department of Interior's "no surprises policy" which shields landowners from future restrictions on the use of their land if they set aside property to preserve an endangered species. The coalition of groups argued the no surprises policy violates the intent of the ESA by disallowing wildlife officials from restricting land use should it become necessary to protect other species. Beissinger and Perrine, Chapter 4 of this volume, and Innes, Polasky, and Tschirhart (1998) discuss Habitat Conservation Plans in which the Clinton administration is including the no surprises policy.

- In February 1999, New York wildlife officials found the bodies of 800 double-crested cormorants (*Phalacrocorax auritus*), a federally protected but not listed species, which were shot on their nesting ground on Little Galloo Island in Lake Ontario. Officials suspect the birds' preying on smallmouth bass, which threatens the livelihood of bait shop owners, motivated the slayings.

- In March 1999, a coalition of environmental and Christian groups sued the USFWS and U.S. Department of Interior Secretary Babbit for refusing to designate critical habitat for seven species in California listed under the ESA.

- In May 1998, federal officials rejected a plan by Colorado to protect four endangered fish species in the Colorado River, stating that the plan left too little river water for the fish. A plan by the USFWS would keep more water in the river but was criticized by Denver water officials who argue it would hurt development in the western part of the state. See Watts et al., Chapter 10 of this volume, for a careful study of the benefits and costs of protecting these four fish.

- In February 1998, the New Mexico livestock industry filed two lawsuits, one to overturn the USFWS designation of 600 miles of critical stream habitat for the endangered willow flycatcher (*Empidonax traillis*), and another to overturn plans by the U.S. Forest Service to remove cattle from nesting areas of the same bird.

- In May 1997, U.S. District Court Judge Forester allowed timber sales to go forward in the Daniel Boone National Forest, but stated that his previous ruling, following a suit filed by environmentalists to stop a 199-acre timber sale, would stand because the habitat of the endangered Indiana bat (*Myotis sodalis*) would be jeopardized otherwise.

- In December 1994, the USFWS decided not to list the lynx (*Felis lynx*) as endangered although field offices admitted that only a few hundred remain in the lower 48 states. Thirteen environmental groups sued USFWS in January 1996, to force a listing, and U.S. District Court Judge Kessler in March 1997, ordered the USFWS to reconsider. In May 1997, USFWS announced that listing is warranted but precluded by lack of funds, and other species have higher priority. To date the lynx has not been listed. In Colorado, a listing would put at risk plans by the Vail ski resort to expand its slopes onto prime lynx habitat. In 1998, a clandestine organization calling itself Earth Liberation claimed responsibility for arson that destroyed several of Vail's buildings.

Table 1.3 shows the total number of court opinions in the United States between 1973 and 1995 by the species involved (from Cash et al., Chapter 19). The interest groups responsible for lawsuits and other actions are motivated by the trade-offs they perceive being fostered on them by the ESA. Some groups may envision their wealth or lifestyles being threatened by too many ESA mandates, while other groups may envision their natural heritage being

Table 1.3. *Number of court opinions on the ESA (1973–1995)*

Species	Number of court opinions
Eagle, Bald	78
Owl, Northern Spotted	70
Darter, Snail	70
Bear, Grizzly or Brown	61
Palila (Honeycreeper)	40
Wolf, Gray	21
Woodpecker, Red-Cockaded	21
Murrelet, Marbled	18
Crane, Whooping	17
Ocelot	15
Alligator, American	13
Tortoise, Desert (Mojave)	13
Whale, Bowhead	12
Whale, Humpback	12
Whale, Sperm	12
Bat, Indiana	12
Turtle, Green Sea	10
Whale, Right	9
Whale, Gray	9
Salmon, Sockeye	8
Squirrel, Mount Graham Red	7
Crane, Mississippi Sandhill	7
Pelican, Brown	7
Turtle, Loggerhead Sea	7
Cui-ui	7
Lion, Mountain	6
Owl, Mexican Spotted	6
Smelt, Delta	6
Trout, Lahontan Cutthroat	6
Wolf, Red	5
Plover, Piping	5

Source: D. Cash et al., "The Database on the Economics and Management of Endangered Species (DEMES)." *Protecting Endangered Species in the United States: Biological Needs, Political Realities, Economics Choices*. J. Shogren and J. Tschirhart, eds. Cambridge University Press, New York, 2001.

Table 1.4. *Total expenditures on endangered species. Federal and state governments (1989–1993)*

Taxonomic group	Federal ($ thousands)	All states ($ thousands)	Total ($ thousands)
1. Mammals	742,828.7	66,260.5	809,089.2
2. Birds	268,388.6	120,233.4	388,622.0
3. Reptiles	50,794.2	18,139.5	68,933.7
4. Amphibians	1,257.4	141.8	1,399.2
5. Fish	222,744.1	5,195.1	227,939.2
6. Snails	1,322.4	86.1	1,408.5
7. Mussels	7,533.3	1,145.4	8,678.7
8. Crustaceans	627.6	78.5	706.1
9. Insects	11,365.6	2,939.6	14,305.2
10. Arachnids	3,035.7	21.3	3,057.0
11. Plants	18,014.6	4,142.4	22,157.0
All Groups	1,327,912.2	218,383.6	1,546,296.0

Source: D. Cash et al., "The Database on the Economics and Management of Endangered Species (DEMES)." *Protecting Endangered Species in the United States: Biological Needs, Political Realities, Economics Choices*. J. Shogren and J. Tschirhart, eds. Cambridge University Press, New York, 2001.

jeopardized by too few ESA mandates. Meyer (Chapter 8) categorizes these trade-offs into: (i) economic activity, (ii) sense of community, (iii) political autonomy and local control, (iv) private property rights, and (v) community natural heritage. Categories (i) and (iv) are discussed at length in Chapters 10–13 and Chapters 14–17. Categories (ii) and (v) concern how local communities identify themselves and whether ESA helps protect or destroy that identity. A timber community in the Pacific Northwest may lose its identity if logging is halted to protect the spotted owl, or a Florida community that depends on tourists viewing endangered manatees (*Trichechus manatus*) may lose its identity if manatee numbers dwindle.

Category (iii) addresses communities losing control to state and federal governments. Although the federal government devotes a small portion of its budget to the ESA, the dollars it does spend can be overwhelming to local communities against ESA policies, or highly prized by local communities in favor of ESA policies. Table 1.4 shows spending by federal agencies on endangered species broken down by taxonomic groups. Because listing and habitat designation in the ESA are supposed to focus on science, one might hope that these funds are well spent in the sense that they are allocated according to the biological needs of preservation. However, according to empirical examinations by Cash (Chapter 7), funding is more consistent with theories of interest group politics and "pork" spending (also see Metrick and Weitzman 1996).

Because both political realities and biological needs guide ESA policies, understanding the political environment and identifying key variables that explain political choices can be enlightening and useful. Cash (Chapter 7) and

Ando (Chapter 6) apply econometric models to these ends. The authors show how the decision to list a species, and the time between proposing a listing and the actual listing, are determined in part by political variables. These political determinants include political party affiliations of the people living near the species in question, number of written comments received from people affected by a listing, environmental ideology of the U.S. senator on the interior subcommittee from the state the species inhabits, and the number of newsprint articles about the species. Institutions matter for effective species protection (also see Lueck 1995).

IV. ECONOMIC CHOICES

Political questions of listing and habitat protection ultimately come down to the fundamentals of decision making – accurately assessing the risks of extinction, weighing benefits against opportunity costs, and understanding impediments and incentives for voluntary species protection (also see the work of Ciriacy-Wantrup 1952; Krutilla 1967; Randall 1988). The need to understand these fundamental issues has pushed economics, whether welcomed or not, into the middle of the reauthorization debate. Why economic behavior needs to be better integrated into the ESA still puzzles many noneconomists who equate economics with financial and commercial concerns. The fact is that economics and conservation biology have the same underlying guiding principle – choice under scarcity. Better accounting for the basics of economic behavior in the formation of species protection policy can aid in reversing the trend that has often led to ineffective and, in some instances, counterproductive conservation policy. For example, a few days before USFWS listed the golden-cheeked warbler, a firm owned by Ross Perot hired workers to destroy hundreds of acres of oak and juniper – habitat to the warbler (Mann and Plummer 1995). Pointing out that we can save more species with fewer resources once economics is addressed may seem obvious to economists, but it is not to many people.

In this light, critical questions that must be addressed include deciding what policies can be adopted that satisfy biological needs while simultaneously decreasing costly interest group conflicts. If economic losses and restrictions on private property use brought on by satisfying biological needs are two major sources of political conflict, can we develop policies that mitigate the losses and lessen the impact of restrictions?

The message of Terry Anderson (Chapter 12) is that private markets can do more to restore and protect critical habitat. Government is not the only solution to preserving endangered species when those species have clear marketable value or when they share a habitat of species that have clear marketable value. Critical habitat that allows open access provides little incentive for anyone to preserve, but if the same habitat is in private hands, and if the owners can restrict access, then an incentive to preserve is created. For example, ranchers who reduce their cattle herds to protect habitat for elk (*Cervus elaphus*) or other big game animals may be more than compensated with hunting fees for harvesting elk. If endangered grizzly bears (*Ursus arctos*) use the same habitat, they too benefit.

Listing decisions and habitat protection must weigh benefits against costs. Assessing the costs of species preservation, while difficult enough, is usually less problematic than measuring the benefits. This is so in part because costs and benefits operate on different time scales – costs often are incurred immediately, while benefits accrue over decades. What are the benefits of saving the endangered Dehli Sands flower-loving fly in California? The costs have included $4 million to relocate the site of a new hospital in San Bernardino County. Many people probably would echo the words of Colton, California city attorney Julia Biggs: "I consider myself an environmentalist, but this is offensive to me. This is not some sylvan glen.... This is not a lion, tiger or bear. Or even an owl. This is a fly" (*Washington Post*, April 4, 1998).

Estimating the social value of endangered species is a challenge. When considering endangered species values, many people mistrust the primary tool used to measure these preferences – contingent evaluation surveys. These public opinion surveys use a sequence of questions to put a monetary value on personal preferences. But since people respond to a survey rather than facing their own budget constraint and actually spending their own money, no market discipline exists to challenge their statements. For instance, if one summed the stated preferences from various endangered species surveys as a crude measure of benefits, the average person was willing to pay about $1,000 to protect eighteen different species. Multiplying $1,000 by the number of U.S. households suggests that we would be willing to pay over 1 percent of GDP to preserve less than 2 percent of the endangered species (Brown and Shogren 1998). Many will find these values to be suspiciously high. Despite the challenge in measuring the value of preservation, determining a plausible range for these values is needed for helpful judgments. Coursey discusses these challenges in detail in Chapter 11. He uses government expenditures as a measure of this willingness, and contrasts his results to contingent valuation results on species values.

A far-reaching benefit-cost analysis is conducted by Watts et al. (Chapter 10) to examine critical habitat designation for four species of fish in the Colorado River. The authors point out that previous studies, such as those conducted for the spotted owl in the Pacific Northwest, have focused on losses to local industries, and this makes for catchy headlines. But the benefits and costs are often widely dispersed geographically, and a regional analysis is more appropriate. They find that while states in the upper Colorado River basin would experience losses owing to habitat designation, states in the lower Colorado River basin would experience offsetting gains. The difference in economic output for a region with and without critical habitat designation is relatively small, often measuring in the range of one-fiftieth of a percentage point. The impact of critical habitat designation on regional income, tax revenues, and employment is similar.

Much work remains in developing and implementing economic incentives for species preservation, especially with respect to instances when endangered species inhabit private property (Eisner et al. 1995; Bean 1999). Perhaps nothing is more controversial in the ESA debate than "taking" of private property for species preservation. Innes (Chapter 14), Polasky (Chapter 15), and Smith and Shogren (Chapter 16) all investigate different aspects of the private property conundrum. The problem is central because private land shelters numerous species at risk (U.S. Fish and Wildlife Service 1997). In a study of endangered species hotspots, Dopson et al. (1997) found endangered species clusters in a number of areas in which competing private land uses are very valuable, including Hawaii, coastal California, and southern and central Florida. The high costs of preservation in these and other areas will exist regardless of whether government pays for the land directly, or whether the costs are imposed on private landowners through "takings."

The "taking" issues arises under the Fifth Amendment to the U.S. Constitution, which ends with the words, "nor shall private property be taken for public use, without just compensation." Many scholars have debated the appropriate limits of this "takings" clause: Under what circumstances (and for what types of government actions) must compensation be paid? How much compensation must be paid? As it stands, the Endangered Species Act does not require compensation for private property owners who suffer financial losses from habitat protections on their land. But both law and jurisprudence are in a state of flux. A variety of legislative initiatives in recent years, some of which passed the full House of Representatives, have aimed at requiring compensation for government actions, including the ESA, that diminished the value of a private property by a minimal percentage, typically ranging from 20 to 33 percent.

Not compensating landowners for takings may prove to be very counterproductive for species preservation. Landowners may choose not to cooperate with government biologists who propose to inventory private lands for their habitat potential. Or landowners who know their property harbors endangered or threatened species may follow a "shoot, shovel and shut up" policy.

Based on the lessons learned during the conference "Endangered Species Protection and Social Order" that produced this volume, the contributing authors offer three reasons why economic behavior matters more to species protection than many people think (see Chapter 18). First, the decision to list a species as endangered can be improved by accounting for economic circumstances in species risk assessment. Human actions and reactions help determine risk and its consequences; omitting these factors from risk assessment can bias estimates of risk. Most people agree with one side of this argument. The common perception is that people's quest for development and commercial profits destroys habitat and endangers species – full stop, end of discussion. But this sentiment gives only half of the story. On the other side, people like nature, a preference that leads to the private creation or protection of habitat. Relative land prices and wealth influence private landowners' ability to set aside land for habitat protection. Risk assessment that does not account for private citizen and community response to wealth or relative land prices, as they make habitat preservation decisions, will underestimate risk in some regions and overestimate risk in others.

This fairly contentious point says that economics has a bigger role to play than helping find cost-effective solutions. We are saying that the biological sciences cannot ignore economic parameters in their models of risk – a point that is not obvious or acceptable to many people. But it is correct if you believe that economic and ecological systems are jointly determined. We are pointing out a problem of omitted variable bias that exists in the prevailing risk assessment–risk management bifurcation underlying ESA policy. One can justly characterize current ESA mindset as following three linear steps: (1) financial and commercial quests put a species at risk; (2) biology determines whether a species should be listed as endangered; and (3) economics then can be used to find cost-effective remedies to reverse this trend. We question step 2 – listing decisions based on only biology. We contend that the precision of species risk assessment can be increased by using both biological and economic parameters as determinants of endangerment. Whether the extra precision is worth the costs of more information is an empirical question.

Second, the benefits and costs of protection should frame the policy debate over species protection. Reality dictates that the net benefits of preservation be weighed against the net benefits of other important societal objectives. Even very intangible, difficult-to-measure values, such as moral imperatives to protect Earth's inhabitants, must be recognized. Policy makers and regulators already implicitly weigh benefits and costs. Explicitly incorporating more formal methods to help discriminate between and among species and other programs will provide greater openness and transparency in how we choose to rank listing decisions and implement recovery plans.

Third, species protection will be more effective by creating the economic incentives to implement the desired level of species preservation in a least cost manner. Economic incentive schemes can and have worked. Currently, the ESA provides some regulatory incentive for landowners to cooperate with species conservation policy through Habitat Conservation Plans – plans that allow a landowner to alter habitat under certain management restrictions. Making these schemes more cost-effective will require additional information on economic opportunity costs and biological effectiveness. But we also recognize that sometimes compensation is not enough – landowners want their privacy respected, their prior stewardship efforts acknowledged, and their ability to protect their investment flexible.

V. CONCLUDING COMMENT

As we begin the new millennium, many scientists believe that our biological systems could undergo profound and rapid changes resulting in accelerated extinction and the mutation of social order. As such, the protection of species at risk must remain a maxim of modern society. In the United States, Congress addressed species risk by enacting the Endangered Species Act twenty-five years ago. And while a quarter century is a short time to judge the overall effectiveness of the act, enough data and knowledge exist now to suggest how we can help improve the ESA in both listing decisions and recovery plan development. Better let it be said that we were not adrift in a sea of interest groups and political infighting, but rather that we used the best biological and economic knowledge we had to chart our course. In the chapters and commentaries that follow, the collection of well-reasoned authors helps us better understand what we know and why we must learn to protect endangered species more effectively.

References

Bean, M. 1986. The Endangered Species Program. Pages 347–71 in R. L. DiSilvestro ed. *Audubon Wildlife Report* 1986. New York: National Audubon Society.
— 1999. Endangered species? Endangered Act? *Environment* 41: 12–38.
Belovsky, G. E., Bissonette, J. A., Dueser, R. D., Edwards Jr., T., Lueke, C. M., Ritchie, M. E., Slade, J. B., and Wagner, F. H. 1994. Management of small populations: Concepts affecting the recovery of endangered species. *Wildlife Society Bulletin* 22: 307–16.
Benton, M. J. 1995. Diversification and extinction in the history of life. *Science* 268: 52–58.
Brown, G. and Shogren, J. 1998. Economics of the Endangered Species Act. *Journal of Economic Perspectives* 12: 3–20.
Carroll, R., Augspurger, C., Dobson, A., Franklin, J., Orians, G., Reid, W., Tracy, R., Wilcove, D., and Wilson, J. 1996. Strengthening the use of science in achieving the goals of the endangered species act: An assessment by the Ecological Society of America. *Ecological Applications* 6: 1–11.
Caughley, G. and Gunn, A. 1996. *Conservation biology in theory and practice*. London: Blackwell Science.
Ciriacy-Wantrup, S. 1952. *Resource conservation: Economics and policies*. Berkeley: University of California.
Clark, T., Reading, R., and Clarke, A., eds. 1994. *Endangered species recovery. Finding the lessons, improving the process*. Washington, D.C.: Island Press.
Crocker, T. and Tschirhart, J. 1992. Ecosystems, externalities and economies. *Environmental and Resource Economics* 2: 551–67.
Daily, G. C. 1997. What are ecosystem services? In G. C. Daily, ed., *Nature's Services*. Washington, D.C.: Island Press.
Daily, G. C., Alexander, S., Ehrlich, P. R., Goulder, L., Lubchenco, J., Matson, P. A., Mooney, H. A., Postel, S., Schneider, S. H., Tilman, D., and Woodwell, G. M. 1997. Ecosystem services: Benefits supplied to human societies by natural ecosystems. *Issues in Ecology* 2: 1–16.
Dopson, A., Rodriguez, J., Roberts, W., and Wilcove, D. 1997. Geographic distribution of endangered species in the United States. *Science* 275: 550–53.
Eisner, T., Lubchenco, J., Wilson, E. O., Wilcove, D., and Bean, M. 1995. Building a scientifically sound policy for protecting endangered species. *Science* 268: 1231–32.

Franklin, J. F. 1993. Preserving biodiversity: species, ecosystems, or landscapes? *Ecological Applications* 3: 202–05.

Gordon, R. E., Lacy, J. K., and Streeter, J. R. 1997. Conservation under the endangered species act. *Environment International* 23: 359–419.

Heywood, V. ed. 1995. *Global Biodiversity Assessment* (United Nations Environmental Programme), Cambridge University Press, Cambridge.

Hunter, M. L. Jr. 1996. *Fundamentals of conservation biology*. Cambridge, MA: Blackwell Science.

Innes, R., Polasky, S., and Tschirhart, J. 1998. Takings, Compensation and Endangered Species Protection on Private Lands. *Journal of Economic Perspectives* 12: 35–52.

Jablonski, D. 1991. Extinctions: A paleontological perspective. *Science* 253: 754–57.

Krutilla, J. 1967. Conservation reconsidered. *American Economic Review* 57: 787–96.

Losos, E. 1993. The future of the U.S. Endangered Species Act. *Trends Ecology Evolution* 8: 332–36.

Lueck, D. 1995. Property rights and the economic logic of wildlife institutions. *Natural Resources Journal* 35: 623–70.

Mann, C. and Plummer, M. 1995. *Noah's choice*. New York: Knopf.

May, R., Lawton, J., and Stork, N. 1995. Assessing extinction rates. Pages 1–34 in J. Lawton and R. May, eds., *Extinction rates*. New York: Oxford University Press.

Metrick, A. and Weitzman, M. 1996. Patterns of behavior in endangered species preservation. *Land Economics* 72: 1–16.

Myers, N. 1979. *The sinking ark: A new look at the problem of disappearing species*. New York: Pergamon Press.

— 1992. Tropical forests: Present status and future outlook. Pages 3–32 in N. Myers, ed. Tropical forests and climate. Dordrecht, Netherlands: Kluwer.

NRC (National Research Council). 1995. *Science and the Endangered Species Act*. Washington, D.C.: National Academy Press.

Nilsson, G. 1983. *The endangered species handbook*. Washington, D.C.: The Animal Welfare Institute.

Nott, M., Rogers, E., and Pimm, S. 1995. Modern extinctions in the kilo-death range. *Current Biology* 5: 14–17.

Perrings, C., Maler, K.-G., Folke, C., Holling, C., and Jansson, B.-O. 1995. *Biodiversity loss: economics and ecological issues*. Cambridge: Cambridge University Press.

Pimm, S. L., Russell, G. J., and Gittleman, J. L. 1995. The future of biodiversity. *Science* 269: 347–50.

Postel, S., Daily, G., and Ehrlich, P. 1996. Human appropriation of renewable fresh water. *Science* 271: 785–87.

Randall, A. 1988. What mainstream economists have to say about the value of biodiversity. Pages 217–23 in Wilson, E. O., ed. *Biodiversity*. Washington, D.C.: National Academy Press.

Roughgarden, J. 1995. Can economics protect biodiversity? Pages 149–54 in T. Swanson, ed. *The economics and ecology of biodiversity decline*. Cambridge: Cambridge University Press.

Scott, J. M., Csuti, B., Jacobi, J. D., and Estes, J. E. 1987. Species richness: a geographic approach to protecting future biological diversity. *Bioscience* 37: 782–88.

Shogren, J. ed. 1998. *Private property and the Endangered Species Act: saving habitats, protecting homes*. Austin: University of Texas Press.

Simpson, R., Sedjo, R., and Reid, J. 1996. Valuing biodiversity for use in pharmaceutical research. *Journal of Political Economy* 104: 163–85.

Souder, J. 1993. Chasing armadillos down yellow lines: Economics in the Endangered Species Act. *Natural Resources Journal* 33: 1095–139.

Stork, N. E. 1997. Measuring global biodiversity and its decline. Pages 41–68 in M. L. Peaka-Kudla, D. E. Wilson, and E. O. Wilson, eds., *Biodiversity II: Understanding and protecting our biological resources*. Washington, D.C.: Joseph Henry Press.

Tear, T. H., Scott, J. M., Hayward, P. H., and Griffith, B. 1993. Status and prospects for success of the Endangered Species Act: A look at recovery plans. *Science* 262: 976–77.

— 1995. Recovery plans and the Endangered Species Act: Are criticisms supported by data? *Conservation Biology* 9: 182–95.

Tracy, C., and Brussard, P. F. 1994. Preserving biodiversity: Species in landscapes. *Ecological Applications* 4: 205–07.

USDA (U.S. Department of Agriculture), Forest Service. 1995. *Wildlife, fish and sensitive plant habitat management*. Washington, D.C.: USDA Forest Service.

USFWS (Fish and Wildlife Service). 1990. Report to Congress: Endangered and threatened species recovery program. Washington, D.C.: U.S. Government Printing Office.

— 1994. Report to Congress: Endangered and threatened species recovery program. Washington, D.C.: U.S. Government Printing Office.

— 1997. *1996 National survey of fishing, hunting and wildlife – associated recreation: National overview*. Washington, D.C.

Vitousek, P., Ehrlich, P., Ehrlich, A., and Matson, P. 1986. Human appropriation of the products of photosynthesis. *Bioscience* 6: 368–73.

Wilson, E. O. 1992. *The diversity of life*. Cambridge, MA: Belknap Press of Harvard University Press.

PART 1

BIOLOGICAL NEEDS

CHAPTER 2

Endangered Thought, Political Animals
Boyd Gibbons

ALEXIS, WE HARDLY KNOW YE

In April 1997, the television network C-Span set out on a nine-month bus tour to retrace the travels and intellectual terrain of Alexis de Tocqueville. Television is seldom a medium for serious education, but here was an effort that has potential for opening our minds.

It was nearly 166 years ago that this twenty-five-year-old French aristocrat arrived in New York and set off by steamer, coach, horseback, and on foot to absorb and analyze the character of our nascent democratic society. Tocqueville did so with a clarity and eloquence unmatched by any other observer before or since. The painful irony is that his classic work is such a stranger to American education. We could make no greater progress against the momentum of specialization and fad in our institutions of higher learning than to require, as a condition of graduation, the study of Tocqueville's *Democracy in America*.

In this book on preserving endangered species, it is especially appropriate that we revisit Tocqueville, for we are engaged on yet another political issue of great weight that is being clouded by the struggle for public opinion, and it behooves us to understand why candor has such difficulty surfacing in American politics.

Tocqueville was a liberal in the true sense of the word, that is, a man passionate on the question of individual liberty, especially liberty of the mind. While there was much in American democracy that held his admiration, he was troubled by how majorities lead to a constriction on independent thinking. Here is what he wrote:

> In the United States the majority undertakes to supply a multitude of ready-made opinions for the use of individuals who are thus relieved from the necessity of forming opinions of their own ... it may be foreseen that faith in public opinion will become a species of religion there, and the majority its ministering prophet ... the majority raises formidable barriers around the liberty of opinion; within these barriers an author may write what he pleases, but woe to him if he goes beyond them ... His political career is

closed forever, since he has offended the only authority that is able to open it . . . He yields at length, overcome by the daily effort which he has to make, and subsides into silence, as if he felt remorse for having spoken the truth.

And then, in a sentence likely to shatter glass in the National Archives, Tocqueville concludes, "I know of no country in which there is so little independence of mind and real freedom of discussion as in America."

It seems to me that these constraints on free expression are equally as formidable within each interest group contending to become the majority. As positions harden and the grapeshot flies, it is a bravo and exceedingly rare voice that ever rims above the din of propaganda to question the assumptions of one's own faction. We may speak of compromise, but, in the political world in which we live – goaded on by a television industry caught up in celebrity, trivia, and exaggeration – we demonize to crush the opposition upon the altar of public opinion. Politics is for winning. This makes it difficult to shape sensible policy and find common ground for its support.

The real quandary of endangered wildlife – of all wildlife in America – is how to achieve their protection on private land. The stakes are profoundly high, the solution unclear, and yet open and civil discourse is as rare as some of the species. Property rights advocates claim that the Endangered Species Act (ESA) is science run amok through the Constitution, that any regulation to protect species is an unconstitutional "taking," that science is mostly suspect and extinction highly exaggerated, and that if the public wishes to protect species on private land, they had better well buy the habitat and pay full price.

Environmentalists tend to imbue the ESA with Biblical stature, proclaiming that the sky is falling, that humans cannot suffer the loss of a single species (for therein may lie the cure for cancer), that protecting endangered species cannot be a "taking," and that landowners deserve the severity of the law. Who wants to speak otherwise and get clobbered by one's peers? Farmers and ranchers can become ostracized from their groups – or seen as foolishly dreamy – if they argue for greater restraints on the plow and cow, and God help the environmentalist who openly questions the equity of the powerful law that has become so useful in stopping projects in the neighborhood.

In my experience, I have found that ESA, or something like it, is essential on large water projects, where political influence is often heavily arrayed against the environment, and on federal land projects, where the national interest coincides with national responsibility.

Nevertheless, on private land ESA inverts the roles of fairness. Instead of spreading the burden of protecting species across all the citizenry, ESA drops it almost entirely on the particular landowner whose property holds a listed species. There is not only little incentive for private landowners to protect species; the law even creates disincentives against voluntary conservation, and by protecting all species may eventually erode public support for wildlife diversity. The ESA was a bold initiative at a time when wildlife had little protection, and it is still about all we have. But twenty-four years of experience trying to protect species and their habitat by federal prohibitions largely on the use of one's private land exposes the weakness of imposing conservation without rewarding it.

On the pollution front, we have achieved a great deal of progress in creating public institutions, laws, and measurable reductions in pollution. Since the first great environmental awakening of the late 1960s and early 1970s, pollution control has commanded the agenda. The programs are not perfect – far from it – but there is at least some general agreement about means and ends. Yet because of the near absence of anything like a workable system of shaping land use and growth on the two-thirds of America that is privately owned, we still remain largely in the dark as to how to create an equitable and efficient means of conserving habitat and wildlife on private lands.

Into this vacuum stepped the ESA, allowing the federal government, among other things, to regulate land use for biological ends. ESA, however, is a clumsy and politically inept tool for shaping private land use across America, and in this respect an extraordinary use of federal authority. The federal government is simply too remote and ill-equipped to assume so vast a responsibility over all the myriad of private landowners. With our capability of rapidly transforming natural surroundings, it is not difficult to foresee a great deal of aesthetic and biological wreckage over the American landscape in the next fifty years if we don't think fresh now. To secure wildlife diversity across this nation against the inevitable press of development and growth, we will need to candidly reexamine how to integrate the public interest fairly and efficiently with the complex dynamics of politics, economics, science, and private land ownership. This is an undertaking so daunting as to make pollution control look easy, for at the heart of this political agony is democracy's eternal tension between private rights and public duty.

WHY WE CARE ABOUT SPECIES

The case for species is that they are the taxonomic reservoirs of the genetic diversity of life, the irreplaceable pools of uniqueness that have accumulated over hundreds of millions of years. Many of our medicines derive from plants and animals, and all that feeds and energizes us – including the oxygen we inhale – comes from the photosynthesis of green plants, which in turn are fertilized by nitrogen-producing microorganisms.

The current rate of species extinction is not comforting. In the last 500 million years, Earth has seen a number of mass extinctions of species, yet nothing at the rate and breadth now caused by human development of habitat – perhaps up to 1,000 times that which occurs, often by gradual changes in climate, over geologic time (Pimm et al. 1995; Jablonski 1991; May et al. 1995).

The rate of species extinction is no matter to take lightly, yet I must admit to discomfort over some of the arguments advanced on their behalf. Are we that dependent on every single species of life, when maybe 90 percent of all species that have ever lived on Earth have long since passed to extinction? I doubt it. We could probably extinguish many species in this country without an appreciable affect on the human lifespan. But quite apart from the ethics and stupidity of such behavior, who wants to live in that sterile an environment?

The premise of ESA is that species diversity equals stability of ecosystems, extinction is irreversible, thus all species must be saved. But this scientific premise obscures the more commanding claim on biodiversity that we too often shrink from admitting, much less advancing: the human yearning for beauty.

Far more than any material benefits that wildlife confer upon us, it is their beauty, the exquisite mystery of nature and life itself, that draw our affection – and, for that matter, the curiosity of scientists – to wild firings and the landscapes they animate. Cures for disease is only one reason we should care about wildlife. Bless the rosy periwinkle's contributions to oncology, but for too long we have leaned on the utility of species to justify their protection. Something far more powerful and inexplicable than utility is driving our passions and sentiments. Wild cranes in flight over a marsh are more than genetic diversity and physics on the wing; nevertheless the language of aesthetics can sound so effete to the practical American mind that political debate rarely admits its importance.

This is why no other environmental issue is more emotionally charged and deeply felt, and none is more intractable – knotted as it is to the larger issue of land use – than the protection of wildlife in danger of extinction.

IN THE FARMER'S BOOTS

While there are vast reaches of public lands particularly in the western United States, much of the habitat in this country on which wildlife depend for survival is privately owned land, from large corporate timberlands to farms and ranches, where decisions to saw, plow, or subdivide can have permanent consequences to wildlife. Unlike polluted air and water, which can be cleaned up, habitat converted to asphalt and cinder block is habitat irretrievably lost. And unlike water and air, private land is the antithesis of the commons, armored with property rights that are as culturally formidable as they are constitutionally fortified, and their regulation for the public good, such as by zoning, has been historically and tenaciously local.

Organizations like The Nature Conservancy, The Conservation Fund, and a growing number of local land trusts make the most of the tax code, altruism, and good bedside manner in helping convince private owners to donate, sell, and otherwise protect unique landscapes.[1] Government policy has only begun to tap the usefulness of such private efforts. Although important for such critical areas as refuges, government acquisition of habitat will always be a marginal tool, constrained by budgets and the social and political imperative

---

[1] The number of land trusts has doubled in the 1990s; they are currently protecting about 4.7 million acres in the United States according to a survey by the Land Trust Alliance, Washington, D.C.

that much of the rural landscape of this country should continue to remain privately owned.

Consequently, any public strategy for protecting endangered species must make common purpose with (and common sense to) the family who owns the meadow and the cows grazing there. To succeed, such strategies must be more than scientifically justifiable – they must be fair.

PROBLEMS WITH ESA

The ESA did not arise in a vacuum. With half the animals and a third of the plants eventually listed under ESA dependent on wet habitats, the United States had lost more than half of its wetlands (excluding Alaska); in California, nearly 95 percent were gone. ESA quietly became law in 1973 when the public was in high alarm about the condition of the environment, there were few laws and institutions for its protection, and there was a long history of local land use controls being bent to favor development of land at the expense of wildlife habitat. By expanding federal powers well beyond the traditional policing of migratory birds, however, Congress little appreciated the controversial nature of the extraordinary authorities it was investing in ESA.

In the day-to-day workings of this law, a landowner with listed species on his land may be required to buy as "mitigation" three or four (or more) times as much additional habitat as he proposes to alter. If this is real estate on the urban fringe, the costs can be considerable. To keep using his land without running afoul of ESA's prohibition against "take," the landowner may have to engage in the expensive and cumbersome process of a "Habitat Conservation Plan," requiring the biological survey of his property and extensive negotiations. A large developer may be able to pass on these costs in the price of house sales, but small businesses, and especially farmers and ranchers, more likely have to absorb the burden.[2]

As ESA imposes sanctions for its violation, it should not be surprising that in species-rich states like California, landowners look out on their fields and anticipate trouble rather than opportunity. Given the costs of mitigation, and with their lobby groups making the most of scare stories, farmers and ranchers genuinely fear entanglement with the statute, some of them plowing up their fallowed fields to preclude an endangered species from seeking refuge there. Their anger is especially acute if the listing was pushed – as it often is – by a group having a surrogate agenda.

MANNERS IN THE FIELD

The ESA has thrust federal wildlife officials into the cultural, economic, and political milieu of local land use decisions for which they are inadequately

---

[2] In Chapter 8, Meyer (2000) makes the case that the trade-offs engendered by the ESA fall on local communities.

trained, sometimes temperamentally unsuited, and often resented. That should come as no surprise. It is difficult to imagine a more extraordinary testing of the tensile strength of our federal system than to create national controls over the use of private land, robe the authority in scientific ermine, and hand the police power to the U.S. Fish and Wildlife Service.

Compared to engineering, the biological sciences are relatively new to American government, exceedingly more complex, and the pains of adjustment are evident. By and large, wildlife biologists seek their profession out of an understandable desire to be in the field studying the objects of their affection. They are not likely to study zoology and ecology out of a preoccupation with the human condition – and it is a rare university that prepares them for the political life of conservation. Consequently, biologists are inclined to view politics as the prostitution of science, and their attitude at the rancher's gate may show it.

Beyond the economic costs that ESA may impose on landowners, what deeply irritates the viscera of many farmers and ranchers is a belief that they are caught in the class divide between city and country. They tend to think of environmentalists – and the biologists who carry their water – as city people removed from the land who are unsympathetic with anyone trying to make a living from livestock and crops. This resentment is deep and underestimated in its power to retard the progress of wildlife conservation.

Environmental groups cling to the Fish and Wildlife Service as the regulatory cop: How else to stop projects they detest? In a different world, I wonder what advances we might have made in real conservation on private lands had the federal approach to protecting species on the rural estate been less penal and more like the services provided farmers by the former Soil Conservation Service. At least we would have matched like cultures, and reduced hostility on the farm.

THE CROWDED ARK

By protecting all species, ESA weighs down the political ark. As more and more species are listed, especially those like the Delhi Sands flower-loving fly that children do not tuck under their pillows as cuddly dolls, taxonomic egalitarianism can bring resistance to the law, if not ridicule. The National Research Council of the National Academy of Sciences has conceded that unless society is to preserve all taxonomic ranks of species and subspecies in trouble, we have to identify the significant groups of organisms. As difficult as that may be to do, it is worth trying.

The case for protecting all species is defensible as a scientific ideal, but carried to its logical ends this ideal strains the limits of effective government. The ESA has largely concentrated on birds and mammals, probably because these are the creatures most people care about. (See Coursey, Chapter 11, for evidence.) Yet science would likely admit to the greater importance of plants and the lower orders of organisms, and at that level, taxonomic discoveries and listings will eventually overload the political patience. Science may press the case for beetles, while the public embraces eagles. The landowner pleads for fairness, respect for his property rights, and relief.

We seem to have great difficulty in plain speaking about this, but when we attach social consequences to creatures, and apply police power to their conservation, they become, in the best sense of the adjective, political animals. Species protection is more than a scientific imperative; it is a choice about the public good. Aristotle defined that as politics, which he believed was humankind's highest calling, namely the improvement of society.

FINDING THE MEANS TO FAIRNESS

The first step in any rethinking of ESA should be to insist on equity for private landowners. This is tricky, as one can think of developers whose attitude about the land has all the sentiment of a casino – they can and should pay for conservation. Nevertheless, habitat is in trouble if farmers and ranchers have to carry virtually all the costs and restrictions. They must have incentives for conservation.[3]

Unfortunately, compared to pollution, research on economic solutions to habitat and wildlife conservation has been lightly occupied territory. Michael Bean at the Environmental Defense Fund has consistently explored economic incentives, and a few organizations like The Nature Conservancy, Resources for the Future, and The American Farmland Trust are now grasping the nettle, but on the whole, this subject has lacked academic cohesion and innovation, leaving the research diffuse and the larger problem unaddressed.

As all invention begins with the familiar, the known options range from direct subsidies (not likely these days) to those indirect, such as deductions, credits, and deferrals under the federal income and estate tax laws, and the trading of development rights and conservation credits, on out to the more conjectural ideas about insurance.

The limitations in using tax policy for conservation or any other social end is that its capacity for inducing desired conduct – as a deduction, a tax credit, or in tax deferral – is constrained by the particular circumstances of each taxpayer and the economic potential of the land. Although the Treasury resists use of tax law for social ends, especially if it diminishes revenues, various bills have been before Congress to ease the estate and income tax burden on lands being used to conserve wildlife at risk.

It took a number of years, and a considerable shift in thinking among environmental groups, before the trading of pollution credits was accepted as a valid way to reduce sulfur oxide emissions from power plants and thus reduce acid rain. Except for the experience of the New Jersey Pinelands Commission and some mitigation banking (mostly wetlands), however, the

---

[3] See Smith and Shogren (Chapter 16) and Innes, Polasky, and Tschirhart (1998) for discussions of property rights and takings issues with the ESA.

trading of development fights for protecting habitat has little widespread practice. Novelty and experimentation are desperately needed.

Although the Supreme Court has yet to clarify the extent to which ESA restrictions may be unconstitutional regulatory "takings," various bills have been introduced in the Congress to establish statutory takings schedules. By helping relieve ESA burdens on the landowner and more equitably placing the financial obligation on the general public, economic incentives could help lessen the pressures for such legislation, which strike me as inviting excessive bureaucracy and boundless litigation.

THE FEDERALIST PAUPERS

Federal preemption through the ESA continues to erode the functions of state wildlife agencies, and this is good for neither federalism nor for wildlife conservation. All that I have said about the difficulty of inserting biology into government and biologists into land-use decisions is as true of state agencies as it is of the Fish and Wildlife Service. Nevertheless, historically state wildlife agencies have managed resident species of wildlife, and their field staffs tend to have better working relationships with private landowners and a greater familiarity with local problems.

Federal agencies resist giving up their own primacy in ESA matters, arguing, not without some justification, that state officials are more susceptible to being compromised by powerful economic and political interests in the state. In the long run, however, a continued federal dilution of state authority over wildlife will only exacerbate the growing estrangement of private landowners from habitat conservation and weaken the sinews connecting citizens to their nearer government.

The federal government should delegate ESA authority to those states that have an effective conservation plan for endangered wildlife, authority to enforce it, and a range of tangible economic incentives to encourage private landowner cooperation. This gets administration somewhat closer to the ground, but of course doesn't answer the larger questions I have been raising. And it leaves local government, the great strength of our democracy that so interested Tocqueville, where it has been too long: bereft of revenues, attracted all the more to the siren of development, yet the one best opportunity for citizens to have a say in public matters that directly affect them.

FINAL THOUGHTS

I wish I had a clear solution to this puzzle, but I have not. My main purpose is to break down the rhetorical prison in which this subject places us, to offer a few modest observations, and, I hope, to stimulate some fresh thinking. To succeed, wildlife conservation must eventually suffuse our habits and manners. In many ways it has begun to, but time is not on our side, as growth has its necessity and momentum. In whatever ways our laws are shaped to conserve habitat on private lands, they must tie together wildlife with the interests of the landowner. We need a new economics, as we need a new politics.

At least by bringing candor to the debate, we may draw harmony out of dissonance, thereby tapping our nobler character, our generous passions, and arriving at a political resolution that bears with it an enduring moral energy.

References

Coursey, D. 2001. "The Revealed Demand for a Public Good: Evidence from Endangered and Threatened Species." Chapter 11 in *Protecting Endangered Species in the United States: Biological Needs, Political Realities, and Economic Choices*, eds. J. Shogren and J. Tschirhart. New York: Cambridge University Press.

Innes, R., S. Polasky, and J. Tschirhart. 1998. "Takings, Compensation and Endangered Species on Private Lands." *Journal of Economic Perspectives* 12 (Summer): 35–52.

Jablonski, D. 1991. *Science* 253, 754.

May, R., J. H. Lawton, and N. E. Stork. 1995. *Extinction Rates* (Oxford: Oxford University Press).

Meyer, S. M. 2001. "Community Politics and Endangered Species Protection." Chapter 8 in *Protecting Endangered Species in the United States: Biological Needs, Political Realities, and Economic Choices*, eds. J. Shogren and J. Tschirhart. New York: Cambridge University Press.

Pimm, S., G. Russell, J. Gittleman, and T. Brooks. 1995. *Science* 269 (July 21): 347–50; National Research Council, *Science and the Endangered Species Act* (National Academy Press, Washington, D.C., 1995).

Smith, R. B. W. and J. F. Shogren. 2001. "Protecting Species on Private Land." Chapter 16 in *Protecting Endangered Species in the United States: Biological Needs, Political Realities, and Economic Choices*, eds. J. Shogren and J. Tschirhart. New York: Cambridge University Press.

CHAPTER 3

A Market Solution for Preserving Biodiversity: The Black Rhino

Gardner Brown and David F. Layton

I. INTRODUCTION

Economic principles guiding human behavior have a minimalist role in the framing of the Endangered Species Act (ESA) in the United States (Brown and Shogren 1998). Its principles and procedures make sense only if the individuals adversely affected by the ESA simply acquiesce, making no effort to avoid the cost of compliance. Illustratively, if my land has habitat characteristics for a species about to be listed, regardless of the cost imposed on me by the listing, I will not remove the specific flora in order to preserve the value of my land which will be lost when the species is listed. Such an assumption is empirically false and the species are the worse for it (Brown and Shogren 1998; Mann and Plummer 1995).

The formal procedures taken to manage the black rhinoceros exhibit the same shortcoming. The consequence for the black rhino of disregarding economic incentives guiding human behavior has been profound, as we portray below. We show how fairly simple economic reasoning can be exploited to restore the black rhino population from its current endangered status. We hope this dramatic example of mismanagement and our antidote will lead to the inclusion of more economic reasoning in setting policies for managing endangered species in the future.

Recent years have witnessed a growing public antipathy toward trade in parts of popular animals, particularly megafauna such as the elephant and rhinoceros. Conservation groups such as World Wildlife Fund (WWF) and the International Union for the Conservation of Nature were instrumental in instituting a ban on trade in rhino horn since 1977 and a ban on ivory since 1989. The animals and products are listed in Appendix I of CITES, the Convention on International Trade in Endangered Species of Wild Fauna and Flora, a treaty in effect since 1975.

It may come as a surprise to economists to learn that the ban on ivory trade has been more successful than we might have expected. The reasons for

We thank the reviewers and editors for helpful comments.

Table 3.1. *Decline of Black Rhino Population*[a]

1960	100,000
1970	65,000
1980	14,000–15,000
1984	9,500
1985	6,000
1987	3,800
1991	3,450
1992	2,480
1994	2,162
1998	2,600

[a] Milliken et al. (1993), except for the most recent estimates. The 1994 estimate was obtained in interviews with the rhino specialist group, Mombassa, Kenya, 1994. See footnote 9 in the text for the source of the 1998 estimate.

success seem to be threefold. First, much of the demand for ivory was to produce tourist-type trinkets, for which there are many substitutes. Second, a continuous flow of gruesome pictures of hacked off heads of dead elephants poached only for their ivory, grieving family members of the dead standing with heads bowed, and the bonfire of ivory in Nairobi Park seem to have informed and shocked many, if not most, people to change their tastes. Third, WWF launched a successful research project to find a substitute material in color, texture, and feel for ivory piano keys.

In contrast, the ban on rhino horn trade has been disastrous for the African black rhino (*Diceros bicornis*). The population has fallen continuously and precipitously from around 65,000 to about 2,600 in two decades (see Table 3.1). Poaching rhinos has provided a ready substitute for formerly legal trade with the result that black rhinos are locally extinct over substantial areas in Africa. The reason for the ban's apparent success for ivory and failure for rhino horn is surprisingly simple. African rhino horn has no close substitutes. A very large fraction of the sales are used by millions in China and Korea as a traditional medicine, primarily to treat persistent fever.[1] Much horn has also been used for dagger handles in Yemen, which for cultural reasons seems to have few substitutes either. Demand is inelastic and real prices have risen by a factor of six or more since the ban was anticipated. The reward for poaching has increased faster than resources allocated to protect rhinos and capture poachers.

While increasing the quality and quantity of effort to reduce poaching is a theoretical solution, the fact is that the effort to date has been inadequate for the task.[2] Draconian measures such as shoot-to-kill (suspected poachers) have

[1] Traditional Korean medicine has sixteen rhino horn prescriptions; in Taiwan there are at least fifteen different horn medicines (Milliken et al. 1993).

[2] See Dublin, Milliken, and Barnes (1995). The most important outcome of this study has been the documentation of chronic and frequently dramatic declines in law enforcement operating budgets throughout the range states surveyed.

been introduced in Zambia, Zimbabwe, and Kenya (see Milliken, Nowell, and Thomsen 1993), but their effectiveness depends on the enthusiasm for administering the policy and on the expected rewards of the poaching activity.[3]

Our prescription for restoring black rhino populations to their former levels does not depend critically on increasing antipoaching activity. The costs of this policy largely have been incident on some of the poorest countries of the world. The benefits of saving endangered species almost certainly are located in the richest countries of the world. To be sure, this makes preservation more difficult. Nevertheless, if *productive* side payments from "us" to "them" have not occurred while the black rhino population plummeted by a factor of twenty-five, we see no reason to expect a reversal of the status quo.

The alternative approach to rhino conservation we utilize has previously been suggested by a number of authors. The basic idea is simple: Cut off the horns of rhinos. This can be accomplished without injury to the animal. Without their horns, there is little reason for poachers to kill rhinos. Fortunately, or unfortunately depending on how one views the problem, rhino horns grow back. Milner-Gulland, Beddington, and Leader-Williams (1992) first studied the problem, and the idea of using dehorning to deter poaching goes back at least to 1980.[4,5] The results of Milner-Gulland et al. (1992) suggest that since rhino horn is so valuable (at current world prices), poachers would poach rhinos more frequently than resource managers would wish to dehorn them, leading to the probable failure of dehorning as an antipoaching technique. Of course, it is recognized that even if dehorning wouldn't deter poaching, allowing the legal sale of dehorned rhino horn could still raise considerable funds for rhino protection.

An important feature in the debates about the profitability and efficacy of dehorning rhinos has been a failure to distinguish between the aggregate or macro impacts of dehorning many rhinos, causing prices to fall, and the impacts of dehorning a small population of rhino which would not cause prices to fall. The literature, written mostly by noneconomists, often has agents like poachers who face local prices acting as if they were the direct suppliers in wholesale markets. To get the story right, there must be both local and world markets, properly connected. Market structure cannot be assumed but must be consistent with observed facts.

---

[3] Milliken et al. (1993) estimate that in their study area there were 167 poachers killed and forty-eight wounded.

[4] See Milliken et al. (1993) for a discussion and history of the concept. Under the assumption of no poaching risk, Loon and Polakow (1997) assess the profitability of dehorning. Rachlow and Berger (1997) consider horn regrowth in white rhinos, and comment on dehorning intervals from the perspective of profit maximization and as a poaching deterrent.

[5] Naturally, calls for dehorning wild rhinos raise questions about dehorning's impact on rhinos. This has led to a raging debate over the biological implications of dehorning, if any, on rhinos and whether dehorning would actually deter poachers. See Berger et al. (1993); Berger, Cunningham, and Gawuseb (1994); Loutit and Montgomery (1994); Macilwain (1994); Berger and Cunningham (1994a,b,c).

We build a rigorously justified economic model of the world market for rhino horn that acknowledges the inelastic demand function for horn, recommends free trade, and supplies the market with horn at a price below the opportunity cost of the poachers. Our economic model consists of all the important actors, poachers, African range states, consumers, speculators, and the relevant data that each considers. This model allows us to see the macro impacts of a policy of allowing free trade in rhino horn supported by a dehorning effort that is large enough to support world demand at a price low enough to deter poaching.[6] To preview our results, we show that such a policy is in fact very likely to work. Before turning to the model, a few more details are necessary.

Substantial stocks of rhino horn are held by the African range states. Other inventories, relevant for the empirical analysis, are held by speculators located in Asian countries. Speculative stocks are held with the expectation that rhino horn is a nonrenewable resource because the population either will continue to decline or horn flows from existing stocks will be inadequate to meet demand at current prices. In either case, the return on speculative holdings is earned through the expected price rise. If these expectations are not fulfilled, holding speculative inventories at current levels cannot be a good investment. Suppose the African range states can credibly commit to a policy of drawing down their inventories and further augment the flow of horn by dehorning operations. Insofar as these policies have been imperfectly forecasted, the time path of horn prices expected by the speculators is wrong. Price will not rise as fast as they anticipated. Therefore, profit-oriented speculators will have to adjust to the changed expectations by bringing some of their inventories on the market.

Not surprisingly, we will show that horn price drops when the African range states behave strategically, and then rises at the rate of interest. The price for the inventory flows is the same for all parties and for this reason we treat the inventories from the range states and Asia as one. For present purposes, we assume that the African states act as if they purchased the inventories of the speculators. We could also have assumed that the speculators purchase the inventories of the range states. The policy consequences would be qualitatively the same in either case.

In recent years, managers of rhino populations have cropped their horns to dissuade poachers. Rhino horn cropped systematically adds to the annual supply. Finally, there is a substantial white rhino population whose horn is a perfect economic substitute for black rhino horn, and it turns out that white rhinos are a far more economical supply of African rhino horn. White rhinos can be dehorned alone, or in combination with black rhinos to keep the market price of horn at a strategically low level.

---

[6] See C. Fernandez and T. Swanson (1994) for a model with some of these features.

II. MODEL

Readers who prefer to read an explicit model should turn to Appendix 3.1. Let us start with inventories. Inventories are drawn down by sales and augmented by horn from dead or cropped rhinos. We imagine the African states can act in unity, not in competition. Most of the rhinos are in South Africa, Namibia, and Zimbabwe and the inventories currently are held mostly by South Africa; a smaller share is owned by Zimbabwe.

The horn-cropping feature is simplified in this analysis. One might treat horn cropping as a maximization problem in which the solution closely resembles the Faustmann approach to determine the optimal time to harvest trees because horn regrow (Milner-Gulland et al. 1992). However, this is not the correct approach in this model because under legal trade with cropping, rhinos are not scarce. In reality, the optimal quantity supplied can be met by minimizing the cost of harvest, achieved by letting the horn grow to its approximate maximum size in about six years. As it turns out, the estimated horn growth function is such that the practical results are insensitive to a reasonable range of dehorning times.

Rhino population dynamics is governed by a logistic growth function (Milner-Gulland and Leader-Williams 1992) whereby "population grows very rapidly when the population is small, and then the rate tapers off as the population increases." Losses occur as a result of natural mortality and poacher kill. African states and poacher kill both supply the market. In this model, poachers take on the role of agents and the African authority is the principal. Poachers are assumed to maximize profit in each period by selling their horn. The poacher is assumed to maximize revenue net of cost taking sales by the African states as known and given. The standard rule follows: Poach until marginal revenue = marginal cost. Obviously, if marginal cost is greater than the poacher's marginal revenue because the African states have supplied enough to drive price sufficiently down, then the poachers will be out of the picture.

African States

It is assumed that the African states want to maximize revenues from cropping rhino horn, less cropping costs and the cost of collecting horn from dead rhinos. This specification has the advantage of simplicity without doing much injustice to reality. It is doubtful that the African states possess very strong altruistic attitudes toward the consumers' surplus of foreigners. However, if the African states maximize profit, less horn would be sold, which slows the drawdown of horn inventories. That is good. Such a goal will imply higher prices charged and that could be bad for conservation if the higher prices attract poachers into the market. We can offset this outcome by introducing a willingness to pay more to have more rhinos preserved, reflecting the preferences of the rest of the world. Having done this, we have to crop horn strategically to keep horn yield so low that poachers will not have an incentive to enter. The rest of the world will then have to pay the African countries to keep prices low. Let us see whether the results of the simple objective function are agreeable before pressing for a revision to incorporate world preservation values into it. A more complete statement of the objective function is to maximize the present value of net willingness-to-pay, using some discount rate.

A Solution

Using standard intertemporal maximization procedures, we obtain two solutions. Case 1, which conservationists hope is empirically true, refers to the solution when inventories and cropping yields are high enough and rhinos grow fast enough so that there is never any poaching, $s_t = 0$. We show in the empirical section that this is true and limit our analysis to Case 1. Case 2 occurs when the supply of horn is inadequate to supply the market at prices low enough to keep poachers out for some periods.

There are two important management regimes for the rhino: the transition period when inventories are being drawn; and the steady state when the flow of rhino horn on the market, obtained from removing horn from rhinos dying naturally and cropped horn, is constant. A discussion of the steady state is a natural starting point.

Steady State

Rhinos start out at the initial low level, B_0, and grow to their steady-state level $B_T^* = \bar{B}$, the carrying capacity, after $\hat{T}$ amounts of time have passed.[7] $\hat{T}$ is routinely solved from the maximization procedure. Remember, poaching kill equals 0 in Case 1. Formally solving the model guides the steady-state price which is less than the threshold entry price of poachers, the condition for being in Case 1.

The steady economic state occurs when the flow of horn from natural mortality and from cropping, if necessary, reach a price just below the entry price of the poachers. The steady biological state occurs later, in general. Of course, in the steady state, inventories are a fiction because harvest equals sales. The maximization procedure also confirms standard reasoning that horn will be sold at a price which reflects the marginal cost of cropping horn or collecting it from dead rhinos when these activities occur. Since inventories represent an investment from an economic perspective, the only reason to make such an investment is that the price of sales from inventory must rise at the rate of interest. If this were not true, then the representative investor should divest some inventory and invest the proceeds where they will earn the market rate of interest. We label the annual value of a kilogram of horn in inventory λ_t and in this model it is the same as the price of horn on the

---

[7] Actually rhinos get very close to but do not achieve $\bar{B}$ in finite time.

market. Once inventories are exhausted, dehorning is used to supply the market. It is a routine calculation to determine the fraction of rhinos annually dehorned.

III. DATA

Much of the data needed to parameterize our model are not available in a form suitable for statistical analysis. This is not due to a lack of interest, as considerable effort has been made by rhino experts to describe all of the facets of the poaching crisis that has decimated rhino populations around the world. It is instead attributable to the fact that the trade in rhino horn has long been illegal, meaning that data have to be covertly acquired. When this is accomplished, the data are typically "best estimates" made by knowledgeable people as opposed to actual records that would support econometric estimation. Before the advent of the trade ban, there were some official records, but these have substantial gaps in coverage, and of course with customs data there have always been strong incentives to underreport sales so as to avoid duties. This does not mean that we can not build a model that represents what is known about the illicit trade in rhino horn. Quite a lot is known about rhino horn trade, but this knowledge is just more qualitative than economists would typically like. Next we describe how we generate parameters for our model. Importantly, despite the fact that there are uncertainties associated with parameter assumptions, the qualitative results of the model are robust.

Population Parameters

The intrinsic rate of growth (r) for rhinos is estimated to be 0.16.[8] The value of the coefficient which creates asymmetry in the growth function $\alpha = 7$, is estimated by Milner-Gulland and Leader-Williams (1992) drawing on analysis by Fowler (1984). By 1992, the black rhino population had fallen to 3,000 (Leader-Williams 1992). A more recent estimate is 2,600, which we adopt.[9]

Estimating the carrying capacity of the rhino population is a place where care and judgment are essential. Carrying capacity is the equivalent of a fixed factor that causes decreasing returns in a production function. In the biological production function for rhinos, the fixed factor is the land which is the source of the food supply. Rhinos actually and potentially are spatially distributed. The population dynamics in one area is independent of the population dynamics in another area. The empirical analysis requires a choice of the number of areas and the size for each one. One provisional solution is the following. From Leader-Williams' (1985) estimate of rhino density at carrying capacity in the

---

[8] Milner-Gulland and Leader-Williams (1992), drawing on data in Hall-Martin (1986) and Hitchins and Anderson (1983).

[9] From the International Rhino Foundation, Internet address www.rhinos-irf.org (citing IUCN/ SSC African & Asian Rhino Specialist Groups and T. J. Foose 1998).

Luangwa Valley, Zambia and data on elephant densities and population in that region (Milner-Gulland and Leader-Williams 1992, Annex 4), the rhinos at carrying capacity are estimated at 6,700. It is assumed that the goal is to restore black rhinos to a population of 67,000, which approximates the estimated population of 65,000 twenty-five years ago (Berger and Cunningham 1994c). Thus, we assume that rhinos will be restored in ten separate areas. Increasing the number of areas shortens the time until the goal is reached. Decreasing the density lengthens the time until the goal is reached. Suitable habitat to achieve this goal does not appear to be a binding constraint. Poaching, not habitat removal, is the source of the decline in black rhino population.

Inventories

Estimated stockpiles of horn held by the producing nations were about 3,600 kilograms based on data collected between 1980 and 1990 (Leader-Williams 1992). An updated estimate, considering additions to inventories by the Natal Parks Board, puts the current level at 5,200 kilograms.[10]

Stocks of rhino horn held by the consuming countries are less easy to document. Inventories held in Taiwan are estimated to be about 10,000 kilograms (Nowell, Wei-Lien, and Chia-Jai 1992). State medical corporations and manufacturers in China had an estimated 8,500 kilograms in 1992 and the private sector in China was believed to hold 4,883 kilograms (Milliken et al. 1993). If accurate, total world inventories of rhino horn exceeded 25,000 kilograms in the early 1990s. Over the remainder of the decade, stocks have been drawn down through consumption, but additions have no doubt been made through poaching. Further stocks are probably scattered throughout Yemen, Korea, and the rest of Asia. With this in mind, we use 20,000 kilograms as a rough estimate for world inventories. The qualitative nature of the results does not hinge on this assumption. If stocks are smaller, then dehorning simply begins earlier, and if stocks are larger, then dehorning can be delayed.

Poacher's Reservation Price

A potential poacher seeks another income-earning activity if the opportunity cost of poaching exceeds the expected benefits from poaching. If a policy lowers the returns from poaching such that the returns are lower than the expected costs, then poaching will cease. So the reservation price (or wage) for poaching rhinos is crucial to our analysis. Unfortunately, it is essentially impossible to come by. Instead, we use simple economic reasoning to suggest a reasonable number for the reservation price for poaching.

There should be relatively free entry into the market for poachers, and therefore poachers will be paid their opportunity costs. These costs will depend

---

[10] Personal communication with N. Leader-Williams, March 31, 1997.

upon three main factors: prevailing wages, antipoaching enforcement, and poaching productivity. Ascertaining prevailing wages in alternative employment seems straightforward enough, at least conceptually. Enforcement consists of two main components that are both hard to estimate: the probability of being caught and the severity of punishment. Punishment can range from fines, to jail time, to death, and the associated opportunity cost depends critically on the value of a poacher's life and risk preferences, neither of which is known. Finally, poaching productivity depends upon the population levels of rhinos, but also may depend upon the population levels of other relevant species such as elephants, and could be affected directly by enforcement as well.

Given the considerations above, we think it is unlikely that the poacher's reservation wage can be built up from data on each of the above factors, and instead use estimates of what poachers actually receive when they sell rhino horns to middlemen. This is not without its own difficulties, as some poachers are essentially paid wages with a bonus for delivering horn, while others self-organize and are only paid when they sell their horn. It is this latter group that will best shed light on the poachers' reservation wage. There are a number of estimates for the amount poachers receive for delivery of a rhino horn. Using figures from Milliken et al. (1993), we take the 1998 reservation price for rhino poaching to be $140 per kilogram.[11] Finally, one needs to relate this figure to the Asian wholesale prices upon which our demand curve is based (discussed below). The available evidence summarized in Milliken et al. (1993, Table 11, page 60), leads to the conclusion that poachers are probably not receiving more than 40 percent of the wholesale price. So in terms of wholesale prices, the reservation price is taken to be approximately $350 per kilogram in 1998 dollars.

Demand

Wholesale quantities purchased and prices paid by importing countries are available for four principal countries (Japan, Korea, Taiwan, and Yemen) for selected years during the 1951–1986 period (Leader-Williams 1992). These data include significant gaps, and do not cover the entire world market. Using these data would result in a very significant underestimate of world demand. The best qualitative estimates are that 8,000 kilograms of rhino horn were exported annually from Africa during the 1970s and that this number fell to around 3,000 kilograms annually during the early 1980s [Leader-Williams

[11] All monetary amounts are in 1998 U.S. dollars. This is the high end of the estimates listed on page 59 of Milliken et al. (1993), which we take to be most likely for a self-organized poaching gang. The low number would not appear to even cover the basic costs of a poaching trip, as described for instance by Milner-Gulland and Leader-Williams (1992), who parameterize models based on data collected in the Luangwa Valley, Zambia in 1985. Given that we desire numbers that are applicable across a variety of locales, and under different enforcement regimes than were in place in the Luangwa Valley in the early 1980s, we think it more prudent to use informed estimates of the prices that poachers receive for horn, and then consider the sensitivity of our results.

(1992), citing work by Martin]. These numbers are based on biologists' estimates of the number of rhinos poached during the period. To form a crude demand curve, we match these quantity estimates to average wholesale price during the period. Our underlying model is that at any point in time, all quantities traded should be traded at roughly the same price. Assuming that the prices of recorded trades were honestly reported, then we can use these prices as an estimate of average prices during the period. Using the weighted average of prices from 1969 to 1971 for Taiwan and Japan, and prices in Yemen from 1980 to 1984 from Leader-Williams (1992), we estimated that 8,000 kilograms were traded at about $168, and 3,000 kilograms were traded at a price of $1,351 (1998 dollars). Using this information, a simple isoelastic wholesale demand curve is parameterized as:

$$Q = 89160^* P^{-.47}$$

Cropping

Horn growth is believed (Milner-Gulland et al. 1992) to follow a von Bertalanffy growth curve used commonly in fisheries literature:

$$v(\tau) = \hat{v} \left(1 - \alpha_1 e^{-\alpha_2 \tau}\right)^{\alpha_3}$$
$$\hat{v} = 3\,\text{kg}$$
$$\alpha_1 = 0.8$$
$$\alpha_2 = 0.87$$
$$\alpha_3 = 3,$$

where $v(\tau)$ is the horn mass in τ years and $\hat{v}$ is the maximum horn mass. The von Bertalanffy growth function captures rapid, smooth growth at first and then the growth tapers off, which the following helpful calculations indicate.

	$v(\tau)$	$v(\tau)/\tau$
$\tau = 1$	.88	.88
$\tau = 2$	1.91	.96
$\tau = 4$	2.78	.70
$\tau = 6$	2.96	.49

The model to be empiricized requires that a choice be made about the fraction of the rhino population to crop annually. Recall that dehorning is a good idea if the price of horn exceeds the cost per kilogram of dehorning. The estimated cost falls with the number of rhinos dehorned at one time, rhino density, and the experience of the crew (Milliken et al. 1993). We use the lower estimates in Milliken et al. (1993) as dehorning costs have fallen since the first largely experimental dehorning efforts. This results in a figure of $395 per rhino (1998 dollars). To translate to a per kilo number, we need to know the rotation length. It will turn out that we can use a maximal rotation of six years, which for black rhinos yields 2.2 kilograms (2.96 kilograms times .75 as one can not take the whole horn).[12] For white rhinos, we assume the same basic growth pattern, but they yield more horn at any point in time. Milliken et al. (1993, p. 50) cite work in which fifty-nine white rhinos yielded 240 kilograms of horn, or approximately 4 kilograms per animal.[13] So at maximum rotation length, the marginal cost of dehorning in per kilo terms is $180 for black rhinos, and $99 for white rhinos (1998 dollars). Therefore, economic considerations dictate that white rhinos should be dehorned before black rhinos. For use in the analysis section, we note that there are currently more than 8,400 African white rhinos (in addition to the 2,600 black rhinos).[14]

IV. ANALYSIS

Instead of a fully faithful empirical analogue to the formal model in the Appendix, in this section we demonstrate that existing rhino populations and horn inventories are adequate to solve steady-state demand. We next check the solution for sensitivity to parameter uncertainty and then discuss the results. Our strategy is to find a "steady-state" solution, albeit at existing population levels. As stocks build up, however, horn available from natural mortality will become available and diminish the need for dehorning.

The derivation of the results can be described in the following manner. We first use the demand curve to find the quantity of horn that the world market demands at the poacher's reservation price (or just under the poacher's reservation price). This is the quantity that the African range state cartel must be able to supply in perpetuity in order to deter poaching. The next step is to determine if there are sufficient rhinos to supply the necessary quantity. As rhino populations will grow if poaching ceases, a sufficient condition is that the current rhino population is large enough. If it isn't, then one could do the much more complex calculation to check if the population will grow enough by the time the current inventory of horn is exhausted to supply the market with sufficient horn to maintain a price below the poacher's reservation price. Next we check to see if at the poacher's reservation price, there are sufficient rhinos to use the maximum rotation length. If this is the case, then this yields a fixed marginal cost of dehorning. Finally, if the marginal cost of dehorning is less than the poacher's reservation price, then the policy is profitable for the African range state cartel.

[12] 70–80 percent of the actual horn can be taken when dehorning without hurting the animal, as discussed in "Dehorning" by Dr. Mark Atkinson, from the International Rhino Foundation, Internet address www.rhinos-irf.org.

[13] These estimates are sufficient for our purposes. Should the need for a much more detailed analysis arise, Rachlow and Berger (1997) provide von Bertalanffy growth curves for white rhinos for horn size and basal circumference as a function of age for anterior and posterior horns for both sexes.

[14] From the International Rhino Foundation, Internet address www.rhinos-irf.org (citing IUCN/SSC African & Asian Rhino Specialist Groups and T. J. Foose 1998).

First we find the quantity of rhino horn demanded at the poacher reservation price of $350 per kilogram (in terms of wholesale prices). The wholesale demand curve yields 5,681 kilograms per year. Next we note that if we rotate the available 8,400 white rhinos on a six-year rotation, we can crop 1,400 white rhinos per year. This will yield 5,600 kilograms per year, leaving just 81 kilogram to be supplied by the 2,600 black rhinos. Using these numbers, we need to crop an additional 37 black rhinos per year, on a six-year rotation. The operation should be profitable as the marginal cost of dehorning the 1,400 white rhinos every year is $99 per kilograms and the marginal cost of dehorning the 37 black rhinos is about $180 per year, as compared to a price of $350 per kilogram. This would yield over $1.4 million per year in profits in addition to deterring poaching.[15]

In terms of sensitivity analysis, we see that we could have underestimated the marginal cost of dehorning significantly without affecting the fact that the policy should work. As long as the cost of dehorning is lower than the poacher's reservation price, then the policy is profitable for the African cartel. In terms of uncertainty over the poacher's reservation price, profitability is more sensitive than the ability of the policy to deter poaching. If we have underestimated the poacher reservation price, then the rhinos are in even better shape. If we have overestimated the poacher reservation price, then we need to defend an even lower price, which means delivering even more horn every year. The worst case scenario, which can still be supported by this policy, can be found as follows. Looking at the horn growth curve for black rhinos shows that a two-year rotation results in maximum yields of 1.91 kilogram per rhino, which after taking only 75 percent of the horn yields 1.43 kilogram per year. For white rhinos, if we assume the same pattern of growth and scale appropriately, we estimate about 2.6 kilograms per white rhinos.[16] At current population levels for both species, this will provide a total of 12,779 kilograms per year. This would drop the world wholesale price to $62. This indicates that we could very substantially have overestimated the poacher reservation price without endangering rhinos. Of course at this price, substantial subsidies would be needed to yield the necessary amount of horn.

In terms of demand sensitivity, we are doubtful that demand is much greater than we have used here, as it is based on the best estimates of rhino poaching as opposed to incomplete trade records. In fact, we suspect that consumptive demand is much lower, because rhino poaching has been supplying both large stockpiles as well as yearly consumption, and therefore our wholesale demand curve includes both stockpiling and consumption. Milliken et al. (1993) provides estimates of the yearly quantity demanded for China, Taiwan, and South Korea. The low end of the range for these three

---

[15] We do not discuss the transition to the steady state in quantitative terms during which inventories are drawn down. The transition likely is short, with demand exhausting inventories in a few years.

[16] We could use results from Rachlow and Berger (1997) to derive a more exact estimate.

countries yields 1,158 kilos per year, and the high ends equals 1,891 kilos per year. Adding in the 75 kilos estimated traded in recent years from Yemen (Martin, Vigne, and Allan 1997), would yield a total world demand of less than 2,000 kilograms. For a sense of our conservatism, note that at the recent Yemeni wholesale price of $982 (Martin et al. 1997), our wholesale demand curve suggests that approximately 3,500 kilograms would be demanded. The figure from our demand curve is 40 percent larger than sales estimated by rhino specialists. Either real demand is much lower than we are supposing or the real wholesale prices are much higher than is reported, but they would have to be off by a factor of two to yield 2,000 kilograms a year.

It appears that if anything, demand will be lower than indicated by our demand curve. This is excellent news for the policy, and to anyone with concerns about potential biological implications of dehorning. The work of Berger and Cunningham (1994a) suggests that one should avoid dehorning female rhinos when they are sympatric with predators. If we have overestimated the level of demand by a factor of two, then roughly speaking, we would only have to harvest horn from half of the currently available white rhinos on a six-year rotation. The other half could be left entirely alone. We very likely can avoid dehorning at least some of the white rhinos, and probably all of the black rhinos. As rhino populations grow, a smaller and smaller fraction would have to be dehorned.

So in terms of meeting market demand while deterring poaching, it is clear that we can do so. Further, we can probably achieve this while dehorning rhinos on a relatively long rotation of every six years, while still leaving a large and growing fraction of the population untouched. It also appears likely that significant sums of money could be raised to further support conservation activities.

V. CONCLUSION

The present policy for preserving black rhinos has never worked, for reasons that follow from first principles in economics. The trade ban on rhino horn has driven up the price of horn, making poaching profitable. Moreover, the demand for rhino horn is very unresponsive to price change, because much of the horn is used in traditional medicine. People are not quickly and easily persuaded to change medicines that doctors have prescribed to them and their family for times extending beyond living memory. There is a piece of economic discipline which has explained theoretically and documented empirically the grave difficulty encountered when efforts are made to control demand by legislative fiat. It rarely has worked, and the rhino population bears the loss because of this most recent folly, which replaced careful thought and fact with wish, however noble intentions may be.

We propose to save black rhinos by removing the ban on trade in rhino horn and to use the substantial stocks of existing horn inventories plus the cropping of rhino horn to drive down the price of horn. Drawing on various parameter estimates in the literature, always choosing "conservative" values, we estimate that a wholesale price of \$350 per kilogram (1998 dollars) or the equivalent of \$140 per kilogram received by the poacher is his reservation price. Inventories can be utilized to supply the market at and below this price. Given our conservative estimates of demand and recorded estimates of cropping costs, more than one-third of \$1 million in profit can be earned by cropping under 20 percent of the white rhinos and a handful (37) of the black rhinos, assuming no yield from natural mortality. While there is an obvious biological distinction between white and black rhinos, fortunately there is not an economic distinction inasmuch as the horn from either species is believed to be equally effective. With insignificant poaching pressures, the black rhino population could grow to more than 11,000 in ten years' time, or more than 30,000 in twenty years if there were population concentrations in ten areas as we have assumed.

If we allow a price low enough (\$62 per kilogram) to generate annual sales of about 13,000 kilograms, larger than any recorded in the literature, *current* rhino populations can meet the demand. The costs of cropping will not be covered by sales price in this special case, so the international community will have to cover the loss in order to save the black rhino. If the contribution is not forthcoming, the policy set forth above will have delayed the extinction of the black rhino. This is better than the current failed policy.

Far more likely, the strategic use of rhino horn inventories to drive out poachers and restore the black rhino population is an extremely attractive experiment with imperceptible downside risk. Its strategic introduction cannot cause more poaching. It will earn badly needed revenues for some of the poorest countries in the world. The results of the policy can be readily monitored because the market is now legal. Illegal markets are difficult to observe accurately. Sales can be tracked and the flows of horn can be adjusted, if necessary, as the accumulating years of observations grow.

APPENDIX 3.1

The model verbally discussed in the text is put more explicitly below.

Let us start with inventories, I, the linchpin of our model. Time subscripts are omitted unless necessary to avoid ambiguity. Inventories are drawn down by sales and augmented by horn from dead or cropped rhinos,

$$\dot{I} = -n + (\epsilon_1 m + \gamma v)B, \tag{A3.1}$$

where $\dfrac{dI}{dt} = \dot{I}$, I_0 known,

> $n =$ sales by African states authority,
> $B =$ black rhino population,
> $v =$ the horn per rhino (in kg) cropped,
> $\gamma =$ the fraction of the rhino population whose horns are harvested annually,

$m =$ the natural mortality rate of rhinos,[17]

$\epsilon_1 =$ the horn yield per rhino at death.

Rhino population dynamics is governed by a logistic growth function (Milner-Gulland and Leader-Williams 1992) less natural mortality (m) and poacher kill (ds):

$$\frac{dB}{dt} = \dot{B} = f(b) - mB - ds, \tag{A3.2}$$

$$f(B) = rB\left[1 - \left(\frac{B}{\overline{B}}\right)^{\alpha}\right], \quad r > 0, \ \alpha \geqslant 1, \tag{A3.3}$$

$r =$ intrinsic rate of growth,

$\overline{B} =$ carrying capacity,

$\alpha =$ a parameter introduced because of asymmetric growth. Maximum sustained yield does not occur at $\frac{1}{2}\,\overline{B}$ for black rhinos.

$s =$ total of poacher take (kg) and sales,

$d =$ reciprocal of horn weight per rhino poached.

From these definitions, the quantity (q) brought on the market by the African states and the poachers is

$q = n + s,$

and the inverse demand function is

$$P = g(q). \tag{A3.4}$$

In this model, poachers take on the role of agents and the African authority is the principal. Poachers are assumed to maximize profit in each period by selling their horn. Poacher total revenue is

$sg(n, s)$

and the total cost of harvesting s kilogram of horn is expressed simply as

$C(s) = cs.$

The poacher's maximization problem is

$$\underset{s}{\text{Max }} V(s) = sg(n, s) - cs \tag{A3.5}$$

---

[17] Insofar as there is mortality due to cropping, it can be absorbed into the estimate of m.

which is solved from

$$\frac{\partial V}{\partial s} = \psi(n, s) - c \leqslant 0, \quad s \geqslant 0$$

where $\psi(n, s) = g(n, s) + s\partial g(\cdot)/\partial s$. The poacher takes n as a known and given in this maximization problem. Whenever marginal revenue, $\psi(n, s)$, is below marginal cost, poaching activity ceases.

African States

African states maximize the total willingness-to-pay for rhino horn, less cropping costs,

$$G(n, s, B) = \int_0^{n^*} g(n, s)\, dn - c_1 \gamma B - c_2 Bm$$

where c_1 is the cost of cropping a rhino and c_2 is the cost of collecting horn from dead rhinos. See the text for more explanation.

More accurately, maximize the net present value of willingness-to-pay in (A3.6):

$$\int_0^{\infty} G(n, s, B)e^{-\rho t}\, dt, \tag{A3.6}$$

where ρ is the discount rate. The problem is reduced to maximizing the current value of the Hamiltonian,

$$\begin{aligned} H = G(n, s, B) &+ \lambda[-n + (\epsilon_1 m + \gamma v)B] \\ &+ \theta[f(B) - mB - ds] \\ &+ \mu[\psi(n, s) - c], \end{aligned} \tag{A3.7}$$

with variables λ, θ, and μ attached to the inventory, population dynamics, and poacher behavioral constraints respectively. The formulation places the African states in the position of a Stackleberg leader. In each period, the African states explicitly account for the impact of their activity on the poachers' optimal behavior.

A Solution

Key necessary conditions for this analysis are:

$$\frac{\partial H}{\partial n} = g(n, s) - \lambda + \mu(\psi_n(n, s)) = 0, \tag{A3.7.1}$$

written as an equality because a continuous interior solution with $n > 0$ is contemplated,

$$\frac{\partial H}{\partial \gamma} = -c_1 + \lambda v \geqslant 0, \quad \gamma \geqslant 0, \tag{A3.7.2}$$

$$\dot{\lambda} - \rho\lambda = -\frac{\partial H}{\partial I} = 0, \tag{A3.7.3}$$

$$\dot{\theta} - \rho\theta = -\frac{\partial H}{\partial B}$$

$$= -[-c_1\gamma - c_2 m + \lambda(\gamma v + \epsilon_1 m) + \theta(f'(B) - m)]. \tag{A3.7.4}$$

Assume inventories and cropping yields are high enough and rhinos grow fast enough so that there is never any poaching, $s_t = 0$.

There are two important management regimes for the rhino: the transition period when inventories are being drawn; and the steady state when the flow of rhino horn on the market, obtained from removing horn from rhinos dying naturally and cropped horn, is constant. In the steady state, rhinos start out at the initial level, B_0, and approach their steady-state level $B_T^* = \bar{B}$, the carrying capacity, after $\hat{T}$ amounts of time have passed.[18] $\hat{T}$ is obtained from solving (A3.2). Remember poaching kill $= s = 0$.

Since Case 1 requires an equilibrium without poacher activity because the market price is too low, the poacher's reaction function is nonbinding, so

$$\mu = 0.^{[19]}$$

Equation (A3.7.2) establishes the marginal value of horn,

$$\lambda^* = c_1/v, \tag{A3.8}$$

assuming cropping in steady-state equilibrium. The marginal value of horn establishes the level of African sales (n^*) from (A3.7.1):

$$P^* = g(n^*, o) = \lambda^*. \tag{A3.9}$$

---

[18] Actually rhinos get very close to but do not achieve $\bar{B}$ in finite time.

[19] When $\dot{\theta} = 0$, from (A3.7.4) and (A3.7.3),

$$\theta = \frac{(\lambda\epsilon_1 - c_2)m + (\lambda v - c_1)\gamma}{\rho - f'(B) + m}$$

if there is cropping and

$$\theta = \frac{(\lambda\epsilon_1 - c_2)m}{\rho - f'(B) + m}$$

if there is no cropping. θ is the marginal economic value of a rhino.

The inventory equation (A3.1) establishes the fraction (A3.8) of the population (B) to harvest annually since

$$n^* = (\epsilon_1 m + \gamma v)B.$$

Holders of stocks of inventory at the end of the transition period will have to receive exactly λ_T per unit; otherwise, arbitragers will enter to drive the value of inventories toward the market price, P^*. Necessary condition (A3.7.2) is used to determine the fraction of rhinos (γ) annually dehorned.

In the steady state, in fact, at all times, the value of μ, the adjoint variable on the poacher reaction function, equals 0 under Case 1.

Having solved for the steady state, the behavior of the system during the transition is straightforward. From (A3.7.3),

$$\frac{\dot{\lambda}}{\lambda} = \rho;$$

and solving to obtain

$$\lambda_t = \lambda_0 e^{\rho t}. \tag{A3.10}$$

Since λ_t has been computed from (A3.7.2), λ_0^* is solved from (A3.10). The price of rhino horn starts out at λ_0^* and grows at the rate of interest until it hits its steady-state value. Inventories are like a nonrenewable resource. More sales take place in the early years compared to later, as the inventory stocks are drawn to zero. Note that cropping does not occur while the inventories are being drawn down.

References

Berger, J. and C. Cunningham (1994a). "Phenotypic Alterations, Evolutionary Significant Structures, and Rhino Conservation." *Conservation Biology* 8: 833–40.

— (1994b). "Black Rhino Conservation." *Science* 244: 757.

— (1994c). "Active Intervention and Conservation: Africa's Pachyderm Problem." *Science* 263, March.

Berger, J., C. Cunningham, A. Gawuseb, and M. Lindeque (1993). "Costs and Short-Term Survivorship of Hornless Black Rhinos." *Conservation Biology* 7: 920–24.

Berger, J., C. Cunningham, and A. Archie Gawuseb (1994). "The Uncertainty of Data and Dehorning Black Rhinos." *Conservation Biology* 8: 1149–52.

Brown, G. M. and J. Shogren (1998). "Economics of the Endangered Species Act." *Journal of Economic Perspectives* 12: 3–20.

Dublin, H. T., T. Milliken, and R. F. W. Barnes (1995). "Four Years After the CITES Ban: Illegal Killing of Elephants, Ivory Trade and Stockpiles." A Report of the IUCN/SSL African Elephant Specialist Group.

Fernandez, C. and T. Swanson (1994). "The Role of a Controlled Rhino Horn Trade as a Means to Control Illegal Trade." Mimeo, University of Cambridge, November.

Fowler, C. W. (1984). "Density Dependence in Cetacean Populations." *Report of the International Whaling Commission* (Special Issue 6).

Hall-Martin, A. (1986). "Recruitment in a Small Black Rhino Population." *Pachyderm* 7: 6–7.

Hitchins, P. M. and J. L. Anderson (1983). "Reproduction, Population Characteristics, and Management of the Black Rhinoceros in the Hluhluwe/Corridor/Umfolozi Game Reserve Complex." *South African Journal of Wildlife Resources* 13: 78–85.

Leader-Williams, N. (1985). "Black Rhino in South Luangwa National Park: Their Distribution and Future Protection." *Oryx* 19: 27–33.

— (1992). *The World Trade in Rhino Horn: A Review*. Traffic International, Cambridge, UK.

Loon, R. and D. Polakow (1997). "A Conceptual Model for Assessing the Economic Feasibility of Harvesting African Rhinoceros Horn." *South African Journal of Science* 93: 237–40.

Loutit, B. and S. Montgomery (1994). "The Efficacy of Rhino Dehorning: Too Early to Tell!" *Conservation Biology* 8: 923–4.

Macilwain, C. (1994). "Biologists Out of Africa Over Rhino Dispute." *Nature* 368: 677.

Mann, C. and M. Plummer (1995). "Noah's Choice." New York: Knopf.

Martin, E. B., L. Vigne, and C. Allan (1997). *On Knife's Edge: The Rhinoceros Horn Trade in Yemen*. Traffic International Report, Cambridge, UK.

Milliken, T., K. Nowell, and J. B. Thomsen (1993). *The Decline of the Black Rhino in Zimbabwe: Implications for Future Rhino Conservation*. Traffic International, Cambridge, UK.

Milner-Gulland, E. J. and N. Leader-Williams (1992). "A Model of Incentives for the Illegal Exploitation of Black Rhinos and Elephants: Poaching Pays in Luangwa Valley, Zambia." *Journal of Applied Ecology* 29: 388–401.

Milner-Gulland, E. J., J. R. Beddington, and N. Leader-Williams (1992). "Dehorning African Rhinos: A Model of Optimal Frequency and Profitability." *Proc. R. Soc. Lond.* 249: 83–7.

Nowell, K., Chyi Wei-Lien, and Pei Chia-Jai (1992). *The Horns of a Dilemma: The Market for Rhino Horn in Taiwan*. Traffic International, Cambridge, UK.

Rachlow, J. T. and J. Berger (1997). "Conservation Implications of Patterns of Horn Regeneration in Dehorned White Rhinos." *Conservation Biology* 11: 84–91.

CHAPTER 4

Extinction, Recovery, and the Endangered Species Act

Steven R. Beissinger and John D. Perrine

I. INTRODUCTION

The Endangered Species Act (ESA) is one of the most important pieces of conservation legislation ever passed in the United States. This act grants a legal protection for plant and animal species and populations to persist. The Endangered Species Act of 1973, and its weaker precursors of 1966 and 1969, were passed at a time of unprecedented economic well-being and expanding civil rights in the United States. Perhaps it was that era and climate that afforded the opportunity to think and care about the future in ways that recent economic and sociological conditions now make it difficult to do. As we begin a new millennium, the United States is struggling to find its political, moral, and economic path, and it is struggling to reauthorize the ESA. Since 1992, the act has been temporarily funded on an annual basis because of a lack of a political consensus for weakening or strengthening it.

The United States is not the only country that has passed legislation to protect imperiled species. The European Union, several of its member nations, and the Australian state of Victoria also have legislation that prohibits the take of imperiled species and the destruction of their habitat (de Klemm and Shine 1993; Bouchet, Faulkner, and Seddon 1999). But the comparative strength, scope, and flexibility of the ESA has led to its description as "the most comprehensive legislation for the preservation of endangered species ever enacted by any nation" (U.S. Supreme Court 1978). The ESA, therefore, stands as a model to be emulated by other countries. Significant changes in the ESA, as a result of the congressional reauthorization process, will likely affect the future mechanisms for conserving biological diversity throughout the world.

This chapter will focus on three themes that are important for understanding extinction, the problems in recovering threatened and endangered species, and the ESA. First, we briefly examine the processes involved in endangerment that lead to either extinction or recovery. Second, we focus on what is known about threatened and endangered species and extinction in the United States. Finally, we discuss why the ESA must change from an act that mostly lists and protects species to one that actually recovers them.

II. THE PROCESS OF ENDANGERMENT AND EXTINCTION

All species, no matter how large their populations may be or how fast these populations have been growing, have a chance of becoming extinct. Catastrophic events, such as prolonged or intense droughts, floods, freezes, or even thermonuclear war or a meteor slamming into Earth may result in the death of all individuals of a population or species. Earth's fossil history is replete with examples of species that have disappeared despite enjoying wide geographic ranges and large population sizes (Jablonski 1991, 1995). The most likely estimates of 3–10 million species currently on Earth may represent only 2–4 percent of all species that have ever lived (May, Lawton, and Stork 1995).

The processes that lead to extinction are often difficult to observe. Processes that cause the local extinction (extirpation) of a population or the global extinction of a species are basically the same, except that species become extinct with the extirpation of the last local population (Andrewartha and Birch 1954; Lawton 1995). We can divide the general process of endangerment into three phases (Figure 4.1). Usually at some time in its history, the population will be near its carrying capacity. The Declining Phase occurs when the population experiences progressive declines. Populations throughout a species' range become very small, and individually they may either go extinct or recover. Often the rate of decline slows and the population may experience low numbers for many years or generations. During this Bottleneck Phase, the population's viability may decline due to a steady loss of genetic diversity. Populations that are reduced to smaller bottleneck sizes and

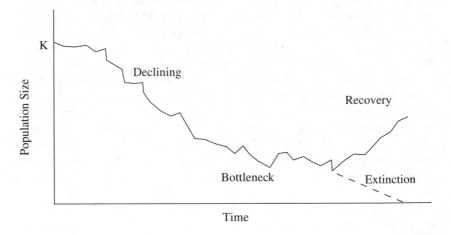

Figure 4.1. Phases in the process of endangerment, recovery, and extinction. At some time during the species' history, its population is near carrying capacity (K). Populations are reduced steadily during the Declining Phase, remain for a period of years or generations in the Bottleneck Phase where genetic diversity is eroded away, and then either recover or go extinct.

that spend more generations in a bottleneck will experience a greater loss of genetic diversity. Finally, the population may either increase to recovery (Recovery Phase) or go extinct.

Extinction is a complex process that can be caused by many factors acting independently or in concert. These forces are often divided into two general types. Deterministic forces such as habitat destruction, overharvesting, or pollution can greatly reduce a population in size and make it susceptible to extinction. Deterministic forces are often the "ultimate factors" that produce the Declining Phase of endangerment (Figure 4.1). Caughley (1994) called the actions of deterministic forces the "declining population paradigm."

Extinction is also caused by stochastic forces, which are chance events. Four main types of stochastic factors can affect the likelihood of extinction and have vastly different effects depending on population size: genetic stochasticity, demographic stochasticity, environmental stochasticity, and catastrophe (Shaffer 1981, 1987). Genetic stochasticity refers to the mortality and loss of fitness that can result from the expression of deleterious recessive genes resulting from inbreeding of close relatives, and the loss of genetic diversity that can occur from the random fixation of genes known as genetic drift. Genetic factors often have their greatest effect during the Bottleneck Phase of endangerment. Genetic stochasticity is primarily expressed when populations become reduced in size to thirty to fifty breeding individuals or less. Demographic stochasticity is the chance that normal birth and death processes will become unbalanced when populations are reduced in size. For example, twelve of the last thirteen surviving Dusky Seaside Sparrows (*Ammodramus maritimus nigrescens*) observed in the wild in 1979 were males (Ehrlich and Ehrlich 1981). Demographic stochasticity acts upon each individual independently and primarily affects vital processes that often take on a binomial distribution. For example, by chance the sex of newborns could become skewed, or by chance all adults may die from normal causes in a given year despite an average annual mortality rate of 50 percent. Demographic stochasticity primarily affects populations with less than fifty to one hundred individuals, when populations approach or are in the Bottleneck Phase of endangerment. Environmental stochasticity refers to the year-to-year variation in birth and death rates that naturally occurs, often as a result of changes in resources or weather. It affects populations of all sizes, but its effects are thought to diminish linearly as population size increases. For example, reproduction of the endangered Snail Kite (*Rostrhamus sociabilis*) is highly affected by year-to-year variation in water levels (Snyder, Beissinger, and Chandler 1989; Beissinger 1995). Catastrophes, like hurricanes, fires, extreme cold or heat, disease outbreaks, and the like, affect populations of all sizes. The effects of catastrophe diminish as population size increases but only to a point, because even large populations are susceptible to catastrophes (Mangel and Tier 1994). Chance catastrophic events are distinguished from environmental stochasticity primarily by the magnitude of their effects on vital rates. Catastrophes are not necessarily rare events but can occur regularly (Beissinger 1986, 1995). The role of stochastic factors in the process of extinction has been called the "small population paradigm" by Caughley (1994).

The demise of the Heath Hen (*Tympanushus cupido cupido*) in 1932, as reconstructed by Shaffer (1981) and Simberloff (1988), illustrates how stochastic and deterministic factors may often act in concert and become magnified once a population has been reduced in size. Once widespread and common in the sandy scrub-oak plains of northeastern United States, overhunting and habitat destruction were the two ultimate, deterministic factors that lead to the Declining Phase and caused this bird to be extirpated from the U.S. mainland by 1870. Only one population remained (Bottleneck Phase) on the island of Martha's Vineyard off the coast of Massachusetts, and by 1908, only fifty individuals were thought to remain in a 1,600-acre refuge. The population grew to 2,000 by 1915 (Recovery Phase) as a result of management to improve the habitat. But then two stochastic events greatly reduced population size. In 1916, a wind-driven fire killed many birds and destroyed their habitat; during the following winter mortality was probably high due to unusually harsh weather and an influx of predatory Goshawks (*Accipiter gentilis*). Thus, the effects of catastrophe and environmental stochasticity reduced the population again to 150 birds, mostly males. In the Bottleneck Phase once again, the population further declined in vigor due to demographic stochasticity from the skewed sex ratio and due to genetic stochasticity from inbreeding depression. In 1920, many birds succumbed to an exotic disease of poultry. By 1927, only thirteen Heath Hens remained, of which eleven were males (demographic stochasticity), and the last one died in 1932. Although hunting and habitat destruction, which had caused the original population decline, were minimized by 1908, catastrophes, environmental stochasticity, skewed sex ratio (demographic stochasticity), inbreeding (genetic stochasticity), and other chance events doomed the Heath Hen after it had been reduced to one population of relatively small size.

The fossil record provides an enormous, albeit incomplete, historical database on extinction. During the course of Earth's history, most species enjoyed long lifespans; the average time from origination to extinction varies from one to four million years for mammals to eleven to thirteen million years for marine invertebrates (May et al. 1995). There were five great mass extinction events in Earth's history, apparently caused by catastrophic events such as the impact of an asteroid or global climate change, where 70–95 percent of the extant species went extinct (Jablonski 1995). Despite the magnitude of these events, they account for only about 10 percent of all extinctions during geologic time (Jablonski 1995). A very rough estimate for the typical extinction rate from the fossil record, not including the five mass extinction events, is approximately one species per year (May et al. 1995).

Modern rates of extinction appear to be much higher than historic rates. Since 1600, approximately 485 animals and 584 plants have been certified as extinct (WCMC 1992). This yields an estimate of 2.67 species per year.

Table 4.1. *The number of species and number and percentage "at risk" for well-known taxa in the United States**

Taxonomic group	Number of species	Number of species at risk	Percentage at risk
Vertebrates	2,536	648	25.6
Mammals	418	69	16.5
Birds	776	113	14.5
Reptiles	278	50	18.0
Amphibians	242	98	40.4
Freshwater Fish	822	318	38.7
Invertebrates	1,795	581	32.4
Butterflies	600	101	16.8
Crayfish	330	168	51.0
Freshwater Mussels	305	207	67.9
Dragonflies	450	83	18.4
Tiger Beetles	110	22	19.9
Plants	16,108	5,292	32.9
Flowering Plants	15,447	5,144	33.3
Conifers	115	30	26.2
Ferns	546	118	21.5
Total	20,439	6,521	31.9

Source: Stein and Flack (1997).
* "At risk" species were determined by the Natural Heritage Network.

However, this figure certainly underestimates the rate of extinction. The great majority of extinctions were documented in well-known taxa like vertebrates, mollusks, and flowering trees. Documented extinctions of insects, the most species-rich taxa that may contain over 3 million species, are two orders of magnitude less than among vertebrates. Even for relatively well-known groups, rates of extinction are underestimates because of the stringent requirements for documenting extinction used by the International Union for the Conservation of Nature (IUCN). Also, nearly half of the recorded extinctions have taken place during this century (Smith et al. 1993), which may reflect an increasing rate of extinction and more attention focused on discovering species and documenting extinction. An even higher estimate of the current rate of extinction can be extrapolated from the rate of extinction of birds and mammals, two relatively well-known groups, during the past century. May et al. (1995) estimated the expected lifespan of the average bird or mammal species at about 10,000 years. This is about two to three orders of magnitude shorter than the average lifespan estimated for these groups from the fossil record.

Perhaps the most sobering way to examine the magnitude of the current situation is to examine the percentage of species thought to be at risk of extinction. Here we focus on recent information for well-known taxonomic groups in the United States produced by The Nature Conservancy and the Natural Heritage Network (Table 4.1). We analyze this list instead of the

Endangered Species List because the criteria for inclusion are more clearly defined and the inclusion of species was not subject to the political process that haunts listing under the ESA (see below). Incredibly, between one-half and two-thirds of the species of freshwater mussels and crayfish are at risk of extinction, along with one-quarter of all vertebrates and over one-third of the plant species considered. Even in the United States, where conservation efforts have been paramount, nearly one-third of the 20,439 species evaluated are at risk of extinction.

The previous analysis does not address how the number of imperiled species in the United States compares to other nations. Using slightly different criteria, the United States ranks sixteenth in terms of the number of imperiled mammals, ninth for birds, second for reptiles and amphibians, and first for fishes and invertebrates (IUCN 1996). These figures must be interpreted with caution, however, as countries differ greatly in size, numbers of species they support, and efforts invested in determining the status of their biological diversity.

III. WHAT IS AN ENDANGERED SPECIES?

The ESA includes two levels of protection for declining species, depending upon the imminence of the extinction threat. An "endangered" species is in danger of extinction throughout all or a significant portion of its range, whereas a "threatened" species is likely to become endangered within the near future. Species, subspecies, and distinct populations may be listed under the ESA as needed [ESA Section 3(15)]. This allows a species to receive different levels of protection in different portions of its range. For example, gray wolves (*Canis lupis*) in Alaska are not listed, while those in Minnesota are listed as threatened, and natural populations in Idaho, Michigan, and Wisconsin are considered endangered (USFWS 1996). Gray wolves recently reintroduced in Yellowstone National Park, Wyoming, Montana, and Idaho are legally considered to be an experimental population that was not essential to the survival of the species [ESA Section 10(j)]. When these individuals are on National Wildlife Refuges or National Park lands, they are treated as if they were listed as threatened; otherwise, they are treated as if they had merely been proposed for listing.

There has been a misconception that the Endangered Species List is dominated by subspecies and populations as opposed to full species. Actually, about 80 percent of the taxa listed or proposed for listing by 1991 were full species, and 20 percent were subspecies or populations (Wilcove, McMillan, and Winston 1993). Vertebrate subspecies are more likely to be listed or proposed for listing than invertebrate or plant subspecies: 80 percent of the birds and 70 percent of the mammals listed or proposed for listing were subspecies or populations compared to 5 percent of the mollusks and 14 percent of the plants (Wilcove et al. 1993). Nevertheless, some of the most contentious conservation problems revolve around listed subspecies such as the northern

Table 4.2. *Number of species listed under the ESA as of April 30, 1999**

Taxonomic group	Endangered U.S.	Endangered Foreign	Threatened U.S.	Threatened Foreign	Total species	Species with recovery plans
Vertebrates	228	513	93	37	871	255
Mammals	61	251	8	16	336	49
Birds	75	178	15	6	274	77
Reptiles	14	65	21	14	114	30
Amphibians	9	8	8	1	26	11
Fishes	69	11	41	0	121	88
Invertebrates	129	7	30	0	166	109
Snails	18	1	10	0	29	20
Clams	61	2	8	0	71	45
Crustaceans	17	0	3	0	20	12
Insects	28	4	9	0	41	27
Arachnids	5	0	0	0	5	5
Plants	568	1	135	2	706	522
Flowering Plants	540	1	132	0	673	494
Conifers	2	0	1	2	5	2
Ferns and Others	26	0	2	0	28	26
Total	925	521	258	39	1,743	886

*Eight species with separate U.S. populations listed both as threatened and endangered are tallied only as endangered. Recovery plans are tallied only for U.S. species.
Source: USFWS (1999).

spotted owl (*Strix occidentalis caurina*) and the Florida panther (*Felis concolor coryi*).

As of April 30, 1999, a total of 1,183 species occurring in the United States and 560 species occurring in other countries were listed under the ESA (Table 4.2). Of the species in the United States, approximately 78% were categorized as endangered and 22% were categorized as threatened. Foreign species primarily made it onto the list if they were endangered, as over 93% of the listed species found in other countries were ruled as endangered. For U.S. species, approximately 71% of the listed vertebrates, 81% of the listed invertebrates, and 81% of the listed plants were considered endangered. Plants account for approximately 60% of all U.S. listed species, whereas vertebrates and invertebrates represent approximately 27% and 13%, respectively. In comparison, over 98% of the species listed from outside the United States were vertebrates. Of the 321 listed vertebrate species found in the United States, approximately 34% are fishes, 28% are birds, 22% are mammals, and 16% are reptiles or amphibians.

Unlike other assessment schemes used by conservation organizations, such as The Nature Conservancy and The World Conservation Union (IUCN 1996), the ESA contains no explicit biological criteria to determine if a species is "threatened" or "endangered" (Rohlf 1991). Instead, Section 4(b)(1)(A) of the act merely stipulates that the decision should be made "solely on the basis of the best scientific and commercial data available." Despite the lack of explicit criteria, the number of surviving individuals of a threatened species at the time of listing is generally an order of magnitude higher than that for an endangered species of the same taxa (Wilcove et al. 1993). Median population sizes for threatened and endangered animals listed or proposed for listing as of 1991 were 4,161 and 515, respectively. The absolute population size, however, may differ significantly between taxa. Although no differences were detected between invertebrates and vertebrates, animal populations at the time of listing were significantly larger than the median size of threatened (2,500) and endangered (99) plants (Wilcove et al. 1993). Differences can also be seen for the number of populations remaining in the wild (Wilcove et al. 1993). Endangered and threatened animals had fewer populations (median = 2.5) compared to plants (median = 4).

IV. CAUSES OF DECLINE AND POPULATION TRENDS OF LISTED SPECIES

Four general causes are responsible for the decline of most listed species (Figure 4.2). Usually several factors may interact to cause a species to decline, so the categories in Figure 4.2 sum to more than 100 percent. Habitat

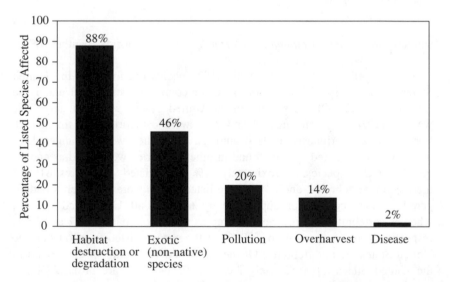

Figure 4.2. The percentage of U.S. species listings or listing proposals that cites a category of threat as a cause of imperilment. Categories sum to more than 100 percent because species are often affected by multiple, interacting threats. Data are from the Federal Register notices for all U.S. species listed or proposed for listing through 1995 and summarized by Wilcove et al. (1996).

destruction and degradation was the most prevalent category of threat, contributing to the decline of 88 percent of listed or proposed species (Wilcove et al. 1996). Within this category, rural/residential/industrial development was the most frequently cited cause of decline for listed plants, amphibians, insects, and arachnids. Agricultural development and modification of free-flowing waterways by reservoir construction also emerged as important causes of habitat destruction for virtually every taxon evaluated (Flather, Joycer, and Bloomgarden 1994; Flather, Knowles, and Kendall 1998; Wilcove et al. 1998). The effects of exotic species represented the second most prevalent cause of declines, threatening 46 percent of all listed species (Wilcove et al. 1996). Interaction with exotic species was the most common threat for fish and birds, and was tied with habitat destruction and degradation for arachnids (Flather et al. 1994). Pollution and overharvesting were noted for 20 percent and 14 percent of listed species (Wilcove et al. 1996). Disease was a factor in only 2 percent of listings. However, disease may be locally important, such as for Hawaiian birds (Wilcove et al. 1998), and its effects elsewhere may be underestimated due to the difficulty of detecting this cryptic factor.

The most recent comprehensive assessment of population trends for all listed species was compiled by the U.S. Fish and Wildlife Service (1996) in a summary report to Congress. Of the 943 listed U.S. species for which the U.S. Fish and Wildlife Service (USFWS) had jurisdiction at the time of the report, 8% were improving, 29% were stable, 35% were declining, and the status of the final 26% was unknown (Figure 4.3). Only 2% of the listed species had gone extinct in the wild, although this figure does not include seven species that were removed from the list because they were determined to be fully extinct. Several of these seven species, however, may have already been extinct at the time of their listing under the ESA (USFWS 1996).

In general, species that have been listed under the ESA for longer periods of time seem to have more encouraging population trends. Of the 108 U.S. species listed between 1968 and 1973, 58 percent were stable or improving by 1996, compared to 31 percent of the 294 species listed between 1989 and 1993 and 20 percent of the species listed between 1994 and 1996 (USFWS 1994, 1996). In some cases, the causes of decline have been addressed with some success for species that have been on the list for a longer time. The percentage of species with unknown population trends does not show such clear pattern over time. Approximately 29 percent of the species listed between 1968 and 1973 are of uncertain status, as compared to 41 percent listed between 1974 and 1978, and 33 percent listed between 1994 and 1996 (USFWS 1996).

Population trends also vary greatly among listed taxa (Figure 4.3). Almost half of listed vertebrate species were improving or stable, while 33 percent were declining. In comparison, slightly more than one-quarter of the invertebrate species were improving or stable and over half were declining. Approximately one-third of the listed plant species were improving or stable, roughly one-third were declining, and the status of the remaining third was

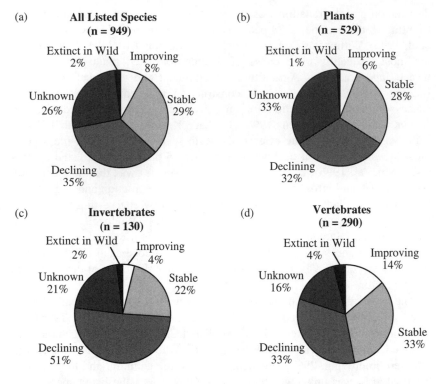

Figure 4.3. Population trends for listed species by taxa as of 1996. This analysis does not include sixteen U.S. species under the jurisdiction of the National Marine Fisheries Service as of 1996, nor species that had been removed from the list due to recovery, extinction, or new data indicating listing was not warranted. Data from USFWS (1996).

unknown. The percentage of species that have become extinct in the wild was approximately equal across taxa, ranging from 1 percent to 4 percent.

One of the primary goals of the ESA is to recover listed species to the point where the act's protections are no longer needed to forestall the threat of extinction [ESA Section 2(6), Section 3(3)]. The USFWS is required to develop and implement a recovery plan for each listed U.S. species. As of April 30, 1999, the service had finalized 519 recovery plans, which encompass approximately 75 percent of the listed species in the United States. Some plans address multiple species, and this approach has been implemented more often as the momentum for ecosystem management in conservation planning has increased. Also, some species have multiple plans addressing different portions of their ranges (USFWS 1999).

Despite these plans, relatively few species have recovered sufficiently to warrant their removal from the list of threatened and endangered species. Prior to 1998, less than a half dozen species had been recovered to the point of delisting. In comparison, seven species had been removed from the list due to extinction, as stated above, while at least eight had been delisted because the original listing data was found to be erroneous (Mann and Plummer 1995). But a relative surge of downlistings may be pending. According to the USFWS, at least a dozen species have recovered to the point where they could soon be removed from the lists of threatened and endangered species (USFWS 1996). The American Peregrine Falcon (*Falco peregrinus anatum*) was delisted in August 1999 amidst much fanfare, and similar actions have been proposed for the Bald Eagle (*Haliaeetus leucocephalus*), Aleutian Canada Goose (*Branta canadensis leucopareia*), Pahrump poolfish (*Empetrichthys latos*), Island night lizard (*Xantusia riversiana*), Virginia roundleaf birch (*Betula uber*), and several other species (USFWS 1996). Although recovery has not equaled the number of new species listed every year, it has apparently outpaced extinction.

V. WHERE ARE EXTINCT AND LISTED SPECIES FOUND?

Figure 4.4 shows the number of species that became extinct and the number of listed species currently found in each state. Historically, at least 110 U.S. species are known to have gone extinct and an additional 416 are presumed extinct (Stein and Flack 1997). Many of these extinctions occurred prior to the passage of the ESA. Species listings and extinctions, however, have much in common. Both occur most frequently in areas with high numbers of endemic species, high levels of human population growth, and high levels of anthropogenic habitat destruction, alteration, and fragmentation (Flather et al. 1994; Dobson et al. 1997; Stein and Flack 1997; Flather et al. 1998; Wilcove et al. 1998).

Hawaii has the dubious distinction of recording more extinct species and listed species than any other state. The small size of the Hawaiian Islands and their isolation produced a tremendous array of unique species, many of which were poorly adapted for the state's rapid human population growth and the introduction of exotic predators and competitors (Scott et al. 1988). California supports many endemic species, many of these plants adapted to the coastal Mediterranean climate that have been highly impacted by agriculture and urbanization (Flather et al. 1994; 1998). Florida ranks third in number of listed species but has suffered comparatively few extinctions to date.

Perhaps the "hotspot" location that most surprises observers is the Southern Appalachian region of Alabama and Tennessee, which ranks high in both listed and extinct species. Until recently, the hundreds of thousands of miles of rivers and streams in this region were home to one of the world's most diverse freshwater assemblages of mussels, crayfish, and freshwater fishes. Over the last century, construction of dams and water impoundments has disrupted hydrological regimes throughout the region, resulting in slowed water flows, increased sediment accumulation, and blocked migratory routes for fish species (Lydeard and Mayden 1995).

a) Extinct Species

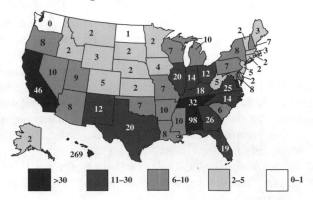

b) Listed Species

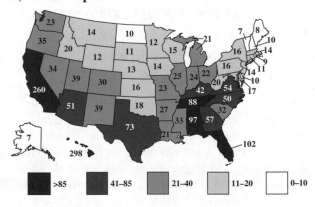

Figure 4.4. The number of global species extinctions and listings for each state in the U.S. State totals are not additive. *A*. Approximately 526 U.S. species may now be extinct, but many of these extinctions probably occurred prior to the passage of the ESA (from Stein and Flack 1997). *B*. The distribution of listed U.S. species as of May 31, 1999. Excludes whales and non-nesting sea turtle species occurring in state coastal waters, species listed due to "similarity of appearance" and some extirpated species (from USFWS 1999).

The Northeast, Midwest, and Great Plains regions of the United States have experienced relatively few extinctions and contain relatively few listed species (Figure 4.4). This is not to say that habitats in these areas have not been greatly altered. For example, of the original 58 million hectares of tall-grass prairie in the Midwest and Great Plains states, approximately 90 percent has been destroyed and the remaining portions are highly fragmented (Noss, LaRoe, and Scott 1995). However, these changes have not resulted in as many listed or extinct species as in other regions, because lower levels of endemism and retention of sufficient residual habitat likely prevented many extinctions (Pimm and Askins 1995). The Pacific Northwest has suffered relatively few extinctions and contains relatively few listed species. However, this region is probably in worse shape than these data indicate. An estimated hundred distinct populations of salmon and other anadromous fish are believed to have been lost even though few full species have gone extinct (Stein and Flack 1997).

State maps of species occurrence can give misleading impressions because most listed species do not occur throughout the state for which they are recorded. Unlike the Bald Eagle and American Peregrine Falcon, which are widely distributed and migratory, the ranges of many listed species are often reduced to small areas, sometimes even to only a single county. Forty-eight percent of the listed plant species have had their ranges so reduced that now they occur only in a single county, as do 40% of arthropods, 36% of birds, 31% of fish, 26% of mammals, 14% of reptiles and amphibians, and 57% of snails (Dobson et al. 1997).

There is little overlap in the distributions of most listed taxa. Nevertheless, two counties in California are hotspots for three taxa: San Diego County (fish, mammals, and plants) and Santa Cruz County (arthropods, reptiles, amphibians, and plants). Nine counties are hotspots for two taxa: four in Hawaii, two in California, two in Florida, and one in Georgia (Dobson et al. 1997). Conservation of these hotspots is likely to provide important benefits only for species whose range does not expand beyond these counties.

VI. THE IMPORTANCE OF LAND OWNERSHIP

The pattern of land ownership throughout the range of a listed species may influence the causes of its decline, as well as the potential for its recovery. Management for listed species is reasonably straightforward on federal lands because all federal agencies are required to avoid activities that would jeopardize the survival and recovery of listed species. However, the ranges of many listed species extend beyond the boundaries of federal lands (Table 4.3). Only 9 percent of the listed species are found exclusively on federal lands, whereas two-thirds of the listed species have most (> 60 percent) of their habitat on nonfederal lands. Fully one-third of listed species are found exclusively on nonfederal lands (USGAO 1994).

The proportion of federal versus nonfederal lands varies widely between states. For example, among the states with the greatest numbers of listed species, 45% of the land is federally owned in California, 16% in Hawaii, 9% in Florida, and 3% in Alabama (U.S. Bureau of Census 1996). Although these figures do not necessarily reflect the distribution of lands used by listed species in these states, it seems reasonable to assume that management and recovery strategies based solely on federal lands are likely to be insufficient.

Privately owned lands are the largest component of nonfederal land, which also includes state, county, city, and tribal lands (USGAO 1994). Over three-quarters of listed species occur at least in part on private lands, and

Table 4.3. *Percentage of listed species apportioned by the percentage of their habitat on nonfederally owned lands, as of May 1993*

Percentage of habitat on nonfederal lands	Vertebrates ($n = 276$)	Invertebrates ($n = 114$)	Plants ($n = 388$)
0	9.1	5.3	9.0
1–20	11.2	3.5	8.8
20–40	8.7	5.3	4.1
40–60	14.5	6.1	8.5
60–80	14.5	4.4	7.7
80–99	26.1	47.3	13.4
100	15.9	28.1	48.5

Source: U.S. GAO 1994; Wilcove et al. 1996.

seventy six listed species occur only on private land (Wilcove et al. 1996). In general, private lands may be more susceptible than federal lands to the dominant cause of species imperilment: habitat destruction due to agriculture, urbanization, and industrialization. Section 9 of the ESA prohibits taking of listed animals, but not plants, on private lands, but strict enforcement of this provision is rare. The vast majority of the legal actions undertaken by the U.S. Fish and Wildlife Service pursuant to the ESA involved the illegal import or export of listed species, with less than 3 percent of violations involving illegal taking of listed species within the United States (USGAO 1994). Although habitat modification and destruction can be considered a "taking," it is arguable whether this provision can be enforced so that it confers significant benefits to listed species (Bean 1998).

Under the current law, private landowners may have little incentive to manage their property for the survival and recovery of listed species (Bean and Wilcove 1996). Landowners, fearing that land-use restrictions would accompany any listed species on their lands, might actively destroy habitat on their property or passively refrain from activities that could benefit listed species (Bean 1998). A comparison of population trends, based on species listed as of May 1993, suggests that listed species occurring exclusively on private lands are faring worse than those occurring exclusively on federal lands (Table 4.4). Of the listed species found exclusively on federal land, more than half were improving or stable, compared to only 22 percent found entirely on private lands. However, these results are not particularly conclusive because they are affected by another more important trend: The status is unknown for more than half of the species found entirely on private lands, compared to only 15 percent found entirely on public lands. It is unlikely that "ignorance is bliss" for these species. Instead, it becomes almost impossible to recover them without being able to determine their status or implement field recovery programs.

Table 4.4. *Comparison of the status of listed species occurring exclusively on federally owned and privately owned lands as of May 1993**

Status of listed species	Federally owned lands ($n = 66$)	Privately owned lands ($n = 75$)
Improving	18	3
Stable	39	19
Declining	28	27
Unknown	15	51

* Species with habitat on both federally and nonfederally owned lands (e.g., privately owned lands, state or local government lands, and lands owned by Native American groups) were excluded from this analysis. "Privately owned lands" exclude lands owned by nonprofit conservation groups.
Source: Wilcove et al. (1996).

Although most threatened and endangered species are found on both federal and nonfederal land, private lands and therefore private landowners are crucial for the survival and eventual recovery of many listed species. Conservation of hotspots for listed species on private lands may be especially critical. As Bean and Wilcove (1997: 1) stated, "Conserving rare species on privately owned land is the most challenging and politically volatile aspect of the U.S. Endangered Species Act. It may also be the most important task facing conservationists."

VII. TOWARD AN ESA THAT RECOVERS SPECIES AND ECOSYSTEMS

The ESA has provided an important safety net for species whose numbers and populations have been reduced to very small sizes. Dedicated recovery efforts by field biologists (e.g., Snyder and Snyder 1989) and ESA provisions prohibiting take have probably been the difference between survival and extinction for many species, and these species might never have received such attention if not for the ESA. Nevertheless, less than a dozen listed species have recovered sufficiently to be delisted, while a nearly equal number have left the list due to extinction. These statistics, however, do not entirely reflect the ESA's successes. Several listed species are now widespread and plentiful, and have populations that are no longer threatened, such as the American alligator (*Alligator mississippiensis*) and Bald Eagle. Instead of celebrating delisting when species have recovered, some conservationists are hesitant to delist the species for fear that they will lose protection and public attention (Pagel, Bell, and Norton 1996; Cade et al. 1997; Pagel and Bell 1997).

There are several reasons why the ESA has been unable to fulfill one of its primary goals of recovering listed species. By the time most species were listed, their population size and number of populations were so greatly reduced that it becomes very difficult and expensive for field recovery efforts to diagnose and reverse the factors that caused the decline (Wilcove et al. 1993). Although the factors causing a species to decline often appear to be known, for many species the causes of imperilment are based on educated guesses and many factors are likely to be interacting (Flather et al. 1998; Wilcove et al. 1998). Delays in correctly identifying and reversing the causes of decline provide more opportunity for the synergistic effects of stochastic forces to erode a species' viability and increase its likelihood of extinction.

Rapid identification and reversal of the factors that caused species to decline have occurred for several listed species threatened by pollution, such as the Brown Pelican (*Pelecanus occidentalis*) and the Bald Eagle. Another example is the American alligator, which recovered rapidly once excessive legal and illegal hunting was reduced (Woodward and Moore 1995). In these cases, recovery was successful partly because the factors that limited population growth were properly identified and reversed relatively quickly by policy decisions to ban the use of organochlorine-based pesticides or to halt hunting and poaching. Implementing these policies strictly and on a large scale was relatively straightforward, especially as compared to regulating the protection of habitat for listed species. Regulation of habitat is often approached on a landowner by landowner basis, especially on nonfederal lands, rather than simultaneously considering the status of all private and public lands throughout the range of a listed species. This often creates problems in protecting species against the cumulative effects of development from many small projects in a region over time (Takekawa and Beissinger 1989).

It may be especially challenging to recover species that are threatened by habitat destruction or exotic species, the two most prevalent causes of endangerment (Figure 4.2). Restoring ecosystems and controlling introduced species are difficult, expensive, and time-consuming. Such situations may be exacerbated for species found mostly on private lands, because inadequate access and a lack of information hamper federal recovery efforts and private landowners may have little incentive to initiate such efforts themselves. Given the dominance of habitat loss as a factor that threatens nearly all listed species (Figure 4.2), it seems logical that protecting key habitats is essential to survival and recovery of many listed species. Critical habitat was incorporated into the ESA in 1973 to protect habitats of special significance in the range of listed species. Yet critical habitat has been declared for less than one-quarter of the listed species (Sidle 1987; Bean et al. 1991). Critics of critical habitat designation have suggested that not only is the process unruly, but the designation may not provide any more protection than is already accorded by the requirements of ESA (Sidle 1987; Bean, Fitzgerald, and O'Connell 1991). Hesitancy to establish critical habitat for listed species may be due primarily to politics, fear of land-use restrictions that come from the designation, and the potential for backlash to directly impact the safety of the listed species. Nevertheless, it is difficult to protect or restore habitats that are not designated as critical to the survival of the species.

Most listed species occur at least in part on private lands, but information on the status, trends, and management of these species on private lands may be difficult to obtain. As mentioned above, the ESA currently offers limited incentives for landowner cooperation or habitat conservation on private lands. One of the few provisions is Section 10(a) of the act, which permits landowners to destroy habitat for listed species and take some individuals of these species during the course of otherwise lawful activities, provided that the landowners develop and adhere to a plan to minimize and mitigate these impacts to the greatest extent practicable. The number of "habitat conservation plans," or HCPs, has grown greatly during recent years, from less than 15 prior to 1992 to over 425 during the Clinton administration under the leadership of Secretary of the Interior Bruce Babbitt (Karieva et al. 1998). These plans can serve as compromises, allowing the destruction of some habitat on private lands in exchange for the protection of other habitat that might have otherwise been lost as well (Bean et al. 1991). However, the scientific rigor of many HCPs has been questioned and concerns have been raised that these plans may actually facilitate destruction of habitat instead of protecting it (Honnold, Jackson, and Lowry 1997; Shilling 1997; Hood 1998; Karieva et al. 1998).

Providing incentives to increase private landowner participation in conservation activities is among the changes that have been discussed or proposed in relation to reauthorizing the ESA. Such incentives include: (1) reforms in the federal, state, and local tax codes to defray the costs to private landowners of keeping wildlife habitat intact (Williams and Lathbury 1996); (2) "safe harbor" agreements that allow private landowners to conserve, create, or improve some habitat for listed species on their lands in return for development of others and guaranteed freedom from additional obligations if more listed species are attracted to their lands; and (3) a "no surprises" policy that would provide landowners who develop HCPs the assurance that no additional land or financial requirements will be expected of them in the future regardless of any new biological information that may arise (Shilling 1997). With few exceptions, policy changes that increase incentives for private landowners to cooperate with recovery efforts and conserve the habitats of listed species are unlikely to handicap conservation efforts more than they already are on private lands. Nevertheless, it remains to be demonstrated whether these incentives will result in an increased recovery rate for listed species.

To move the ESA toward an act that recovers species, the listing process must begin before species have declined so greatly that they become vulnerable to extinction and difficult to recover (Figure 4.1). It is likely to be more cost-effective to prevent the loss of species than to recover them. Making long-term investments in preventive medicine for human health systems is cheaper than the costs of surgery, and the same may be true for managing biological diversity. Surgery in endangered species management takes the form of single species recovery programs that are often implemented as a reaction to crisis situations when a species' numbers become seriously low. Single species recovery programs often cost $50,000–500,000 a year and can run $500,000–1 million a year if captive breeding must be undertaken (Leader-Williams 1990; Derrickson and Snyder 1992; Snyder et al. 1996). Such programs will be absolutely necessary for recovering highly endangered species, but by their nature will conserve only a few species at a time.

On the other hand, a landscape conservation approach simultaneously considering the needs of tens or hundreds of species would be a proactive equivalent to preventive medicine. Landscape conservation approaches include the establishment of parks and reserves, conservation of corridors, designation of buffer zones, and the implementation of ecosystem management plans that comprehensively examine land uses throughout a bioregion. Landscape conservation approaches range in costs from modest planning efforts to more ambitious land and data acquisition campaigns. For the ESA to become cost-effective and result in delisting of more species, it must emphasize proactive approaches that can act as an exit on the road to extinction (Figure 4.1). Prelisting agreements have been developed for a handful of species to promote conservation without the increased regulatory burden associated with listing. In addition, developing a new listing category of "vulnerable" would allow such species to be considered in the economic and ecological impact analyses that comprise landscape conservation approaches before they reach the brink of extinction.

While they may act to prevent listing, landscape conservation approaches alone are unlikely to recover most listed species. The Heath Hen example recounted earlier in this chapter stands as a testament that species can go extinct even when their habitats are protected, if their population size has been greatly reduced. The ESA will need to provide more funds for reactive management to field recovery efforts if we hope to recover species to the point of delisting.

A renewed social commitment to conservation is required if the ESA is to prevent the extinction of hundreds of species in the United States. Relatively little is spent annually on implementing the ESA and only a percentage of these funds goes directly to recovery programs. The ESA cannot be expected to fulfill its goals without the funding it needs. In the long run, species are driven to extinction because of expanding human population growth and resource use. The ESA is a proximate solution that we hope can prevent most extinctions until we find ways to stem human population growth and to use our resources more wisely.

References

Andrewartha, H. G., and L. C. Birch. 1954. *The distribution and abundance of animals*. University of Chicago Press, Chicago.

Bean, M. J. 1998. The Endangered Species Act and private land: Four lessons learned from the past quarter century. *Environmental Law Reporter* 28: 10701–710.

Bean, M. J., S. G. Fitzgerald, and M. A. O'Connell. 1991. Reconciling conflicts under the Endangered Species Act: the habitat conservation planning experience. World Wildlife Fund, Washington, D.C.

Bean, M. J., and D. S. Wilcove. 1996. Ending the impasse. The Environmental Forum, July/August, 22–28.

Bean, M. J., and D. S. Wilcove. 1997. The private land problem. *Conservation Biology* 11: 1–2.

Beissinger, S. R. 1986. Demography, environmental uncertainty and the evolution of mate desertion in the Snail Kite. *Ecology* 67: 1445–59.

— 1995. Modeling extinction in periodic environments: Everglades water levels and Snail Kite population viability. *Ecological Applications* 5: 618–31.

Bouchet, P., G. Falkner, and M. Seddon. 1999. Lists of protected land and freshwater molluscs in the Bern Convention and European Habitats Directive: Are they relevant to conservation? *Biological Conservation* 90: 21–31.

Cade, T. J., J. H. Enderson, L. F. Kiff, and C. M. White. 1997. Are there enough good data to justify de-listing the American peregrine falcon? *Wildlife Society Bulletin* 25: 730–38.

Caughley, G. 1994. Directions in conservation biology. *Journal of Animal Ecology* 63: 215–44.

Derrickson, S. R., and N. F. R. Snyder. 1992. Potentials and limitations of captive breeding in parrot conservation. Pages 133–63 in S. R. Beissinger and N. F. R. Snyder, eds., *New world parrots in crisis: solutions from conservation biology*. Smithsonian Institution Press, Washington, D.C.

Dobson, A. P., J. P. Rodriguez, W. M. Roberts, and D. S. Wilcove. 1997. Geographic distribution of endangered species in the United States. *Science* 275: 550–53.

Ehrlich, P. R., and A. H. Ehrlich. 1981. *Extinction: the causes and consequences of the disappearance of species*. Random House, New York.

The Endangered Species Act of 1973 (as amended through the 100th Congress).

Flather, C. H., L. A. Joyce, and C. A. Bloomgarden. 1994. Species endangerment patterns in the United States. USDA Forest Service General Technical Report RM-241. U.S. Department of Agriculture, Forest Service, Fort Collins, Colorado.

Flather, C. H., M. S. Knowles, and I. A. Kendall. 1998. Threatened and endangered species geography. *BioScience* 48: 356–76.

Honnold, D., J. A. Jackson, and S. Lowry. 1997. Habitat conservation plans and the protection of habitat: Reply to Bean and Wilcove. *Conservation Biology* 11: 297–99.

Hood, L. C. 1998. Frayed safety nets: Conservation planning under the Endangered Species Act. Defenders of Wildlife, Washington, D.C.

IUCN – The World Conservation Union. 1996. Red list of threatened animals. IUCN, Gland, Switzerland.

Jablonski, D. 1991. Extinctions: a paleontological perspective. *Science* 253: 754–57.

—1995. Extinctions in the fossil record. Pages 25–44 in J. H. Lawton and R. M. May, eds., *Extinction rates*. Oxford University Press, Oxford.

Karieva, P. K., and the NCEAS HCP Working Group. 1998. Using science in habitat conservation plans. National Center for Ecological Analysis and Synthesis, Santa Barbara, California and the American Institute of Biological Sciences, Washington, D.C.

de Klemm, C., and C. Shine. 1993. Biological diversity conservation and the law: Legal mechanisms for conserving species and ecosystems. IUCN environmental policy and law paper number 29, IUCN – The World Conservation Union, Gland, Cambridge, U.K.

Lawton, J. H. 1995. Population dynamic principles. Pages 147–63 in J. H. Lawton and R. M. May, eds., *Extinction rates*. Oxford University Press, Oxford.

Leader-Williams, N. 1990. Black rhinos and African elephants: Lessons for conservation funding. *Oryx* 24: 23–29.

Lydeard, C., and R. Mayden. 1995. A diverse and endangered aquatic ecosystem of the southeast United States. *Conservation Biology* 9: 800–805.

Mangel, M., and C. Tier. 1994. Four facts every conservation biologist should know about persistence. *Ecology* 75: 607–14.

Mann, C. C., and M. Plummer. 1995. Is the Endangered Species Act in danger? *Science* 267: 1256–58.

May, R. M., J. H. Lawton, and N. E. Stork. 1995. Assessing extinction rates. Pages 1–24 in J. H. Lawton and R. M. May, eds., *Extinction rates*. Oxford University Press, Oxford.

Noss, R. F., E. T. LaRoe, and J. M. Scott. 1995. Endangered ecosystems of the United States: A preliminary assessment of loss and degradation. Biological Report 28. National Biological Service, U.S. Department of the Interior, Washington, D.C.

Pagel, J. E., and D. A. Bell. 1997. Reply to Cade et al. regarding de-listing the American peregrine falcon. *Wildlife Society Bulletin* 25: 739–42.

Pagel, J. E., D. A. Bell, and B. E. Norton. 1996. De-listing the American peregrine falcon: Is it premature? *Wildlife Society Bulletin* 24: 429–35.

Pimm, S. L., and R. A. Askins. 1995. Forest losses predict bird extinctions in eastern North America. *Proceedings of the National Academy of Sciences USA* 92: 9343–47.

Rohlf, D. J. 1991. Six biological reasons why the Endangered Species Act doesn't work – and what to do about it. *Conservation Biology* 5: 273–82.

Scott, J. M., C. B. Kepler, C. van Ripper, III, and S. I. Fefer. 1988. Conservation of Hawaii's vanishing avifauna. *BioScience* 38: 238–53.

Shaffer, M. 1981. Minimum population sizes for species conservation. *BioScience* 31: 131–34.

—1987. Minimum viable populations: coping with uncertainty. Pages 69–86 in M. E. Soulé, ed., *Viable populations for conservation*. Cambridge University Press, Cambridge.

Shilling, F. 1997. Do habitat conservation plans protect endangered species? *Science* 276: 1662–63.

Sidle, J. G. 1987. Critical habitat designation: Is it prudent? *Environmental Management* 11: 429–37.

Simberloff, D. 1988. The contribution of population and community biology to conservation science. *Annual Review in Ecology and Systematics* 19: 473–511.

Smith, F. D. M., R. M. May, R. Pellew, T. H. Johnson, and K. S. Walker. 1993. Estimating extinction rates. *Nature* 364: 494–96.

Snyder, N. F. R., S. R. Beissinger, and R. Chandler. 1989. Reproduction and demography of the Florida Everglade (Snail) Kite. *Condor* 91: 300–16.

Snyder, N. F. R., S. R. Derrickson, S. R. Beissinger, J. W. Wiley, T. B. Smith, W. D. Toone, and B. Miller. 1996. Limitations of captive breeding in endangered species recovery. *Conservation Biology* 10: 338–48.

Snyder, N. F. R., and H. A. Snyder. 1989. Biology and conservation of the California Condor. *Current Ornithology* 6: 175–263.

Stein, B., and S. Flack. 1997. 1997 species report card: The state of U.S. plants and animals. The Nature Conservancy, Arlington, Virginia.

Takekawa, J. E., and S. R. Beissinger. 1989. Cyclic drought, dispersal and the conservation of the Snail Kite in Florida: Lessons in critical habitat. *Conservation Biology* 3: 302–11.

U.S. Bureau of the Census. 1996. Statistical abstract of the U.S.: 1996. U.S. Department of Commerce, Economics and Statistics Administration, Washington, D.C.

U.S. Fish and Wildlife Service (USFWS). 1994. Report to Congress: Endangered and threatened species recovery program. U.S. Department of the Interior, Fish and Wildlife Service, Washington, D.C.

—1996. Report to Congress on the recovery program for threatened and endangered species. U.S. Department of the Interior, Fish and Wildlife Service, Washington, D.C.

—1999. [http://www.fws.gov/r9endspp/endspp.hmtl].

U.S. General Accounting Office (USGAO). 1994. Endangered Species Act: Information on species protection on nonfederal lands. GAO/RCED-95-16. U.S. General Accounting Office, Washington, D.C.

U.S. Supreme Court. 1978. Tennessee Valley Authority v. Hill. 437 U.S. 153, 180.

World Conservation Monitoring Centre (WCMC). 1992. Global biodiversity: Status of the Earth's living resources. Chapman & Hall, London.

Wilcove, D., M. Bean, R. Bonnie, and M. McMillan. 1996. Rebuilding the ark: toward a more effective Endangered Species Act for private land. Environmental Defense Fund, Washington, D.C.

Wilcove, D., M. McMillan, and K. Winston. 1993. What exactly is an endangered species? An analysis of the U.S. endangered species list: 1985–1991. *Conservation Biology* 7: 87–93.

Wilcove, D., D. Rothstein, J. Dubow, A. Phillips, and E. Losos. 1998. Quantifying threats to imperiled species in the United States. *BioScience* 48: 607–15.

Williams, C. E., and M. E. Lathbury. 1996. Economic incentives for habitat conservation on private land: Applications to the inland Pacific Northwest. *Wildlife Society Bulletin* 24: 187–91.

Woodward, A. R., and C. T. Moore. 1995. American alligators in Florida. Pages 127–29 in E. T. LaRoe, ed., *Our living resources.* U.S. Department of the Interior, National Biological Service, Washington, D.C.

CHAPTER 5

Some Economic Questions about the Biology of Biodiversity Protection: Comments on Gibbons, Brown and Layton, and Beissinger and Perrine

Thomas D. Crocker

I. INTRODUCTION

The three chapters the editors asked me to review are composed by specialists in biology, economics, and the law, but each casts its presentation in a multidisciplinary mold. Though the chapters are heterogeneous in intent and in content, the authors apparently could not make personal sense of the biodiversity issue without mixing their own discipline with other disciplines. Either they needed the other knowledge to implement their own knowledge or they could not resist the temptation that the biodiversity issue offers to fudge traditional disciplinary boundaries. This notion that a multidisciplinary perspective is the optimal way to think about environmental issues currently pervades both scientific and policy discussions (Arrow et al. 1995). Environmental issues are said to be broader than the content of any academic discipline. Federal funding of environmental research says so. Disciplinary mixing is therefore thought necessary to develop knowledge that will help society systemize and resolve these issues.

The form of disciplinary mixing differs widely among the three chapters. In Chapter 4, Bessinger and Perrine offer incidental remarks on morally appropriate worldviews toward the environment and on the design of environmental preservation incentive systems as they use their biological expertise to review succinctly the United States' biodiversity experience under its Endangered Species Act (ESA). In Chapter 2, a delightfully written essay, Gibbons, a lawyer with high profile, frontline federal and state bureaucratic experience in developing and implementing United States' environmental and land-use policies, artfully integrates an impressive array of biological, economic, and historical-political learning to compare the extent to which the ESA and its implementation on the ground reflect the public interest or the special interest theories of government. In Chapter 3, Brown and Layton provide the most technical of the three chapters. They make obvious the merit of at least one

Comments by Mark Agee, Greg Hayward, and the editors have improved the content and the presentation of this chapter.

form of a multidisciplinary perspective, where by merit is here meant that the introduction of prior knowledge from other disciplines lends precision to the insights the tools of one's own discipline can provide an issue. In order to support empirically their unique economic explanation of the sources of population decline of the black rhino and the relative efficacies of alternative policy instruments to restore that population, these authors had to apply quantitatively explicit biological knowledge about black rhino population dynamics and qualitative ethnological information on the medicinal and decorative uses of the rhino horn. Otherwise they could not make their economics do its work very well. Their empirical results would have been less precise and the policy suggestions that followed could well have been counterproductive.

Though the social delights of a multidisciplinary approach to environmental issues are surely widely promoted and funded, questions are rarely asked about how the appropriate mix of the academic division of labor varies with the structures of the research problems the issues raise. Bessinger and Perrine choose a form that allows them to apply their biological knowledge in an uncompromising fashion to the biodiversity issue, while offering asides upon suitable economic incentives and moral correctness for the same issue. One hopes that no reader attaches equal credibility to these two treatments. Gibbons uses an overarching theme, the tension between special interest and public interest government inherent in the U.S. political system. As only an adroit and shrewd editorialist and teacher can, he mines selected knowledge from a variety of disciplines to grow reader worries about the larger societal consequences of special interests who favor biodiversity while also arguing that others should pay for it. Brown and Layton adopt a form their discipline – economics – dictates. They use received biological, economic, and institutional knowledge to construct a choice set for agents interested in the black rhino and they assign reasonable motivations to these agents. Having thus constructed their problem, they use selected analytical and empirical tools of their discipline to solve it in a fashion that even economics skeptics must respect. Their seminal research will require any skeptics who continue to believe economic analysis has little if anything to offer black rhino preservation to justify rather than simply assert this position. The defense will now be intellectually taxing.

Not one of these three chapters suggests that interventions in other disciplines by its particular disciplinary home can change the basic terms on which the other disciplines approach their research problems. If only by default, each chapter firmly advocates intellectual specialization. The authors assiduously avoid any hint of involving themselves in designing the research activities of disciplines not their own. Their approaches are indeed multidisciplinary, but only in the sense that one cannot do good resource and environmental economics if one knows only economics. Other disciplines such as biology and the law must inform the economics. The identical point holds for the resource and environmental aspects of biology and the law. To work with environmental problems like biodiversity so good academic manners and tradition would have it, one must know what other relevant disciplines do and the "solidly verified" results and insights they can provide for one's own work. In principle, if not in practice, consilience is good (Wilson 1998), but one must never question what these other disciplines do or instruct them how they may sometimes do it better.

This reviewer feels that these three chapters adhere too faithfully to this code. All authors could have contributed more to our grip on the trade-offs and complementaries on matters of social order and endangered species by also probing the intellectual supports for perceived disciplinary boundaries. The next section describes some of the boundary supports the authors could usefully have probed, with particular attention to the implications of alternative biological perspectives and their associated models for the operational meaning and the societal value of biodiversity. My perspective is that of an economist trying to understand how biological models affect the terms on which his own discipline addresses the biodiversity issue. Whatever their disciplinary origin, models are metaphors, and one should know any limits to and ambiguities about their terms of use rather than taking the models at face value. Biologists appear to have had considerably more influence on the terms with which people from other disciplines, like economics, have joined the biodiversity issue, but other disciplines seem to have had little systematic influence on the biologist's terms. The focus of the next section is therefore on cautions other disciplines should exercise in passively letting biologists set terms.

As Gibbons suggests, one must look in the right place for a problem. Because of ambiguities in biology about where to look, why we should care about what we find, and how we get it when we find it, other disciplines must be circumspect about what biological information they insert into their own analyses of the biodiversity issue. Causal images are guides for what can and should be done, but the causal images that biology generates about the sources of and the consequences of biodiversity change are ambiguous guides about what to do, what to blame, and what to change. A third section speaks to conditions under which the mutual mixing of biology and economics would likely add positively to our knowledge of the place of biodiversity in biological and economic systems. A summary and conclusions follow.

II. BOUNDARY PROBING

Biodiversity is the Holy Grail of modern commentary on environmental policy, even though Loucks (1985), Ludwig, Hilborn, and Walters (1993), Peters (1991), Westmann (1990), and other leading ecologists are openly skeptical of unvarnished generalizations about what biodiversity is and how it behaves.[1] It is no small wonder then that the three chapters under review

---

[1] Biodiversity is mostly a local phenomenon, so efforts to protect it must be tailored to local circumstances. The tailoring may well require policies which sustain rather then discourage applications of intuitive, unsystematic, historical, local knowledge about the behavior of neighborhood habitats (Agee and Crocker 1998). Developing the capacity to use this local, unlettered knowledge may be integral to preserving biodiversity.

mostly beg these questions. Bessinger and Perrine remark that taxic biodiversity can be defined as numbers of types present at any one place along a multidimensional hierarchy of life forms and the intertemporal and spatial connections among them, including genes, phyla, species, habitats, and ecosystems, though these authors opt for species diversity in most of their discussion. They never mention exactly why – except for the ESA legal fiat – more richness of types, however placed in the hierarchy, is always a good thing. The word biodiversity appears only in the title of Brown and Layton. This title implies that preventing the extinction of the black rhino will enhance biodiversity, and that therefore preserving this animal will be a worthy act, given that the direct costs of doing so are not excessive. These authors probably need not have made the biodiversity connection since the black rhino's romantic appeal in the Western world is sufficient to justify taking action to enhance the continuing viability of its populations. Only Gibbons wonders about the uncontested intellectual status of the value of any biodiversity enhancement whatsoever. In addition to weighing the direct costs of enhancement, he asks that biodiversity advocates put less destabilizing pressure on the body politic by admitting that there are bad as well as good species when humans are allowed to be part of nature. Some species are just plain bad (e.g., the HIV virus), while others might be bad in particular contexts (e.g., bats in one's belfry). He then raises the crux of the matter: Though individual species may be valued for their intrinsic uniqueness, their use values and their life support contributions, what is it that a collection or aggregate of species which constitutes a degree of biodiversity provide? He suggests stability of nature and leaves the matter to rest, then to discuss the gross asymmetries in cost burdens between those who profess to value species' protections and the landowners who end up paying for it via governmental restrictions on their land-use discretion. Under the ESA, the beneficiaries of species preservation can treat biodiversity enhancement as more or less a free good. They have little incentive to enter arcane debates about the analytical and the empirical foundations of the positions they advocate. Yet the debates are hot and the side one chooses can structure the questions asked.

The biodiversity that has evolved into existence at any time and spatial scale is the result of natural selection. Those forms and traits "best" adapted to their abiotic and biotic environment are sorted for or selected.[2] Initial conditions and random events along the way determine what ultimately remains. Biologists have achieved consensus neither on how natural selection works

---

[2] This statement hides at least two difficulties. First, selection is held to preserve, from one generation to the next, the better adapted of the available variations in forms and traits. It thus narrows the formerly available domain of variations (Eldredge and Grene 1992). That is, it narrows biodiversity and restricts the domain of variations on which further selection can work. Second, organisms and their environments can be jointly determined (Lewontin 1983). Adaptation can mean actively adapting one's environment as well as passively adapting to an existing environment.

nor on the management and operational principles, which follow. At the level of the paradigm, they dispute whether evolutionary change is "punctuated," in which it proceeds in short bursts of random, unpredictable change (Gould 1986), or whether it moves in a steady, continuous fashion (Williams 1966). To the unpracticed eye, punctuated change suggests more fidelity to a given steady biodiversity state over some time interval than does continuous change. A propensity toward greater discontinuity hints at a different ability to withstand shocks than under a regime of continuous change. Moreover, if evolutionary change is truly unpredictable in the sense that not even a probability function can be adequately characterized, then it is hard to see what is being accomplished by protecting current biodiversity.

Again at the paradigmatic level, biologists are ambivalent about whether gene reproduction alone (Trivers 1985), or gene reproduction interacting with whole organisms (Fablonka and Lamb 1995), or even ecosystem survival through organismic interactions in the acquisition of matter and energy (Johnston and Gottlieb 1990) drives adaptation – genotypic evolution versus phenotypic evolution. These differences can confuse the outsider about exactly what biodiversity protection involves. The differences also may invoke very unlike strategies for managing biodiversity. Genetic reductionism uses a metric for biodiversity that is the number of groups of actually or potentially (organisms may migrate) interbreeding populations of organisms. Matter and energy reductionism employs the physical and perhaps the behavioral characteristics that organisms share in Darwin's (1979 [1859]) "struggle for life." Obviously, one kind of diversity may change while the other is unchanged: A Wyoming toad may go extinct but there are numerous amphibians who share similar physical characteristics and behavioral habits. One saves the toad if only genes matter; one lets go of the toad if plenty of organisms with its physical and behavioral characteristics are available.

To connect biodiversity to ecosystem performance, most biologists profess a close linkage between biodiversity and ecosystem resilience. A resilient ecosystem state is robust – it better accommodates surprises and shocks than does a less resilient state. Loss of resilience is especially damaging because it makes irreversible losses of adaptation options more likely, implying that shocks to the environment are progressively magnified (Gundersson, Holling, and Light 1995). Holling (1973) used the idea of resilience to describe the ability of a dynamic multispecies ecosystem to keep its structure when stressed.[3] However, biologists disagree whether biodiversity accentuates or attenuates ecosystem resilience. May (1972) says that high biodiversity implies species specialization, thus greater interdependence among species, and hence less resilience with more species. Rodgiguez and Gomez-Sal (1994)

---

[3] Resilience is not stability. Holling (1973) points out that some ecosystems are unstable because population densities vary over wide ranges. These same systems may be highly resilient because they persist in spite of these population variations.

provide empirical support for this hypothesis. Holling (1986) argues the opposite: When one species is lost, having more remaining species increases the likelihood that a remnant species will pick up the ecosystem functions of the lost species. Empirical validation of this thesis is found in Tilman, Wedin, and Knops (1996).[4] The factors, if any, that might flip an ecosystem from behaving in accordance with May (1972) to behaving as Holling (1986) says or vice versa are not evident, though King and Pimm (1983) suggest that disparities in species populations may play a role.

These two opposing different perspectives carry over into the specifics of biodiversity–ecosystem linkages and therefore into the details of management strategies for endangered species. For example, consider that dimension, habitat fragmentation, which Bessinger and Perrine rightly say can endanger a listed species. It is far from clear, however, that fragmentation will always do so for all species in all circumstances. What happens depends on a wide portfolio of deterministic and stochastic factors including the migration and the dispersal behavior of the species and its interaction with other species and with members of its kind (Andren 1994). While using a density-independent model in which species' individuals live independently of one another, Färvinen (1982) concluded that it is unclear whether one large or several small populations will be more secure. Quinn and Hasting (1987) conclude that the mean time to extinction for a density-dependent species decreases with the increasing fragmentation under environmental stochasticity. Burkey (1989) draws the opposite conclusion for demographic stochasticity. In general, until biologists establish consensus, it seems that the only fully responsible procedure for an outsider studying biodiversity who must use biological information to make his own discipline work well is to perform distinct studies under each combination of perspectives and operational propositions that biology offers him. Otherwise one should be explicit about which perspective and propositions one is using and also indicate as well that alternatives exist. None of the three chapters being reviewed live up to either the admittedly onerous ideal or to its less demanding counterpart. All embraced the genetic reductionism perspective, though in Brown and Layton because of these authors' singular focus on the black rhino, the adoption could not have affected results or conclusions. One wonders whether the inferences that Berringer and Perrine draw about biodiversity states and the concerns that Gibbons expresses about biodiversity management would differ if they embraced Darwin's (1979 [1859]) original struggle for life paradigm. Bessinger and Perrine's and Gibbons' remarks seem more consistent with the Hollings (1986) rather than the May (1972) perspective on biodiversity contributions to resilience. However, the Brown and Layton presumption in their model of homogeneous and unconstraining rhino habitat is problematic. Black rhinos are not exempt from the rigors of expending effort to acquire matter

---

[4] Note that both Rodgiguez and Gomez-Sal (1994) and Tilman et al. (1996) study grassland systems.

and energy, their relative ease of this acquisition likely differs across land-scapes, and their resilience must be somewhat sensitive to these differences.

By recognizing issues of value in biodiversity, each paper grants that all elements of human social order do not arise as simple functions of basic bio-logical activity. Human preferences and knowledge have a role. Biology is not destiny for the social order. However, the perfectly valid recognition of the role of human preferences leads in Bessinger and Perrine to a strong hint that every variational trait is worth preserving because every such trait is poten-tially adaptive. That is, the future is uncertain and the extinction of a trait is held to be an irreversible event that may harm the ability of ecosystems to produce whatever those properties of biological systems are which humans value. Three not altogether mutually exclusive responses seem appropriate, beyond the obvious idea that the money cost of preservation matters.

First, the preserve-every-trait value perspective disregards the work of biologists (e.g., Crozie 1992) and economists (e.g., Weitzman 1992) which allows that some genetic traits may be redundant because they have the same evolutionary and ecosystem effects. Any mechanism that selects for effects cannot discriminate among differing structures having identical effects. Second, the preserve-every-trait perspective fails to consider a large body of economic work on quasi-option value, starting with Arrow and Fisher (1974) and more recently thoroughly expounded in Dixit and Pindyck (1994). These quasi-option value results show that preservation of adaptation opportunities may be worthwhile in the presence of temporal uncertainty and irreversibility because subsequent information may dictate a decision different than what initially seemed appropriate. The results do not imply that all adaptation opportunities are worth preserving whatever the cost, however. Not every contingency is worth a hedge. Third, none of the three chapters take account of the possibility that biodiversity loss and the loss of adaptation opportuni-ties or of resilience may not be synonymous. Hanemann (1989) shows, for example, that the prevention of irreversibility may have a negative quasi-option value if the object of choice is in a continuous metric. The reason is that though biodiversity loss itself may be irreversible, a large share of its impact may not be. Natural and human adaptations may soften and even negate the impact. In fact, few would deny that at least some biodiversity loss has improved and still could improve the human condition. Moreover, consis-tent with Miller and Lad (1984), prevention of local or temporary biodiversity loss may cost the opportunity to procure information about the uncertain value of this loss on a larger spatial or temporal scale. It may be worthwhile to let a portion of something go so that we will know more about how much we will miss it if the rest were to go.

All of the preceding remarks take multidisciplinarity to be the feeding of the results of one discipline into the work of another, particularly the feed-ing of economics and the law by biology. But such feeding can be mutual and it is often likely to be so for the biodiversity issue. For example, Bessinger and Perrine worry about the transition probability of moving from one biodiversity state to another. The other two chapters do the same, though less directly. There are, however, two sides to this probability. The first is the regime of shocks that perturb the system and the second is the manner in which the system uses its resources, including feedbacks to the biological system from such economic artifacts as the price system. If differential success in longevity or in acquiring flows of matter and energy partly determines reproductive success in nonhuman biotic settings and if human social order influences this acquisition process, then explanations of biodiversity states could demand attention to the social order. That is, biodiversity states and states of the human social order can be jointly determined.[5] Of the three chapters being reviewed, only Brown and Layton recognize this possibility. As do the other two chapters, they consider the impact of a shock (poaching) originating in the social order upon the biological system. In addition, Brown and Layton also weigh how the response of the economic system to the shock and to the adjustment of the biological system affects and could affect the biological system. For their black rhino preservation problem, they clearly display the relevance of this feedback. Serious policy mistakes have been and will likely continue to be made in black rhino preservation if the feedback for which Brown and Layton account is dismissed. Though they choose not to do so, their recognition of jointly determined village economic systems and black rhino population dynamics could readily have been extended to the provision and protection of black rhino habitat. Neither these authors nor anyone else have yet taken up the task of providing criteria to determine when serious errors of commission and of omission might take place if the possibility of joint determination is arbitrarily dismissed. The next section lays out some preliminary thoughts on these criteria. That specification of how these systems and their parts fit together matters for understanding the relation between biodiversity and economy is the basic, simple point.

III. JOINT DETERMINATION

All it should take to force a recognition that ecological systems and economic systems can be jointly determined is an admission that whether a species is endangered or not or whether ecosystem resilience is degraded depends on human land-use decisions. The admission amounts to an acknowledgment that ecological systems are open systems, are thus spatially and temporally contingent, and are embedded in larger systems of which the economic system is a part. The biodiversity effects of human activities depend upon both the intensive and the extensive margins of land uses. At the extensive margin, people decide how to use land; at the intensive margin, they select the

---

[5] A few mainly analytical studies have used Norgaard's (1981) original coevolutionary insight to explore details of how biological and economic systems may be jointly determined. Shogren and Crocker (1991), Crocker and Tschirhart (1992), Crocker (1995), Kremer (1996), Swallow (1996), Munro (1997), and Perrings (1998) come close to exhausting the list.

intensity of uses. The extensive margin is conditioned upon the structure of the received ecosystem, human technology and capital, including knowledge of local ecosystem behaviors and the relative returns from alternative land uses; the intensive margin is conditional upon the same behaviors and technologies and the extensive margin. Both margins have a role in determining ecosystem structure and habitat, and thus biodiversity and ecosystem resilience. In turn, the ecosystem structure helps determine these margins.

A parsimonious two-step model readily shows that one cannot get far in understanding the relationship between biodiversity and ecosystems if the possibility of jointness between ecosystem resilience and the economic determinants of land use is disregarded. Biodiversity is considered to be a means to the end of protecting ecosystem resilience (Perrings 1998).

Assuming for simplicity that the landowner in question has already set the extensive margin, the first step considers the impact of his activities on this single site upon biodiversity. Biodiversity is measured in the manner of Weitzman (1992). The second step involves the effect of biodiversity upon resilience of the site's ecosystem or habitat.

In the first step, realized biodiversity is

$$B = \pi(X)B^*, \tag{5.1}$$

where B^* is the maximum biodiversity that the inherited abiotic conditions of the site and the exogenous conditions dispatched from neighboring sites will allow, X is a measure of the intensity of human production activities on the site, and π is the proportion of maximum diversity that remains after these activities. Only a single activity within a given time period is considered. Negative biodiversity is not possible. It seems reasonable that $B_{B^*} \geqslant 0$ – a subscript denotes a partial derivative. Expression (5.1) says that realized biodiversity is a function of inherited site conditions and extant human activities. Note that $\pi(0) = 1$, $\pi(X) = 0$, and $\pi(X) > 1$ are all feasible. Respectively, an absence of human activities causes realized and inherited biodiversity to be identical. However, human activities, say mining or acidic pollution, could make the site a moonscape. Finally, these same activities could improve upon the site's inherited biodiversity. The owner might ". . . try to do every little thing [he] can do to enhance what nature can produce" (Bowley 1998, pp. B1, 8).[6] Whatever human activities do to biodiversity, their impact is likely to be spatially and temporally contingent (Ludwig et al. 1993), that is, site- and time-specific.

In the second step, the impact of realized biodiversity upon the realized resilience, R, of the site's ecosystem is

$$R = \theta(B)R^*, \tag{5.2}$$

where θ is the proportion of the maximum resilience, R^*, which remains. As earlier noted, biologists do not agree on the sign of θ_B though economic

---

[6] See also Ricardo ([1817] 1973, 34) on the use of capital to "ameliorate" the quality of the land.

analysis of the biodiversity issue usually assumes that it is positive, as in for example, Perrings (1992). Even so, the sign of θ_{BB} is unclear – whether $\theta(B)$ is convex or concave is unknown and is usually not even discussed.

Upon substituting the realized biodiversity function in (5.1) into the realized resilience function in (5.2), one gets

$$R = \theta[\pi(X)B^*]R^*, \tag{5.3}$$

which defines a resilience production function (Arrow et al. 1995). Realized resilience thus depends on inherited resilience, inherited biodiversity, and human activities. A $\pi(X) \neq 1$ such that biodiversity is not what was inherited need not imply that resilience is affected since species already present or migrants may substitute for an endangered or removed species (Holling 1986).

Human activities may directly affect maximum ecosystem resilience rather than acting through the biodiversity variable as, for example, when plowing the prairie alters the relative populations of already present species (Holling 1973). The altered relative populations may subsequently affect realized resilience. That is, from (5.2)

$$R_{R*} = \theta(B). \tag{5.4}$$

Realized resilience may also be influenced by variations in inherited biodiversity. From (5.3) and (5.1),

$$R_{B*} = R^*\pi(X)\theta_B. \tag{5.5}$$

Together expressions (5.4) and (5.5) imply that inherited biodiversity and inherited resilience can affect the resilience realized at all levels of human activities. They also impact the effect of realized biodiversity upon realized resilience. The sign of (5.4) is arguably positive but because of the earlier noted differences among biologists about the sign of θ_B, the sign of (5.5) is indeterminate. Unless people apply X to produce a moonscape such that π is zero, a positive θ_B results in a positive sign for (5.5), given that inherited resilience is positive. If θ_B is positive, (5.5) implies that human activities which encourage resilience may be substituted for realized biodiversity to maintain the marginal effect that inherited abiotic environments have upon realized resilience. If, on the other hand, θ_B is negative, applications of X will simply amplify any reduction that more realized biodiversity induces in the marginal contribution of the inherited abiotic environment to realized resilience.

Again from (5.3), the marginal impact of human activities on realized resilience is

$$R_x = R^*B^*\theta_B\pi_x. \tag{5.6}$$

This marginal impact is thus dependent upon inherited resilience, inherited biodiversity, the marginal effect of realized biodiversity upon realized resilience, and the marginal effect of human activities upon realized biodiversity. If May's (1972) hypothesis that $\theta_B < 0$ is accepted, then human activities which "enhance what nature can produce" will reduce realized resilience while activities that reduce biodiversity will increase resilience. Adherents of Holling (1986) will conclude the opposite in each case. Given that ecosystem resilience is desired, the May (1972) hypothesis favors human activities that reduce biodiversity and regrets activities that enhance it. In contrast, Holling (1986) suggests that we help nature by actively encouraging biodiversity and by refraining from actions that would reduce biodiversity.

Now, consider the problem of the policy maker who wishes to produce that magnitude of R_x which maximizes some value, whether it be financial or environmental. The policy maker must then set (5.6) equal to the unit value of resilience relative to the unit cost of human activity. Whatever the value objective, its maximization also requires that the second derivative of expression (5.3),

$$R_{xx} = (\theta_B \pi_{xx} - B^* \theta_{BB} \pi_x^2) R^* B^*, \tag{5.7}$$

be nonpositive if any value function proportional to R_x is to be convex. Convexity implies that the value function will not sacrifice all human activity to the inherited environment *or* all of the inherited environment to human activity. Even if consensus exists for θ_B being positive, as much conservation biology and economic commentary would have it, and even if π_{xx} and π_{BB} are negative and are thus "well-behaved," nonpositiveness for R_{xx} requires that the negative magnitude of the first term in the parentheses exceed the second term. Since B^*, R^*, and π_x^2 must all be nonnegative, setting R_x to maximize value then requires that $|\pi_{xx}| > |\theta_{BB}|$, that is, that the responsiveness of realized resilience to realized biodiversity be less than the responsiveness of realized biodiversity to the intensity of human activities. I am unaware of any analytical results or empirical findings that would suggest how likely this is.

Alternatively, if all of θ_B, θ_{BB}, $\pi_{xx} < 0$, then convexity of the value function is impossible. Value maximization under the May (1972) conjecture that $\theta_B < 0$ then obliges the policy maker to choose either a moonscape or the inherited environment. But no particular reason exists to presume θ_{BB}, $\pi_{xx} < 0$. If so, the convexity of the value function remains indeterminate even if $\theta_B < 0$. In general, whether or not the value function will be convex depends in quite complex fashion upon the sign of θ_B and upon the signs and the relative magnitudes of θ_{BB} and π_{xx}. In short, using biological knowledge alone while being an adherent of either May's (1972) or of Holling's (1986) views on the sign of θ_B is insufficient to know what human activities imply for ecosystem resilience and its valuation.

As the papers in Vitousek (1997) amply enumerate, it is the very rare ecosystem that is not affected by human activities. Given the seeming difficulty of using biological propositions alone to capture properties of the linkage between ecosystem resilience and biodiversity, a combination of biological and economic analysis might provide insight about these properties. The following simple framework is intended to do no more than suggest the possibilities for doing so.

Consider the problem that the landowner referred to in expression (5.1) has about deciding the intensity of production activities on his site. He derives utility

$$U = U(Q, R) \tag{5.8}$$

in a weakly separable fashion from his current on-site consumption, Q, and the realized resilience of the site's ecosystem. Recall from expressions (5.1) through (5.3) that $R = R(B(X), R^*, B^*)$. $U(Q, R)$ is twice differentiable and concave. The landowner maximizes $U(Q, R)$ subject to the constraint

$$W + R(B(X), R^*, B^*) = p(X)Q, \tag{5.9}$$

where W is his exogenous money wealth and p is the landowner's unit cost of his on-site consumption, including his opportunity cost of not investing in ecosystem resilience. Off-site consumption is presumed separable from on-site consumption. The unit value of resilience is set at one. On the left-hand side of (5.9), the presence of R (.) implies that more resilience increases the landowner's wealth. More resilience means that the backdrop the ecosystem provides for the landowner's on-site consumption is better protected and can persist longer.

The equilibrium levels of Q and R obtained from the primal optimization problem in (5.8) and (5.9) will vary with the landowner's demand, $\hat{X}$, for the intensity of his production activities. Substitution of $\hat{X}$ into $U(Q, R)$ yields an indirect utility function

$$V = [p(\hat{X}), R(B(\hat{X}), R^*, B^*), W], \tag{5.10}$$

which suggests the landowner will choose that level of on-site production activity which equates the money equivalents of his marginal utilities of consumption and ecosystem resilience, given only that he is wealth constrained. Therefore, expression (5.10) implies that the landowner engages in on-site production activities until his marginal return on these activities equals his substitution rate between consumption and ecosystem resilience. This substitution rate is the landowner's shadow cost of wealth (Hirshleifer 1970), that is, $r = U_Q/U_X$. The landowner's demand for on-site production activities can then be written in terms of this shadow cost

$$\hat{X} = \hat{X}(r(W; R^*, B^*)R^*, B^*) = \hat{X}(r(W)R^*B^*). \tag{5.11}$$

Let $\hat{X}$ be the equilibrium level of activities that produce nonextractive recreational and aesthetic experiences (e.g., restoring a riparian area, blocking motorized access) *or* the equilibrium level of extractive activities (e.g., clearcut logging, mining, monoculture agriculture) which produce commodities that the landowner can sell. Note that expression (5.10) requires

$$V_p p_{\hat{X}} + V_R R_B B_{\hat{X}} = 0. \tag{5.12}$$

Presume reasonably that $p_{\hat{X}} > 0$ such that increased activity of either sort (nonextractive or extractive) increases the opportunity costs of foregoing the other sort of activity. By construction, $V_p < 0$ and $V_R > 0$. If nonextractive activities increase biodiversity or preserve it over a longer time interval such that $B_{\hat{X}} > 0$, then expression (5.12) requires that R_B – which is equivalent to the earlier θ_B – be positive. Thus, consistent with Holling (1986), increasing biodiversity causes increased resilience when humans engage in activities that encourage greater biodiversity. It follows that the Holling (1986) hypothesis would then apply to settings where man has treaded lightly. However, when, $B_{\hat{X}} > 0$, then expression (5.12) requires that $R_B < 0$, which is consistent with the May (1972) hypothesis. Increased intensity of extractive activities reduces realized biodiversity which then raises realized resilience, which implies that the May (1972) hypothesis is apt when human activities have over time substantially altered the landscape. Interestingly, the conclusions of this purely theoretical exercise on jointly determined biological and economic systems conform exactly to the empirical conjecture of Rodgiguez and Gomez-Sal (1994). They speculate that the source of observed empirical differences on the sign of R_B in the grassland ecosystems of the Cantabrian Mountains in Spain and the Yellowstone Park area of North America is that the history of human use of the park has been light such that $R_B > 0$, while the long history of human-guided cattle and sheep grazing in these Spanish mountains has irretrievably altered their ecosystems such that $R_B < 0$.

If human activity decisions have a role in the relation between the resilience and the biodiversity that an ecosystem exhibits, then it appears worthwhile to ask what influence inherited resilience will have upon the intensity of human activities, whether nonextractive or extractive. To evaluate this, substitute $\hat{X}$ from (5.11) into the landowner's Marshallian demand, $\hat{Q}$, for consumption and differentiate with respect to R^* to obtain

$$\frac{d\hat{Q}}{dR^*} = \frac{dQ}{dR^*} + \left[\frac{\partial Q}{\partial p} p_x + \frac{\partial Q}{\partial R} R_B B_x \right] \frac{d\hat{X}}{dR^*}. \tag{5.13}$$

The first term on the right-hand side of (5.13) is the direct effect of the change in inherited resilience upon the landowner's consumption; the second or indirect term is the activity effect of the change in inherited resilience upon the landowner's demand for consumption that is induced by a change in the optimal level of activity. From (5.11), this change in the optimal level of activity and realized resilience are linked through an economic parameter, the landowner's shadow cost, r, of wealth. Equilibrium landowner activities and realized resilience are then jointly determined.

IV. CONCLUDING REMARKS

As Alfred Marshall (1920, 636) noted, "Specialists who never look beyond their own domain are apt to see things out of true proportion." The three chapters here reviewed resort to disciplinary mixing to try to see things about biodiversity in their true proportion. All repudiate an immaculate conception view of either biological systems or economic systems. In varying degrees, each succeeds. Bessinger and Perrine intuit the importance of doing so, Gibbons explicitly acknowledges it, and Brown and Layton actually practice a limited form of it. In particular, Brown and Layton have incorporated important insights from biology into their economic analysis – which is as it should be, since biology has many salient things to say about biodiversity. Equally important, as a moment's reflection about the results of Brown and Layton will demonstrate, is inducing biologists like Bessinger and Perrine and policy makers like Gibbons to bring back insights from economics into the core *structures* of their analyses. I have shown it is unlikely that biological analysis alone can explain how to arrive – once more how *best* to arrive – at biology's chosen desideratum of ecosystem resilience. However, my simple framework, which allows ecological and economic systems to mediate each others' behaviors, easily generates propositions consistent with empirical observations that biologists who study ecosystem resilience and biodiversity view as anamolous. Diversity in disciplinary mixing can therefore lead to better servicing of resilience in ecosystems and in social order.

References

Agee, M. D., and T. D. Crocker. (1998). Environmental Change, Institutions, and Human Capital. In E. T. Loehman and D. M. Kilgore, eds. *Designing Institutions for Environmental and Resource Management*. London, U.K.: Edward Edgar Publishing.

Anderson, S., and P. Francois. (1997). Environmental Cleanliness as a Public Good: Welfare and Policy Implications of Nonconvex Preferences. *Journal of Environmental Economics and Management* 34: 256–74.

Andren, H. (1994). Effects of Habitat Fragmentation on Birds and Mammals in Landscapes with Different Proportions of Suitable Habitat. *Oikos* 71: 355–66.

Arrow, K. J., B. Bolin, R. Costanza, P. Dasqupta, C. Folke, C. S. Holling, B.-O. Jansson, S. Levin, K.-G. Maler, C. Perrings, and D. Pimentel. (1995). Economic Growth, Carrying Capacity, and the Environment. *Science* 268: 520–21.

Arrow, K. J., and A. C. Fisher. (1974). Environmental Preservation, Uncertainty and Irreversibility. *The Quarterly Journal of Economics* 88: 312–19.

Bessinger, S. Roy and J. D. Perrine. (2001). Extinction, Recovery and the Endangered Species Act. Chapter 4 in J. F. Shogren and J. Tschirhart, eds. *Protecting Endangered Species in the United States: Biological Needs, Political Realities, and Economic Choices*. New York: Cambridge University Press.

Bowley, D. (1998). Utility Spiffs Up Kennebec Salmon Spawning Site. *Bangor (ME) Daily News*. August 28.

Brown, G., and D. Layton. (2001). A Market Solution for Preserving Biodiversity: The Black Rhino. Chapter 3 in J. F. Shogren, and J. Tschirhart, eds. *Protecting Endangered Species in the United States: Biological Needs, Political Realities, and Economic Choices*. New York: Cambridge University Press.

Burkey, T. V. (1989). Extinction in Nature Reserves: The Effect of Fragmentation and the Importance of Migration Between Reserve Fragments. *Oikos* 55: 75–81.

Crocker, T. D. (1995). Ecosystem Functions, Economies, and the Ability to Function. In J. W. Milon and J. F. Shogren, eds. *Integrating Economic and Ecological Indicators*. Westport, CT: Praeger Publishers.

Crocker, T . D., and J. Tschirhart. (1992). Ecosystems, Externalities and Economies. *Environmental and Resource Economics* 2: 551–67.

Crozier, R. H. (1992). Genetic Diversity and the Agony of Choice. *Biological Conservation* 61: 11–15.

Darwin, C. (1979 [1859]). *The Origin of Species by Means of Natural Selection or the Preservation of Favored Races in the Struggle for Life*. New York: Avenel Books.

Dixit, A. K., and R. S. Pindyck. (1994). *Investment Under Uncertainty*. Princeton, NJ: Princeton University Press.

Eldredge, N., and M. Grene. (1992). *Interactions: The Biological Context of Social Systems*. New York: Columbia University Press.

Fablonka, E., and M. F. Lamb. (1995). *Epigenetic Inheritance and Evolution: The Lamarckian Dimension*, Oxford: Oxford University Press.

Färvinen, O. (1982). Conservation of Endangered Plant Populations: Single Large or Several Small Reserves? *Oikos* 38: 301–07.

Gibbons, B. (2000). Endangered Thought, Political Animals. *Protecting Endangered Species in the United States: Biological Needs, Political Realities and Economic Choices*. Chapter 2 in J. F. Shogren and J. Tschirhart, eds. New York: Cambridge University Press.

Gould, S. F. (1986). Evolution and the Triumph of Homology, or Why History Matters. *American Scientist* 74: 60–69.

Gundersson, L. H., C. S. Holling, and S. Light. (1995). *Barriers and Bridges to Renewal of Ecosystems and Institutions*. New York: Columbia University Press.

Hanemann, W. M. (1989). Information and the Concept of Option Value. *Journal of Environmental Economics and Management* 16: 23–37.

Hirshleifer, J. (1970) *Investment, Interest and Capital*. Englewood Cliffs, NJ: Prentice-Hall.

Holling, C. S. (1973). Resilience and Stability of Ecological Systems. *Annual Review of Ecological Systems* 4: 1–24.

—(1986). The Resilience of Terrestrial Ecosystems: Local Surprise and Global Change. In W. E. Clark and R. E. Munor, eds. *Sustainable Development of the Biosphere*. New York: Cambridge University Press.

Johnston, T. D., and G. Gottlieb. (1990). Neophenogenesis: A Developmental Theory of Phenotypic Evolution. *Journal of Theoretical Biology* 147: 471–95.

King, A. W., and S. L. Pimm. (1983). Complexity, Diversity and Stability: A Reconciliation of Theoretical and Empirical Results. *American Naturalist* 12: 229–39.

Kremer, M. (1996). Integrating Behavioral Choice into Epidemiological Models of AIDS. *The Quarterly Journal of Economics* 111: 549–74.

Lewontin, R. C. (1983). Gene, Organism, and Environment. In D. S. Bendall, ed. *Evolution from Molecules to Men.* New York: Cambridge University Press.

Loucks, O. L. (1985). Looking for Surprise in Managing Stressed Ecosystems. *Bioscience* 35: 428–32.

Ludwig, D., R. Hilborn, and C. Walters. (1993). Uncertainty, Resource Exploitation, and Conservation: Lessons From History. *Science* 260: 17, 36.

Marshall, A. (1920). *Principles of Economics*, 8th ed. London, U.K.: Macmillan Publishers.

May, R. (1972). Will a Large Complex System Be Stable? *Nature* 238: 413–14.

Miller, J. R., and F. Lad. (1984). Flexibility, Learning and Irreversibility in Environmental Decisions. *Journal of Environmental Economics and Management* 11: 161–72.

Munro, A. (1997). Economics and Biological Evolution. *Environmental and Resource Economics* 9: 429–49.

Norgaard, R. B. (1981). Sociosystem and Ecosystem Coevolution in the Amazon. *Journal of Environmental Economics and Management* 8: 238–54.

Perrings, C. (1992). *Biotic Diversity, Sustainable Development and Natural Capital.* A paper presented at the International Society for Ecological Economics. Stockholm, Sweden.

— (1998). Resilience in the Dynamics of Economy-Environment Systems. *Environmental and Resource Economics* 11: 503–20.

Peters, R. H. (1991). *A Critique for Ecology.* New York: Cambridge University Press.

Quinn, J. F., and A. Hastings. (1987). Extinction in Subdivided Habitats. *Conservation Biology* 1: 198–208.

Ricardo, D. ([1817] 1973). *The Principles of Political Economy and Taxation.* London, U.K.: Everyman.

Rodgiguez, M. A., and A. Gomez-Sal. (1994). Stability May Decrease with Diversity in Grassland Communities: Empirical Evidence from the 1986 Cantabrian Mountains (Spain) Drought. *Oikos* 71: 177–80.

Shogren, J. F., and T. D. Crocker. (1991). Risk, Self-Protection, and Ex Ante Economic Value. *Journal of Environmental Economics and Management* 20: 1–15.

Swallow, S. (1996). Resource Capital Theory and Ecosystem Economics: Developing Nonrenewable Habitats with Heterogeneous Quality. *Southern Economic Journal* 63: 106–23.

Tilman, D., D. Wedin, and J. Knops. (1996). Productivity and Sustainability Influenced by Biodiversity in Grassland Ecosystems. *Nature* 379: 718–20.

Trivers, R. (1985). *Social Evolution.* Menlo Park, CA: Benjamin/Cummings.

Vitousek, P., ed. (1997). Human Determination of Earth's Ecosystems. *Science* 277: 494–525.

Weitzman, M. L. (1992). On Diversity. The *Quarterly Journal of Economics* 107: 363–405.

Westmann, W. E. (1990). Managing for Biodiversity: Unresolved Science and Policy Questions. *Bioscience* 40: 26–33.

Williams, G. C. (1966). *Adaptation and Natural Selection*. Princeton, NJ: Princeton University Press.

Wilson, E. O. (1998). *Consilience. The Unity of Knowledge*. New York: Knopf.

PART 2

POLITICAL REALITIES

CHAPTER 6

Interest Group Behavior and Endangered Species Protection

Amy Whritenour Ando

I. INTRODUCTION

In the face of growing concern over species extinction rates, national and international decision-making bodies have become increasingly aware of the need to establish effective, efficient policies to protect endangered species and their habitat. The task faced by these policy makers is complicated by the fact that policies and institutions may not function in practice as their creators intend. Political forces and human nature may yield patterns in the administration of such policies that are at odds with official doctrine. Political-economy theory describes the sorts of patterns one may expect to see in practice, and even investigates whether the influence of politics over policy can be expected to be a good thing. Citizens, scholars, lawmakers, and administrators can use the ideas that have emerged from this field in their attempts to anticipate, and later quantify, some elements of the divergence between policy *de jure* and *de facto*.

This chapter illustrates how classic political-economy theories are relevant to understanding some aspects of how endangered species policies play out. As part of that exercise, it describes three empirical studies of part of the administration of the United States' Endangered Species Act (ESA). These studies serve as examples of the kinds of empirical work one might do in order to quantify the political-economic forces at work in a policy arena, and mine the information about policies those forces implicitly provide. They also provide particular insight into the role played by political pressure in the process by which species are added to the endangered species list in the United States, and into the costs and benefits associated with those listings.

II. POLITICAL ECONOMY AND ENDANGERED SPECIES PROTECTION

There are many types of conservation policies. Some species are protected by hunting restrictions, whether that hunting is driven by a desire to exploit the creatures, as is the case with big game animals and fish, or by a perception that the species are nuisances that must be eliminated; the latter motive has driven wolves in the United States to the brink of extinction. Hunting restrictions are sometimes accompanied by supporting prohibitions on trade of the species and any products derived from them; famous restrictions have been placed on commerce in ivory and rhinoceros horn.

In other cases, intentional taking may not be entirely, or even partially, responsible for a species' endangerment. Rather, habitat conversion and degradation may threaten a species' survival by eliminating the resources it needs to survive. The Northern spotted owl, for example, dwindled entirely because of logging practices in its home forests. And while salmon in the United States do suffer from overfishing, their endangered status is also in large part due to river diversion and damming in the American West. A variety of policy tools are available for use in such situations. Outright restrictions may be placed on land use in endangered species habitat, and incentives for private landowners to engage in conservation practices may be created with tools like targeted tax breaks. Conservation reserves may be established through land purchases or through conservation easements that leave habitat in private hands.

In order to understand the political-economic forces at work under these varied policy alternatives, one can draw on a school of thought that began with the work of Stigler (1971) and Peltzman (1976).[1] This literature is rich and diverse, but at least one fundamental idea runs through it. Policies and decisions are not made by disinterested automatons, or even by benign public servants determined to maximize societal welfare. All decision makers are economic agents in pursuit of their own interests. Groups with stakes in the decision-making outcomes can influence the policy makers by appealing to those interests. The stronger the appeal of one group over the others, the more likely decisions are to be pushed in the direction of that group's interests.

Thus, to anticipate or explain the political forces that are generated by a given policy, one must understand the gains and losses that are created by the policy, and the nature of the interest groups to whom those gains and losses accrue. Note that interest groups as discussed here should not be confused with the "special interest groups" that populate political rhetoric about issues such as campaign finance reform. An interest group is any group of individuals, corporations, or other economic agents that stand to be similarly affected by a policy decision. In this sense, everyone is a member of many interest groups.

However, groups are heterogeneous, and elements of that heterogeneity may affect how influential they are. For example, large groups may have more resources to devote to influencing government decisions. However, if a benefit of a fixed size is spread out among too many beneficiaries, free riding may limit the efficacy of the group; no one agent has an incentive to devote

---

[1] For some general background in this area, see Posner (1974) and Noll (1989). The ideas set forth in this section are drawn from the literature described in part therein.

resources to the cause, especially since other group members might take up the fight themselves.[2]

When a policy to protect endangered species and/or their habitat is implemented, the set of winners is broad. There is some local concentration of benefits (the thrill of seeing the species, or the advantages of ecosystem health that may be linked to conservation), but much of the gains accrue to an extremely large population. Nonuse benefits, like the warm glow one gets from knowing that giant pandas exist even if one never expects to see them, may be experienced by anyone on the globe. Biodiversity also holds out the promise of breakthroughs in pharmaceutical research; a cure for AIDS, for example, would surely yield an improvement in the quality of life of humanity as a whole. Thus, the interest group of beneficiaries is big, and the benefits are extremely diffuse. One might argue that environmental groups exist in large part because of this kind of diffusion of interests. They work to compensate for the free-rider problem in environmental policy, providing a coherent voice for the benefit side of issues with environmental import.

The losses associated with conservation policy may be concentrated or diffuse. For policies that involve uncompensated restrictions on activity (for example, the ESA in the United States, trade restrictions under CITES), the losses are borne in large part by the agents whose choice sets are limited by the restrictions (traders, hunters, loggers, developers, etc.). True, the policy may produce ripple effects through the economy[3] that have economic implications for a large set of firms and citizens. However, the initial, easily identifiable costs are reasonably concentrated, and so the interest group comprised of the primary losers tends to be pretty well defined.

Other policies, however, have costs that are more broadly dispersed. Incentive schemes and conservation reserves that are paid for out of government funds still have economic costs associated with them. The public money used to fund such programs could be dedicated to other uses (including the funding of alternative conservation programs, or the reduction of revenue-raising taxes). Also, land that is set aside for conservation purposes could be used for other purposes; there is an opportunity cost equal to the loss to society of the value of that use. Those costs, however, are spread over the whole population, and thus "losers" are less easily identified.

The influence of an interest group in a policy arena is likely to depend on the size of the costs or benefits generated by the policy at hand, in addition to how widely dispersed those economic impacts are. The more the winners, for example, can expect to benefit from a policy decision, the more motivated they will be to exert pressure on the policy makers to put that policy into effect, and the greater the support those policy makers can expect to reap from that interest group as a result of putting the policy in place.

---

[2] Stigler (1971) initiated thinking along these lines.

[3] See, for example, Watts et al. (Chapter 10 in this volume).

The magnitudes of expected costs and benefits vary tremendously among potential policies or regulatory decisions. The costs of restrictive policies rise with the value of the uses of the species or its habitat that are now precluded, like the profit to be made from development, or the value of recreational hunting. As the stringency and scope of such restrictions increases, so do the corresponding economic losses. Nonrestrictive policies also have variable costs (albeit, as discussed earlier, quite diffuse). For example, the opportunity cost to society of the nonconservation uses of protected land rises with the total market value of the land set aside.

The benefits of specific measures for protecting species and habitat are heterogeneous as well. Some of that variation stems from differences in the protected species themselves; aesthetic value and popular appeal, genetic distinctness, and degree of endangerment all influence the potential gain from preserving a species from extinction. The expected benefit of a policy also depends on how effective the policy is likely to be.

Interest groups and their motives, in the form of benefits gained or costs avoided, are only half of the equation, however. Patterns of influence in policy making and administration also depend on the decision makers and on the institutions within which they work. What are their objectives, and who affects their ability to achieve those objectives? Elected officials may strive to stay in office, and rely on voters and contributors to election-campaign funds to do so. Nonelected administrators may work for bigger budgets or wider mandates, and are likely to rely on members of government (or even multiple governments, in the case of international law) for those budgets and mandates.

All decision makers are likely to have authority which is circumscribed by legislation, treaty, or other body of law. Thus, they do not have unlimited ability to make decisions that court the favor of their constituents. United States lawmakers, for example, can not pass wildlife protection legislation that explicitly violates the Constitution. In any search for patterns of influence of interest groups over decisions, one must establish the ways in which that influence may feasibly manifest itself. Examples will be presented in Section III of this chapter.

Much of the political-economy literature is positive rather than normative – descriptive rather than judgmental. Decisions are likely to be affected by the pressure of interest groups, but is this process good or bad? Much of the public debate over the power of "special interests" to sway lawmakers and administrators presumes that such influence is undesirable. However, theory set forth by Becker (1983) shows that under some circumstances, the process through which interest groups compete strategically with each other for influence over policy may yield policy outcomes that are more efficient from the viewpoint of society as a whole. In the process Becker describes, any group that lobbies in favor of a policy that imposes a net loss on society is at a competitive disadvantage (relative to those who oppose the policy) when it comes to influencing the decision makers. Thus, highly inefficient policies are relatively unlikely to be implemented. In any given policy arena, however, interest groups may or may not behave in a fashion consistent with Becker's assumptions. Only empirical studies can ascertain whether Becker's model is relevant to the real world.

III. EMPIRICAL STUDIES OF ENDANGERED SPECIES LISTINGS

The ESA has provisions that call for the protection of critical rare-species habitat and the design of recovery plans for species officially designated as endangered or threatened. However, the simple regulatory act of adding a species to the list of those so designated confers strong, basic protection and is the necessary first step toward other forms of protection and rehabilitation. This section presents three empirical studies of the behavior of regulators and interest groups in the political battles over adding new species to the list.

The act allows economic balance in decisions about critical habitat and recovery plans, but it maintains that listing decisions should be made on the basis of scientific evidence of endangerment alone. But are those decisions really immune to the influence of economic considerations? Which species induce interest groups to exert the most pressure on the administrative agencies when proposals are made to add those species to the endangered list? Do the interest groups compete strategically with one another in a manner consistent with Becker's theory? Many official actions are taken by the Fish and Wildlife Service each year in the course of adding new species to the endangered species list. This makes it possible to compile a data set with enough species and regulatory actions to conduct meaningful empirical research designed to answer these questions.

Before such research can be carried out, one must understand the basic elements of this decision-making arena. First, what are the interest groups involved? As mentioned in Section II, protection under the ESA very often entails uncompensated restrictions on the use people can make of land inhabited by endangered species. Thus, the interest group comprised of those who stand to lose as a result of a new listing is often well defined. Since the bulk of the costs accrue to those who live and work near the species, this group is largely local and thus varies in composition among listing proposals.

On the other side, there is sometimes a local component to the benefits of a listing, since those who live near a protected species may take pleasure in seeing it, gain from its contribution to the ecosystem in which it lives (like mussels filtering a river), or derive recreational enjoyment from the open land that is preserved as an ancillary outcome of the listing. However, many of the benefits of a listing are diffuse. In cases with minimal local benefits, support for listings might never coalesce because of benefit dispersion. However, the United States has a number of environmental groups that act to fill the breach in such cases; it is not uncommon to find such groups as active members of the interest group in favor of a listing. Thus, the administrators of the ESA are regularly buffeted by pressure from effective interest groups both for and against the addition of new species to the protected list. It is worth noting, however, that in a nation with no well-organized and active environmental groups, political pressure from the opposition to species protection might face relatively little competition from the beneficiaries of that protection, and the administration of endangered species legislation might look very different.

Next, one must identify the decision makers, their objectives, the groups to which they must appeal on behalf of those objectives, and the discretion afforded them in the decision-making process. The ESA is administered primarily by the Fish and Wildlife Service.[4] Only the members of the Service in charge of this administration know what their underlying goals are. However, it seems likely[5] that the Service is seriously concerned with protecting species under the auspices of the current act, and with garnering political support to increase the strength with which the act is likely to emerge from re-authorization debates.

The structure of Congress is such that particular subcommittees in the House and Senate have disproportionate influence over reauthorization of the ESA; these subcommittees also have the power to exert oversight authority over the administering agencies. It is in the Service's best interests to curry favor with members of those subcommittees, and with the voters and campaign contributors who help keep those legislators in office. If a legislator's power base is in the business community, he and his constituents are unlikely to look favorably upon costly new listings in his state or district. On the other hand, subcommittee members who draw strength from pro-environment interests may want to see evidence that the ESA is being aggressively upheld, and his supporters may be pleased by the addition of local rare species to the endangered species list.

The ESA shapes the routes taken by pressure on the agency. Outside individuals and groups may petition the agency to list a species, and the agency must respond in some way to such petitions in a timely manner. Also, before the agency can add a new species to the list of those protected under the act, it must publish a proposal to do so in the Federal Register. Then follows a comment period, during which the agency must hold local hearings on the issue if so requested. Its decision whether to grant endangered status to the proposed species must respond to all comments received. These mechanisms allow interest groups to pressure the agency directly, rather than just through legislators.

The act also affects the ways in which the agency's decision making may respond, intentionally or not, to that pressure. It mandates that listing decisions should be based only on scientific information about whether species

---

[4] The National Marine Fisheries Service handles marine species and anadromous fish; this agency is not a focus of the studies outlined in this chapter and will thus be neglected, perhaps unjustly, in the text that follows.

[5] These speculations are based on personal communications with members of the Service and scholars familiar with the Service's work, as well as inspection of the official statements and activities of the branch of the Service responsible for administering the ESA.

are in danger of becoming extinct. Congress later directed the Fish and Wildlife Service to develop a listing priority system, but priority is to be determined only on degree of threat and taxonomic distinctness. Thus, the agency may not officially refuse to list a species because the timber industry will be damaged by that determination, nor may it opt to put a species on the list explicitly because local tourism will be bolstered by the species' new status. However, interest groups may present scientific evidence that either strengthens or muddies the case for listing a species. In addition, the agency may respond to political pressure regarding a species by altering the speed with which it moves to place the species on the list.

With this sort of institutional knowledge in hand, a useful data set can be compiled. For the purposes of the three studies described below, data were collected on listing activities during the period 1990–1994. The data set includes hundreds of species that were candidates for addition to the list. For a given species, the data record: features of the species itself such as life-form type, taxonomic distinctness, degree of endangerment, whether it is in conflict with development; the dates of administrative and regulatory decisions regarding the species (when its serious candidacy began, when it was proposed for listing, when it was listed); how much pressure was exerted on the agency in the form of petitions, hearing requests, and comments (both supporting and opposing); whether the species was proposed for listing in conjunction with any others, and if so, how many; features of the counties in which the species is found, such as the number of previously listed endangered species, and whether it overlaps with the state or district of a member of one of the oversight subcommittees with jurisdiction over the ESA. Below, three studies are described which use these data in very different ways to answer political-economy questions about the listing process.

III.1.   What Influence Does Pressure Have on the Agency's Listing Decisions?

In order to answer this question, one must pick a dimension of the decisions in which to look for influence. One could look at the set of all species, and analyze which of them get listed.[6] However, that approach does not isolate patterns in administrative behavior from patterns in scientific research. If the grizzly bear is listed but an obscure beetle is not, that may be either because the agency has favored the bear, or because scientists have compiled more compelling evidence for the endangerment of the bear than of the beetle. To circumvent this problem, the study described here[7] examines decisions made by the Fish and Wildlife Service regarding species that have made it to relatively advanced stages of the listing process. The agency has compiled enough scientific evidence regarding these species, known as Category 1

---

[6] See Cash (Chapter 7), and Metrick and Weitzman (1996) for examples of this approach.
[7] See Ando (1999).

candidates, to feel justified in listing them; it is only a matter of time before the agency formally proposes the species for listing, and then makes a final decision about whether or not they deserve to be added to the list.

Political-economy studies often examine the influence of various factors on the content of decisions. Cropper et al. (1992), for example, look for patterns in EPA decisions of whether or not to ban pesticides. In the case of endangered species listings, this type of analysis would try to quantify factors that influence whether or not a Category 1 species is proposed for listing, and whether or not the agency finally decides to list a species that has been proposed. However, the data reveal that there is relatively little variation in the basic content of actions taken by the Fish and Wildlife Service on the cases of species that have gotten this far in the listing process. Over 85 percent of the Category 1 species are proposed for listing (rather than shunted back to a more primitive stage of the process), and over 98 percent of proposed species are listed (rather than having their proposals withdrawn).[8] If interest groups influence agency decisions, where might that influence manifest itself?

One possibility is revealed by inspecting a different dimension of the decisions: timing. Category 1 candidate species wait anywhere from one day to six years for the agency to either propose them for listing or drop them back in the process. Once proposed, a species can wait as little as five months and as much as three years for the agency to make the final listing decision. This sort of delay can be extremely important, since species are not protected by the act until they have been listed. Meanwhile, species populations may decline naturally or be destroyed directly by hunters, and the land species rely on as habitat may be paved over, cut down, flooded, or drained.

Those who perceive themselves as the beneficiaries of species protection will want to reduce delay as much as possible; indeed, environmental groups have occasionally sued the Fish and Wildlife Service for dragging its heels on listing a species. Conversely, those who stand to lose when a species is granted protection will be better off if the listing is postponed. If nothing else, the costs associated with the listing are delayed. Moreover, land owners and users can make irreversible changes to the land (harvesting timber, laying the foundation of a building) before they are forbidden by the provisions of the act.

Econometric techniques known collectively as duration analysis can be used to estimate how various explanatory factors influence the amount of time the Fish and Wildlife Service takes to move candidate species forward in the listing process.[9] In the study at hand, one set of variables measures direct pressure from interest groups in the form of petitions, comments, and hearing requests. Another set of variables aims to capture unobservable pressure from oversight-subcommittee members, either "pro-development" or

---

[8] These percentages are of the species in the data set that had been the subject of decisions by the point in time when data collection ceased.

[9] Kiefer (1988) is a good basic reference; Lancaster (1990) gives a much more extensive treatment of these methods. For details of the particular econometrics used here, see Ando (1999).

"pro-environment," and their constituents. Provisions are made to look at whether the agency does indeed act more quickly on species that have high-priority rankings under the priority system Congress forced the agency to adopt. Finally, some variables are included to capture any tendencies the agency may have to favor species based on life-form type (vertebrate, invertebrate, or plant?), taxonomic distinctness, or degree of endangerment.

The results of the duration analyses indicate that the Service's administrative behavior is in some ways consistent with the mandates from Congress set down in the act. Species that rank high in the listing-priority system do tend to be proposed for listing relatively quickly. The agency does not seem to favor vertebrate Category 1 species over the less charismatic invertebrates or over plants; such favoritism was once built into the Service's internal priority system, but was later proscribed by Congress. Finally, time limits built into the act do seem to contain the amount of time that passes between when a species is proposed for listing and when the Service makes a final listing decision.[10]

However, the results also show that interest groups do influence the agency's listing process. Institutions that inject direct public input into the process seem effective. Species that are the subject of supporting petitions move on average over a year earlier from Category 1 to being proposed for listing (a reduction in waiting time of 27 percent). Public hearings, often requested by parties concerned about the economic impacts of a proposed listing, add an average of six weeks to the wait between proposal and final listing (an increase of 12 percent). The influence of comments depends on whether they come from supporters or detractors of a listing. Half of all listing proposals receive no opposition at all, but the submission of even one opposing comment in response to a listing proposal delays that listing by an average of fourteen weeks (26 percent). On the other side, the vast majority of proposals receive at least some supporting comments. Low levels of support have little effect on the wait for final listing (perhaps because the diffusion of benefits renders that interest group less influential), but strong pressure from supporters can speed up the final listing decision substantially; 1,000 supporting comments can reduce the proposal period by twenty-five weeks (77 percent).

It is also possible that interest groups influence the listing process through members of Congress who are positioned to have particular control over the form and administration of the act. Category 1 candidates spend less time waiting to be proposed for listing if their habitats overlap the districts of "pro-environment" oversight-subcommittee members. Conversely, candidate species in areas represented by "pro-development" oversight-subcommittee members wait longer for proposal, and even run a higher risk of being sent back to less advanced stages of the listing process. The precise mechanism at work here can not be determined. It may be that the subcommittee members

---

[10] In contrast, there are no time limits on how long a species can spend in Category 1 before the Fish and Wildlife Service has to either propose it for listing or drop it back in the process; perhaps as a result, many species spend years in this stage of the process.

themselves exert unobservable pressure on the agency to drag their heels or make haste on the case of a local species. Alternatively, it may be the constituents of those subcommittee members who stand ready to hassle the agency directly should its actions be too rapid or slow for their tastes.

Whether directly or indirectly, interest groups with strong preferences in the species-protection debate do seem to affect the rate at which the Fish and Wildlife Service lists species local to them. This is true even of groups that support new listings; though benefits may be more diffuse than costs, beneficiaries are not without influence over the listing process.

III.2.   Which Species Attract Interest Group Pressure?

The duration analyses of listing decisions seem to reveal that interest group pressure affects at least the rate at which species progress through the late stages of the listing process. What does this do to the implicit criteria that determine which species are on the list at any point in time? Recall that the ESA mandates that only scientific evidence of endangerment should enter into listing decisions. The empirical results just discussed, however, imply that at a given moment in time, the list will contain more species that get support and fewer that attract opposition than if the process were completely immune to public pressure. Thus, whatever drives interest group pressure influences the composition of the endangered species list as well. If such groups respond rationally to variation in the costs and benefits expected to be associated with listings, then economic factors do play a part in the listing process despite the mandate against that in the law. This scenario can be confirmed or rejected by an empirical exploration of what features of candidate species generate the most pressure from the interest groups.

Such a study can be useful for another reason. Recent discussion of how to reform the ESA has emphasized the use of multispecies protection and recovery plans. Beneath this trend lies the growing conviction of scientists and policy makers alike that there are economies of scope in species protection. In other words, it may be more efficient to protect a number of different species together, rather than to protect the same number of species in widely disparate physical locations.[11] If interest groups are rational (as the political-economy theory discussed in Section II assumes them to be), then a study of patterns in the intensity of their lobbying may reveal interesting things about their perceptions of which listings are likely to generate the highest costs and benefits. In particular, since species are often proposed for listing in multispecies groups,[12] and since the ranges of proposed species often overlap with those of previously listed species, such a study may provide clues to the

---

[11] For an example of a paper that focuses on this point, see Dobson et al. (1997).

[12] This bundling is fairly weak. Species in the same proposal package need not have their cases decided at the same time (though they usually do). Even when all are listed, their protection need not be managed as a group.

payoff involved in shifting endangered species policy to work in terms of multispecies clusters.

To carry out an empirical study[13] of the determinants of interest group pressure, proxies for the intensity of such pressure are generated. The proxies use data on the numbers of supporting and opposing comments that were submitted to the Fish and Wildlife Service with regard to each proposed listing in the data set.[14] No comments from a given side of the debate implies "low" pressure, one or two comments imply "medium-low" pressure, three to ten comments indicate "medium-high" pressure, and more than ten comments are taken to indicate "high" pressure. Separate indicators are created for support and for opposition. The goal of the analysis is to see how features of a listing proposal influence the probabilities that the intensities of support and of opposition will fall into the four categories.[15]

The econometric estimation includes a variety of explanatory variables. A few attempt to capture the influence of political ideology on interest group pressure, while most of the others are designed to pick up variation in the costs and benefits that interest groups perceive to be associated with the proposed listings. Two variables serve to test the theory of economies of scope in the costs of species protection, and to explore how the incremental benefit of a new listing changes with the number of species already or concurrently listed in the same area.

First, a measure is made of the number of previously listed species per acre in the range of the species newly proposed. If economies of scope can exist, and if species found in the same counties tend to overlap in ways that invoke those economies, then opposition may be lower for proposals in areas already packed with listed species. Second, the analysis includes the number of species being proposed for listing in the same package. If the Service bundles species into proposal packages in ways that exploit economies of scope, then opposition to a package with N species may be less than N times as intense as opposition to a package with one species.

The results do not particularly indicate that political ideology and other noneconomic factors have great influence over the intensity of interest group pressure on the agency.[16] The study does, however, support the hypothesis that interest group pressure responds rationally to variation in the expected

---

[13] See Ando (1998a), still a work in progress.

[14] In fact, only proposals of species found in the United States are included in this study.

[15] The particular econometric methodology used is a bivariate ordered probit with heteroskedasticity. See Ando (1998a) for a complete explanation. Greene (1993) provides a good explanation of the ordered probit, which is the core of the method used.

[16] This does not rule that possibility out, however. Political ideology is particularly difficult to measure with proxy variables. Just because the proxies tried in this study were not significant (things like citizen involvement in national environmental groups, median household income, county-level voting outcomes in presidential elections, and the environmental rating of an area's Senators and Representatives) does not mean that ideology and other noneconomic factors do not have any affect on interest group behavior.

costs and benefits of listings. Opposition is greater for proposed species that are known to be directly in conflict with development. Also, both opposition and support are heightened when a proposed species is a vertebrate rather than an invertebrate or plant. Vertebrates tend to have larger ranges than species of the other two types. Thus, more land is likely to be the subject of use restrictions as a result of such listings. This raises the costs associated with the listing. The same feature of vertebrates also raises the benefits, to the extent that supporters of the species benefit from the preservation of open land. In addition, the public may simply like vertebrates better, and derive more pleasure from protecting them than species of the other types.

Opposition is no greater for multispecies packages than for a proposal to protect a single species. This implies that there are some economies of scope associated with protecting the species chosen by the Fish and Wildlife Service to be bundled together. However, the intensity of opposition is unaffected by the number of previously listed species per acre of the range counties of the newly proposed candidates. This may mean that economies of scope do not necessarily exist in species protection just because the species in question can be found in the same counties. Some counties are quite large, and the species found in one may not be located on the same land or be helped by the same land- and water-use restrictions. In such cases, opposition to new listings may actually be greater if the region is dense with previously listed species. The old listings may have tied up much of the available land in the area; thus, restrictions on the remaining area resulting from a new listing may impose heightened opportunity costs.

As with opposition, support for a proposal is no greater if the proposal package includes many species than if it includes just one. Furthermore, support is significantly lower for proposals in areas with many previously listed species per acre. These findings may reflect the existence of beneficial spillovers from the protection of one species to that of a neighbor. If a candidate species is already shielded from the threat of extinction by provisions put in place to protect another species nearby, then the benefits associated with adding the candidate to the list may be relatively small. This explanation is consistent with the existence of economies of scope in species protection.

It may also be, however, that public willingness to pay for species protected in a given county diminishes with the number of species already protected. If this is true, then one must question whether the goal of ESA administration should be to protect as many species as possible at the lowest possible cost, without regard to where those species are located. Social welfare may be greater if protected species are distributed among a variety of geographic locales, rather than clustered together in a small number of "hotspots."

III.3.   Do the Interest Groups Compete Strategically?

The empirical study just described makes the implicit assumption that the interest groups in question do not compete strategically for influence with the

Fish and Wildlife Service. For example, it assumes that if support is relatively high for vertebrate species, that reflects fundamentally high public willingness-to-pay to protect such species, rather than a strategic response to anticipated high levels of opposition to vertebrate listings. This means that the study has assumed that Becker's model of interest group competition does not obtain in this policy arena. Is that assumption valid? Only an empirical study can ascertain this.

Becker's model of strategic competition is a Cournot model, in which the two interest groups decide at the same time[17] how much pressure to exert on the agency. They behave noncooperatively; thus, neither side can directly control the amount of pressure chosen by the other. The structure of this "game" yields reaction functions for both sides. A reaction function describes the optimal amount of pressure for a group to exert as a function of how much pressure the other side musters, as well as of factors (such as whether the species is a vertebrate) that affect the payoff to the group of changing the agency's behavior (in this case, altering the amount of time that passes before a final listing is made). The model assumes that the two sides choose Nash equilibrium levels of pressure; in other words, the pressure exerted by each group is the best response it could have made to the pressure chosen by the other side.

A preliminary empirical study evaluates the relevance of Becker's model to interest group comment submissions regarding the addition of new species to the endangered species list. It tests the most basic hypothesis of the model: that each interest group takes the likely commenting behavior of the other side into account when deciding how much effort to exert in its attempts to influence the Service. Because so many proposals attract no comments at all (especially from the interest group that stands to lose from the listing), this study focuses on observations of whether or not each of the two sides opts to submit any comments to the Service. The goal is to see whether those discrete choices reflect strategic behavior consistent with a Cournot model.[18]

The results of the analyses seem to confirm that the interest groups are not completely irrational; opponents and supporters seem more likely to exert pressure on the agency when the costs and benefits (respectively) of a listing are likely to be high. However, there is no evidence that one group's actions are influenced by its expectations of what the other group will do. These results support the assumption of no strategic competition maintained by the analysis described in Section III.3. However, the findings also mean that one

---

[17] The specification of simultaneous moves seems appropriate for the comment-submissions game at hand here. However, in some applications there may be a good argument that one side moves before the other. This is a qualitatively different model than that analyzed by Becker, and his conclusions about the welfare effects of competition do not automatically apply.

[18] The model tested by this study is not precisely Becker's model. Rather, it is a more flexible Cournot model. For details of the model and of the econometric methodology, see Ando (1998b).

can not rely on the results of Becker's theory for assurance that interest group competition is improving this particular decision-making process.

IV. CONCLUSIONS

Taken together, the results of the three empirical studies described herein reveal interesting patterns in the process of adding new species to the endangered species list. Interest group pressure influences at least one dimension of Fish and Wildlife Service decision making in the late stages of the listing process – timing. Furthermore, levels of pressure from the groups seem motivated at least in part by variations in the costs and benefits expected to result from the listings. Thus, costs and benefits influence the listing process, despite the fact that the act clearly specifies that this part of ESA administration is supposed to be devoid of economic balance.

Is society better or worse off for the impact interest groups have on the listing process? Parties on one side of the debate over the ideal form of the act may be concerned that the endangered species list is not a pure Noah's ark. However, others may be heartened to find that priority may be given implicitly to listings that are expected to have relatively high benefits and low costs. Becker's model of interest group competition finds that competition among interest groups for influence yields policy decisions that are more efficient. There is no evidence, however, that the groups in this arena are competing strategically in keeping with that model. For this reason, the strong results of the model need not apply.

Every act of species protection generates losses and windfalls, and those economic impacts are often felt by different groups. Thus, similar forces are likely to be exerted upon any decision makers charged with managing species protection policy. The effect of interest group involvement will likely vary, however, with policy and institutional details. If, for example, the policy spreads the costs of species protection over an entire nation's population, there may be little in the way of pressure opposed to that protection, and costly species may achieve protected status more rapidly than they do currently in the United States. Interest group influence might in theory be thwarted entirely, but only in a legal and political milieu that provides administrators with no incentives, formal or otherwise, to respond to interest groups.

Observers often bemoan the political battles that surround endangered species protection. However, the products of these battles may be of use to researchers. As illustrated in this chapter, one can use data on political pressure to reveal at least qualitative patterns in public expectations of the costs and benefits that are likely to result from government regulations. This type of empirical work is made possible by the economic insight that the intensity of interest group pressure is likely to vary with the gains and losses created by a policy. Economic theory also provides a framework in which to anticipate the form that *de facto* conservation policy may take, and a helpful base for empirical work designed to quantify the influence of political forces on that policy.

References

Ando, Amy W. (1998a) "Scale Economies in Endangered-Species Protection: Evidence from Interest-Group Behavior." Revision of Resources for the Future Discussion Paper 97–44.

—(1998b) "Do Interest Groups Compete?" Resources for the Future Discussion Paper 98–14.

—(1999) "Waiting to be Protected under the ESA: The Political Economy of Regulatory Delay." *Journal of Law and Economics* 12 (April): 29–60.

Becker, Gary. (1983) "A Theory of Competition among Pressure Groups for Political Influence." *Quarterly Journal of Economics* 98: 371–400.

Cropper, Maureen L., William N. Evans, Stephen J. Berardi, Maria M. Ducla-Soares, and Paul R. Portney. (1992) "The Determinants of Pesticide Regulation: A Statistical Analysis of EPA Decision Making." *Journal of Political Economy* 100: 175–97.

Dobson, A. P., J. P. Rodriguez, W. M. Roberts, and D. S. Wilcove. (1997) "Geographic Distribution of Endangered Species in the United States." *Science* 275: 550–53.

Greene, W. H. (1993) *Econometric Analysis*, 2nd ed. New York: Macmillan.

Kiefer, Nicholas M. (1988) "Economic Duration Data and Hazard Functions." *Journal of Economic Literature* 26: 646–79.

Lancaster, Tony. (1990) *The Econometric Analysis of Transition Data*. Econometric Society Monographs No. 17. New York: Cambridge University Press.

Metrick, Andrew, and Martin L. Weitzman. (1996) "Patterns of Behavior in Endangered Species Preservation." *Land Economics* 72: 1–16.

Noll, Roger G. (1989) "Economic Perspectives on the Politics of Regulation." In *Handbook of Industrial Organization*, vol. 2, eds. R. Schmalensee and R. Willig. Amsterdam, Elsevier Science Publishers, 1253–88.

Peltzman, Sam. (1976) "Toward a More General Theory of Regulation." *Journal of Law and Economics* 19: 211–40.

Posner, Richard. (1974) "Theories of Economic Regulation." *Bell Journal of Economics* 5: 335–58.

Stigler, George. (1971) "The Theory of Economic Regulation." *Bell Journal of Economics and Management Science* 2: 3–21.

CHAPTER 7

Beyond Cute and Fuzzy: Science and Politics in the U.S. Endangered Species Act

David W. Cash

1. INTRODUCTION

The Endangered Species Act (ESA) and its implementation are at the center of some of the most controversial and divisive debates concerning the role of the federal government in environmental protection and in the regulation of the use of natural resources (Bornemeier 1995; Mann 1995; Metrick and Weitzman 1998; Stevens 1995). The controversy surrounding the act raises fundamental questions about a wide variety of social, political, legal, scientific, and ethical considerations that face government policy makers, regulators, and the public.

Recent concerns about the implementation of the ESA and the current debate over reauthorization have provided the impetus for this research. Critics from a variety of different perspectives, for example, have raised questions about the divergence between stated priorities and standards and actual patterns of allocation of resources for species protection (General Accounting Office 1988; Metrick and Weitzman 1996b, 1998; Simon, Leff, and Doerksen 1995). In addition, despite the heavy reliance in the statute on the use of scientific research in guiding the process of species identification and recovery, it is clear that at least some aspects of implementation are not appropriately informed by scientific research as prescribed by law (Clark, Reading, and Clarke 1994; General Accounting Office 1988; Minta and Kareiva 1994; National Research Council 1995; Metrick and Weitzman 1998). Furthermore, from an economic perspective, analyses of spending patterns for recovery efforts suggest an absence of cost-effective resource allocation which reflect both potentially counterproductive departures from official and mandated

Helpful comments were provided by Stephen Breyer, William Clark, Cary Coglianese, Andrew Metrick, Richard Newell, Todd Schatzki, Stuart Shapiro, Robert Stavins, Richard Zeckhauser, and participants in the Environmental Policy and Analysis Ph.D. Seminar at Harvard University. I am particularly grateful for the support of Andrew Metrick, who included me in a National Science Foundation funded project (#SBR-9422772) on the economics of biodiversity conservation, and for J. R. DeShazo's guidance and intellectual support. Naturally, I am responsible for any and all errors contained in this study.

spending priority systems, and a system which itself has potential flaws (Metrick and Weitzman 1996b, 1998; Simon et al. 1995; Yaffee 1982). Simple analysis, for example, reveals a major concentration of resources for only a few species slated for recovery – 40 percent of total recovery spending on vertebrate species from 1989 to 1993 was allocated to only 12 out of 236 species. It is this kind of analysis that suggests the simplistic interpretation of a proclivity for saving "cute and fuzzy" species, or "charismatic megafauna" (Metrick and Weitzman 1996b; 1998). Part of the goal of this chapter is to illuminate the more complex dynamics involved in implementation of the ESA.

In this chapter I explore two areas related to the above concerns: (1) the use of scientific information in the implementation of the act by the U.S. Fish and Wildlife Service (USFWS); and (2) the political economy of funding decisions for species recovery. In order to address these topics, I present analyses of the *listing* and *funding* decisions under the ESA. Using data on listing decisions between 1973 and 1993, funding expenditures between 1989 and 1993, a range of scientific characteristics of species, and a variety of political and bureaucratic variables, I employ statistical analyses to test the following hypotheses:

1. *The ESA Amendments of 1982, which prohibited FWS from making listing decisions based on the taxonomic class of species (i.e., giving preference to mammals), resulted in listing decisions that were more consistent with scientific determinants of species endangerment.* This analysis tests the efficacy of congressionally mandated use of more narrow scientific guidelines in agency decision making.

2. *The amount of funding allocated for recovery efforts is correlated less with scientifically based considerations of endangerment and correlated more with a variety of political considerations.* This analysis explores theories of congressional-bureaucracy relationships and political economic theories of "pork" politics.

The results of these analyses provide support for the notion that scientific inputs are important in implementation of the ESA, but may vary in importance at different stages of the policy process. Perhaps more important, however, results suggest a blurring of the boundary between science and politics in which the choices about what kind of science to do and what species to study are driven by a myriad of political factors. The results also suggest a complex interaction of political variables at both the congressional and agency levels which can help explain patterns of funding for recovery that diverge from both economically and ecologically normative prescriptions.

Since the methodology employs a statistical analysis in a reduced form, it does not allow a determination of causal relationships, and therefore, conclusions that can be drawn from the results are necessarily limited. In addition, as noted in the concluding section of this chapter, there are compelling reasons to statistically examine the listing and funding decisions jointly (as opposed to separately, as they are done in this study). It is hoped, however, that the results of this empirical analysis will provide beginning and tentative answers to the question of the roles of science and politics in regulatory decision making, and provide a foundation from which a structural model can be developed to better allow predictive conclusions.

Section 2 provides a theoretical overview of the foci of this study: the role of science in public policy; and the political economy of environmental policy and agency implementation of environmental statutes. Section 3 of this chapter outlines a description and a brief history of the Endangered Species Act. Section 4 describes the data, methodology, and results of the analysis. In Section 5, conclusions are presented.

2. THEORETICAL BACKGROUND

As science and technology have become an increasingly important part of industrialized society, their roles in the development and implementation of public policy have become more intensively scrutinized. Science has been, and continues to be, critical in providing knowledge and techniques to address a range of public issues. These issues can encompass a continuum of problems from the purely technical in nature, to problems with multiple dimensions and where the technical element is only one of many components. Particularly in these more complex problems, a dynamic balance exists between scientific and political inputs. In discussing the roles of expert advice and science in the process of democratic policy formation, Dahl concludes:

> Decisions about crucial public policies rarely, if ever, require knowledge only of the technically most efficient means to ends that can be taken as given because they are self-evidently right or universally accepted. Because "scientific" knowledge about the empirical world cannot be a sufficient qualification for ruling, pure empirical "science" is not and cannot be enough to constitute a "royal science" of ruling ... Because both moral understanding and instrumental knowledge are always necessary for policy judgments, neither alone can ever be sufficient. (1989, 68–69)

As science is undertaken increasingly in the service of solving controversial and complex environmental problems, it is claimed that the boundaries between science and policy become increasingly blurred (Brooks and Cooper 1987; Jasanoff 1990, 1995). The emerging school of thought of science and technology studies has convincingly argued that, as opposed to being "objectively" separate from social and political forces, science is socially constructed, embedded in the cultural, political, economic, and legal context in which it takes place (Funtowicz and Ravetz 1993; Gieryn 1995; Guston 1998; Jasanoff 1987). Thus, the injection of values into the scientific process is seen as an inevitable part of current science. For example, in an analysis of risk assessment and risk management in the Occupational Safety and Health Administration's regulation of toxicants, Whittemore (1983) asserts:

> Values unavoidably enter virtually every aspect of toxicant risk analysis. This complex intermingling of facts and values is worrisome, because recent evidence suggests that human judgments concerning questions of fact and value are inconsistent and extremely sensitive to the way such judgments are elicited. (23)

While the influence of values and interests has been explored only minimally in the context of science's influence in policy arenas, there is a rich history of the study of these influences in the political realm. The relationship between Congress, interests, and agency decision making, for example, has been the subject of extensive and ongoing research in the areas of the political theories of regulation (Arnold 1979; Fiorina 1974; Mayhew 1974; Shepsle 1978; Smith and Deering 1990) and economic theories of regulation (Alvarez and Saving 1995; Buchanan and Tullock 1975; Calvert, McCubbins, and Weingast 1989; Hahn 1990; Joskow and Schmalensee 1995; Peltzman 1976; Stigler 1971; Weingast and Moran 1983).

Much of the early political science literature focused on the mutually supportive relationship that evolves between congressional oversight or appropriations committees and the agencies for which they have responsibility:

> Bureaucrats appear to allocate benefits strategically in an effort both to maintain and to expand their supporting coalitions. When it furthers their purposes, they broaden their program's geographic scope and increase the number of shares of benefits so that more congressmen can be brought into their supporting coalitions ... Congressmen can claim credit for whatever benefits flow into their districts, but at the same time they have insulated themselves from their constituents' anger when certain benefits cannot be secured. (Arnold 1979, 207–208)

Committee members use their positions on committees to attain benefits that improve their chances of reelection (Fenno 1973), but they also follow a policy of "universalism" in which projects with specific benefits but diffuse costs are distributed among the members of Congress regardless of party affiliation or seniority (Mayhew 1974).

Given the importance of congressional committees in agency behavior, studies have also focused on the process of committee assignment. Shepsle (1978), for example, notes that a member's interests are central to decisions to request and ultimately obtain placement on committees:

> For all major legislative committees, "interest" variables exert a strong independent effect on request likelihood. This effect, moreover, is most pronounced in those committees for which the intuitive linkage between committee jurisdiction and constituency-clientele interests is most obvious ... It is least pronounced in those committees with jurisdictions of general interest to many constituencies. (232)

In an attempt to integrate both political and economic theories of government regulation, Stigler (1971) and Peltzman (1976) laid the groundwork for the subsequent development of positive political economy analyses of government regulatory behavior. Exploring the demand for regulation, Stigler attempts "to explain who will receive the benefits or burdens of regulation, what form regulation will take, and the effects of regulation upon the allocation of resources" (3). Recent empirical studies suggest complexities in a political economy analysis of a wide range of federal outlays. Alvarez and Saving (1995) observe "considerable evidence that congressional committees and politics play a major role in the allocations of federal benefits across congressional districts" (2), but these patterns of allocation are not always in ways predicted by conventional wisdom.

Much of this vein of research has also explored the influence of congressional interest and preferences in the behavior of agencies. Weingast and Moran (1983) observe, for example, that activities of the Federal Trade Commission are "sensitive to changes in subcommittee composition" (793), and that decision making within the bureaucracy is fundamentally influenced by the subcommittee's preferences. Likewise, Calvert et al. (1989) present a model of agency discretion in which policy making in the bureaucracy is driven largely by the preferences of Congress. In this view, bureaucrats are constrained by congressional appointments, agency structuring, and allocations of resources that force the alignment of agency actions with committee preferences. Research has also explored the role of capture and ideology in the behaviors of members of Congress. For example, in an analysis of strip mining legislation, Kalt and Zupan (1984) conclude that members' voting behaviors are determined by a complex dynamic between personal ideology and the preferences and interests of constituents.

Although it is beyond the scope of this chapter to provide a synthesis of these disparate fields, the empirical analysis presented here represents a step toward such a synthesis. Ultimately, a formal conceptual model of the role of science and politics in endangered species conservation will be constructed from which we can derive and empirically test refutable hypotheses and suggest causal relationships.

3. THE ENDANGERED SPECIES ACT: HISTORY, ADMINISTRATION, AND RECENT RESEARCH

3.1. Administration of the ESA and the Listing and Funding Decisions

Reflecting concern over decreasing populations and the extinction of North American species (Littell 1992), Congress passed the Endangered Species Act of 1973 to "provide a means whereby the ecosystems upon which endangered species and threatened species depend may be conserved, [and] to provide a program for the conservation of such endangered species and threatened species" (U.S. Fish and Wildlife Service 1994, Section 2.b). The FWS in the Department of Interior and the National Marine Fisheries Service (NMFS) in the Department of Commerce[1] are charged with implementing the act.

State or federal agencies, individuals, or nongovernmental organizations can petition the FWS or NMFS for a species to be *listed*.[2] This petition sets into motion a well-defined process of review, analysis, and public input (e.g., a public comment period). The culmination of this process is a decision by the respective secretary to not list, or to list the proposed species as threatened or endangered. The act stipulates that this determination shall be made " . . . solely on the basis of the best scientific and commercial data available" (USFWS 1994, Section 4.b.1.A).[3] Though this requirement was in the act when it was first passed, it has not always been strictly followed. Noting the disproportionate number of listed mammals and birds, Congress prohibited the use of taxonomic class to give preference to species during the listing process (and recovery efforts) through amendments to the act in 1982. Prior to this, FWS had given higher priority to classes of organisms that are more closely related to humans (e.g., mammals) than those more distantly related (e.g., amphibians) (Littell 1992). The goal of this amendment was to require listing decisions to be based more firmly on scientific grounds of species endangerment, as opposed to human preferences. One aspect of this study tests whether or not the amendment was effective in reaching this goal.

Once a species is listed, it is entitled to a broad range of protections and recovery efforts. This study focuses on one of these efforts – the mandate of FWS and NMFS to design and implement recovery plans "for the conservation and survival of endangered species and threatened species" (USFWS 1994, Section 4.f.1). The recovery program is central to the implementation of the act, and accounts for approximately 30 percent of the total FWS endangered species program budget. In 1992, this amounted to $18.9 million out of a total budget of $60.7 million. Recovery is implemented in several steps following the listing decision: drafting and approving a recovery plan; implementing the requirements of the recovery plan; and evaluating the success of the recovery effort.

---

[1] The FWS is charged with protecting terrestrial and freshwater species; the NMFS is responsible for marine organisms. This study focuses primarily on the FWS.

[2] The definition of a "species" is more broadly interpreted in the act than it is in standard biological discourse. A "species" includes both traditionally biologically defined species (denoted as full species), as well as subspecies or a clearly defined population. Thus, whooping cranes (a full species), Columbia white-tailed deer (a subspecies of white-tailed deer), and two populations of gray wolf are all defined as "species" under the act (U.S. Fish and Wildlife Service 1994).

[3] As defined in the act, an endangered species is "any species which is in danger of extinction throughout all or a significant portion of its range," and a threatened species is "any species which is likely to become an endangered species within the foreseeable future throughout all or a significant portion of its range" (USFWS 1994, Sections 3.6 and 3.19). "Commercial data" does not mean economic data, but data such as population trends, supplied by industries associated with a species (e.g., the fisheries industry).

Table 7.1. *U.S. fish and wildlife service recovery priority ranking system*

Degree of threat	Recovery potential	Taxonomic uniqueness	Priority rank	w/Conflict
	High	Monotypic genus	1	1C
				1
		Species	2	2C
				2
High		Subspecies	3	3C
				3
	Low	Monotypic genus	4	4C
				4
		Species	5	5C
				5
		Subspecies	6	6C
				6
	High	Monotypic genus	7	7C
				7
		Species	8	8C
				8
Medium		Subspecies	9	9C
				9
	Low	Monotypic genus	10	10C
				10
		Species	11	11C
				11
		Subspecies	12	12C
				12
	High	Monotypic genus	13	13C
				13
		Species	14	14C
				14
Low		Subspecies	15	15C
				15
	Low	Monotypic genus	16	16C
				16
		Species	17	17C
				17
		Subspecies	18	18C
				18

Source: Adapted from Fay and Thomas (1983).

In an attempt to effectively allocate recovery resources among species, Congress, through amendments to the act in 1979, mandated that the FWS create and utilize a recovery priority ranking system. The published system is a three-tiered, lexicographic, eighteen-point system ("1" having highest priority) which ranks species based on degree of threat, recovery potential, and taxonomic uniqueness. The ranking system also takes into account whether the species is in conflict with economic development. A higher priority is assigned to those species in conflict (Fay and Thomas 1983). (See Table 7.1.)

The priority rank of each species is developed by the assigned lead region and used by each region to create a budget for the scientific research and recovery efforts of species in its charge. This budgetary information is used by the FWS budget office in its budget request. Given that the majority of the funds appropriated for recovery are directed to agencies within the Department of Interior, the Interior Subcommittee of the Appropriations Committee is the focus of this study.[4]

3.2. Recent Research on the ESA

Still in the midst of debate in Congress over reauthorization (authorization expired in 1992), the ESA has been the focus of research from both government and academic spheres. In 1988, the house oversight subcommittee, the Subcommittee on Fisheries and Wildlife Conservation and the Environment, of the Committee on Merchant Marine and Fisheries, requested a General Accounting Office analysis of the implementation of the Act (GAO 1988). The report highlights strengths and weaknesses of the act's recovery programs, and recommends a variety of remedial measures for the two implementing agencies. In 1995, the National Research Council (NRC), responding to a request from both the House and Senate, completed an analysis of the use of science in the implementation of the act. The general objective of the NRC was to explore the question: "Is the ESA soundly based in science as an effective method of protecting endangered species and their habitats?" (2–3). The NRC's overall answer to this question is "yes," acknowledging, however, the need for improvement in several areas (National Research Council 1995).

Recent academic empirical research has also addressed a variety of aspects of the act and its implementation. Yaffee (1982) provides a thorough examination of the prohibitive nature of the ESA and the role of prohibitive policy, in general, in democratic policy making. Noting the particular political salience of biological diversity preservation, Tobin (1990) offers a survey of political factors which influence and are influenced by the ESA. Another, more specific, avenue of this research has focused on the determinants of listing and funding decisions, and is the springboard for this current study. Metrick and Weitzman (1996b, 1998) examine both listing and funding decisions by comparing the relative contributions of "scientific" determinants (e.g., level of endangerment) and "visceral" determinants (e.g., size and relative relatedness to humans). The authors conclude that particularly in funding decisions, "visceral" characteristics dominate scientific inputs in the decision-making process. Simon and his colleagues (Simon et al. 1995) investigate the

---

[4] In 1991, 72 percent of federal funds allocated to endangered species recovery was appropriated through the Interior Subcommittees. The rest was appropriated through subcommittees responsible for the Department of Agriculture (except for the Forest Service), the Department of Defense, the Department of Commerce, and the Environmental Protection Agency.

relationship between FWS's own priority ranks for species listed under the ESA and funding decisions. They find no relationship between the overall ranking system and allocation of resources, but they do find that components of the ranking system, such as recovery potential and whether the species is in conflict with economic development, are important determinants of funding. Finally, a legal analysis of the ESA explores how closely FWS and NMFS follow legislative mandates defined in the act, its amendments, and court cases related to the act (Houck 1993). Noting the use of regulatory discretion on the part of FWS and NMFS, large discrepancies are found between the requirements of the act and the actual implementation of it. Houck concludes, for example, that "the ESA has accommodated the overwhelming majority of human activity without impediment" (279).

4. EMPIRICAL ANALYSIS

In an effort to test the two specific hypotheses outlined above, statistical analyses of determinants of the outcomes of the listing and funding decisions are employed in this study. The statistical model used in this analysis draws upon and extends the work of Metrick and Weitzman (1996b). This section is divided into two subsections, each focusing on one of the two hypotheses.

4.1.

Hypothesis 1. The ESA Amendments of 1982, which prohibited the FWS from making listing decisions based on the taxonomic class of species (i.e., giving preference to mammals), resulted in listing decisions that were more consistent with scientific determinants of species endangerment.

In order to test this hypothesis, I begin with a presentation of analyses contributed by Metrick and Weitzman. In their study, the authors capture both scientific and nonscientific measurable determinants of both the listing and funding decisions. While political factors per se are not included in the Metrick/Weitzman analyses, variables that might capture society's subjective valuation of species, and thus influence political decisions, are used. (See Table 7.2 for a chart of variables described below.)

Using data from The Nature Conservancy's Natural Heritage Conservation Database (1993), which includes all vertebrate species and salient features of their natural history, the authors created a dataset that includes over 500 full species of vertebrates in North America (Metrick and Weitzman 1996a).[5] The most important species-specific variable constructed by The Nature Conservancy biologists with respect to this study is an "endangerment" rank.

---

[5] Only vertebrate species are analyzed in this and all other analyses in this chapter. Vertebrates account for the vast majority of recovery funding. In 1991, for example, expenditures on vertebrates were 95 percent of the total (U.S. Fish and Wildlife Service 1992a).

Table 7.2. *Variables used in the analysis*

Variable (*NOTATION IN REGRESSION*)	Description	Source
Listed status (*LISTED*)	Dummy variable: 1 = listed under the Endangered Species Act; 0 = not listed	(USFWS 1992b)
Total federal and state funding for FY 1989–1991 (*LNTOTAL1*)	Natural log of the spending allocated for direct recovery measures from all state and federal agencies.	(Metrick and Weitzman 1996a)
Total funding appropriated by the Interior Subcommittee for FY 1989–1991 (*LNTOTAL2*)	Natural log of the spending allocated for direct recovery measures from all federal agencies under the control of the Interior Subcommittee of the Senate Appropriations Committee.	(USFWS 1990, 1991, 1992a)
Taxonomic class (*MAMMAL, BIRD, REPTILE, AMPHIB*)	Dummy variables that indicate whether the species is a mammal, bird, reptile, amphibian, or fish. (FISH is the benchmark and thus is not included directly in the regressions.)	(USFWS 1992b)
Endangerment rank (*NC-RANK*)	Rank on a 5-point scale established by the Nature Conservancy: 1 = most endangered; 5 = least endangered.	(National Heritage Data Center Network 1992, 1993)
Length (*LNLENGTH*)	Natural log of the length of the species.	(Metrick and Weitzman 1996a)
Monotypic species (*MONOTYPIC*)	Dummy variable: 1 = monotypic species (that is, a full species that constitutes the sole representative of its genus); 0 = not monotypic species. Also part of the 3rd component of the Priority Rank lexicographic ranking system.	(Metrick and Weitzman 1996a)
Subspecies (*SUBSPECIES*)	Dummy Variable: 1 = if taxonomic unit is below full species (i.e., a listed subspecies or population); 0 = not subspecies. Also part of the 3rd component of the Priority Rank lexicographic ranking system.	(Metrick and Weitzman 1996a)
Conflict (*CONFLICT*)	Dummy Variable: 1 = in conflict; 0 = not in conflict. The FWS priority system recognizes species that are judged to be in conflict with economic development. Species in conflict do not receive a higher priority rank than those not in conflict, but they are given a tiebreaking preference between species with the same priority rank.	(Metrick and Weitzman 1996a)

Table 7.2 *Continued*

Variable (*NOTATION IN REGRESSION*)	Description	Source
Priority Rank (*PRIORITY*)	FWS recovery priority rank on an 18-point scale: 1 = highest priority; 18 = lowest priority.	(Metrick and Weitzman 1996a)
Degree of threat (*DEGREE*)	1st component of the Priority Rank lexicographic ranking system. 1 = high degree of threat; 2 = medium degree of threat; 3 = low degree of threat.	(USFWS 1992b)
Recovery potential (*RECOVERY*)	2nd component of the Priority Rank lexicographic ranking system. 1 = high potential; 0 = low potential.	(USFWS 1992b)
Subcommittee Membership in the Senate in 101st and 102nd Congresses (1989 and 1991) (*HAS-SCM*)	Dummy variable: 1 = At least 1 Subcommittee member on the Interior Subcommittee of the Appropriations Committee from state in which species exists (1989 and 1991); 0 = no Subcommittee member.	(Congressional Quarterly News Features 1989, 1991; Riemer 1971; Stebbins 1966; Page and Brooks 1991; Lee et al. 1980; Conart and Collins 1991)
Special earmark (*EARMARK*)	Dummy variable: 1 = special earmark was made for the species during the budget markup process (1989–1991); 0 = no earmark	(USFWS 1996)
Environmental ideology of subcommittee member in the Senate and House (*LCV*)	Average League of Conservation Voters score based on Subcommittee members' voting record for environment-related legislation for each state (1989 and 1991)	(League of Conservation Voters 1989; 1991)
Public Comment Data (*COMM-PRO; COMM-CON; COMM-NEUT*)	Number of comments received by FWS during the official Public Comment Period as part of the listing process. *COMM-PRO* = number of comments in support of listing; *COMM-CON* = number of comments against listing; *COMM-NEUT* = number of comments neither in support of nor against listing.	(Federal Register 1973–1991)
Print media coverage (*NEWS*)	Number of newspaper and magazine articles in the U.S. from 120 sources for each species from 1988–1991.	(Lexis/Nexis)

These ranks range from "1" (critically endangered) to "5" (not threatened).[6] This rank is determined by analyzing "a species' rarity, its population trends, and known or suspected threats to its existence" (The Nature Conservancy 1996). Species included in the Metrick/Weitzman dataset are all vertebrate species that have a rank of 3 or less (indicating that they are threatened to some degree).

The dependent variable in Regression #1 is a dummy variable which indicates whether or not the species was listed (*LISTED*) under the ESA as of 1991 (U.S. Fish and Wildlife Service 1992b). Variables that capture the scientific input in the listing decision are species' degree of endangerment and how genetically unique the species is. NC-RANK is a variable between 1 and 3 that denotes The Nature Conservancy's endangerment rank described above. *MONOTYPIC* is a dummy variable that indicates whether a species is the sole representative of its genus and thus genetically more distinct than a non-monotypic species (USFWS 1992b).

Two nonscientific, or "visceral," characteristics were tested as determinants of the listing decision. These are the taxonomic class of the species and the size of the species. The variables *MAMMAL, BIRD, REPTILE,* and *AMPHIBIAN* are dummy variables (fish is the benchmark) which capture the taxonomic class. The use of these variables addresses the notion that one component of society's valuation of endangered species might derive from how closely a species is related to humans. The more closely a species is related to humans (e.g., a mammal), the higher the value we might place on it, and thus we might be more likely to protect it. *LNLENGTH* is the natural log of the adult length of the species. Physical size also appears to be a characteristic of an animal that might influence the value placed on it. One might expect, for example, a positive coefficient on *LNLENGTH* if the notion is correct that we place higher values on "charismatic megafauna" (Metrick and Weitzman 1996b; Metrick 1998).

The original regression presented by Metrick and Weitzman indicates that the probability of listing is associated with both scientific and "visceral" variables (see Table 7.3, Regression #1). The coefficients on *NC-RANK* and *MONOTYPIC* are both in the expected direction and are both significant. Greater endangerment is associated with a greater likelihood of listing, and monotypic species have a higher probability of being listed than nonmonotypic species. Based on this regression analysis, the nonscientific characteristics also seem to be important in the listing process. Those species that are

---

[6] 1 = critically imperiled throughout their range and have fewer than six occurrences in the world, or fewer than 1,000 individuals; 2 = imperiled throughout their range and typically have between six and twenty occurrences, or fewer than 3,000 individuals; 3 = vulnerable throughout their range and typically have fewer than 100 occurrences, or fewer than 10,000 individuals; 4 = apparently secure throughout its range (but possibly rare in parts of its range); 5 = demonstrably secure throughout its range (however, it may be rare in certain areas) (National Heritage Data Center Network 1993).

Table 7.3. *The listing decision*

Independent variable	Dependent variable = LISTED	
	Regression #1 Metrick/Weitzman (standard error)	Regression #2 corrected for 1982 Amendment (standard error)
MAMMAL	1.11**	0.41
	(0.42)	(0.69)
BIRD	1.21**	−0.40
	(0.38)	(0.82)
REPTILE	0.92**	0.85
	(0.44)	(0.61)
AMPHIBIAN	−1.51**	−1.70**
	(0.45)	(0.77)
LNLENGTH	0.25*	0.13
	(0.14)	(0.23)
NC-RANK	−1.47**	−1.28**
	(0.16)	(0.24)
MONOTYPIC	0.84**	0.96*
	(0.39)	(0.52)
CONSTANT	1.07	0.04
	(0.42)	(0.70)
Logit estimation	N = 511	N = 409
	Log likelihood = −220.4	Log likelihood = −105.9

** = $p < 0.05$; * = $p < 0.1$.

more closely related to humans (mammals, birds, and reptiles) are associated with increased probabilities of listing relative to amphibians and fish.

One shortcoming of this analysis is that it includes species that were listed both prior to the 1982 Amendments to the ESA *and* since 1982. Prior to these amendments, it was FWS policy that "higher" taxonomic classes (e.g., mammals) were given priority over "lower" classes (e.g., fish) in the listing decision. The 1982 Amendments stipulated, however, that this criterion could no longer be used in the prioritization of species for the listing process. This major policy shift is not accounted for in Regression #1. Thus, a bias may exist which overestimates the effect of taxonomic class on more recent listing decisions.

To test the existence of this bias and the efficacy of the 1982 Amendment, I ran the regression including only those species listed after 1982 (see Table 7.3, Regression #2). The results of this analysis are significantly different from those in the Metrick/Weitzman analysis.[7] The two scientific variables are still in the expected direction, and are still both significant. The nonscientific variables, however, have lost their explanatory power. Except for the

[7] The unrestricted log-likelihood function = −220.4; the restricted log-likelihood function = −114.5; $\lambda = -229$; $p < 0.005$.

coefficient on *AMPHIBIAN*, which maintains a negative and significant value, all the other taxonomic variables are not significantly different than zero. Likewise, the coefficient on *LNLENGTH* has become insignificant.

While this model would be more complete with variables that capture more purely political or economic aspects of the listing decision process, as a first assessment it seems that scientific variables have greater explanatory power for the listing decision than do the nonscientific considerations that were measured. Also, it appears that following the Amendments of 1982, taxonomic criteria for listing became insignificant – evidence that FWS, in fact, responded to the Congressional mandate.

4.2.

Hypothesis 2. The amount of funding allocated for recovery efforts is correlated less with scientifically based considerations of endangerment and correlated more with a variety of political considerations.

As noted in Section 3, once a species is listed, funds may be allocated for its recovery. To explore determinants of the funding decision, Metrick and Weitzman completed a tobit analysis of the funding decision[8] (see Table 7.4, Regression #3). The species included in this dataset are all the listed vertebrate species and subspecies (236) as of the end of 1991.

The dependent variable is the natural log of total government spending (federal and state) from 1989 through 1991 on direct recovery efforts (*LNTOTAL1*).[9] All of the same scientific and nonscientific variables that were used in the logit analysis for the listing decision were used in this analysis, with one exception. Since subspecies can be listed as a "species" under the ESA, the dummy *SUBSPECIES* was included in the analysis, like *MONOTYPIC*, to assess the importance of genetic uniqueness in the funding decision.

Unlike in the listing decision, the scientific variables are not significantly correlated with changes in funding in ways that would be normatively predicted. *NC-RANK*, for example, is *positively* correlated with funding and significant. This is the *opposite* of what might be expected. It suggests that the more endangered a species is, the less funding it receives. Certainly this seems to run counter to how FWS has constructed its priority system. Likewise, neither *MONOTYPIC* nor *SUBSPECIES* are significantly different than zero. Thus, it seems that the genetic uniqueness of a species is not associated with different levels of funding.

---

[8] A tobit model was used in this case because the data is censored at $100; spending data is not observed for expenditures less than $100.

[9] The 1988 Amendments to the ESA required the FWS to publish annual reports that delineated per-species expenditures for all species listed under the ESA. This amendment was partially in response to the fact that relatively few listed species received large percentages of the total allocation of funding. 1989, 1990, and 1991 represent the first years these reports were made available.

Table 7.4. *The funding decision*

Independent variable	Regression #3 Metrick/Weitzman	Regression #4 with added political variables	Regression #5 comparing NC-RANK and components of PRIORITY	Regression #6 with added public comment and news variables
	LNTOTAL1	LNTOTAL2	LNTOTAL2	LNTOTAL2
MAMMAL	0.75*	0.11	−0.19	0.04
	(0.44)	(0.47)	(0.54)	(0.59)
BIRD	0.27	0.90**	0.91**	0.42
	(0.37)	(0.42)	(0.43)	(0.62)
REPTILE	−1.72**	−1.64**	−1.66**	−1.31*
	(0.50)	(0.56)	(0.56)	(0.68)
AMPHIBIAN	−0.94	−0.35	−0.41	0.30
	(0.66)	(0.73)	(0.73)	(0.92)
LNLENGTH	−1.03**	0.60**	0.66**	0.37
	(0.15)	(0.17)	(0.18)	(0.23)
NC-RANK	0.65**	0.47**	0.41*	0.48*
	(0.19)	(0.22)	(0.22)	(0.28)
MONOTYPIC	−0.37		0.29	
	(0.50)		(0.53)	
SUBSPECIES	−0.35		−0.47	
	(0.30)		(0.33)	
PRIORITY		−0.10**		0.19**
		(0.04)		(0.06)
CONFLICT		0.86**	1.05**	0.11
		(0.33)	(0.34)	(0.49)
HAS-SCM		1.29**	1.05*	1.53*
		(0.62)	(0.62)	(0.81)
EARMARK		2.04**	2.15**	1.46*
		(0.59)	(0.60)	(0.90)
LCV		−0.0003	0.004	−0.006
		(0.014)	(0.01)	(0.02)
DEGREE			−0.036	
			(0.28)	
RECOVERY			1.70*	
			(0.91)	
COMM-PRO				0.003**
				(0.001)
COMM-OPP				−0.002**
				(0.0009)
COMM-NEUT				0.04*
				(0.02)
NEWS				0.0003**
				(0.0001)
CONSTANT	7.69	7.98	7.97	8.65
	(0.45)	(0.56)	(0.62)	(0.81)
Tobit estimation	N = 236	N = 236	N = 236	N = 136

** = $p < 0.05$; * = $p < 0.1$.

Although the scientific considerations seem to be less significant in this stage of the policy process, nonscientific or "visceral" factors seem to be more important. The coefficient on *LNLENGTH* shows that the size of the animal is positively correlated with spending and is significant. In addition, *MAMMAL* is positively correlated with funding while *REPTILE* is negatively correlated. Coefficients on *BIRD* and *AMPHIBIAN*, while not significant, have the expected signs if taxonomic class influences the funding decision as discussed above – organisms more closely related to humans are valued higher and thus receive preferential treatment. This spending pattern is also illustrated in an analysis of per-species funding by taxonomic class in which mammals and birds receive much higher per-species funding than do reptiles, amphibians, or fish (see Figure 7.1).

4.2.1. New Models

Departing from this re-analysis of the Metrick/Weitzman model and collecting data that captures political variables as well as additional FWS information, I will present further analysis of the funding decision. Again, tobit models are used in these analyses (Regressions #4, #5, and #6) for the same reasons as explained above. (Again, see Table 7.2 for a chart of variables described below.)

The dependent variable in these analyses is still funding levels. However, since some of the new variables capture characteristics of the Interior Subcommittee of the Appropriations Committee, the funding variable (*LNTOTAL2*) was revised to include per species funding from 1989 to 1991 only for those agencies whose appropriations are controlled by the Interior Subcommittee[10] (U.S. Fish and Wildlife Service 1990, 1991, 1992a).

4.2.1.1. New Political Variables. In an effort to capture how political actions in Congress might be correlated with funding decisions, data on several congressional variables were collected and included in the model. *HAS-SCM* is a dummy variable that represents whether or not a species' range includes a state from which there is a subcommittee member (SCM) on the Interior Subcommittee in the Senate during the years in which funding was tracked (1989–1991) (Congressional Quarterly News Features 1989, 1991).[11] Descriptive statistics that provide a comparison of per-species funding for species associated with an SCM ($1.45 million per species) and those not associated with an SCM ($220,000 per species) suggest that increased funding levels for

---

[10] These include all Department of Interior Agencies with species recovery efforts (FWS, Bureau of Mines, Bureau of Land Management, National Park Service, Bureau of Indian Affairs, Bureau of Reclamation), as well as Forest Service in the Department of Agriculture.

[11] These data were collected for the Senate only, because species range data are provided by FWS only at the state level.

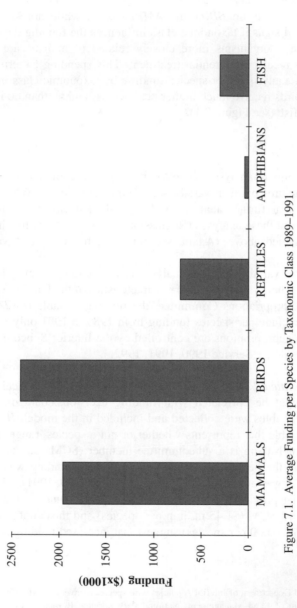

Figure 7.1. Average Funding per Species by Taxonomic Class 1989–1991.

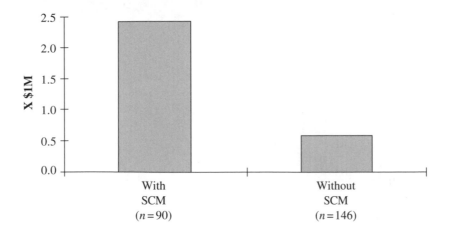

Figure 7.2. Average per Species Funding Associated with Subcommittee Membership 1989–1991.

an endangered species are associated with the presence of an SCM in the state in which that endangered species resides (see Figure 7.2).

An additional variable that might elucidate the role of Congress in the allocation of recovery funding is that of congressional earmarks for specific species. During the budget markup process, members of Congress can submit requests to the Interior Subcommittee for recovery funding earmarked for specific species (Lohoefener 1996). These earmarks are often included in the final markup and, in fact, make up a substantial proportion of the total recovery spending allocated to the FWS. In 1991, for example, $3.6 million of the total $14.9 million (or 24 percent) was the result of congressional earmarks. *EARMARK* is a dummy variable that indicates whether or not a species was specifically earmarked funds (U.S. Fish and Wildlife Service 1996, June 11). Displaying a similar pattern as species associated with an SCM, species that are earmarked funds tend to have much larger per-species funding than those species that do not receive earmarked funds (see Figure 7.3).

To get greater insight into how a subcommittee members' history of voting for environmental legislation might be correlated with present funding allocations, the variable *LCV* was constructed. This variable is derived from the League of Conservation Voters' annual ratings of members for Congress from 1989 and 1991 (the years in which funding was tracked). Each year the League of Conservation Voters assigns a score for members based on key votes on environmental issues.[12] *LCV* is the average League of Conservation Voters score for the Interior Subcommittee Member(s) present in the state(s)

---

[12] The rating is on a 100-point percentage scale. A score of 100 percent, for example, represents a member voting "pro-environment" on all of the bills tracked by the League of Conservation Voters.

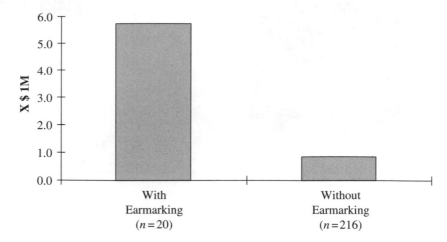

Figure 7.3. Average per Species Funding Associated with Earmarking 1989–1991.

where a species exists (Congressional Quarterly News Features 1989, 1991; League of Conservation Voters 1989, 1991).

Several additional variables were added from FWS databases to illustrate different aspects of the decision-making process. *PRIORITY* is the priority ranking assigned to each species by the FWS as introduced in Section 1. This is an eighteen-point score constructed from a lexicographic ranking system which includes measures of "degree of threat" (3 levels: high, medium, and low), "recovery potential" (2 levels: high and low), and "taxonomic uniqueness" (3 levels: monotypic species, full species, and subspecies). A "1" priority rank indicates the highest priority for recovery efforts, while "18" indicates the lowest priority (Fay and Thomas 1983). (Again, see Table 7.1.)

In an effort to determine the potential differential influence of the three components that are used in constructing the priority rank, I disaggregated the rank into its constituent parts. *DEGREE* is a three-point variable denoting the level of threat to a species – "1" representing the highest degree of threat, "3" the lowest. *RECOVERY* is a dummy variable that captures whether the species has a high or low potential for recovery – "1" represents a high recovery potential. *MONOTYPIC* and *SUBSPECIES* are dummy variables identical to those explained above (Fay and Thomas 1983; USFWS 1992b).

CONFLICT is a dummy variable that indicates whether or not a species is in conflict with economic development. The FWS includes this measure in the priority ranking system by adding a "C" to the assigned priority ranking number.[13] The notation of being in conflict is meant only to distinguish between

---

[13] The rationale for this system is that species in conflict will generally require greater funds to undergo more in-depth consultations with other federal agencies, to administer more extensive public participation (e.g., more numerous hearings), and to draft more contested recovery plans. It is also assumed that species in conflict are in greater threat of extirpation than similarly ranked organisms (Houck 1993).

two species that otherwise would have the same numerical rank. This designation confers on the species in conflict a higher priority than a similarly ranked species not in conflict. There are, therefore, a total of thirty six different ranks (in descending order of priority): 1C, 1, 2C, 2, ... 18C, 18 (Fay and Thomas 1983).

As part of different stages during the implementation of the ESA, the FWS is required to have a public comment period prior to making a final decision. While there is no comment period prior to funding decisions, there is a comment period prior to the listing decision. *COMM-SUPP, COMM-OPP, COMM-NEUT* are continuous variables that denote the number of comments received during the public comment period prior to listing in support of listing the species, opposed to listing, and neutral about listing, respectively. (Neutral comments tend to be from scientists who note particular ecological information about the species without stating an opinion on its need for listing.)[14] The inclusion of these variables in the funding decision analysis is designed to attempt to capture crude political influences in the decision-making process reflected in the general level of public support for each species.

In an additional effort to analyze public interest in different species, the variable *NEWS* was constructed. This variable is the number of news articles in newspapers and magazines throughout the United States that mention the species in the text of the article from 1988 through 1991.[15]

4.2.1.2. New Regressions. The first specification which includes some of these new variables is displayed in Table 7.4, Regression #4. Supporting much of the theoretical and empirical research which suggests that agencies and subcommittee members (SCMs) target the allocation of funds to SCM districts, the coefficient on *HAS-SCM* is positive and significant. Thus, species whose habitat is in a state that is represented on the Senate Interior Subcommittee receive, on average, increased funding.[16]

The coefficient on *EARMARK* suggests a similar political influence. This coefficient is also positive and significant. On one hand, it is trivial to note this relationship, as it is self-evident that species which are earmarked funding are going to have increased allocations of funding. However, it is important to include this variable in the analysis because it shows a clear way in which political behavior influences the funding process.

---

[14] Under the statute, FWS is obliged to publish a summary of all comments as part of the Final Rule. Thus, data for these variables were collected by analyzing all Final Rules published in the Federal Register for each species (Federal Register 1973–1991). Since comments are received from a wide variety of sources (e.g., state agencies, governors' offices, individual citizens, independent scientists, and nongovernmental organizations), this analysis cannot distinguish among the influences of these different perspectives.

[15] Data were collected through keyword searches on the electronic Lexis/Nexis database of 120 newspapers throughout the United States.

[16] Similar results are not found for Senate members who are on the subcommittees that have oversight responsibility for the implementation of the ESA. There is no significant relationship between membership on these committees and funding levels. (Data not shown.)

Although this initial analysis supports an interpretation that is consistent with traditional "pork" politics, it appears as if the issue is more complex, particularly since the recovery of species may not have high levels of local public support nor might the senator be historically pro-environment. To illustrate this, it is instructive to examine the actions of Senator Jim McClure from Idaho. Senator McClure, who sat on the Interior Subcommittee during the time period examined, also made a variety of earmark requests for species in Idaho. Despite this, McClure has always been supportive of lobbies in Idaho that are resistant to endangered species legislation. He has also consistently received low League of Conservation Voters scores; in fact, his 1989 score was 0 percent (Federal Register 1973–1991; League of Conservation Voters 1989; U.S. Fish and Wildlife Service 1996). How can these kinds of seemingly inconsistent behaviors be understood?

A window into this kind of puzzle can be seen in analysis of the role of economic conflict. The coefficient on *CONFLICT* is positive and significant – species in conflict receive more spending than species not in conflict. Furthermore, conflict is somewhat correlated with the presence of an SCM. This phenomenon is seen in an analysis of conditional probabilities of being in conflict and being associated with an SCM. For example, of species associated with an SCM, 43% are in conflict. Of species not associated with an SCM, 28% are in conflict. Likewise, of species in conflict, 49% are associated with an SCM. Of species not in conflict, only 33% are associated with an SCM.

Several political mechanisms could lead to these results. First, SCMs might voice constituents' concerns of the negative economic repercussions of a listed species and thus push FWS to designate a species as one in conflict. This would have several benefits for the SCM. It would improve the possibility that there would be greater public input from his or her constituents in the recovery planning process resulting from the greater number of hearings and other avenues of public comment that are afforded species in conflict. It could also result in increased funds being spent in the state (as noted in the above discussion of *CONFLICT*). It is possible that increased funding for research on species in conflict could serve to delay economically restrictive actions taken by the FWS, or actions that anger a significant or vocal constituency.[17] Third, causality could be in the opposite direction. That is, members of Congress who represent districts in which there is conflict with the ESA might disproportionately request to be on committees and subcommittees that directly oversee or appropriate funding for ESA implementation. This mechanism would be in accord with studies in the committee assignment literature in which legislators request assignments on committees that are particularly important for their constituents (for example, see Shepsle 1978).

---

[17] In fact, this might be what operated with Senator McClure. Among the many ways environmentalists accused Senator McClure and other members of the Idaho and Wyoming delegations of delaying wolf reintroduction was through requesting more research (Williams 1990).

Economic conflict might play an important role in *agency* decision making as well. From an efficiency perspective, the fact that *CONFLICT* is positively correlated with funding, while consistent with FWS policy, seems counterproductive. It can be argued that for equally endangered species, those that are in conflict should receive *less* not more funding, as there are already opportunity costs associated with the preservation of the species. In a one-time static decision-making scenario, this kind of decision rule might make sense. However, this kind of scenario might be seen by the regulator as a multiperiod game in which the regulator must signal to developers and other economic interests that economic conflict will not result in a reduction of recovery efforts. Signaling otherwise might create perverse incentives for increased development.[18]

Further characteristics of the politics of SCMs were analyzed with the use of the variable *LCV*. One might expect to see a positive relationship between *LCV* and funding. That is, increased funding might be expected for those species that live in states represented by an SCM with a higher League of Conservation Voters score (i.e., a "pro-environment" SCM). This, however, is not the case. The coefficient on *LCV* is not significantly different than zero. In a situation such as this, in which public floor votes are not taken, this might be expected.

When comparing how the coefficients on the "visceral" variables in this regression compare with those from the original Metrick/Weitzman analysis (compare Regression #4 and #3), mixed results are evident. Essentially, however, the findings that "higher" taxonomic class and size of the organism are correlated with funding is supported.[19]

As in Regression #3, *NC-RANK* has a positive and significant coefficient in Regression #4. Again, this is counter to what might be expected if FWS were allocating resources to those species that are most endangered. Metrick and Weitzman argue that this counterintuitive result stems from one kind of omitted variable bias. This omitted variable would be a measure of animals' charisma or appeal that is not captured by the "visceral" variables included in the analysis. If this bias does exist in this way, it suggests that *NC-RANK* and charisma would be positively correlated (that is, species with great appeal tend to be less endangered), and "charismatic" species would tend to get

---

[18] Interestingly, the current system also creates perverse incentives – developers have increased incentive to develop land as soon as possible, before endangered species are officially "found" on their property or a resident species is listed as endangered.

[19] The value of the coefficient on *LNLENGTH* has decreased but is still positive and significant. In Regression #3, a 1% increase in length is correlated with a 1% increase in funding. In Regression #4, a 1% increase is correlated with a 0.51% increase in funding. This reflects the positive but weak multicollinearity between *LNLENGTH* and two of the newly added variables, *HAS-SCM* and *CONFLICT*. In addition, in the new regression, the coefficient on *MAMMAL* has changed from being significant to not significant. The coefficient on *BIRD* has changed from being not significant to significant. The coefficient on *AMPHIBIAN* has changed sign from negative to positive but remains insignificant. The coefficient on *REPTILE* has remained both negative and significant. It is not clear how to interpret these changes, but one conclusion remains the same – differences in taxonomic class are correlated with differences in funding.

higher funding. Another possible left-out variable is one that captures the different requirements that different species have for their protection. For example, if larger animals require larger areas of habitat protection, or migratory animals such as birds have more expensive monitoring requirements, or protecting several species of fish that live in the same tributary is relatively inexpensive, the statistical results described above might not necessarily represent a departure from FWS stated policy. Unequal marginal costs of recovery and protection across species might, in fact, result in the same output as that generated from an underlying preference for larger animals that are appealing to humans (i.e., mammals and birds), if in fact species that are more expensive to save are also those more valued by people. Alternatively, it is possible that highly endangered species, whose populations are small, might in fact be less expensive to protect than less endangered species with larger populations and broader distributions. This also would result in a negative correlation between level of endangerment and funding.

Complicating these interpretations, however, is the fact that the coefficient on *PRIORITY* is negative and significant. This indicates that, on average, species with lower priority ranks receive greater funding. This is what one would expect if FWS followed its priority rank when deciding to allocate funding. How could the coefficients on both *NC-RANK* and *PRIORITY*, which ostensibly measure the endangerment of a species, be of opposite sign? Recall that *NC-RANK* captures a more purely scientific assessment of species endangerment and does not consider management issues. *PRIORITY*, however, is a composite ranking derived from three components. One of these, recovery potential, is heavily influenced by management concerns. FWS explicitly designed the priority system so that it did not take into account only the degree of threat faced by a species. There is an attempt to address issues of cost-effectiveness by including the recovery potential of a species in its priority system. It is true, however, that in the lexicographic system, the overwhelming weight of the allocation of resources is supposed to be on the degree of threat. In actuality, this does not appear to be the case, given the coefficient on *NC-RANK*.

To explore the relationship between *NC-RANK* and *PRIORITY* more in depth, another specification of the model is employed in Table 7.4, Regression #5. In this model, *PRIORITY* has been disaggregated into its three component parts: degree of threat (*DEGREE*); recovery potential (*RECOVERY*); and taxonomic uniqueness (*MONOTYPIC* and *SUBSPECIES*). By disaggregating the priority rank in this manner, we can examine the implicit effect of each of the component parts of the ranking system.

Coefficients on these four variables, *DEGREE, RECOVERY, MONOTYPIC,* and *SUBSPECIES*, have the sign one would predict if FWS were using its priority system as required, though only the coefficient on *RECOVERY* is significant. Thus, this could be interpreted that, on average, *RECOVERY* is a more powerful explanatory variable for funding than is *DEGREE*, even though in the lexicographic priority system, *DEGREE* should have relatively greater weight. It appears, therefore, that the scientific component of the priority ranking system captured by *DEGREE* is less correlated with funding decisions than is recovery potential.

Clearly, the different signs on the coefficients of *NC-RANK* and *DEGREE* (and the fact that the coefficient on *DEGREE* is not significant) in Regression #5 raise additional questions. These are supposed to be comparable measures of the degree to which a species is threatened with extinction. However, as noted by Metrick and Weitzman, these two measures are only slightly correlated. They also note that whether or not a species is in conflict has a negative and significant correlation with *DEGREE* (correlation coefficient = −0.331). *CONFLICT*, however, is not correlated with *NC-RANK* (correlation coefficient = 0.0018.) Thus, it appears as if economic conflict determined by the FWS might influence its assessment of degree of threat while it does not seem to influence The Nature Conservancy's measure of threat. It is impossible to determine with the data available in this study which measure more accurately reflects current scientific understanding of species' endangerment, but there is clearly not a consensus.

Final variables that are examined in order to explore political dimensions of the funding decision are public comments made during the listing of each species and the amount of news media coverage devoted to species. In Table 7.4, Regression # 6, the variables *COMM-SUPP, COMM-OPP*, and *COMM-NEUT* and *NEWS* have been included in the analysis.[20] Again, while causal relationships cannot be determined from an analysis of this regression, significant associations between public comments and funding are evident. The coefficients on the comment variables are significant. Both *COMM-SUPP* and *COMM-NEUT* are positively correlated with increased funding, while *COMM-OPP* is negatively correlated. Those species that receive more supportive input or more informational input in the public comment period during the listing process receive greater funds in the later funding process. Likewise, those species that receive comments opposed to their listing receive fewer funds. This can be interpreted as either the FWS or subcommittees responding to public preferences, or alternatively, that administrators in FWS or subcommittees share the same preferences as expressed during the public comment period, or that there is a correlation between public preferences expressed in the comment period and threat of endangerment. It is clear that more detailed analysis of the source and nature of comments would provide greater insight into the nature of the relationship between public comment and funding decisions.

NEWS is also significantly correlated with funding in this model, being positively associated with funding levels. One interpretation of this relationship is that the variable *NEWS* is a rough measure of public interest in a

---

[20] This is run as a separate regression instead of including these variables in Regression #4 because 100 species are dropped from the sample. This is because these 100 species were listed under the Endangered Species Preservation Act of 1966 or the Endangered Species Conservation Act of 1969, which did not require a public comment period. Species listed under these two acts were automatically listed under Endangered Species Act of 1973, without an additional comment period.

species, and that like public comments, the level of public interest influences allocation decisions for species preservation. Another possible interpretation depends on the endogeneity between funding and news. That is, one might expect the number of news articles to increase with more highly funded species because the recovery efforts resulting from spending decisions become the subject of media attention.

It is also important to note that the relationship between *CONFLICT* and comments and news is characterized by collinearity. In this regression, the coefficient on *CONFLICT* has become insignificant (compare with Regression #4). Species in conflict, not surprisingly, are more likely to be the subject of greater public commentary (both in support of and against listing). Likewise, a similar relationship exists between *LNLENGTH* and comments and news. In this specification the coefficient on *LNLENGTH* has become insignificant. This collinearity could be explained if, in fact, larger animals hold more public appeal, and animals with greater appeal receive more comments.

4.2.2.   Implications of the New Models

While definitive conclusions cannot be drawn about *causal* relationships between the dependent and independent variables examined, it seems apparent that a variety of different political variables are correlated with the funding of recovery efforts. The presence of a subcommittee member, economic conflict, media coverage, and public comments can explain changes in funding levels. In addition, it appears that the priority ranking system utilized by FWS emphasizes nonscientific components more than it was designed to do: Measures of the degree of threat are ambiguously correlated with funding decisions; and genetically unique species are not associated with increased funds as is required under the stated FWS policy. This is consistent with the overall inference that it seems that scientific inputs are relatively less important in the funding decision. This analysis would be more complete, however, if it included a better treatment of the demand side of the decision-making process. Variables that capture interest group (i.e., environmental groups, industry groups, etc.) lobbying, donations, and other political activity would result in a more comprehensive analysis of the decision-making process.

As a beginning test, therefore, these analyses seem to support Hypothesis 2: The amount of funding is correlated less with scientifically based considerations of endangerment and correlated more with a variety of political considerations.

5.   CONCLUSIONS

5.1.   Policy Implications for the Endangered Species Act

Given the Endangered Species Act's fundamental reliance on scientific research, the contentious nature of the political debate that surrounds the act, and the nature of the risks and uncertainty of species extinction, the ESA has proved to be a useful case in examining the role of science and politics in regulatory decision making. Based on a variety of studies from government and academia, it is clear that FWS is struggling with how to construct the boundary between science and politics. One might frame the recommendations from such agencies as the GAO and NRC as an attempt to encourage FWS to reclaim the legitimacy of its actions through strengthened scientific input (with a firm boundary between science and politics) and more cogent risk analysis and risk management in its decision-making process. On the other hand, mounting criticisms of the act, particularly from conservative political factions, bespeak an insensitivity of the act to political considerations and to economic efficiency or cost-effectiveness considerations.

By studying two discrete and measurable decision nodes in the implementation process of the ESA, the listing and funding decisions, this study attempts to gain better understanding of how science and politics might influence policy decisions. While my reduced form model only allows inferences about correlations and not causation, the results suggest the following tentative conclusions.

The decision to list a species under the ESA is more highly correlated with scientifically determined characteristics of species (i.e., how endangered they are and how genetically unique they are) than it is with nonscientific variables that attempt to capture aspects of the animals' charisma or appeal (i.e., how closely related it is to humans and how large it is). The importance of scientific input at this stage is also highlighted by the finding that the Amendments of 1982, which called for greater reliance on scientific findings of endangerment and less reliance on subjective valuation of a species' taxonomic class, resulted in a commensurate shift in listing decisions. In this case, where the mandated use of science is judicially reviewable (as it is under the ESA), scientific input influences management decisions.

Alternatively, funding levels are more highly correlated with a host of political inputs and less with scientifically determined characteristics. Clearly, the interaction of the different political inputs and different scientific inputs require complex interpretations of how funding decisions for species recovery are made by FWS. One conclusion that could be drawn from these findings is that the final allocation of funding is not wholly consistent with FWS guidelines, and particularly with its science-based components. Several nonmutually exclusive phenomena might lead to this result.

First, congressional influence through both subcommittee "pork" and special earmarking override FWS guidelines. This influence was noted in the GAO report on implementation of the ESA which concluded, "Congressional earmarking of funds for individual species has contributed to the agency's deviation from its established priority system" (GAO 1988, 4). One curious factor, however, that complicates this kind of "pork" politics is that the pork that is being distributed is not the traditional kind. New highways, hospitals, or sewer systems often garner widespread local support because of both the immediate and long-term benefits they will bring in terms of local jobs and new amenities.

Money for the recovery of endangered species, however, cannot be characterized this simply. Oftentimes the implementation of a recovery plan results in the *blocking* of economic development and other direct amenities for local constituencies. It is possible, however, that increased funding in a state in which endangered species are in economic conflict with development could benefit a senator's constituencies in other ways. For example, as described above, if the money is spent on extended research or more numerous public hearings, the allocation of funding can be used as a stalling tactic in the recovery process (see Ando, Chapter 6 of this volume). In the analysis of the decision to denote critical habitat by FWS, Yaffee (1982) notes that "allegations of strategic delay and footdragging in designation of critical habitat have been prevalent since ... 1975" (92). Likewise, the money can sometimes go toward placating concerned constituencies in terms of monetary compensation for land acquisition or for such actions as animal damage control programs, as has been the case where wolves have been reintroduced. These kinds of actions are consistent with the relationship between conflict, subcommittee membership, and funding, as noted in the previous section. Funds can also be funneled to local research organizations. This is also exemplified by an earmark by Senator McClure for the Peregrine Fund – a nonprofit raptor research center located in Boise. Obviously, distribution of endangered species funds also can address concerns of pro-environment constituencies in the more traditional mode of committee politics.

Second, how close a species is to full recovery might be more heavily weighted than FWS priority ranking system suggests, as is evidenced by the coefficient on *RECOVERY*. This might be caused by both the desire for cost-effectiveness as well as a desire to show successes in the endangered species program. FWS (1992b) notes the importance of this aspect of recovery in its 1992 report to Congress:

> Some otherwise low priority species that need only one or two low priority tasks to complete recovery might receive resources to expedite their reclassification or delisting.
> Thus, given the existing resources with the Service, the primary focus of recovery implementation activities is often placed on "threshold" species. Threshold species are those that, due to current situations, are about to go extinct or those that are close to recovery. (7)

Third, the FWS might be allocating funds strategically to animals with high public appeal in an effort to garner public support for the endangered species program. This was also noted in the GAO (1988) report which stated, "we believe FWS' desire for a positive public perception of its program" (32) contributes to a funding regime that does not follow its stated guidelines. In this regard, the disproportionate allocation of recovery monies to only a few publicly appealing species can be posed as a "poster child" effect[21] – FWS garnering public support for the endangered species program through

---

[21] In the latest FWS report to Congress on the Recovery Program, on the page after the title page is the reproduction of a poster available from the FWS that featured five animals including gray whales, grizzly bears, bald eagles, salmon, and a species of butterfly.

heightened efforts to save symbolic species that have substantial public value, but perhaps low endangerment.[22]

These observations are also consistent with political economy theories in which interests, in this case environmentalists, are able to effectively demand protection for species that serve their needs. These needs could include responding to clientele, setting precedent, creating symbolic value, and increasing opportunities for increasing donations. In addition, certain species can act as surrogates for different but related agendas, and thus act as powerful symbols, or links to other issues. For example, several species serve as "spotlights" for endangered species conservation as well as other environmental issues such as habitat protection, or wilderness preservation. This is noted, for example, in work by Satterfield, Waddell, and Bowden (1993):

> There is no question that opponents of development or a particular activity affecting the environment have at times used the ESA to further their own interests. One well-publicized illustration was the statement by Andy Stahl of the Sierra Club Legal Defense Fund: "The northern spotted owl is the wildlife species of choice to act as a surrogate for old growth protection". (14)

Thus, for environmental advocates, and perhaps the regulators, symbolic value of a designation of a species as endangered or the allocation of funds for its recovery might be an important variable in their objective functions, eclipsing at times more short-term values of saving a particularly endangered but non-symbolic species.

It is likely that some kind of combination of the above interpretations would accurately describe the mix of science and politics that results as FWS attempts to maintain legitimacy with many stakeholders while balancing a variety of scientific and political inputs. It is also clear that like other government agencies that deal with uncertain causes of problems and uncertain outcomes of policies, there is pressure for FWS to more effectively assess risks and provide cogent and efficient responses to them. This is already seen in changes in FWS policy with regard to strengthening the role of science in the listing and funding processes, providing avenues for multiple listings of organisms under the ESA, involving stakeholders in some recovery processes (e.g., through habitat conservation plans), and pursuing a more comprehensive ecosystems approach to biodiversity conservation.

Finally, these findings illuminate a boundary between science and policy that is shifting and fuzzy. The results of the 1982 Amendments suggest, for example, that Congress, through political decisions, attempted to more clearly demarcate the boundary between science and politics, and avoid FWS listing decisions guided by "non-scientific values." However, political decisions about funding recovery efforts strongly influence what science is

---

[22] The top ten species that received funding in 1991 were bald eagle, Florida scrub jay, northern spotted owl, manatee, red-cockaded woodpecker, peregrine falcon, Florida panther, grizzly bear, desert tortoise, and the whooping crane. Four of these ten are listed as threatened, and not the more urgent listing of endangered.

undertaken, what species are studied, and thus what species are afforded attention. Moreover, in the structure and implementation of the priority ranking system, FWS seemed to utilize politically derived criteria (such as conflict, or ease of recovery) embedded in a scientifically "objective" ranking system, blurring science and politics in a single measuring tool. Thus, we see a dynamic science-policy boundary, constantly being negotiated by FWS, Congress, the courts, and the public.

5.2.   Agenda for Future Research

Although this analysis provides a preliminary examination of the role of science and politics in endangered species conservation, the ultimate goal of this research effort is to construct a formal conceptual model derived and synthesized from the fields of science studies, political economy, and resource economics. This model will provide hypotheses that can be rigorously tested in a way that is beyond the scope of what is presented in this chapter.

While the most important aspect of future research will be the derivation of this theoretical framework, testing of this framework will necessitate a more statistically sophisticated approach. The most obvious next step will be to treat both the listing and funding decisions jointly. The current analysis and other studies (for example, Metrick and Weitzman 1996b; Simon et al. 1995) treat the two decisions separately, which introduces selection bias. Since the right-hand variables in both the listing and funding equations affect both listing and funding decisions, but the funding model only includes those species that have been listed, the coefficients on the funding decision will be biased and inconsistent. This is due to an incidental truncation of the funding data. That is, we only observe spending for those species that are listed, and those factors that affect the probability of listing are likely to affect the level of funding received. These kinds of selection bias issues can be addressed with a two-stage estimation as developed by Heckman (1976) in which the two equations are treated simultaneously and consistent and efficient coefficients can be estimated.

Finally, testing of this new conceptual model will require the inclusion of more comprehensive variables of the endangered species decision-making process. This would include, for example, panel data analyses of listing and allocation decisions (as opposed to the static analysis presented in this chapter), and a more complete treatment of the politics of the listing decision. In the context of the ESA, such an econometric analysis would involve tracking changes in congressional makeup, changes in scientific understanding, changes in media content, and changes in interest group activities and how they influence listing decisions and recovery spending decisions.

References

Alvarez, M., and Saving, J. (1995). Deficits, Democrats, and Distributive Benefits: Congressional Elections and the Pork Barrel in the 1980's. *California Institute of Technology Social Science Working Paper* (928).

Ando, A. W. (2001). Interest Group Behavior and Endangered Species Protection. Chapter 6 in *Protecting Endangered Species in the United States: Biological Needs, Political Realities, Economic Choices* (J. Shogren and J. Tschirhart, eds.). New York: Cambridge University Press.

Arnold, R. D. (1979). *Congress and the Bureaucracy: A Theory of Influence*. New Haven, CT: Yale University Press.

Bornemeier, J. (1995). Bipartisan Bid to Revamp Endangered Species Act Introduced in House; Backers Say Bill Will Curb Over Regulation. Foes See an Attempt to Gut Landmark 1973 Law. *Los Angeles Times*, September 8.

Brooks, H., and Cooper, C. L. (Eds.). (1987). *Science for Public Policy*. Oxford: Pergamon Press.

Buchanan, J. M., and Tullock, G. (1975). Polluters' Profits and Political Response: Direct Controls Versus Taxes. *The American Economic Review 65*(1), 139–47.

Calvert, R. L., McCubbins, M. D., and Weingast, B. R. (1989). A Theory of Political Control and Agency Discretion. *American Journal of Political Science 33*(3), 588–611.

Clark, T. W., Reading, R. P., and Clarke, A. L. (Eds.). (1994). *Endangered Species Recovery: Finding the Lessons, Improving the Process*. Washington, D.C.: Island Press.

Conart, R., and Collins, J. T. (1991). *A Field Guide to Reptiles and Amphibians: Eastern and Central North America*. (3rd ed.). Boston: Houghton Mifflin.

Congressional Quarterly News Features. (1989). Congressional Quarterly Almanac. Washington, D.C.: Congressional Quarterly.

—(1991). Congressional Quarterly Almanac. Washington, D.C.: Congressional Quarterly.

Dahl, R. A. (1989). *Democracy and Its Critics*. New Haven, CT: Yale University Press.

Fay, J. J., and Thomas, W. L. (1983). Endangered Species Listing and Recovery Priority Guidelines, *Federal Register* (Vol. 48, pp. 43098–43105). Washington, D.C.: U.S. Government Printing Office.

Federal Register. (1973–1991).

Fenno, R. F. J. (1973). *Congressmen in Committees*. Boston: Little, Brown and Company.

Fiorina, M. P. (1974). *Representatives, Roll Calls, and Constituencies*. Lexington, MA: Lexington Books.

Funtowicz, S. O., and Ravetz, J. R. (1993). Science for the Post-Normal Age. *Futures 25*(7), 739–55.

General Accounting Office. (1988). *Endangered Species: Management Improvements Could Enhance Recovery Program* (RCED-89-5). Washington, D.C.: General Accounting Office.

Gieryn, T. F. (1995). Boundaries of Science. In S. Jasanoff et al. (Eds.), *Handbook of Science and Technology Studies*. Thousand Oaks, CA: Sage Publications.

Guston, D. H. (1998). Stabilizing the Boundary between Politics and Science: The Role of the Office of Technology Transfer as a Boundary Organization. *Social Studies of Science 29*(1), 87–112.

Hahn, R. W. (1990). The Political Economy of Environmental Regulation: Towards a Unifying Framework. *Public Choice 65*, 21–47.

Heckman, J. (1976). The Common Structure of Statistical Models of Truncation, Sample Selection and Limited Dependent Variables and a Simple Estimator for Such Models. *Annals of Economic and Social Measurement 5*, 475–92.

Houck, O. A. (1993). The Endangered Species Act and Its Implementation by the U.S. Departments of Interior and Commerce. *University of Colorado Law Review 64*(2), 277–370.

Jasanoff, S. (1990). *The Fifth Branch: Science Advisors as Policymakers.* Cambridge, MA: Harvard University Press.

—(1995). *Science at the Bar: Law, Science, and Technology in America.* Cambridge, MA: Harvard University Press.

—(1987). Contested Boundaries in Policy-Relevant Science. *Social Studies of Science*, 17, 195–230.

Joskow, P. L., and Schmalensee, R. (1995). The Political Economy of Market-Based Environmental Policy: The 1990 U.S. Acid Rain Program. Draft manuscript.

Kalt, J. P., and Zupan, M. A. (1984). Capture and Ideology in the Economic Theory of Politics. *American Economic Review 74*(3), 280–300.

League of Conservation Voters (1989). *1989 – National Environmental Scorecard.* Washington, D.C.

— (1991). *1991 – National Environmental Scorecard.* Washington, D.C.

Lee, D., Gilbert, C., R., Hocutt, C. H., Jenkins, R. E., McAllister, D. E., and Stauffer, J. R. (1980). *Atlas of North American Freshwater Fishes.* North Carolina: North Carolina State Museum of Natural History.

Littell, R. (1992). *Endangered and Other Protected Species: Federal Law and Regulation.* Washington, D.C.: The Bureau of National Affairs.

Lohoefener, R. (1996). Deputy Administrator, Endangered Species Program, U.S. Fish and Wildlife Service, May 30.

Mann, C. C. (1995). *Noah's Choice: The Future of Endangered Species.* New York: Alfred A. Knopf.

Mayhew, D. R. (1974). *Congress: The Electoral Connection.* New Haven, CT: Yale University Press.

Metrick, A., and Weitzman, M. L. (1996a). Endangered Species Database: Department of Economics, Harvard University.

—(1996b). Patterns of Behavior in Endangered Species Preservation. *Land Economics 72*(1), 1–16.

—(1998). Conflict and Choices in Biodiversity Preservation. *Journal of Economic Perspectives 12*(3), 21–34.

Minta, S. C., and Kareiva, P. M. (1994). A Conservation Science Perspective: Conceptual and Experimental Improvements. In T. W. Clark, R. P. Reading, and A. L. Clarke (Eds.), *Endangered Species Recovery: Finding the Lessons, Improving the Process.* Washington, D.C.: Island Press.

National Heritage Data Center Network. (1993). Conservation Data Base. Arlington, VA: The Nature Conservancy.

National Research Council. (1995). *Science and the Endangered Species Act.* Washington, D.C.: National Academy Press.

Page, L., and Brooks, M. B. (1991). *A Field Guide to Freshwater Fishes of North America.* Boston: Houghton Mifflin.

Peltzman, S. (1976). Toward a More General Theory of Regulation. *Journal of Law and Economics 19*, 211–40.

Riemer, W. J. (Ed.). (1971). *Catalogue of American Amphibians and Reptiles.* Bethesda, MD: American Society of Ichthyologists and Herpetologists.

Satterfield, W. H., Waddell, G. G., and Bowden, M. W. (1993). Who's Afraid of the Big Bad Beach Mouse. *Natural Resources and Environment 8*(1), 13–16, 62–63.

Shepsle, K. A. (1978). *The Giant Jigsaw Puzzle: Democratic Committee Assignments in the Modern House.* Chicago: The University of Chicago Press.

Simon, B. M., Leff, C. S., and Doerksen, H. (1995). Allocating Scarce Resources for Endangered Species Recovery. *Journal of Policy Analysis and Management 14*(3), 415–32.

Smith, S. S., and Deering, C. J. (1990). *Committees in Congress.* Washington, D.C.: Congressional Quarterly.

Stebbins, R. C. (1966). *A Field Guide to Western Reptiles and Amphibians.* Boston: Houghton Mifflin.

Stevens, W. K. (1995). Future of Endangered Species Act in Doubt as Law Is Debated. *New York Times,* May 16.

Stigler, G. J. (1971). The Theory of Economic Regulation. *Bell Journal of Economics 2,* 3–21.

The Nature Conservancy. (1996). *Priorities for Conservation: 1996 Annual Report Card for U.S. Plant and Animal Species.* Arlington, VA.

Tobin, R. (1990). *The Expendable Future: U.S. Politics and the Protection of Biological Diversity.* Durham, NC: Duke University Press.

U.S. Fish and Wildlife Service. (1990). *Federal and State Endangered Species Expenditures – Fiscal Year 1989.* Washington, D.C.: U.S. Department of the Interior, Fish and Wildlife Service.

—(1991). *Federal and State Endangered Species Expenditures – Fiscal Year 1990.* Washington, D.C.: U.S. Department of the Interior, Fish and Wildlife Service.

—(1992a). *Federal and State Endangered Species Expenditures – Fiscal Year 1991.* Washington, D.C.: U.S. Department of the Interior, Fish and Wildlife Service.

—(1992b). *Report to Congress: Endangered and Threatened Species Recovery Program*: U.S. Department of Interior, Fish and Wildlife Service.

—(1994). Endangered Species Act of 1973 as Amended through the 100th Congress: U.S. Government Printing Office.

—(1996, June 11). Information on Congressional Earmarks (compiled on request): Division of Budget.

Weingast, B. R., and Moran, M. J. (1983). Bureaucratic Discretion or Congressional Control? Regulatory Policy Making by the Federal Trade Commission. *Journal of Political Economy 91*(5), 765–800.

Whittemore, A. S. (1983). Fact and Values in Risk Analysis for Environmental Toxicants. *Risk Analysis 3*(1), 23–33.

Williams, T. (1990). Waiting for Wolves to Howl in Yellowstone. *Audubon 92,* 32–39 November.

Yaffee, S. L. (1982). *Prohibitive Policy: Implementing the Federal Endangered Species Act.* Cambridge, MA: MIT Press.

CHAPTER 8

Community Politics and Endangered Species Protection

Stephen M. Meyer

I. INTRODUCTION

Federal and state laws protect endangered species – at least for now.[1] But a new voice may be joining the political chorus threatening both past gains and future progress in U.S. biodiversity policies. It is the voice of local communities mobilizing in opposition to strong government measures to protect wildlife and habitat.[2] Unless we try to understand and address the sources of community-level disenchantment with these policies, the Endangered Species Act (ESA) and similar laws may themselves become extinct.

My argument is fourfold. First, politics has permanently eclipsed science as the main determinant of what can be achieved in endangered species policy, and this is as it should be. Second, an array of issues that goes beyond simple economic interests is mobilizing community politics against government efforts to protect biodiversity in general, and against the ESA in particular. Third, anti-ESA community politics has the potential to be a more formidable and vexing challenge to biodiversity policy than traditional economic interest group opposition. Fourth, an enduring and robust endangered species policy requires that federal and state governments address the non-economic trade-offs imposed on communities by bringing communities into the policy process.

II. POLITICS ECLIPSES SCIENCE

If there is any single point of agreement among proponents and opponents of endangered species protection, it is that politics routinely dominates science

The author is professor in Political Science and director of the MIT Project on Environmental Politics and Policy at MIT. The author is indebted to project research associate Debbie Dineen for comments on drafts of this chapter.

[1] Besides the federal Endangered Species Act, some forty five states have their own endangered species laws that extend protection above and beyond the federal statute. See Defenders of Wildlife (1998).

[2] Throughout this chapter I use the term "wildlife" to connote animals and plants.

in ESA policy and decision making – a situation they both claim to deplore.[3] Instead, they call for "better" science, each confident that better science will strengthen their respective hands in the policy process. Supporters of a strong ESA and similar state legislation believe that better science will prove that we will suffer a severe biodiversity loss unless government intervenes to protect wildlife and habitat. Science, they are sure, will not only prove that we need to restrict further natural resource consumption and human impact on the land but that it will also convince the public to accept whatever economic, social, and political trade-offs might prove necessary. Conversely, ESA opponents assert that better science will show that we can practice "wiser use" of natural resources while saving those species that need to be saved with fewer constraints on land use and development and without the need for undesirable social and political trade-offs.

But the belief that "better science" can take the politics out of endangered species policy and quell the intensifying storm swirling around wildlife and habitat protection is misguided. It reflects fundamental and all too common misunderstandings about the basic nature of science and politics in public policy making, and in particular the inherent link between science and politics in biodiversity policy making. Science is nothing more than a methodology of discovery – a systematic way of finding out about things.[4] Wildlife biology can help us to understand better the habitat and survival requirements of spotted owls, desert tortoises, and karner blue butterflies. Conservation science can direct us in designing better old growth forest reserves to improve biodiversity. And the social sciences can aid us in assessing the economic, political, and social trade-offs that we might confront in implementing conservation plans.

Science, however, cannot tell us whether or not we want to do these things, especially when they compete with other societal goals and values for attention and resources. Science has little to say about which values and interests our society should place above others – for example, whether we should make biological diversity a priority over improving rural healthcare, investing in inner-city schools, or housing the homeless.[5] It cannot tell us the

---

[3] Some students of endangered species policy note that listings decisions seem to correspond fairly well with scientific documentation and cite this as evidence that science appears to be the determining factor in policy making. This inference is incorrect. What they fail to note is that during the last decade, the U.S. Fish and Wildlife Service (USFWS) intentionally held up those listings fearing political repercussions. Legal actions by environmentalists forced those listings. For example, the Center for Biological Diversity is reported to have filed over 120 suits against USFWS since 1989, winning more than 80 percent, for failing to implement the ESA as required by law. See *Greenlines* (1999a).

Although the scientific data were instrumental in determining court rulings, the process was fundamentally political from start to finish. Science was merely instrumental.

[4] Too often science is something less. See Ozawa (1996).

[5] This is not to say that science does not have a role to play in such discussions. It clearly does. Science can inform us about the costs and benefits of the choices we make, but it does not tell us how to weigh those costs and benefits against other options.

degree to which we should treasure the public interest in preserving wildlife (resources held in common) over the public interest in preserving property rights (liberty).

Reaching societal consensus in a sea of competing values, ideas, and interests is the stuff of politics. Politics is the never-ending public "clash" over differing visions of how things ought to be – the essence of democratic governance.[6] It underlies debates about what issues should (and should not) be considered a "problem" worthy of government attention; what types of government action are necessary and appropriate to address the problem; and how the costs and benefits of policy should be distributed among the affected parties. In an age of booming aquaculture, is the loss of the last wild Atlantic salmon really a problem?[7] Is it fair that Maine communities that depend on cranberry growing and aquaculture would be forced to shoulder the weight of likely restrictions to protect the fish (if it is listed under the ESA) merely because the other New England states wiped out their native Atlantic salmon runs 100 years earlier?

In short, science lets us know what needs to be done to preserve wildlife and habitat if we value biodiversity above all else (or if no trade-offs are necessary), but it cannot tell us whether we should value it above all else. When other important values and interests are at stake, it is politics that lets us know how far we can go in trading off competing and conflicting societal goals, of which biodiversity is only one of many contenders.

This division of labor helps to account for a curious paradox in the history of the ESA: how today's most embattled among all our environmental laws passed through Congress with virtually no opposition in 1973.[8] In the decades leading up to the enactment of the federal ESA the social, political, and economic trade-offs associated with protecting America's wildlife seemed to be virtually nonexistent (unless one considers eschewing bird plumes in women's hats socially significant). What wildlife specialists presumed to be likely "species at risk" comprised a handful of charismatic creatures. Thus, in 1973 it was easy for ESA advocates to build into the law the principle that science should be the sole determining factor in ESA actions. Knowledgeable authorities assumed that "the list" would not swell beyond a few dozen animals and that sufficient protection was possible by regulating only federal lands. Endangered species protection could be viewed largely as a technical exercise with few if any public or private interest spillovers.[9]

---

[6] Stone (1997), Reich (1988).

[7] The Governor of Maine, for example, argues no – reported in Allen (1999).

[8] One notable exception was the fur industry, which did raise concerns about its ability to import exotic furs. Protection for domestic wildlife was not the issue.

[9] Although the ESA confrontation over the Tellico dam should have laid such naïve thinking to rest, it was widely misinterpreted as an anomaly that could be handled by an ad hoc arrangement. The "God Squad" was created to handle those presumably rare and special instances of difficult trade-offs.

That belief proved wrong. By the 1990s, unrelenting pressures from natural resource exploitation, land development, and other forms of habitat alteration and incursion drove the list of federally protected species over 1,000. The number of species awaiting review for listing topped several thousand. Scientific research improved our grasp of the complex dynamics of biodiversity and it soon became clear that saving endangered species involved much more expansive and intrusive efforts than the original proponents of endangered species protection ever imagined. In particular:

- far larger swaths of land needed to be regulated;
- private property (not just federal lands) had to be regulated;
- plants and noncharismatic creatures required protection;
- a broader range of activities on both public lands and private property had to be regulated in ways that were previously unthinkable; and
- the time scales for "recovery" – and hence restrictions on land use – were going to be of the order of decades rather than years and therefore so would time scales for regulatory restrictions.

As policy and the law tried to keep up with a growing pool of scientific knowledge, the reach of the ESA and related biodiversity protection efforts began to cast an enormous shadow over the landscape, raising the specter of wide-scale social and economic impacts. For example, saving Pacific salmon populations might require the breaching of dams that supply nonpolluting and low-cost electric power to the high-tech industries of the Pacific Northwest. This would also drain the impounded waters that offer cheap and reliable transportation to and from ports in Idaho. In the southeast a number of military bases face the prospect of significantly curtailed training exercises in order to protect resident populations of red cockaded woodpeckers. Reintroducing wolves, condors, and black-footed ferrets back into the wild may threaten long-standing recreational uses of public lands and some private properties as well.

Not surprisingly, as the scale and scope of possible trade-offs grew, the number and diversity of stakeholders, values, and interests affected by and relevant to endangered species policy exploded. In an ironical twist better science inexorably forced biodiversity policy to pose more significant trade-offs, which in turn generated more intense politics. In biodiversity and conservation policy "better science" pushed politics inevitably to the forefront. Endangered species policy was transformed permanently from a technical process to a political one.[10]

---

[10] Secretary of the Interior Bruce Babbit has taken considerable heat from environmentalists for letting "bad" politics, rather than "good" science, guide endangered species policy. In particular, environmentalists are offended by the Secretary's permitting landowner habitat conservation plans to replace federal agency plans, exempting small properties from ESA regulation, and implementing a "no surprises" policy that reduces the risk of future restrictions on private property for current concessions. From the perspective of this chapter, Secretary Babbit's actions seem almost prescient.

III. COMMUNITY TRADE-OFFS AND COMMUNITY POLITICS

If politics is effectively the controlling force in U.S. biodiversity policy, we must then ask: what kind of politics? Traditional interest group politics would describe well what we have seen for the past decade or so. Economic interests pushed unrelentingly to weaken the stringency of the ESA's prohibitory clauses, reduce the scale and scope of ESA implementation and enforcement actions, and obtain compensatory relief (through payments, tax credits, land purchases, and property rights reform). Meanwhile, environmental interests attempted to expand the law's scope and jurisdiction and pressed to secure additional funding for policy implementation and enforcement.

The push and pull of these two powerful interests created a political stalemate of sorts. ESA opponents were able to chip away at the edges of the endangered species policy, but without being able to muster enough support to significantly change the way the ESA works. ESA supporters prevented the law from being substantially altered, but failed to get it reauthorized. Nor did they get the funds needed to fully carry out policy.

This stalemate has endured because neither "side" was able to mobilize a political majority within the polity, having failed to raise the public "salience" of the ESA and biodiversity policy much above the background noise of ordinary Washington politics. Salience refers to the extent to which an issue is on the public mind and is a direct cause of political action.[11] On the one hand, the concerns of the many disparate economic interests allied against the ESA have not convinced the public that an economic disaster looms on the horizon unless the ESA is weakened. Polls showed, for example, that 63 percent of Alabamians favored federal protection for the Alabama Sturgeon, with only 14 percent opposed, even after a year of intense propagandizing by state economic interests and top political leaders claiming that the proposed listing would cause regional and perhaps national economic devastation.[12]

On the other hand, although the public clearly has signed onto the agenda of protecting biodiversity the issue has – much to the chagrin of environmentalists – very low political salience. It does not mobilize the electorate to political action. Without disputing the possible scientific and ecological significance of the extirpation of the Delhi Sands Flower-Loving Fly, the average person has trouble imagining any personal loss should this species, and many others, disappear forever. Thus, in this stalemated setting the vast majority of politicians do not find it worth their time, effort, or the political risk to push endangered species policy off the current track.[13]

---

[11] For an excellent analysis of salience in environmental affairs and very useful survey results, see Dunlap (1989). See also Downs (1972) on cycles in the political salience of environmental issues.

[12] Finch (1999).

[13] A few senators and members of Congress have consistently pushed ESA reform bills. The fact that these efforts have languished in committee demonstrates the general unwillingness of their colleagues to take on the issue.

The stalemate, however, may soon be broken. A new force – community politics – may enter the equation with the kind of broad-based political appeal that neither economic interests nor environmental interests have been able to muster. The grass-roots mobilization of entire communities against the ESA could seriously cripple biodiversity policy.

So why is the possibility of community mobilization suddenly an issue? As described above, the growing reach of ESA and related laws (driven by advances in conservation science) has expanded both the perceived scale and scope of trade-offs and deepened their penetration into the public realm. Beyond the traditional concern over economic impact (which, interestingly enough, has not had a political mobilizing effect), there are four social and political issues worthy of attention. These are community identity (community culture); community political autonomy and local control; the local culture of property rights, and community attitude toward wildlife. These factors acting together, and in concert with economic impacts, represent a potent mobilizing force at the community level.

Economic Trade-offs and Community Mobilization

Until the mid-1990s, the "problem" of ESA-economics collisions has been confined mostly to individual properties, projects, or firms. (The spotted-owl case is a notable exception.) Although these cases attracted media attention, they failed to mobilize the electorate. A significant political divide is crossed, however, when a community at large ceases to view the economic impact of an ESA listing as involving "unfortunate" individuals and instead starts to anticipate a threat to the collective economic entity: the community itself.

Indeed, a community is more than the simple aggregation of the individual economic preferences of its members. It is more than a local market. A community is a collective social entity that is bound by a web of relationships that alter the nature and characteristics of all the interests that define it, including economic ties.[14] (By analogy, the influence of economic preferences in a business run by twenty family members is different from that in a corporate business run by twenty unrelated shareholders.) Politically, community "economic impact" is both greater and more complex than the simple sum of its individual parts. This is why it is misleading to approach the issue of economic trade-offs in biodiversity policy solely as an individual property owner (compensation) problem, or as a problem of aggregating individual economic harms. It is much more a problem of collective perceptions.

Economic impact is intuitively perceived at the local level in basic terms of *immediate or near-term* job loss, declines in local commerce, reductions in incomes, and decreases of local government services. And these effects need not be direct. Indirect indicators of collective loss can be just as disturbing collectively. These might be something as simple as passing shuttered

[14] See Stone (1997, chapters 1 and 2).

storefronts on the way home from work, no longer hearing the shift whistle at the local mine, or noticing the empty seats at the local diner at lunch time. Small wonder, then, that economic concerns are raised immediately and speculatively by economic interests opposing a species listing or critical habitat designation. The expectation of collective economic impact is the story for galvanizing community action.

Of course, this begs the question of whether endangered species protection actually has harmful economic effects, collective or otherwise. National and state-level studies raise serious doubts about the assertion that the ESA has caused significant economic losses measured at those levels.[15] However, few studies have systematically examined economic impacts at the community level, which is where the significant and enduring dislocations might presumably occur.[16] For example, in Oregon timber-related employment represents about 4–6 percent of the nonfarm jobs. Yet in some seventy-nine towns with populations under 3,000 people, timber-related jobs accounted for the majority of work. In sixty-two of those towns, timber-related production accounted for 80 percent of manufacturing jobs.[17] Intuitively, the threat of community-level *immediate and near-term* economic losses seems real, and in the politics of policy making, perceptions and the short term are what matter most.

More to the point, locally harmful economic impact is a credible "story" – even without data to back it up – especially if the economic activity that is threatened is a cornerstone of the local economy. In politics, "stories" are often more potent in affecting perceptions and expectations than scientific studies and tables of statistics. Indeed, some have suggested that success in politics can be defined as getting one's story accepted by the public, regardless of its validity.[18] Political mobilization arises out of public fear and concern (that is, expectations) as stories appear in the media describing how restrictions on forest cutting, mining, fishing, and farming imposed to protect rare species *might* produce immediate economic losses. The issue is especially galvanizing, of course, when the community is economically dependent on a specific industry.[19]

Amplifying the political potency of the community economic impact "story" is the fact that the cost versus benefit framework that invariably worms its way into policy discussions is inherently biased against wildlife and habitat preservation.[20] First, the description of what the community might lose economically is simple, intuitive, and derived by conventionally accepted methods

---

[15] See, for example, Meyer (1995a,b), and (1998).

[16] Freudenburg et al. (1998) have examined the impact of the spotted-owl listing on employment in Oregon and Washington logging communities and found no effect.

[17] Dumont (1996, 280–81).

[18] See Stone (1997), especially chapter 6. See also Reich (1988).

[19] For a useful description of local dependencies, see Powers (1996). Gould, Schnaiberg, and Weinberg (1996) discuss the inhibiting effects of local economic dependency on local environmental policy making.

[20] Even the very framing of the issue is biased. The question is always asked: How much loss in economic performance are we prepared to accept to protect some increment in

of valuation. Regardless of whether the measure is dollars, jobs, or raw commodity output, the presumed economic impacts of most species protection efforts have a lot of "face validity" for the public, regardless of how reliable the estimates of loss may be. They have the authority of familiarity. Such losses are perceived as certain, immediate, direct, tangible, and horrifying (i.e., lifestyle threatening).

Conversely, the benefits of species and habitat preservation (or, the costs of biodiversity loss) to the community collectively are difficult to imagine, let alone measure. Preservation benefits are speculative, future-oriented, far-term, intangible, and commonly believed to be of little direct consequence. Although one can compute an economic impact of lost salmon runs in Oregon, most endangered species and wildlife do not have obvious commodity value. What, for example, is the economic loss imposed by the extirpation of the Pacific Pocket Mouse or Anthony's Riversnail?

Of course, methods such as contingent valuation exist for such situations and produce numbers, but they are unconventionally derived, have huge error margins, and offer no intuitive sense of value. Although such methods may animate interesting discussions at economics symposiums, they are virtually meaningless in public discussions because they do not translate into income, jobs, tax revenues, etc. When the U.S. Fish and Wildlife Service banned motorized vehicles along a stretch of Plymouth Beach, Massachusetts, for thirty days each spring to protect breeding piping plovers, the town revolted. The local Chamber of Commerce tabulated expected loss in revenue from dune buggy enthusiasts to the dollar, while vague notions of the tourist-attracting value of wildlife were readily dismissed. Similarly, California developers can tally the foregone income and enumerate jobs lost because a rare fairy shrimp prevents the filling of hundreds of acres of vernal pools. But even the most green-minded economist is going to be hard-pressed to come up with a valuation scheme that convinces a community that an aquatic invertebrate should be preferred to tax revenue and jobs.

The cost-benefit framework is distorted further by the fact that the biological "benefits" of a listing and recovery plan are often far from certain. According to a recently released federal report, an option to aid Pacific salmon recovery that involves breaching four hydropower dams on the lower Snake River will require, among other things, replacing lost electric-generating capacity to the tune of $250 million per year. However, it is not certain that the action will be sufficient to bring back salmon populations.

This is an irreconcilable asymmetry in cost-benefit analysis associated with a preservation policy that increasingly finds biological and ecological significance in animals and plants that are, in every other way, insignificant.

---

biodiversity? What if the question were reversed: How much loss in biological diversity are we prepared to accept for some increment in economic performance? The first form of the question presumes that economic performance is the thing of value and that biodiversity is discretionary. The second form flips the priority.

And it is why the "economic impact" of endangered species protection generates such an intense response at the community level. For locals what "will" be lost is obvious: Ted's job, Martha's income, the Rock Creek Mill down the road. It is not so obvious what will be gained.[21] Consequently, anti-ESA rhetoric can speak convincingly about devastating the economy, shutting down entire industries, and crippling commodity markets and in doing so generate real fear at the local level – regardless of whether it is true or not.

Moreover, even if it could be shown that ESA-related local economic losses are only temporary and are overshadowed by broader state economic gains, the fact is that communities do not like being thought of as fungible statistics. The possible loss of several hundred logging and milling jobs among the rural counties of Washington and Oregon may represent a "statistically insignificant" deviation in the context of the state economy, but such losses can be extremely "politically significant." The closing of the only diner in town is not compensated for by the opening of three restaurants in the state capital. For state politicians and congressional representatives, the plight of even a small number of individuals and their communities is the heart of election politics in small, nonurban districts. "Jobs vs. Owls" can be a powerful political metaphor locally.

This focus on communities cautions that it would be a mistake for policy to view economic trade-offs as a single landowner or single land-user problem. Providing monetary or land-swap compensation to a timber company for curtailed production as part of an endangered species conservation effort will not save jobs in the community. Even the prospect of direct government payments to rural governments to replace revenues lost from declining timber production and employment fails to excite local officials, who realize that schools and roads are irrelevant if the people leave for lack of work.[22]

Sense of Community Identity

Self-identity is the glue that binds a community together. Community residents perceive a shared sense of place, history, and even what we might call local culture (a common way of seeing the world and doing things). In the Pacific Northwest we talk about timber communities. In the Northeast we speak about the fishing communities. The Midwest has its farming communities and the Rockies has its ranching and mining communities.

These are more than economic designations. They denote a local culture and life style organized around and defined by *a shared fate* with a particular natural resource, commodity, or landscape. If traditional patterns of access to and use of that resource, commodity, or landscape are substantially changed, then the community's collective sense of self is threatened. A study of the

---

[21] Survey studies suggest that rural communities – those who live among wildlife – harbor great skepticism that people can have a significant impact on nature. See Kellert (1996), chapter 3.

[22] Kronholz (1999).

impact of proposed grazing cutbacks on federal land in Idaho concluded that the action "... would hurt the social networks that tie together rural communities," even though there would be little overall economic impact. Among other things, the ranching community ethic of volunteerism, which provides critical community services such as fire protection and search and rescue, would evaporate as ranches scale down operations.[23]

Seen from the perspective of community culture, it is not difficult to understand why the timber communities threatened by the listing of the Northern Spotted Owl found little comfort in the promise that "ecotourism" might replace lost forestry work. Ecotourism is not what those people and communities are about.[24] Similarly, the New England towns that for centuries breathed to the ebb and flow of each tide find little solace in the prospect that safer and perhaps more lucrative casino work might replace the fishing industry that defined their lives. Residents of Pasco, Washington, oppose the breaching of the lower Snake River dams to aid salmon recovery even though studies show that their community would reap major economic benefits. Why? Because it would harm other farming communities farther upstream.[25]

The great irony here is that many of these community cultures are a product of earlier government policies that promoted natural resource exploitation and land development, and encouraged and subsidized wildlife destruction. The government wanted the land tamed and occupied. Nurtured for decades by paternalistic government policies and financing, these communities now find themselves orphaned as government priorities change. Ecosystem protection and biodiversity preservation replace commodity production as priorities for federal agencies and the *raison d'être* of these communities is threatened, so political backlash should not be surprising.

Interestingly, in the past several years ESA supporters have acknowledged appeals to community identity and local culture when absolute prohibitions on "taking" species ran afoul of native American and Eskimo community traditions. Among others, whale hunts and bald eagle takings have been approved in recognition of certain cultural and historical ties to the land and wildlife. Yet more modern analogues, such as timbering and ranching communities, do not garner much sympathy. This apparent inequity in public policy creates yet another rallying point for community mobilization.

Political Autonomy and Local Control

Political autonomy and local control are issues tightly connected to community identity. This is a community's belief that it retains the ability to make its own choices and decisions, reflecting local values and interests. The concern – real or imagined – is that community public interests and values should prevail over

---

[23] *Idaho Falls Register* (1999).
[24] See Dumont (1996, 282–88).
[25] Mapes (1999).

state and national public interests and values. Even when community identity is not directly threatened, its sense of political autonomy and local control may be.

One need only consider the ferocity of local control politics pertaining to the governance of public schools and libraries to gauge the significance of this issue. Some communities, for example, have pushed to require biology classes to offer "Creationism" as a theoretical alternative to "evolution." Others have removed literary classics such as *Catcher in the Rye* from the shelves of their public libraries citing a clash with local values. Often derided as "parochialism," the prerogative to act in a manner consistent with community views remains a powerful force in American politics.

The disconnect between local and national perspectives on the public interest is exacerbated by the fact that the preservationist perspective takes a long-term view while the community perspective is almost entirely oriented to the "here and now." So environmental activists in Washington, D.C., see protecting the Pacific Yew as having the possible long-term payoff of treating cancer, but local county officials see intense logging of those very same slopes as generating funds today to pay for a much-needed modern medical facility for the community. Both concern public health, but point to very different policies and actions.

Then too, a community may agree almost entirely with state and federal policy on wildlife protection but still resist strongly the decisions imposed on them. The "greater good" has difficulty emerging from local politics when it is defined by parties outside the community. Independence from state and federal politics – resisting the influence of outsiders – is a force to be reckoned with in community politics, especially in communities with a strong sense of identity.[26]

Indeed, this "we–they" dichotomy has grown considerably in recent years because of the near total estrangement between federal land agencies [i.e., the Forest Service, the U.S. Fish and Wildlife Service (USFWS), the Bureau of Land Management (BLM), and the National Park Service (NPS)] and the communities with which historically they have had a close working relationship. Previously a sense of common history and purpose sustained a feeling of shared values and goals. There was a comfortable client-patron relationship and the "feds" were considered members of the community. However, changing organization values – in particular, a shift to a more ecological orientation in all the agencies – have destroyed that relationship and replaced it with one defined by hostility and anger (even a sense of betrayal).[27]

---

[26] In Texas, for example, communities mobilized to create their own water resources districts in order to prevent the state regulating water use, even though it was clear that state control would be more efficient and effective. The issue was local control.

[27] The hostility and distrust that now characterizes federal land agencies' relationships with local communities was illustrated in the sudden resignation of Forestry Service Supervisor (Humboldt-Toiyabe National Forests) Gloria Flora in November 1999. She reported that Forest Service workers were routinely denied service in restaurants, local businesses, etc. as a display of local distain for more ecologically mindful Forest Service policies (See *Greenwire* 1999a).

The political mobilization of communities around the theme of political autonomy is already percolating through western state houses. One of the basic principles of the Western Governors' Association ENLIBRA policy is the need for local control and political autonomy in environmental policy, and in particular, amending the ESA to allow for local control.[28]

Private Land Rights and Public Land Rights

Land property rights has been a banner issue in endangered species politics for the past decade. There are two dimensions to consider. The first is private property rights: the relative authority of the government to impose land-use restrictions on privately owned acreage. The second is public land property rights: the relative authority of the government to favor certain uses over others on public lands and thereby provide (or, withhold) privileges from certain segments of the public.

Traditionally, private property rights have been about "takings" as defined by the Fifth Amendment to the U.S. Constitution. The government cannot take property away from a citizen – that is, physically occupy or use it – without just compensation. However, in contrast to public programs such as highway construction, flood control projects, and military base siting, the government does not physically confiscate land when enforcing the ESA (or other environmental laws). Rather, wildlife preservation is accomplished by placing certain restrictions on the property to safeguard habitat and wildlife – but the property remains in private ownership. The term "regulatory taking" refers to this situation, where the property remains legally in private hands but the government imposes what is basically a use easement that prohibits certain activities in order to protect the public interest. Private property rights advocates claim that this is still a taking protected by constitutional rights. Environmental advocates argue the notion of a regulatory taking is a misconception: The Constitution gives the government the right to regulate without compensation private property use that might harm the public interest.[29]

For the most part ESA–property rights collisions have been limited to big corporate property owners – timber companies, developers, etc. – who turned to the courts hoping for vindication and support. The courts were largely unsympathetic and so these economic interests turned to the political arena, in particular the Congress and state legislatures to secure regulatory takings legislation. That the issue resonates better at lower political levels is demonstrated by the fact that property rights compensation legislation

---

[28] See the ENLIBRA page on the Western Governors Association web site: www.westgov.org.

[29] Biodiversity advocates face the difficulty of demonstrating that destroying habitat and extirpating species represents a true threat to public interests, or comprises a public nuisance. The right of government to regulate clear and present dangers – such as a toxic waste dump – is well established. Why the loss of the hoary elfin butterfly would pose a threat to public interests is not as obvious.

has systematically failed at the national level, but passed a number of state legislatures.[30]

As long as the ESA–property rights fight remained centered on corporate properties, the issue had little community mobilization potential. But again, by the late 1990s the ever-widening circle that species protection seemed to require made small-property owners fearful of the possibility that their lands might be swallowed up in "critical habitats." For example, in the mountain states pressure is building on U.S. Fish and Wildlife to expand the 5 million acres of federal land already protecting the grizzly bear to include another 4 million acres of surrounding private property.[31] A National Wildlife Federation petition for the emergency listing of the Black-tailed Prairie Dog encompasses millions of acres spanning ten states.[32]

For the corporate property owner, economic solutions – buyouts, financial compensation, property swaps, tax incentives – to property rights restrictions may be sufficient, since all that matters is the financial bottom line.[33] However, in many communities individual property rights is often regarded as more than an instrument of economic activity or a simple government entitlement. For many Americans, and rural Americans in particular, property rights represent a social and political investment, a part of the political culture representing an "inalienable" right that transcends government. These are things that cannot be bought off by economic solutions.

The particulars matter as well. The burdens imposed to protect 100 acres of sparrow habitat offer up a very different story depending on whether they are placed on several dozen 10-acre parcels or a single 1,000-acre property. The former can generate considerable community anxiety and galvanize opposing political action, where the latter might spawn a simple law suit.

Perhaps in recognition of this fact, the Interior Department during the last few years devised a series of measures designed to defuse ESA–property rights collisions. Habitat conservation plans employing safe-harbors/ no-surprise policies, and small-property exemptions were added to ESA implementation rules as a nod to these values, trading off habitat and species protection at the margin.[34] Whether or not these kinds of ameliorating

---

[30] Property rights infringements from regulatory actions remains a special interest issue at the national level that is countered by other special interest (environmental and municipal) opposition. It also has low political salience with the general electorate: Urban and suburban voters just do not connect with it.

[31] *Greenlines* (1999b).

[32] *Greenwire* (1998).

[33] Of course this may still leave the resource-dependent community in a bind. If, for example, the government swaps land with a mining company the community is left behind without the prospect of employment, or the workers and families must move.

[34] In essence, these policies offer assurances to property owners that once they devise a habitat conservation plan acceptable to the USFWS, they will not have to worry about additional restrictions on the land should other endangered species or preservation needs become known in the future.

policies will defuse the private property rights issue for the public is questionable.[35]

The second dimension of the property rights issue involves public properties. Many communities have grown up in the shadow of public lands. Their identities are intrinsically tied to patterns of public land use and especially natural resource extraction and recreation. This history has translated itself into a perception of conferred rights – rights that now seem threatened by government biodiversity policies. Bureau of Land Management (BLM) lands that have been leased for grazing for 150 years by generations of a single family are suddenly closed because the cattle are destroying riparian habitat. National park lands that nurtured the recreational needs of a community now prohibit dirt bikes and snowmobiles, while other areas are closed to all entry.

Particularly galling to communities living in the midst of Forest Service and BLM properties is the fact that, as already noted, government policies used to encourage and subsidize actions to domesticate these lands. The community culture was based on people controlling nature and the ideology that they had a special *right* to do so. Now suddenly animals and plants seem to be controlling people on public lands – a reversal of roles. For communities that were born out of policies encouraging open access to public lands, endangered species policies seem like an unnatural act.

Community Attitudes toward Wildlife

Generic attitudes toward wildlife matter as well. They affect how we weigh the trade-offs confronted in preserving habitat and wildlife. And here the evidence suggests that there is a perceptual divide between urban and suburban dwellers on the one hand, and rural communities – those most likely to be significantly affected by an ESA listing – on the other.

Survey studies reveal that *native* residents of rural communities – that is, those people born and raised in rural communities – tend to believe that nature is wild, robust, and resiliently capable of surviving disturbances by man – including species "takings."[36] They are also more likely to have a commodity (utilitarian) view of wildlife and land and feel that they have a better understanding of local wildlife than do visiting scientists. Indeed, there is a general skepticism among wildlife consumers about scientific warnings of ecological problems, such as population declines. For example, in the spring of 1999, the National Marine Fisheries Service moved to restrict the cod catch off New England to twenty pounds per trip in accordance with scientific studies showing that the cod population was crashing. Fishermen, however, were continuing to have high catch rates and dismissed the research

---

[35] It is worth noting that many environmental groups oppose these special provisions, believing they trade off too much in the way of future biodiversity protection needs.
[36] Kellert (1996, chapter 3).

studies: "The science is going to start coming into line with our anecdotal information," one fisherman observed.[37]

For these people "better science" connotes findings that fall into line with what they know to be true from personal experience – from living with wildlife. It is also true that local governments in general, and rural community governments in particular, have very little capacity to assimilate new scientific information. Combined with a basic distrust of the federal government this means that "better science" used in justifying policies imposed from above are unlikely to sway community leaders.

The issue is complicated still further by the fact that many of the very species of wildlife that urbanites and suburbanites want protected are considered to be pests in communities with identities built around fishing, ranching, and agriculture. In Wyoming and Montana, ranching communities are calling for a reopening of grizzly bear hunting season. At the urging of its farmers, Minnesota state authorities are considering removing protections for the gray wolf and allowing hunting. Fishers on the West Coast want permission to shoot federally protected sea lions raiding their nets. Animals historically labeled by the government as pests and systematically exterminated with government funds are now protected in the public interest, but the attitudes in the communities where these traditional government approaches were manifest still linger. These attitudes at the community level, which incidently do not vary with age, simply make the perceived "burdens" of wildlife and habitat protection seem all the more unnecessary and unfair, and government policy inexplicable and unacceptable.[38]

The Other Side of the Community Coin

It would be misleading to leave the impression that all the forces acting at the community level drive politics toward opposing biodiversity policy. There are at least four countervailing forces, which may be relevant over the longer term.

The first is the ongoing long-term economic decline taking place in many natural resource-dependent communities. Even without wildlife and habitat restrictions, the global competition in natural resources, the evolution of the U.S. economy to a services and high-tech foundation, and ever-changing cultural patterns (such as the shift away from smoking, beef consumption, etc.) continue to erode the competitiveness of these communities. Although one might be tempted to argue that government regulations to protect biodiversity may accelerate this trend, the evidence on ESA actions and economic growth

---

[37] *Boston Globe* (1999).

[38] The values conflict here is illustrated by a lawsuit filed by loggers in Minnesota charging that the new ecologically based policies of the Forest Service represent the unconstitutional support of a religion by government, that is the "new age" worship of nature, trees, and animals. See *Greenwire* (1999b).

suggests that there is no reason to expect a reversal even if the ESA was eliminated. Thus, it is likely that the economic and political importance of these communities within their own states will also continue to decline over the longer term.

A second, and related, change is demographic. Young people from rural communities head off to college and do not return in large numbers. Certainly, part of the explanation is the lack of appropriate occupational opportunities. Regardless, the human "capital" that defined rural community values and identity is shrinking. Meanwhile, some of these towns are experiencing an in-migration of urbanites and suburbanites seeking vacation homes or rural lifestyles. These new part-time and full-time residents are bringing with them values and ideals – including wildlife values – that differ significantly from those that traditionally defined the community.[39]

In fact, the Interior Department attempted to capitalize on this incremental "greening" of western communities in the early 1990s. Soon after taking office, Interior Secretary Babbit moved to broaden participation on public lands grazing advisory boards (which set policy for local BLM lands).[40] The idea was to reconstitute the boards that were previously run exclusively by ranchers to include other "voices" from the community – in particular, environmental voices. The effort was only partially successful, however, for although one can certainly find other voices at the regional or state level, it is still difficult to find them at the community level. Ultimately, the extent, magnitude, and timeframe for these values, revolution is speculative, but it is certainly a long-term trend.

Third, we should consider those instances, albeit much less common, where biodiversity policy actually reinforces community economics and identity. In the Pacific Northwest, for instance, downstream salmon fishing communities are pressuring the government to list several salmon species in order to force upstream watershed protection. (Not surprisingly, the timber communities upstream do not want restrictions on river-side forest cutting and so they have rallied to oppose the salmon listings.) Over the longer term, as species disappear and some communities come to realize the losses incurred, we may see greater sympathy for government intervention.

A fourth factor that can put the community on the side of stronger biodiversity policy – NIMBY (not-in-my-back-yard) politics – is, perhaps, more relevant to nonrural communities. In NIMBY politics, the community is interested in blocking some objectionable facility, development, or land-use project. Concern about endangered species protection is strictly instrumental and utilitarian. Species protection is merely a vehicle for derailing the project, with little or no true substantive concern for biodiversity. So, for example, concerned citizens in Lancaster, Massachusetts, began mobilizing to find state-listed endangered species on a development site when it was announced

---

[39] Kellert (1996), Powers (1996).
[40] See *Greenwire* (1993).

that an asphalt plant might be constructed there. Prior proposals for the same location to build schools or homes did not elicit community objections.

Of course when the scientific and ecological criteria for extending regulatory protection to a species or habitat exists, the motivations of the proponents are not policy relevant. If the species warrants protection, the cause of discovery is irrelevant. Nevertheless, NIMBY actions do add to the intensity and complexity of biodiversity politics because some communities can use these laws and regulations instrumentally to protect their property rights, exercise "local" control (against development project proponents), and preserve community identity.

IV. WHY COMMUNITY POLITICS MATTERS

At least for the foreseeable future, "better science" and the balance of forces operating at the local level seem to be directing biodiversity policy and community politics on a collision course. This is likely to occur even if the presumed economic impacts of future species listings could be fully mitigated through compensation, tax benefits, subsidies, etc.

All of which begs the question: So what? How could small, politically disconnected, and geographically isolated communities have any meaningful impact on endangered species policy when powerful economic interests such as the timber and mining industries have been so unsuccessful?

The potential political power of communities in national policy making rests on four elements: grass-roots nature of community mobilization; the low salience of endangered species policy to the electorate; institutional advantages; and tacit support from state wildlife agencies.

Grassroots

First, the mobilization of community politics considered in this chapter is truly grassroots – activism from below.[41] Spawned by a sense of outrage, injustice, and government failure, grassroots politics can have an energy that is uncompromising and unyielding – unlike special interest politics.[42] And although grassroots politics usually has a long gestation period (especially compared to economic interest politics) before it becomes politically potent, once it becomes established it matters, especially in low-population and rural districts.

In particular, grassroots politics carries a mantle of public interest legitimacy that economic interest group politics lacks. When anti-ESA voices were

---

[41] This stands in stark contrast to the situation in the 1980s and early 1990s when mining, timber, and ORV manufacturers funded phony grassroots "wise use" groups in the West. See Dowie (1995, chapter 4).

[42] Ironically, essays on contemporary environmental policy that predict that the "next wave" in environmental politics is going to be pro-environment grassroots activism totally ignore the potential for grassroots opposition. Dowie (1995, chapter 8), Sabel, Fung, and Karkkainen (1999).

"merely" grazing associations, timber companies, and agricultural lobbies, their arguments could be readily discounted as special pleading. But when ordinary people as a community organize to oppose a species listing, the question of legitimacy is reflected back on the policy. Is policy fair? Why should one segment of the population (i.e., small natural-resources dependent communities) be singled out to bear a disproportionate burden in biodiversity policy? Indeed, there is a conceptual similarity here to the issue of environmental justice as it has been applied to the skewed siting of environmentally objectionable (polluting) facilities in communities of color.[43]

The legitimacy of grassroots mobilization among communities is enhanced further by organization. For politicians, organization is what distinguishes a legitimate political actor worthy of attention from a one-shot protest that must simply be endured. Organization provides leadership, resources, and the effectiveness that comes from a division of labor. This is where both corporate economic interest groups and national political interest groups reenter the picture. National "wise use" and property rights organizations (sponsored by economic and political interests) offer financial, legal, and other forms of assistance to communities already mobilizing against government efforts to protect a species. Playing on deep-seated American political mythologies – the preeminence of the individual, the inviolability of property rights, the danger of expanding government, man taming nature, etc. – they also provide an intellectual and political framework around which community politics can organize. At the same time, the political agendas of special interests gain greater political legitimacy by piggybacking on community fears and community politics.

Community mobilization's political impact on biodiversity policy is aided by complementarities between the nature of grassroots activism and the ESA's species-by-species implementation. Grassroots politics focuses on addressing a local issue at the local level. For example, hundreds of grassroots organizations today watch over individual tracts of old growth forest in their backyards – and their backyards alone. By working only at the local level, they fight only local opposition and strike local compromises. Yet, cumulatively their impact might be larger than if a single overarching law or regulation were put in place.

Similarly, ESA listing decisions are prepared, listing areas are designated, critical habitat may be delineated, etc. on a species-by-species basis. Each listing decision is, in a sense, its own isolated case (even in multi-species plans), which leaves it vulnerable to local political opposition. In this respect it is more likely that several dozen communities opposing one or more distinct listings decisions will have a greater impact on the overall implementation of the ESA than would several dozen communities banding together to fight for ESA reform in general. This is because it is easier to deflect bureaucratic behavior on any given decision than it is to get legislative action. This is, in fact, just what we see happening now. The

---

[43] For a discussion of the basic argument of environmental justice in environmental policy, see Bullard (1994).

USFWS tailors individual listing decisions in attempting to avoid major conflicts with local communities.[44] Therefore, the grassroots strategy of fighting many small-pitched battles is likely to be especially effective against the ESA approach of individual listing decisions, resulting in a significant reduction in meaningful overall protection for wildlife and habitat.

Low Salience for the Public

The second element favoring community politics is the pattern of distribution of the costs and benefits resulting from ESA actions. Specifically, strong biodiversity policies confer diffuse benefits across the public but impose (perceived) concentrated costs on communities in the regulated area.[45] Thus, the latter are much more strongly motivated to undertake political action.

Yes, a majority of Americans claim to care about wildlife preservation, endangered species, and habitat protection. Everyone benefits an intangibly small amount from the preservation of a given species or habitat. Although some may derive a general feeling of well-being knowing that wildlife exists "out there somewhere," the average citizen senses no significant change in their life resulting from protection of the Indiana bat. Thus, biodiversity policy is a low salience issue among the public; attitude does not translate into focused political action.[46] Candidates for office do not rise or fall on this issue.

In contrast, the perceived burdens of ESA implementation and enforcement fall quite specifically on certain industries, firms, and projecting into the future, communities. For these actors biodiversity policy has high salience and it shapes their political behavior accordingly. Although environmental groups have been successful in countering efforts by economic interests to weaken biodiversity policies, they may not be as effective if their opponent is communities of ordinary citizens.

Here again the issue of environmental justice – environmental policy placing an unfair burden on a segment of the citizenry – adds to the politics. It took national environmental organizations and federal officials more than a decade to figure out that they had to take into account how environmental costs and benefits were distributed differentially among communities. This realization only came about because communities of color mobilized and organized to make the point. The next chapter in environmental justice awakenings may be natural resources dependent communities "burdened" by biodiversity policy forcing the advocates for stronger biodiversity policies to recognize the uneven distribution of burdens inherent in these efforts.

---

[44] Again, evidence that ESA listings follow pretty much scientific need misses the point. USFWS routinely postpones controversial listings and tailors restrictions in response to political opposition, unless forced by the courts to do otherwise.

[45] This basic framework is described in Wilson (1980, 357–94).

[46] Lober (1995) finds that the distinction between attitude and behavior is crucial in public actions on environmental issues. In particular, only a small fraction of people who claim to be bothered by an environmental issue actually express it in any form of political action.

Institutional Advantages

Third, the very design of the U.S. political system magnifies the ability of small resource dependent communities to affect policy in significant ways. In particular, the committee structure of Congress vests considerable agenda setting and decision power in the hands of committees and subcommittees. More to the point, committee members with seniority, and especially committee chairs hold great sway over matters that come before their committees and have considerable influence on the agencies that are responsible for matters under their jurisdiction. Therefore, influencing critical issues before Congress and putting pressure on executive branch agencies is often most effectively done through the appropriate legislative committee and its staff.

Now consider that the committees and subcommittees responsible for legislative action on natural resource policy, public lands management, and overseeing the operations of corresponding executive agencies also control legislative action on biodiversity policy, including authorization of the ESA. These committees are populated by, and are often chaired by, legislators from districts and states with the highest concentrations of natural resource dependent communities. This is hardly surprising since politicians from these areas have an obvious political interest in securing committee assignments that reflect the dominant interests in their districts. A congressman from Alaska would find the House Resources Committee a useful assignment; a congressman from Manhattan would not.

This pattern of assignment is enhanced by the fact that there are fewer local issues in competition in rural, natural resource dependent districts. The one "big" issue usually revolves around the regional commodity. Politicians from farming districts in Nebraska are concerned with farming issues, while politicians from Washington's rural forest areas want to help timber communities. Although there may be nuanced differences between Republican and Democratic candidates for office, they do not amount to major policy differences when it comes to local trade-offs in endangered species policy. Meanwhile, politicians from industrialized states and urban and suburban districts (where voters may be more favorable toward strong biodiversity policies) have a wider range of problems to focus on, all of which compete for their attention. Therefore, through preference and presence politicians sensitive to the natural resource community interests and values come to control directly the legislative institutional mechanisms that affect policy, including biodiversity policy. They also hold great influence over the bureaucracy that implements policy.[47] They acquire the political power to affect policy far beyond the numbers they represent.

---

[47] A clear indicator of the indirect effect on policy is the large number of lawsuits filed by local environmental groups compelling federal agencies – USFWS, the Forest Service, and the BLM – to enforce existing biodiversity laws and regulations. These agencies are deterred from implementing policy in the hope of avoiding clashes with powerful representatives and senators from likely affected areas.

Add to this the fact that biodiversity is a low salience issue for most of the electorate and the situation is ripe for *vote trading*. Since votes for or against endangered species protection do not affect the political fortunes of the vast majority of legislators, they can freely "trade" their votes on issues like amending the ESA for votes they want on issues that are more salient to voters in their districts or states. A representative from Connecticut might agree to support a bill proposed by a Wyoming congressman that reduces funding for ESA enforcement if the representative from Wyoming will support her amendment to add money to the defense budget to buy another attack submarine. Thus *local* public interests often overshadow national public interests.

Sympathetic State Agencies

Last, consider that fact that most state fisheries, wildlife, and forestry agencies are still dominated by a commodity view of nature. For a variety of organizational and cultural reasons, state agencies have been slow to join the ecological revolution that is transforming federal agencies. State agencies are also more acutely sensitive to the pressures imposed by local politicians and interests. They are also concerned about protecting their professional and organizational autonomy and, therefore, resent federal agency intrusion into state affairs.

Consequently, as local communities mobilize to oppose federal efforts to protect wildlife and habitat, state agencies frequently align with local interests in opposition. State agencies can and do provide local opponents with "counterinformation" – the other side of the scientific coin. They lend professional and scientific credibility to arguments against federal action. The directors of state wildlife agencies from Alabama, Georgia, South Carolina, Tennessee, and Virginia all opposed federal efforts to keep 750,000 acres of woodlands in the Southern Appalachian national forest roadless, claiming that the action would hurt species that depend on new growth that follows disturbance.[48]

In sum, there is good reason to expect that meaningful endangered species protection will feel the rising heat of community political resistance unless the trade-offs – real or perceived – and the communitywide fears they generate can be moderated. Community mobilization could overturn the prevailing political stalemate in ESA policy that has existed since the early 1990s, seriously weakening biodiversity protection and preservation.

V. CONCLUSION

The potential for mobilized community opposition to ESA actions represents a real and serious challenge to biodiversity policy. As science pushes policy to broaden the scale and scope of protection for wildlife and habitats, the

---

[48] *Greenwire* (1999b).

economic, political, and social trade-offs – real and perceived – increase commensurately.

"Better science" cannot be the foundation on which a broader consensus on acceptable policies for protecting biodiversity can be built. The problem is not that the public and its politicians are ignorant of the significance of the loss of wildlife and habitats. They do understand it, more or less. The problem is that the long-term and intangible implications of preserving biodiversity are simply not as salient politically as are the immediate and tangible concerns of economic growth, consumer comfort, and social well-being. There is little that better science can do to change that.

Instead, science should be considered one component in a broader political strategy to preserve biodiversity. Most important, it can be instrumental in separating the myths from the realities in popular perceptions of the issue. Science can help communities challenged by wildlife and habitat protection policies to understand and plan for the inevitability of change, only part of which is driven by environmental concerns. Better biological science can offer communities a view of wildlife and the landscape that is different from local tradition. Ecological science can help to dispel false notions of the invulnerability and resilience of nature. It can help communities to understand better what will be gained or lost biologically and ecologically if certain policies are followed, or ignored. The social sciences can present the intellectual case for the ecological connection between social well-being and wildlife – one that differs from prevailing values in the community – as well as focus community attention on longer-term social and economic trends. Science can help communities to place the real trade-offs in perspective and context.

This can only happen, however, if the transfer of information occurs within a decision-making framework that includes communities as active and equal participants. "Better science" cannot be force fed to communities by patronizing federal authorities or self-righteous environmentalists. Education in this form is condescending and ineffective. Rather, communities need to become part of a process that allows them to develop the capacity to absorb, evaluate, and manipulate the rapidly growing cache of scientific information on biodiversity.

To tie the fate of biodiversity policy to the desperate hope that a fundamental value change will occur sometime soon among the public in general, and affected communities in particular, that will rocket support for more vigorous wildlife and habitat protection to the top of the political agenda would be a fatal mistake. And even over a longer policy-relevant timeframe, it is highly unlikely that affected communities will ever adopt the trade-off view of the most ardent urban and suburban environmentalists, especially since the latter incur no social, political, or economic price for their advocacy. However, it is possible to dampen the intensity of community opposition to strong biodiversity policies, allowing for more creative and effective solutions.

Specifically, we need to consider changing the *decision-making process* that imposes protections under the ESA and other laws. The analysis presented in this chapter suggests that reconciling strong biodiversity protection with community politics is fundamentally a problem of policy *legitimacy*. Legitimacy is a question of who has the right and authority to decide what trade-offs are acceptable in policy making and who gets to decide how those trade-offs are distributed across the affected parties.[49] Recognition of the legitimacy of a policy means that people will abide by a policy and its rules even if they disagree with the policy itself, in a manner similar to accepting as our president someone for whom we did not vote.

Where "science-only" advocates for biodiversity policies err is in believing that scientific knowledge alone confers legitimacy on policy.[50] Certainly professional (scientific) knowledge is an aspect of policy legitimacy. Professional knowledge refers to whether or not decision makers know what they are talking about and whether or not the public believes they know what they are talking about. Part is scientific competence: Do those in charge have the technical know-how and the data to make the right (informed) substantive policy choice? Specialized knowledge about a public problem confers some right to address that problem. Part is trust: Do we believe that those in charge are using their technical knowledge properly? This is political, and on issues where trade-offs are perceived as significant people and communities are often not prepared to grant trust. Studies of rural community governments consistently reveal significant distrust of higher government authorities, even though it is clear that higher level agencies have vastly greater scientific and technical resources.[51] If the information itself is not tainted, then its use in policy is assumed to be biased.[52]

Yet even where professional knowledge is accepted, this "technical" aspect of legitimacy only addresses one small part of the problem, and, from a political perspective, it may be the least important. In democratic societies, legitimacy is determined primarily by perceptions of the fairness of the process by which decisions are made.[53] That is, legitimacy is not about whether your side wins or loses the clash of values and interests, but about *perceptions* of how the game was played. Did all sides of the issue *appear* to have the opportunity to voice concerns, doubts, preferences, etc.? Did all sides *seem* to have equal access to information and resources? Were the rules

---

[49] Stone (1997, chapter 12) describes legitimacy as the political scientist's equivalent of the economist's "invisible hand" as a force in public policy. On the importance of process in arguing a policy legitimacy, see Reich (1988) and Majone (1989).

[50] The idea of technocracy, where decisions are placed in the hands of technical experts, is an old one, but continues to reemerge in various forms. See, for example, Breyer (1993).

[51] See Somma (1997), McBeth and Bennett (1998), Kraft and Clary (1991).

[52] Interestingly, most of the evidence available suggests that in the overwhelming number of cases where the USFWS manipulates the data to achieve a desired outcome, it is directed toward avoiding a listing. For example, in the case of the failure to list the lynx, a federal court judge found that the USFWS ". . . applied an incorrect legal standard, relied on glaringly faulty factual premises and ignored the views of its own experts." See *Greenlines* (1998).

[53] Lober (1995).

by which information was gathered and analyzed and values and interests assessed *perceived* to be fair and unbiased?[54]

Although no polls have been taken, when it comes to ESA implementation decisions and related actions, affected communities would probably answer these questions with a resounding "NO!" The listing and comment process *seems* biased against communities because it appears that everything of consequence has already decided when community input is requested. I stress the word *appears* because perceptions are key. As currently practiced, stakeholders in endangered species cases are defined as the relevant federal agencies, the state wildlife agency, and the affected private landowner or public land user. Regional and extraregional environmental advocates often participate as stakeholders and seem to have early and influential access to policy deliberations and implementation decision making. Frequently they are the parties that initiate the action to list an animal or plant under the ESA to close a forest to logging, or to restrict grazing on public lands. Meanwhile, communities are kept at arm's length, relegated to the role of commentator sitting on the sidelines petitioning federal agencies, but never key players in the process. [55] From the community perspective, biodiversity policy, no matter how soundly grounded in good science, can never be legitimate if it is imposed by outsiders.

And if the decision process is not perceived as fair, then the policy itself must be perceived as unfair. This raises again the issue of environmental justice. Does biodiversity policy impose an unfair burden on certain communities merely because they do not have the financial, legal, or political resources to effectively oppose government action? And there is the moral dimension: If government natural resource policies created these communities and nurtured the values and interests that define them today, does government have an obligation to assist these communities in the transition when policies change?

This focus on policy legitimacy suggests that there may be considerable wisdom in the frequently voiced scheme of bringing communities into the decision-making process from the beginning.[56] Imagine the creation of a working group for each proposed species listing, or more practically for a multispecies habitat conservation plan. The working group would review the data on biological status, habitat requirements, alternatives for implementation, and recovery goals. It would set performance standards, goals, timetables, and requirements in accordance with the available scientific evidence. Community representatives, recognized as key stakeholders, would be engaged from the beginning in the discovery process. Federal resources – money, training, education, etc. – would be needed to build the local capacity to absorb and use the information.

---

[54] For a clear discussion see Stone (1997, chapter 12).

[55] One exceptional example is the involvement of Orange county and San Diego city officials in the development of a multispecies, multihabitat conservation plan. See *Greenwire* (1997a). See also Bernton (1999) for a description of a similar effort by the NMFS in Oregon and Washington.

[56] The Western Governor's Association ENLIBRA policy is a prominent example.

Once species status, performance standards, recovery goals, etc. had been agreed to, the effort would turn to alternative strategies for meeting those goals. Community representatives should not have the power to veto plans, or preempt protection requirements.[57] However, they would be a player at the table in deliberations and a participant in "collective learning" in every step as the policy unfolds. In some ways, the relationship between local and state governments on the one hand and federal authorities on the other would parallel those under the Clean Air Act, which allows the Environmental Protection Agency to approve state implementation plans that are pegged to the performance standards set by federal rules. An example of how this might work is the recent agreement between the National Marine Fisheries Service (NMFS), and state, county, and local governments in Oregon and Washington to attempt to restore salmon and steelhead trout populations in the region. NMFS is setting the protection and recovery standards and state and local authorities are devising rules and procedures to meet those standards.[58]

In general, federal agencies loathe the idea of granting local governments stakeholder status. They believe that excluding "irrelevant" parties such as community representatives will limit extraneous considerations, shorten the permitting time, lessen the politics, and improve the environmental (science-based) outcome.[59]

Similarly, environmentalists cringe at the notion of local community participation because they assume – correctly – that short-term economic, social, and political objectives will be inserted into what they would like to keep as a scientific discussion. The evidence suggest that this fear is justified: Local governments and state agencies are far more attuned to short-term economic and political issues, and more willing to trade off long-term environmental needs, especially those involving wildlife and habitat preservation, than are federal agencies.[60] There is an advantage to having a nonlocal viewpoint in biodiversity policy making because the influence of any given interest is diluted.

Nevertheless, preventing community stakeholders from participating in the unfolding of the scientific evidence from the start of the process merely because they are likely to question the preeminence of ecological values and interests over others undermines the legitimacy of the entire policy. The dominant goal for those interested in biodiversity protection should be "better policy," not "better science" (that is merely an instrument), which in this context means community participation.

As currently practiced, community concerns are crammed into the "comment period," which creates the perception that community issues are, at best,

---

[57] The right of local and state governments to veto federal protection of wildlife is a reckless element of the ESA bill introduced by congressman Don Young of Alaska (cosponsored by 38 republicans): Common Sense Protection of the Endangered Species Act. See Armijo (1999).
[58] Bernton (1999).
[59] Several cases of local-state-federal environmental policy making are described in John (1994).
[60] Koontz (1997), McBeth and Bennett (1998, 584).

footnotes. Early, direct, and substantial involvement by community representatives in the formulation of preservation plans and recovery alternatives would allow community concerns to surface incrementally in the context of the accumulating scientific data. Although participation may not nullify community opposition to an ESA listing, it may lessen the *mobilizing* effect of the listing and dampen the intensity of the politics considerably by increasing policy legitimacy.

Looking out over the next fifty years it is clear that many natural resource- and agricultural-dependent communities will continue to fade socially and economically. Others will undergo a wrenching change in local culture. These changes will proceed regardless of endangered species policy, since they are driven by much more significant social forces. Greatly compounding these societal losses would be the unnecessary loss of biodiversity in these localities caused by short-term political efforts to keep these communities afloat at the expense of sound endangered species protection policies. The only way to prevent both of these tragedies is to confront directly their inherent linkages and integrate our policies to preserve both natural heritage and community heritage. Programs to help these communities make the transition to other social and economic community models are needed. Putting such programs in place before endangered species restrictions become enmeshed with already declining local fortunes could greatly reduce the politics of biodiversity protection.

References

Allen, Scott (1999) "Salmon Safeguard Called Overkill in Maine." *Boston Globe* (December 3).

Armijo, Patrick (1999) "Species Act Changes Proposed." *Albuquerque Journal* (October 29).

Bernton, Hal (1999) "Saving Salmon Is Local Burden." *The Portland Oregonian (online)* (December 15).

Boston Globe (1999) "Fisherman: Rules Killing Livelihood." (June 6).

Breyer, Stephen (1993) *Breaking the Vicious Circle: Towards Effective Risk Regulation* (Cambridge: Harvard University Press).

Bullard, Robert (1994) "Overcoming Racism in Environmental Decision-making." *Environment* 36, no. 4 (May): 10–44.

Defenders of Wildlife (1998) *State Endangered Species Acts* (Washington, D.C.).

Dowie, Mark (1995) *Losing Ground* (Cambridge: MIT Press).

Downs, Anthony (1972) "Up and Down with Ecology: The Issue Attention Cycle." *Public Interest* 28: 38–50.

Dumont, Clayton W. (1996) "The Demise of Community and Ecology in the Pacific North West." *Sociological Perspectives* 39, no. 2: 277–300.

Dunlap, Riley (1989) "Public Opinion and Environmental Policy," in James P. Lester, ed. *Environmental Politics and Policy* (Durham, NC: Duke University Press.)

Finch, Bill (1999) "Alabamians very Concerned." *Mobile Register* (July 11).

Freudenburg, William, Lisa Wilson, and Daniel O'Leary (1998) "Forty Years of Spotted Owls? A Longitudinal Analysis of Logging Industry Job Losses." *Sociological Perspectives* 41, no. 1: 1–26.

Gould, Kenneth A., Alan Schnaiberg, and Adam S. Weinberg (1996) *Local Environmental Struggles*. (New York: Cambridge University Press).

Greenlines (1998) "Biology vs. Politics." (February 17).

— (1999a) "FWS Dragging its Feet Again." No. 953 (August 30).

— (1999b) "Millions of Acres of Grizzly Habitat Unprotected." (November 29).

Greenwire (1993) "Interior Department: 92 Land Advisory Councils Get the Ax." (December 16).

— (1997a) "Natural Resources – Habitat: Southern CA Program Reaching Critical Stage." (February 18).

— (1997b) "Wetlands: Democratic Fundraiser at Center of Controversy." (April 17).

— (1998) "Prairie Dogs: Enviros Petition for ESA Protection." (August 4).

— (1999a) "Society and Politics – USFS: Dombeck Hears NV Workers' Worries." (November 19).

— (1999b) "Natural Resources – National Forests: Loggers Say Ban Is Illegally Based On Religion." (November 30).

— (1999c) "National Forests: Logging Reduction Not a Problem – Scientists." (December 22).

Idaho Falls Register (1999) "Study Shows Effect of Grazing Cutback." (May 10).

John, DeWitt (1994) *Civic Environmentalism* (Washington, D.C.: CQ Press).

Kellert, Stephen R. (1996) *The Value of Life* (Washington, D.C.: Island Press).

Koontz, Tomas M. (1997) "Differences Between State and Federal Public Forest Management: The Importance of Rules," *Publius* 27, no. 1(Winter): 15–37.

Kraft, Michael and Bruce Clary (1991) "Citizen Participation and the NIMBY Syndrome: Public Response to Radioactive Waste Disposal." *Western Political Science Quarterly* 44, no. 2(June): 299–327.

Kronholz, June (1999) "Rural School Districts Get a Taxing Primer in Politics of Timber." *The Wall Street Journal* (December 14).

Lober, Douglas (1995) "Why Protest? Public Behavioral and Attitudinal Response to Siting a Waste Disposal Facility." *Policy Studies Journal* 23, no. 3: 499–518.

Majone, Giandomenico (1989) *Evidence, Argument, and Persuasion in Public Policy"* (New Haven, CT: Yale University Press).

Mapes, Lynda (1999) "Fish vs. Humans: A Northwest Debate." *Boston Globe* (December 19).

McBeth, Mark and Keith Bennett (1998) "Local Elected Officials and Environmental Policy: Does Rural Matter Anymore?" *Social Science Journal* 35, no. 4: 577–88.

Meyer, Stephen M. (1995a) *Endangered Species Listings and State Economic Performance* (MIT Project on Environmental Politics and Policy, Working Paper #4).

— (1995b) *The Economic Impact of the ESA on the Agricultural Sector* (MIT Project on Environmental Politics and Policy, Working Paper #5).

— (1998) "The Economic Impact of the Endangered Species Act on the Housing and Real Estate Markets." *NYU Environmental Law Journal* 6, no. 2: 450–79.

Ozawa, Connie P. (1996) "Science in Environmental Conflicts." *Sociological Perspectives* 39, no. 2: 219–30.

Powers, Thomas (1996) *Lost Landscapes and Failed Economies* (Washington D.C.: Island Press).

Reich, Robert (1988) *The Power of Public Ideas* (Cambridge: Harvard University Press).

Sabel, Charles, Archon Fung, and Bradley Karkkainen (1999) "Beyond Backyard Environmentalism." *The Boston Review* 24, no. 5(October/Novemeber): 4–11.

Somma, Mark (1997) "Institutions, Ideology, and the Tragedy of the Commons: West Texas Groundwater Policy." *Publius* 27, no. 1 (Winter): 1–13.

Stone, Deborah (1997) *Policy Paradox and Political Reason* (New York: W.W. Norton).

Wildlines (1999) "Texas Agency Misuses Wildlife Funds" (November 8), no. 49.

Wilson, E. O. (1992) *The Diversity of Life* (Cambridge: Harvard University Press).

Wilson, James Q. (1980) *The Politics of Regulation* (New York: Basic Books).

CHAPTER 9

On Political Realities: Comments on Ando, Cash, and Meyer

Clifford Nowell

I. INTRODUCTION

Stephen Meyer, David Cash, and Amy Whritenour Ando make a strong case in Chapters 6 through 8 in this volume for the importance politics and interest group behavior play in the implementation of the ESA of 1973 (ESA). Each of these chapters addresses the relative role of science, economics, and politics on the implementation of the ESA. Although each of the authors agrees that politics has an impact on ESA implementation, the authors have varying opinions on the relative importance of politics compared to the other factors.

The conclusions drawn by the authors are diverse. Meyer suggests that science "can never be the dominant force in endangered species protection because other factors, broadly subsumed in the term 'politics', will ultimately determine which lands are included or excluded in a habitat recovery plan."

Cash reaches a different conclusion: "It seems that scientific variables have greater explanatory power for the listing decision than do the nonscientific considerations." Cash does not completely discount the impact of politics on ESA implementation. When it comes to funding the ESA, he concludes (p. 131) "funding is not wholly consistent with FWS [Fish and Wildlife Service] guidelines, and particularly with its science-based components."

Ando reaches a conclusion similar to Cash: both politics and science matter. She concludes that: "Species that rank high in the listing-priority system (*science based*) do tend to be proposed for listing relatively quickly.... However, the results also show that interest groups do influence the agency's listing process."

Put together, these three chapters clearly demonstrate that despite the intentions of the act to have decisions on the listing of species be based solely on scientific evidence, listings are made on the basis of a combination of economics, politics, and science. What is not clear from these three chapters, however, are the implications for society from this deviation. Will the consideration of factors such as economic impact and individual preferences for species reduce the benefits of the ESA, or will these factors focus the ESA on species from which the benefits from preserving are greater than the costs?

In this chapter I will first review the most important aspects of the works presented by Ando, Cash, and Meyer. After comparing the conclusions drawn by the authors on politics and ESA implementation, I will take a more general look at the relationship between interest group behavior, welfare, and implementation of the ESA.

II. CHAPTER REVIEWS

In Chapter 8, "Community Politics and Endangered Species Protection," Meyer makes a strong case for redefining some of the traditional notions in economics of what constitutes a cost to a community, and what is likely to motivate interest groups to organize and operate effectively. Because local communities are most impacted by the ESA, local politics will be what determines the success of the ESA. Meyer starts with the assertion that small, directly impacted communities will be able to organize and lobby more efficiently than larger, more diffuse groups. He suggests that what drives local community involvement in the politics that determine ESA implementation is more than is normally considered by economists when conducting cost/benefit analyses. Meyer argues that what drives local interest group involvement are issues such as economic impact, alteration of private property rights, and a revision of community identity, culture, heritage, and political autonomy.

Perhaps no single author has been more influential in analyzing the motivation for interest group behavior than Mancur Olson, who in his text *The Logic of Collective Action* (1965) suggests which type of interest groups are likely to be most effective in achieving their goals. First, Olson believes that it is easier for interest groups to organize when the number of affected individuals is small rather than large. Second, Olson draws a parallel to a group's ability to be an effective advocate with a group's ability to fund a public good. The goal of the group is a public good for the group. Because of this, when any member of the group puts forth effort to achieve this goal, all members benefit. Thus, all members of the group have the incentive to free-ride on the actions of others. Free-riding is likely to be greater when the group becomes large, when the individual cost of action is large relative to the benefit of action, and when individuals in the group have different levels of commitment to the goal.

These are the exact same issues raised by Meyer in explaining why local communities will be the milieu that will determine the success of the ESA. Large national and international groups will be rendered ineffective in the debate over ESA implementation because of the free-riding generated from the differing levels of commitment to the cause, and due to the ambiguity of the benefits received by individuals. Because of this, if local communities do not support the goals of the ESA, implementation will be extremely difficult.

Of the issues Meyer considers to be most important to local constituents, economists are familiar with the first of these issues, the traditional "jobs versus environment" argument. If an economy is operating efficiently, more environmental quality implies less of some other good. Meyer notes that economists are somewhat proficient at estimating these costs, and more important, local communities have no trouble in identifying these impacts. Benefits to a local community from saving a species from extinction are more nebulous and may accrue at some point in the future, whereas the costs of saving a species will be borne by local groups.

The loss of private property rights is something more difficult for economists to measure, partly because of the ambiguity of who initially "owns" the property right and to what extent the property right extends. Still, economists recognize the value of property rights as a legitimate cost and recognize that any revision of private property rights is likely to generate interest group efforts to capture the benefits of the property right (Stroup 1997; Bromley 1997).

The last category of items that Meyer postulates are likely to provoke community activism are rarely considered in economic analysis in part because they are difficult to measure. These items are best described as community identity issues. Pointing out the importance of these issues is a valuable contribution, and the possibility that ignoring these issues will result in the failure to protect endangered species is critical.

Consider a community with a strong local identity, which revolves around the forest products industry. Local industry injects a sum of money into the economy, but a community member's well-being depends on both income and self-identity. Suppose an individual is asked to choose between two states of the world: State A with income $= x$, and a self-identity as a logger; or State B, with income $> x$ and a self-identity as a tour operator. If the individual chooses State A, she has made clear that a trade-off exists between income and self-identity.

Issues such as community identity are typically ignored in cost-benefit calculations designed to analyze welfare effects of public policy. As an example, consider Duffield, Neher, and Brown (1992), who analyze the benefits to recreationists from increasing stream flow in two blue ribbon trout streams in western Montana. Increased stream flows result in benefits to anglers from improved fishing conditions, but also impose costs to the local community from a decline in water available for crop irrigation. No mention is given to a change in community identity that will result from the region becoming more of a tourist attraction and less of an agricultural community. These costs are real and, Meyer argues, are important in determining the intensity of interest group pressure.

When Meyer concludes that politics, and not science or economics, will determine ESA implementation, what he is claiming is that local communities are less motivated by scientific considerations than personal issues. Science still has a place in local politics, and many would argue with Meyer's proposition that science is unimportant in the process. It may be that better science alone will not be enough to influence the politics surrounding ESA implementation; however, I suspect it is the lack of communication between scientists and the public that is at the root of the problem. If scientists were better able to communicate why an apparently inconsequential species is important, local citizens may be more willing to include science in their own values, and as a result local opposition to the listing of species may be tempered.

In Chapter 7, Cash's "Beyond Cute and Fuzzy: Science and Politics in the U.S. ESA" attempts to determine the importance of scientific information and the political economy on two aspects of ESA implementation: listing and funding.

As background, it is important to remember that the ESA leaves no doubt that science is the only criterion that should be considered in the decision to list a species as threatened or endangered. In an informative discussion of the act, Smith, Mooter, and Schwalbe (1993, 1,037) quote directly from the Act: status determinations must be made solely on evidence from the "best scientific and commercial data available." The word solely was added in 1982 to "remove from the process of the listing or delisting of species any factor not related to the biological status of the species ... [E]conomic considerations have no relevance to determinations regarding the status of the species." Cash goes beyond the listing decision and examines whether funding of those species listed are influenced by political and economic considerations. Although his study suffers from not allowing interaction between the funding and listing decisions, it still provides meaningful information for those studying the act.

Cash's work may be most appropriately viewed as an extension on the work of Metrick and Weitzman (1996) who, using data prior to the 1982 amendment to the ESA, find that both scientific and visceral variables influence both the listing and funding decisions (see Chapter 19 for the database). Cash considers post–1982 data to see if the 1982 amendment was effective in its intent to remove from consideration all but scientific evidence. Using this new data, Cash finds that scientific variables become more important and visceral variables become less important than had been determined by Metrick and Weitzman (1996). It would be interesting to consider an alternative specification that may help illuminate the impact of the 1982 amendment and the relative influence of scientific and political factors on ESA implementation. By combining the datasets of Cash and Metrick and Weitzman, one could easily test for structural change using a series of dummy variables. Using the full dataset and this specification, one could test which of the political and economic variables seemed to gain or lose importance after the 1982 amendment.

One nice aspect of analyzing the listing decision is that the mandate given by Congress to the Fish and Wildlife Service (USFWS) is very specific: consider only scientific evidence. It is often the case that authors studying agency behavior have difficulty defining the agency's goal, and as a result have difficulty in determining factors which influence the agency (Nowell and Tschirhart 1993; Crone and Tschirhart 1998). Because the mandate given to the USFWS does not require the agency to weigh the welfare impacts of policy on competing individuals and interest groups, the listing decision is an excellent policy to analyze, and Cash's results imply that (in light of Metrick and Weitzman's findings) the 1982 amendment was effective. In addition, post–1982, it appears scientific variables did play an important role in listing.

The analysis of funding the recovery of a listed species is much more problematic. Scientific data needed for each species include genetic importance of each species, probability that the species can be saved, and finally, the cost of saving each species. To judge the political influence on funding, data are needed on the political support for saving each species. Cash has good data on political support, probability of saving species, and the genetic importance of each species. Unfortunately, data on the cost required to implement ESA programs for each species is not available. The Office of the Inspector General estimated that $4.6 billion would be required to implement the act. Smith et al. (1992) note that this is equivalent to a minimum of $300 million annually. During five fiscal years, 1989–1993, Congress authorized only a total of $900 million annually for ESA activities (Metrick and Weitzman 1998), far below that necessary to fund recovery of all species.

In his analysis of funding decisions, Cash recognizes the limitations of his data by noting that data are not available on the cost of recovery for individual species. In addition, he cautions that correlation between variables, and questions on the direction of causality, make interpretation of results difficult. Although he finds greater evidence that funding is driven significantly by political considerations, he suggests more research in this area is needed. Because of the data limitations it is difficult to measure what level of individual species funding is optimal from a scientific point of view, given total funding is inadequate to save all species. As a result of this, the conclusions presented in the listing analysis are much more convincing than the results in the funding analysis.

In Chapter 6, "Interest Group Behavior and Endangered Species Protection," Ando summarizes three empirical studies that analyze the behavior of regulators and interest groups with respect to listing a species once the species has been proposed for listing by the USFWS. In addition, she inquires into what factors are likely to motivate interest groups into action. Ando argues that this is an important question because if factors that motivate interest groups are the same factors that would be considered in a traditional cost-benefit analysis, we may have little to fear from interest group involvement.

One of the studies Ando summarizes uses a time-to-failure analysis to attempt to isolate interest group behavior as a "separate, distinct force." Her regression model postulates that the time it takes a species to be listed once it has been proposed can be explained by scientific and political factors. If only scientific data are considered, as required by the act, one would expect that listing times would be shorter for species whose probabilities of saving are extremely time-sensitive. If economic and political variables have no relation to this probability, we would expect to find these types of variables ineffective in explaining the length of time required to list a species. Political factors are proxied by the number of comments (if any) for or against the proposed listing. Although we have no perfect measure for scientific variables and the impact delay has on the likelihood of species survival, Ando does use some reasonable proxies.

Results indicate that political variables do add to the explanatory power of the regression model. In particular, the number of comments for or against a proposed listing do impact the probability of a species being listed given it is currently not listed. Ando interprets this as meaning political pressure as a distinct force is important in the listing decision.

Ando summarizes a second study that analyzes what factors influence political pressure, measured by an index based on the number and intensity of comments received for or against a proposed listing. Again, she uses a series of scientific, political, and economic variables to explain political support or opposition. The model is complicated by the desire to test how interest groups react to each other's activities and test the theory that interest groups do in fact change their level of effort in response to changes in an opposition group's effort.

Ando finds some evidence that economic and political variables influence the political pressure brought by groups for or against species listing, but she finds no evidence to suggest that one group's level of effort is impacted by changes in the other group's efforts. In sum, Ando finds that interest group's are motivated by factors that would typically be included in a cost-benefit analysis, although she stops short of claiming that political ideology is an important determinant of interest group action because of the difficulty in creating suitable proxies for political ideology.

III. INTEREST GROUP BEHAVIOR AND WELFARE

Do interest groups impact ESA implementation? Yes. Is this in the best interest of society? If interest group pressure is simply a reflection of society's preferences, then we should not worry about the influence special interest groups have on public policy. In this instance, interest group pressure may be in the best interests of society. Becker (1983) and Noll (1989) suggest that interest group competition for resources may result in an efficient allocation of resources. Following this logic, one could conclude interest group involvement in ESA implementation is in the best interests of society. This would certainly be a mistake, and the reason why can be found in Mancur Olsen's (1965) analysis.

Individual preferences are translated into interest group influences through an imperfect filter. This filter twists and distorts according to the ease of group organization. Benefits from saving species are distributed widely, are uncertain, and are likely to take place in the future. Costs of ESA implementation are local, immediately identifiable, and happen now. As a result, national groups benefitting from ESA implementation are not able to organize effectively, while local groups who bear the brunt of ESA implementation are better able to organize. The imperfect filter dilutes the political support from the national groups relative to local groups. Meyer is correct in Chapter 8. This filter causes local politics to be the driving force in implementation. To the extent that local communities are successful, it is likely that interest group impacts are not in the best interest of society.

References

Ando, A. W. (2001) "Interest Group Behavior and Endangered Species Protection." Chapter 6 in J. Shogren and J. Tschirhart, eds. *Protecting Endangered Species in the United States: Biological Needs, Political Realities, Economic Choices.* New York: Cambridge University Press.

Becker, G. (1983) "A Theory of Competition Among Interest Groups for Political Influence." *Quarterly Journal of Economics* (97), 371– 400.

Bromley, D. W. (1997) "Constitutional Political Economy: Property Claims in a Dynamic World." *Contemporary Policy Issues* (15), 43–54.

Cash, D. (2001) "Beyond Cute and Fuzzy: Science and Politics in the U.S. Endangered Species Act." Chapter 7 in J. Shogren and J. Tschirhart, eds., *Protecting Endangered Species in the United States: Biological Needs, Political Realities, Economic Choices.* New York: Cambridge University Press.

Crone, L. and J. Tschirhart (1998) "Separating Economic from Political Influences on Government Decisions." *Journal of Economic Behavior and Organization* (35), 405–25.

Duffield, J. W., C. J. Neher, and T. C. Brown (1992) "Recreation Benefits of Instream Flow: Application to Montana's Big Hole and Bitterroot Rivers." *Water Resources Research* (28), 2169–181.

Metrick, A. and M. L. Weitzman (1996) "Patterns of Behavior in Endangered Species Protection." *Land Economics* (72), 1–16.

Metrick, A. and M. L. Weitzman (1998) "Conflicts and Choices in Biodiversity Protection." *Journal of Economic Perspectives* (12), 21–32.

Meyer, S. (2001) "Community Politics and Endangered Species Protection." Chapter 8 in J. Shogren and J. Tschirhart, eds. *Protecting Endangered Species in the United States: Biological Needs, Political Realities, Economic Choices.* New York: Cambridge University Press.

Noll, R. (1989) "Economic Perspectives on the Politics of Regulation." In R. Schmalensee and R. Willig, eds. *Handbook of Industrial Organization.* North Holland: New York, 1253–87.

Nowell, C. and J. Tschirhart (1993) "Testing Between Theories of Regulatory Behavior." *Review of Industrial Organization* (8), 653–68.

Olsen, M., Jr. (1965) *The Logic of Collective Action.* Harvard University Press: Cambridge.

Smith, A. A., M. A. Moote, and C. R. Schwalbe (1993) "The ESA at Twenty: An Analytical Survey of Federal Endangered Species Protection." *Natural Resources Journal* (33), 1027–75.

Stroup, R. L. (1997) "The Economics of Compensating Property Owners." *Contemporary Policy Issues* (15), 55–65.

Replies by Authors

David W. Cash

While Cliff Nowell notes that the three chapters he reviews present diverse conclusions, he also paints a synthetic picture where decision making about endangered species is a dynamic mix of science and politics in which both arenas influence the outputs and texture of the other. In an effort to try to understand this mix, my chapter examined two discrete decisions in the ESA process – listing and funding. As Nowell observes, the analysis of the listing decision is more convincing than the analysis of funding decisions for a variety of statistical and methodological reasons outlined in both the *Empirical Analysis* and *Agenda for Future Research* sections of the chapter. While I have not extended this avenue of research on the ESA, a colleague who was instrumental in constructing our dataset, J. R. De Shazo (currently a faculty member at the University of California, Los Angeles' School of Public Policy and Social Research), is currently undertaking an analysis of the listing and funding decisions in which they are modeled jointly (a more statistically appropriate method), and with a more complete dataset.

Since writing this chapter, much of my research has focused on the relationship between science and policy through the lens of the social studies of science, which provides a more nuanced understanding of science as a socially constructed phenomenon, deeply rooted in the social, political, and cultural context in which it is used. The demarcation between science and politics, therefore, is not inherent or even easily identifiable or defined. Rather it is continually negotiated between the two spheres. As such, both my chapter and Nowell's response present a too simplistic caricature of the relationship between science and politics. For example, Nowell writes that while the ESA and its amendments "leave no doubt that science is the only criterion which should be considered in the decision to a list a species," there is an implicit assumption that "science" is somehow separable from the social and political context in which it is used. In fact, part of what my findings suggest is that the use of science in the ESA is testimony to the notion that political decisions (how recovery funds are allocated and earmarked) drive what science is used and for what kinds of species (which in turn influence future political decisions). Thus "science" is not something discrete or apart from the political process. Its purview and its methods are determined by political processes.

Clarification: Nowell comments that "Cash's work may be most appropriately viewed as an extension of the work of Metrick and Weitzman (1996) who, *using data prior to the 1982 amendment to the ESA*, find that both scientific and visceral variables influence both the listing and funding decision" (my emphasis). Unfortunately, due to lack of clarity in the original draft of this chapter, the scope of the Metrick/Weitzman data was misunderstood. In fact, Metrick and Weitzman did use data from both before (when USFWS was "allowed" to make listing decisions based on taxonomic class) and after the 1982 amendment (when taxonomic class was no longer a permissible criteria for listing), *but the authors did not distinguish between the two time periods*, and therein lay the problem. Because they did not distinguish between the two periods, they did not account for a major policy shift, and a bias exists which *overestimates* the effect of taxonomic class and animal size on more recent listing decisions. My analysis focused on listing decisions after the amendment and essentially eliminates the bias found in the Metrick/Weitzman analysis. When this correction is made, the "visceral" variables (taxonomic class and size) become insignificant, thus leading to my conclusion that scientific variables hold greater explanatory power in the listing decision.

Reference

Metrick, A., and M. L. Weitzman (1996) Patterns of Behavior in Endangered Species Preservation. *Land Economics* 72(1), 1–16.

ECONOMIC CHOICES

PART 3.1 CURRENT APPROACHES

The Endangered Species Act and Critical Habitat Designation: Economic Consequences for the Colorado River Basin

Gary Watts, William R. Noonan,

Henry R. Maddux, and David S. Brookshire

I. INTRODUCTION

The Endangered Species Act (Act) of 1973, as amended, assigns the U.S. Fish and Wildlife Service (USFWS) the responsibility for listing species of plants and animals in the United States whose existence is either threatened or endangered. After a species is listed, the Service is responsible for, among other things, developing recovery plans, reviewing proposed federal actions to ensure that they do not compromise recovery efforts, and designating critical habitat for listed species. Such critical habitat designations, at least in certain situations, can alter economic activity in critical habitat areas that might otherwise be of detriment to certain species. Although the Act has no provisions for studying the economic consequences of listing threatened and endangered species, it does require the Service to assess the economic impacts of all proposed critical habitat designations. As a result, economists have been participating in the ongoing process of designating critical habitat for endangered species and assessing the economic impacts of such designations.[1]

Critical habitat designations impose use restrictions on lands that can change the way in which economic resources are allocated. Threatened and endangered species are usually listed because the current allocation of resources has resulted in excessive habitat degradation. Such adverse modification of natural

The individuals who contributed time, effort, and data to this study are far too numerous to list here. A complete list can be found in the project reports by Brookshire, McKee, and Watts (1993, 1994), and Brookshire, McKee, and Schmidt (1995). We owe a special debt of gratitude to Mel Schamberger, Larry Shanks, Kristen Kingery, Reed Harris, Bob Williams, and Margot Zallen. The authors also acknowledge the contributions of Michael McKee.

[1] It has been argued that the process of listing a species as endangered or threatened has far greater economic consequences than subsequent critical habitat designations, an argument that has some merit with respect to the examples discussed in this chapter. As a practical matter, however, most economic studies of critical habitat designations attempt to estimate the combined effects of both listing and critical habitat designations, and then allocate a proportion of effects to each administrative action.

habitat is generally due to economic activity that has occurred as a result of human settlement and economic development. Resources are allocated to particular uses as a result, and stabilizing and/or reversing this development requires that these resources be allocated to other uses. For example, trees may not be harvested that provide habitat for birds, water may not be used for irrigation so that stream flows are returned to more historic levels, and land may not be developed for housing so that habitat for plant species is preserved. However, by not harvesting trees or building houses, recreational uses may be enhanced and setting aside minimum stream flows in one area may imply that more water is available for development elsewhere. Assessing the economic impacts of designating critical habitat thus requires a general equilibrium analysis to fully capture the range of potential activities created by the designation as well as the range of activities that are eliminated or reduced. In short, the reallocation will yield economic impacts that are benefits as well as costs.

This chapter reports the methodology and results from a study that measured the economic impacts of designating critical habitat for four endangered fishes along a 2,100-mile stretch of the Colorado River and its major tributaries. A second case study covering two fishes and eighty-seven miles of the Virgin River is also discussed. The two studies analyze the impacts of critical habitat designation on two regions greatly differing in size. For the Colorado River study, designation affects all seven states in the Colorado river basin: Arizona, California, Colorado, Nevada, New Mexico, Utah, and

Table 10.1. *Summary of the two case studies*

	Colorado River study[a]	Virgin River study[b]
Listed species	Colorado squawfish, humpback chub, bonytail, razorback sucker	Woundfin, Virgin River chub
Designated critical habitat	2,100 mi of river	87 mi of river
Direct impacts	Operational pattern of federal reservoirs, recreational activities, agricultural output, water re-allocations, new power facilities	Timing of flows, agricultural output, expedited water project construction, water conservation
Affected region	Arizona, California, Colorado, New Mexico, Nevada, Utah, Wyoming	Three counties in Arizona, Nevada, and Utah
Time horizon	1995–2020	1995–2040
Regional impact model	Input–Output, Computable general equilibrium	Input–Output
Number of economic sectors	20	16
Number of impact scenarios	1	2

[a] From Brookshire et al. (1993).
[b] From Brookshire et al. (1995).

Wyoming. The critical habitat analyzed in the Virgin River study affects three counties in Arizona, Nevada, and Utah. In both cases, the study region was determined on the basis of habitat needs and direct economic impacts.

Two study regions differ considerably in the sizes of their economies. The output of the region in the Colorado River study is approximately $1.3 trillion annually, compared to $28 billion for the Virgin River study region. The Colorado River study region constitutes a diversified economy that has experienced growth above the national average during the last several decades. The region of the Virgin River study is currently one of the fastest growing areas in the United States, with continued high population growth rates projected for the time horizon of the study. The time horizons of the studies coincide with the timespan of the proposed recovery plans for the species: 1995 to 2020 in the Colorado River study, and 1995 to 2040 in the Virgin River study. The major characteristics of the two studies are summarized in Table 10.1.

To recover the endangered fishes in these two river systems, the river systems must be protected and/or altered to more closely represent the natural conditions that are believed to be biologically necessary for species survival. Alteration of biological conditions, through listing and the designation of critical habitat, will in turn restrict or alter human uses of the river systems and thus generate direct and indirect economic impacts. The methodology used in the Colorado River and Virgin River studies to measure such impacts involves the following steps:

1. determining how the biological needs of endangered fishes will affect the allocation of resources among river users;
2. assessing the direct economic impacts of resource reallocations on river users; and
3. using a general equilibrium model of the affected region to capture all of the direct and indirect effects of resource reallocations.

Approaching the estimation of critical habitat impacts in this fashion can avoid pitfalls that arise when the focus is on the losing sectors of a local economy. Perhaps the most publicized economic analysis of proposed critical habitat designations was that for the northern spotted owl (Schamberger et al. 1992). That analysis presented a thorough assessment of the impacts of critical habitat designations on the timber industry utilizing public forest resources in the Pacific Northwest, and at one time was designated as a "model for subsequent analysis" by the Service (ECO Northwest 1994). Yet the spotted owl study did not address some of the basic economic questions that arise when resources are reallocated, such as how the rate of timber harvesting on private lands and noncritical habitat lands would change in response to critical habitat designations on federal lands, or how labor resources formerly used to harvest lumber of public lands would be redeployed. The case studies described in this chapter attempt to address issues such as these in the context of critical habitat designations for endangered fish.

II. FROM BIOLOGICAL NEEDS TO RESOURCE REALLOCATIONS

The first step in both the Colorado River and Virgin River studies was a bio-logically based determination of potential critical habitat needs[2] (Maddux, Fitzpatrick, and Noonan 1993; Maddux et al. 1995). In many instances, critical habitat studies are conducted for a single species. Since there are several endangered fishes in each river system and their habitat needs are similar, both studies cover multiple species. The four listed fish species in the Colorado River basin are the Colorado squawfish (*Ptychocheilus lucius*), the razorback sucker (*Xyrauchen texanus*), the humpback chub (*Gila sypha*), and the bonytail (*Gila elegans*). The Virgin River listed species are the woundfin (*Plagopterus argentissimus*) and the Virgin River chub (*Gila seminuda*).[3]

Endemic fish populations in both study regions have been declining since the turn of the century. The declines are a result of physical and biological changes in the river systems: stream flow alterations, habitat fragmentation and modifi-cation, contaminants, and competition with and predation by introduced non-native fish. The natural hydrography of the systems has been significantly altered by the construction of dams and increasing consumptive water uses. A total of forty-three major dams and diversions have been constructed in the Colorado River system. Current consumptive water uses include agricultural, municipal, and industrial, and reservoir evaporation (Maddux et al. 1993, 1995).

Determination of critical habitat requires consideration of physical and biological features that are essential to species conservation. These features, referred to as constituent elements, include: (1) space for populations; (2) food, water, or other nutritional or physiological requirements; (3) cover or shelter; (4) sites for breeding, reproduction, and rearing of offspring; and (5) habitats that are protected from disturbance or are representative of the historical and ecological distribution of species.

In the Colorado River study, about 2,100 miles of the river and its tributaries were designated critical habitat to provide one or more of the constituent elements described above. These designations protect river flows deemed necessary for species survival and recovery as well as riparian areas in the flood plain that are used as backwater breeding areas during periods of high spring flows. The designations also affect how water is released from federal reservoirs along the river system. For example, all four Colorado

---

[2] The administrative procedures of the Endangered Species Act prescribe certain steps in the evaluation of the economic impacts of critical habitat. These have been widely discussed else-where (see Berrens et al. 1997).

[3] The Colorado squawfish and the humpback chub were listed as endangered species on March 11, 1967 (32 Federal Register 4001), and thus were originally listed under the auspices of the Endangered Species Preservation Act of 1966. The razorback sucker was listed as endangered on October 23, 1991 (56 Federal Register 54957), the bonytail on April 23, 1980 (45 Federal Register 27713). The listing of the woundfin occurred on October 13, 1970 (35 Federal Register 16047), and the listing of the Virgin River chub on August 24, 1989 (54 Federal Register 35305).

River fishes require high spring flows for successful breeding and the survival of juvenile fish. Storage of peak flows in federal reservoirs for later release to downstream users could thus be considered an adverse modification of critical habitat in violation of the Endangered Species Act (ESA).

The effect of the designations on the reallocation of resources among other river users is a function of geography. In the Colorado River study, a substantial amount of critical habitat was designated in the state of Colorado on the upper Colorado River and its tributaries, the Gunnison and Yampa Rivers. Along these river reaches, the effect of the designations is to limit further consumptive uses of waters that would reduce peak spring flows needed to provide breeding habitat for fish. These restrictions may inhibit or prevent the state of Colorado from proceeding with plans to divert more Colorado River water to front range communities for municipal and industrial uses. They may also restrict Wyoming's ability to develop and use water in the Little Snake River, a tributary of the Yampa. Water that would otherwise have been consumptively used in Colorado and Wyoming would instead be stored in Lake Powell and eventually released for use by lower basin states.

Critical habitat designated along the San Juan River in New Mexico, a major tributary to the Colorado River, could have negative impacts upon agricultural production. In this case, the existence of critical habitat could prevent the Navajo Tribe from implementing plans to expand the Navajo Irrigation Project near Farmington over the next two decades. As a result, water that would otherwise have been put to irrigational use in New Mexico may also flow into Lake Powell and eventually be released for use by lower basin states.

Substantial amounts of critical habitat were also designated along the lower Green River below Flaming Gorge Reservoir in Colorado and Utah and along the Colorado River between Lake Powell and Lake Mead. These designations have caused the U.S. Bureau of Reclamation to alter its operating plans for those reservoirs. Prior to listing and critical habitat designations, these reservoirs were operated primarily to maximize hydropower production subject to the restrictions of meeting downstream demands and maintaining flood control storage space. This operational regime resulted in relatively constant monthly releases with extreme diurnal fluctuations to provide peaking power for electricity consumers. To provide the constituent elements of critical habitat, however, both Glen Canyon and Flaming Gorge Dams are being reoperated to increase spring releases and decrease fall releases with fewer diurnal fluctuations to provide for breeding habitat for endangered fish.[4] These new operating plans have, in turn, affected hydropower production and recreational uses of the river.

Critical habitat was also designated on the Lower Colorado River below Lake Mead. To provide the constituent elements of habitat needed in this area, a different reallocation of resources was needed than for the upper and middle sections of the basin. Along the lower river, the primary threats to endangered

---

[4] Other tributary reservoirs on the Gunnison and San Juan Rivers are also being reoperated to enhance habitat for endangered fish.

fish consist of competition from nonnative warm-water fish species and bank-side developments such as recreational vehicle parks that can impinge upon backwaters and spawning areas. In many cases, future game-fish stocking and management programs and stream-side developments will be altered or prohibited in critical habitat areas.

In the Virgin River study area, water is being redirected from the currently dominant use, irrigated agriculture, to municipal and industrial uses in order to satisfy the demands of a rapidly growing population. The demands for the endangered fishes will compete with municipal and industrial demands for water currently used in agricultural production. The designation of critical habitat is not the primary cause of declining agricultural production in the area, but will accelerate the ongoing conversion from agricultural uses to other, predominantly municipal and industrial uses.

III. ESTIMATING DIRECT ECONOMIC IMPACTS

Colorado River Study

The resource reallocations described above were translated into estimates of output changes in directly affected sectors of local and regional economies dependent upon the river. In the Colorado River study, prohibitions upon further water depletions in critical habitat reaches along the upper river were modeled by reducing the projected output of the agricultural sectors of Colorado and Wyoming. The rationale for this approach is that in lieu of developing Colorado River waters for municipal and industrial uses, the municipalities in the two states will increase the rate at which irrigation water rights are being purchased and transferred to other uses.[5] Future agricultural production was reduced to match the equivalent amount of water depletions foregone due to critical habitat designations. Foregone depletions were estimated from water use projections contained in state water planning documents. The value of agricultural output foregone was computed using estimates of crop consumptive irrigation requirements, field irrigation efficiencies, cropping patterns, and yields, all taken from published sources.

The effects of critical habitat designations on water users below Flaming Gorge and Glen Canyon dams were modeled in two ways. First, a sample of outfitters providing rafting, fishing, and other recreational services to the public was interviewed in person to assess their reactions to the flow changes needed to enhance spawning habitat for endangered fish. Each outfitter was shown visual hydrographs of average river flows by week, both before and after critical habitat designations, for reaches of the river where he operated. Each outfitter was then asked to identify periods of the year when his operations would be

---

[5] Institutional arrangements vary by state, but both Colorado and Wyoming water laws allow transfers of agricultural water to municipal and industrial uses if the transfer is deemed in the public interest.

affected by the new operating regimes. In most cases, the outfitters were able to identify some negative impacts of the new operating regimes on their operations. These consisted primarily of an increased frequency of high-flow periods in the spring when river boating and rafting would be too dangerous and an increased frequency of low-flow periods in the late summer and fall when boating and rafting would be impractical. Outfitters would not be able to shift trips to other times of the season because of launch restrictions imposed by federal resource management agencies.

Because the most likely substitute sources of similar recreational experiences are outside the Colorado River basin, it was assumed that regional output in the recreation and tourism sectors of the economy would decline relative to precritical habitat conditions. The amount of the decline was estimated using Colorado River recreational usage and expenditure data assembled by federal agencies, adjusted to reflect the estimated percentage of time that the river would have unusable recreation flows.

The second direct effect of new operating regimes on the middle Colorado River system would be to limit the amount and timing of hydropower production. Estimates of the direct economic effects of this resource reallocation were developed by Stone and Webster Management, Inc., on behalf of the Bureau of Reclamation. The results indicate that the new operating plans would result in a need for an additional 121 megawatts of electrical generating capacity in the basin, a somewhat higher average market price for electricity, and somewhat lower consumption.

Estimates of direct impacts for critical habitat reaches on the Lower Colorado River below Lake Mead involved several sectors of the regional economy. Because Wyoming and Colorado will forego some future consumptive uses of Colorado River water to protect endangered fish, the states of California and Nevada likely will be the net beneficiaries of that foregone consumption. At present, none of the upper Colorado River basin states (Colorado, New Mexico, Utah, and Wyoming) utilize their full allotment of water under terms of the Colorado River Compact. Instead, the water is stored in Lake Powell until it is released for hydropower production or to create storage space for flood control purposes. Once released, it is available for use by the lower basin states of Arizona, California, and Nevada. Foregone water uses associated with critical habitat designations in the upper basin would also be available for use by the lower basin states. For this study it was assumed that California would benefit from foregone upstream developments, as would Nevada to serve the burgeoning need for municipal and industrial water in the Las Vegas area.

The direct benefits to the California economy from critical habitat designations will be the inverse of the impacts to Colorado and Wyoming. Instead of increasing the rate of irrigation water rights transfers to municipal and industrial uses, critical habitat designations will allow California to experience a decrease in the rate of such transfers relative to baseline conditions. As a result, they will experience higher agricultural output relative to precritical habitat conditions. The amount of this increase was estimated using a similar approach and data sources were used to estimate the magnitude of agricultural output declines in Colorado and Wyoming. River transit and reservoir evaporation losses in moving water from the upper to the lower basin were estimated using information provided by the Bureau of Reclamation.

In Nevada, the principal economic activity associated with municipal and industrial water use is gambling. The growth of this industry in the Las Vegas area has been constrained by severely limited sources of water. The principal direct impact of critical habitat designations on the Nevada economy would be to allow additional growth in this sector of the economy.

The other direct economic impact that was quantified for the lower basin was a decrease in sport fishing activity at Lake Mead and Lake Mohave relative to precritical habitat conditions. This decrease will come about because state plans to enhance warm-water recreational fisheries in the two reservoirs may be restricted or prohibited because of potential negative impacts on endangered fishes. The magnitude of this effect was estimated using data on fishing activity and fishing expenditures supplied by state officials. Although there may be other direct impacts to the lower basin involving development restrictions in riparian areas, they were not quantified during this study.

Virgin River Study

For the Virgin River study, three types of direct impacts were identified as attributable to efforts to recover the endangered fishes. The first type of impact involves additional transfers of water from agricultural to municipal and industrial uses. Agricultural production in the two-county study area of Utah and Nevada has been declining as municipalities have been purchasing agricultural water rights to meet the demands of a growing urban population. Recovery efforts for endangered fish will accelerate this trend since there will no longer be opportunities to reduce flows in the Virgin River to meet urban needs. The magnitude of the accelerated demand for agricultural water rights transfers was estimated from river flow goals put forth by the USFWS and population projections for communities in the study area. Resulting changes in agricultural output were estimated using methods similar to those used in the Colorado River study.

The second type of impact is a change in the timing of municipal and industrial water development projects that have been planned to meet the region's projected future growth. Because of the need to maintain water in the Virgin River for endangered fishes, alternative water sources will need to be developed sooner than otherwise would be the case. Since these alternative sources are more costly than Virgin River water, the direct effect will be to increase the unit cost of municipal and industrial water relative to the no-impact scenario. To model this latter impact, a simplifying assumption was made that increased expenditures on water would crowd out expenditures on other goods and services throughout the regional economy in proportion to each sector's share of final demand.

The third type of impact involves implementing water conservation measures to meet part of the region's future water needs. Communities in the region now have very high per capita water use rates, which could be significantly reduced by installing more efficient appliances and xeriscaping.[6] The cost of implementing water conservation measures was modeled in a manner similar to that used for increased expenditures on new water projects.

IV. REGIONAL IMPACT MODELING

Two classes of applied general equilibrium models were developed for the analysis of the economic impacts associated with the protection and recovery of endangered species in the Colorado River study.[7] The first class consists of a set of conventional Input–Output (I–O) models of the entire region and of the subregional units (e.g., one for each of the seven states). The second class is a Computable General Equilibrium (CGE) model of the entire region. For the Virgin River study, separate I–O models for each of two impacted counties and a three-county regional model were developed.

CGE models offer several advantages over I–O models, but the central advantage is that CGE models admit factor substitution in production in response to changes in relative prices, while the conventional I–O model employs a fixed proportion (Leontief) production function. The usual production function employed in CGE models consists of a nested form involving either Cobb-Douglass/Leontief or Constant Elasticity of Substitution (CES)/ Leontief forms. The intermediate inputs (outputs of the other sectors in the economy) enter the production function in fixed proportions with coefficients from a regional I–O table. The primary inputs (labor and capital along with land, energy, etc., if these are modeled) enter the top level of the production function along with the composite input produced as intermediate goods. CGE models are, however, much more data demanding than I–O models. Thus, only a single CGE model was constructed for the Colorado River study and none for the Virgin River study.

The I–O Models

The methodology for constructing regional I–O models is widely discussed in the literature.[8] I–O models are a device for organizing the basic accounting

[6] Per capita water use in the St. George, UT area is considerably greater than in other southwest urban areas. Current use is 465 gallons per capita per day (gpcd). For the conservation scenario rate, this was reduced to approximately 260 gpcd, which is comparable to Phoenix and well above Tucson, AZ, which has a use rate of 160 gpcd. Conservation requires expenditures, which raises the effective cost of water, and this was incorporated into the scenario.

[7] The detailed accounts of the modeling are found in Brookshire, McKee, and Watts (1993, 1994), and Brookshire, McKee, and Schmidt (1995). This section draws upon and is taken in part from Chapters 7, 8, and 15 (section K) of Brookshire et al. (1993) and was utilized in Brookshire et al. (1994, 1995).

[8] See Miller and Blair (1985) for a complete development of the theoretical and empirical foundations of I–O analysis.

relations that describe the production sector of the economy. The I–O method assumes all sectors of the economy are tied together by virtue of economic relations called "linkages." Further, the production of a good or service can be described by a "recipe" with the ingredients being the outputs of the other sectors of the economy as well as the primary inputs such as labor, capital, and other raw resources.

Defining $\mathbf{I}$ as the identity matrix, $\mathbf{A}$ the interindustry matrix, $\mathbf{X}$ the vector of outputs, and $\mathbf{Y}$ the vector of final demands, the I–O model equations can be represented as:

$$(\mathbf{I} - \mathbf{A})\mathbf{X} = \mathbf{Y}$$

and the outputs necessary to satisfy intermediate and final demand may be solved for as:

$$\mathbf{X} = (\mathbf{I} - \mathbf{A})^{-1}\mathbf{Y}$$

where $(\mathbf{I} - \mathbf{A})^{-1}$ is known as the Leontief inverse.

Given exogenous shocks to a local economy, changes in gross outputs required to satisfy changes in final demands and/or resource availability are determined. Through its multiplier impact analysis, the I–O model is capable of generating estimates of the changes in output of given commodities, changes in employment, and changes in income.

The primary database for the construction of the initial I–O models was the IMPLAN data.[9] For the Colorado River study, the baseline matrices were constructed from 1982 databases. The Virgin River study utilized 1990 databases. The original 528 IMPLAN sectors were aggregated to twenty for the Colorado River study and sixteen for the Virgin River study. This aggregation reduced the dimensionality of the analysis to manageable levels and enabled the sectors that were affected by direct impacts to be analyzed.

To update the Colorado River model to the 1989 baseline used for analysis, the Gross State Product data from the Department of Commerce, Bureau of Economic Analysis (BEA) were used to update final demand levels for each of the twenty sectors of the I–O model. These data are available at the state level for the period from 1982 through 1989 for seventy-three sectors which can be matched (via SIC codes) to the twenty sectors represented in the I–O models constructed for the Colorado project. In this way, the economic activity reported in the 1982 IMPLAN dataset was updated to 1989.

[9] The IMPLAN modeling and database project were initially undertaken by the U.S. Forest Service to provide regional I–O modeling capability (see U.S. Department of Agriculture 1993). The database management and development and the software development are now conducted by the Minnesota IMPLAN Group (MIG). For these projects, the use of IMPLAN was confined to the construction of the input datasets to the I–O models that were developed in the GAUSS programming language (see Brooke, Kendrik, and Meeraus 1992).

The updated gross output levels were used to update the remaining components of the I–O models based on the 1982 ratios and coefficients. The analyses' results were reported as output changes.[10]

The CGE Model

The approach used in constructing the CGE model of the Colorado River seven-state region follows from the work of Sherman Robinson and his colleagues.[11] This model assumes that the economy is competitive; all prices are presumed to be able to adjust to clear factor and goods markets; all consumers maximize utility; and all producers maximize profits (or, equivalently, minimize costs). Production is characterized by constant returns to scale so that factor payments exhaust the value of the product. Supply (domestic production plus imports) equals demand (domestic consumption plus exports) in all markets.

The household sector is represented as utility-maximizing consumers; the production sector is represented as profit-maximizing firms whose decisions determine the supply of goods and the demand for factors of production (primary and intermediate inputs); international (interregional) trade is represented; there is a government sector collecting taxes and providing collective goods; and there are the market clearing conditions (may be based on assumptions concerning equilibrium or disequilibrium outcomes).

The Social Accounts Matrix (SAM) provides a link between the National Income and Product Accounts (NIPA) data, and the input–output accounts data. As such, it serves as a cornerstone of the CGE models constructed using the Robinson method.

For the Colorado River study, a nineteen sector model was constructed with the benchmark dataset for 1982. The outputs of the nineteen sectors of the economy are produced with inputs of labor, capital, land (where applicable), and an intermediate good. The intermediate good is a composite commodity with the weights determined by the input–output coefficients from the baseline dataset. The production function was defined as a constant returns Cobb-Douglas over the primary factors.[12]

The input data for the CGE model were derived from three sources. The IMPLAN databases (1982) provided the data necessary to construct the

---

[10] Impacts on employment, wages, and taxes are also presented for the region and by sector in Brookshire et al. (1993, 1994, 1995).

[11] Models constructed via the "Robinson" approach are typically solved using computer programs designed to solve large-scale systems of nonlinear equations. The GAMS (General Algebraic Modeling System) software was adopted to solve the model of the seven-state region. This package offers considerable flexibility in the construction of the CGE model and in conducting simulation analyses. See Dervis, De Melo, and Robinson (1982); Berck, Robinson, and Goldman (1991); and McKee et al. (1996) for a discussion of this class of CGE model.

[12] Space does not permit a detailed description of the Colorado River basin CGE model here. A complete specification of the model is given in Brookshire et al. (1993).

inter-industry flows matrix (the input–output table) and the national accounts data which are required to construct the Social Accounts Matrix (SAM). In addition, the production sectors required capital stock data and labor data. The labor data were included in the IMPLAN database, although adjustments were required to convert these data to full-time equivalents (FTEs). The capital stock data were obtained from the *Census of Agriculture* and the BEA Wealth Data disks. Tax data for household and business taxes were included in the national accounts portions of the IMPLAN databases.

The test of the accuracy of the CGE model was its ability to reproduce the benchmark dataset as the equilibrium of the model. The 1995 direct impacts were scaled to reflect the level of economic activity in the 1982 benchmark dataset. These direct impacts were introduced as changes in the components of final demand for the various sectors.

V. IMPLEMENTING THE STUDIES IN THE CONTEXT OF THE ACT

The Recovery Implementation Program (RIP) (U.S. Department of Interior 1987) for the endangered species set a goal of recovery by 2020 for the Colorado River fishes. The USFWS office in Salt Lake City estimated recovery by about 2040 for the Virgin River fishes. To fully capture the economic activity changes due to recovery efforts over time, a comparison was made to a baseline economy where no recovery actions are undertaken. The building blocks for the construction of the baseline were the Bureau of Economic Analysis (BEA) state level projections to 2020 (2040 for the Virgin River study).[13] These projections were augmented with such local information as was available.

The BEA projections include data on employment by sector and state and were used to project gross output by sector on the basis of the 1982 or 1990 coefficients and ratios. The employment/output ratios for each sector calculated from the 1989 baseline model were used to generate the sector output levels for the baseline projections. The generated gross output figures were then used to generate the remaining baseline forecast data. This baseline formed the benchmark against which the impacts due to the critical habitat effects on economic activity within the respective region were compared.[14] A recovery projection was developed utilizing the direct effects of the resource reallocations as inputs to the models. The impacts associated with

---

[13] Forecasting economic conditions forty years or more into the future is obviously fraught with perils that are not enumerated here. The requirements of the Act make such forecasts necessary in spite of their associated uncertainty.

[14] The Virgin River flows through one of the fastest growing regions in the United States. Recent and projected population growth in this region is significantly above the state average levels for Utah and Nevada. Recent population projections undertaken by the local public agencies in the St. George, Utah area were used to modify the BEA data.

listing and the designation of critical habitat were measured as the present value of the differences between the baseline and recovery scenarios.

The Act draws a distinction between economic impacts arising from the listing of the endangered species and those arising from the designation of critical habitat. Only the latter are to be considered in the final determination of the critical habitat. After critical habitat is proposed, and an economic analysis is conducted, an exclusion process is conducted in which the economic impacts of designating critical habitat are evaluated. The Act directs the Secretary of the Interior to consider economic and other relevant impacts based upon biological and economic findings in determining whether to exclude proposed areas from the designated critical habitat. In this process, the USFWS may exclude areas from critical habitat designation when the benefits (economic impacts avoided) of such exclusion outweigh the benefits (species preservation) of specifying the area as part of the critical habitat.

In many cases it is difficult to distinguish between economic impacts attributable to listing a species as threatened or endangered and the economic impacts associated with designating critical habitat for that species. Technically, listing impacts are those associated with protecting individual members of a species from harm, while critical habitat impacts are those associated with protecting the species' habitat from harm. A plan to drain a pond filled with endangered fish, however, would harm both individual species members and their habitat, thus posing the dilemma of how to allocate the impacts of not draining the pond to listing versus critical habitat designation.

Because it is difficult to separate the impacts of listing from the impacts of critical habitat designation, the standard approach is to estimate the combined impacts of both and then judgmentally allocate a proportion of total impacts to each cause.[15] The rationale for the allocation method used in the Colorado River and Virgin River studies revolves around the timing of critical habitat designation relative to listing.

In the Colorado River case, there was a substantial lag between listing the fish as endangered and designating critical habitat (ranging from twenty-six years for the Colorado squawfish and humpback chub to two years for the razorback sucker). As a result, most of the recovery plans for the fish that generate impacts were either already prepared or in the planning stage before critical habitat was designated.[16] For this reason, only 10 percent of all combined impacts associated with resource reallocations for the fish were attributed to critical habitat. In the Virgin River study, however, the relatively close concurrence of listing and critical habitat designation led to assigning 50 percent of combined impacts to each cause.

---

[15] This approach was used in the critical habitat study for the northern spotted owl (Schamberger et al. 1992), and to our knowledge all critical habitat studies that have taken place since then.

[16] At the time that each of the four Colorado fishes were listed, the Service reported that their habitat needs were not determinable. Critical habitat designations were undertaken later as the result of a lawsuit filed by environmental groups.

VI. REGIONAL AND SUBREGIONAL IMPACTS

Colorado River Study

Estimates of the direct economic impacts of critical habitat designations for the four Colorado River endangered fishes are presented in Tables 10.2, 10.3, and 10.4. These impact estimates reflect annual output changes in directly affected industrial sectors in the various states without considering indirect effects on production in other sectors of the state economies. The impacts are a direct reflection of the resource reallocations described in Section III.

Critical habitat designations in the upper basin (Table 10.2) would tend to shift irrigation water use to lower basin states relative to baseline conditions. As a result, Colorado and Wyoming would experience reduced output in the livestock feed and other crop sectors totaling about −$2 million annually by the year 2020. New Mexico would suffer a −$10 million annual output

Table 10.2. *Colorado River study direct economic impacts – annual output changes (1991 $millions)*

| | Year | | | | | |
Sector	1995	2000	2005	2010	2015	2020
Colorado						
Livestock feed	−0.345	−0.690	−1.015	−1.072	−1.293	−1.652
Other crops	−0.063	−0.126	−0.174	−0.223	−0.272	−0.320
Recreation	−0.229	−0.457	−0.457	−0.457	−0.457	−0.457
Electric power	−0.256	−0.436	−0.949	−0.501	−0.880	−0.033
Nonpetrol mining	0.153	0.232	0.364	0.162	0.188	0.166
Oil and Gas mining	0.203	0.020	0.056	0.121	0.531	0.077
Construction	0.804	0.804	0.804	0.804	0.804	0.804
Combined mfg.	0.576	0.576	0.576	0.576	0.576	0.576
Total direct impacts	0.843	−0.077	−0.795	−0.590	−0.803	−0.839
New Mexico						
Livestock feed	0.000	−0.324	−1.186	−1.909	−2.697	−3.312
Other crops	0.000	−0.657	−2.402	−3.875	−5.476	−6.725
Electric power	−0.277	−0.556	−0.595	−0.594	−0.593	−0.598
Total direct impacts	−0.277	−1.537	−4.183	−6.378	−8.766	−10.635
Utah						
Livestock feed	0.000	−0.017	−0.038	−0.076	−0.079	−0.083
Recreation	−0.289	−0.289	−0.289	−0.289	−0.289	−0.289
Electric power	−0.608	−0.600	−0.620	−0.648	−0.688	−0.717
Nonpetrol mining	0.109	0.159	0.165	0.147	0.148	0.159
Total direct impacts	−0.788	−0.747	−0.782	−0.866	−0.908	−0.930
Wyoming						
Livestock feed	0.000	−0.038	−0.038	−0.038	−0.038	−0.038
Recreation	0.000	−0.011	−0.011	−0.011	−0.011	−0.011
Electric power	−0.050	−0.050	−0.050	−0.050	−0.050	−0.050
Nonpetrol mining	0.000	0.000	0.005	0.001	0.012	0.009
Total direct impacts	−0.050	−0.099	−0.094	−0.098	−0.087	−0.090

Table 10.3. *Colorado River study direct economic impacts – annual output changes (1991 $millions) for the lower basin*

Sector	Year					
	1995	2000	2005	2010	2015	2020
Arizona						
Recreation	0.000	−0.028	−0.065	−0.098	−0.130	−0.163
Electric power	−0.235	−0.253	−0.152	−0.195	−0.403	−0.326
Total direct impacts	−0.235	−0.281	−0.217	−0.293	−0.533	−0.489
California						
Other crops	0.525	1.908	4.374	5.817	8.387	10.935
Livestock feed	0.100	0.362	0.827	1.100	1.586	2.054
Total direct impacts	0.625	2.270	5.201	6.917	9.973	12.989
Nevada						
Recreation	0.000	−0.028	−0.065	−0.098	−0.130	−0.162
Electric power	−0.114	−0.114	−0.114	−0.114	−0.114	−0.114
Local amusements	1.863	1.863	1.863	1.863	1.863	1.863
Total direct impacts	1.749	1.721	1.684	1.651	1.619	1.587

Table 10.4. *Colorado River study direct economic impacts – annual output changes (1991 $millions) for the Colorado River basin*

Sector	Year					
	1995	2000	2005	2010	2015	2020
Colorado River basin						
Livestock feed	−0.205	−0.882	−1.680	−2.217	−3.022	−3.720
Other crops	0.552	0.967	1.438	1.372	2.336	3.530
Recreation	−0.243	−0.372	−0.409	−0.435	−0.461	−0.487
Electric power	−1.752	−1.806	−2.372	−1.961	−2.546	−1.465
Nonpetrol mining	0.277	0.398	0.561	0.433	0.262	0.457
Oil and gas mining	0.128	0.093	0.295	0.213	0.688	0.143
Construction	0.788	0.804	0.844	0.844	0.844	0.844
Combined mfg.	0.753	0.768	0.807	0.807	0.807	0.807
Local amusements	1.863	1.863	1.863	1.863	1.863	1.863
Total direct impacts	2.161	1.833	1.347	0.919	0.771	1.972

decline in those sectors by the year 2020. Those declines would be more than offset in the lower basin (Table 10.3), however, by a $13 million increase in California's agricultural output by 2020. This result is a reflection of the fact that water can be used to grow higher value crops in the lower basin relative to the upper basin.

Most of the Colorado River basin's states would suffer declining output (relative to baseline) with respect to electric power production and the recreation and tourism sectors of their economies. These results stem from reoperating federal reservoirs in the basin to provide flows for endangered fish at the expense of recreation and hydropower production. Colorado, however, is expected to see increased construction and manufacturing activity relative to baseline because it is the likely site for adding thermal power production capacity to replace lost hydropower generation. There also will be increases in coal production (nonpetrol mining) and oil and gas production in the upper basin to supply energy for increased electric power production.

Overall, projected direct impacts are negative for five states (Arizona, Colorado, New Mexico, Utah, and Wyoming) and positive for two states (California and Nevada). California will benefit from increased agricultural output relative to baseline conditions because of constraints on water development in the upper basin. Nevada will benefit from increased municipal and industrial water supplies for the same reason.

Table 10.4 shows the direct economic impacts of critical habitat designation for all seven states combined. The results show that total direct impacts attributable to critical habitat designation are slightly positive for the whole basin. This result is largely attributable to the fact that water uses that are constrained by critical habitat will be replaced by alternative uses with higher valued outputs.

The overall direct and indirect sectorial impacts of critical habitat designations in the basin are presented in Table 10.5 in terms of present values (PV) over the study period (1995–2020). These impacts include the direct and

Table 10.5. *Direct and indirect impacts by economic sector: critical habitat – Colorado River study*

Sector	Output impacts (PV @ 3%) (1991 $millions)
Livestock	−1.898
Other crops	62.755
Livestock feed	−66.913
Miscellaneous ag.	3.853
Nonpetrol mining	19.360
Oil and gas mining	5.766
Construction	43.963
Food products	−0.245
Wood products	5.102
Petro. and coal products	−16.760
Other manufacturing	52.088
Trans., comm., and util.	−8.505
Recreation services	−16.506
Electricity products	−113.447
Wholesale and retail	1.819
Fire	7.659
Hhold and bus. svcs.	13.984
Local amusements	136.538
Hlth., ed., and soc. svcs.	0.617
Gov. production	0.173
Total	129.403

indirect effects of critical habitat as estimated from an I–O model for the seven-state region. The impacts are both positive and negative across sectors, reflecting the reallocation process of resources that is required for the recovery of the endangered fishes. Thus, one outcome of the analyses is that there are sectorial distributional consequences. The largest negative impacts were projected for the electric power production sector and the livestock feed sector. The electric power sector must adjust to the changes in the flow regimes of the river system and the livestock feed sector represents a low valued water use that would be partially retired. The present value of net impacts over the study period is $129.4 million.

Table 10.6 presents the present value of direct and indirect impacts by state for the Colorado River study. These projections give an additional perspective on the distributional consequences of the resource reallocation. For the upper basin states, total output changes are negative. However, for the lower basin states the changes are negative for Arizona but positive for Nevada and California. Although basinwide impacts are positive, impacts differ considerably across the different states within the study region. Among the seven states, the largest positive impacts accrue to California, resulting in an increase in output of 0.0013 percent over the baseline. This corresponds to an increase of $335.0 million. Impacts to New Mexico result in a reduction of output by −0.0280 percent, equivalent to lost output of −$245.5 million. In either case, changes over the baseline are still very small. The impacts of the other states lie between these two values.[17]

Table 10.6. *Direct and indirect spatial distribution of critical habitat impacts for the Colorado River study*

	Output: P.V. @ 3% (1991 $millions)	Percentage deviations from baseline
Upper basin		
Colorado	−17.0	−0.0006
New Mexico	−245.5	−0.0280
Utah	−72.6	−0.0060
Wyoming	−7.2	−0.0020
Lower basin		
Arizona	−21.0	−0.0008
California	335.0	0.0013
Nevada	140.3	0.0150
Colorado River basin		
Colorado	129.4	0.0003

[17] The regional impact and the sum for the individual states will not match exactly since the state impacts were computer generated from state-level I–O models, while the region was modeled as a complete entity as well. The differences are due to leakages at the state level that are captured by the larger region.

These results summarize the changes in economic activity that are expected to result from forcing more water from the upper basin to the lower basin because of critical habitat designations for endangered fishes. Because of existing institutional arrangements governing water use in the basin, there is no a priori reason to believe water has been allocated to its highest valued uses in the baseline scenario. The study results support this possibility by suggesting that total economic output in the basin will increase slightly relative to baseline conditions because of water reallocations needed to enhance critical habitat for endangered fishes.[18]

Virgin River Study

For the Virgin River study, two impact scenarios were developed. The construction scenario meets increased instream water demand for endangered fishes by bringing proposed structural water projects on-line earlier than previously planned, and accelerating the ongoing conversion of agricultural water to municipal and industrial uses. The conservation scenario, in addition to some accelerated construction of water delivery projects, assumes that increased water demands are partially met by reducing per capita water consumption through a series of water conservation measures. These measures include more efficient appliances and plumbing as well as xeriscaping.

Table 10.7 presents the Virgin River critical habitat direct and indirect impacts for subregions and the region. The subregional impacts were determined for two counties: Clark County, Nevada and Washington County, Utah. The impacts in Clark County include those to a small section of Mohave County, Arizona, that is included in the study region. Under the construction scenario, the net present value (NPV) of output losses in Clark County is −$10.6 million, a deviation of −0.00001 percent from the baseline. For Washington County, impacts under the construction scenario are slightly larger, but still small. The NPV of lost output is −$47.5 million, a reduction in economic activity by −0.0016 percent from the baseline.

Under the conservation scenario, no direct impacts accrue to Clark County. Thus, only impacts in Washington County are presented. Implementing the conservation scenario will reduce the NPV of output by −$13.7 million, a change of less than −0.00046 percent from the baseline. In terms of output, impacts are actually positive after the year 2025, when increased construction costs for more efficient buildings are offset by reduced expenditures on water.

In summary, the regional impacts due to the designation of critical habitat for the Virgin River study are a net output decrease of $59.8 million (present value) for the construction scenario, a deviation of −0.0001 percent from the

---

[18] Although total impacts are positive, it should be noted that the impacts are extremely small. The percentage deviations from the baseline are reported to illustrate this point. Neither the data nor the models are sufficiently precise to allow us to flatly state that these percentage values are statistically different from zero.

Table 10.7. *Virgin River direct and indirect regional impacts of critical habitat designation*

	Output changes PV @ 3% (1990 $millions)	Percentage deviations from baseline
Subregional results		
Construction scenario[a]		
Washington county	−47.5	−0.0016
Clark county	−10.6	−0.00001
Conservation scenario[b]		
Washington county	−13.7	−0.00046
Regional results		
Construction scenario	−59.8	−0.0001
Conservation scenario	−20.9	−0.0000

[a] The construction scenario (ST) for the Virgin River study meets the increased needs on behalf of the endangered fishes by accelerating the construction of reservoirs and accelerated retirement of agricultural land.

[b] The conservation scenario (CO) for the Virgin River study meets the increased water demands primarily by reducing per capita consumption through investment in water conservation measures, e.g., low-flow shower heads, xeriscaping, etc., for residential and commercial buildings.

baseline. For the conservation scenario, the present value of lost output is −$20.9 million, a deviation from the baseline by less than −0.0001 percent. Both of these impact estimates represent relatively small negative deviations from baseline conditions, in contrast to the Colorado River study where impacts were small but positive. The negative results for the Virgin River study suggest that existing (baseline) water uses in the study area have higher economic value than will be the case with the designation of critical habitat.[19]

VII. COLORADO RIVER NATIONAL EFFICIENCY EFFECTS

The CGE model used in the Colorado River study incorporates explicit accounting of the exchanges between the region and the remainder of the country (and the world) through the small open economy (SOE) assumption. The CGE model treats the Colorado River basin region as an SOE. Through the external trade sector, the implications for the national economy are accounted for in the results. Thus, the impacts are effectively measures of net national efficiency effects of the resource reallocation.

[19] It should be noted, however, that neither the Colorado River study nor the Virgin River study attempted to measure the nonmarket benefits associated with preserving endangered fishes. Inclusion of such measures would alter the relative values of alternative water allocations.

The CGE model reports changes in levels of output by sector, earnings, employment, gross regional product (GRP),[20] and government revenues. These measures are reported as deviations from the baseline. In this analysis, labor supply is free to grow within the region. Economic links with the rest of the United States (and the world) take place through imports and exports of goods and services, foreign borrowing (investment), and employment payments from outside.

To evaluate the national economic consequences of critical habitat designation, the analysis must be conducted in such a manner that the following assumptions are violated to a minimum degree. First, the use of market prices to value the resources displaced by the impact requires that the market for the good in question be free of distortions so that the prices truly reflect the opportunity costs of the resources used to produce it. Second, all other markets in the economy must be operating completely free of distortions. That is, the price paid by consumers must be identical to the cost of producing the good in all markets.[21] Third, the entire national impact must be identical with the regional level impact.

The analyst must still make judgments concerning the extent to which regional impacts are, in fact, national impacts or whether they are pure transfers of resources from elsewhere in the country. This is particularly important in the case of direct impacts relating to large-scale investment in new facilities. If the construction and capital equipment sectors are operating at capacity, then newly installed thermal capacity within the Colorado River basin region will displace capacity expansion activities elsewhere in the U.S. economy. Furthermore, if the value of the displaced activities is very close to the value of the thermal generation plants, the net national impact of the additional thermal capacity would be close to zero. On the other hand, if there is sufficient excess capacity in the construction and capital equipment sectors, then the investment in expansion of the thermal capacity is a pure addition to the national economy.[22]

Another sector for which the possibility of offsetting effects outside the region is important is the recreation services sector. If recreation opportunities are reduced within the Colorado River basin region, it may be that there are substitute activities that will be undertaken outside the region. This is, again, an excess capacity argument. The extent to which recreation substitutes are available is debatable. In this analysis, the recreation resources in the basin are assumed to be unique and the loss of these recreation opportunities

[20] It is important to note that although the results are reported for the regional economy, these incorporate national impacts through imports and exports and labor mobility.

[21] An alternative to this assumption is that the economic consequences of the listing and proposed critical habitat designation are confined to the markets in which the direct impacts occur. That is, there are no indirect effects that are felt in related markets.

[22] The hydropower capacity that is lost due to the changes in the hydrographs in the fish scenario is a sunk cost. The owners of the resources in this sector will experience a loss, but not the national economy.

cannot be replaced within the U.S. economy. The results are only slightly different if this assumption does not hold.

Two scenarios were analyzed with the CGE model to estimate national efficiency effects:

Scenario A. There exists sufficient underutilized capacity in the construction and capital equipment sectors (within the basin or elsewhere in the national economy) that all additions to thermal electric capacity are a net positive addition to the level of national economic activity. The recreation resources within the basin are unique and the loss of these recreation opportunities cannot be replaced within the U.S. economy.

Scenario B. There is no underutilized capacity in the construction and capital equipment sectors (within the basin or elsewhere in the national economy) and all additions to the thermal electric capacity within the basin are constructed with resources that must be displaced from elsewhere in the national economy. Thus, there is no net positive impact from this expenditure on thermal expansion. The recreation resources within the basin are unique and the loss of these recreation opportunities cannot be replaced within the U.S. economy.

Aggregate percentage changes in economic activity relative to the baseline are reported in Table 10.8. For Scenario A, regional gross product is projected to increase by 0.0009 percent as a result of listing and the proposed critical habitat. Since the national effects are accounted for in the CGE model, this would represent an increase in the gross national product. Employment is projected to increase by 0.0015 percent, earnings by 0.0018 percent, and government revenues by 0.0007 percent. In Scenario B, the additions to the thermal generation capacity are treated as a transfer from the rest of the national economy; expenditures are the result of a pure shift of resources from outside the region. Gross regional product is projected to decline from the without-fish baseline value by -0.0008 percent. Employment is projected to decline by -0.0010 percent, earnings by -0.0002 percent, and government revenue by -0.0016 percent.

Table 10.8. *CGE results as percentage deviations from a baseline economy: the case of thermal generation, Scenarios A and B (Critical Habitat)*

	Scenario A (%)	Scenario B (%)
Real gross regional product	0.0009	-0.0008
Employment	0.0015	-0.0010
Earnings	0.0018	-0.0002
Total government revenues	0.0007	-0.0016

Finally, under Scenario A, aggregate consumer surplus increases by $1.95 million. Producer surplus is projected to decline by $0.41 million. Under Scenario B, aggregate consumer surplus decreases by $-$2.59 million and producer surplus decreases by $0.50 million. The total surplus changes for Scenarios A and B respectively are $1.55 million and $-$3.09 million. Overall, national efficiency impacts depend on whether the expansion in thermal generating capacity is a net addition to the level of economic activity or is a simple transfer from other sectors in the national economy.

VIII. SUMMARY AND CONCLUSIONS

The applied general equilibrium approach forces recognition of potential offsetting effects as resources are reallocated to preserve critical habitat for endangered species. Thus, in the Colorado River study, the flow changes required for the endangered fishes decreases agricultural activity in the upper basin of the Colorado River but increases this activity in the lower basin. A partial equilibrium analysis ignores such effects. Further, reallocating water uses causes some activities to decline while others increase. The partial equilibrium analysis omits such effects. The exclusion process utilizing the economic analyses for both the Colorado and Virgin studies resulted in all of the proposed critical habitat being designated. No areas were excluded for economic reasons.

The economic impacts associated with critical habitat designation arise from the required resource reallocation. The impacts are typically regional, rather than local, and thus necessitate regional economic modeling. The appropriate modeling framework must capture both the aggregate and distributional consequences resulting from resource reallocation caused by the designation of critical habitat. Applied general equilibrium models, either input–output (I–O) models or computable general equilibrium (CGE) models, are suitable for these purposes. Partial equilibrium models are inappropriate as they assume that resources not employed in the sectors constrained by the critical habitat will simply cease to exist instead of being reallocated within the regional economy. By the same token, focus on local impacts will obscure potentially offsetting (or magnified) impacts at a regional level. Applied general equilibrium models circumvent this problem by explicitly incorporating the resource reallocation within the regional economy.

The consequences of adopting a narrow region for analysis and an essentially partial equilibrium framework are most apparent in the case of the critical habitat assessment for the northern spotted owl. In that case, the exclusion process resulted in approximately 40 percent of the critical habitat initially proposed being excluded. It is by no means certain that the outcome would have been different had the northern spotted owl study utilized an applied general equilibrium model. Perhaps, however, less habitat would have been lost as a result of the exclusion process.

References

Berck, P., S. Robinson, and G. Goldman. 1991. "The Use of Computable General Equilibrium Models to Assess Water Policies." In Dinar and Zilberman (eds.), 489–509.

Berrens, R. P., D. S. Brookshire, M. McKee, and C. Schmidt. 1997. "Implementing the Safe Minimum Standard Approach: Two Case Studies from the U.S. Endangered Species Act." Unpublished manuscript, The University of New Mexico.

Brooke, A., D. Kendrik, and A. Meeraus. 1992. GAMS: A User's Guide (release 2.25). The Scientific Press, San Francisco, CA.

Brookshire, D. S., M. McKee, and G. Watts. 1993. *Draft Economic Analysis of Proposed Critical Habitat Designation in the Colorado River Basin for the Razorback Sucker, Humpback Chub, Colorado Squawfish, and Bonytail*, Volume II. Prepared for U.S. Department of the Interior, U.S. Fish and Wildlife Service, Salt Lake City, UT.

Brookshire D. S., M. McKee, and G. Watts. 1994. *Economic Analysis of Proposed Critical Habitat Designation in the Colorado River Basin for the Razorback Sucker, Humpback Chub, Colorado Squawfish, and Bonytail: Final Report*. Prepared for U.S. Department of the Interior, Fish and Wildlife Service, Salt Lake City, UT.

Brookshire, D. S., M. McKee, and C. Schmidt. 1995. *Economic Analysis of Critical Habitat Designation in the Virgin River Basin for the Woundfin and Virgin River Chub: Final Report*. Prepared for U.S. Department of the Interior, Fish and Wildlife Service, Salt Lake City, UT.

Dervis, K., J. De Melo, and S. Robinson. 1982. *General Equilibrium Models for Development Policy*. Cambridge University Press, New York.

Endangered Species Act. 1973. And amendments.

ECO Northwest. 1994. *A Method for Estimating the Economic Effects of Habitat Protection, Final Report*. ECO Northwest, Eugene, OR.

Maddux, H. R., L. A. Fitzpatrick, and W. R. Noonan. 1993. "Colorado River Fishes Critical Habitat: Draft Biological Support Document." U.S. Fish and Wildlife Service, Salt Lake City, UT.

Maddux, H., J. Mizzi, S. Werdon, and L. Fitzpatrick. 1995. *Overview of the Proposed Critical Habitat Designation for the Endangered and Threatened Fishes of the Virgin River Basin*. Prepared for U.S. Department of the Interior, U.S. Fish and Wildlife Service, Salt Lake City, UT.

McKee, M., S. Robinson, L. Waldman, and F. Ward. 1996. "A CGE Model of New Mexico." Unpublished manuscript, University of New Mexico.

Miller, R. E., and P. D. Blair. 1985. *Input–Output Analysis: Foundations and Extensions*. Englewood Cliffs, NJ: Prentice-Hall.

Schamberger, M. L., J. J. Charbonneau, M. J. Hay, and R. Johnson. 1992. *Economic Analysis of Cultural Habitat Designation Effects for the Northern Spotted Owl*. U.S. Fish and Wildlife Service, Washington, D.C.

U.S. Department of Agriculture. 1993. *IMPLAN*, IMPLAN Development and Applications Group. University of Minnesota, St. Paul, MN. March.

U.S. Department of the Interior, U.S. Fish and Wildlife Service. 1987. *Recovery Implementation Program for Endangered Fish Species in the Upper Colorado River Basin*.

CHAPTER 11

The Revealed Demand
for a Public Good: Evidence
from Endangered and
Threatened Species

Don L. Coursey

INTRODUCTION

In the environmental arena, it is difficult to put a value on resources, as such values often vary from person to person. Biologists and ecologists value ecosystems in a certain way, often arguing for preservation of the balance of nature, genetic information and its potential future value to the public, and the right of every species to exist.[1] The U.S. Supreme Court echoed this natural science perspective in *Tennessee Valley Authority v. Hill.*[2] The Court concluded that the language of the Endangered Species Act (ESA) "shows clearly that Congress viewed the value of endangered species as 'incalculable' or in practical terms infinite."[3] Therefore, both expert natural science and legal opinion suggest that implementation of the ESA ought to be carried out in a manner more consistent with the biblical chronicle of Noah.

Despite the apparent consensus that environmental resources cannot be accurately valued, there has been a recent push toward justifying all environmental initiatives through cost-benefit analysis.[4] Yet in environmental cases, cost-benefit analysis is often skewed, since the costs are easily measured but the benefits are difficult to estimate. Many environmental public goods do not have an immediately referable market price and may be valued in esoteric

---

This chapter is reprinted with permission from *N.Y.U. Environmental Law Journal* 6 (1998): 411–49.

[1] *See* Charles C. Mann and Mark L. Plummer, The Butterfly Problem, *The Atlantic Monthly*, Jan. 1992, at 47–70.

[2] *Tennessee Valley Authority v. Hill*, 437 U.S. 153 (1978) (holding that the Tellico Dam project, into which the government invested millions of dollars, could not go forward because it would destroy the habitat of the endangered snail darter).

[3] Ibid., at 187. Note, however, that §7(h) of the ESA was enacted in response to *Tennessee Valley*, and allows an endangered species committee (a.k.a. The God Squad) to grant exceptions to the act's prohibitions when the benefits of a development project would outweigh the costs and there is no reasonable and prudent alternative. 16 U.S.C. §1536(h) (1994).

[4] See Exec. Order No. 12,291, 46 Fed. Reg. 13,193 (1981) (requiring all agency decisions to undergo cost benefit analysis prior to promulgation); Exec. Order No. 12,866, 3 C.F.R. 638 (1993) (requiring agencies to assess all costs and benefits of available regulatory alternatives).

ways by individuals. A prime example is the benefits that accrue from protection and preservation of endangered and threatened animals.

Opponents of cost-benefit analysis argue that it is impossible, if not repugnant, to put a price tag on saving an endangered species.[5] After all, how can an analyst put a sterile economic dollar value on the magnificence of seeing a whooping crane? It may be argued that the value of such an experience is infinite, that it is lexicographically more important than other consumptive experiences, or that economic valuation is simply an irrelevant exercise. At this level of discussion, the debate is not about whether an endangered species is valuable, but rather whether it is more appropriate to use philosophical and ethical tools instead of economic ones to describe its value.

Although the argument against pricing species is valid, it fails to acknowledge the reality that public policy, speaking in ethical or philosophical terms, will do nothing to save one species or to protect one habitat. Only economic initiatives will accomplish these goals.[6] Economic resources, however, are finite. At a practical level of analysis, the country must decide how much to spend on protecting endangered species and how to distribute this amount among each endangered plant and animal.

The economic valuation of nonmarket goods is often assessed through contingent valuation methodology (CVM), a controversial yet promising method of determining the public's "willingness to pay" to preserve an environmental good.[7] A typical question from a contingent valuation survey might be: What is the maximum dollar amount your household would be willing to pay for a program that will lead to a 10 percent increase in the whooping crane population? Total public value for such a program would then be obtained by summing the responses of the population. Advocates of the CVM assert that this technique is tailor-made to address the issue of an endangered species' valuation.

The quantitative measures obtained in a given setting are, however, acutely sensitive to the framing of the willingness-to-pay question.[8] Taking a somewhat

---

[5] *See* Mann and Plummer, *supra* note 1, at 47–70.

[6] *See* Michael Hanemann, Valuing the Environment Through Contingent Valuation, 8 *J. Econ. Perspectives* 19, 19 (1994) ("placing a monetary value on . . . [risk reduction, population maintenance of species, or visibility in national parks] can be essential for sound policy").

[7] Ibid. In contrast to contingent valuation methodology, another body of economic research that attempts to determine nonmarket economic value is the literature of hedonic value of life studies. This research values an implicit, statistical human life by looking at what the public does, or does not do, to save lives. The hedonic value of life literature consistently places the value of an average, statistical life at between $2 million and $7 million. Although the method is not without controversy, over the years policy makers have tended to place more credence in the numbers generated using this technique. The primary reason for this increased trust is the fact that the hedonic technique measures what people do while a survey technique most often measures what they say they will do.

[8] *See* Walter J. Mead, Review and Analysis of State of the Art Contingent Valuation Studies, in *Contingent Valuation, A Critical Assessment* 305 (J. A. Hausman, ed., 1993). (This includes an explanation of the results of various contingent valuation methodology (CVM) studies and concluding that measuring people's willingness to pay may not be a suitable means for allocating public and private resources.)

cynical view, existing research indicates that if a surveyor wants a particular monetary value for a species, there is a way of framing the question to obtain this answer. More charitably, the research indicates that different wordings of the same question will produce different measures of value.[9] These measures of value are often orders of magnitude apart. The problem then is that CVM can easily produce many answers to the same basic question. This leaves the policy maker in the position of having to decide which number is most accurate and applicable.

Since CVM is generally used to measure values that do not have independent market measures, it is impossible to determine the accuracy of a CVM study. Since consistency is always a harbinger of accuracy in scientific measurement, this study creates an independent value for species preservation through an analysis of public expenditures on each species, which can then be compared with the values produced by CVM studies. Public expenditures were chosen as a comparison because the expenditure patterns, which are determined through a competitive political process engaged in by Congress and various federal and state departments and agencies, generally reflect the revealed public demand for each animal. While the process may be complicated, disjointed, subject to manipulation by special interest groups, bundled with other issues, and plagued by other side effects of the U.S. democratic process, in most cases the competition within the political system will generate a most preferred expenditure pattern across all endangered and threatened animals.

Until now, there has never been a set of independent measures of value for endangered species that could be used to calibrate those obtained from contingent valuation. Demonstration of a strong consistency between two independent endangered species' value measurements has implications not only for endangered species research, but for the contingent valuation method in general.

This chapter begins with the results of a 1991 public expenditure study, focusing on endangered and threatened species of animals.[10] Section I describes the economic, biological, and policy information collected for each endangered and threatened animal. The value estimates for each endangered animal and the results of statistical analyses that explain expenditure patterns across these animals is then presented.

Section II examines how expenditure patterns may be explained by animal-specific variables, such as the species' group, its listing as either endangered or threatened, its estimated remaining population, its recovery priority, and its perceived importance by the public.[11] Through a national survey on the public's preferences for endangered species, the study tries to explain why public

[9] See Baruch Fischoff, Value Elicitation: Is There Anything There? American Psychologist, Aug. 1991, at 835, 835–47.

[10] U.S. Dept. of the Interior, 102nd Cong., Endangered and Threatened Species Recovery Program 77–267 (1990).

[11] See Don Coursey, Endangered and Threatened Species: How Important Is Animal Preservation to You? (Jul.–Aug. 1993). (Survey results on file with author.)

expenditures have been distributed in the way that they have. Analysis of this survey indicates that public expenditures closely mirror the public's attitudes toward endangered species.

In Section III, the chapter concludes that one specific contingent valuation question frame holds the most promise for generating values consistent with those obtained from a revealed preference approach. By providing an independent variable with which CVM results can be compared, this study will allow future researchers to design more accurate and meaningful CVM analyses.

I. SCIENTIFIC AND POLICY DATA CONCERNING ENDANGERED SPECIES

In 1991, the U.S. Department of the Interior published, through the U.S. Fish and Wildlife Service, "Federal and State Endangered Species Expenditures."[12] A description of the 247 animals examined in this study is provided in Table 11.1. The animals are listed by their common name.

A.   Biological Information

The study assigned each species to one of nine groups: mammals, birds, reptiles, amphibians, snails, clams and mussels, crustaceans, insects, and arachnids. Data were collected on the weight and size of each species, and a quantitative scale was constructed to allow for interspecies size comparisons. Based on the qualitative and quantitative descriptions provided for an animal, each species was assigned to one of eight size groups: the size of a fly or smaller, the size of a snail, the size of a mouse, the size of a rat, the size of a cat, the size of a dog, the size of a deer, or the size of a horse or larger.[13]

B.   Policy Information

The study also classified each species as either threatened or endangered, reporting the species formal listing date. A small number of species are classified as both threatened and endangered because they are threatened in some areas and endangered in others.[14]

Further, the health of each species' population was assigned to one of five categories. A species may be defined as having declining, improving, stable, extinct, or unknown population status.[15] The Department provided each species

[12] The expenditure data reported in this study was combined with scientific and policy data outlined in the Department's 1990 summary report on endangered and threatened species. U.S. Dept. of the Interior, 102nd Cong., Endangered and Threatened Species Recovery Program 77–267 (1990).

[13] Ibid., 12.

[14] Ibid., 10.

[15] Ibid., 11. For some species, the total population of remaining animals is used to measure recovery. For other species, the total habitat acreage is used.

Table 11.1. *Mean Importance of Each Endangered Species; Species Ranked from Most to Least Important*

	Common name	Mean importance		Common name	Mean importance
1	Bald eagle	1.480	43	Virginia N. flying squirrel	2.180
2	Whooping crane	1.570	44	Nukupu'u (Maui population)	2.200
3	Green sea turtle	1.720	45	Olive ridley sea turtle	2.200
4	Leatherback sea turtle	1.890	46	Desert tortoise	2.200
5	Southern sea otter	1.920	47	Nukupu'u (Kauai population)	2.210
6	Grizzly bear	1.940	48	California least tern	2.210
7	Arctic peregrine falcon	1.950	49	Dugong	2.210
8	Hawaiian hawk	2.020	50	Masked bobwhite	2.220
9	Key deer	2.040	51	Laysan duck	2.220
10	Eastern cougar	2.040	52	Attwater's greater prairie chic	2.220
11	Woodland caribou	2.040	53	Mississippi sandhill crane	2.220
12	Florida panther	2.060	54	Eskimo curlew	2.230
13	Aleutian Canada goose	2.060	55	Golden-cheeked (wood) warbler	2.230
14	Kemp's ridley sea turtle	2.060	56	Maui 'akepa	2.240
15	Jaguarandi	2.060	57	Mariana mallard	2.240
16	Red wolf	2.080	58	Bachman's warbler	2.250
17	Northern aplomado falcon	2.080	59	Molokai thrush	2.250
18	Loggerhead sea turtle	2.090	60	'Akiapolaau	2.260
19	California condor	2.100	61	Florida scrub jay	2.280
20	Columbian white-tailed deer	2.120	62	Bay checkerspot butterfly	2.280
21	American peregrine falcon	2.120	63	Piping plover	2.290
22	Brown pelican	2.120	64	Gopher tortoise	2.290
23	Red-cockaded falcon	2.120	65	Hawaii 'akepa	2.300
24	Sonoran pronghorn	2.130	66	West Indian Manatee	2.300
25	Kauai 'akialoa	2.130	67	Yellow-shouldered blackbird	2.300
26	Hawaiian duck	2.130	68	Plymouth red-bellied turtle	2.300
27	Hawaiian dark-rumped petrel	2.130	69	Schaus swallowtail butterfly	2.300
28	Hawaiian stilt	2.130	70	Florida grasshopper sparrow	2.300
29	American crocodile	2.130	71	Roseate tern	2.300
30	Guam Micronesian kingfisher	2.130	72	California freshwater shrimp	2.300
31	Northern spotted owl	2.130	73	Oregon silverspot butterfly	2.310
32	Hawksbill sea turtle	2.140	74	Palos Verdes blue butterfly	2.310
33	Ocelot	2.150	75	Mt. Graham red squirrel	2.310
34	Carolina N. flying squirrel	2.150	76	Black-footed ferret	2.320
35	Ringed sawback turtle	2.150	77	Laysan finch	2.330
36	Indiana bat	2.160	78	Yuma clapper rail	2.330
37	Delmarva peninsula fox squirrel	2.160	79	Kirtland's warbler	2.330
38	Puerto Rican parrot	2.170	80	Nightingale reed warbler	2.330
39	Ivory-billed woodpecker	2.170	81	Small Kauai thrush	2.340
40	Alabama red-bellied turtle	2.170	82	Saltwater crocodile	2.340
41	Hawaiian goose	2.180			
42	Wood stork	2.180			

Table 11.1. *Continued*

	Common name	Mean importance		Common name	Mean importance
83	Audubon's crested aracara	2.340	126	Flattened musk turtle	2.510
84	San Joaquin kit fox	2.350	127	Mariana gray swiflet	2.530
85	Everglade snail kite	2.350	128	Houston toad	2.540
86	Least tern (interior population)	2.350	129	Hawaiian common moorhen	2.550
87	Squirrel Chimney cave shrimp	2.350	130	Cape Sable seaside sparrow	2.550
88	Lange's metalmark butterfly	2.360	131	Mission blue butterfly	2.550
89	San Clemete sage sparrow	2.360	132	Mariana crow	2.550
90	Least bell's vireo	2.360	133	Alabama cave shrimp	2.560
91	Large Kauai thrush	2.370	134	Puerto Rican plain pigeon	2.570
92	Nihoa finch	2.380	135	Lotis blue butterfly	2.580
93	California clapper rail	2.380	136	San Clemente loggerhead shrike	2.580
94	Hawaiian crow	2.390	137	Cave crayfish	2.580
95	Inyo brown towhee	2.390	138	St. Croix ground lizard	2.590
96	Dusky seaside sparrow	2.400	139	Tan riffle shell	2.590
97	Culebra Island giant anole	2.400	140	Texas blind salamander	2.600
98	Black-capped vireo	2.400	141	Puerto Rican nightjar	2.600
99	Pink mucket pearly mussel	2.410	142	Nashville crayfish	2.600
100	Lower Keys rabbit	2.410	143	Blunt-nosed lizard	2.610
101	Maui parrotbill	2.420	144	Tinian monarch	2.610
102	Micronesian megapode	2.420	145	Desert slender salamander	2.620
103	Molokai creeper	2.420	146	Mona boa	2.620
104	Hay's spring amphipod	2.420	147	San Marcos salamander	2.640
105	Crested honeycreeper	2.430	148	Sand skink	2.640
106	Kern primrose sphinx moth	2.440	149	Madison Cave isopod	2.650
107	Alabama beach mouse	2.440	150	Curtis' pearly mussel	2.660
108	Hawaiian coot	2.450	151	Golden coqui	2.660
109	Utah prairie dog	2.450	152	NM ridgenose rattlesnake	2.660
110	El Segundo blue butterfly	2.460	153	Puerto Rican boa	2.670
111	Smith's blue butterfly	2.460	154	Virgin Islands tree boa	2.670
112	Oahu creeper	2.470	155	Blue-tailed mole skink	2.670
113	Po'ouli	2.470	156	Appalachian monkeyface pearly mussel	2.680
114	Gray bat	2.470	157	Ozark big-eared bat	2.680
115	Nihoa millerbird	2.480	158	Coachella valley fingered-toe lizard	2.680
116	Light-footed clapper rail	2.480	159	Kentucky cave shrimp	2.680
117	Hawaiian creeper	2.480	160	Fresno kangaroo rat	2.680
118	Tubercled-blossom pearly mussel	2.480	161	Louisiana pearlshell	2.680
119	Guam rail	2.480	162	Shasta crayfish	2.690
120	Rough pigtoe	2.490	163	Hawaiian hoary bat	2.700
121	Yellow-blossom pearly mussel	2.500	164	White warty-black pearly mussel	2.700
122	Palila	2.510	165	Tar River spinymussel	2.700
123	White cat's paw pearly mussel	2.510	166	Marshall's mussel	2.700
124	San Bruno elfin butterfly	2.510	167	Santa Cruz long-toed salamander	2.720
125	Mona ground iguana	2.510			

Table 11.1. *Continued*

	Common name	Mean importance		Common name	Mean importance
168	Choctawatchee beach mouse	2.720	206	Little-wing pearly mussel	2.860
169	Cumberland bean pearly mussel	2.730	207	Fat pocketbook	2.880
170	Curtus' mussel	2.730	208	Virginia big-eared bat	2.880
171	Giant kangaroo rat	2.740	209	Virginia fringed mountain snail	2.890
172	Speckled pocketbook	2.740	210	Puerto Rican crested toad	2.890
173	Morro Bay kangaroo rat	2.750	211	American burying beetle	2.890
174	Green-blossom pearly mussel	2.750	212	Shenandoah salamander	2.900
175	Higgins' eye pearly mussel	2.750	213	Puritan tiger beetle	2.900
176	Guam broadbill	2.750	214	Salt marsh harvest mouse	2.910
177	Penitent mussel	2.750	215	Fine-rayed pigtoe	2.910
178	Stirrup shell	2.750	216	Noonday snail	2.910
179	Dromedary pearly mussel	2.760	217	Monito gecko	2.910
180	Bridled white-eye	2.770	218	Key Largo cotton mouse	2.910
181	Concho water snake	2.790	219	Cheat Mountain salamander	2.910
182	Orange-footed pearly mussel	2.800	220	Socorro isopod	2.920
183	Ring pink mussel	2.800	221	Chittenango ovate amber snail	2.920
184	Cracking pearly mussel	2.800	222	Key Largo rat	2.920
185	Dwarf wedge mussel	2.800	223	Little Marianas fruit bat	2.930
186	Perdido key beach mouse	2.810	224	Southeastern beach mouse	2.930
187	Pawnee montane slipper	2.810	225	Northeastern beach tiger beetle	2.930
188	Newell's Townsend's shearwater	2.820	226	Stock Island tree snail	2.940
189	Pale lilliput pearly mussel	2.820	227	Valley elderberry longhorn beet	2.940
190	James River spiny mussel	2.820	228	Hualapi Mexican vole	2.940
191	Anatasia island beach mouse	2.820	229	Red Hills salamander	2.950
192	Purple cat's paw pearly mussel	2.820	230	San Francisco garter snake	2.960
193	Ash Meadows naucorid	2.830	231	Atlantic salt marsh snake	2.960
194	Magazine Mountain shagreen	2.830	232	Judge Tait's mussel	2.960
195	Birdwing pearly mussel	2.840	233	Tooth Cave ground beetle	2.960
196	Turgid-blossom pearly mussel	2.840	234	Island night lizard	2.970
197	Shiny pigtoe mussel	2.840	235	Dismal Swamp S.E. shrew	2.970
198	Wyoming toad	2.840	236	Flat-spired 3-tooth land snail	2.980
199	Mexican long-nosed bat	2.840	237	Amargosa vole	2.980
200	Arkansas fatmucket	2.840	238	Marianas fruit bat	3.000
201	Fanshell	2.840	239	Stephens kangaroo rat	3.030
202	Inflated heelsplinter	2.850	240	Tooth Cave pseudoscorpion	3.030
203	Cumberland monkeyface mussel	2.860	241	Painted snake coil forest snail	3.040
204	Delta green ground beetle	2.860	242	Oahu tree snail	3.060
205	Sanborn's long-nosed bat	2.860	243	Eastern indigo snake	3.111
			244	Bee Creek Cave harvestman	3.140
			245	Tipton kangaroo rat	3.200
			246	Tooth Cave spider	3.280
			247	Kretchmarr cave mold beetle	3.420

with a recovery plan, which outlines strategies for a species that may focus on captive propagation, habitat protection, and/or animal translocation. The study reports the percentage of recovery achieved for each species, from listing date until December 1990. The report also indicates whether each species does, or does not, conflict with economic development. Of the 247 total species, 31 percent are reported as conflicting with economic development.

C.   Economic Information

Total expenditures for each species are reported for the 1990 fiscal year. This total includes both federal and state expenditures on the species. Total expenditures for all 247 animals amounted to $84,894,000 in 1990.[16]

D.   The Implied Value of an Endangered Species

Based upon the compilation of public expenditures, one can determine the implied value of an endangered species. By comparing the money spent on these species' recovery programs with the number of animals saved, it is possible to calculate the implicit monetary value placed on saving *a single animal* within a species.[17]

Table 11.2 reports the results of this computation for the 131 animals whose recovery program involves population increase.[18] The numbers reported in Table 11.2 do not represent the implicit value placed upon all members of a given species, but rather the implicit monetary value placed upon saving one member of that species. They range from a low of no expenditure for many of the animals to a high of almost $5 million for a single Florida panther.

Using the same assumptions about expenditure patterns and discounting as those used for the animal propagation programs, it is possible to calculate the implicit monetary value of saving a single acre of habitat for a given species. Table 11.3 reports the results of this computation for the eleven animal species whose recovery program involves increasing habitat. They range from a low of no expenditure for three of the animals to a high of almost $75,000 for a single acre of Hualapai Mexican vole habitat.[19]

---

[16] Ibid., 77.

[17] The two most common recovery strategies used to preserve endangered and threatened species are captive propagation programs (these emphasize and measure total population increase) and habitat protection programs (these emphasize and measure habitat acreage increases).

[18] Using data from the 1990 study, with a 10 percent discount rate, and assuming that expenditures were the same in all years before the 1990 listing.

[19] However, this value may be considered somewhat of an anomaly because the remaining habitat of the Hualapai Mexican vole is only about one acre. The expenditures on this animal have been devoted to increasing its available habitat by a fraction of an acre.

Table 11.2. *Monetary value per animal in a given species*

	Common name	Total expend(\$)/ animal		Common name	Total expend(\$)/ animal
1	Kauai ʻakialoa	0.00	39	Wood stork	42.42
2	Crested honeycreeper	0.00	40	Flat-spired 3-tooth land	
3	Nukupuʻu (Kauai			snail	46.93
	population)	0.00	41	Laysan finch	51.69
4	Palila	0.00	42	Puerto Rican crested	
5	Maui parrotbill	0.00		toad	59.22
6	Dusky seaside sparrow	0.00	43	Chittenango ovate amber	
7	Small Kauai thrush	0.00		snail	60.92
8	Maui ʻakepa	0.00	44	Hawaiian creeper	119.92
9	Large Kauia thrush	0.00	45	Roseate tern	133.67
10	Molokai thrush	0.00	46	Virginia big-eared bat	155.25
11	Desert slender		47	Puerto Rican nightjar	158.27
	salamander	0.00	48	Fat pocketbook	198.26
12	Poʻouli	0.00	49	Brown pelican	233.27
13	Mariana mallard	0.00	50	Socorro isopod	256.87
14	Palos Verdes blue		51	NM ridgenose rattlesnake	281.57
	butterfly	0.00	52	Hawaii ʻakepa	302.48
15	Delta green ground		53	Nihoa finch	362.39
	beetle	0.00	54	Green sea turtle	475.43
16	Monito gecko	0.00	55	Lange's metalmark	
17	Schaus swallowtail			butterfly	675.67
	butterfly	0.00	56	Cave crayfish	708.96
18	Tinian monarch	0.00	57	Florida grasshopper	
19	Inyo brown towhee	0.00		sparrow	796.24
20	Painted snake coil forest		58	Least tern (interior	
	snail	1.17		population)	848.86
21	Golden coqui	1.66	59	Houston toad	954.34
22	Olive ridley sea turtle	2.08	60	Loggerhead sea turtle	1,073.20
23	Gray bat	2.98	61	San Clemente sage	
24	Louisiana pearlshell	4.93		sparrow	1,083.21
25	Utah prarie dog	7.81	62	American crocodile	1,088.09
26	San Marcos salamander	8.59	63	Columbian white-tailed	
27	Mexican long-nosed bat	10.11		deer	1,178.45
28	Audubon's crested		64	Northern spotted owl	1,210.90
	caracara	10.16	65	Kentucky cave shrimp	1,210.90
29	Birdwing pearly mussel	10.56	66	Sanborn's long-nosed bat	1,213.68
30	Alabama beach mouse	14.99	67	Ozark big-eared bat	1,239.39
31	Indiana beach mouse	17.50	68	Hawaiian dark-rumped	
32	Shasta crayfish	20.80		petrel	1,249.03
33	Choctawatchee beach		69	Nihoa millerbird	1,397.42
	mouse	34.11	70	Laysan duck	1,802.34
34	Plymouth red-bellied		71	Newell's Townsend's	
	turtle	36.49		shearwater	2,017.54
35	Marianas fruit bat	40.09	72	Hawaiian coot	2,024.40
36	Desert tortoise	40.91	73	Yellow-shouldered	
37	Mona ground iguana	40.91		blackbird	2,569.88
38	Oahu tree snail	41.14	74	Black-capped vireo	2,709.62

Table 11.2. *Continued*

Common name	Total expend($)/ animal	Common name	Total expend($)/ animal
75 Aleutian Canada goose	2,962.00	104 Sonoran pronghorn	54,165.06
76 Hawaiian hawk	3,063.98	105 Kemp's ridley sea turtle	64,081.48
77 San Joaquin kit fox	3,592.48	106 Red-cockaded woodpecker	71,157.80
78 Morro Bay kangaroo rat	3,807.79	107 Turgid-blossom pearly mussel	72,765.00
79 'Akiapolaau	4,085.30	108 American peregrine falcon	78,092.11
80 Little-wing pearly mussel	4,368.00	109 Tubercled-blossom pearly mussel	83,160.00
81 Wyoming toad	4,629.10	110 Least bell's vireo	85,048.52
82 Guam rail	6,064.23	111 Little Marianas fruit bat	88,970.00
83 Perdido key beach mouse	6,179.52	112 Yellow-blossom pearly mussel	95,634.00
84 Hawaiian stilt	6,237.99	113 Eastern cougar	101,088.00
85 Hawaiian common moorhen	6,241.79	114 Leatherback sea turtle	104,604.28
86 Guam Micronesian kingfisher	7,178.15	115 Kirkland's warbler	162,258.04
87 Piping plover	7,233.30	116 Woodland caribou	176,635.14
88 California clapper rail	7,373.34	117 Black-footed ferret	178,131.27
89 Yuma clapper rail	8,485.66	118 Grizzly bear	184,078.23
90 Mt. Graham red squirrel	8,971.53	119 Light-footed clapper rail	209,898.78
91 Bald eagle	12,057.58	120 Key deer	216,691.86
92 Everglade snail kite	13,669.63	121 Masked bobwhite	257,782.05
93 Southern sea otter	14,374.95	122 Ivory-billed woodpecker	265,608.00
94 West Indian manatee	15,717.24	123 Whooping crane	329,527.83
95 Hawaiian goose	18,284.26	124 Hawaiian crow	435,565.50
96 Tar River spinymussel	19,117.71	125 White warty-black pearly mussel	525,987.00
97 Attwater's greater prairie chic	19,612.25	126 Bridled white-eye	550,188.00
98 Eskimo curlew	24,284.16	127 Mississippi sandhill crane	576,903.60
99 Florida scrub jay	25,357.00	128 Puerto Rican parrot	633,764.65
100 San Clemente loggerhead shrike	25,960.12	129 Bachman's warbler	1,105,119.00
101 Puerto Rican plain pigeon	39,751.92	130 California condor	1,568,176.33
102 Ring pink mussel	40,392.00	131 Florida panther	4,878,056.92
103 California least tern	51,360.96		

II. NATIONAL ATTITUDES TOWARD ENDANGERED SPECIES: A SURVEY

Total expenditures on endangered and threatened species are dominated by a few animals. Figure 11.1 illustrates the relationship between the cumulative

Table 11.3. *The implied dollar value of a protected acre*

	Common name	Implicit total expend/Acre
1	Red Hills salamander	0.00
2	Key Largo cotton mouse	0.00
3	Pawnee montane slipper	0.00
4	Dismal Swamp S.E. shrew	0.23
5	Gold-cheeked (wood) warbler	0.54
6	Tipton kangaroo rat	1.87
7	Giant kangaroo rat	2.14
8	Stephens kangaroo rat	3.93
9	Key Largo rat	4.09
10	Fresno kangaroo rat	4.09
11	Hualapai Mexican vole	69,094.00

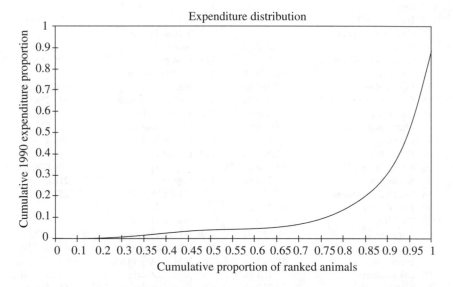

Figure 11.1. The dominance of a few species in overall expenditures.

proportion of expenditures and the cumulative proportion of expenditure-ranked animals. Eight of the 247 animals receive half of the total money devoted to protecting species. At the other end of the spectrum, three-quarters of the animals must share 10 percent of all expenditures. How can this distribution and the distribution of implicit value reported in Tables 11.2 and 11.3 be explained?

In one attempt to explain the expenditure data, a survey of national attitudes toward endangered species was conducted in July and August 1993.[20]

---

[20] *See* Coursey, *supra* note 11.

Table 11.4. *Endangered species survey: summary statistics*

Series	Mean	Std. dev.	Maximum	Minimum
Sex	0.781	0.415	1	0
Child	0.772	1.154	6	0
Age	46.13	15.38	88	19
Education	6.315	1.549	9	1
Urbur	3.073	1.444	5	0
Black	0.055	0.379	5	0
Indalas	0.005	0.068	1	0
Asian	0.009	0.095	1	0
Hispan	0.041	0.199	1	0
Demo	0.338	0.474	1	0
Rep	0.315	0.466	1	0
Polstand	1.727	0.723	3	10
Incomcap	19,778.5	15,271.3	85,000	1,666.66

A random sample of the U.S. population was surveyed by mail to obtain information about the importance of preserving endangered and threatened animals. General information about the importance of preserving animals and information about the specific importance of each animal were collected along with information about the respondents. The 247 animals were divided into five groups of approximately fifty animals each to obtain five different survey instruments. Thus, each respondent was asked to consider approximately fifty animals. The survey instrument is available from the auhor on request. A total of 1,000 surveys were administered with a final response rate of 35.7 percent.

Table 11.4 presents summary statistics for key sociodemographic, political, and economic variables collected from the survey respondents. The survey provided space for respondents to make written comments about endangered species and the survey instrument. The general nature of these comments are available from the author on request.

A.   Animal Preservation: Individual Perspectives

More than 60 percent of the survey respondents indicate that preservation of species in danger of or threatened with extinction is either "important" or "extremely important." Figure 11.2 illustrates this distribution of responses.

Respondents were then asked to indicate why preservation is important. They were asked to evaluate the importance of the existence rights of species, the importance of saving species for future generations, the importance of species in maintaining the balance of nature, the educational importance of species, the recreational importance of species, and the importance of species in maintaining the health of the ecosystem. Figure 11.3 illustrates that the

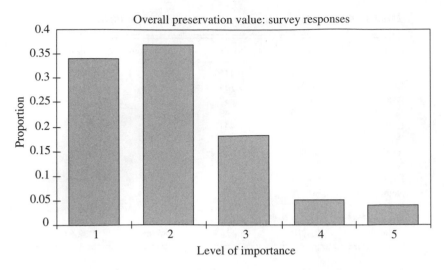

Figure 11.2. The importance of endangered species preservation.
(1 = extremely important; 5 = not important at all).

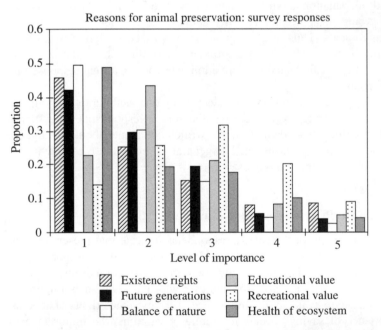

Figure 11.3. Explaining why endangered species are important.
(1 = extremely important; 5 = not important at all).

Table 11.5A. *Explaining overall importance (dependent value: overall importance)*[a]

Variable	Coefficient	Std. error	T-stat	2-Tail sig.
Sex	0.577	0.203	2.842	0.004
Child	0.059	0.079	0.747	0.455
Age	0.022	0.005	4.219	0.000
Education	0.051	0.056	0.909	0.363
Urbur	−0.032	0.060	−0.541	0.589
Black	1.259	0.618	2.037	0.042
Indalas	−0.071	1.049	−0.068	0.946
Asian	0.680	1.060	0.642	0.521
Hispan	−0.180	0.384	−0.468	0.639
Demo	−0.179	0.216	−0.828	0.408
Rep	0.486	0.218	2.235	0.025
Polstand	0.139	0.129	1.078	0.281
Incomcap	−3.66E-07	6.759E-06	−0.054	0.957
R-Squared	0.117			
Adj. R-Square	0.040	Mean of Dep	2.073	
S.E. of Regr	1.023	S.D. of Dep	1.043	
Durbin-Watson	1.990	Sum Sq Resid	143.24	
Loc likelihood	−209.38	F-Stat	1.51	

[a] 150 total observations.

weights placed upon these reasons for animal conservation are not equal. The respondents indicate that maintaining the balance of nature and maintaining a healthy ecosystem are the most important reasons for species preservation. The rights of species to exist and to be enjoyed by future generations are next in importance. Least important among the reasons for preservation are the educational and recreational values provided by the species (although this reason took on greater importance for those respondents placing less importance on protecting endangered species).

Table 11.5A presents a regression that explains the overall importance for preserving endangered and threatened species. The regressors include sociodemographic, ethnic, political, and economic variables collected for each respondent. Table 11.5B reports the result of a regression designed to purge the analysis of marginal variables discovered in the initial regression.

These regressions indicate that females and older respondents tend to place a higher level of importance on preserving animals. Self-reported liberals also place higher levels of importance on preservation. Relative to those that describe themselves as independents, Republicans also place higher value on preservation. No significant effect was found for Democrats.

Tables 11.6A and 11.6B replicate this regression analysis for the variable indicated by the respondents as being of highest mean importance for preserving species: maintaining the balance of nature. Similar to the results found when

Table 11.5B. *Explaining overall importance (dependent value: overall importance)[a]*

Variable	Coefficient	Std. error	T-stat	2-Tail sig.
Sex	0.510	0.185	2.761	0.006
Age	0.024	0.004	5.415	0.000
Black	0.494	0.527	0.938	0.348
Rep	0.737	0.176	4.184	0.000
Polstand	0.197	0.097	2.174	0.030
R-Squared	0.066			
Adj. R-Square	0.042	Mean of Dep	2.082	
S.E. of Regr	1.036	S.D. of Dep	1.059	
Durbin-Watson	1.871	Sum Sq Resid	164.25	
Log likelihood	−227.25	F-Stat	2.720	

[a] 158 total observations.

Table 11.6A. *Explaining the balance of nature (dependent value: overall importance)[a]*

Variable	Coefficient	Std. error	T-stat	2-Tail sig.
Sex	0.380	0.164	2.320	0.020
Child	0.093	0.063	1.459	0.144
Age	0.020	0.004	5.440	0.000
Education	0.065	0.043	1.516	0.129
Urbur	−0.068	0.046	−1.497	0.134
Black	−0.021	0.171	−0.121	0.904
Indalas	0.174	0.953	0.182	0.855
Asian	−0.609	0.685	−0.877	0.380
Hispan	−0.387	0.327	−1.183	0.237
Demo	−0.158	0.159	−0.990	0.322
Rep	0.041	0.168	0.246	0.806
Polstand	0.116	0.091	1.275	0.202
Incomcap	7.084E-06	4.88E-06	1.450	0.147
R-Squared	0.129			
Adj. R-Square	0.078	Mean of Dep	1.800	
S.E. of Regr	0.939	S.D. of Dep	0.977	
Durbin-Watson	1.953	Sum Sq Resid	177.97	
Log likelihood	−284.75	F-Stat	2.500	

[a] 215 total observations.

analyzing overall importance, females and older respondents place higher value on maintaining the balance of nature as a reason for species preservation, yet political identification lacked a statistically significant relationship with a respondent's answer. Tables 11.7A and 11.7B analyze the importance of maintaining a healthy ecosystem – the variable indicated by the respondents as

Table 11.6B. *Explaining the balance of nature (dependent value: overall importance)*[a]

Variable	Coefficient	Std. error	T-stat	2-Tail sig.
Sex	0.404	0.159	2.548	0.011
Child	0.104	0.0613	1.700	0.090
Age	0.020	0.004	5.497	0.000
Education	0.073	0.041	1.770	0.077
Urbur	−0.073	0.045	−1.638	0.101
Hispan	−0.407	0.323	−1.230	0.208
Polstand	−0.073	0.084	0.848	0.396
Incomcap	6.837E-06	4.816E-06	1.419	0.156
R-Squared	0.119			
Adj. R-Square	0.089	Mean of Dep	1.800	
S.E. of Regr	0.933	S.D. of Dep	0.977	
Durbin-Watson	1.95	Sum Sq Resid	180.15	
Log likelihood	−286.06	F-Stat	3.981	

[a] 215 total observations.

Table 11.7A. *Explaining the importance of a healthy ecosystem (dependent value: overall importance)*[a]

Variable	Coefficient	Std. error	T-stat	2-Tail sig.
Sex	0.362	0.173	2.093	0.036
Child	0.042	0.067	0.629	0.529
Age	0.022	0.004	5.523	0.000
Education	0.059	0.045	1.31	0.190
Urbur	−0.058	0.048	−1.21	0.225
Black	0.242	0.179	1.35	0.177
Indalas	−0.958	0.997	−0.960	0.337
Asian	0.368	0.727	0.507	0.612
Hispan	0.104	0.342	0.304	0.761
Demo	−0.078	0.168	−0.466	0.641
Rep	0.522	0.179	2.914	0.004
Polstand	0.094	0.100	0.978	0.328
Incomcap	5.449E-06	5.139E-06	1.060	0.289
R-Squared	0.149			
Adj. R-Square	0.097	Mean of Dep	1.957	
S.E. of Regr	0.98	S.D. of Dep	1.034	
Durbin-Watson	1.734	Sum Sq Resid	191.14	
Log likelihood	−288.97	F-Stat	2.890	

[a] 211 total observations.

being second highest in mean importance for preserving species. Sex and age effects are similar in both magnitude and significance to the results reported above. Additionally, the importance of maintaining a healthy ecosystem is valued more highly by respondents with more education and by Republicans.

Table 11.7B. *Explaining the importance of a healthy ecosystem (dependent value: overall importance)*[a]

Variable	Coefficient	Std. error	T-stat	2-Tail sig.
Sex	0.381	0.162	2.352	0.019
Age	0.021	0.004	5.803	0.000
Education	0.087	0.038	2.320	0.020
Urbur	−0.053	0.046	−1.141	0.254
Black	0.230	0.175	1.315	0.188
Rep	0.530	0.150	3.540	0.000
Incomcap	4.617E-06	4.722E-06	0.978	0.328
R-Squared	0.133			
Adj. R-Square	0.108	Mean of Dep	1.949	
S.E. of Regr	0.974	S.D. of Dep	1.031	
Durbin-Watson	1.729	Sum Sq Resid	196.39	
Log likelihood	−294.46	F-Stat	5.278	

[a] 214 total observations.

B.   Patterns of Animal Importance for a Single Individual

In the survey, respondents were provided with names, complete descriptions, and habitat locations for the animals listed on the Department of the Interior's endangered and threatened species list. They were asked to indicate the importance of preserving each animal, using a five-point importance scale to rank each animal. The responses across species for a single respondent are tabulated in a bar chart, illustrated in Figure 11.4, that measures the proportion of animals the respondent placed into each of these five categories. Individuals are clustered into seven distinct patterns of response distribution.

Twenty-seven percent of the respondents indicated that preservation of all animals is equally valuable. Three quantitative intensity levels are observed. "Noah's Ark" type respondents ranked all endangered and threatened species as "extremely important." To these respondents, each animal is equally and intensely important. "Weak Noah's Ark" type respondents ranked all endangered and threatened species as "important" or "somewhat important." "Disdain" type respondents ranked all endangered and threatened species as "not so important" or "not important at all." To these respondents, the preservation of all animals was equally unimportant. Disdain respondents constitute a small proportion of the respondents who ranked all animals equally.

"Noah's Ark Minus Undesirables" type respondents constitute 5 percent of the survey population. This group ranked most animals "extremely important" and a few animals "not important at all." They expressed preferences similar to the Noah's Ark types, except for a small minority of the animals for which they indicated no importance in preserving.

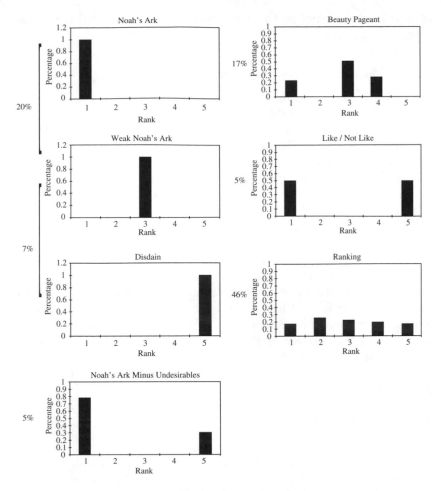

Figure 11.4. A taxonomy of endangered species importance.

"Beauty Pageant" type respondents ranked most endangered and threatened animals as "somewhat important" or "not so important" but had a few favorite animals they designated as "extremely important." This response is observed in 17 percent of the survey population.

"Like/Not Like" respondents were almost evenly bipolar in their response pattern. They either expressed extreme importance or extreme nonimportance in the preservation of animals and made very few responses between the scale endpoints. This type of ranking is observed for 5 percent of the respondents.

The most common response pattern was "Ranking." This type of response was indicated by 46 percent of the survey population. These respondents valued preservation of some endangered and threatened species highly, some not at all, and most somewhere in between. The pattern that emerges is a unimodal distribution of preservation importance that spans the entire range of the response scale.

C.   The Distribution of Importance Across Species

The survey responses may also be averaged across respondents for a single species. Table 11.1 reports the mean importance for preserving each species. These mean values range from a high of 1.480 for the bald eagle to a low of 3.42 for the Kretschmarr Cave mold beetle. Some perspective on the list may be obtained by examining the twenty animals with highest mean importance and the twenty animals with lowest mean importance.

The twenty top-ranked animals are all mammals, relatively large birds, or relatively large turtles. What characteristics do these animals have in common? It is beyond the scope of this chapter to discuss the psychological preference that leads individuals to rank some animals above others; however, it is clear that the twenty top-ranked animals fall well within the bounds of what Murphy has defined as "charismatic megafauna."[21]

Almost all of the twenty bottom-ranked animals are obscure rodents, snakes, insects, or snails. Clearly, they are exactly what Murphy did not have in mind when coining the description "charismatic megafauna." It is safe to speculate that most people would find the twenty bottom-ranked animals neither "charismatic" nor "mega."

The individual patterns of ranking reported in Section IIIB average to produce an approximately normal distribution of mean perceived importance. Figure 11.5 illustrates the distribution of mean importance for the 247 endangered and threatened animal species.

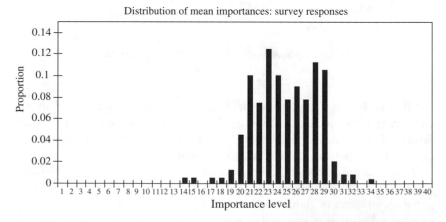

Distribution of mean importances: survey responses

Figure 11.5. The distribution of endangered species importance.
(1 = extremely important; 5 = not important at all).

---

[21] *See* Mann and Plummer, *supra* note 1, at 49.

III. DISCUSSION

The country will never have sufficient resources to save all endangered and threatened species. Practical reality resembles that of Noah managing an ark on a budget constraint. This budget constraint may exclude some animals from the ark. It may also result in unequal berthing accommodations on the ark.

It is hard to define beauty, majesty, largess, grace, power, and a host of other traits that might be used to describe certain species. It is equally hard to define the lack of these traits in other animals. Perhaps, as the entomologist Wilson has argued, it is the presence of these traits that allows people to "anthropomorphize" certain animals. Perhaps, as others have suggested, the public has "vertebrate chauvinism." The large variance in surveyed importance runs directly counter to biological and ecological arguments for species equality. Yet the evidence reported in this study suggests that the public's, rather than the natural scientists', values are translated into policy.[22]

A.   Expenditure Patterns Across Endangered Species

The evidence reported in this study supports the conclusion that Congress is buying protection of animals in a manner consistent with the median desires of the public. Clearly, the high correlation between importance reported in Table 11.1 and implicit value reported in Tables 11.2 and 11.3 plays a role. Animals that rank high on the respondents' scale of importance receive higher degrees of public policy attention and money. The twenty animals with highest implicit monetary value correspond closely, but certainly not exactly, to the twenty top-ranked animals in Table 11.1. Similarly, the twenty animals with the lowest implicit monetary value correspond in many cases to those ranked lowest in Table 11.1.

It may be argued that the money spent to save an endangered or threatened animal may also save other animals. For example, protecting a whooping crane may also lead to the protection of other animals within the crane's ecosystem. Indeed, some might argue that the whooping crane is a symbol of and champion for its ecosystem. If this perspective is taken, the numbers reported in Table 11.1 should be considered either as upper-bounds for the value of each animal or as the total value of the animal and its ecosystem.

The notions of "charisma" and "megafauna" are to some extent quantifiable across animals. Figure 11.6 reports the percentage of different animals that fall within each of the eight size categories used in the study. The modal size of animals on the endangered and threatened species list is about that of a mouse. A few animals are as small as a fly, while a few are as large as a horse. Figure 11.6 may be contrasted with Figure 11.7, which illustrates the percentage of

---

[22] For a similar proposition, *see* Stephen J. Breyer, *Breaking the Vicious Circle: toward Effective Risk Regulation*, Cambridge: Harvard University Press, 1993. (This text analyzes risk perception by the public and the experts and concluding that EPA risk policy responds to the former when it should respond to the latter.)

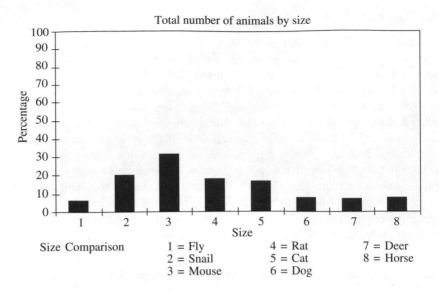

Figure 11.6. The distribution of animal size.

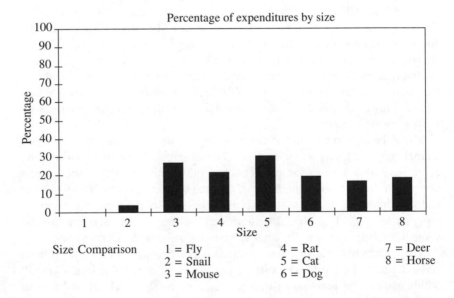

Figure 11.7. Expenditure patterns and animal size.

total expenditures received by a species as a function of species' size. The two smallest categories of animals, while constituting a significant proportion of total listed animals, receive a trivial proportion of total expenditures. Likewise, the larger animals receive a higher share of total expenditures than an equal pro-rated division would imply. "Mega" appears to matter.

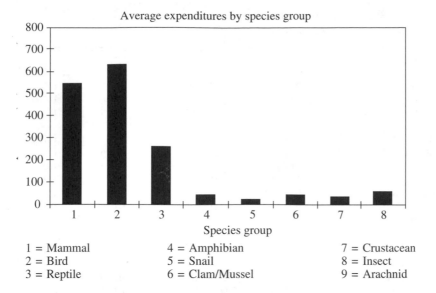

Figure 11.8. Average expenditures across groups.

Charisma is harder to quantify. Figure 11.8, however, examines one notion of what captivates survey respondents and policy makers. In this figure, the average expenditures for each animal species within a given group are illustrated. Mammals, birds, and to a lesser extent reptiles receive average expenditures that dominate those of the other six species groups.

The separate impact of these variables and other policy-related variables are examined in Tables 11.8A and 11.8B. These tables report the results of two regressions explaining total expenditures on a given species in 1990. The explanatory variables include the species' mean importance obtained from the national survey results, the species' size, whether protecting the species interferes with development (a dummy variable),[23] the species' listing date on the endangered and threatened list, the status of the species as either endangered or threatened (a dummy variable), and a list of dummy variables indicating the species' group (birds are eliminated from this list of dummy variables so the species' group effect is measured relative to birds).

These analyses indicate that policy variables are important in explaining the expenditure patterns observed across species. Animals that pose a threat to development receive greater monetary attention than those that do not. Animals that have been more recently listed receive higher funding levels. And, to a somewhat less statistically significant extent, endangered species receive more funding than those that are classified as threatened.

---

[23] A "dummy variable" is one that takes on the value of $+1$ if there is a conflict and 0 if there is not a conflict.

Table 11.8A. *Explaining expenditures across species (dependent variable: total 1990 expenditure)[a]*

Variable	Coefficient	Std. error	T-stat	2-Tail sig.
Meanimp	−826.953	254.798	−3.246	0.001
Sizerank	149.289	58.124	2.568	0.010
Conflict	579.178	169.105	3.425	0.001
Listdate	27.513	8.947	3.075	0.002
Status	−77.644	58.241	−1.333	0.182
Mammal	−319.075	216.140	−1.476	0.140
Reptile	−651.864	253.280	−2.575	0.010
Snail	126.058	429.059	0.294	0.769
Clammuss	−392.930	253.280	−1.551	0.121
Crust	−261.428	410.929	−0.636	0.525
Insect	−225.819	309.793	−0.729	0.466
Arach	−251.931	692.593	−0.364	0.716
Amphid	−328.761	381.094	−0.863	0.388
R-Squared	0.215			
Adj. R-Square	0.171	Mean of Dep	370.250	
S.E. of Regr	1,074.96	S.D. of Dep	1,180.931	
Durbin-Watson	1.574	Sum Sq Resid	2.48E+08	
Log likelihood	−1,908.27	F-Stat	4.914	

[a] 228 Total observations.

Table 11.8B. *Explaining expenditures across species (dependent variable: total 1990 expenditure)[a]*

Variable	Coefficient	Std. error	T-stat	2-Tail sig.
Meanimp	−829.581	237.777	−3.489	0.000
Sizerank	170.698	50.483	3.381	0.001
Conflict	550.165	160.399	3.430	0.001
Listdate	26.191	8.377	3.126	0.002
Status	−88.181	56.634	−1.558	0.119
Mammal	−266.850	205.196	−1.300	0.193
Reptile	−617.681	247.342	−2.497	0.013
Clammuss	−316.587	229.128	−1.382	0.167
R-Squared	0.209			
Adj. R-Square	0.184	Mean of Dep	370.250	
S.E. of Regr	1,066.665	S.D. of Dep	1,180.931	
Durbin-Watson	1.558	Sum Sq Resid	2.50E+08	
Log likelihood	−1,901.129	F-Stat	8.320	

[a] 228 Total observations.

But the analyses also indicate that the natural characteristics and the mean public importance of each species play at least as large a role as the policy variables in explaining expenditure patterns. Controlling for other factors, those animals that are rated highly by the public receive more money. The same is true for larger animals. Birds, mammals, reptiles, and clams and mussels receive different treatment than that received by other animals.

B.   Implications for the Contingent Valuation Method and Public Policy

President Clinton's Executive Order 12866 (September 1993) on regulatory planning and review reaffirms the importance of making accurate assessments of benefits: "Each agency shall assess both the costs and benefits of the intended regulation and, recognizing that some costs and benefits are difficult to quantify, propose or adopt a regulation only upon a reasoned determination that the benefits of the intended regulation justify its costs."[24] For many public policy decisions, this "reasoned determination" of benefits and costs will involve the use of contingent valuation methods. However, scientific knowledge about the accuracy of this methodology is incomplete.

Contingent valuation techniques can be shown to produce accurate measures of value in situations where an independent measure of value is available from a market. But when market value is available, there is little demand for contingent valuation measures. The promise of contingent valuation is for situations where the good in question is a public good, when it is not priced implicitly or explicitly in any market, and when its value is more complex than that derived through standard uses.

The National Oceanic and Atmospheric Administration examined past use of the contingent valuation technique in an attempt to codify guidelines for its application in the above situations.[25] An academic review panel concluded that contingent valuation studies can produce estimates that are reliable enough to be the starting point for a judicial or administrative determination of value.[26] However, one of their recommended guidelines was that researchers remind respondents about alternative expenditure possibilities:

> Respondents must be reminded that their willingness to pay for the environmental program in question would reduce their expenditure for private goods or other public goods. This reminder should be more than perfunctory, but less than overwhelming. The goal is to induce respondents to keep in mind other likely expenditures, including those on other environmental goods, when evaluating the main scenario.[27]

The justification for this guideline was derived from research indicating that when more alternatives are presented, the stated value for the good in

[24] Exec. Order No. 12,866, 3 C.F.R. 639 (1993).

[25] Report of the National Oceanic and Atmospheric Administration Panel on Contingent Valuation, 58 Fed. Reg. 4601–14 (1993).

[26] Ibid., 4610–11.

[27] Ibid., 4613.

question will decrease: the so-called embedding or aggregation effect.[28] Of all the modifications of contingent valuation frames examined to date, the number of alternatives mentioned in the survey instrument most dramatically affects stated respondent value. When more alternatives are mentioned, the stated value of the object in question decreases. This decrease is often many orders of magnitude in size.

The academic review panel did not address two important and related questions. First, is there an optimal number of alternatives to consider? Second, if this optimal number of alternatives is presented to the respondent, will they provide a more accurate or truthful valuation answer? These questions can only be addressed if it can be shown that a given number of alternatives will result in a value estimate that is consistent with an independent measure obtained using another technique.

The implicit values reported for different animal species in this study can play a role in answering these questions. Monetary values are reported for 142 animals that are not traded in markets and most likely have esoteric values that fall into a nonuse category. Further research can explore how contingent valuation survey frames need to be adjusted in order to replicate the revealed public values reported in this study.

The calculus for such an exercise would proceed as follows. Consider again the problem of valuing a 10 percent increase in the whooping crane population. The remaining whooping crane population is 300 birds;[29] thus, a 10 percent increase implies thirty additional birds. Each of these birds has an implicit public value of $330,000 as reported in Table 11.2. Thus, a simple calculation indicates that the implied public value of such a program, based upon past public policy decisions, ought to be $9.9 million. This translates into a mean of $0.99 per household for each of the approximately 100 million U.S. households.

The next step in the calibration process is to determine which type or types of contingent valuation question frames for the whooping crane will produce an average willingness-to-pay of $0.99 per household. Certainly, some number of alternative expenditures can be found that will produce this value. Perhaps other frames that also generate this number will be found.[30]

---

[28] See Don Coursey and Russell Roberts, *Aggregation and the Contingent Valuation Method for Evaluating Amenities* (Wash. U. Olin Sch. of Bus. Working Paper, March 1992). See also Daniel Kahneman and Jack L. Knetch, *Valuing Public Goods: The Purchase of Moral Satisfaction*, 22 J. Envtl. Econ. & Mgmt. 57 (1992) (finding that the contingent valuation method is flawed because a person's willingness to pay for a public good is a reflection of moral satisfaction and not a measure of the welfare gain from the contribution); William H. Desvousges et al., *Measuring Nonuse Damages Using Contingent Valuation: An Experimental Evaluation of Accuracy* (Research Triangle Inst. Monograph 92-1 1992) (presenting subjects with several numbers of birds killed to show that valuations do not vary appropriately with the amount of resource offered).

[29] Data obtained from Department of the Interior.

[30] Perhaps the most promising such frame is aggregation. A highly aggregated survey asks respondents to consider more than the object of interest.

When this process is repeated for other animals, it then will be possible to determine the precise characteristics of a question frame that will consistently produce measures of value equal to the implicit values reported in Table 11.2. If this is accomplished, greater scientific consensus and more well-founded scientific knowledge about optimal contingent valuation design may emerge. In turn, this knowledge can be applied to other situations where revealed public value cannot be independently measured.

CONCLUSION

The problem of valuing human life and the problem of valuing endangered and threatened species share many characteristics. Putting a value on human or animal life makes many people uneasy. Often, the instinctive reaction is that the task is impossible or that life of any form has infinite economic value. Both problems are perceived as being outside of the realm of economic analysis and belonging to another area of discussion. But a claim that the public is doing everything it can to save either human or animal lives is intellectually bankrupt. Constraints and opportunity costs matter in both problems. Some of the species examined in this study will almost certainly become extinct, while others will be saved. As this study shows, the decision as to which species will be saved is dependent upon political and social factors as much, if not more, than scientific concerns. Moreover, while attempts to value species are not precise and often face opposition, studies such as the one presented here can help us to better understand the process through which decisions regarding species protection, as well as perhaps other environmental measures, are made.

CHAPTER 12

The ESA through Coase-Colored Glasses

Terry L. Anderson

When Ronald Coase wrote his seminal article on "The Problem of Social Cost" in 1960, concerns about environmental problems and especially endangered species were held only by a small handful of biologists. The environmental movement had not yet started to impact public policy. Though the Wilderness Act was passed in 1964 prohibiting mechanized vehicle travel, logging, and many other commercial activities on certain public lands, it was not until the 1970s that environmental concerns took center stage with the passage of the Clean Water Act, the Clean Air Act, and the Endangered Species Act (ESA).

Rising incomes, declining numbers of some charismatic species such as the bald eagle and grizzly bear, and the emergence of environmental consciousness through books such as Rachel Carson's *Silent Spring* raised the value of the environment generally and endangered species in particular. Not surprisingly, rising values of these goods led to a struggle for ownership of the environment. The struggle, however, was not over who would pay whom for costs associated with resource use, but over how much and by which agencies would private activities be regulated.

Though Coase's insights have tremendous implications for environmental policy, the debates still focus mainly on the divergence between private and social costs. Indeed, there is almost no discussion of the reciprocal nature of costs. The ESA does not consider the optimal number of species, the ways to minimize the costs of maintaining species, or the issue of who should compensate whom for species loss. Instead, the ESA sets up a framework that regulates private landowners on the ground that they impose costs on society if they take habitat. Nonetheless, the reciprocal nature of costs should be apparent.

Few economists, however, have considered wildlife problems from a Coasean perspective. Two exceptions are Amacher, Tollison, and Willet (1995) and Lueck (1995). Amacher et al. consider the problem of eagle protection in a

I am indebted to Donald Leal for his helpful comments on an earlier draft of this chapter and for allowing me to use examples from our coauthored book, *Enviro-Capitalists: Doing Good While Doing Well*. The chapter was originally drafted while I was a John M. Olin Visiting Fellow at the Cornell Law School.

Coasean context. As they note, "The problem of devising a scheme to protect the eagle is parallel to some extent to that of the pollution example. That is, for the eagle problem, transaction costs and other costs of internalizing the relevant externalities . . . are significant and warrant the investigation of alternative liability assignment schemes" (45). Lueck focuses on the transaction costs of wildlife management determined mainly by the wildlife territory relative to the optimal size of land holdings in other uses (especially agriculture). From the transaction cost paradigm, Lueck concludes that the property rights and regulations over wildlife "exist because they economically mitigate the wealth dissipation that results from incomplete ownership" (21).

This chapter uses Coase's insights to consider how transaction costs vary with alternative property rights regimes and how we might more effectively save endangered species by paying closer attention to the transaction costs associated with these alternative regimes. The next section applies the Coasean framework to different combinations of single and multiple owners of habitat and species, asking how transaction costs might be minimized in each case. By considering the real-world counterparts to these combinations, we can gain insights into how alternative property rights arrangements might reduce transaction costs and improve the way we attempt to save wildlife habitat in general and endangered species in particular.

THE RECIPROCAL NATURE OF WILDLIFE COST

It is important to note at the outset that all bets are off regarding wild species protection if either the species or the habitat are truly an open access resource with no residual claimant. That is to say, if no one owns the species or the habitat, contracting will be impossible. If the habitat has alternative uses that are capturable by a private owner, that owner will try to exterminate species that compete. If those who want more species do not have to pay for any costs borne by others, they want "too many" of the species.

Fortunately, there are few examples of totally open access either because government regulations limit access to the commons or because, when resources get more valuable, people devote effort to defining and enforcing rights to them (see Anderson and Hill 1975). When property rights do evolve, the rights are likely to be for wildlife habitat because it is generally much easier to establish property rights to the habitat than to wildlife themselves. As Lueck (1995) has shown, if the territory of the wildlife is small compared to the optimal size of land holdings, property rights to the wildlife are more likely to be well defined and enforced. The larger the habitat compared to the optimal size of land holdings, the more the costs of defining and enforcing property rights. As Coase explained, fencing can provide a solution to this problem, but fences take a certain amount of the wildness out of wildlife. In some cases, private property rights are quite well defined and enforced as with wildlife on private property in South Africa; in other cases, community ownership mitigates against access from outsiders (see Leal 1996); and in still others, governmental rules restrict access to the resources. The cases that follow show how property rights to wildlife are evolving. In each of these cases, Coase's insights regarding ownership, liability rules, and transaction costs are useful.

The Coase theorem is one of the most written about and perhaps most misunderstood ideas from a Nobel Laureate. His main contribution was the recognition of the reciprocal nature of costs associated with externalities. In other words, when actions by individual A adversely impact the actions of individual B, the locus of liability will depend on the property rights or liability rules that assign those costs. In the case of a domestic cow owned by individual A wandering onto the property of individual B, the property rights can be specified so that the owner of the cow has the right to let his cow wander or so that the owner of the land has a right to be free from wandering cows. The Coase theorem says that, in the absence of transaction costs, the assignment of rights is immaterial to the social efficiency of the outcome; either A bears the costs or B bears the costs. In either case, the costs borne through the distribution of wealth will be quite different. Therefore, at the heart of Coase's proposition is the existence of economic rents whose distribution will depend on the liability rules, but if transaction costs are low, the allocation of resources will be unaffected by the liability assignment.

When transaction costs are positive, however, not only will alternative property rights and liability rules change the distribution of wealth, they will alter the allocation of resources. This corollary has forced economists to focus on the transaction costs as an explanation for why some margins of ownership are not fully accounted for in contracts. This is one explanation for why firms evolve to combine ownership into one entity and thereby lower some of the transaction costs (see Coase 1937).[1] As we will see in the examples, integration of wildlife and habitat ownership into a single firm offers a way of overcoming contracting costs between separate owners. In other cases where transaction costs are high enough to preclude contracting, governmental regulation may be useful, but this raises the possibility of public choice problems.

The transaction costs framework also opens a normative door through which economists are tempted to pass and draw conclusions about the superiority of alternative rights assignments. We will step through that door as we consider several combinations of species and habitat ownership.

The matrix in Figure 12.1 specifies seven combinations of habitat ownership and species ownership determined by single or multiple ownership of species and habitat and by the separability of costs. In the case of multiple ownership, there is the possibility that the reciprocal costs are separable, meaning that they can be assigned to individual land or species owners, or that they are nonseparable, meaning that they cannot be easily determined and therefore assigned.[2] As we will see, multiple ownership raises the possibility of the

---

[1] Of course, firms have other costs of measuring and monitoring performance. See Alchian and Demsetz (1972).

[2] Two sections are blocked out because the reciprocal nature of costs means that costs are either separable or nonseparable. They cannot be separable for one side and not the other. Therefore,

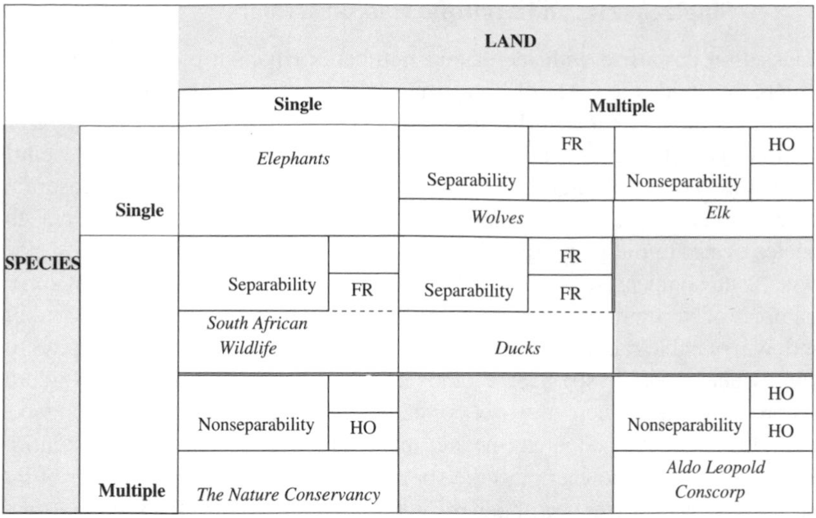

		LAND				
		Single	**Multiple**			
SPECIES	**Single**	*Elephants*	Separability	FR	Nonseparability	HO
			Wolves		*Elk*	
		Separability	FR	Separability	FR	
		South African Wildlife		*Ducks*	FR	
		Nonseparability	HO		Nonseparability	HO
						HO
	Multiple	*The Nature Conservancy*			*Aldo Leopold Conscorp*	

Figure 12.1. A Coasean Matrix of Species – Habitat Ownership Combinations.

free-rider (FR) problem or the holdout (HO) problem. Transaction costs associated with the seven different combinations have definite implications for private contracting for habitat for endangered species and for the possibilities of public (i.e., political) ownership of species or habitat. The examples in each cell of the matrix refer to the case studies discussed in the next section.

Single Species and a Single Habitat Owner

Begin with the simplest combination of one habitat owner and one species owner. Like Coase's and later Ellickson's (1986) wandering cattle or like Cheung's (1973) orchard owners and bee keepers, the allocation problem is a matter of two owners contracting with transaction costs a function of measuring and monitoring the contractual terms. Assuming that the measurement and monitoring costs are low, the assignment of rights or liability makes little difference. In Lueck's (1995) framework, the allocation question in this case depends on the value of the habitat in alternative uses, say agriculture, vis-à-vis its value to the species owner. Assuming that the two uses are mutually exclusive, the land will be used for agriculture if its value exceeds the value of the species and for species if the opposite values hold. If there are trade-offs at the margin, various combinations of agricultural and species output will be produced, and the combination will be determined through private bargaining.

under combinations of multiple ownership, there can be multiple ownership of species and land with separable costs or multiple ownership of species and land with nonseparable costs.

Single Species and Multiple Habitat Owners

Transaction costs rise with increasing numbers of habitat owners and species owners and with the costs of measuring and monitoring the costs associated with the spillovers between habitat and species. First, suppose that there are multiple habitat owners with a single migrating species owned by one entity and that the impact of migrating species on alternative land uses are measurable or separable. In the Coasean context, the habitat owners can either pay the species owner to mitigate losses in alternative uses of the habitat or the species owner can compensate the habitat owners for their losses. As with Coase's example of a train emitting sparks and burning crops, however, making landowners liable raises the problem of the free rider. If one landowner pays the train owner to reduce sparks, the other landowners can free ride. To overcome this problem, landowners must act collectively, and the transaction costs associated with collective action can negate the possibility of a contractual solution. Similarly, if one landowner pays the species owner to reduce the number of that species, other landowners will benefit without having to pay. Even if the impact of the species on each piece of land is easily separable, the greater the number of landowners, the greater the costs of collective action to overcome the free-rider problem. Hence, as Coase pointed out, the assignment of liability can lower transaction costs. In the case where the species migrate among multiple properties, assigning liability to the species owner can reduce transaction costs by eliminating the potential free-rider problem among habitat owners.

The case of multiple habitat owners and a single species owner is complicated further if the species depends on all the habitat but the contribution of each property is not separable. Joint production without separability implies that each landowner contributes to the overall production of the species, but the individual contributions cannot be easily measured or separated. This is similar to joint inputs in any production process wherein separating contributions of individual inputs is costly or where withholding the services of a specialized input reduces the rents from production. In this situation, the owner of a nonseparable input can engage in postcontractual opportunism and hold out for a higher share of any rents from production. Such a case begs for integration of ownership, as in Klein, Crawford, and Alchian (1978). Therefore, when a single species owner contracts with multiple landowners for whom contributions are nonseparable, transaction costs are lowered if habitat owners integrate and bargain as a unit with the species owner.

Multiple Species and Single Habitat Owner

Now switch the example to multiple species owners and a single habitat owner.[3] Assuming species cannot be restricted from the habitat, the free-rider

---

[3] This assumes that species are compatible, that is, they do not impose costs on one another. If they do, then there are potential contracting problems among species owners.

problem flips to the species owners. If any single species owner contracts with the habitat owner for provision of habitat, other species owners can enjoy the fruits of the contract without paying. In the Coasean context, this is equivalent to open range with multiple cattle owners. One cattle owner paying a crop owner for damages when other cattle cannot be excluded allows the others to free ride.[4] Making the crop owner bear the cost of grazing or pay each cattle owner to keep out his cattle reduces transaction costs associated with the free-rider problem. Hence, in this case we would expect liability to reside with the landowner so that he would negotiate individually with each species owner to obtain the optimal number of species.

Suppose, however, that the costs to the single habitat owner of hosting multiple species are nonseparable, meaning that it is not possible to discern the impact of an individual species on the output of land. If the habitat owner is required to pay owners to keep each species off his property, postcontractual opportunism raises its ugly head on the side of the species owners, each of whom can hold out for a larger share of any production rents. Under these circumstances, integration of ownership is a way to eliminate the holdout problem.

Multiple Species and Multiple Habitat Owners

The highest transaction costs occur when there are multiple owners on both sides of the transaction. If costs are separable, multiple owners of species and multiple owners of habitat all have an incentive to free ride. If costs are nonseparable, multiple owners of species and multiple owners of habitat have an incentive to act opportunistically and hold out for a larger share of the rents. In this situation, complete vertical integration is the solution. Though the transaction costs may be high, this integration can be done privately, or as Cheung (1983) points out in his discussion of "The Contractual Nature of the Firm," the ultimate form of vertical integration is the state where all inputs and outputs are owned by the sovereign government.

Integration of wildlife and habitat ownership via the political sector, of course, raises the prospect of other transaction costs. Often there are multiple owner/agencies for both species and habitat. For example, the ESA essentially assigns species ownership to the U.S. Fish and Wildlife Service, but state fish and wildlife agencies also claim some authority over species. The habitat, on the other hand, is controlled by the Forest Service, the Bureau of Land Management, the National Park Service, and state land agencies, to mention a few. Like private parties, the agencies can act as free riders or holdouts. Moreover, these owners/agencies are often restricted from contracting with one another to reduce species – witness the problem of reducing the number of bison migrating out of Yellowstone National Park into Montana – or

---

[4] Of course, in the case of cattle, branding is a way of lowering the cost of identifying who has paid.

from contracting to increase habitat – witness the difficulty of reintroducing species such as wolves or grizzly bears onto public lands. To make matters worse, the owner/agency is not a residual claimant with a clear objective function such as profit maximization or species maximization. This makes it difficult to hold agencies accountable and to reward them for producing the optimal number of species. Finally, the principal-agent problem is exacerbated in the political sector where it is difficult to know whether the agency is producing what the citizen/agents desire. In short, vertical integration through governmental ownership overcame the transaction costs of markets, but it still is no panacea.

OF COASE AND WILDLIFE

The various combinations outlined above can be illustrated with case studies of how contracting can solve wildlife habitat problems even in a world of positive transaction costs.[5] Each case shows how transaction costs have been overcome to assign rights and liability, engage in contracts, and measure and monitor contract performance. Because the real world is not as simple as the analytical framework outlined above, the examples do not dovetail exactly with the combinations in Figure 12.1, and they do not necessarily involve endangered species. Nonetheless, the examples show how Coasean bargaining results in integration of species and/or habitat ownership. Moreover, these examples do not imply that markets can overcome all transaction costs; in some cases, collective action will be necessary. But these examples do suggest that markets may be able to do more than we give them credit for.

Before considering some specific examples, we should recall that Coase did account for the possibility of fencing, which can be a solution to the species problem. Whether parties will use fencing depends on the cost of fencing relative to the value of the damage caused to land in other uses and the value of the wildlife. Zoos and wildlife parks are cases of the fencing solution applied to wildlife where the value of the land as "habitat" is greater than the value in alternative uses, where the wildlife owner is liable for damage caused by the wildlife to neighbors, and where the owner can exclude potential free riders to capture the value of the wildlife. Under these conditions, fencing becomes a viable mechanism for internalizing the externalities. Similarly, fencing is a way of excluding species that do damage to habitat or excluding species that have not paid for access. In the cases examined below, fencing can play an integral role in the private solution to habitat provision.

Single Species and a Single Habitat Owner

The first example of a single species and single owner comes from the Fort Apache Indian Reservation in eastern Arizona. The reservation boasts a herd of

---

[5] These case studies are drawn from Anderson and Leal (1997).

7,500 free-ranging elk on 750,000 acres of diverse habitat ranging from oak chaparral at lower elevations to mixed conifer forests at higher elevations.

Hunting records over two decades give some idea of the success elk hunters enjoy on the Fort Apache Reservation. From 1977 to 1995, nontribal hunters took ninety bull elk that made either Boone and Crockett or Safari Club record books. One of these, in the "nontypical" category, scored 445 points and ranked second in the world in 1996. By comparison, this is about the same number of record elk that have been taken from the entire state of Montana since record keeping began in 1932. Since 1980, nontribal hunters have enjoyed a 90 to 95 percent success rate on guided trophy elk hunts, with an average score hovering around 366 Boone and Crockett points.

Let there be no misunderstanding; the trophy elk population on Fort Apache is not solely the work of mother nature. The resource base is large, the habitat is prime, and, according to reservation biologists, the genetics of the herd are ideal for producing trophy elk. But management has also played a pivotal role in producing trophy elk on the reservation.

Prior to 1977, elk hunting on the reservation provided good hunting in relation to nearby national forest lands. Still, it was nowhere near the quality it is today. Then, the Arizona Game and Fish Department maintained responsibility for wildlife management on the reservation. It used its personnel to patrol the reservation during hunting season. Typical of state game policies, the state agency increased hunter opportunities by issuing 700 nontribal hunting licenses priced at $150 each for any size antler elk. The revenues from license sales went to the state rather than the tribe, and management left residents of the reservation totally out of the equation.

Though the Arizona Game and Fish Department might have maximized hunter numbers, it did not maximize hunting quality. For the period 1970–1976, only three record-book elk were harvested on the reservation. Moreover, the situation was likely to get worse considering the evidence from other states such as Montana, Idaho, and Washington where large numbers of hunters result in overharvesting of immature bulls, the seed crop for future trophy bulls (see Wenders 1995).

Fortunately for both the tribe and the reservation's elk, tribal leaders recognized that they could do a better job and earn significant returns for the tribe by integrating their ownership of the habitat with ownership of the elk. To capture these potential benefits, the tribe assumed control of hunting on the reservation and implemented its own management philosophy. In 1977, with the backing of Tribal Chairman Ronnie Lupe and the eleven-member Tribal Council, Phillip Stago, director of the Fort Apache recreation department, informed the state that the tribe was assuming complete control of all hunting and fishing on the reservation. Eventually, the state acquiesced, removing state wardens from the reservation for the 1977 hunting season.

The tribe's first step toward quality management was the reduction of hunting pressure on immature bulls. It accomplished this by ending the general (any antler) state-sanctioned bull elk hunt and replacing it with the trophy elk hunt.

Elk hunting permits declined dramatically from 700 under state management in 1977 to thirty under tribal control in 1979. At the same time, the tribe increased the price of a permit tenfold from $150, the price charged by the state, to $1,500 in 1979, and revenues from the sale of permits were retained by the tribe.

It took the tribe several years and a U.S. Supreme Court case to get the state completely out of wildlife management, but by 1981, the tribe finally had complete control. Under tribal ownership of the species and the land, the quality of hunting blossomed. Mature bulls as a percentage of all bulls observed on the reservation increased dramatically and now stands at sixty bulls for every hundred cows. Not only did the number of mature bulls increase significantly, the number of record-book elk also increased dramatically.

On the other side of the globe, African tribes are using property rights to solve wildlife and habitat conflicts. And as the following story suggests, the conflicts can be significant when they involve elephants.

> Darkness comes quickly to the East Caprivi, being so close to the Equator. Bevan Munyali, a village game scout, appointed by his community who live in this region of Namibia, helps light the fires.
>
> Together with the other men, they will spend the night in this farmer's corn field, trying to protect their food crops from the elephants. Usually it is the lone bulls that come, as they have each night this week, trampling the crops and eating hundreds of pounds of corn as they pass through the area. Bevan is worried. He must balance the farmer's concerns regarding the elephant with his own task, which is to help his community to conserve their natural resources and the wildlife in the area.
>
> Hours slip past. Bevan and the farmer doze beside the glowing embers. But then the crack of dry branches wakes them, indicating that something big is moving in their direction. Two fully grown bull elephants crash into the field. The farmer shouts to wake the others, and in unison they start banging steel pots together. The elephants turn to face the noise, their sensitive ears flapping in aggravation. Then they charge. Three tons of muscle standing eighteen feet high at the shoulder, the bulls rush forward, sending the farmer and his family running for safety.
>
> Realizing the danger, Bevan fires two blasts from his shotgun into the air, in the hope that the elephants retreat. Instead, one of the bulls wheels around and heads straight toward him. Defenseless, Bevan retreats from the field. The elephants continue on their way, eating and trampling the ripe corn underfoot. No doubt, the farmer and his family will be short of food for the remainder of the year. (Victoria Hylton, Southern Wild Productions, n.d., 5)

This account of a peasant farmer's struggle against wild animals is rarely portrayed in Hollywood versions of African wildlife, but it shows the potential costs to Africans trying to sustain a living off their land. Wildlife management problems result because indigenous people trying to live off the land often have to compete with wildlife; in other words, wildlife is a liability rather than an asset. These people generally resent the fact that land is being set aside for animals rather than for people. Moreover, out of the parks and reserves come lions, leopards, elephants, and hippopotamus that range onto communal lands where they can destroy crops, livestock, and occasionally people.

Inspired by wildlife experts and environmental groups such as the World Wildlife Fund, the Zimbabwe government changed the incentives by changing the ownership. The government's innovative wildlife management program is known as CAMPFIRE (Communal Area Management Plan for Indigenous Resources). This "entrepreneurial approach to rural development" (Environmental Consultants (Pvt) Ltd. 1990, 3) is based on the principle that the benefits from wildlife must go to those who pay the financial and social costs of coexisting with wild animals. The CAMPFIRE concept essentially devolves ownership of wildlife to local communities that can profit from them.

The Nyaminyami District Council with a human population of 35,000 and communal lands totaling 363,000 hectares offers a prime example of how CAMPFIRE works. In 1989, its inaugural year, Nyaminyami's CAMPFIRE project generated Z$272,000 from safari hunting and another Z$47,000 from culling to keep local wildlife populations under control. With the major capital costs of Z$201,933 covered by funds donated by conservation groups, the district had Z$16,000 to distribute among the twelve separate communities after paying operating and administrative costs and allocating 12 percent for capital investment and reserves (Thresher 1993, 45).[6]

Another early CAMPFIRE success came in the Beitbridge District. However, unlike Nyaminyami, the Beitbridge project was financed completely by the returns from wildlife. Recognizing that different communities within the district make more sacrifices to provide wildlife habitat, the Beitbridge Council distributed wildlife profits unequally to communities within the district, giving more to those communities that produced more, higher-valued animals.

In 1990, the Beitbridge District CAMPFIRE project generated Z$50,235 from hunting. Of that amount, the community of Chikwarakwara received Z$43,930, or 87 percent of the total, because it was the top wildlife producer. Two other neighboring communities received much smaller amounts because of lower animal numbers. National parks also paid the Beitbridge District Council Z$46,000 for revenues accrued from past safari hunting, from which Chikwarakwara received another Z$20,000. Free to determine how their proceeds would be used, the people of Chikwarakwara decided to pay each of the 149 households in the community Z$200 as a wildlife dividend. The remainder of the earnings went toward building a school and purchasing a corn grinding mill. Though the Z$200 dividend may not seem like a lot to wealthy westerners, it represented nearly a doubling of average annual income for each family. Changing attitudes toward wildlife are becoming apparent among the people involved with CAMPFIRE. "Now the people of Beitbridge are reported to be talking seriously about how to control poaching. They are considering the possibility of reducing a household's cash payment

---

[6] At the time one Zimbabwean dollar was equivalent to U.S. $0.20.

by the value of any animal poached by any of its members, e.g., Z$75 for an impala" (Thresher 1993, 50).

CAMPFIRE projects in other districts have taken their cue from these early successes. The Binga District project capitalizes on its long shoreline at the western end of Lake Kariba and the adjacent Chizaria National Park that forms a repository for wildlife that roam onto communal lands. The project includes a lease with a private hunting safari operator and joint ventures with two photographic safari operators. Plans are also under way for a commercial fishing venture. The Hwange District is developing the "scenic attractions and natural resources" near the Zambezi River and Victoria Falls by forming joint ventures with two photographic safari operators who are building tourist camps in the areas (Environmental Consultants (Pvt) Ltd. 1990, 23). Bulalima Mangwe District has set aside a marshy area west of the Natal River for an elephant herd that forms the basis for safari hunting agreements between the district council and private operators.

Single Species and Multiple Habitat Owners

Separability

A perfect example of multiple landowners interfacing with a single species owner is the unlikely case of a predator, the wolf. Realizing the wolf reintroduction into the northern Rockies was so controversial because it would require livestock to bear some costs from predation, Hank Fischer, Northern Rockies representative for Defenders of Wildlife, took an innovative tack. He and his group claimed liability for the potential predator. In 1987, Fischer raised a fund of approximately $100,000 by selling prints by a well-known Montana artist depicting wolves howling around the geysers of Yellowstone National Park. There may still be some free riders among people who value knowing wolves are roaming the mountains of Montana, but voluntary contributions tied to a poster were sufficient to put a compensation fund in place. Defenders hopes to keep a least $100,000 in the fund at all times.

Fischer announced that his group would use these funds to compensate livestock owners for losses due to wolf predation. From 1987 to October 1999, the compensation program paid approximately $96,310 to approximately 100 producers for 132 cattle, 280 sheep, and 10 other. In each of these cases the offending wolves have been controlled and the predations stopped. Says Fischer, "We hope this solid record of responsiveness brings the one thing we seek in exchange: tolerance on the part of ranchers and other members of the public for wolves that do not bother livestock. We remain committed to upholding our side of the bargain."

Of course, some controversy arises over the burden of proof that claimed livestock predation is due to wolves. Defenders of Wildlife defers to the Montana Department of Livestock's predator control officer whose responsibility it is to investigate livestock kills. If he says it is a wolf, the fund pays;

if he is not sure, it does not. For livestock owners who experience losses and who are convinced wolves are the culprits, this is seen as a flaw in the system. But any system of liability requires proof and will therefore have doubters who bear uncompensated losses because the burden of proof is not met. The important part of this story is that it shows how assignment, or in this case acceptance, of liability for the species provides a Coasean solution to the single species, multiple habitat owner problem.[7]

Nonseparability

Elk provides an example of a single species interfacing with multiple habitat owners whose contributions are nonseparable. The elk species migrate among properties, spending spring on one property raising their young, summer and fall on another property grazing, and winter on another struggling to survive until the spring thaw. Separating and measuring the contribution of each parcel of land is impossible because each is important to their survival. Migrating elk provide a classic single species–multiple landownership case where contracting is costly and some form of vertical integration is useful.

Ted and John Flynn, third-generation brothers who live on their family cattle ranch near Townsend, Montana, have overcome the multiple habitat owner problem by organizing hunters and ranchers into a group called Greyson Creek Meadows Recreation, Inc. Through this organization, recreation members pay a fee for access to the land owned by several different ranchers. In former days, hunters could range for miles in any direction without seeing other people and without worry about trespass. But this began to change in the 1980s. Hassled by increasing hunting pressure, landowners began to restrict access to their private lands. With only a few hunters seeking access, landowners could be neighborly and provide free access, but population and hunting pressure were increasing the cost to the landowner of providing access. Facing more restrictions on access, the Flynns and their friends had to adjust if they wanted to preserve habitat and access. Unlike the Fort Apache Reservation that is one contiguous ownership unit, land ownership around the Flynn ranch is fragmented, ranging from small cabin sites to thousands of acres, and these smaller units cannot provide the habitat diversity the elk need.

Obtaining access to the land in fragmented ownership at a reasonable price required that the Flynns overcome the transaction costs by organizing Greyson Creek Meadows Recreation, Inc., in 1987. According to the organization's rules, members pay a fee, and Greyson Creek corporation pays ranchers

---

[7] Of course, this solution is not a true property rights solution because Fischer is not legally liable for all wolves. If the wolf population grows, there is some point at which economics would say there are enough wolves, but will Fischer be willing to bear the liability for this many wolves? And if he is, he might decide that some wolves should be shot, but the U.S. Fish and Wildlife Service may not let him. Hence there is no pressure toward the optimal number.

for access and, in some cases, an additional fee if animals are harvested on a specific piece of property. The group also posts and patrols the land against trespass, carries liability insurance, and agrees to abide by several other rules including restrictions on driving on the properties. For the landowner, this arrangement removes most of the hassles of managing hunters and provides additional income. In 1998, members of Greyson Creek paid an annual fee of $450 for individuals and $500 for families for combined fees of approximately $15,000 for approximately 30,000 acres of private land.

While not as productive as large, contiguous properties, the Greyson Creek properties have abundant numbers of elk and deer, and increasing populations of black bear, mountain lions, coyotes, and eagles. With vehicular access restricted, both game and nongame species are being found in areas where previously there was too much human pressure. Members are encouraged to harvest the more mature elk and deer so as to improve the quality of the herds. The Flynns have cut some timber on their property, but they did so selectively to balance timber profits, cattle grazing, and wildlife habitat. Though there are no annual game censuses, Greyson Creek members agree that the restricted access and more systematic management of the properties have increased the number of species they see and improved the quality of the recreation experience.

Multiple Species and Single Habitat Owner

Separability

Game ownership rules in South Africa encourage land management that accommodates multiple species on single land units. In South Africa, landowners who fence their land according to governmental requirements own the wildlife species within the fences, even if the wildlife had been free ranging prior to the fences. Under these rules the single landowner can become the owner of multiple species as well. This integrated owner then often contracts with professional hunters who carry out management practices and provide paying customers.

Angus Brown and Clive Perkins are professional hunters who have contracted with Piet Lamprecht, the owner of approximately 20,000 acres in the northern Transvaal Province of South Africa. According to their contract, Angus Brown Safaris provides the accommodations and guide services while Piet provides the habitat. In this case the accommodations include beautiful African huts with walls woven from reeds and roofs thatched from grass. Horns from animals indigenous to the area adorn the walls, and skins cover the floors. Food in the camp is typical South African fare highlighted by the wild meat killed by the hunters. Natural pans and developed water holes provide water for the animals in this land on the edge of the Kalahari Desert. At these water points, archery hunters sit for hours in tree stands or ground blinds waiting for animals to come for their daily drink. Of course, all of these capital improvements are possible only because hunters are willing to pay a fee for the services.

Perhaps more important, however, is the impact that hunting revenues have on land management. As land owner, Piet Lamprecht gets a share of the daily hunting fees paid by the customers. He also gets nearly two-thirds of the trophy fees paid for each animal. These trophy fees are crucial to the incentives faced by Angus, Clive, and Piet, for unlike most hunting in North America where hunting fees generally go to state or federal agencies, fees in South Africa go to the people who have the largest stake in wildlife management. Like a menu at a restaurant, the hunter faces a price list for the animals available: Tsessebe $1,500; Zebra $750; Kudu $700; Wildebeest $700; Blesbok $250; Warthog $100; Impala $80; and the list goes on.[8] Angus, Clive, and Piet mutually agree on these prices that reflect the relative scarcity of the species. With warthogs and impala abundant, their prices are low; with tsessebe and waterbuck scarce in the region, their prices are high.

What impact do these fees have? On the demand side for the hunter facing a budget constraint, the trophy fees force a careful weighing of preferences against price. Hunters might think a tsessebe would make a nice addition to the trophy room, but the price of $1,500 translates into two or three of the less scarce big animals such as zebra or kudu. Indeed, though not available on Piet's property, Angus Brown Safaris can arrange hunting for elephant or rhino, the two more scarce of the hunted species, at a price of $12,000 and $28,000. Needless to say, this reduces the quantity demanded by pricing most hunters out of the market.

The supply-side impacts of these incentives are important because they compensate the landowner for providing a home for the wildlife. Piet's ranch used to be mainly a cattle operation with some cultivated fields of peanuts and cotton, but the potential for hunting profits has changed this. All but a handful of cattle have been removed from the land. Interior fences necessary for cattle management are removed to give wildlife a freer range, and water points are converted from troughs to more natural water holes. Because of hunting revenues, instead of carrying several hundred brahma cattle, the land supports approximately 500 impala, 150 kudu, 100 wildebeest, 150 gemsbuck, 50 tsessebe, 50 waterbuck, and numerous other species. Angus, Clive, and Piet begin each hunting season with an estimate of the number of harvestable animals and agree on prices for each species. They consider ways to improve the habitat and whether it would be profitable to invest in importing other species, such as cape buffalo, indigenous to the region, but now largely absent. Without the profits from hunting, less habitat would be available for the indigenous species of the Kalahari, and fewer animals would survive.

Well-known safari writer Peter Hathaway Capstick captured the important nexus between hunting and habitat management in South Africa.

> The interesting thing is that untold hundreds of thousands of hectares and *morgen* that even a few years ago were scrub grazing for a mix of game and

---

[8] These are 1996 prices.

cattle have now been entirely allocated to game. Why? Economics, as always. Game pays its own way, eats nearly anything, is more resistant to disease and predators and generally produces a higher and better use for the land.... Even the old enemies become assets to the farmer who switches from cattle to game. One friend of mine used to lose as many as thirty calves a season to leopards.... Now, those same leopards are worth a cool $1,000 to $1,500 [in 1999 the values would be approximately $2,600 to $3,000] each to sport hunters, not a bad trade-off for animals that caused a liability of well over ten grand and had to be poisoned! Tell me, is that bad for leopards?... This sort of thinking is, then, the basis of the modern mechanics of the safari industry in Africa, whether in South Africa or Sudan. Once again, the elemental economic rules apply, whether to the garment district of New York City or the wait-a-bit thorn of the Luangwa Valley or the Okavango Swamp: What can justify its existence stays, what can't must go, whether a skirt-manufacturing plant or a herd of impala. Sorry, I don't make the rules. (1983, 18–19)

Nonseparability

An 18,000-acre area known as the Pine Butte Swamp in central Montana is an ecosystem that provides the last remaining prairie grizzly bear habitat in the lower forty-eight United States. Because of interconnections between all of the species, especially the plants eaten in the early spring by the grizzlies descending from their snow-covered hibernation habitat to the lowlands to replenish lost reserves and the livestock that might be preyed upon by the grizzlies, separating the reciprocal Coasean costs would be virtually impossible. If grizzly bears eat livestock, there are clear costs, but if livestock eat vegetation valuable to the grizzlies, the costs go in the opposite direction. When other species such as deer, big horn sheep, eagles, and many others are added to the equation, separability is even more difficult.

To avoid negotiating over these costs, The Nature Conservancy (TNC) purchased the entire 18,000 acres and manages them as a unit so that the costs are internalized to the firm known as the Pine Butte Swamp Preserve. As owner of the preserve, TNC attempts to maximize the ecosystem value as seen by the conservancy, but it also cannot ignore the opportunity cost of commodity values. Therefore, TNC leases grazing to nearby ranchers for approximately $10,000 per year, but it does not allow cattle in the preserve when the grizzlies are there. This minimizes the potential cost if a bear were to prey on livestock. TNC also operates a guest ranch on the property, offering guided nature tours and access to hiking trails, fishing, horseback riding, animal viewing, and even paleontological excursions to the famous Egg Mountain. In effect, by taking ownership of the land and responsibility for the costs of grizzly bears while on their land, the conservancy has become a joint owner of the resources for whom costs are internalized. This example shows how ownership integration can reduce Coasean transaction costs and encourage more efficient resource allocation.

Multiple Species and Multiple Habitat Owners

Separability

Migrating waterfowl provide an example of multiple species utilizing habitat owned by multiple landowners with impact of species identifiable and separable. For example, ducks migrate over vast territories, nesting in Canada, flying across the United States, and wintering in Mexico. While all the habitat contributes to the survival of duck, the nesting habitat is critical. Between the 1950s and the 1990s, North American duck migrations fell from over 100 million to less than 50 million due to the loss of nesting habitat, mainly on thousands of private farms in the upper midwestern United States and in southern Canada.

Recognizing there was a problem, Charles Potter, then director of the Delta Waterfowl Foundation, essentially claimed "liability" for the ducks while they were nesting. Potter recognized that farmers in the region known as the prairie pothole region were draining potholes to create additional farmland. This was creating a classic reciprocal cost Coasean problem; draining the potholes was impacting waterfowl, but keeping the habitat meant less farmland. To internalize the costs, Delta Waterfowl Foundation, supported entirely from private contributions from individuals, companies, conservation organizations, and private foundations, contracts with farmers to produce ducks by protecting the nesting habitat around prairie potholes on their land. Delta Waterfowl believed that the Adopt-A-Pothole program could make a significant impact because 95 percent of the ducks raised on the prairies of the upper Midwest and southern Canada are produced on private farmlands. Prior to the program, the landowner had little or no economic incentive to maintain or restore pothole habitat and may have even faced a disincentive from government farm programs that subsidized draining potholes.[9] As a result, over the last fifty years, hundreds of thousands of acres of potential duck factories were lost.

The Adopt-A-Pothole program created a way of raising capital from hundreds of individual contributors in the United States and Canada by giving them a sense of ownership in a pothole. Each contributor receives an aerial photograph of his or her adopted pothole, a quarterly report on its status, and an annual estimate of duck production. Adopt-A-Pothole achieves its goal through innovative contractual arrangements consisting of multiyear land leases and production contracts. The land leases pay farmers approximately $7 per acre to maintain pothole habitat and $30 per acre to restore pothole habitat. Production contracts, on the other hand, pay directly for duck production, thus giving the farmer an incentive to invest in improving nesting habitat.

The program has been overwhelmingly successful both in terms of raising capital and increasing duck production. Contributions totaled nearly $1 million after only two years of operation, and the list of supporters grew from 250

---

[9] See Anderson and Leal (1991, 57) for further discussion of the impact of farm subsidies.

to over 1,000 individuals and organizations. By 1994, some 18,000 pothole sites had been enrolled from farms in Manitoba, Minnesota, and North Dakota, providing nesting habitat for Mallards, Canvasbacks, Shoveler, Bluewinged Teal, Greenwinged Teal, Gadwalls, Lesser Scaup, Redheads, and Pintails. These adopted potholes are fast becoming North America's duck factories. For instance, nest density is twice as great for adopted sites compared to unadopted sites, and nesting success averages 51 percent for adopted sites compared to 10–15 percent for unadopted ones. Moreover, for those adopted potholes using a special Delta Waterfowl Foundation nesting device affording greater protection from predators, nesting success was an astounding 90 percent (Delta Waterfowl Foundation 1993). Such early accomplishments have earned the program accolades from the conservation community. On June 8, 1994, the U.S. Wildlife Service named the Adopt-A-Pothole program the winner of its National Wetlands Conservation Award for the prairie pothole region.

Nonseparability

As a father of modern ecology, Aldo Leopold understood very well the problems associated with multiple species and multiple landowners. Throughout his career, Leopold wrestled with how economics "both motivates and constrains land use decisions" (Palmini 1993, 38). He was by no means sanguine that markets could address all of conservation's ills,[10] but he did recognize the role of the individual landowner. Leopold challenged "the growing assumption that bigger buying [of public land] is a substitute for private conservation practice" (quoted in Flader and Callicott 1991, 196–97). In his essay "Conservation Economics," Leopold concludes that "conservation will ultimately boil down to rewarding the private landowner who conserves the public interest" (quoted in Flader and Callicott 1991, 202).

Today the Leopold legacy lives on through the entirely private 1,500-acre Leopold Memorial Reserve owned and managed by The Sand County Foundation. The reserve includes the farm from which Leopold's ideas emanated. The Sand County Foundation, a private, nonprofit organization established in September 1965, created the reserve and oversees its restoration. The reserve itself serves as an experimental laboratory for testing new methods for restoring natural ecological processes on lands that have been intensively farmed or logged, damaged, and abandoned. Included are cultivated lands, oak savannas, sedge meadows, prairie grasslands, and wetlands that provide habitat for wildlife.

In addition to the original farm, tracts of land have been incorporated into the reserve's management system through agreements with neighboring landowners. Each of the owners participating in the reserve has agreed to refrain from certain land-use practices detrimental to the restoration of natural habitats. Landowners retain title to their property and agree to manage

---

[10] Neither did he blindly accept government as the only response. See Leopold (1966, 249).

individual parcels in concert with the objectives of the entire reserve. The original agreement bound landowners to a five-year term, to be extended indefinitely unless formally terminated by a majority of the landowners party to the agreement. By the agreement, participating landowners take a proactive approach toward restoring the natural amenities. They maintain a prescribed fire management program to enhance soil vitality and forest under story growth; carry out selective timber cuts to increase biological diversity; conduct planting programs to supplement natural habitat and wildlife foods; sponsor baseline inventory and peer-reviewed research; and carry out a coordinated trespass control program to protect the area from vandalism, poaching, and littering. In addition, the landowners allow the Sand County Foundation's scientific team of ecologists, biologists, and hydrologists to monitor and manage the reserve as a single unit. In establishing these arrangements with its neighbors, the foundation took Leopold's words on compensating landowners to heart. Reed Coleman, Sand County's chairman, describes how this was done.

> A couple of us decided we ought to do something about curtailing development near the shack. We went to seven or eight landowners of various types and convinced them to enter into a voluntary agreement.... As compensation, we would pay that landowner's property taxes. We developed these agreements in 1965, before conservation easements had been discovered, and they have lasted almost thirty years. (Coleman 1994, 19)

The Sand County Foundation uses the reserve as an important vehicle to convey its message of land stewardship. According to its brochure (1989), the foundation is "in the practice of healing the biologic community, with its human population on the lands and waters of the northeastern Sand County, Wisconsin. We do so to provide one model of effective stewardship. This is not to generate precise replicas, but in order to enable other private landowners and committed conservationists to find their own way back to the good earth."

Education on the reserve includes primary school visits, invited conservation "working tours," and seminars for corporate leaders. At every level, emphasis is placed on participating in active conservation work on private lands. Adult visitors to the reserve enjoy Leopold's practical approach to conservation, meaning they get their hands dirty. Recent projects include picking and sacking of prairie seeds for prairie restoration, surveying of tracts for weedy plants and removing them, and assisting with the prescribed fires.

The success of the ongoing restoration program is quite impressive compared to the paucity of wildlife in the 1930s. The reserve now boasts resident bald eagles, otters, black bears, and deer. Meanwhile, continual monitoring of the reserve and the various conservation practices provides a long-term experiment in land management. By virtue of private, voluntary action, the landowners are finding ways to enhance the biological diversity of their land through good stewardship. For other landowners interested in protecting natural amenities and enhancing the long-term productivity of their land, the reserve provides an effective tool for practical environmental education.

In the spirit of Leopold, the foundation continues to test new ideas in restoration under the direction of Brent Haglund, executive director of the foundation. One of Haglund's recent creations is the "Quality Hunting Ecology Program" linking wildlife management to ecosystem restoration. Recognizing that too many deer can disrupt the ecological balance and that most hunters want to shoot buck deer, the program controls deer population on the reserve by requiring that hunters earn a buck by first harvesting two does.[11] The success of the program is demonstrated by (1) the increase in the number of indicator species such as white pine and white oak whose recruitment is essentially nil throughout the Midwest because deer overbrowse the saplings; (2) the improved age and sex ratio of the deer population; and (3) better resource stewardship practiced by landowners who take more interest in wildlife habitat and hunters who litter and vandalize less. Under Haglund's leadership, the program is being implemented on thousands of acres of Wisconsin Power and Light company lands where the company has reduced land management costs and improved hunting opportunities.

Another example of an innovative contractual approach to multiple species–multiple landownership problems is found in South Africa. "We are asking companies to invest in conservation not to donate to it," says Dave Varly, co-founder of Conservation Corporation, a company founded in South Africa in 1990. Mr. Varly and deputy chairman Alan Berstein make no apologies for the fact that they are trying to turn a profit from wildlife. To the contrary, they, along with many other conservationists in southern Africa, believe that having profits as the driving force is the key to ensuring that wildlife and wildlife habitat will be around in the future. Messrs. Varly and Berstein created one of the first large-scale businesses to invest in wildlife conservation. Prior to forming Conscorp, Varly owned Landolozi Reserve, one of South Africa's most successful commercial private wildlife ranches, and Berstein was managing director of a company that raised money for investment in sub-Saharan Africa. As of 1995, the partners had raised $40 million[12] and had plans for a $20 million expansion project. In addition to Landolozi, Conscorp opened Phinda Reserve comprising 17,000 hectares of private land; negotiated an innovative contract with Kruger National Park that incorporates the 14,000-hectare Ngala private reserve on the western boundary into the park, but gives Conscorp exclusive operating rights; and established Singita Reserve with 15,000 hectares where the big five (elephant, rhinoceros, cape buffalo, lion, and cheetah) can be seen. The corporation is also diversifying beyond its initial four game lodges in South Africa by developing new game reserves in other southern African countries.

---

[11] Telefax transmittal from the Sand County Foundation dated July 28, 1995.
[12] All dollar figures were computed assuming a ratio of 3.66 South African rand to the dollar.

Though wildlife ranching is not new to South Africa, the innovative con-tracting that Conscorp uses to make wildlife pay is. The corporation generally owns only small land parcels, enough to accommodate its lodges. For the rest, Conscorp contracts with surrounding landowners for conservation ser-vices. Rather than having to tie up capital in vast tracts, Conscorp has con-tracted for access to private lands for game viewing and hunting. The articles of association that Conscorp developed to contract with private landowners included in the Mun-Ya-Wana Game Reserve in South Africa's northern Transval illustrates their innovative approach to contracting. Mun-Ya-Wana encompasses 30,000 hectares. Among other purposes, the articles state that the purposes of the reserve are "to promote and conserve endemic wildlife and habitat within the confines of the area ... ; to establish the Reserve as a sanctuary in perpetuity for endemic wildlife and habitat so as to enable sustainable resource utilisation ... ; to endeavour to increase the area of the Reserve ... ;" and "to maximise the long term economic and ecological value of the properties .... "[13] Above all, the company tries to minimize congestion because "large numbers of persons on the Reserve are undesirable."

Because Conscorp is catering to tourists who want to enjoy game in the natural African bush, the company strives to keep all development on the reserve "congruent with the principle of minimal environmental impact and minimal aesthetic impact." Road use is strictly limited to those specified in the Articles of Association. Game drives must avoid residential areas and are coordinated through a radio network, with each member responsible for erecting and maintaining a base station. The number of game drive vehicles and boats is controlled by the company to avoid congestion problems. The architecture of all the structures erected on the reserve must be "ecologically and aesthetically sympathetic," and "the siting of structures and services on and to the reserve are placed in unobtrusive places so as not to have an adverse effect on the surroundings." To promote wildlife and maintain a nat-ural setting, landowners agree not to keep domestic animals, including dogs and cats. They can build structures on their property, but only with written consent from the company and only after submitting detailed drawing and artist's impressions. To maintain the integrity of the reserve, landowners cannot subdivide their properties, cannot undertake other commercial activi-ties such as prospecting or establishing tent villages or caravan parks without agreement from the company.

Why would landowners be willing to agree to all of these restrictions by including their lands in the reserve? In a word, profits. Conscorp estimates that dry land cattle ranching earns approximately $21 per hectare per year and cropping earns $68. This compares to nearly $200 to $300 per hectare per

---

[13] All references to terms of agreement between Conscorp and the landowners come from the Articles of Association available from Conscorp.

year in Conscorp reserves. Conscorp director, Howard Greach, says, "We are demonstrating a form of land use involving wildlife as a sort of cash crop."

The perimeters of Conscorp properties are fenced with eight-foot-high game fence made of twelve strands of high-tensile smooth wire, and game within cannot be "tethered or enclosed in any cage or fence" and "irrespective of that game's ownership, shall be entitled to graze, browse or feed anywhere on a reserve." To guarantee that animals cannot leave the reserve, each landowner is responsible for erecting to company standards a perimeter fence for the land under his control, but maintenance of the fence is the responsibility of the company. By the same token, to ensure the most natural setting and to guarantee free range for the animals, the landowner must "lift and remove the fences which surround or traverse his land, save where the fence in question is a perimeter fence . . . or a protection fence immediately adjacent to a dwelling." The company erects gates and garrisons guards at the gates to control access.

Because game is free to move anywhere on the reserve, Conscorp has written a very detailed contract specifying the rules for culling, hunting, and capturing. Prior to admission into the company, a census is conducted of the number and species of game for each landowner. If this census shows that the landowner's game populations are insufficient to contribute to the overall purposes, "then the prospective member shall be obliged to supplement the species, in kind or in cash as may be agreed with the Company." Each year another census is conducted to determine net changes in game populations, and the company allocates "proportionally to each land controller the overall increase or decrease in game numbers . . . ." Any disagreements over numbers are arbitrated by the state wildlife agency known as the parks board, and decisions are final and binding on all parties. Members are not allowed to introduce any new species to the reserve without prior written consent of the company, but consent may only be withheld if the species is not indigenous to the region. The company can also introduce species with those introduced becoming the property of the company. The agreement allows landowners to "cull, hunt, or capture game" provided the activities follow the laws, regulations, and rules of the parks board and provided the landowner obtains a permit from the company specifying the number of game to be taken. Any member who did not contribute any of a particular specie to the collective herd is not entitled "to hunt, cull or claim ownership or benefit from the proceeds of any sale of that specie except where a separate agreement is in place." The hunt, cull, or capture must take place within the landowner's boundaries. If an injured animal escapes to land controlled by another, "only the leader of the hunt and one tracker may follow the specie of game in question onto the land of another member in accordance with the rules laid down from time to time."

Special provisions are made for the introduction of a species, such as the rhinoceros, for trophy hunting. Again, the animal cannot be prevented from ranging over the reserve, but when it wanders onto land controlled by another, "the landowners will be obliged to agree on a method of resolving this problem and allowing the owner of the introduced animal to hunt the animal on the property where it has moved to. In the event that the parties cannot agree, it will fall upon the disciplinary committee of the directors or failing that the Directors to rule as a matter of urgency in this matter to achieve a speedy solution." Through such contracting, Conscorp has overcome the transaction costs that could preclude a Coasean solution.

IMPLICATIONS FOR THE ESA

Given the reciprocal nature of costs associated with endangered species, the acrimony surrounding endangered species preservation is quite understandable. Though efficiency may be invariant to the assignment of liability in a Coasean world of low transaction costs, the distribution of wealth is not, and it is the distributional issue that fuels the endangered species fire. Unfortunately, the process of settling the distributional issue of who should be liable for endangered species has efficiency implications as well because the rights are up for grabs. Therefore, perhaps the most important conclusion from a Coasean view of endangered species is that the locus of rights should be established as quickly as possible.

But the view of endangered species through Coase-colored glasses has further important implications. In resolving the locus of rights and hence liability, ownership of both habitat and species should be put into the hands of residual claimants who have the ability to trade those rights. The contracting examples presented above occur because private actors have established a residual claim on the rents from wildlife and are able to contract for the relevant inputs to produce those rents. Hank Fischer's wolf compensation scheme, for example, works because Hank has to worry about repeat dealings with ranchers and because he and his group capture some of the benefits associated with the existence of wolves. South African wildlife are thriving because landowners who supply habitat are residual claimants who can contract over inputs. The lesson is that we should do all we can to lower the transaction costs of defining and enforcing rights to species and habitat and of trading those rights. Especially where there is a single species causing identifiable damages for multiple habitat owners, making the species owner liable is a way of eliminating the free-rider problem. This can be applied to the bison problem in Yellowstone. If the National Park Service were liable for any infection of livestock by brucellosis, the agency would become much more innovative in its solutions to the problem. From the examples given, it appears that integration of ownership is often an important way of reducing transaction costs and promoting private contracting, especially if the species can be fenced in and the nonpayers fenced out. Encouraging landowners to consolidate ownership for the purpose of providing species habitat and allowing them to profit from selling access to those species could mimic the approach taken in South Africa (Leal and Grewell 1999). This would mean that state fish and game agencies would have to give up their strong opposition to private claims to species.

Ownership and private contracting are much less likely to work when the rights reside with owners who cannot be made liable, who do not have a claim on the residual, and who cannot negotiate exchanges with other input owners. The National Park Service is not liable for its bison or wolves. The U.S. Forest Service cannot profit from reserving its lands for habitat. In fact, it only profits from leasing habitat to logging companies who want to cut trees or ranchers who want to graze cattle. And even if it could profit, regulations often restrict transfers of habitat to noncommodity uses. Hence, the Bureau of Land Management has been prohibited from letting grazing permittees transfer their permits to environmental groups on a willing buyer-willing seller basis.

The trump card for nearly all endangered species problems is that the benefits of preservation cannot be measured and therefore captured by a residual claimant. Using the free-rider argument, many environmentalists have argued that governmental ownership of habitat and regulation of private land is a necessary solution to species preservation. Though the free-rider problem is no doubt real, its very nature renders it unquantifiable. The above cases, however, suggest that private contracting is working despite positive transaction costs. Facilitating these solutions often requires getting legal restrictions on ownership of habitat and species out of the way so contracting can take place. Perhaps there is still an underprovision of species preservation, but there is no reason to forgo the benefits of private contractual solutions. Because of positive transaction costs, the view through Coase-colored glasses may not be entirely rosy. On the other hand, a Coasean view is one that recognizes the benefits of private contracting for solving all kinds of allocation problems including species preservation.

References

Alchian, Armen, and Harold Demsetz. 1972. Production, Information Costs, and Efficiency. *American Economic Review* 62(5): 777–95.

Amacher, Ryan C., Robert D. Tollison, and Thomas D. Willet. 1995. The Economics of Fatal Mistakes: Fiscal Mechanisms for Preserving Endangered Predators. In *Wildlife in the Marketplace*, ed. Terry L. Anderson and Peter J. Hill. Lanham, MD: Rowman and Littlefield, 43–60.

Anderson, Terry L., and P. J. Hill. 1975. The Evolution of Property Rights: A Study of the American West. *Journal of Law and Economics* 18(1): 163–79.

Anderson, Terry L., and Donald R. Leal. 1991. *Free Market Environmentalism.* San Francisco: Pacific Research Institute.

— 1997. *Enviro-Capitalists: Doing Good While Doing Well.* Lanham, MD: Rowman and Littlefield.

Capstick, Peter Hathaway. 1983. *Safari: The Last Adventure.* New York: St. Martin's Press.

Carson, Rachel. 1962. *Silent Spring*. Boston: Houghton Mifflin.

Cheung, Steven N. S. 1973. The Fable of the Bees: An Economic Investigation. *Journal of Law and Economics* 16(1): 11–33.

— 1983. The Contractual Nature of the Firm. *Journal of Law and Economics* 26(1): 1–21.

Coase, Ronald. 1937. The Nature of the Firm. *Economica* 4(16): 386–405.

— 1960. The Problem of Social Cost. *Journal of Law and Economics* 3(October): 1–44.

Coleman, Reed. 1994. The Land Ethic in Modern Times. *Philanthropy*, fall.

Delta Waterfowl. 1993. *Delta Waterfowl: Adopt A Pothole Summary Report*, August.

Ellickson, Robert. 1986. Of Coase and Cattle: Resolution Among Neighbors in Shasta County. *Stanford Law Review* 38(Feb.): 623–87.

Environmental Consultants (Pvt) Ltd. 1990. *People, Wildlife and Natural Resources: The CAMPFIRE Approach to Rural Development in Zimbabwe*. Harare, Zimbabwe: The Zimbabwe Trust.

Flader, Susan L. and J. Baird Callicott. 1991. *The River of the Mother of God and other essays by Aldo Leopold*. Madison: University of Wisconsin Press.

Hylton, Victoria. N.d. The Wild Harvest. Southern Wild Productions, Johannesburg, South Africa.

Klein, Benjamin, Robert B. Crawford, and Armen A. Alchian. 1978. Vertical Integration, Appropriable Rents, and the Competitive Contracting Process. *Journal of Law and Economics* 21(2): 297–326.

Leal, Donald R. 1996. Community-Run Fisheries: Avoiding the 'Tragedy of the Commons.' *PERC Policy Series*, PS-7. Bozeman, MT: Political Economy Research Center.

Leal, Donald R. and J. Bishop Grewell. 1999. *Hunting for Habitat: A Practical Guide to State-Landowner Partnerships*. Bozeman, MT: Political Economy Research Center.

Leopold, Aldo. 1966. The Land Ethic. Reprinted in *A Sand County Almanac with Essays on Conservation from Round River*. New York: Ballantine Books.

Lueck, Dean L. 1995. The Economic Organization of Wildlife Institutions. In *Wildlife in the Marketplace,* ed. Terry L. Anderson and Peter J. Hill. Lanham, MD: Rowman and Littlefield, 1–24.

Palmini, Dennis J. 1993. The Conservation Economics of Aldo Leopold. *Wisconsin Academy Review* (summer): 37–44.

Thresher, Valerie. 1993. Economic Reflections on Wildlife Utilization in Zimbabwe. Masters thesis, University of California at Davis.

Wenders, John T. 1995. The Economics of Elk Management. In *Wildlife in the Marketplace*, ed. Terry L. Anderson and Peter J. Hill. Lanham, MD: Rowman and Littlefield, 89–108.

CHAPTER 13

On Current Approaches to ESA Analysis: Comments on Watts et al., Coursey, and Anderson

John B. Loomis

INTRODUCTION

The two chapters by Terry Anderson (Chapter 12) and Don Coursey (Chapter 11) illustrate contrasting optimism and pessimism of the first two authors. Anderson is optimistic that privately negotiated agreements can make major contributions to saving endangered species and their habitats. He is pessimistic about "... whether the [government] agency is producing what the citizen/agents desire" (Anderson, pp. 232). In contrast, Coursey appears optimistic that despite what he acknowledges as the shortcomings of the political process, "... competition within the political system will generate a most preferred expenditure pattern across endangered animals" (Coursey, pp. 202). At least this is "the premise entertained throughout the analysis." And a very entertaining premise it turns out to be in his chapter: Coursey tries to convince us that agency expenditures can be used for more than reflecting the agency's priorities among species protection efforts; they can be used for valuation. As discussed below, this suffers from several weaknesses, even if Anderson's pessimism about efficiency of government agency actions is overcome. Coursey's pessimism is directed toward nonmarket valuation techniques, even though they pass many of the tests Coursey sets as his standard.

The chapter by Watts et al. (Chapter 10) reflects the realism of actually quantifying the local economic impacts and national efficiency costs of critical habitat determinations with limited analysis budgets and time. This pragmatic chapter serves as a template for performing economic impact studies and at the same time determining if there is any real net cost to the nation as a whole. At least for the endangered fish in the Colorado River system, Watts et al. find no significant costs at the national level for increased instream flows for fish. By first establishing this on the cost side, arguments over the benefit side become less important. As always, each chapter emphasizes one aspect of the endangered species analysis problem and, as pointed out below, does not address other equally important aspects. The comments below attempt to suggest how the gaps of each chapter could be remedied or at least acknowledged.

TERRY ANDERSON ON COASEAN SOLUTIONS TO THREATENED AND ENDANGERED SPECIES

In "The ESA through Coase-Colored Glasses," Terry Anderson provides a well-thought-out framework and discussion of the applicability and limits to voluntary exchange as a means of protecting endangered species. A large focus of Anderson's chapter is to remind policy makers and managers that we can transform wildlife from being a liability to landowners into a valuable asset for landowners. Anderson's examples drive home a point often overlooked by wildlife managers who have forgotten their Aldo Leopold: incentives matter. Anderson documents several such cases involving huntable big game animals in the United States and Africa. The case of wolf recovery shows just how large the gains from trade can be: It took only about 10,000 of the millions of beneficiaries of wolf reintroduction to compensate for the small losses that were concentrated among a few ranchers. The gains from allowing landowners to be paid for ranching wildlife instead of livestock are significant both from an economic returns and biological standpoint. These examples illustrate that private, negotiated efforts can make an important contribution for certain types of wildlife species.

Unfortunately, Anderson generalizes these case studies on game animals and a high-profile species to make broad conclusions about all endangered species. While a Coasean solution might contribute to the preservation for high-profile species such as the wolf or huntable species such as elk and waterfowl, it will be of little help for the hundreds of less glamorous species on the endangered species list. Only if the habitat protected for elk or the wolf is the very same habitat needed for the hundreds of plant species, nongame fish, and snails that dominate the endangered species list will the Coasean approach make a substantive contribution. Unfortunately, there is often minimal habitat overlap and there are little marketable recreation use benefits associated with hunting and viewing the majority of endangered plants and insects on the endangered species list. Rather, the benefits of protecting nongame wildlife, plants, and insects are off-site public good benefits (Brown and Shogren 1998, 12). These off-site public good benefits relate to the option for future use of the genetic diversity these species provide us, the existence value from just knowing the species exists in its native habitat and knowing that preservation today provides these species to future generations (Bishop and Welsh 1992; Randall and Stoll 1983). As noted by Brown and Shogren (1998) and empirically demonstrated in our own research, the benefits of threatened, endangered, or rare species extend far beyond the local area where the critical habitat is located, and include residents of both the east and west coasts in the United States (Loomis 1996; Loomis and Caban 1996).

As indicated by Brown and Shogren (1998, 12), "Most economists now acknowledge that people might have preferences about protecting species and related services they will rarely ever, if at all, see or use." Since these existence benefits of endangered species are public goods, government has a legitimate role to play, just as it does for the classic textbook example of a public good – national defense. The inability to exclude nonpayors from benefiting and the nonrival nature of consumption make private provision of the economically efficient amount of national defense nearly impossible. This is because private firms cannot force free riders to pay and, therefore, have less than the sufficient amount of resources to provide the optimal amount. We recognize this with regard to national defense. We don't have a B-1 bomber "check-off" on income tax forms to solicit contributions. Voluntary approaches won't work for national defense and are not likely to be the complete answer to provide protection of the majority of endangered species either. Rather, we use mandatory taxes that force all beneficiaries to pay for national defense. Thus, government taxation and provision of habitat and protection for endangered species can contribute to an economically efficient solution and should not be overlooked any more than privately negotiated contributions should not be overlooked.

Anderson also provides a useful framework in his Figure 12.1 to organize the possibilities of ownership of the species and ownership of the land. It may be particularly applicable to endangered species such as plants that are fixed in location. In Anderson's diagram, we may have a single landowner and a single species. At the other end of the spectrum with multiple species and multiple landowner, life for us and Coase gets more complicated. Anderson does seem to downplay the role of government to act as an agent of the public to reduce transaction costs in these multiple-species cases. Rather than the landowner having to negotiate with the millions of people who benefit from continued existence of endangered species, the federal government can act as our agent. Now we are back to a "small numbers" case in which the Coase Theorem would indicate there are gains from exchange. Contrary to my reading of Anderson, I believe the property rights to threatened and endangered (T&E) species had already been established when the ESA was passed. In 1995, the U.S. Supreme Court in *Babbit v. Sweet Home Chapter of Communities for a Greater Oregon* (515 U.S. 687) reaffirmed that the public has ownership of these species and this protection applies to the species habitat as well.

Overall, I commend Terry Anderson's continuing efforts to make policy makers and managers aware that private actions and voluntary negotiations can make valuable contributions to conservation of wildlife species. There is much to be gained by paying private landowners to protect T&E species on their lands. However, the optimum level of protection will require everyone, not just recreation users, to pay. Only government has the power to overcome the free-riding inherent in voluntary provision of a public good like T&E species preservation.

COURSEY AND THE REVEALED PREFERENCES OF GOVERNMENT AGENCIES

In Don Coursey's analysis, it is government actions that are analyzed to see what can be inferred about agency priorities (a fair amount) and society's valuation of individual species and their habitats (perhaps, not much).

Metrick and Weitzman (1996, 1998) as well as Ando (1999) have published similar statistical analyses of the determinants of the listing decision and recovery expenditures. I believe there are some interesting insights into the political economy of species preservation from all of these analyses. However, Coursey's finding: "The evidence reported in this study supports the conclusion that Congress is buying protection of animals in a manner consistent with median desires of the public," stands in contrast to Anderson's skepticism on this same topic.

The desire to use the expenditures of government agencies or contributions to environmental groups as a measure of value has a long history, but it has weak conceptual foundations. Economists since Alfred Marshall have recognized that expenditures do not reflect the full utility or inframarginal value of market or nonmarket goods; there is a consumer surplus (Sassone and Schaefer trace consumer surplus back to Dupuit, in 1844). Even if the government budget process was aimed toward maximization of economic efficiency, it is hard to deny that preservation would provide a value over and above this expenditure to members of society. This point is all the more obvious when the reader inspects Tables 11.7 and 11.8 of Coursey's chapter: There are no reported expenditures for several species, implying a zero value. But this is misleading, as there may be species for which there is little cost necessary to protect them. For example, they exist in National Parks or Wilderness Areas and their preservation does not preclude any legally allowed development, or like the Mexican Spotted Owl, protection of habitat avoids below-cost timber sales. Again, the consumer surplus or net benefits to society are large because there are minimal expenditures to protect them. This reason aside, I question Coursey's empirical finding of zero expenditures since it ignores the thousands of dollars required by the public and the agency to put the species on the endangered species list in the first place.

Coursey suggests these expenditures on endangered species may serve "to calibrate those obtained from contingent valuation" (p. 202). As noted above, reliance on expenditures to calibrate contingent valuation survey estimates of net willingness to pay or consumer surplus is misplaced: Expenditures underestimate maximum willingness to pay. Of course, contingent valuation surveys sometimes (but not always) overestimate actual willingness to pay as well. However, contingent valuation estimates of willingness to pay for air quality (Brookshire et al. 1982) and hundreds of recreation studies (Carson et al. 1996) are actually less than their revealed preference counterparts.

However, in the case of goods with more nonuse values such as endangered species, there is evidence that stated willingness to pay often exceeds actual cash contributions (Brown et al. 1996). In part this may be due to arriving at a valid measure of actual willingness to pay for public goods. The free-riding problem that bedevils fund raising for public goods in the real world also bedevils contingent valuation field experiments (Randall 1998). Nonetheless, if it is calibration of contingent valuation estimates that one wants, there are more conceptually sound ways to do this than using agency expenditures.

See Champ et al. (1997), Bjornstad, Cummings, and Osborne (1997), and Fox et al. (1998) for examples of successful calibration approaches.

Generally speaking, contingent valuation studies have passed the standard set by Coursey. Specifically Coursey states: "Consistency is always the harbinger of accuracy in scientific measurement." As noted by Bailey (1994, 73), "Since reliability by definition means consistency, . . . it would seem better to test for reliability through repeated applications of the same measure." Over the past decade all the referred journal articles that have empirically investigated the consistency or test-retest reliability of contingent valuation estimates have demonstrated such consistency (Loomis 1989, 1990; Carson et al. 1996). This includes articles by an economist working for Exxon (Reiling et al. 1990). Measurement of WTP using the same survey instrument eight months after the original survey administration showed no statistical difference between an individual's WTP over this time period, and correlation of responses that were significant at the .01 level for both visitors and nonusers (Loomis 1989).

Finally, a META analysis of eighteen different T&E species that was published several years prior to this book showed that economic values of protecting these species were sensitive to economic variables but not to unimportant differences in question format. Specifically, WTP increased with the species population change, the type of species, and whether the payment was a one-time or annual amount, but not sensitive to the contingent valuation question format used (Loomis and White 1996). The internal consistency of the values is high, with the economic variables in the META analysis explaining two-thirds of the variability in the economic value of each species.

In sum, Coursey's results on expenditures by species and by acre of habitat provide some insights regarding the priorities of the U.S. Fish and Wildlife Service, but do not provide much in the way of economic valuation estimates to society for T&E species. They may in fact mislead more than inform.

A PRAGMATIC APPROACH TO QUANTIFYING LOCAL IMPACTS AND NATIONAL COSTS OF T&E SPECIES

The need for a balanced and pragmatic approach to the analysis of endangered species is the central theme in Watts et al.'s chapter on Critical Habitat Impacts. As the authors note, most of the focus in previous empirical analyses such as the northern spotted owl has been on losses to local industries. While stories of the "local sky is falling" make great headlines, this is only half the story. As noted by Watts et al. designation of critical habitat necessarily reflects a reallocation of natural resources. As such, there are both losers and gainers. The problem is most traditional county-level economic impacts studies that use input–output models tend to concentrate on the local impacts, and ignore those areas and sectors gaining from the reallocation of resources.

Watts et al. adopt a broader regional analysis, taking into account the entire Colorado River drainage and a general equilibrium approach. As noted by the authors, "The applied general equilibrium approach forces recognition of potential offsetting effects as resources are reallocated to preserve critical habitat for endangered species. Thus, in the Colorado River study, the (river) flow changes required for endangered fishes decreases agricultural activity in the upper basin of the Colorado River but increases the activity in the lower basin" (p. 198).

On the impact side, where effects are measured as output changes, the authors find an overall positive increase in output due to greater instream flows for endangered fish. That is, rather than the traditional view of high costs, there are small net positive gains to the region. In part this is due to ESA requiring water reallocations that make economic sense: Move water from states like Colorado and New Mexico where the water grows livestock feeds (e.g., hay) to a state like California that grows vegetables with it in the Imperial Valley. It takes a powerful law like ESA to overcome the current inefficiencies in our water allocations. This is not the only case where ESA improves efficiency of water use. Whittlesey, Hamilton, and Halverson (1986) found similar results for the Snake River basin: Transferring water from low-valued agriculture to instream uses would increase total economic value as the transferred water would pass through several hydropower dams on the way to the Pacific Ocean. Again, there is little or no net opportunity cost to endangered species recovery; there are net benefits from ESA forcing society to break down the artificial state barriers to efficient water use.

The computable general equilibrium framework also allows for evaluation of the national economic efficiency effects of critical habitat designation. It is important to use this national perspective for two reasons: (a) this is a federal law and a federally listed species so the national level is the appropriate accounting stance; (b) local effects are simply transfers of economic activity across regions and industries.

The main area for improvement in the Watts et al. chapter is omission of the nonmarket benefits of the critical habitat. Surely a quantitative analysis intended to meet the mandate of a law that requires an economic analysis of critical habitat designation would include the benefits of the critical habitat to the species. While measuring the nonmarket benefits of public goods is controversial, it can and has been done (one of the authors of the Watts et al. chapter is one of the pioneers in this area). The valuation methods are not perfect, but neither is the computer general equilibrium model. The computable general equilibrium model relies on a long list of simplifying assumptions, which the authors of this chapter carefully note may not hold. Although benefit studies were not available at the time the authors performed their analysis, they could have adopted the approach used in the Northern Spotted Owl case, and surveyed the existing literature on the economic value of T&E species. Espinosa and V. K. Smith (1995) have incorporated such nonmarket values into computable general equilibrium models as well.

Nonetheless, the Watts et al. computer general equilibrium approach serves as a significant advance in estimating the economic effects of critical habitat. It can be considered a template and building block that future economic analyses of critical habitat can build upon.

CONCLUSION

These authors and their chapters stimulate our thoughts about possible economic approaches to preserving endangered species. Terry Anderson points out the success of privately initiated incentive-based solutions, while Don Coursey suggests perhaps government allocation of expenditures relates to the public's preferences. Once listed, the ESA may be working to rescue and recover the mega-fauna humans adore; however, private actions and current government expenditures are not adequate to meet the requirements of recovery planning and designation of critical habitat for less glamorous species. Without the pragmatic approach of Watts et al. to quantify the national economic costs and without techniques to measure the benefits of less glamorous species, we may be relegating a great deal of genetic diversity to extinction.

References

Anderson, Terry. 2001. The ESA Through Coase-Colored Glasses. Chapter 12 in *Protecting Endangered Species in the United States: Biological Needs, Political Realities, Economic Choices*, eds. J. Shogren and J. Tschirhart. Cambridge University Press, New York.

Ando, Amy Whritenour. 2001. Interest Group Behavior and Endangered Species Protection. Chapter 6 in *Protecting Endangered Species in the United States: Biological Needs, Political Realities, Economic Choices*, eds. J. Shogren and J. Tschirhart. Cambridge University Press, New York.

Bailey, Kenneth. 1994. *Methods of Social Research*, 4th edition. The Free Press, New York.

Bishop, Richard and Michael Welsh. 1992. Existence Values in Benefit-Cost Analysis and Damage Assessment. *Land Economics* 68(4): 405–17.

Bjornstad, David, Ronald Cummings, and Laura Osborne. 1997. A Learning Design for Reducing Hypothetical Bias in the Contingent Valuation Method. *Environmental and Resource Economics* 10: 207–21.

Brookshire, David, Mark Thayer, William Schulze, and Ralph d'Arge. 1982. Valuing Public Goods: A Comparison of Survey and Hedonic Approaches. *American Economic Review* 72(1): 165–77.

Brown, Gardner, and Jason Shogren. 1998. Economics of the ESA. *Journal of Economic Perspectives* 12(3): 3–20.

Brown, Thomas, Patricia Champ, Richard Bishop, and Daniel McCollum. 1996. Which Response Format Reveals the Truth about Donations to Public Goods. *Land Economics* 72(2): 152–66.

Carson, R., N. Flores, K. Martin, and J. Wright. 1996. Contingent valuation and revealed preference methodologies: Comparing the estimates for quasi-public goods. *Land Economics* 72(1): 80–99.

Carson, R. et al. 1997. Temporal Reliability on Estimates from Contingent Valuation. *Land Economics* 73(2): 151–63.

Champ, P., R. Bishop, T. Brown, and D. McCollum. 1997. Using Donation Mechanisms to Value Nonuse Benefits from Public Goods. *Journal of Environmental Economics and Management* 33(2): 151–62.

Coursey, Don. 2001. The Revealed Demand for a Public Good: Evidence from Endangered and Threatened Species. Chapter 11 in *Protecting Endangered Species in the United States: Biological Needs, Political Realities, Economic Choices*, eds. J. Shogren and J. Tschirhart. Cambridge University Press, New York.

Espinosa, Anres and V. Kerry Smith. 1995. Measuring Environmental Consequences of Trade Policy: A Nonmarket CGE Analysis. *American Journal of Agricultural Economics* 77(3): 772–77.

Fox, John, Jason Shogren, Dermot Hayes, and James Kliebenstein. 1998. CVM-X: Calibrating Contingent Values with Experimental Auction Markets. *American Journal of Agricultural Economics* 80(3): 455–65.

Loomis, John. 1989. Test Re-test Reliability of the Contingent Valuation Method: A Comparison of General Population and Visitor Responses. *American Journal of Agricultural Economics* 71(1): 76–84.

— 1990. Comparative Reliability of the Dichotomous Choice and Open Ended Contingent Valuation Techniques. *Journal of Environmental Economics and Management* 18(1): 78–85.

— 1996. How Large Is the Extent of the Market for Public Goods: Evidence From a Nationwide Contingent Valuation Survey. *Applied Economics* 28(7): 779–82.

Loomis, John, and Armando Gonzalez-Caban. 1996. The Importance of the Market Area Determination for Estimating Aggregate Benefits of Public Goods: Testing Differences in Resident and Nonresident Willingness to Pay. *Agricultural and Resource Economics Review* 25(2): 161–70.

Loomis, John, and Douglas White. 1996. Economic Benefits of Rare and Endangered Species: Summary and Meta-Analysis. *Ecological Economics* 18(3): 197–206.

Metrick, Andrew, and Martin Weitzman. 1996. Patterns of Endangered Species Preservation. *Land Economics* 72(1): 1–16.

— 1998. Conflicts and Choices in Biodiversity Preservation. *Journal of Economic Perspectives* 12(3): 21–34.

Randall, Alan. 1998. Beyond the Crucial Experiment: Mapping the Performance Characteristics of Contingent Valuation. *Resource and Energy Economics* 20: 197–206.

Randall, A. and J. Stoll. 1983. Existence value in a total valuation framework. In *Managing Air Quality and Scenic Resources at National Parks and Wilderness Areas*, R. Rowe and L. Chestnut (eds.), pp. 246–53. Westview Press: Boulder, CO.

Reiling, Stephen, Kevin Boyle, Marcia Phillips, and Mark Anderson. 1990. Temporal Reliability of Contingent Values. *Land Economics* 66(2): 128–34.

Sassone, Peter and William Schaefer. 1978. *Cost-Benefit Analysis – A Handbook*. Academic Press: San Diego, CA.

Watts, G., W. Noonan, H. Maddux, and D. Brookshire. 2001. Critical Habitat Impacts: Integrating Biology and Economics According to the ESA. In *Protecting Endangered Species in the United States: Biological Needs, Political Realities, and Economic Choices*, eds. J. Shogren and J. Tschirhart. Cambridge University Press, New York.

Whittlesey, Norman, Joel Hamilton, and Philip Halverson. 1986. *An Economic Study of the Potential for Water Markets in Idaho*. Idaho Water Resources Research Institute, University of Idaho, Moscow, ID.

Replies by Authors

Gary Watts, William Noonan, Henry Maddux, and David Brookshire

Although Dr. Loomis' comments on our chapter are generally favorable, he points to the omission of nonmarket benefits associated with critical habitat designation as an area for improvement. We agree. From a pragmatic perspective, however, incorporating such estimates into our analysis would be difficult. As Dr. Loomis noted, benefit studies associated with preserving such species as the Colorado squawfish, humpback chub, bonytail, and razorback sucker were not available at the time our analysis was performed. Furthermore, time and resources were not available to develop benefit estimates for preserving these species using contingent valuation or other nonmarket valuation techniques. Dr. Loomis suggests that we could have surveyed the literature on the economic value of other T&E species and incorporated such nonmarket values into the CGE model using benefit transfer techniques. That suggestion, however, ignores the unique and controversial way in which some native fishes of the Colorado River system are viewed by various segments of the public and fisheries management professionals.

Prior to passage of the Endangered Species Act, many native fishes in the basin were considered "trash" fishes that competed for habitat with salmonoid species that were introduced for sport fishing purposes. In fact, various species of suckers and chubs were routinely poisoned in the 1950s and 1960s in an attempt to enhance recreational fisheries. Perhaps the best example of such actions is the use of rotenone in 1962 to remove almost all native fishes from Wyoming's Green River system above newly constructed Flaming Gorge Reservoir. While such actions are now prohibited by law, it is clear that the value of native fishes is still not universally accepted by the recreational public and fisheries management professionals in the basin.

Given this situation, incorporating nonmarket benefit estimates for preserving other species into our analysis would be inappropriate because such species usually are not viewed as a nuisance by some segments of the public. (Note: Some T&E species may be viewed as a nuisance after they are listed because of potential localized economic impacts, but that situation differs from one where the species has perceived impacts independent of listing as in the present case.) However, developing direct benefit estimates for preserving the native fishes using nonmarket techniques remains an interesting potential follow-on study and would present some challenges to nonmarket benefit estimation techniques.

TERRY L. ANDERSON

John Loomis's critique of Coasean bargaining to solve endangered species problems falls into three categories: (1) contractual solutions can only be applied to species that have marketable values; (2) most species do not have marketable values; and (3) property rights have been assigned to endangered species through the Endangered Species Act and subsequent court rulings.

The first emphasizes the importance of viewing wildlife generally and endangered species particularly through "Coase-colored glasses." Coase's central insight was that bargaining will occur if transaction costs are low relative to value of the goods that are being bargained for. Contractual arrangements for elk, now one of the higher valued North American game species, would not have existed fifty years ago because the value of the good was not high enough to overcome the transaction costs. As values rise relative to transaction costs, markets will evolve. To be sure, government can play a role in reducing transaction costs so that these markets will evolve sooner, which raises the question of whether governments are doing this. In the case of marketable wildlife species, most state laws stand in the way of, rather than promote, wildlife markets. Hence, my response to Loomis is that we should be asking government to do what it should do best – help define and enforce property rights that will result in Coasean bargaining solutions.

Loomis's second critique is the existence value trump card that is always played to support governmental intervention in the environmental arena. First, let me note that this argument should be carefully separated from option values. If it is the "option for future uses," then there is no need to expect that Coasean bargaining won't work. Pharmaceutical contracts for options on valuable biota in Central American rain forests are a case in point.

For existence values, there clearly is the possibility of free riders and hence underprovision of the good by the market. But this immediately raises at least three further questions that must be addressed by advocates of governmental solutions to this problem. Number one: Doesn't this "market failure" offer an opportunity for the entrepreneur who can figure out a way to market the good for which there is existence value? This is what The Nature Conservancy has been so effective at. Number two: What evidence is there that governmental provision through general taxes improves resource allocation given that its ability to concentrate benefits and diffuse costs is a classic case of the free-rider problem? Indeed, the large number of species on the endangered species list could be taken as evidence that special interests have used government to promote their cause at the expense of others. Number three: What limits are there on the role of government once we let the existence-value camel's nose under the tent? Suppose engineers have existence values for large dams, or animal haters have nonexistence values for extinct species; should the government use general tax revenues to promote those causes?

Finally, no student of the property literature starting with Coase and continuing with volumes in law and economics would agree that the Endangered

Species Act has established property rights to endangered species. To say that the government or the public owns these species begs the question of who has access to them, who can derive benefits from them, and who can make trade-offs over their use. Unless there is a clear residual claimant (and of course this can be a group of people including a government agency) with the ability to buy and sell the species (or its habitat), then it is hard to see what kind of property rights exist. Certainly, absent these characteristics, there is no potential for Coasean bargaining, and this is precisely the problem with the current approach to endangered species. If the government as our agent took ownership of species and were willing to bargain with landowners for habitat, many of the problems of preserving habitat would disappear. Indeed, this is the point of Defenders of Wildlife's wolf recovery program. If the National Park Service or the U.S. Fish and Wildlife Service really owns the wolves released in Yellowstone, why is Defenders paying the bill?

In conclusion, are endangered species markets perfect? Only if we define perfect to mean that contracting will take place as long as the value of the gains from trade exceed the transaction costs. Such a definition is useful only insofar as it focuses our attention on why transaction costs are too high. Thus focused, we can begin to ask either how government institutions can lower transaction costs and encourage Coasean bargaining, or how transaction costs within government can be lowered to improve the efficiency with which public goods are produced and delivered. Debates such as this are the threads from which the fabric of progress is woven.

ECONOMIC CHOICES

PART 3.2 FUTURE INCENTIVES

CHAPTER 14

The Economics of "Takings" in a Multiparcel Model with a Powerful Government

Robert Innes

I. INTRODUCTION

The Fifth Amendment to the U.S. Constitution proscribes government "takings" of private property without just compensation. Beyond constitutional requirements for compensation is a legislative debate on how far the government should go to pay landowners for costs of environmental protections. Recent legislative proposals, for example, would require compensation for diminution in private property values that occurs when the government acts to protect endangered species (under the Endangered Species Act – ESA) or wetlands (under the Clean Water Act and the Farm Bill).[1]

For economists, two sets of issues arise in the takings context – corresponding with the legislative debate on compensation on the one hand, and on the other, the constitutional debate on appropriate limits to the takings clause.[2] In the legislative arena, economic logic can shed light on how compensation affects *private incentives to use property* – and in view of these effects, when and how much compensation should be paid in order to ensure an efficient private use of land. On the constitutional front, in contrast, the question is how to provide the government with incentives to regulate and take land efficiently, using constitutional (compensation) restraints that curb potential government misbehavior.

This chapter is concerned with both of these issues when, contrary to prior economic modeling, the economic setting is one with multiple parcels of private land that can differ in their *levels of private development* and that afford the government a choice of *how much land* to "take" for public uses such as habitat or wetlands preservation. Although there are a variety of "real world"

---

[1] Such compensation requirements were the centerpiece of H.R. 925 (which passed the U.S. House of Representatives in March 1995), S. 605 (the Dole-Gramm-Hatch bill of the 104th Congress), and H.R. 2275 (which required compensation for ESA actions and passed the House Resources Committee in October 1995). Similarly, more recent legislation would make it easier for landowners to challenge environmental and zoning laws in federal courts.

[2] This debate is a long-standing and continuing one among legal scholars. See, for examples, Epstein (1985), Kmiec (1988), Michelman (1988), Rose-Ackerman (1988), and Treanor (1985).

cases that would seem to fit the multiple-parcel specification reasonably well (see Section II below), this feature of the takings problem will also be shown to be central to the efficiency effects of compensation.

The starting point for economic arguments for and against payment of compensation is the classic paper by Blume, Rubinfeld, and Shapiro (BRS) (1984). BRS envision a property owner who chooses the extent of initial private development (or capital investment) on a given piece of property, knowing that there is some probability of a future taking of the property by the government. When a taking occurs, the initial investment is rendered worthless. In this setting, BRS argue that payment of compensation will prevent landowners from internalizing the prospective loss of their investment in the event of a taking, thus leading them to invest too much in their property, relative to what is efficient.

Several counterpoints to this argument can, in principle, restore economic motivations for compensation. The first is a market failure. When there is no private insurance for the risk of a taking, compensation can implicitly provide insurance to risk-averse property owners and thereby enhance welfare.[3] The second is a government failure, which the literature has called "fiscal illusion" (e.g., see BRS; Fischel and Shapiro 1989; and Miceli and Segerson 1994). When it is subject to fiscal illusion, the government places less weight on the private costs of its actions than it does upon the public benefits and budgetary costs. As a result, it has been argued that the government will appropriate private property too often if it is not compelled to fully internalize the private costs of such takings.[4] Compensation adds these private costs to the government's budget and thereby elicits more efficient government behavior.[5,6]

---

[3] Blume and Rubinfeld (1984) develop this point carefully. Kaplow (1986) argues that, to the extent that property owners are risk averse and desire insurance, private insurance markets will emerge for takings risks, and compensation will not be needed to achieve efficient risk-sharing. For further discussion of these issues, see also Fischel and Shapiro (1988) and Farber (1992).

[4] This point dates back to the early work on takings, including Michelman (1967), deAlessi (1969), and Baxter and Altree (1972). See also Berger (1974), Johnson (1977), Epstein (1985), and Burrows' (1989) critique of Epstein.

[5] Kaplow (1986) criticizes this fiscal illusion argument, suggesting that governments are as likely to undervalue public benefits of takings as they are to undervalue private costs. However, in an important paper that builds upon ideas in Fischel (1985) and Ely (1980), Fischel and Shapiro (1989) explain fiscal illusion with majoritarian governance in which political majorities place zero weight, ex-post, on the private costs borne by minorities. Ex-ante, before anyone knows whether he or she will be in the majority or the minority, all will agree on a constitutional rule that requires some compensation and thereby forces the majoritarian government, ex-post, to consider the private costs of its actions.

[6] Miceli and Segerson (1994) have recently argued that, even with fiscal illusion, compensation is not necessary for efficiency. If the courts require compensation only when the government behaves inefficiently, then the government will behave efficiently and compensation will not be required. However, this rule cannot be implemented if, as posited in this chapter, the courts are not equipped to determine whether or not government policy is efficient (a determination which may be reserved for the government that is elected to make it).

In the endangered species context, two additional motives for compensation can be important.[7] First, landowners can often affect the likelihood that their land will be valuable as endangered species habitat. For example, they can cull old growth trees that are preferred by Northern Spotted Owls or Red Cockaded Woodpeckers, or quietly shoot endangered creatures that trespass. Absent any takings compensation, landowners have a powerful incentive to engage in these actions – actively seeking to reduce the prospective public use value of their land and/or not acting to protect or enhance this value, thereby reducing the likelihood that their land will be appropriated for habitat (e.g., see Innes 2000; Stroup 1997; Welch 1994; Lambert and Smith 1994). In order to afford landowners with the needed (efficient) preservation incentive, some compensation is required.[8]

Second, a key paper by Polasky and Doremus (1998) argues that it is often necessary to acquire information about a particular piece of land – using costly field surveys, for example – before its *value* as habitat can be known.[9] Compensating landowners for the lost private use rights, when their land is designated as critical to endangered species habitat, then has two advantages: It makes landowners willing to cooperate in the acquisition of the needed information; without compensation, in contrast, landowners would want to obstruct any field investigation that might lead to a "taking." In addition, compensation confronts the government with both the benefits of a taking (the public use or habitat value) and the private costs of a taking. As a result, the government has an incentive not only to "take" land when it is efficient to do so; it also has an incentive to gather information about the land's usefulness as habitat when and only when the costs of acquiring information are outweighed by the benefits in making a better "takings" decision.

All of these motives for compensation derive from settings in which landowners and governments view a single parcel of land in isolation. This chapter takes a different perspective, and in doing so, develops a different motive for compensation. Specifically, I consider a region with many owners of homogeneous land parcels, each of which can either be developed or not developed at two points in time, ex-ante (before a taking might occur) and ex-post (at the time takings decisions are made). The extent of ex-ante development – or investment – is thus measured by the number of landowners who choose to develop ex-ante, rather than the level of investment on a given piece of property by a given landowner (as in BRS, for example).[10]

---

[7] See Innes, Polasky, and Tschirhart (1998) for further discussion of these arguments.

[8] See Innes (1997) for an analysis of the desired form and level of takings compensation under these circumstances.

[9] See also Polasky, Chapter 15 of this volume, who integrates models in which landowners can affect the value of their land in public use (Innes 2000) and models in which information acquisition is costly (Polasky and Doremus 1998).

[10] The approach and analysis in this chapter formalize and generalize Innes (1997).

The case of *Lucas v. South Carolina Coastal Council* (1992) illustrates the economic environment of interest in this chapter. In 1986, David Lucas purchased two beachfront lots on a South Carolina barrier island. Two years later, a change in state law increased the distance from the high-tide line at which new building was allowed, thus preventing Lucas from building on his property. Houses that were already built – but would otherwise have violated the new law – were "grandfathered" in. Lucas sued, arguing that he was due compensation for a taking.

The central feature of this case, and of the setting modeled in this chapter, is that different owners of homogeneous property make different development choices; some develop their property early on and others wait to develop. Indeed, as economies grow, such heterogeneous development choices are efficient, with development proceeding in response to growing demand for the services that new development can provide. Moreover, government takings do not – and should not – treat developed and undeveloped property symmetrically. Other things equal, the least valuable undeveloped land should be taken first, just as was done in the Lucas case. This practice, however, implies that, if takings are not compensated, landowners have an incentive to develop their land early in order to reduce their risk of government appropriation.

This overdevelopment incentive can be countered if the government pays appropriate compensation to owners of lands that are taken for public uses. However, as is stressed in what follows, it is not government compensation per se that is necessary for the achievement of efficient development incentives, but rather the "equal treatment" of property owners who develop and who do not develop. Incentives to develop early are generated by differences between ex-post profits that are available to owners of developed and undeveloped land, respectively. Hence, by appropriately protecting the *relative* value of undeveloped and developed land – rather than allowing this relative value to fall with takings of undeveloped land – efficient ex-ante development incentives can be provided. For example, the cost of a taking can be distributed more evenly between the owners of the land that is taken (the "burdened") and other landowners (the "unburdened") by requiring some payment from the latter to the former. The relative cost of owning undeveloped property – vis-à-vis developed property – then goes down, which counters the excessive incentive to develop early. In other words, more "equal treatment" is being provided even though the government itself is paying nothing. One regulatory approach that achieves equal treatment in this way – at no government cost – is a tradeable development rights program that requires landowners who wish to retain a full development right to buy up rights from owners of undeveloped land. Those who sell their rights then forego development, turning over their land for the government's taking.

The distinction between compensation and equal treatment is particularly important when one considers the incentives that confront a "political government." Contrary to prior analyses that model government regulatory behavior in response to various exogenous compensation rules,[11] this chapter shows that an unfettered government – one that can freely choose both its regulatory/takings policies and its compensation/tax policies – will generally make *efficient* takings decisions, regardless of its political preferences. However, it will set its compensation policies to suit political ends that, except by coincidence, do not prompt landowners to make efficient ex-ante development choices. A constitutional equal treatment requirement can prevent such distorting political opportunism and, at the same time, preserve the government's incentives for efficient takings. In contrast, if the courts impose a requirement that landowners be fully compensated for takings, this chapter argues that the government's takings decisions will *not* be efficient in general. When the government is averse to budgetary outlays on landowners, a compensation requirement can lead it to curtail its expenditures by allowing excessive levels of development.

The balance of the chapter is organized as follows. The next section develops and analyzes the chapter's benchmark model of land development and takings, abstracting from political considerations that may affect government policies. Section III then incorporates political behavior and explores the need – and desired structure – for judicial restraints on government actions. Section IV discusses several generalizations of the basic model. Finally, Section V closes the chapter with a discussion of three recent takings cases.

II. THE BENCHMARK MODEL

Consider a model of land development and takings in which risk-neutral individuals own a number of homogeneous land parcels, each of which can either be developed initially (at time 1), developed later (at time 2), or not developed at all. As in a number of studies in urban economics (starting with Ohls and Pines 1975), this model embodies the idea that it is efficient for development to proceed gradually through time, with some fraction of the available land developed at time 1 and the possibility of further development at time 2. Unlike these other studies, however, this chapter focuses on the prospect for a government "taking" of land at time 2. Specifically, there is some "external harm" created by development or, equivalently, a public benefit of removing land from private development and placing it in a public use. The public benefits may be the protection of endangered species, or biodiversity in general, for example. These benefits – or the corresponding "external harms" from developing the land for private use – are uncertain at the initial time 1 and revealed to the ruling elected government at time 2. Based upon the revealed level of land's value in public use, the government acts to remove land from private development at time 2. Each property owner decides whether to develop his parcel in time 1 or wait until time 2, knowing that there may be a government "taking" at this time.

---

[11] This perspective is common to the analyses of "fiscal illusion" described earlier, as well as recent work by Brennan and Boyd (1995). A notable exception is an interesting paper by Farber (1992), who discusses "discretionary government compensation."

Initial uncertainty about the nature of external harm, while generally realistic, is also necessary in this chapter because it motivates a separation between the government's regulatory decision (in this model's time 2) and private landowners' development decisions (in this model's time 1). As will be seen in what follows, this separation – and the attendant need to elicit appropriate choices from both government and landowners – is at the crux of the takings issues of interest here.

A rather wide variety of cases may be thought to fit this general description. For example, there may be a number of land parcels on a coastline, where construction on each parcel involves the substitution of storm barriers for sand dunes, increasing flooding and environmental harm. In this case, the potential harm from coastline development increases with the intensity or level of development. As population settlement and recreation patterns are discovered over time, the cost of this harm is learned. Alternately, there may be a number of wetland parcels that, when converted to farmland, reduce floodwater storage, water quality, and wildlife habitat. Again, a greater intensity or extent of wetland development increases the severity of harm to these public resources, and the government learns more about the potential cost of this harm over time. In the suburban development context, more development can create more congestion, less open space, more noise and air pollution, worsened flooding problems, and reduced aesthetic values. Or in the endangered species context, more development reduces the potential habitat for rare animals and plants. Over time, the strength and habitat of animal and plant populations may change, and the potential value of land use as habitat is discovered.

Formally, consider a region in which the total supply of homogeneous land parcels equals $\overline{X}$ and the market for these land parcels is competitive. The amount of land that is privately developed at time 1 will be denoted by x_1. This time 1 development has a per-parcel cost of D_1 and a total private value, between time 1 and time 2, of

$$V_1(x_1) = \int_0^{x_1} p_1(z)\, dz,$$

where $p_1(z)$ is the inverse market demand for time-1-to-time-2 development and $p_1'() < 0$. Thus, when x_1 land is developed at time 1, property owners who develop their parcels obtain a net time 1 rent of $V_1'(x_1) - D_1 = p_1(x_1) - D_1$.

At time 2, more land can be developed or some previously developed land can be "restored" to its natural state. Let X denote the total amount of privately developed land after the time 2 development and/or restoration has occurred. The "external damage" caused by this development (from time 2 onward) is $E(X, \theta)$, where θ is a random variable that has a uniform probability distribution on the unit interval, $[0, 1]$. $E(X, \theta)$ has the following properties: (1) $E_X() > 0$ and $E_{XX}() \geqslant 0$: increases in development raise external costs at a nondecreasing rate; and (2) $E_{X\theta}() > 0$: higher values of θ yield higher marginal (and total) external costs of development. Once the government observes θ, it chooses X to maximize social welfare. This level of development is achieved by: (1) banning development on some or all undeveloped land, and/or (2) requiring that some previously developed land be restored.

The X developed land has a value associated with the services provided from time 2 onward. This value is $V_2(X) = \int_0^x p_2(z)\,dz$, where $V_2'(X) > 0$ and $V_2''(X) < 0 \,\forall\, X$. All values are stated in time 2 equivalents, thus incorporating any discounting. For example, if x_1 land is developed at time 1 and the government does not require that any of this land be restored at time 2, each time 1 developer will receive a per-parcel payoff of

$$(V_1'(x_1) - D_1) + (V_2'(X) - D_{12})$$

where D_{12} is a cost of bringing "old development" up to "new development" standards. Similarly, land that is only developed at time 2 yields its owners per-parcel net rents of $(V_2'(X) - D_2)$, where $D_2 > D_{12}$ is the per-parcel time 2 development cost.

If, at time 2, the government requires restoration of a land parcel that was developed at time 1, such restoration costs the nonnegative amount R and thus yields a private payoff (without any compensation) of $V_1'(x_1) - D_1 - R$. Moreover, when land is not developed, it has zero private value at both times 1 and 2.

I now turn to the intuitive content of this model, and refer the analytically minded reader to the Appendix, where a formal analysis of the model is developed.

Efficient Development. In this model, a government that restricts development at time 2 will want to "take" undeveloped land *first*, before it requires restoration on any developed land. By taking a parcel of undeveloped land, rather than requiring restoration on a parcel of developed land, the government can generate net cost savings equal to $R + (D_2 - D_{12}) > 0$, that is, the restoration cost R plus the time 2 development cost savings obtained by "updating" developed land rather than developing undeveloped land.

In view of this "takings" priority, there are four relevant classes of θ realizations at time 2. I will denote these classes by A, B, C, and D, moving from the highest values of θ (in class A) to the lowest (in class D). If θ is in the high class A, external costs of development are so large that an efficient government policy calls for banning all additional development (beyond x_1) and, in addition, restoring some developed land to its undeveloped state. If θ is in the next highest class B, external costs are large enough to motivate a ban on all additional development (beyond x_1) but not large enough to justify costs of restoring land that is already developed. If θ is in the third class C, external costs only justify a partial ban on additional development (of previously undeveloped land), meaning that some new development is allowed but not the complete development of all land. Finally, if θ is in the lowest class D, external costs are insufficient to justify any regulation on development.

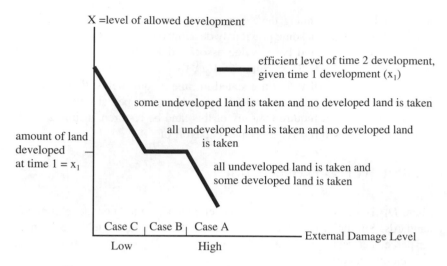

Figure 14.1. Ex-Post Efficient Regulatory/Taking Policy.

For simplicity, class D cases are ignored here. Figure 14.1 depicts optimal time 2 development levels for these different cases (different external damage levels).

Time 1 Development Choices Under No Compensation. Suppose that, although the government regulates time 2 development in an ex-post efficient manner, no compensation is paid to either owners of undeveloped land on which development is proscribed or owners of developed land who are required to restore their property to its undeveloped state (and thus bear the per-parcel restoration costs, R). Without compensation, landowners have an incentive to develop their property early (at time 1) in order to avoid the risk of being denied development rights as the owners of undeveloped property. Because this early development incentive reflects no corresponding societal value, excessive development occurs.

Consider Case A, for example. In this case, only a fraction of developed land is taken, and time 1 development provides a landowner with a *chance* to obtain a valuable development right. Because all undeveloped land is "taken," those who do not develop at time 1 have no such opportunity. The marginal time 1 developer thus obtains, on average, a fractional share of the time 2 rents that go to time 1 developers, $\{V_2'(X) - D_{12}\}(X/x_1)$, and pays only a fractional share of per-parcel restoration costs, $R[(x_1 - X)/x_1]$. In the "A" cases, however, every additional parcel of land that is developed at time 1 leads to one more parcel of land that is "taken" – and restored – at time 2;[12] hence, the time 2 *social* benefit of this development is negative to the extent that costs must be incurred to

---

[12] In the A cases, the optimal level of allowed time 2 development does not depend upon the level of time 1 development at the margin (see Appendix 14.1). Hence, for these cases, a

restore the land to a condition suitable for public use. The difference between private net benefits of investment and social net benefits, $-R$, is thus:[13]

$$\{V_2'(X) - D_{12}\}\left(\frac{X}{x_1}\right) - R\left(\frac{x_1 - X}{x_1}\right) - [-R]$$

$$= \{V_2'(X) - D_{12} + R\}\left(\frac{X}{x_1}\right) = E_X(X, \theta)(X/x_1) > 0. \tag{14.1}$$

To the extent that time 1 developers retain development rights in time 2 (with the probability (X/x_1)), they do not face – and thus ignore – the external costs of their development. This ignored external cost, as described in equation (14.1), favors more development than is efficient.

A similar "rent seeking" incentive for early development exists in Cases B and C as well. In both cases, only undeveloped land is taken, and early (time 1) development thus eliminates a landowner's risk of appropriation entirely.

Theorem 1. When there is no compensation for government takings, initial (time 1) development will be higher than is efficient. (See Appendix 14.1 for proof.)

I next turn to how the "rent-seeking" incentive identified in Theorem 1 can and cannot be corrected.

The Pigouvian Solution. Arguably the simplest path to providing landowners with efficient development incentives is to confront them with precisely the societal costs that are otherwise missing from their optimization calculus, namely, the "external damages" that marginal development creates. This can be done in two ways: (1) Pigouvian taxes, under which all land that remains or becomes developed at time 2 is subject to a tax, or liability assessment, equal to the ex-post marginal external damage from development; and (2) Pigouvian compensation, under which all land that is taken at time 2 is afforded compensation equal to the marginal external damage foregone. Under either of these policies, each parcel of land that is developed as of time 2, rather than diverted to public use, yields its owner net benefits that are precisely equal to the societal (private) benefits that such development affords, net of the societal cost from its foregone alternative (public) use. As a result, landowners will take precise account of all societal benefits and costs when making their time 1 development decisions.[14]

The problem with these solutions is that their implementation requires the observation of the external damage realization at time 2. Clearly, the elected

---

marginal increase in the amount of developed land at time 1 increases the amount of land that is taken at time 2 by exactly the same amount.

[13] The last equality in (14.1) is due to the government's optimality conditions for choice of X (in Case A); in words, this condition equates the value of allowing an additional parcel of (time 1) developed land to remain in private use, rather than be restored ($V_2' - D_{12} + R$), with the external cost of this marginal development ($E_X(\ )$).

[14] Hermalin (1995) notes the efficiency of the Pigouvian approach in a single-parcel takings model.

government that imposes a land-use regulation must observe this value if it is to behave efficiently. Indeed, in the context of the present model, the very purpose of the elected government is to determine these values and provide appropriate amounts of the public goods in accord with its determinations. In part, this chapter is concerned with how the government should make these choices and how it can elicit efficient development choices from landowners. More deeply, however, this chapter is concerned with how the provision of efficient development incentives can be *verified by the courts* and, in view of potential government misbehavior, how to design appropriate restraints on government that are also enforceable by the courts. In this context, a meaningful and realistic distinction between the elected government and the courts is that the external damage realizations, which are determined by the elected government in its decision-making process, are *not* observable to the courts. This distinction motivates an inquiry into mechanisms for allocating the costs of takings that are not directly tied to external damage realizations, but that are instead tied to variables that both landowners and the courts observe, such as the market value of land, construction/development costs, and the *distribution* of external damages. The remainder of this section studies such mechanisms.

Development Incentives Under Full Compensation. A full compensation policy provides a landowner with takings compensation equal to the economic benefits that would accrue to him or her in the absence of a taking. Such compensation has two effects. First, because it eliminates the value of a development right (with landowners indifferent between obtaining a right and being compensated for a taking), there is no longer the rent-seeking incentive to develop. Second, the compensation provides a time 1 developer with construction cost savings in all external damage cases. Equivalently, under a full compensation policy, a developer does not consider the prospective loss of his time 1 development investment in the event of a taking. Excessive development thus results for the same reasons as it does in the single parcel (BRS) takings model.

Theorem 2. When there is full compensation for government takings, the time 1 development level will be higher than is efficient. (See Appendix 14.1 for proof.)

Efficient Compensation and the Equal Treatment Standard. Although full compensation leads to overdevelopment, alternative compensation regimes can provide efficient development incentives. To understand how an efficient compensation regime can be constructed, it is useful to think rather generally about how to ensure a coincidence between the landowner's financial incentives to develop and the societal benefits and costs that such development will bring. One way to ensure such a coincidence is to provide landowners with time 2 payoffs that reflect the "ex-post" social values that result from the various external damage realizations. The following equation defines policies that satisfy this criterion:

$$P_D - P_U = \text{marginal social benefit of developed land at time 2}$$
$$\equiv q \qquad\qquad (14.2)$$

r = Price of a Full Development Right

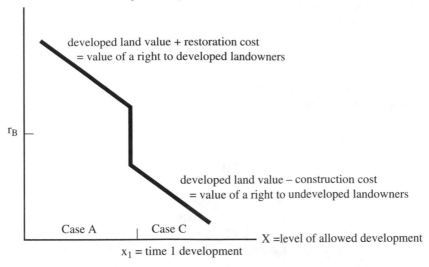

Figure 14.2. Price of a Development Right Under a TDR Policy.

where P_D is the time 2 payoff to owners of developed land (on average across all developed land) and P_U is the corresponding payoff to owners of undeveloped land. The right-hand side of equation (14.2) gives the increase in economic value to society, at time 2, that results from a marginal increase in the amount of land developed at time 1. Equation (14.2) requires that the net private benefit of having a developed land parcel, rather than an undeveloped parcel, equals the net social benefit of developed, rather than undeveloped, land. Equation (14.2) will be said to define an *equal treatment standard* for owners of developed and undeveloped property.

To interpret this standard more precisely, let us express the marginal time 2 benefits of developed land for each of the various external damage cases depicted in Figure 14.1. In Case A, marginal developed land is taken and, hence, yields a time 2 loss equal to any cost required to "restore" a developed land parcel to a condition suitable for public use. Thus, we have, for Case A,

$$q = q_A = -R. \tag{14.3a}$$

In Case B, the amount of time 1 development determines the amount of allowed time 2 development, giving us[15]

$$q = q_B = \text{the marginal private value of development } (V_2' - D_{12}),$$
$$\text{less the average marginal external damage of}$$
$$\text{development in B cases.} \tag{14.3b}$$

---

[15] q_B depends only on an average value of external damages because of this chapter's premise that compensation cannot depend on realizations of these damages that are unobservable to the courts (see earlier discussion on Pigouvian taxation).

Finally, in Case C, marginal undeveloped land is developed at time 2. Hence, marginal time 1 development yields the savings of the time 2 construction costs that would otherwise have to be borne on the property:

$$q = q_C = D_2 - D_{12}. \tag{14.3c}$$

Note that, with optimal policies, the marginal social value of developed land is smaller when external costs of development are larger:

$$q_A < q_B < q_C.^{16} \tag{14.4}$$

Two possible implementations of the equal treatment rule are as follows.

Equal Treatment Compensation. In Case A, wherein both developed and undeveloped land parcels are taken, equal treatment will be satisfied if takings compensation (C_U for undeveloped land and C_D for developed land) is provided to *both* types of land at the *full compensation rate for developed land*:

$$C_U = \{V_2'(X) - D_{12} + R\} = C_D. \tag{14.5}$$

With this compensation, developed landowners will receive the same payoff, whether they retain development rights or they are required to restore their land, forego development benefits, and receive the takings compensation. Undeveloped landowners, however, receive a payoff that is higher to the extent of any "restoration" costs, costs for which they are compensated but which they do not have to bear. Equations (14.2) and (14.3a) are thus satisfied with the proposed compensation.

In Case C, wherein only some undeveloped parcels are taken, *full compensation* yields all undeveloped landowners the same payoff, namely, the time 2 private value of development less the cost of construction, $P_U = V_2' - D_2$. Since developed landowners only face the updating costs, D_{12}, their payoff is $P_D = V_2' - D_{12}$. Full compensation thus satisfies the equal treatment conditions (14.2) and (14.3c), $P_D - P_U = D_2 - D_{12}$.

Finally, in Case B, wherein all undeveloped parcels are taken – and no developed parcels are taken – equal treatment will be satisfied if the undeveloped landowners are compensated for the average value of their land in public use (i.e., the average marginal external damage in B cases), rather than for

---

[16] When only some undeveloped land is taken (Case C), the optimal amount of allowed development equates the net marginal value of development (the marginal private value, less the marginal external damage) with the cost of developing an additional parcel, q_C. Similarly, optimal policy in A cases equates the net marginal value of development with q_A, the restoration costs saved by allowing an additional parcel of developed land to remain developed. B cases occur when the net marginal value of development, with all undeveloped lands and no developed lands taken, is between q_A (which is negative) and q_C (which is positive). Hence, with q_B equal to the average net marginal value of development in B cases, we have equation (14.4).

the lost private value. Note that this "external damage compensation" exceeds the private value of development lost by owners of undeveloped land.[17]

In summary, the equal treatment standard can be satisfied with an appropriate policy of takings compensation. Such a policy provides *more than full* compensation to *un*developed landowners whenever all undeveloped land is "taken" (Cases A and B), thereby countering the overdevelopment incentive created by *exactly full* compensation. Achieving "equal treatment" with compensation is, hence, even more costly to the government than the exactly full compensation called for under an eminent domain doctrine. However, equal treatment can be achieved in ways that are less costly to the government, and more costly to landowners overall. Indeed, tradeable development rights can achieve equal treatment with zero government compensation cost.

Tradeable Development Rights. Rather than compensating landowners for a "taking" – for the denial of the right to develop – the government could distribute costs of its takings using a tradeable development rights (TDR) policy. Under a TDR scheme, the government issues each and every parcel owner tradeable permits that entitle him (or her) to hold the fractional number, $X/\overline{X}$, of developed land parcels. In order to develop a parcel fully, the parcel's owner must buy up some additional rights from other landowners, who then forego the right to develop.

Turning again to the cases depicted in Figure 14.1, competitive prices for a full TDR – the right to develop a full parcel – are as depicted in Figure 14.2. In Case A, when there are fewer rights than land developed at time 1, owners of developed land must buy TDR permits from other owners of developed land. Hence, the price of a full permit will equal the value of the right to these owners, $V_2'(X) - D_{12} + R$, the net gain to a developed property owner from "updating" versus restoring his land. At this permit price, owners of developed land obtain the same payoff, whether they buy up rights in order to keep their development or sell their rights and "restore" their land. This payoff (thinking about the "sell rights" strategy) equals the value of the TDRs that each landowner is endowed with, less any costs of "restoration." Undeveloped landowners, whose return to development is strictly less than the price of a full permit, sell their permit endowment to developed landowners. The difference between the landowner payoffs, $P_U - P_D$, is simply the restoration cost, as required by the equal treatment standard (equations (14.2) and (14.3a)).

In Case B, there is not a deterministic competitive price for development rights, as indicated in Figure 14.2. However, if the government stands ready to buy and sell permits at an appropriate price, r_B in the figure, the equal treatment

---

[17] From (14.3b), the average marginal external damage in B cases equals the marginal private value of development, less q_B. With $q_B < q_C$ (equation (14.4)), compensation for this foregone damage is greater than the value of developed land, less q_C, which is precisely the private value of developing undeveloped land.

standard will be satisfied. The r_B permit price that will satisfy equal treatment is the Case B average level of marginal external damages or, equivalently, the average Case B Pigouvian development tax. At this price, developed landowners gain more from owning a permit, $V_2' - D_{12} + R$, than it costs them to buy one, r_B, while undeveloped landowners gain more from selling a permit, r_B, than it costs them to forego development, $V_2' - D_2$. Hence, developed landowners buy permits from undeveloped landowners at the regulated price, r_B.

In Case C, the story is similar to Case A. Here, there are more development rights than developed land and owners of undeveloped land must buy permits from other undeveloped landowners. Hence, the price of a full permit will equal the value of this permit to undeveloped landowners, namely, the value of developed land, less costs of construction, $V_2' - D_2$. At this permit price, undeveloped landowners all obtain the same payoff, the net value of developing an undeveloped parcel, less the cost of buying up the extra permits needed to obtain a full development right. Developed landowners also obtain the value of retaining their development, less costs of required permit purchases. Because developed landowners need not bear costs of new construction, however, these payoffs differ by the amount of the new construction cost, $D_2 - D_{12}$, as required by the equal treatment conditions (14.2) and (14.3c).

TDRs work because, in essence, they replicate a Pigouvian development tax. In Case A, for example, a developed land parcel is the marginal "taking" and the societal optimization calculus equates the marginal value of land in public use with the marginal private value of retaining development, including any restoration cost savings. A TDR program, in turn, confronts landowners with a price for development that equals the second term in this calculus. Because of society's optimization, this price is precisely the societal cost of development, the marginal external damage. Exactly the same logic applies in Case C, with undeveloped land replacing developed land at the margin.[18]

The TDR program described here is the logical equivalent of efficient compensation *if* the class of landowners that are potentially subject to a taking is identical to the population of potential beneficiaries from a taking – and to the public that may be subject to taxation for the payment of any compensation. Whether taxes are levied on all landowners and used to pay efficient compensation to the owners of taken land, or landowners with development rights are required to pay these taxes directly to the owners of taken land, by buying their TDRs, is irrelevant to the flow of cash and economic benefits. These regimes differ, in an economically relevant sense, only

---

[18] Note also that tax/subsidy programs can be used to replicate the TDR policy outcomes characterized here. A permit policy effectively *taxes land that is not taken* at the per-parcel rate of $r(\theta)(1 - (X/\bar{X}))$ and *subsidizes land that is taken* at the per-parcel rate of $r(\theta)(X/\bar{X})$, where $r(\theta)$ is the relevant permit price. The direct imposition of such taxes and subsidies may be more practical than permit policies in instances where, for example, the government desires contiguous or dispersed tracts of land and, for this reason, wishes to target certain parcels, among many in a given class, for a taking.

when the class of landowners is distinct from the overall body politic that benefits from land-use regulation and pays taxes to support any costs of public good provision. Such is the case for the vast majority of examples that motivate this inquiry and will be the basis for modeling political behavior in what follows. In these cases, TDRs are much less burdensome to the general "taxpaying public" and more burdensome to landowners as a group.

III. POLITICAL BEHAVIOR AND AN EFFICIENT TAKINGS DOCTRINE

I have so far assumed that government acts benevolently to maximize society's economic welfare. A prominent theme in the takings literature is that the government may not be so altruistic and may indeed undervalue the private benefits and costs that accrue to landowners and other victims of takings. If so, it is argued, the government will "take" property more often than is efficient, unless compelled to confront the full costs of its actions by a constitutional requirement that compensation be paid to takings victims.

This section takes a critical look at this argument in the context of this chapter's multiple-parcel takings model. The basic purpose of this inquiry is to shed light on any systematic biases that may characterize the political choice process in which the government is engaged and, in doing so, learn something about how to structure judicial restraints on government behavior in order to enhance society's overall economic welfare. In view of this purpose, government "misbehavior" is not modeled as stupidity or irrationality, but rather as a rational response to potentially unscrupulous political preferences.[19] Judicial restraint on government behavior should, in this context, be designed to ensure that government and individual citizens have the *incentives* to act in society's interest. To study these incentives, this chapter departs from the analytical perspective of prior work that models the government as making its taking decisions in response to various *exogenous* compensation rules. Here, instead, government is assumed to *choose* both its regulatory/takings policy *and its compensation/tax policy*. This distinction is not only important in determining whether and how government behavior may lead to inefficient outcomes. It is also necessary to characterize the types of constitutional restraints that work – and do not work – to correct such inefficiencies.

An Interest Group Perspective on Government. Consider a model of government with two "interest groups": (1) landowners, and (2) the general public

---

[19] I should point out that this analysis is limited to some extent by the absence of explicit government and citizen "mistakes." Epstein (1992) argues, for example, that a "second review" of government policy, by the courts, can be advantageous because it reduces the likelihood of a mistake. However, this argument does not suggest how a "second review" should proceed, given that the actions which the courts take – and the rules that they follow – will provide incentives for government choices at the outset. This analysis focuses on these incentives and their implications for judicial policy.

that pays taxes and bears the "external damage" from development.[20] The government maximizes a political welfare function that depends upon the payoffs reaped by the interest groups,

$$G(W_L, W_T),\tag{14.6}$$

where W_L is the political benefit obtained from landowners and W_T is the total payoff obtained by "taxpayers." To be general, W_L is allowed to depend upon the payoff that each and every landowner obtains. With landowners indexed by i on the interval, $[0, \overline{X}]$, owners of developed land will be assigned index values on the lower interval, $[0, x_1]$, where x_1 is the amount of land developed at time 1, and W_L becomes:

$$W_L = W_L(\{P_i\}; x_1),\tag{14.7}$$

where $P_i =$ payoff to the ith landowner.

The government will choose both its takings policy and its compensation policy to maximize its welfare function, $G(\ )$ in equation (14.6). The takings policy can be represented by the collection of zero-one choices,

$$T_i = \begin{array}{ll} 1, & \text{if landowner } i\text{'s parcel is taken} \\ 0, & \text{otherwise.} \end{array}\tag{14.8}$$

Compensation policy is characterized by the government's choice of payoffs, $(\{P_i\}, W_T)$.

The government's choices are subject to the constraint that the payoffs can be made from the available economic surplus at time 2. This surplus will equal, plus or minus a constant, the private value of the land parcels that the government does *not* take, less construction costs, costs of "restoring" developed land for takings, and "external damages" from development. Formally representing the societal economic surplus by $S(\{T_i\}; \theta, x_1)$, the constraint on government choices is as follows:

$$W_T = S(\{T_i\}; \theta, x_1) - \int_0^{\overline{x}} P_i\, di\tag{14.9}$$

where the subtracted integral is the total amount of surplus allocated to landowners. In essence, the government is assumed to tax away the net private values that accrue to landowners and then hand back payoffs to these landowners in "tax rebates."[21] Although landowner "taxes" and "tax rebates"

---

[20] Section IV below considers the addition of another key interest group, the "environmental lobby," arguing that results from the present two-group model are robust.

[21] The private values that accrue to landowners may include some external costs of aggregate development. These costs may be present even when agglomeration benefits of development accrue to the general public and more than offset *all* external costs of development, including those to landowners. The logic of this analysis thus extends to environments in which no

actually occur in one step, they yield a residual payoff to the general taxpaying public that is as described in equation (14.9).[22]

In the absence of any constitutional restraints on government behavior – the counterfactual case of initial interest here – equations (14.7) and (14.9) can be substituted into equation (14.6) to yield the following government choice problem:

$$\max_{\{P_i, T_i\}} \; G\!\left(W_L(\{P_i\}; x_1), S(\{T_i\}; \theta, x_1) - \int_0^{\bar{X}} P_i \, di \right) \tag{14.10}$$

Inspection of problem (14.10) reveals two key properties of its solution. First, the chosen takings policy, $\{T_i\}$, will be ex-post efficient, maximizing the total economic surplus, $S(\,)$. Because the government's welfare function depends upon the payoffs that it hands out, with higher payoffs increasing its political welfare (ceteris paribus), it will want to maximize the amount of available surplus. Moreover, without constitutional or judicial constraints on the government's choice of payoffs, takings policy only affects the government's compensation policy via its effect on the economic surplus. Hence, the government will make its takings decisions efficiently so that it will have the largest possible economic pie to distribute among its constituents.

Second, the government's choice of landowner payoffs, $\{P_i\}$, will reflect an entirely political calculus, with no account for their effect on ex-ante development incentives. As illustrated in more specific examples below, the government's political calculus may lead to incentives for landowners to develop either more land or less land than is efficient ex-ante (at time 1), depending upon the nature of its political welfare function.

The first result contrasts sharply with prior analyses of takings in which the government's choice of takings policy *determines* the payoffs – or compensation – that landowners receive. In these analyses, a government that places little political value on landowners' welfare will "take" more land than is efficient if such takings reduce landowner welfare and increase the welfare of more politically potent groups who benefit from public use of the land. While such conclusions indicate possible government responses to exogenous compensation rules, they do not reveal the source of governmental inefficiency that calls for corrective restraint. Indeed, in this chapter's model, an unfettered government makes efficient takings decisions, but needs constitutional or judicial restraint to ensure that landowners are provided with efficient development incentives ex-ante. The trick is to construct a restraint that

---

takings are efficient and, yet, landowners might normally be thought to favor development restrictions. This source of political pressure is mitigated here by the government's opportunity to offer landowners other compensations for their costs of growth.

[22] Implicit in equation (14.9) is the premise that the government is able to extract the private value of developed land at time 2. This premise is relaxed in Section IV below.

fixes landowners' development incentives and does not, at the same time, add a distortion to the government's regulatory/takings choice problem.

An Equal Treatment Solution. To give landowners correct ex-ante development incentives, any governmental "restraint" must elicit payoffs that satisfy "equal treatment" on average. Otherwise, the difference between undeveloped and developed landowner payoffs at time 2 will not reflect the net societal benefits of leaving land pristine at time 1.

In some cases, however, the imposition of an equal treatment standard, in the generic form described in Section II above, does *not* achieve efficiency. The reason is that such a standard can potentially distort the government's choice between a "Case A" policy, $X < x_1$, and a "Case C" policy, $X > x_1$, by linking developed and undeveloped landowners' relative compensation to this choice.[23] These distortions can be avoided if the equal treatment constraint (14.2) is collapsed into a *uniform equal treatment (UET)* requirement that does not distinguish between the regulatory cases, A, B, and C,

$$P_D - P_U = \left\{ \int_0^{x_1} P_i \, di/x_1 \right\} - \left\{ \int_{x_1}^{\bar{X}} P_i \, di/(\bar{X} - x_1) \right\} = E(q; x_1), \qquad (14.11)$$

where $E(q; x_1)$ is the expected value of q, the marginal social benefit of developed land, under efficient time 2 regulatory policies (as defined in equation (14.3) above). When the government's choices in problem (14.10) are subject to the UET constraint, (14.11), its takings policy again affects its payoff choices only via the policy's effect on total economic surplus. As a result, the government will choose its takings efficiently, to maximize economic surplus. Moreover, the government's payoff choices, by satisfying (14.11), will elicit efficient time 1 development decisions from landowners.[24]

---

[23] Suppose, for example, that owners of developed land are government "insiders" and owners of undeveloped land are "outsiders," meaning that the government can obtain a political benefit by providing a higher *relative* payoff to the developed landowners. Under the equal treatment standard, the courts distinguish between the different cases (A, B, and C) by observing the government's choice of allowed development, X, and applying the appropriate equal treatment constraint, (14.2)/(14.3a), (14.2)/(14.3b), or (14.2)/(14.3c), accordingly. Since a "Case C" policy affords the developed landowners a higher relative reward than does either a "Case A" or "Case B" ($X = x_1$) policy, the government will have an incentive to increase the level of allowed development from at or below x_1 (Case B or A) to marginally above x_1 (Case C) in order to permit a higher relative compensation for developed landowners. This higher relative compensation, in turn, yields time 1 developers a higher relative reward at time 2 than is matched by the net societal benefits that time 1 development brings. Excessive development thus results at time 1 and sometimes at time 2. Conversely, if the owners of *un*developed land are "insiders" and the owners of developed land are "outsiders," the equal treatment standard will prompt underdevelopment at time 1 and occasional overregulation at time 2.

[24] UET need not be the only equal treatment requirement that can elicit efficient outcomes. However, it is the simplest and requires the least information about government preferences. Moreover, a government cannot, in general, be given a choice between alternative equal treatment standards because such a choice will permit the government to choose payoffs that

There are many ways in which the government can satisfy a UET standard. For example, UET can be achieved with a compensation program that has the following three features: (1) any developed landowner is fully compensated for a taking of his or her land; (2) any undeveloped landowner is provided *more than full* compensation for a taking, with compensation set as follows:[25]

$$C_U = (V_2' - D_{12}) - E(q; x_1) > V_2' - D_2; \tag{14.12}$$

and (3) any new development of undeveloped land is subsidized in order to provide the landowner with the same payoff as he or she would receive if the land was taken. Under this UET compensation policy, all developed landowners receive the same payoff, as do all undeveloped landowners, with the two payoffs differing by $E(q; x_1)$, as required for UET.

Tradeable Development Rights. UET can also be implemented with a tradeable development rights (TDR) approach that is substantially less costly to the government. To implement UET, a TDR program requires the following supplementary policies: (1) in A cases $(X < x_1)$, the government offers to subsidize the cost of restoration on developed land, with

$$\text{restoration cost subsidy} = \text{restoration cost } (R) + E(q; x_1); \tag{14.13}$$

(2) in C cases $(X > x_1)$, the government either subsidizes any new development of previously undeveloped land or taxes any previously developed land that remains developed, at the following rate per parcel

$$\text{per parcel subsidy or tax} = \text{net time 2 development cost}$$
$$(D_2 - D_{12}) - E(q; x_1); \tag{14.14}$$

violate equal treatment *on average* even though they always satisfy one of the allowed equal treatment standards ex-post. For example, a modified equal treatment standard,

$$P_D - P_U = g(X),$$

where $g(X) = q_A$ for some A cases $(X < x_1)$, $g(X) = q_C$ for some C cases $(X > x_1)$, and $g(X)$ is continuous and nondecreasing, can often be designed to elicit efficient outcomes. However, the courts must be able to determine any government interest in affording developed landowners higher or lower relative compensation if they are to design a rule that prevents inefficient regulatory choices in pursuit of relative compensation changes. Moreover, suppose the government is given a choice between UET and the modified equal treatment (MET) rule, and developed landowners are more politically powerful than undeveloped landowners. Then the government will implement MET when it allows higher relative compensation for developed landowners and UET otherwise. On average, the relative compensation afforded developed landowners will thus be greater than is necessary for efficiency. For these reasons, this chapter focuses on a UET approach to the achievement of equal treatment.

[25] The inequality in equation (14.12) follows from $q_A < q_B < q_C$ (from equation (14.3) and the definition of "case B"), which implies that $E(q; x_1) < q_C$.

r = Price of a Full Development Right

Figure 14.3. Price of a Development Right Under the "Three-Pronged" TDR Program.

and (3) in B cases ($X = x_1$), neither of the first two supplementary policies is pursued, but the government stands ready to buy and sell TDR permits at the market price that would have prevailed with both supplementary policies in place.

Figure 14.3 graphs the price of a full development right in the presence of these subsidies and taxes. For each chosen level of allowed development X, developed landowners face a permit price that leaves them indifferent between (i) buying up TDR permits in order to retain their development, and (ii) selling their rights and bearing the restoration cost, net of subsidy. Hence, even when no developed land is actually taken, a developed landowner obtains a payoff equal to the value of his TDR endowment, less the net restoration cost. Undeveloped landowners, in turn, obtain a common payoff equal to the value of their TDR endowment. The difference between these payoffs, $P_D - P_U$, is the (negative of the) net restoration cost, which is precisely the average marginal social benefit of developed land required to elicit efficient time 1 development decisions, $E(q; x_1)$.[26]

Tightening the Uniform Equal Treatment (UET) Standard. Judicial restraints such as a UET requirement are enforced by the courts in three stages: First (in stage 1), a landowner must choose to file a takings claim. Second (in stage 2), the court must decide whether to dismiss the claim or find that a takings violation has occurred. And third (in stage 3), if a takings violation is deemed to have occurred, the court must impose a remedy on the government. Here,

---

[26] Appendix 14.1 formally documents that the three-pronged TDR regime satisfies the UET standard.

efficiency is achieved by using a UET standard to *define* a taking (in stage 2) and requiring appropriate compensation (in stage 3) as a *remedy* for a takings violation, namely, violation of the UET standard.[27]

However, in defining compensable takings, the courts can impose some restrictions on the government that go beyond UET and yet preserve incentives for efficient behavior. For example, efficiency is *not* impeded by requiring the government to offer landowners *uniform payoffs* in order for takings claims to be dismissed. Uniformity means that all owners of developed land receive the same payoff and all owners of undeveloped land also receive a common payoff. The courts could even go a step further by requiring government compensation policy to take a form that is equivalent to this chapter's TDR implementation of UET combined with a homogeneous tax or subsidy per unit of land in the region. Neither a uniform payoff requirement nor a "TDR standard" upsets the separation between the government's takings policy and its compensation policy. Requiring uniformity only changes the variables that the government chooses for its compensation policy from $\{P_i\}$ to P_U and P_D. And by allowing for a redistributive land tax or subsidy, the TDR standard yields the government a landowner payoff choice that again is only linked to the government's regulatory policies by the total economic surplus available for distribution. The government will therefore want to choose its regulatory policy to maximize the surplus. The same can be said for a minimum landowner payoff (or "fairness") requirement that does not link the required minimum payoff to the government's regulatory decision (e.g., a constraint that each P_i be no smaller than some fixed $\overline{P}$). The same, however, cannot be said for a strict compensation requirement.

The Inefficiency of a Strict Compensation Requirement. Let us now suppose that the courts only dismiss takings challenges when the government implements UET with the compensation program described earlier, without any further taxes on landowners. In essence, this requirement imposes two sets of constraints on government behavior: (1) that developed and undeveloped landowner payoffs be uniform and satisfy UET, and (2) that landowner payoffs be at least as high as UET compensation levels.[28] When landowners have sufficient political power, only the first constraint binds because the government would like to offer high landowner payoffs anyway. Moreover, as noted above, the first constraint, on its own, does not distort government regulatory choices.

---

[27] A takings remedy should elicit takings claims by landowners when UET is violated – that is, when a takings violation has occurred. And it should also provide the government with an incentive to meet the UET requirement without court enforcement of the standard (assuming some costs of court proceedings, however small). The following takings remedy has both of these properties: Compensation that yields the claimant the higher of (a) his UET-implementing compensation payoff, and (b) the average payoff that satisifies UET, P_D (if the claimant owns developed land) or P_U (otherwise).

[28] If landowner payoffs satisfy the first constraint and are higher than UET compensation levels, landowners will have no incentive to file takings claims.

When landowners are not politically powerful, however, a UET compensation requirement elicits too little regulation and too much allowed development. Formally, the government's regulatory policy can be characterized here by the allowed development level, X, with this development allocated first to developed land. UET compensation requires that developed landowners each receive their full compensation payoff, $C(X)$. Applying the law of demand to development, more allowed development will lead to a lower marginal (and average) value of developed land and, hence, a lower level of the UET compensation required of government, $C'(X) < 0$. Undeveloped landowners, in turn, receive the same payoff, plus the equal treatment premium, $P_U = C(X) + E(q; x_1)$. The government's regulatory choice problem is thus as follows:

$$\max_{X} \; G(W_L(P_D = C(X), P_U = C(X) + E(q; x_1); x_1), S(X; \theta, x_1)$$

$$- (C(X)\bar{X} + E(q; x_1)(\bar{X} - x_1)) \tag{14.15}$$

Differentiating with respect to X gives the first-order condition,

$$[dG/dC(X)] \; C'(X) + [\partial G/\partial W_T][S_X(X; \theta, x_1)] = 0, \tag{14.16}$$

where $\partial G/\partial W_T > 0$. When landowners are not politically powerful, $dG/dC(X)$ is negative; the government would like to lower landowner payoffs. Thus, with $C'(X)$ also negative, the first term in the above derivative is positive. If X is chosen to maximize the economic surplus, so that $S_X()$ is zero, the government will thus want to increase X further. In order to maximize its objective function, the government will keep increasing X until the marginal efficiency cost of raising X further (the second term in the above derivative) exactly offsets the marginal political gain from reduced landowner payoffs (the first term). In sum, because the government benefits from the reduced landowner payoffs that increased development permits, it will choose a development level X which is higher than is ex-post efficient – that level which maximizes the economic surplus.

The distortionary impact of a compensation requirement is only worsened when a UET standard is not also imposed. Simply compelling full compensation will prompt the government to underregulate under the same circumstances – and for the same reasons – as it does under UET compensation. Moreover, full compensation will prompt landowners to overdevelop at time 1, which they do not do under UET compensation.

Although requiring UET compensation can impede efficiency, it should also be noted that both the UET standard and a uniform payoff standard impose *relative compensation* requirements on the government. UET defines required relative compensation for owners of undeveloped, versus developed, land. And uniformity ensures, for example, that an owner of developed land that is taken receives the same payoff as an owner of developed land that is not taken.

Examples of Political Preferences

The following examples illustrate the range of possible political welfare functions and the outcomes that they would produce in the absence of constitutional restraint.

A Majoritarian Government. As in Fischel and Shapiro (1989), consider a government that represents only the interests of the majority constituency, which we will suppose does not include the landowners. In this case, the government places a zero weight on landowner payoffs. Somewhat more generally, the government may place a uniformly lower weight on the landowners' economic welfare than it does on that of the majority taxpaying public, as in models of fiscal illusion (e.g., BRS and Miceli and Segerson 1994). The government's political welfare function then takes the form,

$$G = w_L \left[\int_0^{\bar{X}} P_i \, di \right] + w_T \left[S(\{T_i\}; \theta, x_1) - \int_0^{\bar{X}} P_i \, di \right], \quad w_L < w_T, \quad (14.17)$$

where the political weight on landowners, w_L, would be zero in a purely majoritarian model. Here, the government can increase its political welfare by lowering landowner payoffs, obtaining a net political gain of $(w_T - w_L) > 0$ for every dollar of benefit that it takes away from the landowner group. Assuming that landowners can always walk away from their property, their economic payoffs cannot be negative. The government will thus maximize its political welfare by setting all landowner payoffs as low as possible, namely, to zero. Under a rather mild regularity condition, such payoffs provide less incentive for ex-ante development than is efficient.[29] In essence, the government expropriates the net time 1 investments that landowners make and thereby deters efficient levels of these investments. A UET requirement in this case, while it will leave owners of undeveloped land with nothing, will protect developed landowners from the ex-post opportunism that would otherwise deny them appropriate incentives for development.

A Jaded Government. Suppose that political support and opposition is generated in the following way: A landowner provides intense political support (of one unit) if she receives at least her expected development payoff (P_D or P_U) and, in addition, there are some other landowners who receive less than their expected development payoff (so that the landowner views the government as doing him or her a favor). Conversely, a landowner provides intense opposition (of one unit) if he or she loses any investment that was made on the property at time 1, and infinite opposition if he or she receives a negative

---

[29] At an optimum, total societal benefits of marginal time 1 development, across times 1 and 2, are set to zero. If this calculus yields a cost in time 1 that is offset by a later benefit at time 2 – so that time 1 development requires some net time 1 investment – then the average difference between the payoffs to developed and undeveloped land at time 2 must be positive in order to elicit efficient time 1 development decisions. A zero difference between these payoffs, as occurs in the majoritarian example, thus yields too little incentive for time 1 development.

payoff. Otherwise, a landowner is politically neutral, providing net support of zero.

In this political setting, the government will maximize the net support (support minus opposition) for a given landowner "payoff budget." Starting from base landowner payoffs of zero, there are three types of landowner rewards that the government can offer, each of which earns the government a net support of one unit either by neutralizing intense opposition or generating intense support by a previously neutral landowner: (1) Increase a developed landowner's payoff from zero to the level of the time 1 development investment, thus neutralizing his or her opposition. (2) Increase a developed landowner's payoff from the time 1 investment level to the expected time 2 development payoff, $\bar{P}_D$. (3) Increase an undeveloped landowner's payoff from zero to the development payoff, $\bar{P}_U$. Under plausible conditions that will be assumed here, the first two of these three landowner rewards each costs the government less than the third.[30] Hence, in order to obtain the greatest political support at least cost, the government will offer rewards to developed landowners [(1) and (2)] before offering any undeveloped landowner rewards [(3)].

In view of this logic, the government will pursue one of two general compensation strategies: (1) offer positive payoffs *only* to owners of developed land, or (2) offer all developed landowners their expected development payoff, $\bar{P}_D$, and also offer some undeveloped landowners their expected development payoff, $\bar{P}_U$, while leaving some remaining undeveloped landowners with nothing. Notably, a jaded government always nails some landowner in order to do a favor to the rest. In the first case, when the government disenfranchises all owners of undeveloped property, the government's compensation policy for developed landowners will depend upon whether the first (time 1 investment) reward is smaller or larger than the second (development payoff) reward. If it is smaller, then all developed landowners will be given their time 1 investment payoff before any landowner is rewarded with the full expected development payoff. However, if the time 1 investment reward is larger, then some or all developed landowners will be given their full expected development payoff and the remaining landowners will be given nothing. Here, the government discriminates against undeveloped landowners for political gain, even when it fully compensates developed landowners.

These payoff choices can, in principle, yield either excessive development ex-ante or too little development ex-ante, although the former outcome (excessive development) is more plausible. For example, if the government offers all developed landowners at least their time 1 investment, then the

---

[30] These conditions are that (i) the time 1 development investment is less than the expected development payoff obtained by undeveloped landowners (i.e., $D_1 < \bar{P}_U$), and (2) total development costs for time 1 developers (including both the time 1 investment and any time 2 costs of "updating" the property) are no less than time 2 costs of construction (i.e., $D_1 + D_{12} \leqslant D_2$). (If $D_1 + D_{12} = D_2$, then a tie-breaking condition is also needed to resolve government indifference in favor of rewarding a developed landowner. For example, an arbitrarily small cost of providing any positive reward to a given landowner will suffice to break such ties).

average difference between the time 2 payoffs offered developed and undeveloped landowners will be at least as large as the difference between the full compensation payoffs, $\bar{P}_D - \bar{P}_U$.[31] In this case, there will be even more time 1 development than is elicited by full compensation – and full compensation already yields excessive development for the reasons described earlier.

IV. EXTENSIONS

In this section, I turn to extensions and generalizations of the simple model developed at the outset, exploring the robustness of this chapter's qualitative conclusions.

1. Site-Specific Attributes of Land. This chapter has modeled land as homogeneous, with the external costs of development – or the public good value of a taking – common across all properties in the region. In some cases, however, specific pieces of property will have particularly high value in public use.[32] Other things equal, such properties should be taken first. In thinking about such lands, there are two cases of interest: When it is known ex-ante (in this chapter's time 1) which specific land parcels will later be of high value in public use, and when it is *not* known ex-ante which sites will be particularly attractive for takings.[33] The latter case has a rather minor impact on this chapter's qualitative conclusions. An efficient ex-post regulatory/takings policy will be somewhat more complicated; for example, the government may optimally take some "high public value" developed property even while it allows development on some "low public value" undeveloped property. However, it will still be efficient to take undeveloped land more frequently than the more expensive developed land, whether the land has a high or a low public use value. Hence, equal treatment is still needed to avoid rent-seeking development incentives.

---

[31] This claim can be verified from three observations: (1) Full compensation payoffs for developed and undeveloped landowners differ by the net saving in time 2 construction costs on a developed parcel, $\bar{P}_D - \bar{P}_U = D_2 - D_{12}$. (2) The time 1 investment level, D_1, is assumed to be at least as large as this difference (see footnote above). (3) When developed landowners obtain at least their time 1 investment payoff, D_1, the difference between the average payoffs offered to developed and undeveloped landowners, respectively, is at least as large as the minimum of D_1 and $P_D - P_U$.

[32] See, for example, Smith and Shogren, Chapter 16 of this volume, who consider the case where added benefits accrue from not developing adjacent private parcels.

[33] When the government desires contiguous land parcels for public use, a combination of these cases may be thought to arise. On one hand, the government may not know ex-ante which set of contiguous parcels it wants. On the other hand, the government's demand for contiguity makes some parcels particularly attractive for takings ex-post. For such a setting, the present analysis might be interpreted as defining parcels so that a single parcel itself contains a critical mass – or sufficient contiguity – to meet a desired public purpose. Going beyond this analysis, contiguity values may require incorporation in ex-post landowner payoffs in order to elicit efficient ex-ante development decisions. For example, a taking of discontiguous development may require treatment similar to that given undeveloped land that is taken in order to prompt efficient contiguity in ex-ante development choices.

Both efficient ex-ante development incentives and incentives for efficient government regulatory behavior can be achieved, as before, with a UET standard that reflects the expected marginal social benefits of keeping land undeveloped initially. However, to achieve efficient takings with a tradeable development rights (TDR) approach, the government will need to compel the sale of TDRs by owners of targeted high public value properties.

If there is ex-ante knowledge about which sites are likely to have high public use value, then these sites should be viewed as a distinct class of land for purposes of this analysis. Indeed, if a particular parcel of land is entirely unique, then the single parcel model of takings may be an apt representation of the regulatory problem.

2. Intensity of Development. When landowners decide not only whether to develop at time 1, but also how much to invest in development at times 1 and 2 – or equivalently, how intensively to develop – there are more "economic margins" to consider in devising an efficient takings doctrine. To understand these margins, let us assume that only the level of development – and not its intensity – affects "external damages." Hence, as before, the government regulates the number of land parcels that may be developed at time 2. And the extent of investment on land that remains developed at time 2, whether it be investment on newly developed land or additional investment on land already developed, only affects social welfare via its impact on private values.

Thinking only about landowner incentives for the moment, three criteria must be satisfied in order to achieve efficiency: (1) Landowners must be provided with equal treatment on average (across the various possible external damage cases) in order to elicit efficient time 1 development decisions. (2) Owners of land that remains or becomes developed at time 2 must be provided with the full marginal private benefits and costs of their time 2 land investments in order to elicit efficient choices of these investments. (3) Time 1 developers must be provided, at time 2, with an average marginal investment payoff that reflects the private value of the marginal investment when this investment is not lost to a taking, and the zero value of this marginal investment when, with an efficient time 1 investment level and an efficient takings policy, the investment is lost to a taking.

This third criterion has been the central focus of extant single-parcel takings analyses, analyses which raise two issues:

1. Overinvestment, it is argued, may occur in order to raise private costs of takings and thereby alter ex-post government policy (e.g., see BRS 1984).
2. Full compensation for a taking will lead those landowners who develop their land at time 1 to ignore the lost value of their exante investments in the event of a taking, thus eliciting too much investment (again see BRS).

In the present multiple-landowner model (and in contrast to the BRS single-parcel model), the government's regulatory policy will not be affected by an individual landowner's investment choice; rather, the government's choice of permissible development, X, will hinge on marketwide investment and development choices that any one individual does not affect. However, if an individual landowner invests more in his land, ceteris paribus, it will be efficient for this particular land to be "taken" less frequently ex-post. Thus, just as time 1 developers need to share in the opportunity costs of taking undeveloped land in order to avoid an incentive for excessive development, property owners who invest more in their land need to share the costs of taking *other* land in order to avoid an incentive for excessive investment. Both the compensation and the permit regulation implementations of this chapter's uniform equal treatment rule can meet this end. Under the permit policy, increased investment – and the associated lower risk of a taking – carries with it the cost of buying up other landholders' development rights. Likewise, under the compensation policy, increased investment carries with it the cost of lost compensation in the event of a taking. If improperly implemented, however, compensation will give developed landowners the full (developed property) value of their marginal time 1 investment, even though this value is lost when a taking occurs. In BRS, the resulting overinvestment incentive can be avoided by making the compensation "lump-sum," that is, invariant to the investment level on a "taken" land parcel. In the present setting, this separation can be achieved by tying compensation to a market outcome (such as average investment on "taken" land or investment on marginal "taken" land) that is beyond the control of an individual landholder.

Turning to the government's incentives, this chapter has argued that, in the absence of restraint, even a very jaded government's self-interest is generally served by maximizing total economic surplus at the time of regulation. Hence, judicial restraint is not needed to compel efficient regulation or efficient time 2 investment choices. However, the government cannot be relied upon to provide landowners with correct time 1 incentives, whether for development or land investment. What is needed, therefore, is a judicial requirement that government takings/compensation policy satisfy both a suitably defined equal treatment standard (such as the UET requirement described above) and the above criterion [number (3)] for efficient time 1 investment incentives. As a practical matter, both of these criteria will be satisfied, and uniform payoffs also achieved, if a government's compensation policy is required to take a form that is equivalent to either (1) this chapter's "UET compensation" program (modified as just described), combined with a homogeneous subsidy or tax per unit of land, or (2) this chapter's TDR implementation of UET combined with a homogeneous land tax or subsidy. As noted above, such policies provide landowners with efficient development and investment incentives. Moreover, by requiring the government to obey this standard in order to avoid a takings violation, the courts will not compromise the government's incentives to behave efficiently at time 2. Unlike a strict UET compensation requirement, this takings standard does not tie landowner payoffs to the government's regulatory decisions and potentially distort these decisions as a result. Rather, by allowing for a redistributive land tax or subsidy, this standard yields the government a distributional (landowner payoff) choice that is only linked to the government's regulatory and time 2 investment policies by the total economic surplus available for distribution.

3. Active Lobbying. The foregoing analysis has modeled government's political welfare function, and the attendant influence of the interest groups, as exogenous. An alternative and richer view of government behavior would encompass "lobbying" activity by the interest groups that produces a political welfare function. This chapter's conclusions about takings and compensation policy, given an arbitrary political welfare function, extend to this richer environment. For example, a UET restraint continues to elicit efficient regulatory and development choices, while a compensation requirement will often lead to underregulation. What is missing, however, is an analysis of lobbying costs and the effects of alternative judicial restraints on both lobbying activity and the resulting political welfare function. While a complete treatment of these issues cannot be attempted here, a couple of observations can be made. With respect to "lobbying costs," this chapter abstracts from losses of economic resources on wasteful lobbying activity. This abstraction comes with little loss in generality when these costs are small relative to the economic costs and benefits that enter the calculus of land development and regulatory policy choices. Casual empiricism suggests that lobbying costs are often very small relative to the economic benefits at stake in the policies that lobbying is intended to affect. In the two-year 1991–1992 period, for example, a total of only $402.3 million was spent by all PACs throughout the United States (U.S. Department of Commerce, Bureau of the Census 1994).[34] However, in some specific cases (e.g., see Fischel 1992), lobbying costs may be substantial and thus merit modeling that is absent here.

Turning to the effects of lobbying on political welfare, a judicial compensation requirement would reduce the incentive for landowners to lobby the government and thereby lead to reduced "political power" of landowners. Recalling that a compensation requirement gives the government an incentive to underregulate land use precisely when landowners are not politically powerful, we can conclude that the incorporation of lobbying activity only reinforces the distortionary impact of a compensation requirement. Relative to a compensation requirement, a UET standard will give landowners a greater incentive to lobby for high payoffs. And a "uniform payoff" requirement, by making landowner interests more homogeneous, may be expected to increase the political effectiveness of landowner lobbying efforts.

4. An Environmental Interest Group. Suppose that, in addition to landowner and "taxpayer" interest groups, there is an "environmentalist" lobby (as posited,

---

[34] Of course, there are other political expenditures above and beyond those by PACs. As an approximation, PAC expenditures might be inflated by the ratio of congressional campaign expenditures to PAC congressional campaign contributions to yield an estimate for total expenditures on political lobbying, broadly defined, of about $2 billion over the two-year 1991–1992 period.

for example, in Brennan and Boyd 1995). Political welfare would then depend on a third argument, the political benefit obtained from the environmentalists, W_E:

$$G(W_L, W_T, W_E) \tag{14.18}$$

W_E will be determined, as with the other interest group political welfare measures, by the "payoff" that the environmentalists receive. Without loss of generality, this payoff can be measured in a monetary equivalent. In fact, the government may be thought to reward the environmentalist lobby in a two-stage process, first setting an environmental "budget" and then allocating the budget across environmental projects in order to maximize the environmental benefit. This process gives rise to both an environmentalist payoff that depends on the environmental budget, call it P_E, and a marginal monetary valuation of environmental benefits that is equated across projects. The marginal valuation of environmental benefits can be applied to the takings policy choice of interest here to yield a monetary value, to the environmentalists, of the "environmental damages" from development. The total "external damage" from development will then equal this environmental damage value, plus any additional external costs to the general taxpaying public.[35] And the environmentalists' payoff can then be measured by the net monetary value of environmental benefits provided,

W_E = environmental budget (P_E)
$\quad$ − environmental damage from development.

With the taxpayer group paying out the environmental budget, P_E, its payoff becomes

W_T = landowner/taxpayer economic surplus − total landowner payoff
$\qquad − (W_E +$ environmental damage from development). $\tag{14.19}$

The total economic surplus, $S(\{T_i\}; .)$, now captures both the landowner/taxpayer surplus and the "environmental damage," leading to the following choice problem for an unrestrained government:

$$\max_{(\{T_i\}, \{P_i\}, W_E)} \quad G\left(W_L(\{P_i\}; x_1), S(\{T_i\}; .) - \int_0^{\bar{x}} P_i \, di - W_E, W_E\right)$$

$$\tag{14.20}$$

As before, the government need not distort its regulatory policy in order to achieve its distributional objectives, even when "environmentalists" are a

---

[35] There are different ways to break up "external costs." Brennan and Boyd (1995), for example, capture the environmental interests of all constituencies – which represent all external effects – in the environmentalist payoff. Here, additional external values are allowed.

beneficiary constituency. All of the results developed above thus extend directly to this enriched setting.

5. Government Behavior Under Asymmetric Information.

5. Government Behavior Under Asymmetric Information. This chapter has so far posited that the government can fully extract any economic rents that would otherwise accrue to private agents. Although the marginal value of developed land – its market value – is clearly observable and taxable, the government may not be able to determine how much private consumer surplus each individual consumer/landowner derives from land ownership, beyond the market value. In what follows, I will characterize circumstances under which the government does and does not act *as if* it could fully extract each consumer's private surplus – choosing an efficient regulatory policy in the absence of any judicial restraint – despite its imperfect information.

To be more specific, suppose the demand for developed land derives from heterogeneous consumer values of owning a unit of developed land, with the demand curve (and associated aggregate value for a given amount of developed land, X) obtained by sequentially ordering the consumer values from highest to lowest. In this setting, a landowner can be characterized by two indeces on the interval of available land, $[0, X]$: First is the i index used above, with index values lower than x_1 representing owners of developed land. Second is an index of the landowner's private value of holding developed land, y, with lower y values associated with higher land values. Landowner y obtains the following time 2 net consumer surplus, given aggregate development of X:

$$g(y;X) = \begin{matrix} V_2'(y) - V_2'(X) & \text{for } y \leqslant X \\ 0 & \text{for } y > X \end{matrix}$$

where $V_2(x)$ is the total time 2 private value of x units of developed land.[36] The government observes the i index values, the marginal (market) land value $V_2'(X)$ and the total net consumer surplus,

$$g^*(X) = \int_0^{\bar{X}} g(y;X)\, dy = V_2(X) - XV_2'(X).$$

However, the government does not observe consumers' y indices and, hence, does not know which particular consumers obtain higher surplus values. The payoff to landowner (i, y) is thus comprised of an observable and government-chosen "base" payoff, P_i, plus the private surplus, $g(y;X)$. Moreover, since the government can directly extract all economic rents other

---

[36] Note that landowner y obtains the surplus value $g(y;X)$ even when his or her land is "taken." Land will trade to those who place highest value on its private use. Note also that, although the mathematical arguments developed here concern the case of private information about the consumer surplus values, $g(y;X)$, these values may be adjusted to include any external costs of development that accrue to landowners and that are hidden from the government. The logic of the ensuing discussion is robust to such adjustments.

than the net consumer surplus, the economic surplus available to taxpayers is as follows:

$$W_T = S(X; \theta, x_1) - g^*(X) - \int_0^{\bar{X}} P_i \, di,$$

where the government's regulatory policy has been reduced (for simplicity and without loss of generality) to the allowed development level, X, achieved in cost-minimizing fashion.

Let us first consider how this structure affects the government's regulatory choice, X, when its political benefit from landowners depends upon the *aggregate payoff* that accrues to landowners,

$$P_L = \int_0^{\bar{X}} P_i \, di + \int_0^{\bar{X}} g(y; X) \, dy.$$

The government's choice problem can then be written as:

$$G\left[W_L\left(\int_0^{\bar{X}} P_i \, di + g^*(X); x_1 \right), S(X; \theta, x_1) - g^*(X) - \int_0^{\bar{X}} P_i \, di \right].$$

Corresponding first order optimality conditions are:

$$P_i: G_L \left[\partial W_L / \partial P_L \right] - G_T = 0 \tag{14.21}$$

$$X: \{ G_L[\partial W_L / \partial P_L] - G_T \} g_X^*(X) + G_T S_X(X; \theta, x_1) = G_T S_X(X; \theta, x_1) = 0 \tag{14.22}$$

where $G_L = \partial G / \partial W_L$ and $G_T = \partial G / \partial W_T$. The first equality in (14.22) follows from condition (14.21). Condition (14.22) implies that the government will maximize its own political welfare by choosing X efficiently, to maximize the total economic surplus $S(\ )$.

More generally, one can envision two types of political mechanisms. First, political benefits (or pressure) may depend upon the inferred average payoff obtained by each landowner i, with the average taken over y values that are possible in the population of landowners:

$$P_i + E(g(y; X)) = P_i + \int_0^{\bar{X}} g(y; X) \, (1/\bar{X}) \, dy.$$

For example, such a process will prevail if the landowners' y values are only revealed to them after policy decisions have been made and political benefits realized. Alternately, if the political benefit function, $W_L(\ )$, is the result of some observable pressure exerted at the time of policy decision making, landowners may send "pressure signals" consistent with this payoff averaging as equilibrium strategies in an adverse selection game among them.

Second, the political benefit derived from landowners may depend upon landowner payoffs realized after policy decisions have been made. In this case, the government may maximize its expected political welfare with the political benefit from landowners taking the random value,

$$W_L(\{P_i + g(y; X)\}; x_1).$$

This value is random to the government because it cannot observe the y indeces and, hence, attaches a probability distribution to y for each consumer/landowner. The assigned probability distribution is assumed to be the population distribution for y, which is uniform on $[0, X]$.

In the first case, the government's choice problem is as follows:

$$\max_{\{P_i\}, X} G\left[W_L(\{P_i + (g^*(X)/\overline{X})\}; x_1), S(X; \theta, x_1) - g^*(X) - \int_0^{\overline{X}} P_i \, di \right].$$

Evaluating first-order conditions for this problem yields the optimality condition, $S_X() = 0$, again implying efficient regulatory decisions.

The second case is more complicated and is formally developed in Appendix 14.1. There it is shown that, if the marginal political benefit of raising a landowner's payoff is invariant to the anticipated level of private surplus that accrues to the landowner, then efficient regulatory choices are again achieved. However, if a lower level of landowner surplus yields a higher marginal political benefit from payoff "dollars" allocated to the landowner (perhaps due to a concave political pressure function), then an unfettered government will have an incentive to overregulate. Overregulation occurs because concavity of the political benefit function implies that a dollar of risky landowner payoff yields a lower political benefit than a dollar of riskless landowner payoff. From the government's point of view, the consumer surplus constitutes risky payoff. Hence, the government places a lower value on the consumer surplus than it does on other sources of economic surplus, including the market value of land. As a result, the government's valuation of marginal development does not include the full benefit of this development in increased consumer surplus and the government allows less development than is efficient.

In sum, there are a variety of circumstances under which an unfettered government will choose an ex-post efficient regulatory policy despite an inability to observe and extract individual consumers' private surpluses, including: (1) When landowners are developers who obtain the marginal (market) land value and the "consumer surplus" accrues to the general public. (2) When landowners are also the recipients of consumer surplus in the land market and the government's political benefit from landowners either (a) depends upon the aggregate landowner payoff (as posited in extant takings analyses), or (b) depends upon the inferred average payoff obtained by each landowner, with an arbitrary functional dependence on the different landowner payoffs. However, if the government's political benefits from landowners depend upon landowner payoffs realized after policy decisions have been made and, in addition, a lower landowner surplus yields a higher marginal political benefit of the economic payoff allocated to the landowner (ceteris paribus), then an unfettered government will undervalue the private surplus that accrues to consumer/landowners and over regulate land use as a result.

V. SUMMARY AND CONCLUSION

This chapter constructs a model of government takings in which some property owners develop their land earlier than others. After some initial development has taken place, the government discovers the value of placing land in a public use. In response to this discovery, the government bans some or all further development and, in some cases, requires that some developed land be restored to its undeveloped state. Because of nonnegative "restoration" costs on developed land and/or costs of developing undeveloped land, it is efficient for the government to "take" undeveloped land *first*, before it "takes" any developed land. As a result, the possibility of *un*compensated takings gives landowners an incentive to develop their land early on in order to reduce the risk that their land will later be appropriated for public use. Efficiency can be achieved if takings are implemented with policies that afford "equal treatment" to landowners, ensuring appropriate relative compensation for owners of this chapter's generic developed and undeveloped land. For example, if government limits on total development are implemented with the issuance of an equal number of tradeable development rights to the owners of each and every land parcel, equal treatment can be satisfied. Such a permit policy compels developed landowners to buy development rights from undeveloped landowners, thus compensating the undeveloped landowners for donating their land to public use and restoring efficient ex-ante development incentives.

Although government failure is not necessary to the argument for equal treatment policies, political behavior can motivate constitutional restraints on government actions. This chapter characterizes the type of judicial restraint that is needed when the government chooses both its regulatory/takings policy and its compensation policy. Because the government can use its compensation/tax policy to redistribute economic rents between landowners and other constituencies, the government's only concern in its regulatory policy is to maximize the size of the overall economic pie that is available for distribution, regardless of its political preferences. Hence, in this chapter, government self-interest is served by an efficient regulatory policy. However, its political motives can often lead to ex-post landowner payoffs that fail to provide landowners with incentives for efficient levels of development ex-ante.

Constitutional restraint is thus needed to restore efficient development incentives. A necessary property of such a restraint is that it provide landowners with "equal treatment," on average. To be efficient, a constitutional restraint must also avoid adding a distortion to the government's regulatory choice problem. A uniform equal treatment (UET) restraint meets both objectives – correcting ex-ante development incentives and preserving efficient government regulatory incentives – by requiring a uniform difference between the average economic payoffs afforded to owners of developed and undeveloped land, respectively, with this difference chosen to reflect the average net societal benefits, ex-post, obtained from marginal ex-ante development. However, if the courts require the government not only to satisfy UET, but to implement equal treatment with a full compensation program, then the government will often have an incentive to underregulate by allowing too much land development. When landowners are not politically powerful, the government will want to lower landowner payoffs, which it can do by increasing the level of allowed development and thereby lowering the land price to which compensation is tied.

The economic logic developed here stresses the careful identification of potential inefficiencies in government behavior and the design of judicial restraints that can correct these inefficiencies, taking account of both the full range of government powers and logical distinctions between the functions and abilities of elected governments and the judiciary. Such logic motivates equal treatment restraint on government behavior and identifies a potential distortionary effect of a strict compensation requirement on government regulatory incentives, even when such compensation is designed to elicit efficient landowner development decisions.

In closing, it is instructive to interpret this chapter's logic in the context of three recent takings cases.

Yee v. City of Escondido (1992). This case revolves around two government regulations of mobilehome parks. The first is a city rent control ordinance under which the rents that the owner of a mobilehome park can charge his tenants are set at below-market levels by the City Council. The second is the California Mobilehome Residency Law (MRL) which confines the circumstances under which a park owner can terminate a lease agreement, effectively endowing tenants with property rights to their leases and any submarket rents that go with them. The MRL increases efficiency by allowing the mobilehome leases to trade at market prices and, hence, allowing tenants and prospective tenants to make their housing choices in response to these prices. Without the MRL, the rent controls inefficiently deter tenants from moving because, when they move, they lose the rent subsidy that they enjoy in the mobilehome park.

This case is interesting not only because it illustrates the government's desire to achieve ex-post efficient outcomes (with the MRL) even when it wants to baldly redistribute economic rents from one interest group (park owners) to a politically more potent constituency (tenants). Perhaps more important, it illustrates the government's failure to provide efficient ex-ante development incentives. To the extent that controlled rents are set below market levels, the rent control statute, with or without the MRL, denies equal treatment to mobilehome park owners.[37] Although this chapter has focused on the relative benefits that are offered developed and undeveloped property owners, equal treatment requires, more generally, that landowners be provided with the net social benefits associated with their initial land development/investment decisions, relative to alternative development/investment decisions. In the mobilehome context, equal treatment requires that park owners be afforded the net social benefits of investing their land in mobilehome use, rather than alternative uses in the area. Without equal treatment, landowners can anticipate ex-post appropriation of mobilehome park rents and will, as a result, invest too little land ex-ante in these parks. The case for constitutional restraint in this instance is clear, not because of the MRL, but because of the unequal treatment that the rent control ordinance affords park owners. Unfortunately, the Supreme Court chose to sidestep the issue of rent control entirely in this case and focus instead on whether the two statutes together affected a taking when the rent control ordinance alone was presumed not to do so. Posed in this way, the takings debate degenerates into a choice between allowing the government to make an efficiency-enhancing policy change (the MLR) or instead, striking down the efficiency-enhancing innovation in order to increase the social costs – and thereby deter the adoption – of a rent control ordinance that should itself be struck down.

Dolan v. City of Tigard (1994). In *Dolan*, and its logical predecessor, *Nollan v. California Coastal Commission* (1987), the Supreme Court has established two tests for exemption of a local land-use restriction (or exaction) from the takings clause. In both cases, a landowner asked the local government regulator for permission to engage in further development of his or her property, and the regulator tied this permission to the landowner's provision of land set asides that were of value to the general public. For such government actions to be exempt from the takings clause – and hence, exempt from an obligation to fully compensate the affected landowners – the Court has ruled that the actions must satisfy both "essential nexus" (*Nollan*) and "rough proportionality" (*Dolan*) standards. "Essential nexus" exists when the permit conditions that are exacted by the regulator can be motivated by a legitimate state interest that would be impaired by the proposed development. "Rough proportionality" requires, in addition, that the government exactions impose a cost on the landowner that is roughly the same (or at least no greater than) the monetary value of the damage that the development causes to the state's interest.

---

[37] Controls on mobilehome rents are sometimes motivated by the claim of monopolistic practices by park owners. Owners, it is argued, may exploit the immobility of tenants' mobilehomes to charge above-market rents. However, as Epstein (1992) points out, there is no reason to believe that rental contracts, signed before a tenant commits his mobilehome investment, are incapable of surmounting this problem. Moreover, even accepting this argument, rents should only be limited to relevant market levels.

In the eyes of an economist (at least this economist), these new criteria represent another notch in a takings jurisprudence that attempts to distinguish between government actions that represent *new takings* of property – or equivalently, *additions* to the government's stock of public goods – and those actions that instead represent protections of property that the public (or others) already owns. The first type of action is viewed as a taking for which the government must pay. The second type of action represents "nuisance" prevention that does not come under the takings clause. Sound economics underlies the exemption of nuisance preventions from takings. If the government must pay every time someone wants to damage public property, its costs of maintaining the property will skyrocket and, as a result, taxpayers will be deterred from providing appropriate amounts of the public resources that require protection. Although satisfaction of the Court's "essential nexus" and "rough proportionality" standards is clearly *sufficient* to conclude that a government action falls under the nuisance rubric, the slope becomes very slippery very fast when moving beyond these criteria. For example, is endangered wildlife a public resource that is harmed by habitat-impairing land development? Or is wildlife habitat a public good that should be paid for?[38]

Not only do the answers to these questions lie largely in the eye of the beholder; the questions themselves may be the wrong ones to ask. This chapter suggests, in essence, that courts should inquire instead about the need for judicial restraint in order to provide *incentives for efficient behavior* by both government and private property owners. If there is not a reasonably clear case for characterizing a government action as nuisance prevention, then the next step in a judicial review should arguably be to ask whether the affected landowner was afforded equal treatment. For example, was Florence Dolan afforded the same treatment and opportunities as were owners of similarly situated properties, or were there other property owners who had obtained development rights akin to those requested by Dolan and who were not confronted with a similar price for these rights? In answering this question, the Court could well have found that Dolan was not afforded equal treatment and, hence, made the same ruling in the end, compelling Tigard to pay compensation. However, the Court did *not* ask this question, instead finding that the absence of "rough proportionality" was *sufficient* cause for awarding compensation. In the context of this chapter, the *Dolan* decision may thus be interpreted as a judicial compensation requirement whenever a nuisance motivation for the government action cannot be clearly shown.[39] Such a requirement, we have seen, will often prompt underregulation by government and overdevelopment by landowners.

---

[38] See Meltz (1994, particularly page 13) for discussion of these and other issues in the extant takings jurisprudence on endangered species protection.

[39] Indeed, *Nollan* and *Dolan* yield a compensation requirement even when a government action counters a nuisance, but mitigates the damage in a way that is different – and perhaps less costly – than mitigation which satisfies the essential nexus criterion.

Lucas v. South Carolina Coastal Council (1992). Although the Court did not apply an equal treatment standard in *Yee* or *Dolan*, it implicitly did so in *Lucas v. South Carolina Coastal Council* (1992). In *Lucas*, the Supreme Court ruled that the takings clause applied when a local authority sought to comply with the South Carolina Beachfront Management Act by prohibiting the plaintiff, David Lucas, from developing two beachfront lots.[40] An important feature of the South Carolina case is that Lucas held undeveloped property on which building was prohibited, while owners of *developed* beachfront property were not prevented from enjoying the fruits of their development. In essence, the Court found that unequal treatment of Lucas and neighboring property owners warranted compensation under the takings clause.[41]

Reacting to the Court's decision in this case, the Environmental Defense Fund (Searchinger 1992) asked: "Must the public pay off landowners to preserve the basic ecological processes on which our environment depends?" This chapter argues that the answer to this question need not – and often should not – be affirmative. The government may regulate land use to achieve environmental objectives in ways that provide "equal treatment" to landowners and do not bankrupt the Treasury. For example, permit programs that are designed to achieve given target levels of wetlands restoration or open space preservation can satisfy the equal treatment requirement defined in this

---

[40] See Epstein (1993a,b) for further discussion of the Lucas case.

[41] This feature of the Lucas case is emphasized in both the U.S. Supreme Court's majority opinion on the case and Justice Kennedy's concurring opinion. In its majority opinion, the Court rules that the government has a duty to compensate property owners for losses sustained due to regulatory actions unless these actions are for the purpose of preventing nuisances or damages to public or private resources. Moreover, the Court argues that such a nuisance motivation for regulation must be supported by common law. In *Lucas v. South Carolina Coastal Council*, the Court concludes that the latter common-law criterion for obviating the government's duty to compensate was absent, writing: "The fact that a particular use has long been engaged in by similarly situated owners ordinarily imports a lack of any common-law prohibition . . . So also does the fact that other landowners, similarly situated, are permitted to continue the use denied to the claimant." The Court also cites this unequal treatment of Lucas to distinguish its *Lucas* decision from its decision in *Penn Central Transportation Co. v. New York City* (1978), wherein the Court sustained New York City's landmarks preservation program against a takings challenge; in the *Lucas* decision, the Court quotes the following passage from its *Penn Central* opinion: "These (Hadacheck, Miller, and Goldblatt) cases are better understood as resting not on any supposed 'noxious' quality of the prohibited uses but rather on the ground that the restrictions were reasonably related to the implementation of a policy – not unlike historic preservation – expected to produce a widespread public benefit and *applicable to all similarly situated property*" (italics added). In his concurring opinion, Justice Kennedy maintains that "the common law of nuisance is too narrow a confine for the exercise of regulatory power" that does not obligate the state to compensate; instead, he argues that a duty to compensate exists when regulations violate a property owner's "reasonable expectations" concerning uses to which the property may be put. "Furthermore," writes Kennedy, "the means as well as the ends of regulation must accord with the owner's reasonable expectations. Here, the State did not act until after the property had been zoned for individual lot development and most other parcels had been improved, *throwing the whole burden of the regulation on the remaining lots*" (italics added).

chapter, even though they require little or no government outlay of funds. However, if an elected government fails to implement "equal treatment" with a budget-saving policy, it is neither reasonable nor efficient to expect the courts to accept a low government cost outcome that, as Justice Kennedy puts it, throws "the whole burden of the regulation on the remaining (undeveloped) lots."

APPENDIX 14.1

A.   The Benchmark Model

To characterize efficient development behavior, it is useful to proceed inductively, first describing efficient government policy at time 2 for a given level of time 1 development, x_1. Then, in view of optimal time 2 behavior, an efficient time 1 investment level can be determined.

Efficient Time 2 Development Case A

With sufficiently high external costs, the government will choose the extent of restoration – or equivalently, the level of total development, $X < x_1$ – to solve the following problem (assuming a non-zero optimum):

$$\max_{X} J_2(X; x_1, \theta) = [V_2(X) - E(X, \theta)] - (x_1 - X)R - XD_{12}. \tag{A14.1}$$

The social welfare function, $J_2()$, includes the net public benefit of development, $V_2 - E$, less (i) the restoration costs borne on the remaining developed land, $x_1 - X$, and (ii) the private "updating" costs borne on the retained development, X. The following first-order condition characterizes the solution to problem (A14.1):

$$(V_2'(X) - D_{12}) + R = E_X(X, \theta) \Rightarrow H(X, \theta) \equiv V_2'(X) - E_X(X, \theta)$$
$$= D_{12} - R. \tag{A14.2}$$

In class A cases, the marginal "taken parcel" is land that has been developed at time 1. Efficiency thus requires equating marginal external damages $E_X()$ (the benefit of a marginal taking) with the private benefits lost by restoring the marginal *developed* land parcel (the cost of a marginal taking). As indicated in equation (A14.2), these lost benefits equal the foregone private land value, V_2', plus the net cost of restoring (vs. updating) a developed land parcel, $R - D_{12}$. The solution to (A14.2) will be denoted $X^A(\theta)$.

Case C

With this low range of external costs, the government will choose the extent of additional development that will be permitted. Its choice problem is thus as follows:

$$\max_{X} \ J_2(X; x_1, \theta) = [V_2(X) - E(X, \theta)] - (X - x_1) D_2 - x_1 D_{12} \quad \text{(A14.3)}$$

with $X > x_1$. The social welfare function now includes the net public benefits, $V_2 - E$, less (i) costs of updating developed land (all of which is retained in development) and (ii) costs of developing $X - x_1$ undeveloped parcels. The corresponding optimality condition is:

$$H(X, \theta) \equiv V_2'(X) - E_X(X, \theta) = D_2. \quad \text{(A14.4)}$$

In C cases, a welfare-maximizing government equates marginal external damages with private benefits lost by taking a marginal *undeveloped* land parcel, per equation (A14.4). The solution to (A14.4) will be denoted $X^C(\theta)$.

Case B

The government will want to neither allow further development nor restore land that has already been developed when the marginal social gain from either of these strategies is negative. Formally, if $H(x_1, \theta) < D_2$, then social gains from increasing allowed development above the level of time 1 development, x_1, will be negative. Likewise, if $H(x_1, \theta) > D_{12} - R$, then social gains from lowering development below current levels (by restoring developed land) will also be negative. Both of these inequalities hold when θ is in class B, implying that X wil be set exactly equal to x_1.

For a given x_1, classes A, B, and C, θ realizations are thus:

Class A $= [\theta_A(x_1), 1]$,   where $\theta_A(x_1)$ solves $H(x_1, \theta_A) = D_{12} - R$

Class B $= (\theta_B(x_1), \theta_A(x_1))$,   where $\theta_B(x_1)$ solves $H(x_1, \theta_B) = D_2 > D_{12} - R$

Class C $= [0, \theta_B(x_1)]$.

The different θ classes, and corresponding optimal X choices, are illustrated in Figure 14.1. In what follows, the three class labels, A, B, and C, will be used to denote either different θ realizations or, as will be convenient later, different X choices. Specifically, when $X < x_1$, "case A" is said to occur; similarly, when $X > x_1$, we have "case C"; and when $X = x_1$, we have "case B."

Efficient Time 1 Development

In view of the above characterization of optimal time 2 government policy, an efficient time 1 development/investment level will solve the following problem:

$$\text{Max}_{x_1} \; J(x_1) = \{V_1(x_1) - D_1 x_1\} \tag{A14.5}$$

$$+ \int_0^{\theta_B(x_1)} \{V_2(X^C(\theta) - X_1)D_2 - x_1 D_{12} - E(X^C(\theta), \theta)\} \, d\theta$$

$$+ \int_{\theta_B(x_1)}^{\theta_A(x_1)} \{V_2(x_1) - x_1 D_{12} - E(x_1, \theta)\} \, d\theta$$

$$+ \int_{\theta_A(x_1)}^{1} \{V_2(X^A(\theta)) - (x_1 - X^A(\theta))R - X^A(\theta)D_{12} - E(X^A(\theta), \theta)\} \, d\theta.$$

The social welfare function, $J_1(x_1)$, includes the time 1 benefits, $V_1(x_1) - D_1 x_1$, plus the expected value of time 2 welfare; the three integral terms in equation (A14.5) express the latter expectation, with the first, second, and third integrals measuring expected benefits in class C, B, and A cases, respectively. Using the definitions of $X^A(\theta)$ (equation (A14.2)), $X^C(\theta)$ (equation (A14.4)), $\theta_A(x_1)$ and $\theta_B(x_1)$, the first-order condition for (A14.5) is as follows:

$$x_1^*: \; \partial J_1(x_1)/\partial x_1 = \{V_1'(x_1) - D_1\} + D_2 \theta_B(x_1) - D_{12} \theta_A(x_1)$$

$$- R(1 - \theta_A(x_1)) + \int_{\theta_B(x_1)}^{\theta_A(x_1)} H(x_1, \theta) \, d\theta = 0. \tag{A14.6}$$

Condition (A14.6) is assumed to have a solution between 0 and $\bar{X}$, reflecting the essential qualitative structure of the model – namely, that it is efficient to have some land, but not all land, developed initially and that a variety of regulatory policies may be efficient later, at time 2.

Private Development Choices Under No Compensation

Private landowners develop their property at time 1 whenever the expected benefit of time 1 development is greater than the expected benefit of waiting to time 2. The privately determined level of total time 1 development, x_1, will be such that landowners are indifferent between these two development strategies, namely, when the net expected private benefit of time 1 development – vis-à-vis waiting to time 2 – is exactly zero.

With no compensation for takings, a landowner's expected payoff from time 1 development, per-parcel, is as follows:

$$\{V_1'(x_1) - D_1\} + \int_{\theta_A(x_1)}^{1} \left[\{V_2'(X^A(\theta)) - D_{12}\} \left(\frac{X^A(\theta)}{x_1} \right) \right.$$

$$\left. - R \left(\frac{x_1 - X^A(\theta)}{x_1} \right) \right] d\theta + (\theta_A(x_1) - \theta_B(x_1)) \{V_2'(x_1) - D_{12}\}$$

$$+ \int_0^{\theta_B(x1)} \{V_2'(X^C(\theta)) - D_{12}\} \, d\theta. \tag{A14.7}$$

The first term in (A14.7) represents the time-1-to-time-2 rents that time 1 developers obtain, given competition in the land market. The second (integral) term gives the expected time 2 profits that are obtained when it is in class A. There are two components to these profits; with the government allowing $X^A(\theta)$ parcels to remain developed, each time 1 developer obtains the development profits, $V_2'(X^A(\theta)) - D_{12}$, with the probability $(X^A(\theta)/x_1)$ (i.e., the probability that the government does not regulate a particular parcel of developed land), and the restoration losses, $-R$, with the complementary probability. The remaining terms in (A14.7) give the expected value of the landowner's payoff when θ is in class B or C.

The corresponding per-parcel benefit of refraining from time 1 development, and instead waiting until time 2 is:

$$\int_0^{\theta_B(x_1)} \{V_2'(X^C(\theta)) - D_2\}\left(\frac{X^C(\theta) - x_1}{\overline{X} - x_1}\right) d\theta. \tag{A14.8}$$

The owner of undeveloped land only obtains a positive profit in time 2 when θ is in class C. In this event, the owner obtains the development payoff, $V_2'(X^C(\theta)) - D_2$, with a probability equal to the proportion of undeveloped land that is allowed for development, $(X^C(\theta) - x_1)/(\overline{X} - x_1)$.

The net private benefit of time 1 development is the difference between (A14.7) and (A14.8), which I will denote by $\pi(x_1)$. The private development level under no compensation, x_1^{NC}, sets $\pi(x_1) = 0$. To relate x_1^{NC} to its efficient counterpart, x_1^*, it suffices to evaluate $\pi(x_1^*)$; if $\pi(x_1^*)$ is positive, then at an x_1^* development level, landowners will strictly prefer development at time 1 to waiting until time 2 and they will thus develop more than x_1^*. Using (A14.6) to evaluate $\pi(x_1^*)$ gives (with some simplification):

$$\pi(x_1^*) = \int_{\theta_A(x_1^*)}^1 \{V_2'(X^A(\theta)) - D_{12} + R\}\left(\frac{X^A(\theta)}{x_1}\right) d\theta$$

$$+ \int_{\theta_B(x_1^*)}^{\theta_A(x_1^*)} E_X(x_1^*, \theta) d\theta$$

$$+ \int_0^{\theta_B(x_1^*)} \{V_2'(X^C(\theta)) - D_2\}\left(\frac{\overline{X} - X^c(\theta)}{\overline{X} - x_1^*}\right) d\theta > 0. \tag{A14.9}$$

where the inequality follows from $E_X() > 0$ and the definitions of $X^A(\theta)$ and $X^C(\theta)$ in equations (A14.2) and (A14.4). Equation (A14.9) implies Theorem 1.

When θ is in class A, for example, the difference between private net benefits of investment and social net benefits, $-R$, is as given in equation (14.1), which gives rise to the first (Case A) integral term in equation (A14.9).

Similarly, in "C" cases, only a fraction of undeveloped land is taken, giving the owner of a developed parcel a *certain* development right, while confronting the owner of an undeveloped parcel with a positive probability of losing his parcel to the government; the latter probability is $(\overline{X} - X^C(\theta))/(\overline{X} - x_1)$. Again, a no-compensation policy gives landowners an incentive to develop at time 1 in order to improve their chances for time 2 development. Formally, without compensation, those who do not develop at time 1 lose the following amount of time 2 expected payoff:

$$\{V_2'(X^C(\theta)) - D_2\}(\bar{X} - X^C(\theta))/(\bar{X} - x_1)), \tag{A14.10}$$

even though the marginal social trade-off between time 2 and time 1 development – fixing total development as of time 2 – balances time 1 development benefits, $\{V_1'(x_1) - D_1\} + \{V_2'(X) - D_{12}\}$, against time 2 development benefits, $\{V_2'(X) - D_2\}$, on a *one-for-one* basis. The third (Case C) integral term in equation (A14.9) follows directly from this logic.

Finally, for realizations in class B, total allowed development at time 2 exactly equals time 1 investment, x_1. Hence, social gains from marginal development equal the private gains, $\{V_1'(x_1) - D_1\} + \{V_2'(x_1) - D_{12}\}$, less the externality cost of this marginal development, $E_X(x_1, \theta)$, where (by the definition of class B),

$$E_X(x_1, \theta) \in (V_2'(x_1) - D_2, V_2'(x_1) - D_{12} + R). \tag{A14.11}$$

The second (Case B) integral term in (A14.9) follows.

The Pigouvian Solution

Pigouvian taxation or compensation reduces the net value of a time 2 development right by $E_X(X, \theta)$. For Case A, the net benefit of time 1 development is thus reduced by this value, multiplied by the fraction of developed parcels that retain development rights at time 2, X^A/x_1:

$$E_X(X^A, \theta)(X^A/x_1) = (V_2'(X^A) - D_{12} + R)(X^A/x_1). \tag{A14.12}$$

Equation (A14.12) follows from the optimality of X^A (equation (A14.2)) and exactly offsets the excess Case A gain to time 1 development described in equation (14.1). Similarly for Case C, a Pigouvian solution increases the average net benefit of having *undeveloped* land at time 2 (rather than developed land) by the tax/compensation rate, $E_X(X, \theta)$, multiplied by the proportion of undeveloped parcels that are "taken":

$$E_X(X^C, \theta)(\bar{X} - X^C)/(\bar{X} - x_1)) = \{V_2'(X^C) - D_2\}(\bar{X} - X^C)/(\bar{X} - x_1)), \tag{A14.13}$$

Equation (A14.13) follows from the optimality of X^C (equation (A14.4)) and exactly offsets the excess Case C gain from time 1 development described in (A14.10). Finally, the Case B tax/compensation, $E_X(x_1, \theta)$, directly offsets the excess Case B gain to time 1 development in (A14.11). With Pigouvian taxation or compensation exactly offsetting all of the excess gains to time 1 development described in equation (A14.9), efficient development incentives will be restored.

Development Incentives Under Full Compensation

Full compensation yields the following landowner benefit from time 1 development:

$$\{V_1'(x_1) - D_1\} + \int_0^1 V_2'(X(\theta; x_1))\, d\theta - D_{12}, \tag{A14.14}$$

where $X(\theta; x_1)$ is the ex-post efficient level of time 2 development (given θ and x_1). The corresponding landowner benefit of waiting until time 2 to develop is:

$$\int_0^1 V_2'(X(\theta; x_1))\, d\theta - D_2. \tag{A14.15}$$

Subtracting (A14.15) from (A14.14) gives the landowner's net benefit of time 1 development,

$$\pi(x_1) = \{V_1'(x_1) - D_1\} + (D_2 - D_{12}). \tag{A14.16}$$

Evaluating this net benefit at x_1^* (by substituting from equation (A14.6)), we have

$$\pi(x_1^*) = (R - D_{12} + D_2)(1 - \theta_A(x_1^*)) + \int_{\theta_B(x_1^*)}^{\theta_A(x_1^*)} (D_2 - H(x_1^*, q))\, d\theta > 0, \tag{A14.17}$$

where the inequality follows from $(D_2 - D_{12}) > 0$ and $D_2 \geqslant H(x_1^*, \theta)$ $\forall \theta \in (\theta_B(x_1^*), \theta_A(x_1^*))$ (by the definition of class B). Equation (A14.17) directly implies Theorem 2.

Equal Treatment Policies

By similar reasoning, any policies that satisfy the following *equal treatment conditions* can also work to provide landowners with efficient development incentives:

$$P_D - P_U = -R \equiv q_A \qquad \text{when } X < x_1 \text{ (class A),} \tag{A14.18a}$$
$$P_D - P_U = -D^* \equiv q_B \qquad \text{when } X = x_1 \text{ (class B),} \tag{A14.18b}$$
$$P_D - P_U = -(D_{12} - D_2) \equiv q_C \quad \text{when } X > x_1 \text{ (class C),} \tag{A14.18c}$$

where P_D and P_U are average developed and undeveloped landowner payoffs, and

$$D^* = \int_{\theta_B(x_1)}^{\theta_A(x_1)} \frac{E_X(x_1, \theta)\, d\theta}{[\theta_A(x_1) - \theta_B(x_1)]} - (V_2'(x_1) - D_{12}) \in (D_{12} - D_2, R)$$

For example, consider a Tradeable Development Rights (TDR) program in which the government issues each and every parcel owner tradeable permits that entitle him (or her) to hold the fractional number, X/X, of developed land parcels. In class A and C cases, the government allows free trading in the permits. In class B cases, however, the government stands ready to buy and sell permits at the fixed price,

$$r_B = V_2'(x_1) - D_{12} + D^* = \int_{\theta_B(x_1)}^{\theta_A(x_1)} E_X(x_1, \theta) \, d\theta' [\theta_A(x_1) - \theta_B(x_1)]. \quad (A14.19)$$

Figure 14.2 in the text graphs the inverse demand for one-parcel permits for varying levels of total development, X. In all cases, the price of a time 2 development right – the permit price – equals the Pigouvian development tax (averaged for B cases). In Case A, the equation (14.2) optimality condition for the regulatory choice, X^A, implies that the permit price, $V_2' - D_{12} + R$, equals the marginal external damages, $E_X(X^A, \theta)$. Equations (A14.4) and (A14.19) imply the same equivalence for C and B cases. Hence, the permit policy replicates the Pigouvian solution and thereby elicits efficient development choices.

A Three-Pronged TDR Policy That Achieves Uniform Equal Treatment (UET)

Consider a TDR program combined with the restoration cost subsidy (in A cases), $s_R = R + E(q; x_1)$, and the new development subsidy (in C cases), $s_D = (D_2 - D_{12}) - E(q; x_1)$. It needs to be shown that this program satisfies UET and achieves an efficient land allocation (by prompting the release of undeveloped land for takings before developed land).

Land Allocation

In all cases, the three-pronged program yields the following price for a single development right:

$$V_2'(X) - D_{12} + (R - s_R) = r(X) = V_2'(X) - (D_2 - s_D), \quad (A14.20)$$

where $r(X) \equiv V_2'(X) - D_{12} - E(q; x_1)$. The left-hand side of (A14.20) gives the value of a development right to developed landowners (in A cases) and the right-hand side describes its value to undeveloped landowners (in C cases). In A cases, developed landowners compete with each other for development rights, yielding the TDR price $r(X)$; undeveloped landowners are not offered the s_D subsidy and, hence, prefer to sell a right, rather than obtain the development value, $V_2' - D_2 < r(X)$ (with $E(q; x_1) < D_2 - D_{12}$ from (A14.16)). In C cases, undeveloped landowners compete with each other for development rights, again yielding the TDR price $r(X)$; developed landowners are not offered the restoration subsidy and, hence, strictly prefer to buy rights from undeveloped landowners (with $E(q; x_1) > -R$ from (A14.16)). In B cases, the government offers the regulated price $r(x_1)$, at which developed landowners prefer to buy and undeveloped landowners prefer to sell.

UET

In Case A, developed landowners all obtain the same payoff, equal to that obtained by selling their permits and restoring their land. Undeveloped landowners obtain the value of their permit endowment. Thus, we have:

$$P_D = \text{value of permit endowment} - (R - s_R)$$
$$= P_U - (R - s_R) = P_U + E(q; x_1). \tag{A14.21}$$

The last equality follows from the definition of s_R. In Case C, all landowners obtain their development payoff, namely, the value of developing their land less the cost of required TDR purchases. Because both developed and undeveloped landowners must purchase the same number of permits in order to acquire a full development right, their payoffs have the following difference:

$$P_D - P_U = [V_2' - D_{12}] - [V_2' - (D_2 - s_D)]$$
$$= D_2 - s_D - D_{12} = E(q; x_1). \tag{A14.22}$$

In Case B, undeveloped landowners sell their permits to obtain the payoff, $P_U = (x_1/\bar{X}) \, r(x_1)$. Developed landowners, in turn, obtain their value of development less the cost of purchasing the $(1 - (x_1/\bar{X}))$ additional permits required for a full development right:

$$P_D = [V_2' - D_{12}] - (1 - (x_1/\bar{X})) \, r(x_1)$$
$$\Rightarrow P_D - P_U = V_2' - D_{12} - r(x_1) = E(q; x_1). \tag{A14.23}$$

Together, (A14.21)–(A14.23) affirm UET condition (A14.11). Identical reasoning affirms UET and an efficient land allocation when an "old development tax" replaces the new development subsidy.

B.   Government Regulatory Incentives under Asymmetric Information, when Political Welfare Depends upon Ex-Post Landowner Payoffs

Measuring expected political welfare now requires discrete values for the indices i and y:

$$i \in \{1, \ldots, \bar{X}\}, \quad y \in \{1, \ldots, \bar{X}\},$$

which yield the following expectation:

$$\sum{}^* \{G[W_L(\{P_i + g(y_i; X)0\}; x_1), W_T] \, (1/\bar{X})^{\bar{X}}\} \tag{B14.1}$$

where $W_T = S(X; \theta, x_1) - g^*(X) - \sum_{i=1}^{\bar{X}} P_i di$ and $\sum^*$ denotes the set of $\bar{X}$ summations, $\sum_{y_{\bar{X}}=1}^{\bar{X}} \cdots \sum_{y_1=1}^{\bar{X}}$. Maximizing the expected political welfare function in (B14.1) yields the following first-order conditions:

$$P_i: \quad \sum^* (G_{L_i})(1/\bar{X})^{\bar{X}} - G_T^* = 0, \tag{B14.2}$$

$$X: \quad \sum_{i=1}^{\bar{X}} \sum^* (G_{L_i} g_X(y_i; X))(1/\bar{X})^{\bar{X}} + G_T^*(S_X() - g_X^*(X)) = 0, \tag{B14.3}$$

where $G_T^* = \sum^* (G_T (1/\bar{X})^{\bar{X}})$, $G_{L_i} = G_L (\partial W_L / \partial P_i)$, and

$$g_X(y; X) = \begin{cases} -V_2''(X) & \text{for } y \leqslant X \\ 0 & \text{for } y > X \end{cases} \tag{B14.4}$$

With $g(y_i; X) = \max(V_2'(y_i) - V_2'(X), 0)$, equation (B14.2) can be rewritten as follows:

$$\sum_{-i}^* \left\{ \sum_{y_i=1}^{X} G_{L_i} + G_{L_i}^0 (\bar{X} - X) \right\} (1/\bar{X}) \bar{X} = G_T^* \tag{B14.5}$$

where $\sum_{-i}^*$ is $\sum^*$ without the y_i summation and $G_{L_i}^0$ equals G_{L_i} evaluated at $g(y_i; X) = 0$. Using (B14.4) and (B14.5), the first term is equation (B14.3) can be expanded as follows:

$$A = \{-V_2''(X)\} \left\{ \sum_{i=1}^{\bar{X}} \left[\sum_{-1}^* \left(\sum_{y_i=1}^{X} G_{L_i}(1/\bar{X})^{\bar{X}} \right) \right] \right\}$$

$$= \{-V_2''(X)\} \left\{ \sum_{i=1}^{\bar{X}} \left[G_T^* - \sum_{-i}^* G_{L_i}^0 (\bar{X} - X)(1/\bar{X})^{\bar{X}} \right] \right\} \tag{B14.6}$$

To evaluate equation (B14.6) – and, in turn, equation (B14.3) – let us consider two possible settings:

Setting 1: $G_{L_i}^0 = G_{L_i}$. Here, holding fixed all landowner payoffs other than that of the ith landowner, the marginal political benefit of raising the ith landowner's payoff, G_{Li}, is invariant to the anticipated level of private surplus, $g(y_i; X)$, that accrues to landowner i. Noting that

$$\sum_{i=1}^{\bar{X}} \sum_{-1}^* G_{L_i}^0 = \sum^* G_{L_i}^0,$$

and exploiting condition (B14.2), G_{L_i} can be substituted for $G^0_{L_i}$ in equation (B14.6) to yield:

$$A = \{ -V''_2(X) \} \{ \bar{X} G^*_T - (\bar{X} - X) G^*_T \} = \{ -V''_2(X) \} X G^*_T. \qquad (B14.6')$$

Substituting (B14.6') for the first term in equation (B14.3), and noting that $g^*_X(X) = -X V''_2(X)$, yields:

$$\{ -V''_2(X) \} X G^*_T + G^*_T (S_X() + X V''_2(X)) = G^*_T S_X() = 0. \qquad (B14.3')$$

Condition (B14.3') implies an efficient regulatory choice.

Setting 2: G_{Li} is decreasing in the anticipated level of landowner i's private surplus, $g(y_i; X)$, so that $G^0_{L_i} > G_{L_i}$ when G_{L_i} is evaluated at $y_i < X$. Here, a lower level of landowner surplus yields a higher marginal political benefit from payoff dollars allocated to the landowner, implying:

$$G^0_{L_i} > \sum_{y_i=1}^{\bar{X}} G_{L_i} (1/\bar{X}). \qquad (B14.7)$$

Substituting (B14.7) into (B14.6) gives:

$$A < \{ -V''_2(X) \} \left\{ \bar{X} G^*_T - \sum_{i=1}^{\bar{X}} \sum{}^* [G_{Li} [(\bar{X} - X)/\bar{X}](1/\bar{X})^{\bar{X}}] \right\}$$
$$= \{ -V''_2(X) \} \{ \bar{X} G^*_T - (\bar{X} - X) G^*_T \} = \{ -V''_2(X) \} X G^*_T. \qquad (B14.6'')$$

Using (B14.6'') in (B14.3) gives

$$0 = A + G^*_T (S_X - g^*_X) < \{ -V''_2(X) \} X G^*_T + G^*_T (S_X + X V''_2(X))$$
$$= G^*_T S_X(). \qquad (B14.3'')$$

From (B14.3''), we can conclude that $S_X()$ is positive at a political optimum here, implying that X is set below its efficient level.

References

Baxter, W., and L. Altree. (1972) "Legal Aspects of Airport Noise," *Journal of Law and Economics* XV, 1–113.

Berger, L. (1974) "A Policy Analysis of the Takings Problem." *New York University Law Review* XLIX, 165–226.

Blume, L., and D. Rubinfeld, (1984) "Compensation for Takings: An Economic Analysis." *California Law Review* LXXII. 569–624.

Blume, L., D. Rubinfeld, and P. Shapiro. (1984) "The Taking of Land: When Should Compensation Be Paid?" *The Quarterly Journal of Economics* C, 71–92.

Brennan, T., and J. Boyd. 1995 "Political Economy and the Efficiency of Compensation for Takings," Working Paper, Resources for the Future.

Burrows, P. (1989) "Getting a Stranglehold With the Eminent Domain Clause." *International Review of Law and Economics* IX, 129–47.

deAlessi, L. (1969) "Implications of Property Rights for Government Investment Choices." *American Economic Review* LIX 13–24.

Ely, J. H. (1980) *Democracy and Distrust: A Theory of Judicial Review* (Cambridge, MA: Harvard University Press).

Epstein, R. (1985) *Takings: Private Property and the Power of Eminent Domain* (Cambridge, MA: Harvard University Press).

—(1992) "*Yee v. City of Escondido*: The Supreme Court Strikes Out Again." *Loyola of Los Angeles Law Review* XXVI, 3–22.

—(1993a) "*Lucas v. South Carolina Coastal Council*: A Tangled Web of Expectations." *Stanford Law Review* XLV, 1369–92.

—(1993b) "The Seven Deadly Sins of Takings Law: The Dissents in *Lucas v. South Carolina Coastal Council*." *Loyola of Los Angeles Law Review* XXVI, 955–78.

Farber, D. (1992) "Economic Analysis and Just Compensation." *International Review of Law and Economics* XII, 125–38.

Fischel, W. (1985) *The Economics of Zoning Laws* (Baltimore, MD: Johns Hopkins University Press).

—(1992) "Exploring the Kozinsky Paradox: Why Is More Efficient Regulation a Taking of Property." *Chicago-Kent Law Review*, LXVII.

Fischel, W., and P. Shapiro. (1988) "Takings, Insurance, and Michelman: Comment on Economic Interpretations of 'Just Compensation' Law." *Journal of Legal Studies* XVII, 269–93.

—(1989) "A Constitutional Choice Model of Compensation for Takings." *International Review of Law and Economics* IX, 115–28.

Hermalin, B. (1995) "An Economic Analysis of Takings." *Journal of Law, Economics and Organization* XI, 64–86.

Innes, R. (1997) "Takings, Compensation and Equal Treatment for Owners of Developed and Undeveloped Property." *Journal of Law and Economics* XL, 403–32.

—(2000) "The Economics of Takings When Land and Its Public Use Value Are in Private Hands." *Land Economics* (May) 76, 195–212.

Innes, R., S. Polasky, and J. Tschirhart. (1998) "Takings, Compensation and Endangered Species Protection on Private Lands" *Journal of Economic Perspectives* XII, 35–52.

Johnson, M. (1977) "Takings and the Private Market." In *Planning Without Prices*, B. H. Siegan, ed. (Lexington, MA: D.C. Heath).

Kaplow, L. (1986) "An Economic Analysis of Legal Transitions." *Harvard Law Review* XCIX, 509–617.

Kmiec, D. (1988) "The Original Understanding of the Taking Clause Is Neither Weak Nor Obtuse." *Columbia Law Review* LXXXVIII, 1630–66.

Lambert, T., and R. Smith. (1994) "The ESA: Time for a Change." Center for the Study of American Business, Policy Study 119.

Meltz, R. (1994) "The ESA and Constitutional Takings." Paper presented at Conference on Regulatory Takings and Resources, Natural Resources Law Center, University of Colorado School of Law, June 13–15.

Miceli, T., and K. Segerson. (1994) "Regulatory Takings: When Should Compensation Be Paid?" *Journal of Legal Studies* XXIII, 749–76.

Michelman, F. (1967) "Property, Utility, and Fairness: Comments on the Ethical Foundations of 'Just Compensation' Law." *Harvard Law Review* LXXX, 1165–258.

— (1988) "Takings, 1987." *Columbia Law Review* LXXXVIII, 1600–29.

Ohls, J., and D. Pines. (1975) "Discontinuous Urban Development and Economic Efficiency." *Land Economics* LI, 224–234.

Polasky, S. (2001) "Investment, Information Collection, and Endangered Species Conservation on Private Land." Chapter 15 in *Protecting Endangered Species in the United States: Biological Needs, Political Realities, Economic Choices*, eds. Jason Shogren and John Tschirhart (New York: Cambridge University Press).

Polasky, S., and H. Doremus. (1998) "When the Truth Hurts: Endangered Species Policy on Private Land With Incomplete Information." *Journal of Environmental Economics and Management* XXXV, 22–47.

Rose-Ackerman, S. (1988) "Against Ad-Hocery: A Comment on Michelman." *Columbia Law Review* LXXXVIII, 1697–711.

Searchinger, T. (1992) "Private Property Rights and Environmental Harm." *EDF Letter*, XXIII (4), 4.

Smith, R., and J. Shogren. (2001) "Protecting Species on Private Land." Chapter 16 in *Protecting Endangered Species in the United States: Biological Needs, Political Realities, Economic Choices*, eds. Jason Shogren and John Tschirhart (New York: Cambridge University Press).

Stroup, R. (1997) "The Economics of Compensating Property Owners." *Contemporary Economic Policy* XV, 55–65.

Treanor, W. (1985) "The Origins and Original Significance of the Just Compensation Clause of the Fifth Amendment." *Yale Law Journal*, XCIV, 694–716.

Welch, L. (1994) "Property Rights Conflicts Under the ESA: Protection of the Red-Cockaded Woodpecker." In *Regulatory Takings, Farmers, Ranchers, and the Fifth Amendment*, B. Yandle, ed. Center for Policy Studies, Clemson University: Clemson, SC.

Dolan v. City of Tigard (114 S. Ct. 2309, 1994).

Lucas v. South Carolina Coastal Council (112 S. Ct. 2886, 1992).

Nollan v. California Coastal Commission (107 S. Ct. 3141, 1987).

Yee v. City of Escondido (112 S. Ct. 1522, 1992).

CHAPTER 15

Investment, Information Collection, and Endangered Species Conservation on Private Land

Stephen Polasky

1. INTRODUCTION

A majority of species listed under the ESA depend on private land for a majority of their habitat (U.S. Fish and Wildlife Service 1997). Conserving endangered species on private land has triggered fierce debates in the courts and in Congress. The courts have wrestled with the question of the reach of the ESA on private land. In *Babbitt v. Sweet Home Chapter of Communities for a Great Oregon*, the Supreme Court ruled that the ESA allowed the government to prohibit otherwise legal land uses on private land if such use significantly modifies habitat in a way that would harm a listed species. Congress has wrestled with the question of whether the government must pay compensation to private landowners who face restrictions on land use to conserve listed species. At present, such compensation is not required.

The current structure of the laws governing species conservation on private land creates several incentives problems that are likely to lead to inefficient outcomes.[1] The fundamental problem with current law is that landowner cooperation with conservation policy is necessary for an efficient result, but such cooperation is unlikely to occur. Before the government can restrict an activity on private land, it must find convincing evidence that the activity will cause "harm" to a listed species. While it is not exactly clear what constitutes convincing evidence, the courts have generally insisted on a showing that a listed species inhabits the area and that the proposed activity would have a detrimental impact on the species (Polasky and Doremus 1998). In some cases gathering the necessary evidence to invoke restrictions under the ESA may require on-site inspection of the property. Trespass law, however, gives a landowner control over access to her property. Even where it is possible to gather biological information off-site, Congress has prohibited using federal

I thank Holly Doremus, Rob Innes, Bruce Rettig, Tommy Stamland, John Tschirhart, participants at the University of Pennsylvania Environmental Law seminar, and the Social Order and the ESA Conference in Centennial, Wyoming for helpful comments and conversations about these issues.

[1] Innes, Polasky, and Tschirhart (1998) contains a summary of incentive issues related to endangered species protection on private lands.

funds to gather such information without landowner consent (Public Law No. 104-134, Section 2901(c)). The landowner may have powerful economic reasons for preventing such information from being collected. With the information, the regulator may be able to restrict economic activity, such as timber harvests or home building, that lessens the value of the property. Without payment of compensation, the landowner has a clear incentive to prevent such information from being collected.

This chapter analyzes the efficiency of equilibrium outcomes for endangered species conservation on private land under the current ESA and possible reforms. In Section 2, the basic model is described. The model includes the possibility of landowner investment, information collection, and land-use decisions for private land that may contain habitat for endangered species. In Section 3, the equilibrium outcomes under the current ESA and several possible reforms are compared. The possible reforms considered include basing compensation on expected (or actual) species conservation value, basing compensation on market value, and including a permitting requirement whereby the landowner must demonstrate that development activity yields a higher value than does conservation before being allowed to develop. Basing compensation on species conservation value is shown to yield an efficient solution. However, several problems with this approach are discussed that make it impractical to implement. The other reforms analyzed do not yield an efficient solution but are more feasible to implement. Each alternative is shown to be an improvement over the current legal structure. In particular, an alternative based on Polasky and Doremus (1998) that combines elements of both permitting and compensation is shown to yield equilibrium outcomes that are superior to simpler schemes that consider only compensation. Section 4 contains some brief concluding remarks.

2. MODEL

The model in this chapter builds on Polasky and Doremus (1998). The analysis focuses on a single parcel of land owned by a single risk-neutral landowner.[2] The parcel can be either developed or preserved in its natural state. Development allows economic activity to occur and generates a flow of rents over time. Let $D \geq 0$ represent the development value of the land, that is, the present value of the rents generated by economic activity. Since the values generated by development are largely derived from marketable goods and services, it is assumed that the landowner receives D with development. Let $P \geq 0$ represent the value of the land if it is preserved. Preservation may generate benefits that have positive externalities or are pure public goods. In addition to possibly providing valuable ecosystem services with far-reaching

---

[2] For issues raised with multiple parcels, see Innes (1997), and in this volume Innes (Chapter 14) and Smith and Shogren (Chapter 16). For issues raised by risk aversion, see Blume and Rubinfeld (1984), Kaplow (1986), and Farber (1992).

benefits (Daily 1997), preserving a land parcel may provide habitat to one or more endangered species. Conserving an endangered species may be a pure public good (e.g., existence value for the species) or may allow for partial rent capture by the landowner (e.g., ecotourism). For simplicity, it is assumed that the landowner receives no return with preservation.[3]

In reality, obtaining an estimate of preservation value may be exceedingly difficult even when the value of preservation is limited to the possibility that the land parcel provides habitat for an endangered species. In this case, there are (at least) two challenges to estimating preservation value accurately, one biological and the other economic. On the biology side, there is the issue of estimating how changes in land use on a particular parcel affect a species survival probability. Whether a species currently inhabits a particular portion of habitat, or whether it will in the future, is often unknown. More general knowledge of a species' habitat preferences can allow use of spatially explicit population biology models to estimate the effect of a change in the landscape pattern on a species survival probability (e.g., Lamberson et al. 1992, 1994; Schumaker 1996). However, such models require understanding species life history characteristics and habitat preferences, along with detailed information on landscape pattern, which is not available for most applications.[4] Simpler approaches, such as combining species habitat relationships with the size of remaining habitat patches, can be used to generate rough estimates (e.g., White et al. 1997).

There is also the economic issue of estimating a value for the survival of a species. For most species, much of the value of continued existence will come from nonmarket and nonuse values. There is debate both within and outside the economics profession about whether economists can estimate nonuse values in a meaningful way (see, for example, the exchange between Hanemann 1994, and Diamond and Hausman 1994). Deriving an estimate for the existence value of a species seems especially problematic (Stevens et al. 1991).

Current endangered species policy avoids the valuation issue altogether. Under Section 9 of the ESA, any activity that causes "harm" is prohibited. As interpreted by the courts, "harm" includes habitat modification that adversely affects a listed species. In theory, "harm" is to be determined by biological not economic factors. An activity that causes "harm" is prohibited no matter what the relationship is between the benefits of the activity and the costs in terms of species loss. In practice, however, the relative value of development versus

---

[3] Incorporating partial rent capure by the landowner is straightforward. As long as rent capture by the landowner with preservation is not complete so that preservation yields positive externalities, the qualitative results derived in the model continue to hold. For more on the difficulty of capturing rents from conservation, see McNeely (1993), Defenders of Wildlife (1993), and Sedjo (1992).

[4] Many of the population biology models to date have focused on the population dynamics of the spotted owl as a function of the forest landscape. The spotted owl-timber controversy in the Pacific Northwest was for population biologists what the Exxon Valdez case was for nonmarket valuation economists.

preservation seems to matter. Several observers have pointed out examples where economic considerations have affected decisions that were supposed to be based strictly on biological considerations (e.g., Houck 1993, 285–96; Thomas and Verner 1992, 628). Ando (2000) and Metrick and Weitzman (1996) find that agency listing and funding decisions are statistically related to factors unrelated to the rules for making listing and funding decisions, but which are related to the perceived value or importance of a species.

Because of the uncertainty surrounding the true preservation value, let the preservation value of the land parcel, P, be a function of a random variable Ω with realized values $\omega \in [\underline{\omega}, \bar{\omega}]$. Define $f(\omega)$ as the probability density function and $F(\omega)$ as the cumulative density function of Ω. If the uncertainty about preservation value is mainly a function of whether the species inhabits the land parcel and how development would affect the species, it may be possible to reduce uncertainty with a biological survey of the property. For simplicity, suppose that for a cost of C, the realized value $\omega \in \Omega$ is learned by both regulator and landowner.

Both the development value and the preservation value of a land parcel may be affected by landowner investment. Three types of investment are considered. Let x represent the cost of investment in increasing the development value of the land, $D(x)$, with $D'(x) > 0$, $D''(x) < 0$. For example, a landowner may build an access road or make other site improvements to increase the market value of the property. Let y represent the cost of investing to increase the preservation value of the parcel, such as the cost of restoring or improving habitat conditions. Let z represent the cost of investing to *decrease* the preservation value of the parcel. A particularly relevant example in the endangered species context is the alleged activity of some landowners to remove listed species from their properties ("shoot, shovel, and shut up"). The resulting preservation value is given by $P(y, z, \omega)$, with $P_y(\cdot) > 0$, $P_{yy}(\cdot) < 0$, $P_z(\cdot) < 0$, $P_{zz}(\cdot) > 0$, where $P_i(\cdot)$ and $P_{ii}(\cdot)$ indicate the first and second partial derivatives with respect to variable i. It is of course possible that x affects $P(\cdot)$, and likewise that y and z affect $D(\cdot)$. For simplicity these effects are not considered.

In reality, the investments that a landowner may undertake are limited by various other regulatory rules. For example, regulatory approval must be granted before building may take place or before draining a wetland. Some actions of the landowner, though, are not regulated. Other actions, though regulated in theory, cannot be effectively monitored by regulators and are *de facto* unregulated (e.g., "shoot, shovel, and shut up").

Given the assumptions of the model, an unregulated landowner would always choose development over preservation. However, sometimes society as a whole would prefer preservation to development. In order to secure preservation, there must be some combination of regulations restricting development and/or compensation for a landowner that preserves her land. In the next section, various sets of rules are considered. First, to provide a benchmark, the efficient solution is characterized. Second, the current set of rules under the existing ESA is modeled. Next, two types of compensation to

Table 15.1. Timing of stages

Stage 0	Nature selects $\omega \in \Omega$
Stage 1	Institutional rules chosen
Stage 2	Investment stage: Landowner selects (x, y, z)
Stage 3	Information collection stage: Landowner/Regulator chooses whether to spend C to learn ω
Stage 4	Land-use stage: Land is developed or preserved

landowners when preservation is chosen are considered: (a) compensation equal to preservation value, and (b) compensation equal to development value. Finally, a close variant of a set of rules proposed in Polasky and Doremus (1998) is considered. Under these rules, if the development value exceeds the expected preservation value, then the regulator must compensate the landowner for lost development value when preservation is mandated. On the other hand, if the expected preservation value exceeds the development value, then the landowner may develop if development value is shown to exceed preservation value but must also pay a development fee. This set of rules was shown to yield an efficient outcome in a model of information collection and land-use decision making, but without the possibility of landowner investment.

The timing of moves in the model is illustrated in Table 15.1. Initially, nature draws a value of ω from the distribution of Ω. Then, in stage 1, the regulatory rules are established. The rules specify the conditions, if any, under which the regulator will mandate the preservation of the parcel. The rules also establish the conditions under which payments from the regulator to the landowner, or from the landowner to the regulator, will occur. In stage 2, the investment stage, the landowner chooses x, y, and z. Stage 3 is the information collection stage. For a cost of C, a survey of the parcel can be undertaken that reveals the actual preservation value, $P(y, z, \omega)$, to both the landowner and the regulator. Without a survey, only the distribution of preservation value, conditional on investment, is known. Either the landowner or the regulator may initiate and pay for a survey. However, because of trespass laws, landowner permission must be granted for a survey to take place. In the final stage, stage 4, a land-use decision is made (preserve or develop). Typically the land-use decision is made by the landowner. However, under the rules set in stage 1, if certain conditions hold, the regulator will mandate preservation.

3. ANALYSIS

A.   The Efficient Solution

The efficient solution is a useful benchmark to measure the outcomes under the alternative sets of rules considered below. Assuming risk neutrality, an efficient solution maximizes the expected value of the land parcel net of costs over the set of feasible solutions. To find the efficient solution, it is easiest to first solve two subproblems: (a) the efficient investment and land-use decisions when information is not collected, and (b) the efficient investment and (conditional) land-use decisions when information is collected in stage 3. Then, using the solution of these subproblems, it is easy to show whether or not it is efficient to collect information.

When no information will be collected in stage 3, an efficient solution can be found by solving the following problem:

$$E(V) = Max \ \lambda D(x) + (1 - \lambda) \int_{\omega}^{\bar{\omega}} P(y, z, \omega) f(\omega) d\omega - x - y - z, \quad (15.1)$$

where λ is restricted to be 0 or 1 (0 if preservation is chosen and 1 if development is chosen). Note that since $P_z < 0$, $z = 0$ is always optimal, that is, it is never efficient to invest to lower preservation value. The optimal choice of x and y depends on the choice of λ. If $\lambda = 0$, then $x = 0$ and y^* is defined implicitly by

$$E[P_y(y^*, 0, \omega)] = 1, \quad \text{for } y^* > 0 \quad \text{otherwise } y^* = 0, \quad (15.1a)$$

where $E[\cdot]$ is the expectations operator. If $\lambda = 1$, then $y = 0$ and x^* is defined implicitly by

$$D'(x^*) = 1, \quad \text{for } x^* > 0, \quad \text{otherwise } x^* = 0. \quad (15.1b)$$

The optimal choice of λ is $\lambda = 1$ if and only if $D(x^*) - x^* > E[P(y^*, 0, \omega)] - y^*$, for x^* and y^* defined above.[5] In words, the efficient solution is one in which the marginal benefit of investment equals the marginal cost, and where land is put to the highest valued use conditional on efficient investment. Note that it is only optimal to invest in increasing value for the type of land use ultimately to be chosen.

When information will be collected in stage 3, development will be chosen if and only if $D(x) > P(y, z, \omega)$ in stage 4. Having information about the preservation value allows the actual preservation value, instead of the expected preservation value, to be compared with the development value. Define $\omega(x, y, z)$ implicitly by $D(x) \equiv P(y, z, \omega(x, y, z))$. For values of ω greater than $\omega(x, y, z)$, it is efficient to choose preservation in stage 4. For values of ω less than $\omega(x, y, z)$, it is efficient to choose development in stage 4. However,

---

[5] Assume throughout that if development and preservation are of equal value, that it is efficient to preserve (ties go to the species).

at the time of investment in stage 2, the value ω is unknown. In stage 2, effi-cient investment levels can be found by solving:

$$E(W) = Max \int_{\underline{\omega}}^{\omega(x,y,z)} D(x)f(\omega)\,d\omega$$

$$+ \int_{\omega(x,y,z)}^{\bar{\omega}} P(y,z,\omega)f(\omega)\,d\omega - x - y - z. \tag{15.2}$$

Efficient investment levels are defined implicitly by:

$$D'(x^{**})F(\omega(x^{**}, y^{**}, z^{**})) = 1 \tag{15.3a}$$

$$\int_{\omega(x,y,z)}^{\bar{\omega}} P_y(y^{**}, z^{**}, \omega)f(\omega)\,d\omega = 1 \tag{15.3b}$$

$$z^{**} = 0. \tag{15.3c}$$

Note that when information is collected in stage 3, that investment levels in stage 2 are intermediate between 0 and the level of investment defined by equations (15.1a) and (15.1b). Knowing information will be collected that may show that either development or preservation is preferred means that it is efficient to invest in increasing the value of both development and preserva-tion. Alternatively, if it were possible to survey prior to investment, the cor-rect level of investment given the actual preservation value could be undertaken. The value of knowing information prior to investment is that investment can then be directed only to the type of land use that will ulti-mately be chosen. In this chapter, however, investment is assumed to take place prior to information collection.

Since it is possible to ignore information and mimic the uninformed solu-tion, having information can never lead to lower expected value so that $E(W) \geq E(V)$. Typically, having information improves the expected value of the solution. It is efficient to collect information whenever the expected bene-fits are equal or greater than the costs of collecting information:

$$E(W) - E(V) \geq C. \tag{15.3c}$$

B.   The Solution Under the Current ESA Rules

Under the current ESA, no compensation is required to be paid to landowners when regulations restrict the use of land to protect a listed species. Before regulations to protect species can be applied on a particular land parcel, how-ever, regulators must show that a listed species uses the area and that a pro-posed activity will have adverse impacts on the species. Though exactly what evidence is necessary to show whether a listed species uses an area is unclear, merely showing that a parcel is within the historical range of a listed species is probably insufficient. Actually observing that a listed species inhabits the parcel may be required. Getting this type of information may require on-site inspection of the property. Because of trespass laws, on-site inspection requires the approval of the landowner.[6] These information requirements are modeled by assuming that the regulator must have evidence that the actual, not just the expected, preservation value is greater or equal to the development value in order to mandate preservation. In other words, collecting information in stage 3 is a prerequisite for mandating preservation in stage 4.

Under these rules, the landowner has both the incentive and the ability to prevent preservation from being mandated. In blocking collection of information in stage 3, by not allowing the regulator access to the property, the landowner can guarantee that development in stage 4 will be allowed. Since the landowner receives no value from preservation and the full value from development, she will always choose to develop. This result is inefficient whenever parameter values are such that preservation yields a higher expected land use value. At the investment stage, the landowner will choose to set x such that $D'(x) = 1$ (or $x = 0$ if $D'(0) < 1$) and to set $y = z = 0$. Note that there is no incentive for the landowner to invest in helping or harming listed species since the preservation value is irrelevant to the landowner.

In reality, it may be possible for the regulator to discover the actual preservation value even without an on-site inspection. In viewing from the edge of the property, or from the air, it may be possible to detect the presence of a listed species. Suppose there is some probability that the regulator may observe the preservation value via off-site inspection methods. In this case, the landowner has an incentive to increase the probability that the development value exceeds the preservation value. The landowner may do this by increasing x above the level at which $D'(x) = 1$, by setting $z > 0$, thereby lowering the preservation value, or both.

In sum, the current ESA creates a number of perverse incentives for private landowners. The investment, information collection, and land-use decisions on private lands are likely to be inefficient as a result.

C.   The Solution with Compensation Equal to (Expected) Preservation Value

Instead of the current set of rules, suppose that all decisions on investment, information collection, and land use are made by the landowner. To give the landowner some incentive to choose preservation, suppose the landowner is compensated an amount equal to either the actual or expected preservation value, depending upon whether information was collected in stage 3, if she chooses preservation in stage 4. Note that under these rules, the landowner's

---

[6] A more complete description of the information required to enforce the ESA and the means available to the regulator to collect this information is contained in Polasky and Doremus (1998).

payoffs are identical to society's payoffs. The maximization problem for the landowner is identical to that shown in section A at each decision stage. Therefore, the landowner will make efficient investment, information collection, and land-use decisions.

From an efficiency standpoint, if this could be done it should be done and there would be little left to say. As with traditional externalities, decision makers will make efficient choices when all of the consequences of their actions are fully internalized. However, as noted earlier in this chapter, it may well be impossible to implement a scheme in which landowners are compensated for preservation value. Polasky and Doremus (1998) state that "(t)he cost of determining this value, the high probability that the regulator and the landowner will disagree about it, and the expense of litigation to resolve these disagreements, make basing compensation on conservation value impractical." It is difficult to imagine that a real compensation scheme could be based on preservation value.

In addition, there may be real resource costs to using government funds to pay compensation. Government funds typically must be raised through use of distortion causing taxation. In this case, the government faces a trade-off between providing proper incentives via compensation and the distortions from raising money to pay for compensation. Paying compensation equal to the full preservation value in this context is inefficient.[7]

To solve the problem of the real resource cost of raising government funds, suppose that instead of compensating a landowner that preserves, that a landowner that develops must pay an amount equal to preservation value. In a model without investment and information collection decisions, whether the government pays compensation for preservation, or the landowner pays for the right to develop, is irrelevant on efficiency grounds. Just as in Coase (1960), defining the initial property rights, which here determine the direction of the payments, will affect distribution but will not affect efficiency. With investment and information collection, however, defining different compensation rules does have efficiency consequences. If the landowner has to pay an amount equal to preservation value when she develops, the landowner will never invest to increase preservation value ($y=0$), and will often choose to invest to decrease preservation value ($z>0$), in order to lower the necessary payment. Of course, any solution that involves $z>0$ is inefficient. When the landowner can manipulate preservation values through investments, it is more attractive to design a regulatory scheme that relies on carrots rather than sticks.

D.   The Solution with Compensation Equal to
Development Value

In most situations in which compensation is paid to landowners, the amount of compensation is set equal to the fair market value of the property. This rule

---

[7] Lewis (1996) discusses this issue applied to environmental regulation in general. Smith and Shogren (Chapter 16, of this volume) discuss this issue in the context of species conservation.

is used in cases of eminent domain. Although this type of compensation can be implemented in practice, it suffers some drawbacks from an efficiency standpoint. In particular, it is possible that both investment and information collection decisions will be inefficient.

Assume that compensation is equal to $D(x)$ whenever preservation is mandated by the regulator. In this case, the landowner receives $D(x)$ regardless of whether the land is developed or preserved. As under the current rules, the landowner will invest such that $D'(x) = 1$ (or $x = 0$ if $D'(0) < 1$) and set $y = z = 0$. This pattern of investment is efficient only if development will always occur. Unlike under the current ESA rules, however, preservation may occur. The landowner has nothing to lose from allowing preservation and so should not oppose efforts to collect information. If the regulator does collect information and finds that the development value is less than the preservation value, the regulator will mandate preservation. In this case, the efficient investment pattern is $x^* = 0$ and $y^* \geqslant 0$. Since there is some possibility of preservation being chosen, the landowner has too much incentive to invest in raising the development value and has too little incentive to increase the preservation value. The first of these results is the standard inefficiency of compensation with prior investment first shown by Blume, Rubinfeld, and Shapiro (1984).

Polasky and Doremus (1998) show that incentives for information collection may also not be efficient when compensation equal to $D(x)$ is paid to landowners when preservation is mandated. If the regulator does not collect information, the default decision is to allow development. When the expected value of preservation exceeds the development value, the efficient default decision is to preserve rather than develop. In order to avoid an inefficient default decision, the regulator may have an excessive incentive to collect information and may collect information when it is inefficient to do so.

E.   The Solution with the Assignment of Property Rights Based on Initial Values

In a model with information collection and land-use decisions, but without the possibility of prior investment by the landowner, Polasky and Doremus (1998) showed that a regulatory scheme that can be loosely characterized as assigning property rights on the basis of an initial comparison of preservation and development value achieved an efficient outcome. In this section, the outcome under a similar regulatory scheme is analyzed. In this scheme, if the expected preservation value is greater than the development value, the regulator is assigned the property rights. The regulator will mandate conservation unless it is shown that the development value exceeds the preservation value. If this is demonstrated, the landowner then may develop but has to pay a development fee equal to the expected preservation value conditional on it being less than the development value. On the other hand, if the development value is greater than the expected preservation value, the property rights would be assigned to the landowner. If the regulator then mandates preservation, the regulator must compensate the landowner an amount equal to the development value.

With investment in stage 2, it is no longer clear whether the comparison between preservation and development values that establishes the property rights is to be done before or after investment has taken place. The analysis begins by analyzing the case where property rights are established at the outset prior to any investment by the landowner. The analysis of the case where property rights are established after investment follows.

With property rights established prior to investment, the assignment of property rights depends upon the comparison of $D(0)$ with $E[P(0, 0, \omega)]$. There are two possible assignment of property rights. First, suppose $D(0) > E[P(0, 0, \omega)]$ so that property rights are assigned to the landowner. The rules in this situation are identical to the situation analyzed in Section D above. The landowner receives $D(x)$ regardless of the eventual land-use decision. As before, the landowner will set x such that $D'(x) = 1$ (or $x = 0$ if $D'(x) < 1$), and $y = z = 0$. As in Section D, this pattern of investment is inefficient if there is a positive probability that preservation will be mandated in stage 4. Conditional on the investment levels, however, the information collection decision will be efficient. Unlike the situation in the final paragraph of Section D, if no information is collected, the default decision (allowing development) is efficient since $D(0) > E[P(0, 0, \omega)]$. Therefore, the regulator does not have excess incentive to collect information.

Now suppose that $D(0) \leqslant E[P(0, 0, \omega)]$ so that the property rights are assigned to the regulator. Without a survey in stage 3, preservation will be mandated in stage 4. With a survey in stage 3, the landowner will be allowed to develop when $D(x) > P(0, 0, \omega)$. The landowner who develops pays a development fee equal to $E[P(0, 0, \omega)|P < D(x)]$. In this case, the problem facing the landowner in stage 2 is:

$$Max \int_{\underline{\omega}}^{\omega(x)} (D(x) - P(0, 0, \omega)) f(\omega) \, d\omega - x - y - z, \tag{15.4}$$

where $\omega(x)$ is defined by $D(x) = P(0, 0, \omega)$. Note that y and z do not affect the outcome in any way except through cost and so will be set equal to zero. The optimal choice of x for the landowner will satisfy $D'(x)F(\omega(x)) = 1$ (or $x = 0$ if $D'(0)F(\omega(0)) < 1$). Since $\omega(x)$ differs from $\omega(x, y, z)$ in the efficient solution (where in general $y > 0$), investment in x will also not be efficient. The probability of preservation as it appears to the landowner is less than it is in the efficient solution shown in section A. In practical terms, though, this inefficiency may not be large. Unless there is large scope for positive investment in increasing preservation value, overinvestment in increasing development value will likely be small. Conditional on investment, Polasky and Doremus (1998) show that the landowner has the correct incentive to collect information.

In sum, the scheme where property rights are set based on the comparison of preservation and development value prior to investment, while not yielding an efficient solution, represents an improvement on section D (paying compensation equal to development value). When it is impossible to pay compensation equal to preservation value, this scheme may be an acceptable alternative, at least on efficiency grounds.

The other alternative case to analyze is where the assignment of property rights is done after the investment stage. When property rights are not assigned prior to investment, the result may be quite inefficient. In choosing investments in stage 2, the landowner knows she can influence the assignment of property rights, which will take place at the beginning of stage 3. The landowner will be assigned the property rights whenever $D(x) > P(y, z, \omega)$. There may be a large payoff to the landowner from being assigned the property rights. Suppose this effect is large so the landowner finds it profitable to invest so she has the property right. The landowner's problem in this case is:

$$Max\ D(x) - x - y - z + \mu(D(x) - E[P(y, z, \omega)]),$$

where μ represents the multiplier on the constraint $D(x) > E[P(y, z, \omega)]$. In order to satisfy the constraint, the landowner may set x above the level for which $D'(x) = 1$, or $z > 0$, or both. This outcome is reminiscent of the outcome under the current ESA with some possibility of detection by the regulator that the preservation value exceeds development value.

Allowing the landowner to manipulate the assignment of property values introduces incentives for the landowner to distort investment, including incentives for the landowner to take actions inconsistent with preservation. As a result, both the investment pattern and the resulting land-use decision may be inefficient. Without the ability to limit investment prior to assignment of property rights, basing the property rights assignment on values subject to manipulation by the landowner is an invitation for trouble. It is greatly preferable to assign property rights before, rather than after, investment.

4. DISCUSSION

In the prior section, the outcome under the current ESA and various alternative reforms were compared. If compensation to landowners who are forced to conserve is based on the preservation value (expected, or actual if known), an efficient solution on investment, information collection, and land-use decisions will be achieved. However, it is unlikely that such a scheme could be implemented. The scheme that defines property rights based on initial comparison, based on Polasky and Doremus (1998), though not perfect fares well in comparison with other schemes that may be feasible to implement. All possible reforms analyzed in this chapter do better on efficiency grounds than does the current ESA.

Several other issues, which were not discussed in any depth in this chapter, are important in the analysis of endangered species policy on private land. First, equity considerations may dominate efficiency considerations in the policy debate. Do landowners deserve compensation when conservation is required or should a landowner reimburse the public when her actions result in damage to a publicly held resource? In the law, there is a thin and somewhat arbitrary line between restricting an action that causes harm to the public, which does not deserve compensation, and restricting an action because it would prevent consumption of a public good, which does deserve compensation. Whether conserving species provides a public good or is a responsibility of landowners has not been sorted out fully in the courts, or in society at large.

Another important set of issues falls under the general heading of "transactions costs." Defining the rules differently may influence enforcement and administrative costs in important ways. Permitting procedures may require extensive paperwork and review. Providing compensation requires the government to raise funds, which may impose real resource costs on society. These costs need to be considered in the consideration of any actual policy reform.

References

Ando, A. 2001. "Interest Group Behavior and Endangered Species Protection." Chapter 6 in J. Shogren and J. Tschirhart, eds., *Protecting Endangered Species in the United States: Biological Needs, Political Realities, Economic Choices.* Cambridge University Press.

Blume, L. and D. Rubinfeld. 1984. "Compensation for Takings: An Economic Analysis." *California Law Review* 72: 569–624.

Blume, L., D. Rubinfeld, and P. Shapiro. 1984. "The Taking of Land: When Should Compensation be Paid?" *Quarterly Journal of Economics* 99: 71–92.

Coase, R. 1960. "The Problem of Social Cost." *Journal of Law and Economics* 3: 1–44.

Daily, G. (ed.). 1997. *Nature's Services: Societal Dependence on Natural Ecosystems.* Washington, DC: Island Press.

Defenders of Wildlife. 1993. *Building Economic Incentives into the ESA.* Washington, DC: Defenders of Wildlife.

Diamond, P. and J. Hausman. 1994. "Contingent Valuation: Is Some Number Better than No Number?" *Journal of Economic Perspectives* 8: 45–64.

Farber, D. 1992. "Economic Analysis and Just Compensation." *International Review of Law and Economics* 12: 125–38.

Hanemann, W. M. 1994. "Contingent Valuation and Economics." *Journal of Economic Perspectives* 8: 19–44.

Houck, O. 1993. "The ESA and Its Implementation by the U.S. Departments of Interior and Commerce." *Colorado Law Review* 64: 277–370.

Innes, R. 1997. "Takings, Compensation and Equal Treatment for Owners of Developed and Undeveloped Property." *Journal of Law and Economics* 40: 403–32.

Innes, R. 2001. "The Economics of 'Takings' in a Multiparcel Model with a Powerful Government." Chapter 14 in J. Shogren and J. Tschirhart, eds., *Protecting Endangered Species in the United States: Biological Needs, Political Realities, Economic Choices.* Cambridge University Press.

Innes, R., S. Polasky, and J. Tschirhart. 1998. "Takings, Compensation and Endangered Species Protection on Private Lands." *Journal of Economic Perspectives* 12(3): 35–52.

Kaplow, L. 1986. "An Economic Analysis of Legal Transitions." *Harvard Law Review* 99: 509–617.

Lamberson, R., R. McKelvey, B. Noon, and C. Voss. 1992. "A Dynamic Analysis of Northern Spotted Owl Viability in a Fragmented Forest Landscape." *Conservation Biology* 6: 505–12.

Lamberson, R., B. Noon, C. Voss, and K. McKelvey. 1994. "Reserve Design for Territorial Species: The Effects of Patch Size and Spacing on the Viability of the Northern Spotted Owl." *Conservation Biology* 8: 185–95.

Lewis, T. 1996. "Protecting the Environment when Costs and Benefits Are Privately Known." *Rand Journal of Economics* 27: 819–47.

McNeely, J. A. 1993. "Economics Incentives for Conserving Biodiversity: Lessons from Africa." *Ambio* 22: 144–50.

Metrick, A. and M. Weitzman. 1996. "Patterns in Behavior in Endangered Species Preservation." *Land Economics* 72: 1–16.

Polasky, S. and H. Doremus. 1998. "When the Truth Hurts: Endangered Species Policy on Private Land with Imperfect Information." *Journal of Environmental Economics and Management* 35: 22–47.

Schumaker, N. 1996. Using Landscape Indices to Predict Habitat Connectivity." *Ecology* 77: 1210–25.

Sedjo, R. 1992. "Property Rights, Genetic Resources, and Biotechnical Change. *Journal of Law and Economics* 35: 199–213.

Smith, R. and J. Shogren. 2001. "Protecting Species on Private Land," Chapter 16 in J. Shogren and J. Tschirhart, eds. *Protecting Endangered Species in the United States: Biological Needs, Political Realities, Economic Choices*. Cambridge University Press.

Stevens, T., J. Echeverria, R. Glass, T. Hager, and T. More. 1991. "Measuring Existence Value of Wildlife: What Do CVM Estimates Really Show?" *Land Economics* 67: 390–400.

Thomas, J. and J. Verner. 1992. "Accommodation with Socio-Economic Factors under the ESA – More than Meets the Eye." *Transactions of the North American Wildlife and Natural Resource Conference* 57: 627–41.

U.S. Fish and Wildlife Service. 1997. News release, June 6, 1997.

White, D., P. Minotti, M. Barczak, J. Sifneos, K. Freemark, M. Santelmann, C. Steinitz, R. Kiester, and E. Preston. 1997. "Assessing Risks to Biodiversity from Future Landscape Change," *Conservation Biology* 11: 349–60.

CHAPTER 16

Protecting Species on Private Land

Rodney B. W. Smith and Jason F. Shogren

1. INTRODUCTION

When passed in 1973, few lawmakers anticipated the firestorms that would surround the Endangered Species Act (ESA). The ESA epitomizes the classic quandary of diffuse social benefits and concentrated private costs. About half of the listed endangered species have 80 percent of their habitat on private land (see Brown and Shogren 1998; Innes, Polasky, and Tschirhart 1998), and many landowners complain that the costs of complying with the ESA are too great.

The lack of satisfactory answers to questions about fair compensation to landowners have helped stall the reauthorization of ESA since 1992. For example, the proposed listing of the Black-Tailed Prairie Dog as a "threatened species" typifies the controversy over how best to protect species at risk on private land. Environmentalists and biologists argue the prairie dog is a keystone species in Great Plains ecosystems. Prairie dogs provide prey for various species of raptors and black-footed ferrets, and they supply habitat for burrowing owls, spotted salamander, and mountain plover. Prairie dogs rework the soil to provide nutrients for plant growth of benefit to grazing animals (Whicker and Detling 1988).

But historically, ranchers and government agencies in many Western states like Wyoming and Montana have considered the prairie dog a pest. Many people believe that prairie dogs compete for livestock forage, create livestock hazards with their burrows, and increase soil erosion. For these reasons, ranchers and government agents have systematically reduced their populations. But now under the ESA, if the current or proposed use of private property violates this directive, the landowner must either rethink his actions toward more benign activities, or apply for an incidental take permit. This idea of restricting private property rights to protect a rodent that many people still consider a pest rubs many landowners the wrong way.

Some landowners argue that if society asks landowners to supply a public good on private land, society should fairly compensate those affected. They contend the ESA has and will unfairly constrain their freedom to protect or enhance their investment. They are upset because no compensation has been forthcoming for what they perceive as a "taking" of their land, that is, the incurred impact from managing private land in ways compatible with the ESA. These impacts include restricted building development projects, agricultural production, mineral extraction, and recreation. In addition, local and regional municipalities can suffer when an economic impact of compliance leads to worker displacement.

Landowners do not expect these costs to fall anytime soon for two main reasons. First, the list of threatened and endangered species continues to expand. The list has increased by an order of magnitude since 1973 – from 114 in 1973 to over 1,200 in 2000. Plus there are thousands of additional species waiting to be added to this list. Second, the act has a broad scope. Protection is required for all species plus any subspecies and unique populations of species even if the species is found elsewhere. Unique populations are protected for their own sake.

But the cooperation of private landowners is vital for the protection of many endangered species. Policymakers and natural scientists now willingly admit that incentives matter to the private landowners, upon whose acres an estimated 90 percent of endangered species rely (GAO 1995). For instance, on March 6, 1995, Interior Secretary Bruce Babbitt and D. James Baker, then Under Secretary of Commerce, announced ten principles to improve ESA implementation; principle #3 was "to create incentives for landowners to conserve species."[1] Beedy (1995) and Eisner et al. (1995) both include "economic incentives" in their wish lists on how best to fix the ESA. Given this opening, various incentive proposals have rushed in to fill the void, including "safe harbors," tax relief, and tradeable habitat permits (see for example Keystone Center 1995; Glickfeld 1996; Polasky, Doremus, and Rettig 1996).

Several cases studies exist in which private landowners in the United States have become partners voluntarily in positive and proactive plans to protect and enhance natural resources on their land. Examples include the preemptive actions taken to protect the Louisiana black bear, habitat conservation plans for the red cockaded woodpecker, safe harbors and no surprise policies, conservation agreements and plum creek timber, and markets for instream flow for aquatic species (see, for example, Turner and Rylander 1998). And while people can disagree over the actual effectiveness of these schemes, most everyone agrees that the net benefits of species protection could be increased if policy makers address how one could use economic rewards to

---

[1] The other nine principles were: treat landowners fairly and with consideration; minimize social and economic impacts; provide quick, responsive answers and certainty to landowners; base ESA decisions on sound and objective scientific information; prevent species from becoming endangered or threatened; promptly recover and delist threatened or endangered species; provide state, tribal, and local governments with opportunities to play a greater role in carrying out the ESA; make effective use of limited public and private resources by focusing on groups of species dependent on the same habitat; and promote efficiency and consistency in the Departments of the Interior and Commerce (Valdes-Cogliano 1995).

landowners for more cost-effective stewardship of actual and prospective habitat and species.

What economic incentive options do we have for voluntary species protection? As society explores new ways to think about endangered species protection on private property, a variety of compensation schemes are possible: direct compensation from the government to owners of land; conservation banking and tradeable rights in habitat, under which those who wish to develop land would buy permits from those who would then not be able to develop; insurance programs under which landowners are compensated if endangered species impose costs on them, like the fund created by defenders of wildlife under which ranchers are compensated when wolves destroy livestock; estate tax relief to allow large chunks of land to be preserved, rather than broken up to pay federal estate taxes; and tax deductions for conservation expenses.

All schemes present their own unique challenge to policy makers. No compensation scheme is simple or straightforward to implement. Compensating private landowners is subject to shaky claims and extensive litigation. Trading habitat requires that we define what quantity and quality of habitat is "equivalent." Widespread use of the insurance mechanism can be curtailed because of the costs to assess the losses to property owners. It is not obvious that tax breaks for preserving large estates would generate more benefits than simply buying the land, or allowing it to be sold with some sort of easement, and the political attractiveness of providing additional tax breaks to wealthy landowners is questionable (Brown and Shogren 1998).

We need an analytical framework to help us understand the behavioral incentives behind protecting endangered species at risk on private land. Understanding underlying economic behavior is fundamental if agencies plan to push harder on promoting cost-effective protection. Protection strategies should address the design of efficient economic incentives to encourage landowners to preserve their property. Agencies or private parties can attempt to buy species protection by providing an incentive for the landowner to cooperate, using either compensation for "takings," or using permits and fines.

This chapter explores the nature of incentive design for endangered species protection on private land. Our goal is to better understand what we know and still need to know about effective voluntary incentive systems for protection. We explore the underlying economic behavior in operation on both private property and government agencies. Herein we outline the basic steps to design a voluntarily incentive scheme for endangered species protection. Our case presumes the critical species habitat cuts across the holdings of several private landowners; and that the likelihood of survival will be significantly enhanced if the landowners create a single large habitat reserve that minimizes "edge effects" (Eisner et al. 1995; NRC 1995).[2]

---

[2] Edge effects occur at the boundaries between different habitats, e.g., the edge between a forest and a field. Some species such as game animals thrive along the edge, while others are driven deeper into the forest. The fragmentation of forests creates more and more edges that can have

A regulator designs a welfare maximizing mechanism that offers each landowner a contract schedule specifying a monetary transfer for acres retired, with the transfer possibly including a conservation bonus scheme to promote acre agglomeration across landowners. The regulator takes an active role by identifying critical habitat for listed and unlisted species, and then designs a voluntary compensation scheme for critical habitat that cuts across the holdings of several private landowners. Our system is voluntary, allows for a minimum probability of species survival, is flexible enough to accommodate a single large or several small reserves through the use of acreage agglomeration bonuses, provides incentives for each landowner to reveal his private information regarding the land's rental structure, and accounts for the deadweight loss of raising the funds used to compensate the landowner for setting aside acres (also see Smith 1995).

Our results suggest that retired acres under asymmetric information should never be more than those retired under the full-information benchmark.[3] Uncertainty about the economic system leads society to underinvest in retired acres, on average. Second, the regulator could implement the full information allocation of retired acres only if no deadweight loss exists. But given the current climate of balanced budgets, the regulator will need to find funds for habitat reserves from some other worthy project. Third, the regulator uses its knowledge about how landowners will react to the agglomeration bonus and adjusts the transfer downward. This implies that regardless of whether the regulator prefers one coordinated single large reserve or several uncoordinated small reserves, the financial cost to society is the same in this class of models.

2. LANDOWNER PREFERENCES

Suppose a regulator discovers an endangered species on the private property of several landowners. Rather than impose some uniform restriction on land use, the regulator instead wants to design a voluntary acreage retirement program that maximizes social welfare. The voluntary program seeks to induce each landowner to enter into a contract with the regulator, with the contract specifying the transfer T^i, he will receive for retiring a^i acres into a wildlife reserve. If the regulator knew each landowner's property rents, the costs of the retirement scheme could be minimized – each landowner would be given a small amount above his reservation price. But a landowner's preference valuation is usually private information. The regulator invokes mechanism design theory to address this information asymmetry.

---

a negative effect on endangered species protection. Working off the theory of island biogeography, the biological community has argued over the net effects of edges and the optimal design of habitat reserves, i.e., the SLOSS debate – Single Large or Several Small reserves (see for example Soulé and Simberloff 1986; Gilpin and Soulé 1986).

[3] Exceptions to this rule are discussed in Smith and Shogren (2001).

Assume n landowners exist within a "habitat region,"[4] and index the landowners by $i \in I = \{1, 2, \ldots, n\}$. Represent the ith landowner's rents by $\Pi^i(A^i, \theta^i)$, where A^i is the landowner's acreage endowment and θ^i is an efficiency parameter called the landowner's type. For notational simplicity we assume $A^i = A \ \forall \ i \in I$. A landowner with type θ^i will often be called a type-θ^i landowner, and unless noted otherwise, each landowner's type is his private information. To simplify, assume each θ^i is distributed uniformly over $[\underline{\theta}, \overline{\theta}]$, where $\underline{\theta} < \overline{\theta}$. Let $\theta = (\theta^1, \ldots, \theta^n)$ represent the vector of landowner types, and denote the set of all possible type vectors by Θ. Let $\theta^{-i} = (\theta^1, \ldots, \theta^{i-1}, \theta^{i+1}, \ldots, \theta^n)$ denote the vector of types of everyone except landowner i and let $\Theta^{-i} = \times_{i=1}^{n-1} [\underline{\theta}, \overline{\theta}]$ be the set of all possible θ^{-i} vectors.

The following assumption requires that rents be increasing and strictly concave in acreage endowments, strictly increasing in types, and that marginal rents be strictly increasing in type.

Assumption 1. Over the relevant region: $\Pi_1^i \geqslant 0$, $\Pi_{11}^i < 0$, $\Pi_2^i > 0$, $\Pi_{12}^i > 0$.

We use mechanism design theory – truthful direct revelation (TDR) mechanisms – to develop the properties of an optimal ex-post efficient incentive scheme.[5] Ex-post efficiency requires that the mechanism implement the full-information or second-best allocation corresponding to each possible vector of types in Θ. Also, implementing an ex-post efficient mechanism requires the communication between landowners and regulator take place in two rounds. In the first round the regulator announces to landowners a contract schedule

$$\Gamma = \{\Gamma(\theta^1), \ldots, \Gamma(\theta^n)\}_{\theta \in \Theta},$$

where $\Gamma(\theta^i) = \{a(\theta^i, \theta^{-i}), T(\theta^i, \theta^{-i})\}_{\theta^{-i} \in \Theta}$ is a state-contingent contract schedule specifying that if landowner i reports a type of $\hat{\theta}^i$ he receives one of the contracts in the schedule $\Gamma(\hat{\theta}^i)$. Exactly which contract he receives depends on θ^{-i}, the vector of types reported by the other landowners. If the vector of types reported by all other landowner types is $\hat{\theta}^{-i}$, then landowner i receives the contract $(a(\hat{\theta}^i, \hat{\theta}^{-i}), T(\hat{\theta}^i, \hat{\theta}^{-i}))$.

Each landowner observes the contract schedule and reports a type $\hat{\theta}^i$ to the regulator. In the second round the regulator observes the vector of reported types $\hat{\theta}^i$ and tells each landowner i they are to receive the contract $(a(\hat{\theta}^i, \hat{\theta}^{-i}), T(\hat{\theta}^i, \hat{\theta}^{-i}))$.[6] The contract defines the terms of trade between the landowner and regulator: the landowner receives a transfer $T(\hat{\theta}^i, \hat{\theta}^{-i})$ for retiring $a^i \equiv a(\hat{\theta}^i, \hat{\theta}^{-i}) \leqslant A$ acres, $i = 1, 2, \ldots, n$. The mechanism is a truthful

---

[4] More than one habitat region can exist, but the notation becomes more cumbersome.

[5] See Smith and Shogren (2001) for a discussion of the properties of an optimal ex-ante efficient mechanism.

[6] See Myerson (1987) for a general discussion of direct revelation mechanisms.

direct revelation mechanism if it is optimal for each landowner to report his type truthfully, that is, he reports $\hat{\theta}^i = \theta^i$.

2.1.   Coordinating Acreage Retirement

The habitat supporting endangered species often falls on more than one tract of private land. A voluntary land retirement scheme similar to the Conservation Reserve Program should allow a landowner the prerogative to chose which acres he will retire. Such freedom of choice in endangered species incentives might serve to fragment retired acres into several small habitat reserves. Although some species thrive on the edges between habitats, biologists have argued that endangered species most likely do not (see Yahner 1988). Biological evidence has accumulated to replace Leopold's (1933) "law of interspersion" – more edge, more population density – with the proposition that edge effects cause extinction (Mills 1995; Paton 1994). Edge effects arise from nest paratism and the penetration of light and wind into the habitat. Species move away from the edge and further into a forest causing a reduction in total area and lower population persistence (e.g., Vickery, Hunter, and Scott 1994; Brittingham and Temple 1983; Bissonette, Fredrickson, and Tucker 1988; Robbins, Dawson, and Dowell 1989).

A voluntary incentive scheme for endangered species should be flexible enough so landowners can retire acres unilaterally to create a coordinated single large reserve. Each landowner thus needs incentives to set aside his acres such that they are adjacent to his neighbor's retired acres. If each landowner agglomerates his retired acres along his fence line voluntarily, edge effects will be minimized. Our mechanism design provides this needed incentive by offering a lump-sum agglomeration bonus to each landowner. The agglomeration bonus serves to induce the landowners to voluntarily coordinate their retirement decisions such that the new habitat reserve is contiguous with minimal edge effects.

Formally, for each $i \in I$, let $(x_k^i, y_k^i) \in \mathbb{R}_+^2$ denote the "coordinates" of the kth acre retired by the ith landowner, $k = 1, 2, \ldots, a^i$. Also, for each $i \in I$, denote the set of all possible ways that a^i acres can be retired by the set $\Sigma^i(a^i) \subset \times_{k=1}^{a^i} \mathbb{R}_+^2$. A coordination strategy for landowner i is denoted $\sigma^i(a^i) \in \Sigma^i(a^i)$, where $\sigma^i(a^i)$ is a set containing the coordinates of each of the a^i retired acres. Denote the vector of n landowner strategies by $\sigma = (\sigma^1(a^1), \ldots, \sigma^n(a^n)) \in \times_{i=1}^{n} \Sigma^i(a^i)$. Given that all other landowners play "border" strategies $\sigma^{j*} \in \Sigma^i(a^j)$, the payoff to landowner i from playing $\sigma^i(a^i)$ is denoted $P^i(\sigma^i(a^i); \sigma^{-i*}) \in \mathbb{R}_+$, where $\sigma^{-i*} = (\sigma^{1*}, \ldots, \sigma^{i-1*}, \sigma^{i+1*}, \ldots, \sigma^{n*})$. For a given a^i, define the lump-sum agglomeration bonus by

$$P^{i*}(a^i) = \max_{\sigma i} \left\{ P^i(\sigma^i(a^i); \sigma^{-i*}) : \sigma^i(a^i) \in \sum^i (a^i) \right\}.$$

The agglomeration bonus is what landowners receive for coordinating their acreage retirements to creat a relatively contiguous land mass. Assume a set of rules exist, R, such that for each landowner i:

$$\sigma^{i*}(a^i) \in \arg \max_{\sigma^i \in \sum^i} P^{i*}(a^i).$$

The landowner's optimal strategy is to coordinate land retirements such that the retired acres are contiguous. As an extreme example, say no landowner's land endowment is valued at more than \$100,000. Assuming that landowners are risk neutral and rational, one such rule would be that each landowner gets \$500,000 if the entire set of retired acres forms a contiguous land mass and zero dollars otherwise.

2.2.   Incentive Compatibility and Voluntary Participation

Given the mechanism Γ, the expected profit to landowner i given that he reports $\hat{\theta}^i$ and all other landowners report $\hat{\theta}^{-i}$ is[7]

$$\Pi^i(A - a(\hat{\theta}^i, \hat{\theta}^{-i}), \theta^i) + t(\hat{\theta}^i, \hat{\theta}^{-i}) + P^{i*}(a(\hat{\theta}^i, \hat{\theta}^{-i})),$$

where $T^i = t(\hat{\theta}) + P^{i*}(a(\hat{\theta}))$. Define "program rents" (or information rents) as:

$$\begin{aligned}\hat{\pi}^i(\theta^i, \hat{\theta}^i; \hat{\theta}^{-i}) = {} & \Pi^i(A - a(\hat{\theta}^i, \hat{\theta}^{-i}), \theta^i) + t(\hat{\theta}^i, \hat{\theta}^{-i}) \\ & + P^{i*}(a(\hat{\theta}^i, \hat{\theta}^{-i})) - \Pi^i(A, \theta^i).\end{aligned} \tag{16.1}$$

Here, program rents are the difference between the expected profit a landowner receives when participating in the program and the profit that he would receive when not participating.

As noted earlier we seek to design a direct-revelation mechanism within which it is optimal for each landowner type to truthfully reveal their type to the regulator. We consider truthful Bayesian-Nash equilibria, where for each $i = 1, \ldots, n$, given that all other landowners report their type honestly, truthtelling is landowner i's optimal response. Truthtelling is optimal (in the Bayesian-Nash equilibrium) only if the direct revelation mechanism satisfies:

$$_{\theta^{-i}}\left\{\pi_2^i(\theta^i, \hat{\theta}^i; \theta^{-i}) \Big|_{\hat{\theta}^i = \theta^i}\right\} = 0. \tag{16.2}$$

The subscripts denote partial derivatives with respect to the jth argument, that is, $\hat{\pi}_2^i = \partial \hat{\pi}^i / \partial \hat{\theta}^i$. A full decomposition of (16.2) reveals the mechanism is

---

[7] We assume that acres entered into the reserve generate no rents for the landowner other than the transfer received from the regulator. The interested reader can accommodate the possibility that retired acres earn nonzero rents by representing the landowner's rental structure as $\tilde{\Pi}^i(A^i - a^i(\hat{\theta}^i; \hat{\theta}^{-i}), a^i(\hat{\theta}^i; \hat{\theta}^{-i}), \theta^i)$, and assume that $\tilde{\Pi}^i$ is nondecreasing and concave in its second argument.

designed so the expected marginal benefit associated with misrepresenting one's type (change in transfer) is exactly offset by the corresponding expected marginal cost (rents lost from retiring acres). Assume that truthtelling is the landowner's optimal response and let the function $\pi^i(\theta^i; \theta^{-i}) = \hat{\pi}^i(\theta^i, \theta^i; \theta^{-i})$ represent landowner i's expected profit when $\hat{\theta}^i = \theta^i$. An equivalent envelope condition for truthtelling is[8]

$$
\begin{aligned}
{}_{\theta^{-i}}\{ \pi_1^i(\theta^i; \theta^{-i})\} \\
= {}_{\theta^{-i}}\{ \hat{\pi}_2^i(\theta^i, \theta^i; \theta^{-i})\} + \theta^{-i}\{ \hat{\pi}_2^i(\theta^i, \theta^i; \theta^{-i})\} \\
= {}_{\theta^{-i}}\{ \Pi_2^i(A - a(\theta^i, \theta^{-i}), \theta^i) - \Pi_2^i(A, \theta^i)\} < 0,
\end{aligned}
\tag{16.3}
$$

implying that program (or information) rents are decreasing in the landowner's type. The landowner has two opposing incentives. He has an incentive to overstate his lost rents and ensure himself of a higher reservation base (i.e., makes the claim that his land earns higher rents), with the expected gains from overstating one's type given by $\Pi_2^i(A, \theta^i)$. But he also has a countervailing incentive to understate his type because lower types retire more acres and receive larger transfers. The expected gains from understating one's type is $\Pi_2^i(A - a^i, \theta^i)$. Given $\Pi_{21}^i > 0$, we have $\Pi_2^i(A - a^i, \theta^i) < \Pi_2^i(A, \theta^i)$: the gains from overstating one's type dominates the gains from understating, hence information rents are decreasing in the landowner's true type.

The second-order condition for truthtelling is, for all $\theta^i \in [\underline{\theta}, \overline{\theta}]$,

$$
{}_{\theta^{-i}}\{a_1(\theta^i, \theta^{-i})\} \leqslant 0
\tag{16.4}
$$

(see Laffont and Tirole 1987). The second-order condition requires the expected acreage retirement function to be nonincreasing in landowner type; the more efficient landowners retire fewer acres.

The mechanism is voluntary if the landowner is at least as well off participating in the program than not participating. For voluntary participation the land retirement program must satisfy

$$
{}_{\theta^{-i}}\{ \pi^i(\theta^i; \theta^{-i})\} \geqslant 0.
$$

By (16.3) landowners' program rents are decreasing for all types (strictly decreasing for positive a^i). Given that program rents are decreasing in θ^i, the participation constraint is satisfied if

$$
{}_{\theta^{-i}}\{ \pi^i(\overline{\theta}; \theta^{-i})\} = 0.
\tag{16.5}
$$

---

[8] To derive equation (16.3), totally differentiate (16.1) with respect to θ^i and $\hat{\theta}^i$ and use equation (16.2).

In summary, truthtelling is the landowner's optimal response if the revelation mechanism satisfies equations (16.3) and (16.4), or equivalently, equations (16.2) and (16.4). Voluntary participation is satisfied if the type-$\bar{\theta}$ landowner earns at least zero program rents. If so, all other landowners also earn nonnegative program rents.

3. THE REGULATOR'S PROBLEM

Now consider the regulator's optimization problem. Let $S(\sum_{i=1}^{n} a(\theta^i, \theta^{-i}))$ represent some measure of species survival in a habitat region, given that $\sum_i a^i$ (possibly contiguous) acres are retired. For example, S could represent the likelihood of survival of a protected species as a function of acres retired (i.e., the safe minimum standard). Or, S could represent the expected number of species protected in the habitat region. We assume S is a smooth, differentiable,[9] nondecreasing function of habitat size (see, for example, Montgomery, Brown, and Darius 1994). The likelihood of species survival must meet the *minimum acceptable probability of survival* (MAPS) criterion $\bar{S} \leqslant S(\sum_i a^i)$, where $\bar{S}$ is the minimum acceptable probability of survival. The MAPS constraint represents how past preferences encoded in the ESA affect present preferences of current citizens. The MAPS constraint says that even if today we have low preferences for certain less-appreciated species (e.g., black tailed prairie dogs), the ESA forces us to achieve some minimum level of survival.

Assume raising transfer revenues entails a per dollar deadweight cost of raising funds equal to λ,[10] and represent the social benefit accorded to S by the strictly concave benefit function $B(S(\cdot))$. Given a vector of types, acreage endowments, and set of contracts, net social welfare is (suppressing the arguments of a^i and t^i):

$$B\left(S\left(\sum_i a^i\right)\right) + \sum_i [\Pi^i(A - a^i, \theta^i) + t^i + P^{i*}(a^i)] - \sum_i (1 + \lambda)\,[t^i + P^{i*}(a^i)]$$

$$= B\left(S\left(\sum_i a^i\right)\right) + \sum_i \{\Pi^i(A - a^i, \theta^i) - \lambda[t^i + P^{i*}(a^i)]\}. \tag{16.6}$$

Net social welfare equals the social benefit of wildlife preservation plus landowner rents less the deadweight cost of raising funds, with net welfare

---

[9] A species survival function could very well be discontinuous, e.g., a step function or a function that is zero until some threshold level of habitat size is reached, after which the likelihood of survival gradually approaches some upper bound less than or equal to one. With modifications, the approach used here can accommodate smooth functions that are continuous almost everywhere (a finite number of jumps) and, when continuous, the rate at which the species survival function changes is not too fast. See Assumption 2.

[10] A problem similar to ours, is where the regulator faces a budget constraint $\sum_i (t^i + P^{i*}) \leqslant M$, with M being the maximum amount that the regulator can spend. In such a case λ could be interpreted as the shadow value of relaxing the budget constraint, and subsequent results are similar to ours.

unambiguously decreasing in the transfers' deadweight costs. Let $a(\theta) = (a(\theta^1, \theta^{-1}), \ldots, a(\theta^n, \theta^{-n}))$. Expected net social welfare is written as

$$_\theta\{W(a(\theta), \theta, \lambda)\},$$

where

$$W(a(\theta), \theta, \lambda) = B\left(S\left(\sum_i a(\theta^i, \theta^{-i})\right)\right) + (1 + \lambda)\sum_i \Pi^i(A - a(\theta^i, \theta^{-i}), \theta^i)$$
$$- \lambda\sum_i \theta^i[\Pi_2^i(A, \theta^i) - \Pi_2^i(A - a(\theta^i, \theta^{-i}), \theta^i)] \qquad (16.7)$$

(see Appendix 16.1). Expected net welfare is equal to the expected benefits of endangered species preservation plus the expected profits to landowners less their expected information rents. Smaller information rents create more expected net welfare.

Assumption 2. (i) $\tilde{B}''(S(\hat{a}))[S'(\hat{a})]^2 + \tilde{B}'(S(\hat{a}))S''(\hat{a}) < 0$ and $\Pi_{211} \leqslant 0$ for all $\hat{a} \in \mathbb{R}_+$, (ii) $\Pi_{212} \geqslant 0$.

Assumption 2 (i) ensures that W is strictly concave in the acres retired and that a unique solution to the regulator's problem exists. Assumption 2 (ii) requires that marginal profits increase in the landowner's type at an increasing rate, and is a sufficient condition for the monotonicity condition, defined by equation (16.4).

To choose the optimal contract schedule Γ, the regulator solves the following optimization problem:

$$\max_a {}_\theta\{W(a(\theta), \theta, \lambda)\}$$

subject to

$$A \geqslant a(\theta^i, \theta^{-i}), \quad i = 1, \ldots, n$$

$$\bar{S} \leqslant S\left(\sum_i a(\theta^i, \theta^{-i})\right).$$

As a comparative benchmark we first define the properties of full-information allocation. A regulator who knows the landowners' types also knows their rental structure. With an interior solution the optimal full-information allocation satisfies the following necessary conditions:

$$(B' + \gamma) S' - (1 + \lambda) \Pi_1^i - v^i = 0, \quad \forall \theta, \ i = 1, 2, \ldots, n \qquad (16.8)$$

$$(1 + \lambda) \Pi_1^i + v^i = (1 + \lambda) \Pi_1^j + v^i, \quad \forall i, j \qquad (16.9)$$

and

$$t(\theta^i; \theta^{-i}) + P^{i*} = \Pi^i(A - a(\theta^i, \theta^{-i}), \theta^i),$$ (16.10)

where v^i is the shadow value of the ith landowner's last retired acre. Acres are retired such that the net marginal cost of retiring acres is equal across all landowners, and the total transfer equals his lost rents – this our comparative benchmark. Let γ be the shadow value of the MAPS constraint.

Now let's return to the asymmetric information problem. The Lagrangian for the regulator's problem under asymmetric information is:

$$\mathcal{L} = \theta \left\{ W(a(\theta), \theta, \lambda) + \sum_i v^i(\theta)[A - a(\theta^i, \theta^{-i})] \right.$$
$$\left. + \gamma(\theta) \left[S\left(\sum_i a(\theta^i, \theta^{-i}) \right) - \bar{S} \right] \right\},$$

where $\gamma(\theta)$ is the shadow value of increasing the MAPS criterion when the vector of landowner types is θ. Pointwise optimization yields the following necessary conditions for ex-post efficiency:

$$\frac{\partial \mathcal{L}}{\partial a^i(\theta)} = (B' - \gamma) S' - (1 + \lambda)\Pi_1^i - \lambda(\theta^i - \underline{\theta})\Pi_{21}^i - v^i \leqslant 0,$$

$$\forall \theta, \quad i = 1, 2, \ldots, n$$ (16.11)

$$\frac{\partial \mathcal{L}}{\partial v^i(\theta)} = (A - a(\theta^i, \theta^{-i}) \geqslant 0, \quad \forall \theta, \quad i = 1, 2, \ldots, n$$ (16.12)

$$\frac{\partial \mathcal{L}}{\partial \gamma(\theta)} = S\left(\sum_i a(\theta^i, \theta^{-i}) \right) - \bar{S} \geqslant 0, \quad i = 1, 2, \ldots, n.$$ (16.13)

And the optimal transfer function is given by

$$t(\theta^i, \theta^{-i}) = \int_{\theta^i}^{\bar{\theta}} [\Pi_2^i(A - a(s, \theta^{-i}), s) - \Pi_2^i(A, s)] \, ds + \Pi^i(A, \theta^i)$$
$$- \Pi^i(A - a(\theta^i, \theta^{-i}), \theta^i) - P^{i*}(a(\theta^i, \theta^{-i})).$$ (16.14)

The first term on the right-hand side of equation (16.14) is the type-θ^i landowner's information rent. As suggested by (16.5), all but the highest type landowner earns such rents. By (16.11), a necessary condition for the optimal acreage decision is that for all $i, j \in I$,

$$(1 + \lambda)\Pi_1^i + \lambda(\theta^i - \bar{\theta})\Pi_{21}^i + v^i = (1 + \lambda)\Pi_1^j + \lambda(\theta^j - \bar{\theta})\Pi_{21}^j + v^j.$$

The net marginal benefit of retiring acres must be the same across all landowners. Under asymmetric information only the least efficient landowner will retire the full-information number of acres. Comparing expressions (16.11) and (16.8) reveals that for all other landowner types the number of acres retired under asymmetric information will be less than the corresponding full-information levels. This result follows from the strict concavity of W.

The generalized ex-post model reveals five results. First, it is clear that addressing the problems associated with imperfect information about economic incentives is as fundamental to effective species protection policy as imperfect information about natural systems. Biologists rightly point out that imperfect information about the population biology of species and their roles in ecosystems confounds the design of preservation policy. In like manner, imperfect information about economic behavior complicates policy design. On private land, the government needs landowner cooperation to gain the information necessary to administer conservation policy. For instance, not only is there likely to be asymmetric information concerning landowner rents, there is likely to be private information regarding the existence or nonexistence of a listed species on a landowner's property. Landowners may have avoided regulation altogether by hiding such information from the government. If so, conservation policy can use compensation to be effective. But the rub is that the regulator should lower the transfer payment to high type landowners to lessen the incentive for low types to take advantage of their private information and mimic the high types. But smaller transfers result in fewer acres set aside for habitat. Unless deadweight loss is zero, asymmetric information will lead to a smaller reserve relative to a reserve implemented under complete information. Since information rents decrease in the landowner's type, and decrease faster as less acres are retired, the regulator can curtail information rents by decreasing acreage retirement levels below full-information levels. In doing so the regulator trades off decreased information rents with the costs of the induced distortion. The net result is that either the realized habitat will be less than desired, or the desired habitat will be more expensive than may be justified.

Second, habitat size falls as deadweight loss (λ) increases. Given that W is strictly concave in each a^i, greater deadweight costs induce the regulator to decrease the size of habitat reserves to reduce the distortions induced by the deadweight costs. To see this, totally differentiate the equilibrium condition (16.11) with respect to λ and a^i, and set the result equal to zero

$$\frac{da^i}{d\lambda} = \frac{\theta^i \Pi_{21}^i + \Pi_1^i}{W_{11}}.$$

Since $\theta^i \Pi_{21}^i + \Pi_1^i$ is positive and W_{11} is strictly negative, it follows that the acreage profiles are decreasing in λ: as deadweight losses increase, acreage retirement levels decrease for each type and for all acreage endowments. The regulator decreases retirement levels for each type because as λ increases, the share of each dollar going to landowners falls, and with less per dollar available for acreage retirement, the regulator is forced to retire fewer acres. Accordingly, one would expect the size of the habitat reserve to decrease given larger values of λ. Since retirement levels fall, the portion of total per-acre costs accruing to landowners falls also.[11]

Third, as deadweight losses increase, total program costs could increase or decrease. The change in total program costs have two components: (i) a per-acre price effect which increases as λ increases, and (ii) an acreage effect where the number of acres retired falls with increases in λ. If the price (acreage) effect dominates, total programs costs will fall (increase) as dead-weight costs increase. When trying to implement a voluntary habit reserve program, it is possible to have a perverse situation where total program costs increase, while landowner transfers and habitat acreage falls.

Fourth, the regulator can use her knowledge about how landowners will react to the agglomeration bonus and adjust transfers accordingly. An increase in the agglomeration bonus is directly offset by a decrease in the transfer payment. This implies that regardless of whether the regulator prefers one coordinated single large reserve or several uncoordinated small reserves, the financial cost to society is the same within our framework. The single large versus several small debate is funding-neutral – the cost is the same either way. Note that a flip side exists to this result. If coordinated and unco-ordinated land retirements cost the same, the regulator cannot save money by giving up on the idea of a single large reserve. Several small reserves will cost the regulator the same amount of resources because as she decreases the agglomeration bonus, because she must increase the transfer.

Finally, when the MAPS constraint binds in both the full-information and ex-post efficient allocations, habitat areas will be the same size and equal to $\bar{A}$, where $\bar{A}$ is the minimum number of land units that set $S(\sum_i a^i) = \bar{S}$. Smith and Shogren (2001) show that if landowner preferences are linear in acres retired and landowner acres are perfect substitutes in creating habitat, the ex-post mechanism takes all of the least expensive land first, then all of the next cheapest land, etc., until the MAPS constraint is satisfied.

4. CONCLUSION

The Endangered Species Act of 1973 (ESA) shelters threatened and endan-gered species from environmental pressures they might encounter on public and private land in the United States. Passed with little opposition in Congress, few lawmakers at the time anticipated the political firestorm the Act has created today. Today people tend to either glorify the ESA as vision-ary or demonize it as invasive. Often the split arises over whether landowners deserve compensation for protecting the public good with private hands.

This chapter has outlined the basic steps behind an optimal incentive schemes for endangered species preservation given asymmetric information. The optimal incentive scheme includes a potential bonus for landowners who coordinate their land retirement decisions. We find that less land is retired on

---

[11] Differentiate (A16.1) with respect to a^i to see that the total transfer is increasing in acres retired.

average under asymmetric information than full-information levels and that acreage retirement levels decrease as deadweight losses increase. We also argued that even though habitat size falls as deadweight losses increase, it is possible for total program costs to increase. Finally, we find that the single large reserve versus several small reserve debate is funding-neutral.

These results provide some insight into the plausibility of implementing voluntary habitat reserves, and when it might make sense to implement non-linear retirement schemes. If the habitat reserve can be discontiguous, or if it must be contiguous and cuts across the entire landholding of relatively few landowners or if small "holes" are allowed, then taking the time to design an efficient nonlinear retirement scheme could be worthwhile. However, the value of implementing a voluntary nonlinear pricing scheme might be limited if the desired habitat reserve cuts across the entire landholdings of many land-holders or "holes" are not allowed. In this case the regulator needs to com-pare the relative pros and cons of paying each landholder top dollar for their land or paying them an average "fair price" and be done with things.

Finally, the funding-neutral result seems counterintuitive if one believes the landowners can exploit a regulator who prefers a single large reserve. If the landowners know their implicit coordination is necessary to satisfy the regulator's preferences, they should extract more rents by holding out on which acres are retired. In the class of models we consider, however, this does not occur because doing so violates the incentive compatibility and participa-tion constraints. One possible extension would be to allow landholders to col-lude on the decision to participate and allow for "holdouts."

But we must recognize that compensation itself is no less controversial. Voluntary incentive systems have supporters and critics from both sides of the debate. Conservationists who support economic incentives see compensation as a practical way to buy cooperation; landowners proponents argue that it is only fair to compensate property owners who are restricted in their ability to protect their investment. Conservationists who oppose economic incentives see compen-sation as a backdoor policy to sabotage the ESA through underfunding; averse landowners see compensation as a lever that will open the door for more federal control over their property, especially given the line of species being considered for listing. Whether any voluntary scheme can be successfully implemented across a wide range of private property remains a challenge for the future.

APPENDIX 16.1

Given a vector of other types θ^{-i}, expression (16.6) can be simplified in three steps. First, integrate Π_2^i between θ^i and 1 to get

$$\pi^i(\bar{\theta}; \theta^{-i}) - \pi^i(\theta^i; \theta^{-i}) = -\pi^i(\theta^i; \theta^{-i})$$

$$= \int_{\theta^i}^{\bar{\theta}} [\Pi_2^i(A - a(s, \theta^{-i}), s) - \Pi_2^i(A, s)] \, ds.$$

Next, set the above equal to (16.1).

$$\pi^i(\theta^i; \theta^{-i}) = \int_{\theta^i}^{\bar{\theta}} [\Pi_2^i(A, s) - \Pi_2^i(A - a(s, \theta^{-i}), s)] \, ds.$$

$$= \Pi^i(A - a(\theta^i, \theta^{-i}), \theta^i) + t(\theta^i, \theta^{-i}) + P^i*(a(\theta^i, \theta^{-i})),$$

and rearrange terms to get

$$t(\theta^i; \theta^{-i}) + P^i*(a(\theta^i; \theta^{-i}))$$

$$= \int_{\theta^i}^{\bar{\theta}} [\Pi_2^i(A, s) - \Pi_2^i(A - a(s, \theta^{-i}), s)] \, ds - \Pi^i(A - a(\theta^i, \theta^{-i}), \theta^i).$$

$$(A16.1)$$

For a given θ and Γ, substituting expression (A16.1) into (16.6) gives

$$B\left(S\left(\sum_i a(\theta^i, \theta^{-i})\right)\right) + (1 + \lambda) \sum_i \Pi^i(A - a(\theta^i, \theta^{-i}), \theta^i)$$

$$- \lambda \sum_i \int_{\theta^i}^{\bar{\theta}} [\Pi_2^i(A, s) - \Pi_2^i(A - a(s, \theta^{-i}), s)] \, ds.$$

Next, integrate the above expression over Θ:

$$_\theta\left\{B\left(S\left(\sum_i a(\theta^i, \theta^{-i})\right)\right) + (1 + \lambda) \sum_i \Pi^i(A - a(\theta^i, \theta^{-i}), \theta^i)\right\}$$

$$- \lambda \sum_i {}_\theta\left\{\int_{\theta^i}^{\bar{\theta}} [\Pi_2^i(A, s) - \Pi_2^i(A - a(s, \theta^{-i}), s)] \, ds\right\}.$$

$$(A16.2)$$

Rewrite the integral term in (A16.2) as

$$\sum_i {}_{\theta^{-i}}\left\{\int_{\underline{\theta}}^{\bar{\theta}} \int_{\theta^i}^{\bar{\theta}} [\Pi_2^i(A, s) - \Pi_2^i(A - a(s, \theta^{-i}), s)] \, ds \, d\theta^i\right\}.$$

By Fubini's Theorem the above expression is equivalent to

$$\sum_i {}_{\theta^{-i}}\left\{\int_{\underline{\theta}}^{\bar{\theta}} \int_{\underline{\theta}}^{\theta^i} d\theta^i \, [\Pi_2^i(A, s) - \Pi_2^i(A - a(s, \theta^{-i}), s)] \, ds\right\}$$

$$= \sum_i {}_{\theta^{-i}}\left\{\int_{\underline{\theta}}^{\bar{\theta}} \theta^i [\Pi_2^i(A, \theta^i) - \Pi_2^i(A - a(\theta^i, \theta^{-i}), \theta^i)] \, d\theta^i\right\}$$

$$= \sum_i {}_{\theta^{-i}}\left\{ \theta^i \{ \theta^i [\Pi_2^i(A, \theta^i) - \Pi_2^i(A - a(\theta^i, \theta^{-i}), \theta^i)] \} \right\}$$

$$= \sum_i {}_{\theta}\left\{ \theta^i [\Pi_2^i(A, \theta^i) - \Pi_2^i(A - a(\theta^i, \theta^{-i}), \theta^i)] \right\}.$$

It follows that expected welfare can be represented by

$${}_{\theta}\{ W(a(\theta), \theta, \lambda) \},$$

where $a(\theta) = (a(\theta^1, \theta^{-1}), \ldots, a(\theta^n, \theta^{-n}))$ and

$$W(a(\theta), \theta, \lambda) = B\left(S\left(\sum_i a(\theta^i, \theta^{-i}) \right) \right) + (1 + \lambda) \sum_i \Pi^i(A - a(\theta^i, \theta^{-i}), \theta^i)$$

$$- \lambda \sum_i \theta^i [\Pi_2^i(A, \theta^i) - \Pi_2^i(A - a(\theta^i, \theta^{-i}), \theta^i)].$$

References

Beedy, E. (1995). Ten Ways to Fix the Endangered Species Act. *Endangered Species Bulletin* 12: 12–14.

Beissinger, S. and M. I. Westphal (1998). On the Use of Demographic Models of Population Viability in Endangered Species Management. *Journal of Wildlife Management* 62: 821–41.

Bissonett, J., R. Fredrickson, and B. Tucker (1988). The Effects of Forest Harvesting on Marten and Small Mammals in Western Newfoundland. Report prepared for the Newfoundland and Labrador Wildlife Division and Corner Brook Pulp and Paper Ltd., Utah State University, UT, May 15.

Brittingham, M. and S. Temple (1983). Have Cowbirds Caused Forest Songbirds to Decline? *BioScience* 33: 31–35.

Brown, G., and J. Shogren (1998). Economics of the Endangered Species Act. *Journal of Economic Prespectives* 12: 3–20.

Eisner, T., J. Lubchenco, E. O. Wilson, D. Wilcove, and M. Bean (1995). Building a Scientifically Sound Policy for Protecting Endangered Species. *Science* 268: 1231–32.

General Accounting Office (GAO) (1995). Correspondence to representative Don Young on estimated recovery costs of endangered species. Washington, DC, B-270461.

Gilpin, M. and M. Soulé (1986). Minimum Viable Populations: Processes of Species Extinction. *Conservation Biology: The Science of Scarcity and Diversity* (M. Soulé, ed.). Sunderland, Mass: Sinauer Associates.

Glickfeld, M. (1996). Beyond Regulation: Creating Incentive Strategies to Promote Endangered Species Conservation in California. Stanford University, photocopy.

Innes, R., S. Polasky, and J. Tschirhart (1998). Takings, Compensation, and Endangered Species Protection on Private Land. *Journal of Economic Prespectives* 12: 35–52.

Keystone Center (1995). The Keystone Dialogue on Incentives for Private Landowners to Protect Endangered Species. Final Report, Keystone, CO, p. 47.

Laffont, J.-J. and J. Tirole (1987) Auctioning Incentive Contracts. *Journal of Political Economy* 95: 921–37.

Leopold, A. (1933) *Game Management.* New York: Charles Scribner's Sons.

Mills, L. (1995). Edge Effects and Isolation: Red-Backed Voles on Forest Remnants. *Conservation Biology* 9: 395–403.

Montgomery C., G. Brown, Jr., and M. Darius (1994). The Marginal Cost of Species Preservation: The Northern Spotted Owl. *Journal of Environmental Economics and Management* 26: 111–28.

Myerson, R. (1987). Mechanism Design. *The New Palgrave: A Dictionary of Economics* (J. Eatwell, M. Milgate, and P. Newman, eds.). New York: The Stockton Press.

National Research Council (NRC) (1995). *Science and the Endangered Species Act.* Washington, DC.: National Academy Press.

Paton, P. (1994). The Effect of Edge on Avian Nest Success: How Strong Is the Evidence. *Conservation Biology* 8: 17–26.

Polasky, S., H. Doremus, and B. Rettig (1996). "Endangered Species Conservation on Private Land." *Oregon State Agricultural Experiment Station Technical paper no. 10918.*

Robbins, C., D. Dawson, and B. Dowell (1989). Habitat Area Requirements of Breeding Forest Birds of the Middle Atlantic States. *Wildlife Monographs* 103: 1–34.

Simberloff, D. (1988). The Contribution of Population and Community Biology to Conservation Science. *Annual Reviews of Ecology and Systematics* 19: 473–511.

Smith, R. (1995). The Conservation Reserve Program as a Least-Cost Land Retirement Mechanism. *American Journal of Agricultural Economics* 77: 93–105.

Smith, R. and J. Shogren (2000). Voluntary Incentive Design for Endangered Species Protection. *Journal of Environmental Economics and Management* (forthcoming).

Soulé, M. and D. Simberloff (1986). What Do Genetics and Ecology Tell Us About the Design of Nature Reserves? *Biological Conservation* 35: 19–40.

Turner, J. and J. Rylander (1998), The Private Lands Challenge: Integrating Biodiversity Conservation and Private Property. *Private Property and the Endangered Species Act: Saving Habitat, Protecting Homes* (J. Shogren, ed.). Austin, TX, University of Texas Press, 92–137.

U.S. Fish and Wildlife Service (USFWS). (1996) *Report to Congress: Endangered and Threatened Species Recovery Program.* Washington, DC: U.S. Government Printing Office.

U.S. Fish and Wildlife Service/National Marine Fisheries Service (US-FWS/NMFS) (1996). Endangered Species Habitat Conservation Planning Handbook. Washington, D.C. (November).

Valdes-Cogliano, S. (1995). Making the ESA Work Better. *Endangered Species Bulletin* 10: 4–8.

Vickery, P., M. Hunter, Jr., and M. Scott (1994). Effects of Habitat Area on the Distribution of Grassland Birds in Maine. *Conservation Biology* 8: 1087–97.

Whicker, A. S. and J. K. Detling (1988). Ecological Consequences of Prairie Dog Disturbances. *Bioscience* 38: 778–85.

Yahner, R. (1988). Changes in Wildlife Communities Near Edges. *Conservation Biology* 2: 333–39.

CHAPTER 17

Compensation for Takings under the ESA: How Much Is Too Much? A Comment

Rob Godby

Twenty-five years ago, when the ESA was enacted with overwhelming support in the Congress and Senate, few legislators would have foreseen the controversy it would create.[1] When signed into law there were believed to be only 109 species needing protection; however, in the interim this has grown to 1,177 species, with 60 percent being plants. Of these, approximately 90 percent are found on private lands.[2] Only twenty-seven species have ever been delisted, sixteen of which have either disappeared or were originally listed by mistake.[3] The ESA (ESA) of 1973 gives government the ability to restrict a landholder's activities on private lands if an endangered species is found upon them. Private landholder actions are restricted in two ways by this legislation. Under current interpretations of Section 9 of the Act, the landholder may not engage in activities that threaten a listed species directly, and landowners are forbidden to "take" without permit any endangered species on their land.[4] Further, they also may not engage in any activity that significantly and adversely modifies the habitat of an endangered species (Innes, Polasky, and Tschirhart 1998). These restrictions have resulted in a number of legal confrontations and the Act has come to symbolize to some all that is wrong with "big government."

Recent legal debate has concentrated on what these controls actually imply. On the one hand, by limiting the activities a landholder can engage in on their own land, the government has effectively "taken" the land even though private ownership is maintained. Such controls may be seen as a *de facto* appropriation of private land by government, and, under the fifth Amendment to the U.S. Constitution, require just compensation by government.[5] On the other hand, the government has always had some right to determine how land will

---

[1] The Endangered Species Act was signed into law by President Richard Nixon on December 28, 1973 after passing the Congress by a vote of 355–4 and the Senate 92–0.

[2] Brown and Shogren (1998).

[3] Hebert (1998).

[4] The allowance for an incidental taking permit was added to the Act in 1982.

[5] The 14th Amendment also ensures due process of law before any state appropriates private property.

be used. Historically, local and municipal governments have set bylaws governing land use, or zoning rules, that are seen to support the public good by avoiding, for example, industrial/commercial versus residential development conflicts. Zoning regulations have generally been applied without compensation for loss of land values due to their usage restrictions. The ESA, by setting restrictions on land use, is like a zoning regulation, and by historic precedent, not applicable to the takings considerations outlined under the Fifth Amendment. Recent legislative initiatives, as described in the preceding chapters, have attempted to address this issue. With the recent ideological shift to the political "right" in the 1990s, governments at all levels seem to have been moving toward the view that legislative control of land is akin to appropriation, and therefore deserving of compensation.[6]

Whether such "takings" will require compensation in the future has important policy relevance. From a government perspective, initiatives like the ESA only attempt to control private actions deemed not in the public interest through legislative constraints and, therefore, should not be considered appropriations. With this perspective, such controls may be assumed to be financially costless by regulators since this type of regulation has historically not required compensation. Economists have termed this "fiscal illusion" as when considering the benefits and costs of a regulatory initiative, planners do not include the opportunity costs implied by the initiative. If such regulations, however, become viewed as governmental "takings," then required compensation will necessitate an outlay of government resources. Further, if the government is forced to pay full compensation for loss of land value, the full opportunity cost of the regulatory decision will be borne by the government, and indirectly the public, to constrain private actions. Compensation consideration would then require decisions within government regarding the policy trade-offs that such outlays would demand and/or the taxation initiatives needed to fund them. A benevolent government, acting to maximize social welfare, would have to make such decisions evaluating the marginal benefits to society of additional species protection against the marginal social costs of reduced government action in other policy areas or increased taxation caused by the required compensation. The outcome of such an analysis may necessitate the reduction of governmental protection of endangered species relative to levels if compensation were not required.[7]

A government would also have to consider the equity issues compensation would create. Since equity is often in the eye of the beholder, how compensation requirements affect government policy decisions would depend on the

---

[6] See Innes et al. 1998, footnote 2 for a description of the most recent compensatory legislative initiatives under the ESA.

[7] Such "crowding out" of endangered species protection may not occur if government takes the view "the value of endangered species is incalculable," as found in the Supreme Court ruling described in footnote 1 of Smith and Shogren (Chapter 16 of this volume); however, it would imply that given a governmental budget constraint, other social programs would be crowded out or reduced in scale or scope. Further, private activities in other areas may be distorted by taxation changes.

political incentives a government faces. Although compensation concerns initially seem to belong to legal and political science scholars, if government decisions are influenced by the incentives they face, the economist certainly has something to add to the debate, given understanding and explaining decisions in the face of incentives is their bailiwick.

The decision of who should pay for the cost of land taken, the private landholder or the government, would seem one easily solved by application of the Coase Theorem. If this were the case, the legal debate would boil down to a question of property right definition. To the economist though, a set of follow-up questions arises. If the property right falls to the landholder, as seems more likely in the current political environment, how does compensation affect individual and governmental incentives regarding preservation and development? In particular, whether compensation is constitutionally required or not, at what level should compensation be set to ensure private agents do not engage in socially inefficient activities? At what level should compensation levels be set to ensure government does not overregulate? Can alternative decentralized regulatory mechanisms be defined that properly align private incentives with society's to ensure preservation when warranted? The chapters in this volume by Innes (Chapter 14), Polasky (Chapter 15), and Smith and Shogren (Chapter 16) address these issues and extend current analysis to the frontiers of economic thought regarding the "takings debate."

Previous research, both by the authors of these three chapters and others, has provided important answers regarding individual incentives and government action. Blume, Rubinfeld, and Shapiro (1984), hereafter BLS, defined the starting point for research in this area. They considered the compensation incentives involved in a taking decision for a single land parcel under uncertainty regarding the value of the land in public use. In their model a landowner is faced with an investment decision and the possibility that some future event will cause their land's public value to exceed its private value. The government takes the land if such an event occurs and the landowner's initial investment and future returns from the land are lost. If no compensation is paid for such takings, private landholders will consider an investment's expected value given that it may be lost if future outcomes lead to a taking. Decisions considering the possibility of loss, the authors find, lead to efficient levels of investment and development. If full compensation (equal to the private use value of the property) is paid, then landowners will receive this value regardless of whether land is taken or not. This distorts marginal private incentives to invest and creates an incentive to overinvest. Further, if the government considers the cost of compensation in its taking decision in the cost-benefit computation to determine the land's public value, a second incentive to overinvest in development to reduce the probability of a taking arises for landowners.[8]

---

[8] The authors also consider a lump-sum compensation, which is invariant to level of investment on the land. As long as this compensation level is unaffected by investment level on the land, it also leads to efficient investment effort.

The results of this model are clear: ". . . no compensation is efficient, while full compensation for the value of the land and structures is inefficient" (BLS, 90). These results, however, do not account for a number of the possible concerns previously outlined. BLS did not allow that private actions could include not only development decisions, but also enhancement (preservation) activities, or intentional actions to reduce the public value of the land. They also did not include the possibility of restoration costs being required, as would be the case if natural habitat were being restored on previously developed land, nor did they account for possible information asymmetries or uncertainties regarding the public use value of land when the taking decision is made. Finally, a practical concern must also be addressed. The definition of private use values may be difficult to determine.

The extensions provided in Chapters 14–16 enrich the original environment modelled by BLS, which was not developed to describe takings under the ESA explicitly. These extensions can be characterized as follows:

(i) Multiple landholder takings decisions (Innes).
(ii) Institutional (trespass law) considerations creating imperfect information regarding actual public land values (Polasky).
(iii) Asymmetric information regarding public and private land values and biological uncertainty (Smith and Shogren).
(iv) Verifiability: Courts must be able to define what "just compensation" is (considered in all three preceding chapters).

Clearly, determination of the optimal level of compensation to induce an efficient land-use outcome may be more problematic than just considering the definition of fairness implied by the Constitution. The information the government and landowners possess regarding the endangered species in question may be asymmetric. Since the purpose of the ESA is to preserve, then the problem facing regulatory designers is to ensure that all agents, including government, choose to act in a manner consistent with the social interest, including where information asymmetries exist. Innes presents the case when information is common knowledge, identifying how compensation affects individual development decisions and government regulatory effort. He also identifies an efficient decentralized regulatory approach to create efficient land-use incentives.

Polasky and Smith and Shogren extend Innes's analysis by allowing that private agents may engage in activities that enhance or preserve habitat (or conversely degrade it) and attempt to identify incentive mechanisms that induce socially efficient levels of development and preservation. Polasky attempts to identify specific types of compensation changes to the ESA that would improve the incentives the legislation creates for efficient land use on single land parcels. Smith and Shogren consider the design of a decentralized regulatory framework to induce preservation across land parcels. They describe how a menu of compensation packages to induce voluntary land preservation could be designed when biological and economic information uncertainties exist for the planner. They also show that such schemes can be designed that create incentives for contiguous land parcels to be set aside when such outcomes are desired.

The following summarizes the results of these chapters, considering comparatively their findings to answer the questions originally posed: at what level should compensation be set to ensure private agents do not engage in socially inefficient activities? At what level should compensation levels be set to ensure government does not overregulate? Can alternative decentralized regulatory mechanisms be defined that properly line up private incentives with society's to ensure preservation when warranted? Concluding remarks are made afterward regarding the results these chapters derive.

COMPENSATION AND INCENTIVES

One problem with the "takings" compensation literature is that the results yielded by particular studies may not be general to environments other than the ones they are developed in. Since endangered species preservation often involves situations that differ in the order of information revelation and development decisions, changes in the structure of the problem can lead to different compensation results than those suggested by BLS. The three preceding chapters all change the model considered by BLS in significant ways as each changes the context within which the takings decision is made. These structural model differences are described in Table 17.1. Extensions to the basic BLS model can be defined in two directions: structural changes to the basic model that account for real-world decision considerations, and institutional problems present in the ESA legislation but ignored in BLS. Innes's chapter describes the former, addressing how considerations of multiparcel takings affect the compensation results. Polasky describes how trespass laws and consideration of preservation incentives influence efficient compensation levels. Shogren and Smith address how voluntary preservation mechanisms can be designed to overcome biological and economic uncertainty.

LANDOWNER INCENTIVES

Since governments rarely face single landowners in a takings decision, the interaction is more complex than BLS model it. In particular, a government must decide *how much* land to take, and *from whom*. Innes considers landowner incentives when takings occur over a number of parcels of land, each possibly differing in amount of initial development. In making its takings decision, Innes proves what seems intuitively obvious: It is always better for society if government takes undeveloped land first. In his model, this occurs for two reasons: Taking undeveloped land avoids loss of investment costs and it also avoids restoration costs required to reestablish lost habitat. With this in mind, three scenarios may occur: some undeveloped land may be

Table 17.1. *Comparative Structures of Takings Models*

Author(s)	Blume, Rubinfeld, and Shapiro (1984)	Innes	Polasky	Smith and Shogren
Game Structure:				
Stage 1:	Nature selects state (value of land in public use)	Nature selects state (marginal external damage due to development)	Nature selects state (marginal external damage due to development)	Endangered species discovered
Stage 2:	Compensation rules determined	Compensation rules determined	Institutional rules chosen for takings and compensation	Regulator offers multiple landowners menu of land retired-compensation level choices
Stage 3:	Single landowner decides level of land development	Multiple landowners make discrete development decisions (Yes/no)	Single landowner decides level of development, preservation and anti-preservation	Land-use decision (level preservation with given compensation, maintained in private use)
Stage 4:	State of nature revealed	State of nature revealed	Information regarding state of nature collected at a cost, and cooperation is required	Not Applicable
Stage 5:	Land-use decision (taken or maintained in private use) contingent on state of nature	Land-use decision across land parcels (taken or maintained in private use) contingent on state of nature	Land-use decision (taken, preserved or maintained in private use) contingent on state of nature	Not Applicable
Stage 6:	Not Applicable	Development, maintenance or restoration of land	Not Applicable	Not Applicable

taken, all undeveloped land may be taken or, for high enough public use value realizations, all undeveloped land and some developed land may be taken. Unlike in BLS, in Innes's framework government may choose among a number of land parcels to take, each of which may be developed or not. This results in landowners having an incentive to overinvest if no compensation is paid. Doing so reduces the public value of taking their land, as restoration costs must be incurred. If full compensation is paid as defined by the value of the private investment returns forgone due to a taking, landowners have an incentive to overinvest for the same reason they do in BLS. Since their investment return is guaranteed, the marginal decision is distorted and landowners invest inefficiently from society's perspective. Regardless of whether compensation is made in full or not at all, landowners have incentives to invest inefficiently due to the optimality of taking undeveloped land first.

In the multiple land parcel setting, the challenge then becomes to determine if any compensation scheme can be defined that restores efficient development incentives to landowners. One possibility is a Pigouvian scheme as described in Hermalin (1995) using a single land parcel model. This requires the marginal damage due to development be determined. Those landowners whose land is taken receive a subsidy of equivalent value while those retaining development pay this value as a tax. Innes shows this can lead to efficient development incentives, but the problem lies in the determination of the marginal external damages. Since only government would be making such a value determination, landowners may have the incentive to challenge their findings in court. As the true social value is not public knowledge, asking courts to adjudicate such a decision would make such a compensation policy problematic. Furthermore, nonbenevolent governments might exploit this information asymmetry. Although Pigouvian methods would therefore be difficult to implement in practice, they do shed light on what is required to achieve efficient incentives. Landowner development payoffs must be aligned with marginal external damages.

Innes outlines two possible compensation schemes with this property. The first is to compensate using what he calls an "equal treatment" criteria. The incentive to overinvest in the presence of full compensation is the result of the higher returns developed land yields to landowners regardless of whether land is taken or not. To correct this, Innes suggests a compensation scheme that pays full compensation to developed landholders, but more than full compensation to undeveloped landholders. In cases where developed and undeveloped land is taken, both types of land would be compensated at the private value of developed land. If all undeveloped land were taken only, all landholders would receive the average value of their land in public use, which by definition is greater than the private value, else the government would not take it. Finally, if only some undeveloped land were taken, full market value compensation would be paid, yielding *all* undeveloped landowners the same payoff. All three compensation schemes eliminate overinvestment incentives by increasing the expected payoff to undeveloped land. Furthermore, these methods do not lead to verification concerns in the courts as all landowners are paid at least the market value of their land, "just compensation" as described by the Fifth Amendment, and therefore have no incentive to challenge the levels in court.

Such compensation programs would be costly to government. Innes's second suggestion is to implement a permit trading scheme, wherein the amount of land described by the number of total permits issued would be equal to the amount of land the regulator wishes to leave in private hands after determining how much land to set aside. If each landholder is initially allotted permits for a fraction of their land, and is required to hold permits equal to the total amount of land they own to retain development rights, trading would lead to undeveloped landholders selling their permits to developed landowners due to differences in land value. Undeveloped land would then be set aside and these landowners compensated by permit revenues. Since developed landowners share in the costs of taking, they no longer have an incentive to overinvest as the expected value of undeveloped land is increased. Competitive markets would ensure the price of permits paid to undeveloped landholders would be equal to the use value of developed land, resulting in an equivalent outcome to Innes' equal treatment compensation scheme.

This model indicates the importance of making landowners aware of preservation concerns, not only for environmental reasons, but also for economic efficiency. Innes's model, as well as BLS's, utilizes the typical rational agent found in most economic frameworks. This assumption implies all agents are aware of all potential states of the world, including those where land is taken, and maximize accordingly. In reality this is obviously not true. Some agents may decide to invest without ever considering the possibility that use of their land could be lost due to government regulation. By definition, this type of landowner would be unaffected by compensation incentives as they would, by assumption, be unaware of them. If such agents exist, purely out of ignorance they will overinvest relative to agents that account for this possibility. Clearly, for overinvestment to be avoided the correct compensation policy must be chosen, while efforts must also be made to ensure landowners are aware of preservation concerns when they make their investment decisions. Not only is this important from a preservation standpoint, but also to ensure that compensation incentives are acted upon.

Polasky addresses the institutional problems particular to the ESA that may lead to inefficiencies in species preservation outcomes. In particular, the implicit costless information assumption used in the BLS model may not be true. If information regarding the marginal external damage of development is costly to acquire, private agents may never have an incentive to collect it. Further, landowners may be able to block the acquisition of such information by society as laws require that government get permission to conduct on-site inspections when attempting to determine if endangered species are present. Since the ESA requires proof, not just conjecture that an endangered species is present to enforce a taking, this complicates the incentives compensation creates. Often such verification can be done from the air or from the edge of private land. Landowners, however, may no longer just consider development choices. They may also choose to pursue strategies to reduce the likelihood such species are present on their land, thereby changing the state of nature as it exists when and if information is collected. Such activities would be costly to society's interests but possibly beneficial to the landowner, depending upon the compensation mechanisms in place.

In general then, without compensation, the incentive exists to overdevelop, contrary to the BLS model (Innes), while landowners may also have the incentive to pursue harmful activities to protect their investments from takings, particularly if off-site verifications of endangered species' presence are possible (Polasky). Compensation plans that align the landowner's payoffs with society's to induce efficient outcomes may also be difficult. Pigouvian solutions are unverifiable as described above and therefore should be expected to be inefficient and/or litigious. Polasky and Innes (2000b) also extend the BLS analysis to include the possibility of preservation effort. If Pigouvian taxes were levied on development after endangered species were discovered, and if preservation efforts (one could consider the choice of using "environmentally friendly" development methods in conjunction with private development) taken prior to discovery increased the marginal external damage development caused, such activities would not take place. Furthermore, full compensation based on private development values would lead to overinvestment as found in BLS, and too little conservation effort if such efforts are costly because they do not influence the compensation level. None of these types of compensation schemes leads to private agents collecting information regarding the state of nature if it is costly to acquire. Polasky argues that in his model's circumstances, assignment of property rights before the investment stage could be useful. If, prior to investment, development value were less than the expected public value of a given parcel of land, the landowner could be asked to pay this difference as a permit to develop. If the opposite were true, the landowner would be allowed to develop with the understanding that if a taking occurred later, they would be fully compensated. This would eliminate the incentive for the landowner to block information collection but would still create the incentive to overinvest as in BLS. Importantly, Polasky's results indicate it may be impossible to define a compensation scheme that always results in efficient land use, avoids destructive activities, and creates cooperation between the landowner and regulator.

Smith and Shogren depart from the standard investment/compensation framework by assuming that an endangered species has already been found and development decisions made. They ask, how can a regulator ensure that an appropriate amount of land be set aside for habitat preservation voluntarily? This is a valuable avenue of future research given Polasky's findings that under command and control regimes there may not be an optimal level of compensation that induces proper investment decisions. Also, given landowners may be unaware of the applicability of endangered species preservation to their land, designing optimal compensation levels to ensure efficient development effort may be more of an academic exercise than a truly relevant policy objective. It is more likely that, as in the case of the Black-tailed prairie dog discussed by Smith and Shogren, development and land-use decisions have already been made when the endangered species is discovered. Unlike the other models that assume the public value of land is calculable, Smith and Shogren consider the problem of designing incentives for voluntary preservation efforts when biological information is uncertain and the private values of land are unknown. They use a menu of compensation contracts for different amounts of land retired to account for information asymmetries regarding private values. To address the biological uncertainty they suggest that a regulator is only likely to be able to define a minimum amount of land necessary to ensure some *minimum acceptable probability of survival*, or MAPS constraint. The problem is then modelled as an agency problem would be addressed, creating an incentive compatible mechanism for agents of different value types to set aside land such that the MAPS constraint is met.

Their results indicate that information asymmetries regarding private values and biological uncertainty create conflicting objectives. Contracts for agents of different productivity types (and therefore different private values) must be specified. To ensure the participation of high productivity landowners, appropriate compensation levels must be chosen. Unfortunately, this creates an adverse selection problem due to the existence of lower productivity agents. To ensure incentive compatibility, some deadweight loss (relative to a full information outcome) is incurred to increase the compensation contracts meant for lower productivity landowners. Given fiscal constraints, increased uncertainty regarding landowner types increases the deadweight loss required to ensure incentive compatibility and therefore less total land retired for a given compensation fund. Increased biological uncertainty increases the amount of land required to ensure the MAPS constraint is met. The greater the information problems, the more serious this conflict could be.

Despite the information conflict, these results suggest workable methods of designing incentive compatible methods of voluntary species preservation are possible. Data needed to design preservation contracts are easily accessible. The system suggested is also flexible. Incentives for large reserves composed of lands set aside by a number of contiguous landowners can be created. Innes and Polasky do not address this issue, but it is clearly important for some species. Finally, this methodology addresses fiscal realities in the face of biological and economic uncertainty, and how species preservation might be accomplished at least cost.

Information and uncertainty problems could cause inefficient outcomes when attempting to use command and control regulatory methods. As Innes has shown, decentralized programs like tradeable permits could create efficient investment incentives. In the presence of imperfect information it may be necessary to avoid command and control regulation completely and attempt to design preservation policies that create incentives for landowners to preserve when there is a possibility of an endangered species living on their land. Smith and Shogren outline such a mechanism for enticing private preservation decisions when biological uncertainty and private land value asymmetries exist. Polasky suggests another, allowing property rights to be permits purchased at their expected value to society combined with compensation programs when development values exceed expected public values. Identifying other decentralized policy mechanisms for species preservation would certainly be a valuable avenue of future research.

GOVERNMENT INCENTIVES

Clearly, compensation levels are relevant to government. One question the debate regarding compensation for takings raises is whether a constitutional requirement for compensation is necessary or efficient. BLS' results indicate compensation should not be required from an efficiency standpoint, but as noted, their model may be too simplistic to deal with the specifics of the ESA. The results of Innes and Polasky indicate some compensation may be necessary to create incentives for efficient levels of preservation and development activity. In this framework, a benevolent government may not need a constitutional compensation requirement. Additionally, such a requirement, especially one for "just compensation," may cause inefficiency if court interpretations of such a phrase imply that full market value be paid. Decentralized incentive schemes may avoid much of this problem by allowing preservation or development choices to be voluntary. Therefore, a constitutional requirement could undermine economic efficiency if governments are benevolent.

Governments may not always be benevolent, however. They may be influenced by democratic incentives, and if governments represent those that elected them, then policy may reflect the preferences of specific interest groups. Innes et al. (1998) provide an overview of these concerns as they apply to the ESA. Fiscal illusion then becomes an important consideration from an efficiency standpoint. If, in enacting policy, government considers the costs and benefits of its decisions, they may only consider financial costs as they apply to the various groups involved. An interest group perspective would say that the benefits to those groups that the government wishes to curry favor with would be weighted more heavily than others. Without consideration of the actual opportunity costs society experiences for given actions, this may lead to the actual costs incurred by affected groups being underweighted in the government's objective function. Whether constitutional compensation requirements are necessary to prevent this may depend on how accurate such interest group models are, and which groups are represented by government. Environmental lobbies might lead to underweighting of landowner costs in preservation efforts, in which case increased compensation may be necessary. If government represents landowner interests, the opposite may be true.

The Constitution functions to restrain governmental activities that may impinge on individual liberties. It also functions to ensure that equal treatment is preserved among citizens. This suggests schemes like Innes's "equal treatment" compensation criteria or permit trading methods may be more acceptable and less litigious than those that require specific levels of compensation. If so, then the former methods should be considered not just on efficiency grounds.

Another question is how compensation levels affect government preservation effort. Given fiscal realities, budgets for preservation are not unlimited, and any regulatory preservation initiatives that minimize the costs of such policies are welcome, as they will allow an increase in the scope of such efforts. The costs and scale of such programs will be affected by information considerations. Smith and Shogren point out that biological uncertainty and economic considerations may work in opposite directions when it comes to preservation effort. When programs require increased expenses to deal with economic incentives and information asymmetries, this will reduce the amount of preservation a given budget can accomplish. When biological uncertainty requires that more land be retired to ensure an acceptable probability of species survival, increased budgets may be required to accomplish preservation goals. Funding of such objectives will then come in conflict with other policy objectives, chasing the limited dollars available in public coffers. The bottom line, as in all environmental economic problems, is defining the optimal trade-off. As Smith and Shogren note, this is really an exercise in social choice.

CONCLUSIONS

Since current legislative debate centers on whether compensation should be awarded, the economist could be called upon to contribute some insight. Essentially this discussion asks "who should pay" and can be answered from the economist's perspective by application of Coasian logic. Such answers, however, are lacking as information problems make the issue more difficult than it first may seem. The seminal model explored by Blume, Rubinfeld, and Shapiro suggests if "just compensation" implies full market value, then from an efficiency perspective, compensation should not be paid. All extensions of their model, as described here, concur in their assessments – full compensation results in individual landowner incentives to overinvest prior to the takings decision. The models, however, disagree in their conclusions regarding the appropriateness of zero compensation. While BLS conclude this will yield efficient development incentives in a general takings model, those authors whose frameworks describe specific characteristics of the takings problem faced under the ESA disagree. Both Polasky and Innes find that without compensation landowners have an incentive to overdevelop too. This occurs because efficient takings outcomes always take undeveloped land first and prior development leads to a lower likelihood of that particular land parcel being taken. Both models find the compensation requirements (or lack thereof) of the ESA could be improved upon. Both models also find that only compensation levels that align society's interests with private landowners' will result in efficient outcomes. When the value of public land is unknown at the time the development decision but becomes public knowledge in time, Innes outlines two possible efficient compensation solutions. Both have the property of equal treatment across developed or undeveloped landowners. Polasky finds in the context of his model there may not be a mechanism that can result in efficient incentives if information is costly to acquire.

Whether the current compensation requirements of the legislation serve to ensure government acts in society's interest are also unclear. Government should consider the actual costs of its preservation decisions when making policy. Fiscal illusion, calculating the cost of policy as equivalent to its financial requirements, may result in overpreservation from a social perspective as it does not account for true social costs. In this light, current legislation does not instill efficient government activity. Models of government in the presence of interest group politics are also undecided as to whether a constitutional compensation requirement is required. If government represents landowner interests, this should not be necessary, while if the opposite is true such a requirement may be needed.

Finally, decentralized preservation mechanisms, those that actually make the choice of preservation effort a landholder decision and create incentives for positive landowner preservation efforts, are a promising avenue of future research. Such mechanisms face the same problems as centralized methods but in some cases may be less costly while preserving efficient incentive structures. Innes's permit trading suggestion is an example. They may, however, be as costly as centralized methods, as Polasky and Smith and Shogren find. All policies suggested here, though, do result in improvements over the preservation incentives currently embodied in the existing ESA legislation. There are no clear answers in the problem of endangered species preservation and compensation. This results from the fact that it is a wide-ranging Act that is applied to many different cases that pose unique regulatory problems. What is clear is that some aspects of the legislation could be improved to incorporate economic efficiency considerations. The current compensation requirement (or specifically the lack thereof) results in judicial conflicts while not inducing efficient development incentives.

References

Blume, L., Rubinfeld, A., and Shapiro, P. (1984) "The Taking of Land: When Should Compensation be Paid?" *Quarterly Journal of Economics* 99, 71–92.

Brown, G., and Shogren, J. (1998) "Economics of the ESA." *Journal of Economic Perspectives* 12, 3–20.

Hebert, J. (1998) "Conflict over ESA Remains." *Casper Star Tribune.* December 28.

Hermalin, B. (1995) "An Economic Analysis of Takings." *Journal of Law, Economics and Organization* 11, 64–86.

Innes, R. (2001) "The Economics of Takings in a Multiparcel Model with a Powerful Government." Chapter 14 in J. Shogren and J. Tschirhart, eds., *Protecting Endangered Species in the United States: Biological Needs, Political Realities, Economic Choices*. New York: Cambridge University Press.

— (2000b) "The Economics of Takings When Land and Its Public Use Value Are in Private Hands." *Land Economics* 76, 195–212.

Innes, R., Polasky, S., and Tschirhart, J. (1998) "Takings, Compensation and Endangered Species Protection on Private Lands." *Journal of Economic Perspectives* 12, 35–52.

Polasky, S. (2001) "Agency Problems in the Efficient Conservation of Species." Chapter 15 in J. Shogren and J. Tschirhart, eds. *Protecting Endangered Species in the United States: Biological Needs, Political Realities, Economic Choices*. New York: Cambridge University Press.

Smith, R., and Shogren, J. (2001) "Protecting Species on Private Land." Chapter 16 in J. Shogren and J. Tschirhart, eds. *Protecting Endangered Species in the United States: Biological Needs, Political Realities, Economic Choices*. New York: Cambridge University Press.

Replies by Authors

Compensation for Takings Under the ESA: Reply and Extension

Robert Innes

Rob Godby provides a wonderful synthesis of the economic issues surrounding compensation for endangered species protections on private land. In this reply, I will comment on some of the conceptual issues left outstanding in this synthesis and, in doing so, describe a relevant extension. My focus here (in contrast to that in my chapter) will be on the single-parcel model of governmental takings that has pervaded the literature.

In standard single-parcel models of takings (starting first with Blume, Rubinfeld, and Shapiro 1984), there is an essential separation between the timing of private land-use decisions and governmental "takings" decisions – decisions that may (or may not) divert private property to a public use. In particular, a landowner makes private investment (or conservation) decisions in some initial period, and at a later time, the government discovers something about the prospective value of the property in a public use that may motivate a "taking" (such as designation of land for endangered species habitat). This sort of specification is clearly an abstraction, though I believe a very useful one. Most important perhaps, it abstracts from concerns about the *optimal timing* of government regulation in order to focus, in the simplest way possible, on a pervasive and very practical concern in the design of any takings doctrine: the *incentives* afforded to private landowners to use their land efficiently. In fact, I believe this concern is essential in any meaningful examination of governmental takings of private property because, virtually by construction, land is in private hands for some considerable period of time *before* regulation takes place. And there are good reasons for this to be the case: Public use values are discovered as time proceeds, motivating post-discovery governmental action.

I belabor this point here for two reasons: (1) When it is found that a particular takings and compensation doctrine leads to inefficient private investment (or conservation) behavior, Professors Godby and Polasky seem to suggest that a possible resolution is to implement a takings/compensation policy *prior* to the time of landowner investment. Such a resolution, however, violates the fundamental spirit of the temporal separation between private and governmental action that must (I believe) be at the core of any takings analysis in which long-run land-use incentives are at issue. (2) In a related vein, Rob Godby questions the foundation upon which virtually every economic analysis of takings rests, writing: The assumption (of rational agents) "implies all agents are aware of all potential states of the world, including those where land is taken, and maximize accordingly. In reality this is obviously not true. Some agents may decide to invest without ever considering the possibility that use of their land could be lost due to government regulation." I confess, as a Neoclassical economist, that this statement is akin to a red flag for a bull. There is nothing obvious about the notion that private landowners behave stupidly, failing to consider what the government may do to them and their property in the future. Such a premise may be thought to motivate direct government regulation of all land-use decisions, at all times, on any and all private lands that may ever be of public use. The point of takings analyses is that such an outcome is ruled out *a priori* (for all the usual good reasons), and that governments must worry about *incentives* that their policies provide private landowners for wise use of their property, in view of the temporal separation between private and public decisions.

This said, let me turn to an outstanding issue in the economics of takings as it relates to endangered species preservation.

INFORMATION ACQUISITION AND CONSERVATION

Polasky and Doremus (1998) add an important dimension to the taking process: At the time of a potential government taking, information about the potential value of the property in public use (as habitat, for example) is not known with certainty. Rather, this value can only be uncovered with costly efforts to acquire information about the property, with field surveys and other investigative efforts. What is more, landowners can often prevent government agents from performing field surveys on their property that can be essential to determining the presence of endangered species and/or the potential value of the property as habitat. Without this information, the government may leave the property in private hands, either because it is efficient to do so (with the private use value exceeding the *uninformed* estimate of habitat use value) or because the government must prove its case before the land can be taken (by gathering the requisite information and using it to show that the *informed* estimate of habitat use value exceeds the property's private use value). If so, landowners will have every incentive to obstruct the government's information collection activities unless the government compensates them if and when their property is designated for habitat.

In the presence of information acquisition activities, incentives need to be aligned to ensure that (i) information is collected when and only when the prospective societal benefits from the information exceed the costs of its acquisition, (ii) landowners cooperate in information collection, so that the collection activities are conducted at minimum cost, and (iii) land is taken only when its public use value (estimated with whatever information has been efficiently collected) exceeds the private cost of the taking. Polasky and Doremus (1998) describe rules that have these efficiency properties. There are two components to these rules: (1) The burden of proof: Must a landowner prove that a taking is inefficient in order to keep his property in private use, or must the government prove that a taking is efficient in order to place the property in public use? (2) Compensation: Must a landowner compensate the government for its lost public use value in order to avoid a taking, or must the government compensate the landowner for his lost private use value in order to condemn the property?

In a private property rights regime, both the burden of proof and the compensation obligation reside with the government. Full compensation gives the landowner a motive to cooperate in the acquisition of information – because he has nothing to lose by cooperating. Locating the burden of proof with the government also implies that a taking does *not* occur when information is *not* collected; the reason is that, without acquiring information, the government cannot prove its case. This outcome is efficient when the uninformed estimate (or expectation) of public use value is *less than* the private use value – that is, when an "uninformed" taking is *not* efficient.

However, suppose instead that an uninformed taking *is* efficient. Then, without information collection, private property rights prevent the government from efficiently designating habitat. The government, in turn, will strive to reduce the efficiency costs that arise in the absence of information, by acquiring information more often than would otherwise be efficient. By instead locating the property right with the government – essentially implementing a Pigovian tax regime by placing both the burden of proof and the compensation obligation with the landowner – Polasky and Doremus (1998) argue that efficiency can be restored. Without information, a taking then occurs, as is efficient. Moreover, by collecting information, the landowner obtains exactly the societal benefits that the information affords, namely, any net positive gain from preventing a taking that would otherwise occur.

The prescription then is for private property rights when the "uninformed" public use value is less than private value, and for government property rights (or Pigovian taxes) when it is above the private value. *The problem with this prescription is that it creates huge incentives for landowners to overinvest in their land's private uses* (or underinvest in conservation).

In thinking about the landowner investment (or conservation) incentives, particularly in the endangered species context, it is important to consider the effect which the landowner's choices may have on not only the value of the land in private uses, but also its value in public uses (see Innes 2000). For example, landowners in the Pacific Northwest and Southeast have been observed moving to shorter forest rotations that cull old growth trees that are potential habitat for endangered birds (Sugg 1993; Lambert and Smith 1994). In view of these effects, both private property rights regimes and Pigovian tax regimes prompt landowners to overinvest (Innes 2000). With full private value compensation – even if it is lump-sum and thus avoids the usual overinvestment problem (Miceli 1991) – landowners do not consider the benefit of lowering their private use investment in raising the likelihood of higher public use values; hence, they do not circumscribe their investment to account for these benefits. With Pigovian taxes, matters are much worse; landowners can lower their tax bill by lowering the public use value that is foregone when they pay the government in order to void a taking; landowners thus overinvest in order to lower the likelihood of high public use values – and associated high taxes.

With the Polasky and Doremus (1998) rule that combines private property rights and Pigovian tax regimes, there are added incentives for overinvestment (Innes and Polasky 1999). Most important, landowners will want to raise the private use value in order to increase the likelihood that an uninformed taking is not efficient (i.e., that the uninformed estimate of public use value is less than the private use value); they can thereby increase the likelihood that they retain private property rights, rather than be subjected to the Pigovian tax regime.

Innes and Polasky (1999) develop an alternative approach that gives landowners an incentive to (1) cooperate with government information acquisition, (2) refrain from inefficiently gathering information on their own, and (3) invest in (or conserve) their property exactly to the extent that is efficient. The government, in turn, has free (and sole) reign to acquire information and take land for public use. Specifically, Innes and Polasky (1999) propose the following set of rules:

1. When a taking occurs, the government obeys a "negligence compensation" rule of the sort proposed by Miceli and Segerson (1994) and Innes (2000). Under this rule, the landowner obtains a given (positive) amount of takings compensation if he has not overinvested (or underconserved); otherwise, no compensation is forthcoming. Typically (the case I am considering here), the needed takings compensation is less than full private land value.
2. When the government decides not to acquire information (because it is too costly), a landowner bears the burden of proof to avoid a taking.
3. Once a government attempts to acquire information, it commits to take the property *unless* information is actually acquired and reveals that the land should not be taken (because the revealed public use value is less than the private use value).

With the last of these rules, landowners will not obstruct the government's information acquisition efforts because these efforts offer the landowner a chance to avoid a taking that he is better off without. Moreover, the first and second rules can deter the landowner from inefficiently acquiring information on his own. The only time that a landowner wants to acquire his own information is when, by doing so, he can sometimes avoid the taking and thereby reap the private land value rather than the lower compensation value. However, with sufficiently high takings compensation – though compensation that is less than "full" private use value – this benefit is smaller than the landowner's costs of gathering the necessary information.

Finally, the first rule gives landowners an incentive to invest efficiently. The landowner's alternative is to overinvest and receive no takings compensation; with sufficiently high compensation for "nonnegligent" (efficient investment) behavior (though compensation which is typically less than full private value), the landowner prefers the efficient course.

In policy language, this approach is akin to the use of habitat conservation plans that require landowners to prove their case in order to void a taking. However, there is an important addition: The government must pay positive compensation to landowners who are "nonnegligent" (because they have acted to efficiently conserve their property). Compensation is necessary to avoid incentives for landowners to overexploit their property and thereby degrade its potential value as an environmental asset. It is also necessary to avoid incentives for landowners to collect information inefficiently and litigate with this information in order to void an uncompensated taking. Notably, however, the rules suggested here *do not rely on direct government regulation of private land-use decisions* at the time when these private decisions are made; instead, they rely on *incentives* provided to landowners by governmental decision and compensation rules at a *subsequent* time when governmental takings/public use decisions are being made. The temporal separation between private and public use decisions is thus respected – a separation that is essentially intrinsic to private property.

References

Blume, L., D. Rubinfeld, and P. Shapiro. (1984) "The Taking of Land: When Should Compensation Be Paid?" *The Quarterly Journal of Economics* 100, 71–92.

Innes, R. (2000) "The Economics of Takings and Compensation When Land and Its Public Use Value Are in Private Hands." *Land Economics* 76, 195–212.

Innes, R. and S. Polasky. (1999) "Takings, Compensation, Information and Conservation." Working Paper, University of Arizona.

Lambert, T., and R. Smith. (1994) "The ESA: Time for a Change." Center for the Study of American Business, Policy Study 119.

Miceli, T. (1991) "Compensation for the Taking of Land Under Eminent Domain." *Journal of Institutional and Theoretical Economics* 147, 354–63.

Miceli, T., and K. Segerson. (1994) "Regulatory Takings: When Should Compensation Be Paid?" *Journal of Legal Studies* 23, 749–76.

Polasky, S. and H. Doremus. (1998) "When the Truth Hurts: Endangered Species Policy on Private Land with Incomplete Information." *Journal of Environmental Economics and Management* 35, 22–47.

Sugg, I. (1993) "Ecosystem Babbitt-Babble." *Wall Street Journal*, April 2.

PART 4

SUMMARY AND DATABASE

CHAPTER 18

Why Economics Matters for Endangered Species Protection and the ESA

Jason F. Shogren, John Tschirhart,

Terry Anderson, Amy Whritenour Ando,

Steven R. Beissinger, David Brookshire,

Gardner M. Brown, Jr., Don Coursey,

Robert Innes, Stephen M. Meyer, and

Stephen Polasky

Evidence suggests that Earth's species may be in the midst of a wave of extinction, disappearing at rates 10 to 1,000 times greater than background or natural rates of extinction (Jablonski 1991; May, Lawton, and Stork 1995; National Research Council 1995; Pimm et al. 1995). If we agree that the extinction problem is due to human action, then modifying human behavior must be part of the solution. And yet the consistent exclusion of economic behavior in the calculus of endangered species protection has led to ineffective and, in some instances, counterproductive conservation policy.

This chapter argues that endangered species preservation must take into account basic principles of economic behavior to avoid wasting valuable resources that yield no gain in species protection. We address why economics matters more to species protection than many people think, and what this implies for the ongoing debate over the reauthorization of the ESA (ESA) of 1973.

A news columnist's quip captures a common reaction to reports of species at risk: "What scientists call endangered most people call bait" (Smith 1996). To others the value of protecting endangered species is so obvious, and so overwhelming, that estimates of costs and benefits seem immaterial. This view is exemplified by Roughgarden (1995), who argues that economics should not be confused with morality: "In fact, we should not take costs into account when setting environmental (or other) objectives, but we should take costs into account when considering how to implement moral objectives as policy" [emphasis in original]. This view attempts to keep the morality of endangered species stewardship "outside the slick [benefit-cost] terrain of the economists and their philosophical allies" (Ehrenfeld 1988).

A version of this chapter appeared in *Conservation Biology*, December 1999.

Many people expect the moral argument alone to suffice in the preservation debate. But election data, government budget allocations, and agency behavior demonstrate that current moral outrage falls short of generating the political will necessary to reverse the loss of biodiversity by strengthening the ESA. Although virtually all people support the goal of protecting endangered species, many would not choose to protect species if doing so would divert too many resources from other noble goals such as providing health care, education, and a decent standard of living. Thus, in reality, endangered species policy is as much a question of social choice as of biology.

And while most people will acknowledge that the ideal of "Noah's Ark" has been replaced with the pragmatism of "Noah's Choice" (Mann and Plummer 1995), this realization forces an unsettling question: Exactly what opportunities are lost when a moral compass directs policy? If the supporters of stewardship of endangered species adhere to their philosophy because they see a social benefit to preservation and a moralistic demand for action, it is reasonable to investigate the opportunity costs and reallocation of resources generated by such ethics (e.g., Epstein 1995). Landowners' desires to protect their investments and maintain their own heartfelt, moral self-determination have demanded as much. Ignoring whether the benefits of preservation outweigh the benefits of commercial use may ultimately cause these landowners, whose property helps shelter many listed species, to reject well-intentioned ESA policy (see, for example, Innes, Polasky, and Tschirhart 1998; Shogren 1998).

If economic analysis cannot be set aside without unfavorable consequences, how can we use such analysis to improve endangered species and biodiversity protection? Appealing to economics does not imply that legions of species must be sacrificed. Indeed, numerous economic reasons exist for preservation. Some species and habitats provide useful goods and services; other species and habitats are valued aesthetically. Further, even seemingly low-value species are linked to high-value species through ecosystem interactions. See Tschirhart and Crocker (1987) and Crocker and Tschirhart (1992) for a discussion of the general equilibrium approach to modeling the integration of economies and ecosystems.

In the discussion that follows, we offer three reasons why economics matters to endangered species protection and the ESA. In doing so, we speak to the following questions: What is the desired level of species protection? And what is the cost-effective way to achieve that protection? Even if the answer to the first question is that we will try to save everything, economic analysis is still relevant because it advises us on how to minimize the costs to achieve that goal.

(i) *Economics matters because human behavior generally, and economic parameters in particular, help determine the degree of risk to a species.*

Establishing whether a species is currently endangered usually is accomplished by assessing its likelihood of extinction or viability, as determined by the present sizes, trends, and distributions of its populations and their likely interactions with the stochastic forces of nature (Gilpin and Soulé 1986; Soulé 1987; Lande 1993). Based on this assessment process, two comments frequently are put forth in endangerment discussions: (a) "A species is either endangered or not – economics has nothing to do with it," and (b) "listing a species as endangered is a biological decision – economics should have nothing to do with it." Both comments are open to challenge. Economics plays a role in determining whether a species is endangered and whether it ought to be listed, because human adaptation to economic parameters affects the odds of species survival.

For example, surrounding human communities, we would expect that more preserved habitat implies greater odds of species survival. Moreover, these human communities are characterized by key economic parameters such as wealth and the relative prices of land. Communities with greater wealth and lower relative land prices can better afford to preserve more habitat. Ignoring wealth, land prices, and other economic parameters when estimating the odds of species survival is to omit relevant variables. There is the question of whether the benefits of gathering economic information to improve the estimation of survival odds exceed the costs of data collection and the resulting delays in decision making. Evidence from parallel efforts with other environmental issues suggests they do – that is, net benefits from economic information are positive (e.g., Milon and Shogren 1995; Bockstael 1996; Agee and Crocker 1998).

Variables in economic and environmental systems are jointly determined; neither nature nor mankind is autonomous. In considering the future trajectory of species' populations, we must account for today's economic parameters. This view challenges the traditional risk assessment-management bifurcation in which risk is first quantified by the natural sciences and then recovery strategies are implemented (Carroll et al. 1996). At the onset, proper risk assessment should incorporate parameters from both the biological and economic systems (e.g., Crocker and Shogren 1998).

Although listing decisions currently examine how forest management, housing development, and other human activities place species at risk, they do not address how people are likely to respond to a listing decision and its concomitant restrictions. Some responses are in the political arena, and we agree that excluding political whims from risk assessment is appropriate; neglecting the economic realities of human responses, however, is not. Economics manifests itself directly into the fundamental science of species protection, not just the normative political process. By explicitly integrating economic parameters into the process, risk assessment will more accurately reflect the unbiased odds of species survival and, as a consequence, will make ESA policy more effective. This is key – everyone acknowledges that human actions affect species risk; most people do not then account for the fact that people react to the risks, and take actions that can either accentuate or attenuate the risk further. This feedback loop of human reaction by both landowners and government is what is consistently underemphasized in species protection policy. Is the marginal benefit of adding omitted variables to improve the estimation of species risk worth the marginal cost? We think the answer is yes – there should not be significant additional delay involved because most of the economic data exists and is readily available.

(ii) *Economics matters because in a world of scarce resources, the opportunity cost of species protection – in terms of the reduced resources for other worthwhile causes – must be taken into account in decision making.*

Scarcity is a reality. The time, labor, and capital available to us are all scarce resources and must be spread over many human desires. Demands that economics "transcend a paradigm of scarcity of value in species" is liking asking biology to surrender its notion of organisms (O'Neal et al. 1995). Because every preservation program has an opportunity cost – the benefits foregone from not spending the resources on other worthwhile causes – society may place more value on other goods and services than on the last species to be preserved. Consequently, as important as species are, choices among and between species and other programs must be made.

Understanding the nature of these choices requires that we explicitly account for the benefits and costs of various proposed programs. Such an accounting is already being conducted implicitly, so incorporating such calculations to discriminate among species achieves greater openness and transparency in how we choose to rank listing decisions and implement recovery plans. Criteria and analyses that discriminate among species will be controversial, but unavoidable. Implementation of the present ESA assuredly has allowed such discrimination, without admitting or examining it openly. Allowing administrators to compare costs and benefits explicitly subjects these factors to formal review (Arrow et al. 1996; Metrick and Weitzman 1996).

Despite this argument, most researchers acknowledge that accurately measuring preservation benefits for endangered species protection is difficult (Brown and Shogren 1998). An alternative to comparing costs and benefits is to adopt as a goal cost-effectiveness, that is, finding the least expensive path to a desired target. Three examples underscore how cost-effective policies can improve resource allocation. First, populations on the domestic endangered species list are dispersed around the United States, thereby creating the problem of allocating limited funds to preserve those sites that will maximize the number of species protected. By taking into account that land values vary across the United States instead of treating land as homogeneous, the costs of protecting half of the species on the list can be cut by two-thirds (Ando et al. 1998). Second, there are diminishing returns to increasing the probability of species survival, and cost-effective policies will stop short of full protection. For example, the northern spotted owl (*Strix occidentalis caurina*) can be saved relatively inexpensively with a reasonably high probability. But the cost to improve the odds of survival to 92 percent from 91 percent has been estimated at $3.8 billion (Montgomery, Brown, and Adams 1994). The ESA must weigh the value of an extra 1 percent survival probability against the value of employing the resources devoted to survival in some other endeavor, which may include saving other species.

Third, the old adage that "an ounce of prevention is worth a pound of cure" is applicable to species protection programs (e.g., Eisner et al. 1995; Babbitt 1997). Single species recovery programs are cures: they often cost $50,000–$500,000 annually, and can run to $1 million if captive breeding must be undertaken (Snyder et al. 1996). Preventive measures such as landscape conservation approaches, including the establishment of parks and reserves, and the enactment of habitat and other conservation planning efforts are more likely to be more cost-effective because they protect multiple species simultaneously. The odds are that the ESA will achieve greater success and better cost-effectiveness by improving its emphasis on proactive approaches such as natural community conservation planning, developing a formal candidate list, and by stressing collaboration through habitat conservation planning (Noss, O'Connell, and Murphy 1997; O'Connell and Johnson 1997; Beissinger and Perrine 2001). The inclusion of economic behavior is vital if the goal is to move toward a more proactive and effective ESA that focuses on strategic risk reduction through prevention rather than cure.

(iii) *Economics matters because economic incentives are critical in shaping human behavior, and consequently the recovery of species.*

When endangered species inhabit private land, incentives are likely to be needed to encourage landowners to preserve their property. Currently, the ESA provides little incentive for landowners to cooperate with species conservation policy. A landowner may have financial incentives to prevent government scientists from finding listed species on his or her lands, to reduce the value of the land as habitat for listed species, or to "take" listed or potentially listed species. These actions are wasteful because they may result in direct harm to listed species, destroy or reduce the value of habitat, and increase the costs of designating habitat and species recovery (e.g., Innes et al. 1998). Agencies or private parties can attempt to prevent such actions by providing an incentive for the landowner to cooperate, using either compensation or permits and fines.

The first of these incentive approaches is to have the government pay full compensation to landowners (Goldstein and Heintz 1993; Innes et al. 1998). For instance, Defenders of Wildlife compensate ranchers for livestock losses to wolves. Doing so removes any financial penalty for cooperating with conservation policy, which should make species conservation policy on private land less controversial and less adversarial. If not implemented properly, however, compensation can introduce its own undesirable incentives, such as prompting excessive levels of investment to increase market value (Blume, Rubinfled, and Shapiro 1984; Innes 1997), or even a de facto repeal of the

ESA if underfunded by Congress. Compensation paid to landowners who anticipate this payout when making their private land investments can prompt excessive levels of land investment. Such incentives can be avoided if the compensation is not tied to private losses, or is tied to the property's habitat value. In these cases, an ESA action does not reward a landowner for higher investment levels, the returns that are lost. This approach coupled with take permits would be consistent with Habitat Conservation Plans and Incidental Take Permits, one of the few provisions in the ESA (Section 10(a)) that provide explicit incentives to private landowners (e.g., Bean and Wilcove 1997; Shilling 1997).

Imperfect information about the population biology of species and their roles in ecosystems confounds the design of preservation policy (Simberloff 1988; Beissinger and Westphal 1998). In like manner, imperfect information about economic behavior exacerbates the government's problem. In particular, information asymmetries between landowners and the government introduce an additional set of issues revolving around the landowners' incentives to reveal information. On private land, the government needs landowner cooperation to gain the information necessary to administer conservation policy, yet landowners may have been able to escape regulation by hiding information from the government. If so, conservation policy may need to use the "carrot" of compensation rather than the "stick" of permits and fines to elicit information. But herein lies the dilemma: Lower compensation is good because it lessens the incentive for landowners to take advantage of their private information, but lower compensation also results in fewer acres set aside for habitat. The net result is either that the realized habitat will be smaller than preferred, or the desired habitat will be more expensive than may be justified (Polasky and Doremus 1998; Smith and Shogren 2001). This suggests that a combination of mechanisms might be needed – including government compensation, verification of habitat as a requirement for a subsidy, government or conservation group purchases of land or development rights, insurance programs, tax breaks, and government-established tradeable rights in habitat conservation or development.

Because government decision makers also respond to incentives, understanding how compensation affects government incentives to carry out conservation policy is likewise important. Government agencies have considerable latitude in making decisions and are susceptible to the influence of special-interest groups. In the absence of compensation, government may undertake more ESA actions than are desirable because it will understate the costs of action to the landowners. Alternatively, if the government must pay full compensation, it can be expected to undertake fewer ESA actions than are desirable, especially if compensation is raised through a tax system that inevitably distorts other decisions in the economy and is politically unpopular. Whether carrots or sticks are used to obtain landowner cooperation greatly affects the incentives and the ability of government to undertake conservation actions.

Just as policy makers cannot ignore the laws of nature, neither can they ignore the laws of human nature when protecting endangered species. Economic behavior matters for protecting and recovering endangered species. Effective federal and local policy requires that we adjust our perspectives, and better integrate both human actions and their reactions to species risk into the mix of viewpoints guiding endangered species policy.

References

Agee, M. and T. Crocker. 1998. Economies, Human Capital, and Natural Assets. *Environmental and Resource Economics* 11: 261–71.

Ando, A., J. Camm, S. Polasky, and A. Solow. 1998. Species Distributions, Land Values, and Efficient Conservation. *Science* 279: 2126.

Arrow, K., M. Cropper, G. Eads, R. Hahn, L. Lave, R. Noll, P. Portney, M. Russell, R. Schmalensee, V.K. Smith, and R. Stavins. 1996. Is There a Role for Benefit-Cost Analysis in Environmental, Health, and Safety Regulation? *Science* 272: 221–22.

Babbitt, B. 1997. To Reauthorize the ESA. Why, Where and How We Should Translate Our Success Stories into Law. Speech to the National Press Club, Washington, D.C. 17 July.

Bean, M. and D. S. Wilcove. 1997. The Private-Land Problem. *Conservation Biology* 11: 1–2.

Beissinger, S. and M. I. Westphal. 1998. On the Use of Demographic Models of Population Viability in Endangered Species Management. *Journal of Wildlife Management* 62: 821–41.

Beissinger, S. and J. Perrine. 2001. Extinction, Recovery, and the Endangered Species Act. Chapter 4 in J. Shogren and J. Tschirhart, editors. *Protecting Endangered Species in the United States: Biological Needs, Political Realities, Economics Choices*. Cambridge University Press, New York.

Blume, L., D. Rubinfeld and P. Shapiro. 1984. The Taking of Land: When Should Compensation Be Paid? *Quarterly Journal of Economics* 100: 71–92.

Bockstael, N. 1996. Modeling Economics and Ecology: The Importance of a Spatial Perspective. *American Journal of Agricultural Economics* 78: 1168–80.

Brown, G. and J. Shogren. 1998. Economics of the *Endangered Species Act. Journal of Economic Perspectives* 12: 3–20.

Carroll, R., C. Augspurger, A. Dobson, J. Franklin, G. Orians, W. Reid, R. Tracy, D. Wilcove, and J. Wilson. 1996. Strengthening the Use of Science in Achieving the Goals of the ESA: An Assessment by the Ecological Society of America. *Ecological Applications* 6: 1–11.

Crocker, T. and J. Shogren. 1998. Endogenous Risk and Environmental Program Evaluation. Pages 255–69 in G. Knaap and T. Kim, editors. *Environmental Program Evaluation*: A Primer. University of Illinois Press, Urbana-Champaign, Illinois.

Crocker, T. and J. Tschirhart. 1992. Ecosystems, Externalities, and Economies. *Environmental and Resource Economics* 2: 551–68.

Ehrenfeld, D. 1988. Why Put a Value on Biodiversity? Pages 212–16 in E. Wilson, editor. *Biodiversity*. National Academy Press, Washington, D.C.

Eisner, T., J. Lubchenco, E. O. Wilson, D. Wilcove, and M. Bean. 1995. Building a Scientifically Sound Policy for Protecting Endangered Species. *Science* 268: 1231–32.

Epstein, R. 1995. *Simple Rules for a Complex World*. Harvard University Press, Cambridge, MA.

Gilpin, M. and M. Soulé. 1986. *Conservation Biology: The Science of Scarcity and Diversity*. Sinauer, Sunderland, MA.

Goldstein, J. and H. Heintz, Jr. 1993. *Incentives for Private Conservation of Species and Habitat: An Economic Perspective*. Office of Policy Analysis, U.S. Department of Interior, Washington, D.C.

Innes, R. 1997. Takings, Compensation, and Equal Treatment for Owners of Developed and Undeveloped Property. *Journal of Law and Economics* 40: 403–32.

Innes, R., S. Polasky, and J. Tschirhart. 1998. Takings, Compensation, and Endangered Species Protection on Private Lands. *Journal of Economic Perspectives* 12: 35–52.

Jablonski, D. 1991. Extinctions: A Palentological Perspective. *Science* 253: 754–57.

Lande, R. 1993. Risks of Population Extinction from Demographic and Environmental Stochasticity and Random Catastrophes. *The American Naturalist* 142: 911–27.

Mann, C. and M. Plummer. 1995. *Noah's Choice: The Future of Endangered Species*. Knopf, New York.

May, R., J. Lawton, and N. Stork. 1995. Assessing Extinction Rates. Pages 1–34 in J. Lawton and R. May, editors. *Extinction Rates*. Oxford University Press, New York.

Metrick, A. and M. Weitzman. 1996. Patterns of Behavior in Endangered Species Preservation. *Land Economics* 72: 1–16.

Milon, J. and J. Shogren, editors. 1995. Integrating Economic and Ecological Indicators. Preager Press, Westport, CT.

Montgomery, C., G. Brown, Jr. and D. Adams. 1994. The Marginal Cost of Species Preservation: The Northern Spotted Owl. *Journal of Environmental Economics and Management* 26: 111–28.

National Research Council. 1995. *Science and the ESA*. National Academy Press, Washington, D.C.

Noss, R., M. O'Connell, and D. Murphy. 1997. *The Science of Conservation Planning: Habitat Conservation under the ESA*. Island Press, Washington, D.C.

O'Connell, M. and S. Johnson. 1997. Improving Habitat Conservation Planning: The California Natural Community Conservation Model. *Endangered Species Update* 14: 1–3.

O'Neal, A., A. Pandian, S. Rhodes-Conway, and A. Bornbusch. 1995. Human Economies, the Land Ethic, and Sustainable Conservation. *Conservation Biology* 9: 217–28.

Pimm, S., G. Russell, J. Gittleman, and T. Brooks. 1995. The Future of Biodiversity. *Science* 269: 347–50.

Polasky, S. and H. Doremus. 1998. When the Truth Hurts: Endangered Species Policy on Private Land with Imperfect Information. *Journal of Environmental Economics and Management* 35: 22–47.

Roughgarden, J. 1995. Can Economics Save Biodiversity? Pages 149–53 in T. Swanson, editor. *The Economics and Ecology of Biodiversity Decline*: The Forces *Driving Global Change*. Cambridge University Press, New York.

Shilling, F. 1997. Do Habitat Conservation Plans Protect Endangered Species? *Science* 276: 1662–63.

Shogren, J. editor. 1998. *Private Property and the ESA. Saving Habitat, Protecting Homes*. University of Texas Press, Austin.

Simberloff, D. 1988. The Contribution of Population and Community Biology to Conservation Science. *Annual Reviews of Ecology and Systematics* 19: 473–511.

Smith, J. 1996. Column. *Las Vegas Review Journal & Las Vegas Sun.* 16 July.

Smith, R. and J. Shogren. 2001. Protecting Species on Private Land. Chapter 16 in J. Shogren and J. Tschirhart, editors. *Protecting Endangered Species in the United States: Biological Needs, Political Realities, Economic Choices.* Cambridge University Press, New York.

Snyder, N., S. Derrickson, S. R. Beissinger, J. W. Wiley, T. B. Smith, W. D. Toone, and B. Miller. 1996. Limitations of Captive Breeding in Endangered Species Recovery. *Conservation Biology* 10: 338–48.

Soulé, M. editor. 1987. *Viable Populations for Conservation.* Cambridge University Press, New York.

Tschirhart, J. and T. Crocker. 1987. Economic Valuation of Ecosystems. *Transactions of the American Fisheries Society* 116: 469–78.

CHAPTER 19

DEMES: Database on the Economics and Management of Endangered Species

Codebook version 2.2

David W. Cash, J. R. DeShazo, Andrew Metrick,

Stuart Shapiro, Todd Schatzki, and

Martin Weitzman

INTRODUCTION

The Database on the Economics and Management of Endangered Species (DEMES) was developed for social scientists and policy analysts interested in the regulations affecting the management of endangered species. A mix of scientific, managerial, political, legal, and economic variables is contained in this database for species meeting one of the following criteria:

1. Species listed as threatened or endangered under the Endangered Species Act (ESA).
2. Species formerly listed under the ESA.
3. Species petitioned or proposed for listing between 1991 and July 1997 whose placement on the list was deemed unwarranted by Fish and Wildlife Service.
4. Vertebrate species with a ranking of N3 to N1 in the Nature Conservancy's (TNC) species database. TNC ranking represents the "relative rarity or endangerment of the species" and is comprised of a 5-point scale – N5 is not endangered; N1 is critically endangered. We included species with ranks between N1 and N3 to capture those species that might conceivably be considered for endangered species conservation. The database thus provides the ability to compare the management received under the ESA for an independently chosen set of endangered species.
5. A few additional species not meeting any of the above requirements with significant government spending.

The database contains variables describing the management of species under the ESA, and the political, legal, and social factors that might affect this decision making. The project hopes to provide an excellent starting point for researchers interested in understanding and improving the decision-making processes and institutional design of the ESA.

For more details and the DEMES data contact J. R. Deshazo, *deshazo@ucla.edu*

Although the database includes records for a large number of species, not all variables are collected for each species. In general, most variables have been collected for vertebrates, while only limited information is available for invertebrate animals and for plants. Likewise, more data have been collected for species under the jurisdiction of the U.S. Fish and Wildlife Service (FWS) than for those under the jurisdiction of the National Marine Fisheries Service (NMFS). Collection of political and legal variables has been limited to vertebrates. Species not regulated by the ESA have no information on federal listing and management status.

The database contains five individual workbooks broken down by areas of interest and their relevant data: (1) General Information, (2) Range, (3) Listing, (4) Habitat Conservation Plan Expenditures, and (5) Scientific/Social/Political/Legal Variables. The following is a brief synopsis of each workbook and the data used to define each category.

Workbook #1 on general information contains data that describe various aspects regarding each species from the database. It covers the species' different names, ranking and dimensions. The types of variables are grouped by data on:

Management Variables: the rankings or indices used by the TNC, NHN, or the FWS, which rank the relative degree of priority that should be given species. These variables also include taxonomic characteristics and variables that capture aspects of ESA implementation (e.g., federal status and the FWS Priority index).

Size Variables: basic statistics regarding a given species' size, weight and genus.

Workbook #2 – the Range. Using predetermined management variables, this dataset lists the incidence of each species by state, territory, and geographic world region. The workbook also includes the previous and current federal status of each species along with their perceived level of conflict with economic development. Data in this section were collected through FWS sources unless otherwise noted. These data are current as of June 1996 unless otherwise noted. A group of these data pertains to the FWS Priority Ranking System for species recovery. This is an 18-point score constructed from a lexicographic ranking system which includes measures of "degree of threat" (3 levels: high, medium, and low), "recovery potential" (2 levels: high and low), and "taxonomic uniqueness" (3 levels: monotypic species, full species, and subspecies). A "1" priority rank indicates the highest priority for recovery efforts, while "18" indicates the lowest priority. In addition, FWS notes whether or not a species is in conflict with economic development. The notation of being in conflict is meant only to distinguish between two species which otherwise have the same numerical rank. This designation confers on the species in conflict a higher priority than a similarly ranked species not in conflict. There are, therefore, a total of thirty six different ranks (in descending order of priority): 1C, 1, 2C, 2, ... 18C, 18.

The particular groups of variables used on this worksheet:

General Management Variables: These data are compiled by the FWS and describe the federal status of each specie, the perceived presence of conflict with economic development, the level of threat each specie faces, the potential for recovery, the state of the habitat, the species' range including states, territory, and global geographic regions.

Workbook #3 – Listing. This section includes data on the number and categorization of comments received by the FWS regarding the proposal to list a species. These comments are broken down by the source of the comment, its position, and then tallied. The particular groups of variables used on this worksheet:

Listing Process Variables: From the final rules on listed species found in the Federal Register, it was possible to find a number of important events in the listing process, such as when petitions were submitted for a species to be listed, and when critical habitat was proposed. By U.S. law, all federal agencies must print their final rules in the Federal Register. Before a rule is finalized, in most cases, individuals and groups who might be concerned must be notified. Anyone is then invited to comment on the proposed rule during a predetermined comment period. When public comments are received by federal agencies, they must be answered promptly. The public comments and replies by the Fish and Wildlife Service are reported in the eventual publication of the final rule. The data in the comment variables section is taken directly from the FWS (or for marine species, the National Marine Fisheries Service) final rule as it was printed in the Federal Register. *DATES OF COLLECTION*: This data covers all listed vertebrates prior to June 1995, in addition to all listed species (of all taxonomic classes) from June 1995 to June 1997.

Comment Variables: These variables represent data on the number and categorization of comments received by the Fish and Wildlife Service regarding the proposal to list a species. These comments are either submitted by mail or presented at public hearings that must be held by the Service if requested. While sometimes the number of people in attendance at these hearings is noted in the Register, only the number of people who made comments is included in this data. The number of people submitting written comments and commenting at public hearings came directly from the Federal Register publication of the final rule on the species' listing. The first species for which this comment data was collected was listed on September 25, 1975.

For each listing, the information given about public comments is broken down into categorizations based on the source of comments and the position the comment took on the listing (for, against, or neutral). In many cases, the sources of comments are not made clear in the rule, so only the total number of comments for, against, and neutral are entered. These are added to create a total comments variable. In the case where the position of a comment is unclear, it is only recorded in the total comment variable. Therefore, the total comments is sometimes greater than the sum of comments for, against, and neutral. The number of comments accounted for in this database for any of the comment variables corresponds to the maximum known number of comments fitting that categorization (e.g., elected officials supporting listing). This number may be less than or equal to the actual number of comments for that category and position. The reason for this is that often the final rule, as it appears in the Register, will hint that more comments that fit a particular category were made than were actually described in the rule. For instance, the final rule may state that several federal agencies commented, but only mention two specifically. In this case, the total number of federal agencies, as shown in the database, will be two. On occasion, the rule notes the quantity of comments as a range ("more than 1,000" for example). Here we have reported the quantity as an inequality ($>1,000$). In cases where the number of comments fitting a particular categorization is described as a majority, majority is interpreted to mean sixty percent of the comments for which it is a majority of.

Data for listing comments was broken down, where possible, into the following categories:

> Elected Officials/States Comments Includes all federally elected officials, comments made by particular states, or comments made by state Governors
>
> Federal Agencies' Comments Includes federal agencies
>
> State/Local Agencies' Comments Includes state, county, or local agencies, towns, counties, or cities and state legislators
>
> Environmental Groups' Comments Includes any comments made by environmental or conservationist groups (for example, the Sierra Club)
>
> Scientists/Scientific Groups' Comments Includes comments made by scientists and scientific organizations and groups
>
> Business/Landowners' Comments Includes comments made by businesses, industry representatives, or private landowners
>
> Organizations' Comments Includes comments by any organization, including those representing business, the environment, or other concerns
>
> Individuals' Comments Includes comments by any individual. Could include scientists, landowners, or elected officials, among others.

Change in Listing Variables: As the condition of a species changes, or more information pertinent to a listing decision becomes available, a species' federal status can be changed by the Secretary of the Interior. This change in a species' listing must be preceded by the same proposal and comment process that accompanies the original listing of a species. The dates for the steps in this process are included in the database when available. *DATES OF COLLECTION*: This section of the database includes all changes in listings that occurred between June 1995 and June 1997 – a total of five species.

CODING KEYS: The last two variables on some variables have to do with possible changes in listing. The variable codes for these various changes in listings are only different in their last two letters. The last two letters identify these changes in listing from endangered to threatened, ET for example. The following is a list of possible two-letter suffixes to the listing variables below and the changes they correspond to:

ET = Endangered to threatened
TE = Threatened to endangered
UL = Removed from list (previously either Endangered or Threatened

Workbook #4 – Habitat Conservation Plan Expenditures details by year, the expenditure on each species by state, aggregate federal and by each federal agency. The types of variables include:

Habitat Conservation Plan Variables: A Habitat Conservation Plan (HCP) is a detailed plan that provides for the conservation of a federally listed endangered species under the federal Endangered Species Act. Section 10 of the ESA provides this mechanism for landowners, enabling them to carry out activities on their lands even though those activities may result in an "incidental take" of an endangered species. In exchange, landowners agree to the provisions of the plan and agree to implement it. Plans are developed by the private landowner and must be approved by FWS (1994). This section includes data collected up to June 1995.

Expenditure Variables: Under Section 18 of the Endangered Species Act of 1973 as amended in 1988, all reasonably identifiable expenditures for a listed species are to be reported by federal and state agencies to Congress (via the Secretary of the Interior and FWS). In a few instances, there is reported spending for nonlisted species. All federal agencies and those states receiving Section 6 grant-in-aid funds are asked to report. This report, entitled *Federal and State Endangered Species Expenditures* has been produced annually since 1989. The data include the years from 1989 to 1993. The 1994 FY has not been published, as of August 1997. Data is grouped by agency (state funds are left aggregated). The expenditures may include a margin of error: When more than one species is involved, an agency might divide expenditures equally among all the species (USFWS 1995).

Worksheet #5 – Scientific/Social/Political/Legal Variables includes data on a range of scientific, social, political, and legal variables that may affect species management. It attempts to detail the relative frequency and public exposure of each species based on scientific articles, news citations, those species earmarked for funding by Senate members, and 'representation' by Senate subcommittee members from the Environmental Protection, Environment and Public Works subcommittees. The particular groups of variables used on this worksheet:

Scientific Documentation Variables. This section includes records of the frequency with which species were mentioned in scientific publications in either a significant or incidental manner. Data have been recorded from 1970 to 1995, with all observations from 1983 missing.

Social Variables: In July and August 1993, a random sample of the U.S. population was surveyed by mail about the importance of preserving endangered and threatened animals. General information about the importance of preserving animals and information about the specific importance of each animal was collected along with information about the respondents. In "The Revealed Demand for a Public Good," Coursey (Chapter 11 of this volume) reports the mean importance of preserving a species. His range runs from 1.48 for the bald eagle (most important) to 3.42 for the Kretschmarr Cave mold. The survey gave possibilities from 1 (extremely important) to 5 (not important at all).

Political Variables:

    i. Committee Membership Data is included on presence of U.S. Senate subcommittee membership on appropriate legislative committees in states where listed species reside. The Senate Interior Subcommittee controls appropriations for FWS. The Senate Environmental Protection Subcommittee of the Environment and Public Works Committee provides oversight for FWS. Data are also included on voting records on environmental matters by Senate subcommittee members and states in which species reside. Data was collected only for terrestrial vertebrates (those under the jurisdiction of FWS, not NMFS).

    ii. Earmarking: Members of Congress can appropriate special earmarks of funds for specific species. These variables account for the total amount of earmarked funding going to each species during the years from 1989 to 1997.

    iii. Other political variables.

Legal Variables: When a species is listed, legal conflicts may arise as development interests see their projects impeded by the restrictions of the Endangered Species Act. Data for this section came from Lexus, an on-line database containing legal and regulatory information. From the file containing environmental case law archives, keyword searches were done on each individual vertebrate species in conjunction with the Endangered Species Act, and the number of court opinions in which they appear is recorded. This number of court opinions is further broken down into cases from various court levels (Lexis-Nexis). These data have only been collected up to June 1995.

Acknowledgments. The creation of this database was made possible by National Science Foundation grant #SBR-9422772. Much of the raw material for this database derived from data made available through The Nature

Conservancy (TNC)/Natural Heritage Network (NHN) with invaluable and much appreciated help from Melissa Morrison of TNC. Any material supplied by the TNC/NHN was up to date at the time of provision. TNC/NHN continually updates and improves its scientific information and thus the data presented in this database may not represent current Nature Conservancy/ Natural Heritage Network scientific information on the ever-changing status of organisms in the United States. We would also like to thank Darlene Lin, Brian Gordon, Bella Sewall, Jeffrey Szeto, and Jean Pierre Batmale for excellent research assistance. Finally, we would like to thank the librarians at Harvard's Museum of Comparative Zoology Library and the Widener Government Documents Library for their assistance. This database and the accompanying coding contained in this documentation is presented here as a "beta" version. We welcome and encourage comments on both substantive data issues and format, style and ease-of-use issues.

References

Coursey, Don. 2001. "The Revealed Demand for a Public Good: Evidence from Endangered and Threatened Species." Chapter 11 in J. Shogren and J. Tschirhart, eds. *Protecting Endangered Species in the United States: Biological Needs, Political Realities, Economic Choices*, New York: Cambridge University Press.

Lexis-Nexis Database.

U.S. Department of the Interior, Fish and Wildlife Service. 1995. "Federal and State Endangered Species Expenditures." Fiscal Year 1989 to 1993, Washington, D.C.

U.S. Department of the Interior, Fish and Wildlife Service. 1994. "Status of Habitat Conservation Plans." Washington, D.C., mimeo.

Index